Russia and Eurasia
at the Crossroads

Springer

Berlin
Heidelberg
New York
Barcelona
Hong Kong
London
Milan
Paris
Singapore
Tokyo

Egor S. Stroev · Leonid S. Bliakhman
Mikhail I. Krotov

Russia and Eurasia at the Crossroads

Experience and Problems of Economic Reforms
in the Commonwealth of Independent States

 Springer

Prof. Dr. Egor S. Stroev
Federal Assembly Federation Council
Chairman of the Russian Federation
Region Administration
Lenina Sq. 2
303900 Orel
Russia

Prof. Dr. Leonid S. Bliakhman
Prof. Dr. Mikhail I. Krotov

CIS Interparliamentary Assembly Council
Taurida Palace
Shpalernaya Str. 47
193015 St. Petersburg
Russia

ISBN 3-540-65721-5 Springer-Verlag Berlin Heidelberg New York Tokyo

Library of Congress Cataloging-in-Publication Data
Die Deutsche Bibliothek – CIP-Einheitsaufnahme
Russia and Eurasia at the Crossroads/E. S. Stroev... – Berlin; Heidelberg; New York; Bar-
celona; Hong Kong; London; Milan; Paris; Singapore; Tokyo: Springer, 1999
 ISBN 3-540-65721-5

This work is subject to copyright. All rights are reserved, whether the whole or part of
the material is concerned, specifically the rights of translation, reprinting, reuse of illus-
trations, recitation, broadcasting, reproduction on microfilm or in any other way, and
storage in data banks. Duplication of this publication or parts thereof is permitted only
under the provisions of the German Copyright Law of September 9, 1965, in its current
version, and permission for use must always be obtained from Springer-Verlag. Violations are liable for prosecution under the German Copyright Law.

© Springer-Verlag Berlin · Heidelberg 1999
Printed in Italy

The use of general descriptive names, registered names, trademarks, etc. in this publication does not imply, even in the absence of a specific statement, that such names are
exempt from the relevant protective laws and regulations and therefore free for general
use.

Hardcover-Design: Erich Kirchner, Heidelberg

SPIN 10721527   42/2202-5 4 3 2 1 0 – Printed on acid-free paper

CONTENTS

INTRODUCTION

This last century of the second millennium has compressed human history to such an extent that whole ages of engineering, economics, social politics and the humanities have been accommodated in decades or even years. Mankind has matured and applied its cognitive and creative genes to advance science and to internationalise future goals, including the vital goal of **sustainable social development**. However, having no control over the new pace of history, twentieth-century civilisation has faced global cataclysms of a frequency and depth unprecedented and inconceivable in the past millennia.

Among the recent "crises" to be "resolved" in the third millennium is disintegration of the Soviet Union, the biggest state and third largest population in the world.

Regretfully, the pace of change in the Soviet Union had been slower than the rates of reform elsewhere. Attempts at economic redecorating instead of radical market-oriented reforms failed.

In Soviet society, general discontent with the progress of *perestroika* in the 1980s provoked the "child complacency" syndrome that is typical of a young mind contemptuous of any adult action: it is convinced that things could have been done much better and much quicker. With the new millennium approaching, the Soviet Union gave way to 15 new states ridden with both inherited and acquired economic, political and social maladies.

It is common knowledge, however, that childhood epidemics are short-lived. Twelve out of the 15 former republics of the Soviet Union joined the Commonwealth of Independent States (CIS) and are using their identity to catch up with the objective historical trajectory in a torturous search for ways and forms of embodying the obvious truths of integration, co-ordination and collaboration. Ignorance of international experience in reform and innovative economic growth with its essential component of integrative action has meant that economic reforms have been far slower and less successful after the disintegration of the former Union than in Central and Eastern European countries or China. Industrial output in the CIS countries has decreased by more than half during the 1990s, in particular in the research-intensive industries that determine national economic competitiveness and in the production of consumer goods and construction materials. Dramatic differences between living standards have triggered social conflicts. While demolishing the previous administrative command system, the CIS countries have failed to establish a legal economy fit to function along the lines of exchange in global economic relationships. This could not be remedied by exclusive exports of raw materials, excessive borrowing and the unsound use of foreign loans.

On the other hand, the CIS countries have gathered experience of reforms that deserves detailed consideration. Trends, conditions and rates of reforms differ significantly in different countries, but towards the end of the 1990s, the countries previously impeding denationalisation and liberalisation accelerated the pace of reforms, while those who had pinned their hopes on the "invisible hand" of the market began to increase State regulation and social orientation. Circumstances beyond reasonable control have pushed their economic complexes towards alignment and integration, even though establishing new economic relations has been far more difficult than dismantling the old ones.

The recognition of the losses entailed by breaking down artificial administrative and traditional historical, geographical, cultural, scientific and economic relations has been evident in new political developments within most of the CIS member states. Using current political science terminology, we can say that **moderate centrism** is gradually coming to dominate Commonwealth politics, acting in the interests of the broad public segment, i.e. the working community and the middle classes, focusing on market values and reasonable pragmatism and initiating economic and social reforms based on thorough analysis, adequate knowledge of natural laws and concepts of strategic perspectives. It is not surprising that today's centrists without an extreme "left" or "right" bias appeal both to the widest possible general public and to those more "advanced" intellectual and academic communities with a knowledge of the deep-seated ongoing processes.

It is the larger public interest, the natural "common sense" view of life that comes closest to the academic view of future promise for the CIS as an inter-state union with unique foundations, collaborative procedures and potential.

The authors' conception of functioning and economic development in the CIS is based on a realistic analysis of the current potential of the CIS and of the great challenges faced by each individual member and the Commonwealth as a whole as they progress from a critical situation towards stabilisation and prosperity. The following assumptions underlie the concept of reform used here:

1. Reforms in the CIS are not meant as a retreat to the capitalism and self-regulating market economy of the turn of the century, but rather as a transition to a socially oriented and diversified economy of a sustainable development society requiring active State regulation, especially in the initial phases.

2. The performance criterion for reforms cannot be represented in rates of privatisation, the number of commercial banks, stock exchanges, etc. but rather

in sustained economic growth and development of the principal productive force in society – human individuals.

3. As the conditions of structural reforms differ significantly in different CIS countries, both Western (mainly liberal and monetary) and Eastern (mainly institutional) experience of reforms should be utilised, although merely imitating these reforms will not work in the CIS.

4. All CIS countries have accumulated some positive experience in individual fields of reforms; this experience should be generalised and shared.

5. As disintegration of the previous administrative pattern of integration is inevitable, structural reforms provide a basis for mutually beneficial economic integration and joint access to the world market.

6. Progress in the new economic integration will have to be long and persistent, starting with the customs and parliamentary union, unrestrained circulation of commodities, capital, information and labour, a unified scientific, technological and educational area, joint investment projects and transnational corporations (TNCs), to be followed by the common currency and transnational government.

7. The most important component of reforms is improved performance and renovation in production to ensure the well-being of present and future generations. Development of the individual, of views and behaviour, morality, culture, science and education – all these represent the goals of reforms and the conditions for their success. The humanitarian aspect of reforms is essential in the CIS, incorporating Western and Eastern, Christian and Islamic civilisations and diverse national cultures.

We assume that the CIS is an inter-state entity of an extremely dynamic nature. This poses considerable analytical difficulties, because innovation in the functional laws and principles of the CIS outstrips recognition. On the other hand, this dynamic quality raises hopes that the CIS may provide an adequate instrument for Commonwealth nations to build a new economic, political and sociocultural pole in the world. In this context, the CIS may well be regarded as *mankind's strategic reserve* within Eurasia. The overall national potential within the Commonwealth, given adequate common goals, restored traditional and new relations of a higher quality and intensity, suggests that CIS mechanisms can be used by the international community in the 21st century as a new motor for progress and effective collaboration in the new civilisation.

This book examines recent political and economic developments both in the individual CIS member states and in the CIS as a whole. Our primary concerns are the implementation of the decisions taken by the CIS Heads of Government and the Interparliamentary Assembly and the theoretical basis for ongoing processes and future perspectives proposed by members of the academic and political communities in the CIS.

Our study refers to the international literature – in particular, the economic growth and balancing theories (e.g. L. Walras, A. Marshall, I.V. Pareto, C. Arrow, F. Hahn, F. Machlup, R. Solow) and the evolutionary theory of economic change (e.g. R. Nelson, S. Winter). The liberal monetary conceptions (e.g. M. Friedman, G. Sachs) provide an insight into the nature of financial flows, while the institutional ones (e.g. J.M. Keynes, A. Hansen, P. Samuelson, V. Leontiev, M. Weber, J. Buchanan, J.C. Galbraith, R. Heilbronner) are of essential importance for State regulatory activities in the CIS economies in general. Of particular value in this context are theoretical works on transitional economy (J. Poridan) and generalisations of the experience of reform in Central Europe (J. Balcerovicz, W. Klaus) and China (e.g. Den Siaoping, Chu Zhunsi).

The book draws on statistical and analytical data provided by the CIS Intergovernmental Statistics Board, the World Bank, international economic organisations and CIS centres.

The book can be used as a textbook on CIS economics, the theory and practice of economic reform, and economics for managers at higher educational establishments and business schools.

Chapter 1

THE CIS IN THE WORLD ECONOMY

1.1 The CIS and Its Economic Potential

General information. Geographically, Eurasia is the Earth's largest continent, covering the two parts of the world, Europe and Asia, and surrounded by the Arctic, Pacific, Atlantic and Indian oceans and their seas. It is also the Earth's most populated one – over 3 billion – with the world's most populated countries China and India accounting for more than half of the population and about 285 million in the 12 independent CIS member states (see Table 1).

The CIS incorporates over 100 nations and nationalities, including 50 traditionally Christian and almost 40 Islamic ones. Among the more numerous are the Russian, Ukrainian, Uzbek, Byelorussian, Kazakh, Tatar, Azerbaijan, Armenian, Georgian, Moldavian, Czuvash, German, Bashkir, Jewish and Mordvinian nationalities.

The CIS is bordered by seas of three oceans. Russia is washed by the Baltic, Arctic (Barents, White, Karsk, Laptevs, East-Siberian, Chukotsk) and Pacific (Bering, Okhotsk, Japan) seas; the Ukraine, Russia and Georgia have access to the Black Sea, the Ukraine and Russia to the Azov and Russia, Azerbaijan, Kazakhstan and Turkmenistan to the Caspian Sea.

Many of the almost 3000 rivers (e.g. the Danube, Dniester, Dnieper, West Dvina, Ural, Kura, Terek, Syrdaria, Amudaria) run in more than one CIS country. There are two salt lakes, the Caspian and the Aral, the world's deepest freshwater lake, Baikal, and the sizeable lakes (more than 5000 km^2) Balkhash, Ladoga, Onega and Issyk-Kul.

There are vast plains and lowlands (East European between the Carpathian and Crimean mountains, the Caucasus and Urals; West Siberian between the Urals and Enisei River, Turansk in Central Asia, and North Siberian), tablelands (e.g. Mid-Siberian south of Taimyr) and mountains (Carpathian, Crimean and the Caucasus in the West; Kopetdag, Pamir, Gissar-Altay, Tyang-Shang, Djungar Alatau, and Tarbagatai in the South; Altay, Kuznetsk Alatau, Sayan, Verkhoyansk, Chersk, Urals, Baykal ridges, Trans-Baykal and Taimyr hills, etc. in the East).

Table 1

Population (as of the beginning of the year, in thousands) and Area (1000 km²) in the CIS Countries

Country	Population									Area
	1991	1992	1993	1994	1995	1996	1997	1998	As of 1 January 1999	1997
Azerbaijan	7187	7297	7368	7431	7487	7535	7574	7632	7700²	86.6
Armenia	3574	3649	3722	3742	3753	3766	3781	3791	3798	29.8
Belarus	10261	10281	10346	10367	10345	10312	10284	10252	10227	207.6
Georgia	5464	5463	5447	5433	5417	5416	5424	5439	5445²	69.7
Kazakhstan	16793	16964	16986	16942	16679	16544	15993	15642	15491	2724.9
Kyrgyzstan	4422	4484	4502	4463	4483	4545	4607	4668	4730	199.9
Moldova	4367	4359	4348	4353	4348	4334	4320	4241	3648¹	33.8
Russia	148543	148704	148673	148366	148306	147976	147502	147105	146714²	17075.4
Tajikistan	5358	5570	5571	5704	5786	5884	5970	6067	6164²	143.1
Turkmenistan	3714	3809	4254	4361	4450	4567	4628	4687	4990²	491.2
Uzbekistan	20708	21207	21703	22192	22562	23007	23444	23867	24232	447.4
Ukraine	51944	52057	52244	52114	51728	51334	50894	50500	50091	603.7
CIS	282335	283844	285164	285464	285336	285300	285421	283831	283230²	22113.1

¹ Except population of the left bank of the Dniester area and Bendery.
² Estimated.

The CIS countries have a common history reaching back 1000 years. As early as the first millennium B.C. there were states in Transcaucasia (Urarty, Kolkhida, Caucasian Albania), in Central Asia (Bactria, Sogdiana, Khoresm) and on the coast of the Black Sea (Bosporia and Scythian kingdoms). In the second half of the ninth century, the Kiev Rus emerged as the hotbed of Ukrainian, Byelorussian and Russian nations. The territory was invaded from the East, South and West. During the great migration, Finno-Ugrian, Asian and Caucasian nations moved westward to the territories of modern Turkey, Hungary, Finland and even Spain. In the sixteenth century, the Russian state emerged (Imperial Russia after 1721), with some nations joining willingly, seeking protection from invaders, and others being conquered.

Until 1991, the CIS countries were Union republics in the USSR and ranked first in Europe and second in the world in terms of gross domestic product (GDP); moreover, they led the world in oil, coal, iron ore, pig iron and steel, fertilisers, cement, saw-timber, woollen cloth, leather footwear, butter and many types of machinery (20% of world-wide industrial output). The USSR also led the world in qualified professionals in natural and engineering sciences, physicists and engineers. On the other hand, its living standards lagged far behind those in Western European countries, the USA and Japan.

Competitive quality of the national economy. Competitiveness of the national economy means the ability to produce and sell both in domestic and world markets the goods and services to meet effective demand and to ensure economic growth and improved quality of life.

International economic organisations (e.g. the World Economic Forum, the World Bank) have set up about 350 guides to indicate national economy competitiveness. These include the following:

– The country's economic potential and its usage (e.g. population, natural resources, contribution of manufacturing and high-tech industries to GDP, proportion of expenditure on final consumption and investments)

– Economic internationalisation (contribution to international division of labour and investment flows, share of GDP accounted for by foreign trade, export/import balance, export share of high technologies, export/import price index ratio)

– Quality of State regulation in social and economic processes (e.g. legislative support, legal order/rule of law, political stability, extent of administrative corruption, ability of the authorities to evaluate an economic situation, national debt as a percentage of GDP)

– Financial stability (size of budget deficit, inflation, national currency exchange rate, gold and hard currency reserves, range and quality of financial services, development of the stock market, arrears, export trade debtor balance)

– Development of the infrastructure (energetics, transport, roads, communications and telecommunications, social welfare, business)

– Quality of management (number of qualified managers, qualification standards, availability of up-to-date training facilities, flexible management structures, computerised management)

– Rates of return, efficiency and level of risk (return on sales and assets, tax share of GDP, evaluation of investments risks, insurance system, performance and its behaviour)

– Standards of science and technology standards (R&D expenditure as a proportion of GDP and the government budget, number and qualifications of research workers, number of patented developments, licence export/import trade balance, standards of science and technology in basic industries, profitability and quality of basic products, consumption of materials and power in production processes per head and its dynamics, pollution and waste recycling)

– Quantity and qualifications of labour resources, quality of life (e.g. ratio of the employed to the unemployed, standards of education and vocational training, range of real incomes, size of middle classes as a proportion of the population, housing conditions, environment and labour conditions, public health, crime, social services)

Some of these guides rely on official statistics, while others are based on expert opinion and specialised surveys. This comprehensive approach is not biased with regard to population or natural wealth. Thus Singapore and Hong Kong rank second and third, respectively, on the list of 48 states in the 1990s due to their high management standards, vigorous enterprising activities and contribution to world economic relations. The USA came to the fore, replacing Japan at the head of the list, due to their achievements in the development and use of advanced technologies as well as their extensive foreign trade. Having lost some competitive merits in performance and wages in the 1990s, Japan now ranks fourth.

The CIS countries were never listed among the more competitive countries before 1995. Russia was the first to be included, coming 48th (below Greece, Mexico, Poland, Hungary and Venezuela). Russia also ranked 42nd in terms of GDP per head, 47th in terms of industrial wages (only ahead of China) and last, although far outperforming other CIS countries, in most socio-economic characteristics.

With respect to the gross national product (GNP) per head in the mid-1990s, the World Bank listed Denmark as the European leader (over $28,000 per year), followed by Germany ($25,500) and Sweden ($23,600). Incomes were lower in Estonia ($2800), Russia ($2600), Poland ($2500), Latvia ($2300) and Lithuania ($1400), immediately followed by Belarus, the Ukraine, Kazakhstan and other CIS countries.

Superior economic development rates in the 1990s (with an annual increase in GDP of over 7%) have been demonstrated by China, Thailand, Malaysia, Vietnam and Indonesia. These countries have formed a new world economic pole. Further economic growth (with an annual increase in GDP of over 1.5%–2%) is evident in the other two economic poles – Western Europe and North America. The contribution made by the CIS to world industrial output decreased from 20% to 10%. However, once the current reforms have been completed successfully, natural and human resources may help the CIS to emerge among the several (three to four) economic poles in the world.

Natural resources. The CIS countries hold almost one quarter of the world's basic natural resources, occupying a prominent place in terms of explored reserves of oil, natural gas, coal, iron and manganese ores, precious, non-ferrous and rare metal ores, potassium chlorides, raw phosphates, diamonds, graphite, mica etc. and in terms of renewable power and fuel resources, fertile land and fresh water.

There are explored reserves of *oil* in Russia (13% of world total), Azerbaijan (over 10%) and Uzbekistan, with exploitation in progress in the Ukraine, Georgia, Moldova and Tajikistan. Since Europe and the USA only have oil reserves to last for 10 years, the Caspian, Tengiz and Karachaganak fields in Kazakhstan and the Sakhalin and Russian Arctic fields are particularly attractive. The Caspian continental shelf (10 billion t oil and 1.9 trillion m^3 gas) may head the world list in the 21st century.

Russia (Yamal Peninsula, Barents and other coastal areas in the North) holds 38% of global reserves of *natural gas*, with more than a further 20% concentrated in Azerbaijan, Turkmenistan, Kazakhstan and Uzbekistan (Caspian and Amudaria oil and gas fields).

Coal supplies in the CIS countries are estimated at 7 trillion t (Donetsk, Pechora, Karaganda, Kuznetsk, Kansk-Achinsk, Tungus, Lena, South Yakutian and other fields). Russia, the Ukraine and Kazakhstan together rank second and third in the world in hard and brown coal output.

There are important deposits of *iron ore* in the Ukraine (Krivoi Rog), Russia (Kursk, Ural, Angara-Ilim and Aldan areas) and Kazakhstan (Kustanai Region), *bauxites* in the Ukraine, Kazakhstan and Russia (North Urals), *manganese* in the Ukraine and Georgia, *copper* in Russia (Siberia), Kazakhstan, Central Asia and Transcaucasia, *nickel* and *cobalt* in Russia (Norilsk and Kola areas), *tin* in Russia (Yakutsk and Magadan regions), *tungsten* and *molybdenum* in Central Asia, North Caucasia and Russia (Far East) and *diamonds* in Russia (Yakutia, North Urals and Archangel region).

Recent years have witnessed the vigorous development of rich *gold* fields: Kumtor in Kyrgyzstan (among the world's ten richest); Vasilkovski in Kazakhstan; Angren and Amaigantau in Uzbekistan; Zeravshan, Aprelevka and

Yakhsu in Tajikistan. Gold fields are abundant in Russia, and exploitation is under way in Armenia and the Ukraine, among others. There is a major *silver* deposit (Bolshoi Kalimansur) in Tajikistan. Russia has the world's richest reserves of *platinum* and *nickel*, and Kazakhstan of *chromium* and *uranium*.

The world's most extensive forest tracts are in Russia and Belarus. Kyrgyzstan, Tajikistan and Russia utilise only 5% of their hydropower potentials.

Of international importance are the reserves of *phosphorites* (Karatau in Kazakhstan), *apatites* (Kola Peninsula), *potassium chlorides* (Belarus and Perm region in Russia) and mineral and clean water (Transcaucasia, Central Asia, Russia).

The world largest tracts of fertile black soils are in the Ukraine, Moldova and South West Russia.

All of the CIS countries are rich in valuable natural resources. However, many essential economic resources (e.g. forest, uranium, manganese, silicon) have been transferred elsewhere.

Human potential in the CIS. According to the CIS Statistics Board, the average annual labour resources (able-bodied and active under- and over-age groups) exceeded 159 million (56% of total population) by 1996. Education and qualification standards are fairly high. The majority (49%) are employed in services, including transport, trade, science and other non-productive spheres (56% in Kazakhstan, 51% in Russia, 49%–54% in Belarus, Azerbaijan and the Ukraine and 38%–42% in Armenia, Uzbekistan and Moldova). Employment rates in industry and construction in 1997 varied between 15% and 20% in Azerbaijan, Moldova and Central Asia and amounted to 34% in Belarus and Russia and 30% in the Ukraine. High employment rates in the agricultural sector (30%–46%) are typical for Azerbaijan, Armenia, Moldova and Central Asia.

Significant changes have been evident in the CIS labour potential and its structure in the 1990s. The period between 1994 and 2000 witnessed the first decrease in the total population, with deaths exceeding births mainly in Russia, the Ukraine and Belarus. Sustained growth was only evident in Armenia, Azerbaijan, Kyrgyzstan, Kazakhstan, Turkmenistan, Tajikistan and Uzbekistan.

Labour migration has been substantial, with the main outflows from Central Asia and Transcaucasia and from the Ukraine and Russia since 1994, although the rates decreased considerably later in the 1990s, in particular from Kyrgyzstan, Armenia and Moldova.

Employment rates have decreased (by 1%–2% in Russia, Moldova, Armenia and Kazakhstan and by 3% in the Ukraine in 1998), with a growing army of unemployed (11% in Kazakhstan and Russia, 8.4% in the Ukraine, with women accounting for 60%–70%).

Employment rates are rising in the private sector, primarily in joint ventures (employing over 1 million in 1998). The private sector was the main employer in Central Asia, Transcaucasia and Moldova in 1998 (60%–72%), accounting for over 47% in the CIS (42% in Russia).

Unlike the rest of the world, the CIS countries have become increasingly rural since 1992. A dramatic decrease in the urban population is evident in Kyrgyzstan (from 38% to 25%), Uzbekistan (from 40% to 38%), Tajikistan (from 31% to 28%) and Armenia. In parallel, absolute rural figures have decreased in Belarus and the Ukraine.

Significantly lower rates of birth and natural growth have been typical for most of the CIS countries in the 1990s. Thus total birth rates in Uzbekistan decreased from 34.5% in 1991 to 29.8% in 1995 (natural growth from 28.3% to 23.4%). Infant mortality (per 1000) varied between 12 and 14 (Belarus, Ukraine) and 32 and 46 (Central Asia, Azerbaijan), as compared to 6 in Japan, Sweden and some other developed countries.

Death rates have been significantly higher in some countries in the 1990s, with a consequent reduction in the population. Between 1991 and 1998, deaths amounted to almost 1.5 million in the Ukraine and 1.440 million in Russia (see Table 1). The population dwindled in Georgia, Kazakhstan, Belarus and Moldova. However, there was a total growth of 2.5 million across the CIS (as against the reduction by 463,000 in 1997).

The CIS offers one of the world's most extensive and least saturated markets. The large proportions of young people in South Central Asia and the Caucasian republics may provide an impetus to further development or, if the reforms fail, social outbursts. The retired account for over 21% in the Ukraine and less than 10% in Central Asia (with more than 40% under 16).

The disintegration of the USSR and armed conflicts in some of the CIS states led to migration, entailing considerable economic losses. Between 1991 and 1996, migration in the territory of the former USSR brought almost 7 million to Russia (e.g. 1.3 million from Kazakhstan, 1.2 million from the Ukraine, 582,000 from Uzbekistan, 306,000 from Azerbaijan and 290,000 from Tajikistan).

The peak outflows (excess of departure over arrival) occurred in 1995 in Azerbaijan (about 25,000 leaving for other CIS or Baltic states and 5,500 arriving), Armenia (10,500 and 3,600), Kazakhstan (208,000 and 68,000), Kyrgyzstan (929,000 and 18,000), Moldova (28,000 and 15,000), Tajikistan (52,500 and 6,500), Uzbekistan (103,000 and 32,000), respectively. Most went to Russia and Belarus. Thus some republics lost many qualified professionals.

With regard to education and professional qualifications, the CIS is ahead of the neighbouring countries, although it does of course differ considerably from more developed countries, in particular the USA, in the number of universities (almost 2000 in the USA) and specialised two-year colleges, training facilities and equipment providing access to the latest achievements in science and technology, as well as in the intensity of undergraduate work. On the other hand, schools and institutions of higher education in Russia and other CIS countries (as the cases of emigrating graduates illustrate) provide superior basic education, comprehensive knowledge, general training in the humanities and team skills.

The CIS countries provide a minimum (modular) standard of required knowledge in each successive stage. As a result, students from Russia and other CIS countries, along with those from Japan and China, often demonstrate superior achievements in various surveys and international comparisons.

In addition, the level of public culture in the CIS is comparatively high. The CIS Statistics Board compared international data of museum visits per thousand population. Museum visits are indicative of reasoned individual demand which cannot be met by television programmes. During the period of reform in the CIS, museum visits decreased one and a half times on average. Nevertheless, in the mid-1990s, the figure in Russia (509) was higher than in Greece or Brazil, in Azerbaijan, Kazakhstan, Moldova and Belarus (205–275) it was higher than in Italy and Spain (105–151), and in the Central Asian countries (43–148) it was far higher than in Iran or Indonesia (20–30).

All these factors benefit science and creative engineering. Scientific and technological potential in the republics of the former USSR actually stems from the post-war period. Thus, between 1940 and 1990, the quantity of research workers per 10,000 increased 8.5-fold in Kazakhstan and the Ukraine, 12-fold in Russia and 21.5-fold in Belarus. In 1990, while engineering standards in some fields of the Soviet economy were lower than in the USA and Western Europe, they were adequate in the military industry complex (MIC) and often superior in the space industry.

1.2 Natural Resources and Production Potential of the CIS Countries

Each of the 12 CIS countries has an abundant supply of natural resources (minerals, fertile land), agricultural and industrial potential and effective communication with adjacent countries.

Azerbaijan (86,600 km^2 in area) borders on Iran, Armenia, Georgia and Russia. One half of its area is taken up by mountains, but conditions in the Kura-Araks and Lenkoran plains are favourable for cotton, subtropical fruit and vegetables, tea and even sericulture.

Among the key industries are oil and gas production (mainly in the Caspian shelf), oil refining, chemical and petrochemical (fertilisers, sulphuric acid, synthetic rubber, and the former USSR's biggest detergent works in Sumgaite), machine building (oil, chemical, electrical engineering), mining (iron ore and alunite), aluminium, light (mainly textile) and food industries. Radio-electronics and instrument-making were well developed in the republic in the 1980s, but the output decreased in the 1990s.

Armenia (29,800 km^2 in area) borders on Turkey, Iran, Azerbaijan and Georgia. Vines, fruit and vegetables are grown in the Ararat valley.

Industry mainly consists of non-ferrous metallurgy (mining plant in Alaverdy, copper-molybdenum works in Kajaran and Agaran, aluminium plant near Erevan), machine building (electrical engineering, instruments, computers, tools, electronics), chemical (synthetic rubber, plastics, synthetic fibres, sulphuric acid, caustic soda, fertilisers), jewellery, light (leather and footwear in particular) and food (wine-making, preserves) industries.

Georgia (69,700 km^2 in area) borders on Turkey, Armenia, Azerbaijan and Russia. Its natural features include the Kolkhida lowland and the forest lands (39% of the total area) in the Major and Minor Caucasus. Conditions on the Black Sea coast and in the mountains are very favourable for citrus plants, tea, vine, fruit and vegetables, recreation and tourism. Oil (Baku-Batumi) and gas mains from Russia (Ciscaucasia) and Azerbaijan have been laid in Georgia. The ports Poti and Batumi are of essential importance both for Georgia and Armenia.

Industry mainly consists of ferrous (Rustavi, Zestafoni) and non-ferrous (e.g. manganese in Chiatura, barite) metallurgy; aircraft (Tbilisi), car (Kutaisi), chemical (Rustavi, Kutaisi), light (Tbilisi, Kutaisi, Gori, Batumi) and food (tea, tobacco, preserves, wine-making, mineral water-bottling) industries.

Georgia abounds in hydropower resources. The electricity transmission line laid in its territory and managed by JV Gruzrosenergo ensures the systematic transmission of electric power between Russia (Stavropol region), Georgia (Inguri hydropower plant – Zestafoni – Idani – TbilGRES), Turkey and, in the future, Armenia, Iran and some other countries too.

Belarus is the sixth largest CIS state (207,600 km^2), bordering on Poland, Lithuania, the Ukraine and Russia. The Polesie lowland constitutes the greater part of the area. Belarus ranks high among the CIS countries both in its industrial and agricultural potential (e.g. milk and meat, potatoes, vegetables, flax).

Among the more developed industries are car and tractor building (Minsk, Zhodino, Mogilev), instrument-making and radio-electronics (including television sets, refrigerators, computers), oil refining and petrochemistry, fertilisers, synthetic fibres (Svetlogorsk, Mogilev, Novopolotsk), potash fertilisers and woodworking (Bobruisk, Borisov, Vitebsk, Gomel). There are developed light (textile, knitted wear, leather, footwear) and food (meat, butter and fat products, preserves, starch and treacle) industries using local raw materials.

Kazakhstan, the second largest CIS country (2,724,900 km²), lies in the Caspian and Turan lowlands on the southern outskirts of the West Siberian plain. It borders on China, Russia, Uzbekistan and Kyrgyzstan. Among the rivers are the Irtysh, Ural, Chu, Syrdaria; in the west the country reaches the Caspian Sea. Among the important natural features are the large Balkhash Lake and the Aral Sea in the south.

Kazakhstan is unique in mineral wealth, including oil (Tengiz and other major fields in the Caspian area), non-ferrous and rare metals (e.g. chromites, copper, lead, zinc, bauxites), iron ores (Sokolov-Sarbai and Lisakovo deposits), coal (Karaganda and some other fields), gold, manganese, uranium, phosphorites and natural gas.

These provide the basis for the development of non-ferrous (Balkhash, Jezkazgan, Ust-Kamenogorsk and Chimkent works) and ferrous (e.g. Temirtau, Aktiubinsk) metallurgy, chemical (Karatau, Chimkent, Jambul), mining and coal industries. Machine building works in Alma-Ata, Pavlodar, Karaganda and some other towns support the industries and agriculture.

Kazakhstan's agricultural complex specialises in grain crops (36 million hectares mainly in northern regions), sheep-breeding (35 million grazing in the steppes in the 1980s) and cotton, rice and sugar-beet (2 million hectares mainly in southern regions). These support the meat and milk, sugar and other food industries and light industry.

Kyrgyzstan (199,900 km² in area) borders on China, Tajikistan, Uzbekistan and Kazakhstan. A large part of the territory is occupied by the Pamir-Altay and Tyang-Shang mountains. Intensive farming is developed in the Chu, Talass, Alai and Fergana valleys. Arable lands comprise 60% of the 1.3 million hectares under crop. While sugar-beet, tobacco and cotton are cultivated, special emphasis is placed on sheep-breeding (10 million in the 1980s).

The republic's wealth lies in its hydropower resources. The most powerful hydroelectric station Toktogul was constructed on the Naryn River. The picturesque Issyk-Kul Lake is navigable.

Among the more important mineral resources are gold, polymetals, mercury and antimony. They support the country's mining industry, mainly gold-mining.

Kyrgyzstan operates several instrument-making and electrical engineering works supplying accessories for the VPK in Russia and large agricultural engineering plants. Among other well-developed industries are meat production, flour and sugar mills.

Moldova is a comparatively small (33,800 km² in area) but densely populated republic bordering on Romania and the Ukraine. The fertile lands (one third represented by black soils) favour cultivation of vines, fruit, berries, vegetables (e.g. tomatoes, pepper, green peas) and tobacco. Meat and milk production is well developed. There are many fish ponds between the rivers Dniester and Prut.

In the 1970s and 1980s, Moldova developed high-technology industries (instrument-making, radio-electronics, electrical engineering), co-operating with MIC enterprises in Russia, the Ukraine and Byelorussia; tractor building (Kishinev), chemical, light, cement and some other industries were also developed. However, Moldova is generally known for its wines and brandies and for preserved fruit and vegetables, tobacco and confectionery.

The energetics involves the Dubossary and Moldavian hydropower stations, but domestic power resources are insufficient. Gas and oil pipelines to Romania and on to the Balkans have been laid in Moldova.

Russia is the world's largest country by area (17,075,400 km^2) and has the fifth largest population (after China, India, the USA and Indonesia); it lies both in Europe and Asia, in the Eastern and in part (in the extreme North-East) in the Western hemispheres. Many areas in Siberia and the Far East are in the permafrost zone. Temperatures in the different regions of Russia average between −1° and −50°C in January, and +1° and +25°C in July.

Russia borders on the seas of three oceans. The main ports are in the Baltic (St. Petersburg, Kaliningrad), Barents (Murmansk), White (Archangel), Black (Novorossiisk) and Far East seas (Vladivostok, Nakhodka, Magadan). There is ship traffic on the major rivers (the Volga, North Dvina, Don, Pechora, Ob, Irtysh, Enisey, Angara, Lena, Amur, Neva), lakes (e.g. Ladoga, Onega, Baikal) and waterways (Belomoro-Baltiisk, Volgo-Don, Volgo-Baltic).

Russia has a fairly extensive (over 4000 km) frontier with China, also bordering on Norway, Finland – the only CIS frontier with a member state of the European Union (EU) – and all the CIS countries except for Moldova, Armenia, Turkmenistan, Tajikistan and Kyrgyzstan.

Russia's mineral wealth is estimated at $15 trillion. Among the more important resources are natural gas (40% of world reserves – West Siberian, Pechora-Timan, Volga-Ural, Sakhalin fields and the Yamal Peninsula), coal (Kuznetsk, Irsha-Borodinsk, South Yakutian and many other fields), iron ore, diamonds (in Yakutia and North European area), non-ferrous, rare and precious metals (in Siberia, mainly in the North, and in the Far East), apatites (Kola Peninsula), phosphorites and potassium chlorides.

Over 44% of the area (749 million hectares) is covered by forest. Russia is among the world leaders in commercial fish and game resources.

Russia has the world's largest available mining industry, with related ferrous (e.g. Magnitogorsk, Chelyabinsk, Nizhni Tagil, Novokuznetsk, Cherepovets, Lipetsk), aluminuim (e.g. Bratsk, Sayanogorsk, Krasnoyarsk, Achinsk) and other non-ferrous metallurgies (e.g. Norilsk, Krasnoyarsk, Irkutsk), chemistry and petrochemistry (e.g. plastics, fertilisers, chemical fibres, tyres).

The more advanced industries include aircraft (Moscow, Saratov, Kazan, Ulyanovsk, Ulan-Ude, Komsomolsk on the Amur, Voronezh, Samara) and space rocket, car (Togliatti, Nizhni Novgorod, Moscow, Myass, Ulyanovsk) and tractor building (e.g. Volgograd, Chelyabinks), shipbuilding (e.g. St. Petersburg, Kaliningrad, Nizhni Novgorod, Severodvinsk), heavy machinery (Yekaterinburg, St. Petersburg, Moscow, Novosibirsk, Krasnoyarsk), instrument-making and radio-electronics (Moscow, St. Petersburg, the Urals, Volga Region, West Siberia).

Russia is among the world's major producers of saw-timber (Ust-Ilimsk, Bratsk, Archangel and some other complexes), cellulose and paper (Archangel, Leningrad, Vologda and some other regions), cement and other building materials, textiles (e.g. Ivanovo, Kostroma, Yaroslav region, Moscow, St. Petersburg), clothes and footwear.

Russia's integrated power system is supplied by hydroelectric power stations (GESs) on the Enisey (Krasnoyarsk, Sayano-Shushenskaia), Volga, Angara, nuclear power stations (AESs) (e.g. Leningrad, Novovoronezh, Balakovo) and thermoelectric power stations (TETs).

The areas under crop comprise over 125 million hectares, although cultivated lands account for only 13% of the total area (47% in the USA and 56% in the EU), including 7% under crop (20% in the USA and 35% in the EU). Major crops include grain (wheat, rye, barley, oats, and rice and maize in the south), potatoes, vegetables (e.g. cabbages, root crops), sugar-beet and sunflower. However, southern regions (Stavropol, Kuban, Volga, West Siberia) are exposed to frequent droughts, and the Non-Chernozem Zone is subject to abundant damp. Commercial poultry- and cattle-breeding received real impetus in the 1980s using imported forage. It was tremendously affected by the transition to a market-oriented economy, due to increased transport and power costs and reduced State subsides.

Tajikistan (143,100 km^2 in area) borders on China, Afghanistan, Turkmenistan, Uzbekistan and Kyrgyzstan. It is a predominantly mountainous country, with the Turkestan, Zeravshan, Gissar and Alay ranges and the Alpine Pamir. Between the mountains lie the fertile Vakhsh, Gissar and other valleys.

The republic is unique in terms of its hydropower reserves, with the rivers Syrdaria, Amudaria, Zeravshan and Pyandj, among others, fed by mountain glaciers. In addition to the functioning Nurek, Varzob, Kairakkum and some other hydroelectric power stations, there are even more powerful ones (e.g. Rogun, Sangutdin), although these are not yet finished. They do not require virgin lands to be flooded to supply inexpensive energy to other Central Asian countries and their southern neighbours; in addition, they control river flow, thus ensuring the well-being of millions of people.

The mere 800,000 hectares under crop include 600,000 hectares of arable land. Fine cotton and volatile oil-bearing plants (including the unusually flavoured Tajik lemons) are cultivated, and sericulture is well developed.

Tajikistan is unrivalled in silver-containing ores (Big Kalimansur), gold, rare and non-ferrous metals, antimony, etc.

The country's industrial potential is based on one of the world's biggest aluminium works (Tursunzade town), advanced chemical (e.g. Yavan town), light (cotton-cleaning, cotton fabrics, silk mills, carpet-making) and food (preserves, butter, fat products) industries and mechanical engineering (transformers, light and food engineering). Over 70% of the industrial potential is within the North Khodjent region with its non-ferrous metallurgy (Chkalovsk town).

Turkmenistan has an extensive frontier with Iran, Afghanistan, Kazakhstan, Uzbekistan and Tajikistan. Most of its 491,200 km^2 area consists of a low plain reaching the Caspian Sea in the west and the Kopetdag mountains in the south. The Karakum Desert forms a large part of the plain.

The main natural resources are oil, gas and various chemical supplies, in particular mirabylite (Kara-Bogaz-Gol Bay). The Turkmenbashi (formerly Krasnovodsk) port facility in the Caspian Sea and the oil and gas pipelines currently being laid support export trade in valuable raw materials.

There are more than 500,000 hectares of arable land, with the topography allowing for extension involving the Karakum canal from the Amudaria River and using both groundwater and desalinated sea water. Fine cotton (the only other CIS country apart from Uzbekistan) and grapes, fruit, melon and gourd plantations are cultivated. Astrakhan sheep-breeding and sericulture are well developed. An advanced grain programme was initiated in the 1990s.

The key industries are the oil/gas, chemical, light (cotton, silk, wool, carpet-making) and food industries and construction materials.

Uzbekistan (447,400 km^2 in area) takes up the largest part of the Turand lowland, Kyzylkum Desert, and Tyang-Shang and Gissar-Altay spurs in the south, bordering on Afghanistan, Tajikistan, Turkmenistan and Kazakhstan. The major rivers are the Amudaria and Syrdaria. The Fergana, Zeravshan, Chirchik-Angren and some other valleys are extremely fertile. Arable land accounts for 3.3 million of the 4 million hectares under crop, ensuring good yields of cotton, kenaf and other industrial crops, along with rice, grapes, garden plants, melon and gourd plants and vegetables. The number of sheep exceeded 7 million in the 1980s.

There are abundant reserves of natural gas (Bokhara and Kashkadaria regions), oil, gold and other non-ferrous and rare metals.

Among the key industries are agricultural engineering, electrical engineering, car and aircraft building, construction and road engineering and metallurgy (including uranium). Uzbekistan has advanced chemical (e.g. fertilisers, synthetic fibres, plastics), light (cotton-cleaning, cotton and wool), food and construction materials industries.

The **Ukraine** is one of the largest (603,700 km^2) and second most populated CIS country, featuring the Volyn, Podol, Dniester and Azov plains, the Polessk, Dnieper and Black Sea lowlands, the Donetsk mountain ridge and the Crimean and Carpathian mountains. The major rivers are the Dnieper, South Boug, North Donets, Prut and Dniester and the Danube estuary.

The area under crop exceeds 33 million hectares, with black soils comprising over half of this. Grain crops (e.g. wheat, barley, millet, rice, buckwheat), sunflower, sugar-beet, fruit and berries are cultivated.

The Ukraine abounds in coal (Donetsk, Lvov-Volyn and Dnieper fields), iron ore (one half of the former USSR's coal output in Krivoi Rog), manganese (one third of the former USSR's supply) and explored reserves of oil and gas (mainly in the marine shelf).

The Ukraine features advanced power engineering (e.g. the Khmelnitsk and some other nuclear power stations, the hydroelectric power cascade on the Dnieper, the Uglegorsk, Zaporozhie, Krivoi Rog, Burshtyn, Zmiev nuclear power stations). The country has major port facilities (Odessa, Ilyichevsk, Kherson, Nikolaev, Izmail, Kerch, Reni, Mariupol). Ship traffic occurs on the Dnieper, Danube, Desna, Pripyat and Dniester. Oil and gas mains from Russia and southern CIS states to Western Europe, the Balkans and Turkey have been laid in the Ukraine.

Particularly well developed are ferrous (Donetsk-Dnieper region) and non-ferrous metallurgies, chemical (fertilisers, sulphuric acid, caustic soda, plastics, chemical fibres, dyes), food (sugar, butter and fat products, meat and preserves), light, woodworking and cement industries. The Ukraine occupies a prominent place among the CIS countries in shipbuilding (e.g. Nikolaev, Kherson, Kerch), heavy and agricultural engineering, car building (e.g. Lvov, Zaporozhie, Lutsk), lathe building, instrument-making and transport engineering (e.g. Lugansk).

High technologies are employed in aircraft (Antonov design bureau with the AN), space-rocket, electronic and other industries.

1.3 Industry in the CIS Countries in the Twentieth Century

Industry as a basis for the economy. Since the first industrial revolution in the late eighteenth century, industry has provided a basis for economic development. The examples of England as the world's workshop in the nineteenth century and the USA as its twentieth-century counterpart look set to be followed by Southeast Asia in the 21st century. The industrial bastions of the past maintain and further develop their high-technology industries, thus retaining their roles as financial, scientific, technological and cultural poles in the world.

Pre-revolutionary Russia was a medium-developed industrial country, neither virgin territory in industrial terms nor an economic miracle. Despite the fairly high industrial growth rates (annual rates of 5%) and the immense natural and human resources of Imperial Russia before World War I, output per capita was eightfold less than in the USA, three- to fourfold less than in England and Germany and twofold less than in France.

There was no industrial diversification at the turn of the century. With the advanced textile mills (e.g. Moscow, Ivanovo, St. Petersburg, Kostroma), metallurgy (the Urals and the Ukraine), petroleum industry (Baku), shipbuilding and engineering (Central Russia and East Ukraine), high-technology industries (by the standards of the time) such as motorcars, tractor-building and instrument-making were typically non-existent. Industrial enterprises were located atomistically, i.e. in central, south and north west regions of Russia, in the Donetsk-Dnieper area and Baku. In the vast expanses of Siberia, the Far East and Turkestan, only domestic crafts were carried out.

The low specialisation and industrial infrastructure standards also deserve mention. Unlike the USA and West European countries, general-purpose and mainly State-owned works such as Izhorski, Putilov and Obukhovski in Petersburg prevailed, producing anything from iron-clads and ordnance to spades, axes and shakos and never co-operating with small- or medium-scale businesses.

A strong dependence on foreign investment and equipment was particularly evident in engineering. Immediately before World War I, more or less up-to-date cotton-cleaning plants, silk mills and repair shops emerged in Turkestan and light and food industries in Byelorussia, Georgia and Armenia.

The GOELRO Plan was the country's first comprehensive programme of industrialisation, designed to create sizeable mechanised industries employing new technologies (overall electrification of the public economy) to guarantee the industrial focus.

Principal phases of industrialisation. Modern CIS member states were subject to several schemes of government regulation of industry after 1917.

One (1918–1921) involved direct control by government departments – chief directorates and centres, actually ignoring market mechanisms ("exchange of commodities"). The "War Communism" was the outcome of the Civil War and the prevailing ideology, an embodied dream of capitalism crushed in a charge by the Red Guards, eliminating market mechanisms and exercising day-to-day centralised control of commodity flows. As a result, output was decimated by 1921, and the people starved.

Another system of governance (the New Economic Policy, NEP, initiated in 1921) involved, in an industrial sense, the following: firstly, multiple ownership types (foreign concessions and small-scale private businesses); secondly, trusts (combining factories, works and design offices generally within a single branch) and syndicates (purchase and sales corporations); and thirdly, overall profit and loss management (economic independence of the State, free choice of suppliers and buyers, partly including international markets).

In the 5–6 years of NEP, output reached that of the pre-war (1914) level again, mainly in the light, food and timber industries, construction materials, fertilisers and primitive agricultural engineering. However, the NEP failed to provide sufficient accumulations and incentives for the extensive industrialisation and development of heavy industry.

Resolutions passed by the Fourteenth Congress of the VKP(b)/All-Russia Communist Party (Bolsheviks) to launch the industrialisation policy provided for the quickest possible elimination of import trade in machinery and equipment, making the country an independent economic entity rather than mere appendage of the international capitalist economy and a powerful revolutionary instrument for the workers of all lands and oppressed colonial and semi-colonial nations. This meant political rather than economic goals. The accelerated pace of industrialisation demanded external rather than internal industrial sources of capital accumulation, i.e. non-equivalent confiscation of agricultural produce, export trade in grain and cultural property, unpaid forced labour.

With some minor modifications, the 1929–1932 pattern of restricted economic autonomy survived into the 1980s. The trusts and syndicates were dissolved, with their economic functions assigned to production units – factories, works, mines, etc. Intermediate administrative units (chief directorates) were established within ministerial departments. Government regulation was replaced by direct administration: rigid planning first of the range of products, supply, sales and prices, then of average wages and in 1932 even of standard output. Since economic autonomy could no longer be extended to capital investments and decisions were now taken by the State, calculating return on assets made no sense. Economic incentives and responsibilities were only related to fulfilling the tasks assigned "from above". Industrialisation involved the following radical changes across the whole economic structure, ensuring the country's engineering and economic independence and subsequent victory in the Patriotic War (World War II):

– Industry became the key element of the public economy (over 70% of GDP), industrial output holding a firm second place in the world between the 1940s and the 1980s, with 99.8% contributed by State-owned enterprises.

– The industries grew in number from 40 in 1914 through 150 in 1940 to 300 in 1970, with heavy industry accounting for over 70% of the total output; under the pre-war 5-year plans, 12,000 sizeable enterprises were built or radically renovated in metallurgy (e.g. Magnitogorsk, Kuznetsk, Nizhni Tagil, Mariupol) and the chemical (e.g. Berezniki, Voskresensk, Novomoskovs, Chimkent), tractor building (e.g. Stalingrad, Kharkov, Chelyabinsk) and motorcar building (e.g. Moscow, Gorky) and other industries.

– The contributions made by the eastern (across the Urals) and southern areas to the total output increased from 8% to 40%, ensuring in 1943– despite the army retreating to the Volga and Caucasus – superiority in tanks, ordnance and aircraft over Germany by utilising almost the entire European potential.

– The engineering staff grew from 90 in the 1930s to 2,800 in the 1960s, with qualified workers increasing more than tenfold, thus ensuring compliance with superior world standards in some fields of precision engineering, high-quality metallurgy and special chemistry.

Industry in the post-war period. On the other hand, industry in the USSR failed to ensure sustainable economic growth and a high quality of life during peace, and much less so under the conditions of the market economy. This was impeded by the following: the predominant extensive development type (more construction projects, more natural resources utilised, more jobs), intensive use of materials, inferior quality of civil products, aggravated by the overall shortages and isolation from the world markets (manufacturing industries contributing to the export market five- to tenfold less than those in the West).

Soviet industry focused on giant enterprises. The post-war Orsk-Khalilov and Cherepovets metallurgical, Shchekino and Nevinnomyssk chemical, Tajik aluminium and many other plants were inefficient by social and environmental criteria. Thus, for instance, raw materials were transported long distances from Central Asia to be processed in the European region. Abortive reforms in the late 1950s and later in the 1970s were not crowned with success, involving the replacement of some projected parameters rather than systematic economic change.

In the post-war period, the country began production of nuclear reactors, space instruments, electronic and micro-electronic devices and laser equipment. However, on the whole, industry ceased to serve as a basis for sustainable economic growth as far back as the 1980s. With almost 70% of the labour force engaged in mining and processing to manufacture military and space equipment instead of means of production and consumer goods (as compared to one half in the USA and one tenth in Japan and Germany), industry was no longer cost-efficient. Industrial structures were characterised by the contribution made by the mining/metallurgy complex being the highest among the developed countries and computer, electronic and instrument-making industries and services being increasingly laggard. The distribution of sites involved long-distant transport of raw materials from Central Asia northward or from East Siberia and Far East westward and then of finished products back. Isolation from the world market meant that the national economy ceased to be competitive, and by the early 1990s the energy, metal and water resources and work costs per unit of profit were two- to threefold higher than in developed industrial countries.

Structural reform was an urgent necessity, because later in the 1980s only 20%–25% of enterprises were able to sell their products at world market prices.

Industry in the CIS in the 1990s. Economic characteristics in the CIS countries deteriorated significantly between 1990 and 1994 (see Table 2). The GDP dropped by 40%, while net product (less all material costs) and industrial output almost halved. A dramatic downturn in production was evident in an almost threefold reduction in freight turnover (excluding pipelines).

The GDP in the CIS increased by 0.7% in 1997. Increases were seen in Armenia in 1994, in Georgia in 1995, in Azerbaijan, Belarus, Kazakhstan, Kyrgyzstan and Uzbekistan in 1996 and in Russia, Moldova and Tajikistan in 1997. However, the past decline was so strong that a comparison between the 1988–1990 and the 1998 GDP in individual CIS countries shows an increase of only 55% (1997 level), including 29% (1968 level) in Georgia, 31% (1970) in Tajikistan, 36% (1965) in Azerbaijan, 42% in the Ukraine (1977) and 58% (1980) in Russia.

As a result, the Commonwealth moved from the second to fifth in the world (below the USA, Japan, China and Germany) in industrial output, ranking at the bottom of the first 100 in GDP per capita (about $1000 per year as compared to $4000 in Czech Republic and Hungary, $20,000 in the EU member states and $25,000 in the USA).

The downturn was due to a range of circumstances. Government purchases of industrial goods were reduced drastically, including both military products and capital construction (almost halved).

The purchasing power of the population and agricultural demand, etc. dwindled. In 3 short years, prices for industrial produce rose by a factor of 2200 (see Table 2), and commodity turnover decreased at over 50% in legal trade (excluding the "shuttle" import traders) and almost tripled in services (see Table 2). According to EU consumers' unions taking the purchasing power of the Austrian population as 100, Switzerland and the USA had a purchasing power of over 120, Japan 106, Australia, Italy, the Netherlands, Germany and France between 90 and 98, Turkey and Greece between 56 and 58, the Czech Republic 44, Hungary 31, Russia 26, Moldova 11, etc.

Table 2

Basic Social and Economic Indices in the CIS from 1992 to 1994
(taking 1991 values as 100 in comparable prices)

	1992	1993	1994
Gross domestic product (GDP)	82	73	61
Net product	80	70	58
Industrial output	82	72	56
Industrial producers' price index (Ч)	21	239	2202
Agricultural output	91	89	78
Investments	61	55	41
Cargo shipped by national transport (excluding pipelines)	74	53	36
Retail trade turnover of legally registered enterprise	65	59	55
Services of legally registered enterprises	62	44	30
Exports[1] to outside the CIS	100	99.7	112
Imports[1] from outside the CIS	100	74	77

[1] As a percentage of 1992 values in nominal prices of that time.

Later in the 1990s, the characteristics of economic development gradually improved. The GDP and industrial output increased in two CIS countries in 1995, in eight in 1996 and in ten between 1997 and 1998 (see Table 3).

In 1998, industrial output increased in Transcaucasia and Central Asia. The 1991 level was regained in Uzbekistan, but Azerbaijan, Armenia, Kazakhstan and Kyrgyzstan only recovered 45%–47%, and Georgia and Tajikistan less than 20% of their respective levels. Belarus attained 60% of the 1991 level. The financial crisis resulted in decreased output in Russia, the Ukraine and Moldova (only 37% of the 1991 level).

The slump was also related to deteriorated markets within the CIS. Export markets were also reduced, although by no means as dramatically as exchange with neighbouring countries.

Table 3

Main Indices of Economic Development in the CIS Countries between 1995 and 1998 (as a percentage of the preceding year)

Country	GDP			Industrial output				Investments				Foreign debt as a % of GDP		GDP	
	1995	1996	1997	1995	1996	1997	1998	1995	1996	1997	1998	1995	1997	1997 (as a % of 1990)	1998 (as a % of 1997)
Azerbaijan	83	101	106	83	94	100.3	102	57	180	167	145	46	68	36	110
Armenia	107	106	103	102	102	101	97.5	...	103	...	...	93	49	55	107
Belarus	90	101	110	88	103	118	111	59	92	120	116	18	16[3]	72	108
Georgia	102	110	111	91	103	108	97	103	110	187	200	69	32	29	103
Kazakhstan	91	101	102	92	191	104	98	63	65	119	113	20	19	63	97.5
Kyrgyzstan	94	105	110	82	111	147	108	182	130	65	47	35	63	60	102
Moldova[1]	97	97	101	94	100	98	89	83	85	94	100	65	105[3]	36	91.4
Russia	96	95	100.4	97	96	102	95	90	82	95	93	34	30	58	95.4
Tajikistan	88	80	101	95	80	97.5	108	75	75	90[2]	...	216	151	31	105
Turkmenistan	90	100	85[2]	93	120	70	...	100	105	104[2]	...	212	114	...	...
Uzbekistan	99	102	105	100	106	106.5	106	104	100	117	115	21	28	87	104
Ukraine	88	93	97	83	96	98.2	98.5	65	85	93	105	29	24[3]	42	98.3

[1] Data of the left-bank Dniester area and Bendery omitted hereafter.
[2] Estimated.
[3] Including outstanding debts for power resources.

Upon disintegration of the USSR, industrial output in the CIS countries decreased more significantly than it had done in the war years 1941–1945 when the Ukraine, Belarus and most of European Russia was invaded. Moreover, the downturn was heterogeneous, having a more significant impact on the research-intensive manufacturing industries that determine overall national economic competitiveness as we approach the 21st century. The CIS countries lost over 300 developments and establishments in aerospace and robot engineering, information and biotechnologies and up-to-date materials. In 1998, the CIS contributed less than 1% of world lathe building, coming fifth on the list (below Japan, Germany, the USA and Italy). Most manufacturers of optical instruments, electronic devices, etc. were closed down. The output of textiles, footwear, clothes and home equipment was decimated. Three quarters of CIS market demand was met by imported and not necessarily top-quality goods.

Nonetheless, output stabilised later in the 1990s, even increasing in the oil and gas, mining, chemical, metallurgical, timber, and cellulose and paper industries, i.e. those involving non-renewable natural resources, most significant pollution and hard labour. The contribution made by the fuel and energy complex (FEC) to CIS output totals doubled (32% vs. 16.5%), with a corresponding decrease in high-tech industries, an opposite trend to that occurring in more developed countries. Two industrial complexes have taken shape to date: the raw materials-based and export-oriented complex and the manufacturing complex have no secure market niche. This has determined the change in the role of the CIS in the international division of labour (to be discussed in more detail in Chaps. 6, 9).

1.4 The CIS in World Economic Relationships

Competitive advantages of CIS economies. The roles played by individual regions or countries in the international division of labour are determined by the competitive advantages of their economies. One absolute merit of the Commonwealth economy is the availability of resources lacking on international markets. Among the most important are oil, natural gas, timber (Russia and Belarus having over one quarter of global forest reserves), iron ore, non-ferrous ores (e.g. nickel, titanium, chromium, manganese, copper, molybdenum), rare and precious metal ores, crude chemicals, land suitable for farming and building construction and fresh water.

The CIS is a large market for goods and services. An important advantage is its geography, having the shortest land and sea (in the Arctic Ocean) passage from Europe to Southeast Asia, with the latter set to become a world economic pole in the 21st century.

The relative competitive advantages include inexpensive labour and energy resources. However, these are only beneficial if qualified and disciplined staff and resource-saving technologies are available; if production is labour, material and energy intensive, particularly with domestic prices for resources approaching world prices, these advantages become negligible.

The CIS is a medium-developed economic region, i.e. listed below many North American, Western European and Southeast Asian countries but above most regions in Asia and South America. For instance, in the mid-1990s, the GNP per head amounted to $25,000 in Japan and the USA, $15,000–20,000 in the EU member states, $10,000–12,000 in South Korea and Taiwan, $4000–5000 in the Czech Republic and Hungary, $3500 in Poland and the Baltic states, $2700 in Russia and $1000–2000 or even less in other CIS countries.

When comparing the GDP in the CIS and developed countries, however, the differences in estimating procedures and available information should be taken into account. Developed countries estimate GDP on the basis of final returns. Such estimates would be incorrect in CIS countries because of inadequate cash flows, banking and other financial statistics, multiple cases of concealed gain to evade taxation (in private trade and services, and often in other spheres, almost every other account is settled in cash, circumventing banks and the tax authorities), mass-scale arrears, etc. As a result, according to the World Bank, the actual GDP decline across the CIS between 1991 and 1996 (accounting for real volumes of exports/imports, unregistered foreign trade intermediaries, the private sector in general) was a quarter below the official statistical data.

Statistical data about the construction materials and electricity consumed are far more indicative than returns reported by the business units themselves. Considerable gains from "shuttle" and border trade are generally omitted in official statistics.

The findings from a comparative analysis across the CIS are shown in Table 4.

In terms of economic scale, since Russia accounts for more than half of the CIS population and over 60% of overall national income (of all the CIS countries), it differs radically from other CIS countries. Five CIS countries (Russia, the Ukraine, Kazakhstan, Uzbekistan and Belarus) contribute 94% of national incomes in the CIS, with only 6% shared by the remaining seven.

In terms of economic development (described here by national income per capita, productivity of labour and consumption of goods and services per head as a percentage of the CIS average), Belarus, Russia and the Ukraine lead the field, with Tajikistan and some of the other CIS countries lagging far behind.

Between 1993 and 1996, the lag decreased in Belarus (with the figure increasing from 54% to 68%) and Uzbekistan (from 28 to 31%), but increased in Georgia (from 51% to 38%), Kazakhstan (from 83% to 65%), Tajikistan (from 15% to 9.4%) and particularly in the Ukraine (from 79% to 45%) and Moldova (from 36% to 19%). In Russia, GDP per capita was 140% of the CIS average in 1993 and 155% in 1996.

Table 4

**Comparative Characteristics of Development in the CIS Countries
in the mid-1990s (as a percentage of the CIS average)**

Country	Popula-tion (mil.)	Includ-ing Russian	National income per capita	National income total	Labour produc-tivity	Consump-tion of goods and services per capita
Russia	148	115	155	61	108	118
Ukraine	59	11.4	44	18	96	102
Belarus	10	1.3	68	4.7	113	129
Moldova	4.4	0.6	19	1.2	75	85
Armenia	3.4	0.05	22	0.6	76	52
Azerbaijan	7.1	0.4	22	1.7	79	58
Kazakhstan	17	6.2	65	5.2	98	75
Uzbekistan	21	1.7	31	5	74	60
Georgia	5.5	0.3	38	...	...	...
Tajikistan	5.4	0.3	9.4	0.6	49	39
Kyrgyzstan	4.5	0.9	20	1	85	54
Turkmenistan	3.7	0.3	21	1	92	65
Total in the CIS	289	138.5	100	100	100	100

Different CIS countries face different challenges. Reforms in some states are impeded by major regional differences and quite often by historical opposition by ethnic cultural groups or clans (in Russia, the Ukraine, Moldova, Kazakhstan, Kyrgyzstan, Tajikistan and Georgia). When aggravated by erratic national policies, these have resulted in dramatic conflicts leading to streams of refugees and forced emigration (e.g. in Azerbaijan, Armenia, Georgia and Tajikistan).

In some CIS states (Armenia, Moldova, the Ukraine and Belarus), energy resources are in very short supply, especially oil products and gas, while the primary concerns in others are transport facilities (Armenia and Tajikistan) or national migration to adjacent states (Russia, Kazahstan, Tajikistan, Uzbekistan and Turkmenistan).

Many CIS countries (the Transcaucasian republics, Tajikistan and Turkmenistan) have a permanent need for imports of basic foodstuffs, in particular grain.

Integration in world economic relationships. Access by the CIS countries to the world market is influenced by the following factors:

– The total volume of export/import transactions, both as a percentage of GDP and per head, and its dynamics

– The export/import ratio (net balance of trade)

– The export structure (share of manufacturing goods, services, research and technology products)

– The import structure (share of research and technology products, equipment, high technologies)

– The production structure of foreign trade (ratio between sales of finished products and transactions of international co-operation in the development, production and sales of goods and services)

– Geographic diversification (distribution of foreign relations)

– The ratio of paid and received money (net balance of payments)

– The amount of export national debt, both as a percentage of GDP and per head, and its dynamics

On the face of it, the integration of the CIS countries in the world economy represents the major achievement of independent economic policies. Exports from the CIS countries totalled $80 billion in the mid-1990s.

However, the total volume of foreign trade is inconsistent with their economic potential. The CIS countries account for only 4.5% of world trade, half as much as their share of world population. Annual exports of goods and services to outside the CIS per head in the Commonwealth in the mid-1990s only averaged $277 ($443 in Russia, $172 in Belarus, $141 in Kazakhstan, $125 in Turkmenistan, $108 in the Ukraine, $85 in Tajikistan, $75 in Uzbekistan, $64 in Moldova, $44 in Azerbaijan, $31 in Kyrgyzstan, $28 in Armenia and $13 in Georgia).

In terms of contribution to international trade turnover, Belarus heads the list, with transactions per head amounting to $1548 in 1997, followed by Russia ($944), Kazakhstan ($669), the Ukraine ($619) and Moldova ($476). The average across the CIS is $734 compared to $4000–6000 in the UK, Germany and Italy.

The share of exported finished goods and services and of accessories decreased, while that of raw materials increased.

The share of imported consumer goods increased (including luxury goods such as luxury cars, jewellery, cosmetics, confectionery, alcohol and other beverages), with investment products and up-to-date equipment both decreasing.

Some CIS countries either depend on imported goods or have lost their independent food supply.

A number of CIS countries have unfavourable balances of trade and payments, importing more goods and services than they export and covering commodity deficits with foreign loans and humanitarian aid.

Export market structure. Goods with high added value constitute a minor part of CIS exports (see Table 5).

Table 5

**Share of Goods with High Added Value in the CIS Export Markets
(as a percentage of total exports) in the mid-1990s**

Country	Machinery and equipment		Transport		Instruments and tools		Plastics, rubber, elastics		Ready-made foodstuffs	
	Total	To CIS countries	Total	To CIS countries	Total	To CIS countries	Total	To CIS countries	Total	To CIS countries
Azerbaijan	7.1	16.1	1.1	1.7	0.3	0.8	2.5	4.9	4.4	9.3
Armenia	14.8	...	4.3	...	1.5	...	4.1	...	4.8	...
Belarus	13.4	18.1	15.9	20.0	1.4	0.8	5.4	5.6	2.3	3.0
Kazakhstan	2.8	4.9	1.1	2.0	0.2	0.2	1.1	1.8	1.2	2.0
Kyrgyzstan	7.3	10.1	1.8	2.6	0.3	0.5	0.5	0.7	20.7	30.0
Moldova	6.2	7.7	1.7	2.3	0.2	0.3	0.6	0.6	51.3	58.6
Russia	4.8	13.4	5.1	5.8	0.3	0.7	1.9	4.3	0.7	1.5
Uzbekistan	1.5	3.2	1.2	2.8	0.0	0.1	0.2	0.4	1.2	2.5
Ukraine	11.8	...	6.4	...	0.5	...	2.8	...	8.5	...

Export trade generally involves raw materials. Crude oil (re-exported from Russia), oil products, fertilisers and chemicals account for almost one third of the volume of exports in Belarus; hard coal, crude oil, oil products, ferroalloys, copper and black copper alloys, nickel and alumina account for 52% in Kazakhstan; cotton fibre, wool and raw antimony for 50% in Kyrgyzstan; crude oil, oil products and natural gas for 42% in Russia; and oil products, cotton fibre and rolled steel plate for 81% in Azerbaijan. Almost the whole (98%) of the volume of exports in Tajikistan is represented by cotton fibre and alumina; 90% by cotton fibre and oil products in Turkmenistan; and 81% by cotton fibre in Uzbekistan. The proportion of machines, equipment, transport and instruments is insignificant (between 1% and 17%).

Patterns of structural change in the economies of developed countries can be inferred from the corporate gains and stock index (exchange rate behaviour) in various branches. In 1996, the *Financial Times* quoted the largest gains (profit rates over 20%) of 44 beverage and tobacco manufacturers, medical services, cosmetics and software and hardware suppliers. These were followed (profitability between 14% and 19%) by 82 corporations specialising in communications, diversified chemical engineering, electronics, heavy engineering and the retail trade. Halfway down the list (profitability between 10% and 14%) were machine building, pharmaceutics, motorcar, aerospace and electrical engineering, as well as advertising, entertainment and recreation, publishing, clothes, footwear and consumer durables. At the bottom (profitability between 5% and 9%, and under 3% in Japan) were oil extraction, electricity, water and gas supply, commercial banks, financial institutions and diversified holdings.

Stock indices went up in computer technologies, aerospace and defence industries (34% in the 1990s), other high technologies, public health (26%) and pharmaceutics; and down in mining (4%), cellulose and paper. Judging by the foregoing, the CIS has been developing industries of little promise in the 1990s, with those of considerable promise stagnating.

Prices for raw materials, as opposed to research-intensive goods, are susceptible to sharp market fluctuations. Thus the highest oil price in the 1990s ($26.8 per barrel) was evident late in 1996 and almost halved as a result of the wide gap between demand and supply in 1997 and 1998. The price for gold also went down due to increased interest from investors in hard currency and the crisis in Southeast Asia. The price for aluminium halved in the 1990s due to unco-ordinated expansion of export in the CIS countries, only to go up again with restricted exports. By contrast, the price for lead went up in 1997 with reduced export markets in the CIS countries (from 233,000 t in 1994 to 150,000 t in 1996), mainly in Kazakhstan.

Later in the 1990s, prices for many metals produced in the CIS countries fell on the London Stock Exchange. Particularly dramatic was the case of uranium (exported from Kazakhstan, Russia and Uzbekistan), for which prices are generally governed by a demand/supply balance (uranium only accounting for 2% of NPS costs). During the oil crisis in the 1970s, prices increased to $16.5 per pound. Between 1988 and 1991, due to the ending of the Cold War and the disintegration of the USSR, export trade in uranium in the CIS countries increased more than tenfold (from 105 to 5600 t). As a result, prices more than halved (dropping to $7–8). They only rose again in 1995, reaching $15.5 in 1997.

These data suggest the following. Exclusive export trade in raw materials can never ensure national economic stability. Moreover, the CIS countries influence world price levels in a significant manner. Finally, joint forecasting and adjustment of prices will benefit all the CIS countries.

The primary concern of export in the CIS countries will be to improve competitiveness. For instance, increased costs and corresponding prices for the

Lada, Aleko-Moskvich and Tavria has resulted in failure on the Eastern European car market. With total sales doubling in the mid-1990s (particularly in the Czech Republic, Poland and Slovakia), the VAZ market share dropped to 1% (from 20% to 6% in Hungary and from 70% to 20% in Bulgaria). This position was immediately occupied by Fiat, Volkswagen (after acquiring Skoda), Suzuki (after starting production in Hungary) and certain South Korean and French corporations.

Other major problems in the CIS countries include certification involving improved quality and compliance with strict environmental regulations, reliable trade agents and disproving the accusations of dumping.

In the late 1990s, the maximum sulphur content in diesel fuels sold in the EU markets was set at 0.05% (fuels exported from the CIS countries contain 0.2%), with concomitant strict requirements concerning gasoline, black oil, etc. Hence liquid fuels from the CIS countries are regarded as crude and require refining, with subsequent significant price reductions. A more reasonable alternative is high refining before export. Converting exports in Russia, Kazakhstan, Turkmenistan and Azerbaijan from crude oil to highly refined petroleum products will increase currency earnings almost tenfold and will also create more jobs. No finished products can be offered for export unless certified (mainly for safety) by internationally authorised centres.

Exporters from the CIS often make consignment agreements without having the counterpart's solvency checked by a servicing agency. This entails great losses.

On the other hand, foreign countries often impose restrictions on CIS export trade. In order to counter "cut-throat" exporters trading metal in dirt-cheap barter transactions, the USA raised tariffs by up to 74%–104% for ferrochrome, ferrosilicon and manganese alloys. The USA and the EU member states initiated anti-dumping procedures concerning essential items of the CIS export trade in finished products (not raw materials) such as fertilisers, ferroalloys, transformer steel, rolled aluminium and other metals, uranium and zinc from Russia, the Ukraine, Kazakhstan and Uzbekistan, etc. Quotas were imposed on metals, rocket and space services, etc.

Urged by competing Western companies, import tariffs were raised from 6.5% to 42% for transformer steel imported from Russia, presumably in an anti-dumping effort. Thus "dumping" meant selling goods at considerably lower prices than those set on the world market or their production costs. Indeed, the mass-scale export trade in aluminium and other non-ferrous metals from the CIS in the early 1990s reduced international market prices, eventually affecting the exporting countries. In some cases, private firms did offer dumping prices for all kinds of non-certified goods from rare earth metals to caviar and vodka.

The situation changed in the mid-1990s. Thus, between 1992 and 1997, for instance, world prices for oil in Russia rose (taking into account export tariffs, excise duties, etc.) from 30% to 90% of international prices. The rise in domestic prices for exported goods doubled the rate of inflation. In such circumstances, CIS export traders should not evade anti-dumping processes. Rather than abandon the market, export prices should be adjusted to correspond to domestic prices (with the CIS countries particularly concerned with polystyrol, polyvinyl chloride, polypropylene, caustic soda, acetone and other chemicals), and production plans co-ordinated to reduce excessive inventories, etc. Dumping can only be claimed when significant losses are entailed for industries in the importing country. In some cases, comparatively low prices are dictated by high standards of technology (e.g. in uranium refining or manganese production). All the CIS countries should be recognised by international trade as transitional rather than State-directed economies, and some should be seen as developing states.

One typical example is related to export trade in uranium. In the 1970s, responding to a claim issued by American titanium corporations, the USA imposed prohibitive import duties (84%). Prices went up accordingly, creating the risk of titanium being replaced by less expensive construction materials. As a result, the duties were reduced in 1997, thus enhancing Russia's and Kazakhstan's export of sponge titanium (with the CIS countries accounting for over three quarters of U.S. imports) and accessories of titanium alloys.

Import market structure. Despite decreased food imports (e.g. grain, sugar, wheat flour, sunflower seed oil) in the 1990s, both ready-made and raw foodstuffs, as well as machinery, equipment, transport and instruments, continue to make up the bulk of CIS import trade. They account for 63% of total imports in Azerbaijan, 54% in Belarus, 70% in Kazakhstan, 79% in Kyrgyzstan, 63% in Russia, 43% in Moldova, 39% in Tajikistan, 58% in Turkmenistan and 81% in Uzbekistan.

The liberalisation of foreign trade is by no means due to indifference on the part of the government to the structure of import. The USA, Japan and the EU countries use non-tariff regulation to import up-to-date know-how, advanced technologies and unique equipment rather than consumer goods and standard equipment that can be produced domestically. Less developed countries restrict imports of finished products and reduce import tariffs for process lines as well as units and components to be assembled using domestic labour.

One typical case is CIS trading with the EU. The CIS had a favourable consolidated balance of trade maintained by Russia, Turkmenistan and Tajikistan. The remaining CIS countries imported more from the EU than they exported (with this difference in Transcaucasia varying between 42% and 65%). Oil and metals dominated in the total volume of import.

Germany, Italy and France still represent the CIS' principal partners in foreign trade (over 70% of turnover), and the EU countries are well known for their engineering achievements. However, their import of equipment continues to dwindle in the CIS, while that of cosmetics, furniture, jewellery, beverages, domestic electric devices is growing (more than tenfold in some cases). The greatest share (over 85%) belongs to Russia and the Ukraine.

The EU countries restrict access to their markets for competitive goods from the CIS. Rigid quotas are imposed on satellite launching with Russian rockets. In this case, the launching price is adjusted to the European *Orion*, depriving Russia of competitive advantages associated with lower costs. The import of magnesium, as requested by rivals in France and Norway, is operated at minimum prices estimated from average European rather than CIS costs (only one tenth of imports can be priced at a 20% reduction). This undermines the competitive strength of CIS exports (with the EU previously accounting for one third of the market). Special charges are imposed on potash fertilisers, an important export item in Belarus.

The CIS countries rarely resort to customs and non-tariff measures to protect their producers. On the other hand, in 1996, Lithuania, although applying for EU membership, raised import duties on sugar (from 35% to 70%), dairy products (from 20%–45% to 30%–50%), eggs (from 30% to 35%), meat products and some other goods where market demand can be satisfied by domestic producers.

Protective measures are even taken by strong advocates of free trade. Thus the U.S. sugar quotas doubled the prices against the world price (from $10–11 to $21–23 per pound) for the benefit of domestic producers. In the EU countries, special certification boards refuse import of obsolete equipment.

Integration in the world economy involves membership in the World Trade Organisation (WTO) representing more than 100 countries, including Eastern European ones. This will ensure some preferences for CIS countries (the import tariff level for WTO members dropped by 90% between 1926 and 1995 and currently amounts to less than 5% in most positions). WTO membership will involve lifting import quotas and other import discriminations as well as privileges for domestic over foreign producers.

The CIS countries should support domestic producers by protecting the domestic market. For instance, corporations such as the Philips, Bosch, Siemens, Eletrolux and Sony have occupied the CIS domestic market for equipment, establishing networks of trade representatives rather than joint venture companies. CIS experience indicates that, in such circumstances, the exporters are generally concerned with tax exemptions. For instance, Kyrgyzstan granted VAT (20%) exemptions in 1996.

In some cases, import duties should be raised for foodstuffs (in 1996 amounting to 21% in the EU, 16% in Russia and even less in other CIS countries). In many cases of unjustified customs policies, raw materials are exported from the CIS and then imported in the form of finished products at high prices. Thus Russia exports cellulose and paper, including special wallpaper, for instance, while importing finished wallpaper, although nine up-to-date facilities stand idle because of a lack of orders.

Construction firms in CIS countries, in particular in Moldova, Belarus and Armenia, should hold their traditional market against competitors from Turkey (in Russia alone, Turkish firms are subcontracted in 75 building projects worth $6 billion) and some other countries. There can be no question (at least in the nearest future) of rapid overall reduction of import tariffs, of their being lifted for aircraft engineering or of mandatory tenders open for foreign companies to major contracts with the government.

On the other hand, the high import duties (up to 20% in Russia) for high-technology equipment are not sensible. With annual imports of equipment amounting to $2.6 billion in the USA, $1.7 billion in China and $1.1 billion in Germany, the CIS – with its operational machinery stock depreciated by 50% – only has annual imports worth $200 million. At the same time, no protective duties are imposed on imported standard, general-purpose machinery produced in CIS countries.

Typical for many CIS countries is the emergence of labour-intensive accessories production. Production units in the EU are generally located in low-cost regions. In this context, border restrictions are not advisable.

In addition, it must be remembered that imported foreign equipment is associated with the import of components, materials and services often exceeding original contracts.

Geographic structure of foreign trade. Some CIS countries have a very limited geographical distribution of foreign trade. Thus Hungary, Germany, Poland and the USA account for almost 40% of export trade, and Austria, Germany, Poland and the USA for 53% of import trade in Belarus; the UK, Germany, the Netherlands, China, the USA and Switzerland account for 67% of export trade, and Germany, Italy and China for over 50% of import trade in Kazakhstan; Romania accounts for 52% of export trade, and Germany, Romania and the USA for 53% of import trade in Moldova; Belgium, the Netherlands and Switzerland account for almost 70% of export trade, and the UK, the USA and Switzerland for over 60% of import trade in Tajikistan; Germany, Italy, Malta, the Czech Republic and Turkey account for 61% of export trade, and Germany, Iran, Turkey, the USA and Yugoslavia for almost 50% of import trade in Turkmenistan; the UK, the Netherlands, China and Switzerland account for over 60% of export trade, and Germany, China, Poland, the USA and Switzerland for 62% of import trade in Uzbekistan.

About two thirds of the export market in Azerbaijan is accounted for by Iran, and one half of its imports by Iran and Turkey. Between 1992 and 1995, commodity turnover between Iran and Armenia increased 15-fold and then increased again with the new Araks bridge. However, along with mutually beneficial projects such as the hydropower station on the frontier river Araks and gas and electricity transmission lines, there have been mass-scale imports of low-quality goods, supplanting national producers. The same is true of foreign trade with China in Kazakhstan and Kyrgyzstan.

Kazakhstan has a favourable balance of trade with China, exporting ferrous metals (37%) and chemicals (13%) and importing sugar (26%), electrical equipment (14%) and consumer goods (10% without illegal trading). The export of power supplies shows great promise (when the oil pipeline to Central China is completed), as do fertilisers (a joint venture company involving the Karatau-Jambul phoshorite field). Construction of the Europe to Asia optic-fibre communications line, railways and pipelines will ensure access to seaports in the south for some CIS countries. However, imports of some consumer goods from China (often duty and tax-free) affect national industries.

During the period of reform, Russia has considerably extended its foreign trade, coming to the fore in world and of course European markets of natural gas, oil and oil products, ferrous and non-ferrous metals, fertilisers, timber, weapons and armaments. Foreign trade turnover increased by 40% between 1993 and 1997, amounting to $139 billion (15th and 16th in the world) and 20% of GDP.

Some Russian companies hold strong positions in international financial markets. Since 1996, the list of the world's 500 leading companies in market capitalisation (issued stocks by their price on the domestic market) includes Gazprom (about $8 billion, with deposit certificates priced fourfold higher on Western stock markets than in Russia). The list of Europe's 500 leaders, along with three Czech firms, contains five in Russia – two oil (Lukoil, Surgutneftegaz) and two power companies (EES Russia and Mosenergo), and a telecommunications operator Rostelekom.

Russia has extended its export market of power and machinery to countries further away. Energomashexport Inc. holds an order pack until 2005 worth over $600 million for equipment for hydroelectric power and thermal stations with an aggregate capacity of 9000 MW to Columbia, Mexico and some other countries (in collaboration with Siemens). Russia ranks next to Germany among the European exporters of equipment to China (annual exports over $3 million), including equipment for nuclear power stations.

On the other hand, machinery and equipment accounted for only 4.5% of Russian export volume in 1997 in contrast to 20% in 1990, due to inadequate competitiveness, marketing and advertising and high costs and prices. This problem can be solved by joint assembly arrangements with firms in importing countries (with AvtoVAZ establishing assembly lines in Finland, Uruguay and Columbia), joint production (e.g. of engines for the ZIL and KAMAZ and aircraft) and foreign sales and services.

Foreign trade in Russia typically focuses on raw materials. Exports are dominated by fuel and power resources (47% in 1996), and the import market is dominated by machinery and equipment and by transport (37%). The import of services, primarily Russians travelling abroad, dominates over exports (e.g. foreign tourists, carrier services). While the balance of trade and net balance of current operational costs are favourable (exports being more expensive than imports), balances of capital are greater and current accounts are negative. This means that Russia is still a net investor for the remaining world, i.e. exporting more capital than it imports (about $15 billion annually).

This is typical for some other CIS countries as well. There continues to be a deficit in Russia's balance of payments as opposed to its trade balance due to the repayment of significant amounts of debts incurred by the former USSR. The 1997 moratorium on discharging domestic and foreign debts resulted in a drastic deterioration of the Russian investment rating and a banking crisis. At the same time, financial results give a negative balance of $15 billion (e.g. non-recovered export gains, purchase of assets abroad). Even greater amounts of foreign currency are exported illegally under simulated export contracts or by purchasing real estate abroad. Forty thousand offshore firms have been established in tax-free zones (e.g. Cyprus, Bahamas, the Cayman Islands). According to expert opinions, almost 40,000 firms are controlled by criminal authorities, including over 500 joint venture companies, with the underground economy accounting for over 40% of GDP.

Russia operates an extensive export of goods and services to the Ukraine (10.2% of total exports in the mid-1990s), Germany (7.2%), China (6.0%) and the USA. The UK, Iceland, Italy, Belarus, Kazakhstan, Japan, Switzerland and the Netherlands account for 3%–4% each, and Poland, Hungary, Slovakia, Turkey, Finland and the Czech Republic for 2%–3% each. By contrast, no substantial reasons can be found for poor Russian exports to Uzbekistan (1.3%) and especially Transcaucasia, Turkmenistan, Kyrgyzstan and Tajikistan (0.1%–0.2% each) – these being several times lower than to Austria, Belgium or the Baltic countries.

With regard to imports into Russia, the Ukraine also comes first (16%), followed by Germany (10.8%), Kazakhstan (6.8%), the USA (6.5%), Belarus (5.7), Italy (4.9%) and Finland (3.4%). Comparatively strong positions are held by Moldova (1.8%) and Uzbekistan (1.3%), while Transcaucasia, Turkmenistan and Tajikistan (between 0.1% and 0.3% each) have almost abandoned their markets in Russia (to be discussed in more detail in Chap. 9).

The unfavourable world market situation in 1998 affected the CIS member countries' export and import rates, finally reducing exports by 16% and cutting imports by 11%. In 1 year, the active trade balance of the CIS has dropped 1.5-fold (more precisely, the active trade balance decrease in the CIS has reached $18.7 billion in 11 months). The non-member countries were the most effective in their export-mport operations (the import rate stood at 73%, and the import rate was 63%). At the same time, it should not be forgotten that the rate of decline of mutual trade between the CIS countries was lower than the rate of decline of mutual trade with other countries of the world. The general importers are Belarus, Georgia and Moldova; their export to CIS member countries is equal to two thirds of all the goods imported to Belarus, Ukraine, Kyrgyzstan and Tajikistan.

Thus the roles played by CIS countries in the world economy are totally inconsistent with their economic and human potential. The economic reform will bring dramatic changes in the CIS nations.

Field of Debate

1. How can the economic potential of the area of Eurasia consisting of the CIS be described? What role does this region play in the world economy?

2. Describe the natural resources, production potential and population in the CIS member states (Azerbaijan, Armenia, Georgia, Belarus, Kazakhstan, Kyrgyzstan, Moldova, Russia, Tajikistan, Turkmenistan, Uzbekistan and the Ukraine).

3. What changes in the CIS economies were related to industrialisation and industrial developments between the 1950s and 1980s?

4. What are the competitive advantages of CIS industries in the international markets?

5. What were the causes of deteriorating industrial output in the CIS in the 1990s? Analyse the effects of recent industrial developments in CIS countries.

6. What is national economic competitiveness? How is it measured? What is the first thing that needs to be done to improve it?

7. Analyse the export market structure in the CIS countries. How can these structures be modified?

8. Analyse the import market structure in the CIS countries. How can these structures be modified?

9. Describe the geographical distribution of foreign trade in the CIS countries.

10. How are the roles played by individual CIS countries and the CIS as a whole in the world economy changing as we approach the 21st century? What ought to be changed, and what goals ought to be attained?

Chapter 2

GENERAL GOALS OF ECONOMIC REFORMS

2.1 Towards Sustainable Development in Society

Sustainable development and the market. Economic reforms in the CIS countries are focused on providing sustainable economic development in the 21st century. While the term *sustainable development* seems rather vague and somewhat inferior to recent conventions such as socialism and capitalism, this multipolar definition best describes the future economic framework.

The first characteristic of sustainable development is *balanced economic growth*, ensuring a new quality of life and effective employment while maintaining and improving the environment. International experience indicates that this growth cannot be based on the development of raw materials alone. This was also demonstrated by a drastic reduction in prices for major export items in the CIS in 1997 and 1998, including oil (40%), nitrogen fertilisers and ammonia (40%–50%), round timber (27%), gold, ferro-alloys, hard coal, copper, natural gas and nickel (10%–18%). Sustainable growth can only be achieved in the framework of an active development policy for the manufacturing industries and high technologies.

The second characteristic of sustainable development is a *social, human orientation of the economy*, focusing on education, public health, science and culture – in short, on the human potential as the basic national source of wealth. Otherwise no informatisation (i.e. the cultivation and widespread public accessibility of information resources) of society will be possible, and without informatisation neither genuine democracy nor new technological frameworks are conceivable. This active social policy will prevent excessive stratification in society, ensuring political stability.

The third characteristic of sustainable development is an *integrated dynamic* and yet *stable ecological and economic framework* involving both the national economy and human potential in the interests of both present and future generations. Many developed industrial countries have achieved superior rates of economic growth by burning immense quantities of fuels produced in less-developed states. As a result, mankind is facing the risks of global climate change, deforestation, desertification and shortage of fresh water. Sewage and flue-gas treatment methods have been inefficient on a world-wide scale. In this connection, some foreign economists have advanced the concept of restricted economic growth and use of material resources. This, however, is only applicable to developed countries with high living standards. The CIS countries need an innovative environmental policy to develop and apply new technologies to prevent or effectively utilise harmful discharge.

The fourth characteristic and prerequisite of sustainable development is *regional economic integration* and the consequent *equal and mutually beneficial integration in international economic relationships*. No issues related to the 21st-century humanitarian society can be dealt with by individual countries, even by those that are large in area or rich in oil or gold. An effective mechanism is required to co-ordinate the interests and policies of many nations.

Last but not least, the fifth characteristic of sustainable development is *purposeful and consistent regulation* of development, following the principles of international law, new business ethics and genuine democracy in a multipolar world of continuous changes and reforms.

Today as never before, the history of society is governed by the progressive and sequential development of productive forces and economic relations towards integration and socialisation initially at a national level and then on a world-wide scale (with all the conflicting trends this entails). This is what is happening in more dynamic regions, such as Southeast Asia, Europe and North America.

Comprehensive development of the needs and abilities of the primary productive force – individual human beings – is gaining particular significance as the main form of public wealth and a guide to progress. In the 21st century, individuals will no longer be subordinate to machinery as a mere element of the production process; the principal sphere of human activity will involve collecting, updating, processing, communicating and analysing information, i.e. research, development and application of innovations. Thus progress in market reforms cannot be achieved unless such reforms guarantee the development of science, education and the health services.

The propelling force of progress is represented by the economic interests of individuals and large social groups. Successful reforms in all countries have employed non-violent methods of conflict settlement and compromises and have made used of available frameworks of restriction and balancing (social and religious organisations, trade unions, consumer and environmental associations, social insurance and security). Neglected social groups will block reforms.

On the other hand, the long-term goal of reform is generally seen in the transition from an administrative command system to a market economy. This definition is fairly ambiguous, because there are different concepts of the *market economy*. On a common-sense level, the market is a place where goods are exchanged for money and money for goods, i.e. a marketplace. However, traditional political economists describe the market as a sphere of commodity circulation (exchange) where immediate social relations are replaced with intermediate commodity/money relations. Hence the view of the market as spontaneous and only effective with underdeveloped productive forces, as an antipode to conformity to established law, opposing and defying plans and immediate social relations.

The different concepts of the market imply the four different ideas of the eventual goal of reform: (1) a commodity market with inherent categories of value, price, profit, etc. but with no capital and labour markets and without privatisation (as proposed by communist parties in some CIS countries); (2) a self-regulating market with free pricing and a minimal share of State-owned property (as proposed by some right-wing liberal economists); (3) a dual-level system with macro-economic ratios regulated from above but the micro-economic level regulated by the market (as proposed by some economists in China); (4) full-scale market economy with active State regulation ensuring its social and environmental orientation.

What distinguishes the administrative command economy from the market one is neither money as a measure of value and means of circulation (surviving through almost all historical stages in the USSR), nor planning (far more effective under current market conditions with the new subjects, object and methods), nor even the socialisation of production. First and foremost, the market economy is characterised by the relations between production and consumption, changing from the vertical links mediated by central authorities to horizontal, immediate consumer/producer relations involving their representative associations (intermediaries).

In an *administrative command economy,* socialisation assumes the form of nationalisation of means of production and State direction (direct administration by the State) of all types of economic activity, with planning appearing in a centralised, totalitarian command form. This type of economy can only be effective under three conditions: (1) limited demands with strict priorities according to relevance (focusing on defence and basic industries); (2) a generally recognised enemy, with broad public segments prepared to survive at the cost of hard work and heavy sacrifice; (3) available labour forces (unemployment or forced labour) and central governance of natural resources. These conditions were given in the USSR between the 1920s and the 1950s. In our opinion, timely conversion to the market economy following post-war reconstruction in late 1950s would have turned the USSR into an effective democratic federation or confederation.

International experience indicates the three forms of *market economy*: (1) a free and self-regulating market (unrestrained competition, pricing determined by demand and supply, non-interference of the State in economic relations); (2) a regulated industrial market (regulated competition and pricing supported by anti-trust legislation, social and environmental security, public-financed science, education and culture, State-owned infrastructure) first emerging in the USA and then in other developed industrial countries during the 1929–1931 crisis; (3) a regulated information market (the prevalent commodity represented by services rather than things; conversion from goods-money to goods-credit relations, with banks acting as national accounting centres; pre-production decision-making about the amount, quality and prices of goods produced on the base of market research and contracting) emerging in the USA, Japan, Germany, etc. in the 1990s.

It is the latter form of market that will ensure sustainable economic development.

Major stages of social development in the twentieth century. As before, the history of society in the twentieth century is a progressive movement of productive forces, economic and other social relations from fragmentation to socialisation first on a national and then on a world-wide scale, from spontaneity of conflicting fragmentary producers and consumers to order, i.e. the recognition control of proportions. Through wars and crises, society continues its onward march from the realm of necessity to the realm of freedom.

Admittedly dealing with productive and proprietary relations, the Soviet political economy described class structure as the only guide to periodicity in the development of society, and history in the twentieth century has strengthened the case of change from the primitive community, slavery, feudal and private-capital relations associated with the anarchic market and hired labour/capital antagonism to a socially oriented society with well-developed frames of sustainable development involving macro-economic and environmental control, redistribution of national income and publicly subsidised education, science and health services.

However, history is not described by class dimension alone, firstly because twentieth-century societies are largely heterogeneous, combining capitalist, socialist, feudal-tribal and primitive-natural characteristics, and secondly, because there are other important dimensions.

Another special twentieth-century feature is the change in *technological systems*. This involves the transition from *domestic crafts* (hand tools, multi-skilled craftsmen, an integrated living/working area, e.g. a workshop, household field) and *manufacturing* (specialised tools, partial division of labour, home/work separation) to *machine production* (including agriculture, construction building and the non-productive sphere) and later in the century to *post-industrial computerised production* (automated instruments, including sensor systems, software and control systems, versatile workers, an integrated living/production area with the majority of people using home computers linked up to corporate networks). Farms, workshops, factories and the automated complex function in diversified social patterns, with this diversity enhancing sustainability (e.g. obsolete minor business forms time and again ensuring survival in the CIS).

A role of some significance has been played by *forms of economy*. These include the *natural economy* and the three market economy forms mentioned above: a *free and non-regulated market* (with perfect competition and a minimal economic role of the State), the *administrative command commodity production* (with central confiscation and re-distribution of the bulk of net income, central supply for production, regulated cash and credit flows), the *regulated industrial market* (dominated by competing oligopolies and monopolies, regulated with anti-trust legislation, with social economic security guaranteed by the State and macro-economic control of structural improvements) and the *regulated information market* (with increasingly long-term contracted production at fixed basic prices, prevalent sales of services, conversion from cash to electronic payments).

To an extent, all the CIS countries have been exposed to each of these forms during the twentieth century. Thanks to the natural economy with its family orchards and vegetable gardens, millions of people have not gone hungry. The free market that emerged after the abolition of serfdom in 1861 prevailed early in this century and existed in the sphere of consumer goods in 1917 and 1918 and between 1921 and 1926. The administrative system functioned between 1914 and 1917 on private capitalist lines and between 1918 and 1990 under State-ownership principles (accompanied in 1918–1921 by severe restrictions on commodity relations).

The *administrative command system* in the former USSR involved central confiscation of the bulk of the surplus product, centralised distribution of production resources, a strict hierarchy of producers, centralised administration and wages paid with the State allocations depending on fulfilled central targets. Not long ago, front-rank workers in a Central Asian country were given bicycles and televisions sets as gifts from the Head of State on his birthday.

In a free and non-regulated market, the elements of competition and price mechanisms are of critical importance. Some components of this market survived in the USSR until late 1920s (subsequently remaining in the background in underground or semi-underground economics) and in developed Western countries until the crisis of 1929–1933. The free market permits the rapid elimination of shortages and queues, while introducing uncontrollable price rises, mass-scale unemployment, large differences between the rich and the poor and overproduction crises. At present, a free market can only be seen in some Asian, South American and African countries having no developed heavy industry and making no independent contributions to international science and technology.

In the past 30 years, according to the UN, the contribution made by the countries in the bottom 20% in terms of wealth (with dominating free markets) to world income dropped from 2.3% to 1.4%, while the contribution of those in the top 20% increased from 70% to 85%. In the latter case, the State has been nationalising the railways, power supply systems and some heavy industries and sponsoring major investment projects since the 1930s. Their example has been followed by Eastern Asian countries, where GDP has increased fourfold between the 1960s and 1990s. Interestingly, the more developed countries generally had fewer natural resources. Their success largely depended on the system of government and on an advanced, valid and effective legislation.

The *regulated industrial market* involves the State interfering with the economy to oppose monopolies (anti-trust legislation, regulated prices for strategic resources), the provision of social guarantees (e.g. minimum wages, pensions, vacations, unemployment benefits, health insurance), environmental security (ergonomic and environmental control) and management of structural improvements (research and technology programmes, subsidised education and culture, social security). Everyone can plan what he or she will pay for. State planning therefore concerns radical technology systems or less developed regions, while corporate planning deals with products, prices and profits.

The *regulated information market* emerged in more developed countries later in the twentieth century. This actually eliminates the Marxian spontaneous market exclusively regulated by price mechanisms. The producer obtains knowledge about effective demand and prices before rather than during production by contracting via world-wide telecommunications networks. Society has found a way to plan, i.e. voluntarily regulated development obviating the State planning directives and the marketplace spontaneity. Using a PC, up-to-date information can be obtained about demand and supply anywhere in the world, contracting terms and the product itself, and an agreement of delivery and payment can be signed.

The long-term goal of reforms involves sustainable development in accordance with the regulated information market principles rather than a retreat to the market forms of the distant past. This means highly effective socialisation of production beginning with informatisation (free access to public databases via telecommunications) and a well-developed production, science, technology, social and institutional market infrastructure. This is a socially and environmentally oriented economy with an advanced framework of allocations for public demand, social and environmental monitoring, income redistribution, social security and investment in human capital. The sequential nature of production is ensured by forecasting, programming and marketing research and by subsequent direct pre-production, long-term contracting for producers and consumers (where necessary mediated) via telecommunications.

Unlike the administrative command system, this system allows for a day-to-day account of diversified and rapidly changing demand and focuses on consumers' interests, initiative, enterprise and individual responsibility, preventing government authorities and interest groups from monopolising the administration and distribution of national wealth.

Another guide to periodicity in the development of society is the *internationalisation of economy*. At the turn of the century, Russia was well on the way from local to advanced regional markets. In some CIS countries, the national market is still non-existent due to the differences in socio-economic conditions (social systems in Chechnia, Dagestan and Tuva have never been the same as in central Russia), poor communications and local barriers of a feudal nature. Prices for basic goods in different regions still differ considerably.

The international literature has been active in investigating another guide – the change of *civilisations*, the prevalent forms of public wealth – from agrarian (land and cattle) through industrial (factories, works and other assets) to a civilisation focusing on knowledge and its application, culture and recreation. This public wealth is personified and cannot be expropriated as was the case in 1917. Primitive privatisation will not make sense here, because it involves a mere transfer of obsolete machinery, with far more valuable team experience and unique specialised knowledge either lost or "emigrating" with their holders.

We would like to describe the **sustainable development society** as a social and economic system emerging in developed industrial countries in the last few decades of the twentieth century, a new phase of civilisation, socialisation and technological, economic and social development. The new civilisation involves comprehensive development of the individual, including individual demands (basic demands secured for all working or disabled individuals) and abilities (involving comprehensive but differentiated education, vocational training, personnel selection and management).

The *socialisation of production* is supported by a global computer network to collect, analyse and communicate all types of information, with unrestricted access for all interested legal and private persons. The principal working instruments, rather than machines acting on the surface lattice of the subject of work, will be represented by automated technological complexes transforming the subject on the atomic-molecular, ion, quantum and gene-cell levels by physico-chemical and biological methods.

The new economic framework, instead of extensive economic growth, provides *environmental/economic balance* with the maximum possible conservation of resources, supported by the global infrastructure, macro-economic regulation of international markets of capitals, technologies, goods and labour and transnational corporations (TNCs) actively co-operating with local small businesses and acting as the main element of production.

Public ownership in this case will evolve in corporate, co-operative and State forms, with the *middle class* – owners and professionals engaged in the marketing, management, development and application of innovation and the maintenance of sophisticated engineering systems and diversified services – coming to the forefront in the social context.

Almost throughout the twentieth century, the former USSR was the focus of competition between two world systems. This should end in convergence rather than victory of one over the other. The CIS countries should not make the fatal error of looking back to the "Russia we have lost", i.e. the capitalism that existed at the turn of the century.

The sustainable development society is an **information society** created by a convergence of market and socially oriented (planned) economies. Superior performance supported by the computerisation, transnationalisation and incorporation of production within a new economic framework will provide material and other conditions of individual growth for employed, unemployed or disabled individuals. Global information networks will be available for individuals and large or small firms as sources and/or users of engineering, commercial, social and environmental information. The prevalent middle class will combine highly qualified work in the development, application and use of new technologies for standard products and customised services with the management of capital, above all of an intellectual nature.

Many models of economic development tested in the 1980s were orientated towards maximum social security (e.g. in Sweden and Germany), a State-supported export market (e.g. in Japan and South Korea) and free market prices with strict control of the rules of competition (e.g. in Singapore, New Zealand and Chile). All these, however, faced tremendous challenges by the late 1990s.

The high taxes required to support the high contingency benefits caused the flight of capitals, fewer jobs, high unemployment rates (particularly in Germany) and a declining rate of exchange (in Sweden). Rates of economic growth fell among the Asian "tigers", including South Korea, spending only 0.2% of GDP on patents, copyrights and other types of intellectual property. Things were particularly bad in Indonesia, with the economy dominated by oligarchic groups closely associated with government authorities.

On the other hand, in the USA, with PCs in over 35% of families in 1997 (15% in the EU countries and 1% in the CIS countries) and 3% of homes with access to the Internet (double the figure in Germany and the UK), over 2 million new jobs are created every year. In addition, there are superior rates of economic growth and controlled inflation.

According to expert opinion, over 15 million American families will have access to the Internet by the year 2002. However, progress also has its dark side. Increased mental strain causes fears of being dismissed and being unable to repay loans for a house or a car or to meet health bills. The U.S. economy loses almost $30 billion per year due to mistakes or miscalculations made by undereducated employees. One quarter of all American adults cannot calculate the amount paid in a supermarket, read a printed form or find a street on a city map. More than half are uneasy about growing crime rates, high college tuition fees (prestigious universities charging over $20,000 per year) and expensive health services. These are acquiring a new significance in the CIS.

In 1997, the seven more developed countries had 24 million unemployed, with 15 million made to work on half-time schedules. The crisis of the 1930s and the war damages of the 1940s developed a spirit of solidarity, joint action and mutual support, contributing to an advanced welfare system. The 1980s and 1990s, however, have been dominated by fierce competition, labour discipline, mistrust and general pretensions. Privatisation of State property was associated with the closure of many social programmes, insecure employment and increasing inequality. Remuneration paid to a senior manager in the 1960s was 30 times, and in the 1990s even 200 times the salary of an ordinary employee.

Towards the end of the twentieth century, there is a growing awareness of the fact that co-operation in a market-oriented economy is more beneficial than confrontation.

Some foreign economists, e.g. the Nobel prize-winner G. Buchanan, predicted economic failure in the USA and other countries where the adequate state of the market is supported by an increasing budget deficit (amounting to 2.1% of GDP in the 1970s, 4.1% in the 1980s and about 5% in the mid-1990s in the USA), increasing national debt (55% in the 1980s and over 70% in 1995) and related interest rates and, consequently, the Federal Government's share as a debtor in the markets of loan capital (17% in the 1960s, 27% in the 1970s, 41% in the 1980s and almost 85% in the 1990s). They propose balanced economic growth, planned restriction of demand and enhanced public regulation of social and economic processes. Otherwise, the developed industrial countries will run the risk of defeat by the growing number of poorer nations, and if the latter attain Western levels of power consumption and pollution, by nature itself.

The market in a sustainable development society requires a high level of regulation, both vertical – by central and local government authorities (e.g. using taxes, economic legislation) – and, more importantly, horizontal – with long-term contracts between the protagonists in the market.

What are the distinguishing characteristics of the market conception of planning? The *subject of regulation* is represented both by physical material proportions (output of specific necessities of life) and, more importantly, by the social and economic interests of producers, consumers, resource holders and their associations, i.e. reproduction of the social system as a whole. The *planning bodies* involve both central and local government authorities and all legal entities acting under long-term and fairly stable contracts. Instead of purely administrative (government orders, specifications, social and environmental standards), the *method of proportion balancing* uses economic factors (taxes, prices, environmental charges, emission fees, health and property insurance, interest and depreciation rates, rate of exchange, customs regulations, budget subventions). Along with directive planning by the owner, the form of *ensuring conformity to plan* involves market research, forecasting, programming and principally long-term contracting. The *planning procedure* is governed by task-programme (with higher authorities only planning structural changes, starting from their sponsored multivariant programmes) rather than hierarchical principles (with the plan devised by a higher authority, to be broken into single-version tasks for subordinates). Instead of fixed targets, the *planning basis* involves standards (intervals of normal public levels of the scope and efficiency of production and the demand for goods and services by homogeneous economic or sociodemographic groups).

Transition from the industrial to the information society triggers a series of new trends in the development of the market relationships.

Conditions of sales are increasingly determined prior to production through long-term contracting, fixed prices and customer's specifications, rather than *ex poste*, when already offered to unidentified buyers.

The commodity is increasingly represented by R&D products (inventions, developments, processes and know-how, pilot specimens, computer algorithms and software), services and small-scale products with a long production cycle rather than standard goods.

Non-priceable resources (intellectual potential, labour quality, environmental conditions) and output totals (social, information, resource, environmental effects) are growing in importance.

Public costs increasingly involve advanced allocations (to fixed capital, R&D, personnel training and insurance, environmental control) and joint allocations (to other branches and spheres of public economy).

Prices are determined by unit utility rather than unit cost (as in the era of approximately agreed range of production and public demand), with normal costs recognised as those of leading enterprises rather than the average weighted level.

National markets will be incorporated in the world market with the exchange of commercial information by computer networks (arranged by commodity, stock and currency exchanges) rather than at the level of the marketplace (between immediate sellers and buyers).

Instead of immediate action in the market, most commodity producers (small-scale plants) are represented by transnational corporations under long-term contracts.

Enhanced interrelation of the markets of consumer goods, producers' goods, R&D products and innovations, investments, currency and labour is accompanied by increasing differences in economic valuation (current profitability, investment return, standard values, social and economic expectations).

Three roads to a sustainable development society. The first road was taken by Western nations. Their contribution to world civilisation is *entrepreneurship*, i.e. activities of independent economic agents undertaking financial risk to make regular profits from the use of property and sales of goods, works and services. They are typically prudent, law-abiding and disciplined, trained by the long (300- to 500-year) market experience and Protestant ethics. They are the strong world leaders in the set of firms, managers, discoveries and inventions per million population. With all the shortcomings of representative democracies, they have attained superior levels of publicity, public control over government authorities, legal independence and freedom of the press.

On the way to the new type of society, utilising the experience of the USSR and the new ideas of economic science, they succeeded in overcoming the multiple defects of capitalism described by K. Marx. There is no relative and much less absolute pauperisation of the working class. The reserve army of industrial labour has come to serve as a reasonable element of economy, with the State securing a minimum wage and working conditions as well as benefits and, more importantly, retraining for the unemployed. Furthermore, there is no evidence of anarchic production in the Marxian sense. The banks are the national accounting centres controlling cash flow under the supervision of the central reserve system. Most producers have information about demand and supply before production begins. Bankruptcy, although a rather unpleasant procedure, is quite ordinary and by no means fatal. The State is an important manager of research-intensive goods and services, the land owner and infrastructure manager. The monopolies, rather than being instruments of economic decay, as predicted, appear as agents of macro-economic regulation, and instead of the small business being ousted, they are using it to their advantage and opening up new perspectives.

On the other hand, while solving a range of problems, the capitalist path to an information society has created other and even greater concerns. There has been a growing dissociation from the Third World currently involving many CIS nations. The world communications network has provided access to information about the way of life in richer countries and how to handle highly sophisticated arms. There is no Soviet bloc today to act as an arbitrator and a counterpoise in a two-polar world. The nuclear power plants, power supply systems and information networks are both components of the information society and targets that are very vulnerable to diversion. If all nations attain the Western level in energy utilisation, mankind will face the risk of environmental suicide.

Mature societies, like mature human beings, are more knowledgeable and closer to their goal. This is what the demographic situation demonstrates. Informatisation and the advances of pharmacology have reduced mortality rates, thus drastically increasing the population in the poorer countries, and birth rates, particularly affecting the richer countries. Increasingly more Western families are incomplete, childless or homosexual, and in some European countries population growth is only ensured by Asian or African immigration.

Afro- and Latin Americans will dominate in the USA in the mid-21st century. The mechanism of natural selection is no longer efficient. Increasingly more children inherit low cultural levels, painful diseases and social handicaps. New labour requirements in the consumer society are coming into grave conflict with genetic and intellectual potentials. G. Buchanan, V. Leontiev and other prominent economists rightly suggest that, without strict public regulation of ongoing socio-environmental and economic processes, more developed countries will also face the risk of financial collapse because their wealth is related to the accumulating budget deficit and national debt.

The second road to the information society was taken by the Asian "tigers". Their contribution is largely associated with new forms of national government (collaborating with business associations and trade unions), long-term planning of structural improvements (by industry and planning ministry departments) and personnel management focusing on team skills, development training, superior performance and new technologies. The "Japanese miracle" modified the ideology of tribal loyalty, strict discipline, mutual aid and respect for elders as a form of modern labour ethics. The requirements of sustainable development have been splendidly met within the framework of long-term employment, mutual responsibility of the firm and the employee, moral and psychological incentives and staff consolidation and continuous development training in a wide range of skills. Of prime importance are the focuses on team work, joint rationalisation and discussion of decision proposals, wages depending on work experience and slow but persistent promotion. The framework starts out from corporate ownership (in contrast to the situation in the USA, 70% of stocks are held by legal entities rather than individuals) and the resulting focus on long-term positioning in the world market rather than maximum current profits.

On the other hand, achievements in many Asian countries depended on restricted consumption by staff, comparatively low wages and intensive labour and tough party and State policies. When wages in South Korea approached European levels in the 1990s, the authors of the country's historic dash were sentenced to long-term imprisonment. With workers no longer willing to work 10-h shifts, the pace of economic growth subsided. With no independent science and technology based on basic research, long-term achievements in the world market can no longer be attained.

The choice of the third road of twentieth-century development by the CIS countries was neither accidental nor blind. The national economies have been typically state-controlled, lacking the civil traditions of modern history, strong legal authority, private land ownership, and presenting a unique fusion of Western and Eastern cultures. As N.A. Berdyaev pointed out at the turn of the century, "Russians are an Eastern nation in their spiritual makeup; Russia is the Christian East for two centuries strongly influenced by the West".[1]

Many of the ideas tested for three quarters of a century were generally impracticable. One utopia involved making the available "human material" Communist. The extremely damaging "class approach" resulted in the actual elimination of more active producers, particularly in rural areas. No improvement was achieved with totalitarian centralised administration of the public economy. Transaction costs of itemising the public economy plan by individual factory sections and products and corresponding reporting and accounting were far greater than necessary to establish and maintain the relations of independent economic agents, and there were indirect losses related to the lack of marketing research, delayed administrative action and suppressed local initiative.

Nevertheless, the CIS nations have taken radical steps on their way towards an information society, even though the sacrifices have been too great. No other sizeable country has attained such great achievements in such a short time in education (from 65% illiterate to the world leader in terms of the number of engineers, technicians and research workers in natural and engineering sciences), public health (defeating many infections), culture (the world's largest number of copies in science, engineering and fiction), physico-mathematical and natural sciences and some fields of engineering (e.g. laser, aircraft and space-rocket technologies, power engineering, new materials and alloys). It was in the USSR that target programmes were first initiated (GOELRO) to be elaborated in other countries, as well as macro-economic prognoses and balances, state ergonomic standards, collective forms of competition and in-house training. This legacy cannot be abandoned.

Post-industrial society, particularly in its Japanese version, has been active in using Russian experience in State support for science, education, public health, culture, social planning, moral incentives, etc. On the other hand, the lack of transnational planning prevents solutions being found for the environmental, sociopolitical and demographic problems of sustainable development, endangering the 21st-century civilisation.

The multinational and multiconfessional country with no schooling in market labour discipline has created a new intellectual potential and further developed the existing intellectual potential at short notice. However, large-scale infringements of law and unjustified restrictions on the freedom of information inhibit the collective democracy that originally differed from the individualistic forms of Western democracy. Command planning for urgent military and political decision-making was not replaced in due time by macro-economic regulation focusing on social and economic efficiency and accounting for radical

---

[1] Berdyaev, N.A. (1990): The Sources and the Meaning of Russian Communism. Nauka, Moscow, 7 (Бердяев, Н.А. (1990): Истоки и Смысл Русского Коммунизма. Наука, Москва, 7) [In Russian]

changes occurring later in the twentieth century in the content of work and capital, the structure of production resources, forms of production management and socialisation.

The planning system involving estimates of output growth by the new natural and labour resources used, a high proportion of savings, levelled distribution and limited demand is not a blind alley but rather a means of transition from primitive market forms combined in Imperial Russia with a feudal or even tribal set-up to an information society. It is pertinent to note that in the course of a few years the CIS nations have attained the level of industrial and cultural development that many of their neighbours failed to achieve for centuries.

The world has rejected not the theory of social orientation and public control of economic development, but rather the eventual fetishistic and antidemocratic manner of implementing Marxist ideas. Pope John Paul II, who has had first-hand experience of totalitarian delights in Poland, highlights firstly the objective conditional nature of the Marxist appeal to those who wish to solve their everyday problems, secondly the positive components of socialist experience in eliminating inequality, poverty and ignorance and thirdly the eventual implementation of some Marxist ideas in more developed countries.

The CIS nations are not establishing capitalism but rather a new social and economic structure, generalising the experience unknown to classical Marxism-Leninism and inconsistent with the capitalism/socialism juxtaposition because it is based on twentieth-century realities. The pattern draws on the analysis and prediction of actual trends emerging in the progress of reform rather than being just another experiment in abstract paper design. The socialist idea today means an end to the separation of management from property (most workers becoming owners of small and medium-sized businesses or lessees, shareholders and managing directors of large enterprises), authority (changing from representative to immediate democracy based on local government and interest co-ordination) and culture (public regulation of the interests and demand priorities depending on their relevance to individual growth).

As this takes place, work will be aimed at process applications of science; human social nature will be further developed and revealed in the immediate communication of information among all producers and consumers; and the role of intellectual, social and environmental (global) productive forces will grow disproportionately faster than working time. The comprehensive development of the human potential as a systemic characteristic of abilities and demands will be an essential condition of an eventual sustainable development of society.

2.2 Structural Economic Reforms.
The Liberal Model

General background of structural reforms. An *economic reform* involves an organisational change in the economy, in the concentration, specialisation and co-operation of production and in the tax, customs, anti-trust and other spheres of economic legislation. Reforms of this kind have taken place in any developing state at all times.

Structural reforms comprise a special class of economic reforms related to changes in the structure of the public economy. They include the transition from a free and self-regulating market to a regulated industrial market in the 1930s in the USA (Roosevelt's New Deal) and some other Western countries; from an industrial to an information market in more developed countries between the 1970s and 1990s; and from the administrative command model of commodity production to various regulated market types in Germany and Japan in the 1950s and in the CIS, Eastern Europe, Baltic, China, Indochina, etc. in the 1990s.

Structural reforms imply a transition to the new economic structure involving new types of ownership, structure of the public economy, role of the national economy in the international division of labour, methods of macro-economic regulation and institutional and legal status of business units.

Structural reforms are generally defined as a means to resolve a severe social and economic crisis. A Russian saying that "a peasant will never cross himself until there is a peal of thunder" is probably also true outside the Christian community. The need for a radical change in organisational forms of the economy was only recognised both "at the top" and "at the bottom" after the crises of 1929–1933 in the West and upon disintegration of the previous *dzaibatsu* system in Japan in late 1940s. Nevertheless, even the most radical structural reforms cannot be defined as a revolution, a forcible and murderous displacement of the old regime. On the contrary, their objective is to prevent revolution, avoiding it by making it unnecessary. A structural reform is not a goal in itself, but rather a means to settle accumulated conflict.

In the last decades of this century, more than 40 countries in Europe, Asia and South America, including all the CIS countries, have been carrying out structural economic reforms in various manners and with different degrees of success. There is no common opinion among economists about the essence and adequate range of national features of reform, the criteria for their effectiveness, their influence on processes of economic integration or the forms and methods of State regulation in a transitional economy.

Depending on their political predilections, different authors in the CIS countries view the initial results and prospects of reform in different ways: as a retreat to capitalism, to Russia, Georgia, Armenia, etc. "we have lost", or as progress to a new socially oriented society; as a disaster pushing most of the nation towards the verge of poverty or as a torturous but necessary process to create a new economy; as casting off the chains of empire and gaining independent access to international markets as another Kuwait, Switzerland, etc. or as the prerequisite for a new and mutually beneficial economic integration.

Structural reforms in the 1980s and 1990s were and are being applied within various social and economic systems. Reorganisation applies both to former "socialist" and less developed market-orientated nations (e.g. Spain, Chile, Peru, Indonesia, Malaysia, Thailand) and even to those we describe as fairly well-off (e.g. the USA, Japan, Germany).

Generally speaking, the reforms involve the following: firstly, a new role of the State in economic regulation and *privatisation* (to be discussed in Chap. 3) – change in the ownership structure (placing State-owned and municipal plants under the jurisdiction of non-public legal entities); secondly, the creation or development of a *market infrastructure* (to be discussed in Chap. 4) along inter-regional or transnational principles (e.g. commercial banks and other financial institutions – holdings, commodity, stock and currency exchanges, insurance companies, telecommunications and information networks, leasing and venture companies, centres for personnel training, selection and evaluation, wholesale and distribution centres, consulting, expert, marketing, certification and auditing firms, scientific and technological pools and technology exchange centres); thirdly, *modification of the branch structure* of production, starting from conversion in the military industry complex (MIC), reducing the share of raw materials and increasing that of research-intensive branches, including those focusing on export trade of consumer and investment goods and services (to be discussed in Chap. 5); fourthly, *financial stabilisation* of the public economy (to be discussed in Chap. 6), investments and tax reforms (closure of the notoriously unprofitable, strengthening of unrewarding but promising, enhanced development of internationally competitive enterprises in all branches); fifthly, increasing *integration in the world economy* (developing the technology and science complexes, increasing export, import and co-operative sales as a proportion of GDP) by regional grouping (to be discussed in Chap. 9); and sixthly, *reorganisation of enterprises* as the main elements of economy (to be discussed in Chap. 8).

The term "structural improvements", extensively used both in Russian and foreign publications, has not been specified in terms of content or measuring principles. Conceptual differences result in a diversity of relevant criteria and indices. We propose the following four principal aspects of structural change in the economy:

1. *Improvements in the national product structure*, i.e. changes in the industrial and product structure of economy, its profile. They are described by the

proportions of total GDP, national income, employment rate, production assets estimations and export and import trade accounted for by different branches of the economy and industry. The improvements are accompanied by changes in the regional structure of the economy and in the intensity and direction of inter-industry relationships.

2. *Institutional improvements* involving the creation and development of new economic institutions and spheres of employment, a change in the market pattern and in organisational forms of business.

3. *Social and economic improvements* stemming from the change in the relations between various types of ownership and management.

4. *Technological improvements* related to the emergence of new technological forms basing on electronification, information, biotechnologies, etc.

Foreign authors mainly discuss the improvements in industrial and technological structures following the two oil shocks (oil price rises), changes in the scope and pattern of international markets, liberalisation of the world capital market, development of micro-electronic technology and the two major economic recessions in the 1970s and 1990s. The Organisation for Economic Co-operation and Development (OECD) analysed structural improvements in the economies of the seven most developed countries (Australia, Canada, France, Germany, Japan, the UK and the USA) between 1960 and 1985. Some authors describe the technological and social improvements related to the scientific and technological revolution, the emergence of an information (post-capitalist, post-industrial) society, efficiency criteria in production and the infrastructure in the new situation. However, none of the countries achieved simultaneous and rapid improvements in production, institutional and socio-economic structures on as large a scale as the successor states to the former USSR. They employed two basic models.

Models of reforms. The model of structural reform is defined as a mode of implementation largely governed by the role of the State and the pace of reorganisation. The twentieth century has witnessed two models of reform, both currently applied in the CIS countries in various modifications.

The *liberal-monetary model* draws on the classical political economy of A. Smith and D. Ricardo, elaborated in the twentieth century by neo-liberal economists led by M. Friedman and others, mainly of the Chicago School (USA) and the International Monetary Fund (IMF).

According to this model, the State devises an overall programme of reforms and proceeds with active macro-economic financial regulation, without interfering with immediate governance and gradually assigning State-owned enterprises (after reorganisation and careful valuation of assets and with legislative and organisational support for the emerging joint-stock companies) to private investors, including foreign ones, at appropriate prices. The reorganisation usually takes several years. The prime object is to cut inflation and interest rates, revoke the laws inhibiting market forces and reduce government expenditure.

The *institutional model* of reforms starts out from some Marxist arguments and the theory proposed by J. Keynes and elaborated by modern neo-Keynesians, evolutionists and institutionalists. According to this concept, the State acts as a strategic investor, the owner of major enterprises in basic industries and the infrastructure. In addition to macro-economic regulation, it devises long-term plans (from advisory, indicative to mandatory ones in the State sector) and target programmes, sponsoring and subsidising their implementation. In this case, reforms are gradual, generally covering the lifetime of a generation (20–30 years). Their main objective is the creation of market-regulating institutes (organisations, systems) and the restructuring of production.

There is some controversy among economists as to whether general monetary policy rules lifting market restrictions and ensuring overall liberalisation or nation-specific market-regulating State institutions constitute the essential prerequisite of reform.

Many proponents of the second model maintain that the starting conditions, the system of values and the organisation of life in the CIS countries are unusual to the extent of defying the general conclusions of macro-economic theory or foreign experience; they necessitate an original specific theory and have original national lessons to be learnt.

The liberal concept assumes that macro-economic laws can be applied to all countries. Accordingly, the progress of reform only depends on consistent compliance with IMF requirements generalising the experience of market economy countries and the conclusions of international research about the rates of economic growth and regulation of economic processes.

It should be noted that the conflict between the two conceptions – of the *"economic man"* responding to change in economic conditions in any country in approximately the same way and the *"national man"* generally relying on ethnic collectivism (the relationship between individualistic and co-operative social psychologies), *value orientation* (relevant material and spiritual values), mentality, the character of human behaviour and group relations – can be traced back to the nineteenth century. The fathers of classical political economy, P. Quesnay, A. Smith, A. Turgot and D. Ricardo, were cosmopolitan and liberal. Chicago University Professor R. Lucas won the Nobel prize for the development and application of the hypothesis of rational expectations, furnishing a means for the statistical evaluation of economic relations between companies, organisations and households and predicting their behaviour using the global theory of economic growth, the theory of capital investment and finance. Non-market motivations divorced from continuous cost and benefit analysis are regarded by adherents to this concept as relics of the past unfit to be used in deciding on appropriate models of reform and easily surmounted as they emerge.

In his *National System of Political Economy* (1841), the German economist F. Liszt was the first to criticise the idea of applying the monetary laws of liberal trade to any nation. In the nineteenth century, G. Boeckl related the "national man" to the specific features of climate, soil, food and landscape. The German school of history (e.g. K. Bücher, W. Sombart) emphasised specific stages of economic development in individual nations rather than natural conditions. Marxists defined the stages by types of ownership and class structure in society (specific economic laws of societal stages), some other economists by forms of labour organisation (individual, family, crafts, manufacturing, factory) and yet others by the development of productive forces and the structure of consumption (with the work of W. Rostow,[2] J. Bell, J. Galbraith receiving wide recognition in the 1960s), civilisation types (O. Spengler, A. Toynbee[3]) or "long waves" (N.D. Kondratiev).

Institutionalists (M. Weber,[4] P. Northrop, A. Kreber, P. Sorokin, S. Bulgakov, N. Berdyaev,[5] P. Heine[6]), like monetarists, relate reforms to national economic culture but, unlike monetarists, they derive them from typical ideology and economic behaviour in social and ethnic communities rather than natural or other objective conditions. These views were elaborated in the Soviet and Russian literature of the 1980s.[7]

World Bank experts[8] believe that liberal economic policy (liberal pricing, dramatic cuts in subsidies, privatisation of State property, abolition of administrative restrictions on foreign and domestic trade) benefits economic growth. Countries employing more liberal strategies of reform (Poland, Slovenia, Hungary, Croatia, the Czech Republic, Slovakia, Macedonia) had minimum average annual decreases in GDP (16%) between 1989 and 1993 and maximum increases (4.3%) between 1994 and 1997. By contrast, in the Baltic countries, Bulgaria, Romania and Mongolia, where the pace of privatisation was slower, the

---

[2] Rostow, W. (1960): The Stages of Economic Growth. A Non-Communist Manifesto. Cambridge

[3] Toynbee, A. (1991): Comprehending History. / Translated from English. Progress, Moscow (Тойнби, А. (1991): Постижение Истории. / Пер. с Англ. Прогресс, Москва) [Cited here from Russian edition]

[4] Weber, M. (1990): Selected Works. / Translated from German. Progress, Moscow (Вебер, М. (1990): Избранные Произведения. / Пер. с Нем. Прогресс, Москва) [Cited here from Russian edition]

[5] Berdyaev, N.A. (1990): The Sources and the Meaning of Russian Communism. Nauka, Moscow (Бердяев, Н.А. (1990): Истоки и Смысл Русского Коммунизма. Наука, Москва) [In Russian]

[6] Heine, P. (1991): The Economic Mentality. / Translated from English. Novosti, Moscow (Хейне, П. (1991): Экономический Образ Мышления. / Пер. с Англ. Новости, Москва) [Cited here from Russian edition]

[7] Zaslavskaia, T.I., Ryvkina, R.V. (1991): Sociology of Economic Life: Essays on Theory. Nauka, Novosibirsk, etc. (Заславская, Т.И., Рывкина, Р.В. (1991): Социология Экономической Жизни: Очерки Теории. Наука, Новосибирск) [In Russian]

[8] (1996): From Plan to Market. World Development Report 1996. Washington

decrease was greater (–4.2% per year), and the increase lower (+4.0%). The CIS countries demonstrated the most substantial decrease between 1989 and 1995 and superior increases in more liberal strategies (e.g. Kyrgyzstan, Kazakhstan, Russia) between 1996 and 1998.

On a world-wide scale, according to D. Guargli, L. Lawson and W. Block (12 countries over 20 years), superior economic freedom calculated on the basis of 17 indicators provided superior growth rates (Hong Kong, Singapore, the USA, Switzerland, Canada, Germany), while intensive government regulation (in 16 countries) caused the GDP to decline (0.6% per year). According to some economists, more intensive State regulation and budget-carried GDP redistribution results in lower rates of economic growth and more dramatic declines. Increasing government revenue will mean an increased burden of taxes, in turn inhibiting private initiative. Moreover, as government investments are less efficient than private, their increased proportion of GDP will reduce the efficiency of production. In addition, the fiscal deficit will enhance inflation (particularly when covered by issuing money), increase external and internal debt (if it is discharged with foreign loans and government securities) and freeze the domestic financial resources for economic development (investment in government bonds being far more profitable and less risky).

According to A. Illarionov, the actual level of tax and other government revenues in the 1990s accounted for 32%–33% of the GDP in the USA, Japan and Australia (with GDP growth rates of up to 1.8%–2.4% per year) and over 60% in Sweden (with the resulting decrease in growth rates to 0.2%). In Russia and other CIS countries, taxes exceed 33% of the GDP, with public expenditure (including internal and foreign loans, as well as tax allocations) amounting to over 5% of GDP. The value was 34%–37% in developed industrial (the USA, Japan, Australia) and 21%–27% in medium-developed countries (South Korea, Chile, Mexico, Turkey, Thailand). In China, aggregate public expenditures between 1979 and 1995 (including financial aid and subsidies) decreased by one third – from 36% to 14% of GDP – and that of the Central Government from 12% to 5% of GDP. Investment of released resources gave an immense impetus to economic growth.

There is another opinion, however. Of course, expenditure related to an ineffective government machine must be reduced. But the lower proportion of public expenditure for social and investment purposes in South Korea, Thailand or even the EU countries and the USA compared with that in the CIS countries is not the cause but rather the effect of the emergence of extensive non-government funds, e.g. investment, pension, insurance. The GDP per capita is much higher. Simple reduction of the part of public expenditures in the CIS from 40%–50% to 24%–26% of GDP in the current situation would put an end to the establishment of the infrastructure and the social benefits traditionally provided in CIS countries (as opposed to countries such as Turkey and India).

The fact that federal expenditure in the USA before the Great Depression in the 1930s only comprised 8%–9% of GDP did not help to prevent the collapse. Many economists rightly suggest that investment and government allocation expenditure in the social sphere amounting to 25%–30% of GDP will stabilise the market economy. Reform is never a cut-and-dried matter.

The CIS countries have yet to elaborate a theory of economic organisation (regulated functioning) to be accepted as an ideology by the government, key political parties, business associations, trade unions and eventually by the majority of the economically active population.

Liberal theories generally summarise the experience of primitive commodity production dominated by small- or medium-scale producers of comparatively simple goods with short pay-back periods. Perfect competition, market equilibrium, the extensive use of debt securities (bonds, bills and notes) as means of payment and circulation – all these are instrumental in proportional economic development with partial or general overproduction crises when overabundant supply causes prices to dropped, producers lacking foresight to face financial ruin and capital to spontaneously transfuse into more profitable spheres of application. To date, the theory applies to the partial regulation of economic activities (transactions) in poor and medium-level agrarian or agro-industrial countries representing the basic IMF clientele.

Many proponents of the institutional theory point out that socialised production, reinforced positions of major enterprises, augmented roles of the industrial infrastructure, R&D complexes offering in-depth diversification and well-developed co-operation and sophisticated machinery with long investment pay-back periods for extensive and remote markets are inconsistent with the individualistic character of economic activities, requiring conformity to plan, i.e. deliberate rather than spontaneous proportion regulation. They advance the theory of transition from private to public regulation of economic behaviour of individuals (households) and firms by concentrating appropriate information in the hands of the government. In the pre-computer age, this also required the centralisation of property and producer's returns, thus drastically reducing economic initiative and market mobility. Transaction costs of planning, resource distribution, accounting and control and, more importantly, maintaining the firms attaining (or willing to attain) planned targets while failing to secure actual return (costs of utilised resources at world market prices exceeding output, common practice in the USSR) were far higher than in the market economy system.

On the other hand, scientific and technological revolution in the second half of the twentieth century enabled banks and exchanges to act as national accounting centres and, in collaboration with producers and consumers (immediate parties in transactions), to process the amount of information, making centralisation of this information ineffective (and, consequently, economic control by the State).

Transaction costs (marketing, advertising, contracting, legal support, hedging technological and commercial risks, strategic management) were significantly lower with direct relations and, more importantly, more efficient than with command administration by the government.

The institutional model of reforms involves private rather than public economic regulation, but also long-term contracts made by legal entities and supported by a civil, financial and economic legislation and supervised by government institutions collaborating with local government authorities and producers', consumers' and other associations. In this case, while retaining the predominantly market character (the bulk of goods and a significant part of services sold under contracts), the system of economy is no longer individualistic. The *contract* acts as a form of planning output, quality and prices prior to production, i.e. deliberately balancing demand and supply, including future development (options and forwards). As this occurs, cost and non-cost valuations are combined. In many instances, the institutional model underlies both general and specific features of inflation in CIS industrial-agrarian countries dominated by large monopolies employing obsolete technologies and therefore uncompetitive (with normal wage rates and environmental standards) on international markets.

It should be noted that an increasing number of prominent economists in the USA are arguing against artificial macro-/micro-economic differentiations, since neither the Keynesians nor the monetarists have been able explain the economic growth or decline of individual nations. Economic science describes the behaviour of economic units (individuals, their associations, firms and the government), involving theories of welfare, enterprise and motivation, and decision-making under uncertain conditions. A model of reform must therefore account for both general macro-economic laws and findings from a micro-economic analysis of conditions in specific countries or regions, i.e. national market economy types. This is precisely the approach employed by many reformers in the past, e.g. S.I. Witte,[9] the narodniks (populists). Modern authors emphasise national distinctions in decision-making, co-ordination, legal support, stimulation of economic activities and ownership patterns.[10]

Radical Western economists believe that a transitional economy implies not reorganisation but rather the closure of most enterprises and an entirely new economy system, the previous industrial structure being "improper".[11] D. Lipton, G. Sachs and some other proponents of the IMF's monetary concept, acting as government advisors in some CIS countries, maintained that reforms should be

---

[9] Witte, S.Iu. (1992): National Economy and F.Liszt. Voprosy Economiki 2–3 (Витте, С.Ю. (1992): Национальная Экономика и Ф.Лист. Вопросы Экономики 2–3) [In Russian]

[10] Gregory, P.R. (1989): Comparative Economic Systems. Boston

[11] Blanrhard, O., Dornbusch, R., Krugman, P., Layard, R., Summers, L. (1991): Reform in Eastern Europe. Cambridge, 65

initiated with the overall liberalisation of prices and markets, the lifting of import quotas, the reduction of customs tariffs and the unrestricted use of hard currency. In their opinion, even the 500 days proposed by S. Shatalin/G. Iavlinski are too long for radical reform, and the privatisation of major enterprises is urgent.

However, not all Western economists accepted this point of view. Many believed that A. Smith's "invisible hand of the market" alone was not strong enough to reform the Soviet economy system.[12] Washington (USA) University Professor J. Philips strongly suggested that blindly copying Western economic principles and an orientation towards Western markets would result in an almost triple reduction in real earnings in four fifths of households in the CIS countries. Prior to privatisation, major plants ought to be reorganised and re-equipped, which is unthinkable without restoring trade within the CIS. Only after that could the government "finance new projects without creating confusion and demonstrating its uselessness".[13]

Institutional and liberal conceptions appeared at the centre of theoretical controversies in the CIS again later in the 1990s. While everyone agreed on unfavourable effects during the first few years of reforms in many CIS countries, the causes of failure were treated very differently.

Six members of the Russian Academy of Science and five American economists, including three Nobel prize-winners, advocated reinforced State regulation conditions of the transitional economy. They proposed the five basic strategies of regulation: (1) co-ordinated establishment of the market infrastructure (e.g. banking system, accounting, insurance, currency control, information networks); (2) crime control and creation of incentives for production with an effective tax system; (3) restoration of consumer demand and non-inflationary economic growth by investing in R&D and the production sphere; (4) social protection of the rights of the population, development of social and ecological funds; and (5) anti-monopoly regulation and support for new competitive firms.

Liberal economists see the main problem of CIS reforms in excessive State intervention and the inadequate extent of economic liberalisation. They suggest that the government should first of all protect the security and property rights of citizens by assigning property to effective owners rather than work teams or directors. In their opinion, equal rights and opportunities, enhanced incentives and initiative and a middle class would only be possible with a drastic reduction of government expenditure, financial aid to agriculture, overall privatisation of heavy industry and restricted administrative control.

The controversy can only be resolved in action.

---

[12] Adams, W., Brock, J. (1993): Adam Smith Goes to Moscow: A Dialogue on Radical Reform. Princeton
[13] In: (1996): Проблемы Теории и Практики Управления (Problemy Teorii i Praktiki Upravlenija) 2, 25 [In Russian]

The Western version of liberal reforms. In the 1980s and 1990s, the USA (Reaganomics), the UK (Thatcherism) and some European Community (EC) countries as well as Japan, South Korea, etc. initiated economic liberalisation. Italy and France are now working towards privatisation of petrochemical, aircraft, automobile and some other corporations in which the state had controlling stakes until the 1990s. There have been reductions of import duties, currency restrictions and subsidies to the agricultural sector.

These are accompanied by the closure of many ministerial departments. In order to discharge the budget deficit, U.S. Republicans propose to eliminate the departments of power engineering, transport, housing and urban development, and education, to merge the trade and labour departments, to decimate the staff in the agriculture department and to cut financial aid to farmers.

Economic support will continue in more advanced branches, though not in the form of subsidies but rather by the transfer of state-owned technologies and information, political and credit support in export trade, tax exemptions, etc.

Western European liberal reforms largely depended on economic integration in the EC.

Spain carried out a liberal structural reform in the 1960s and 1970s, using exports of manpower to other European countries, popular tourism and foreign investments. Between 1960 and 1975, GDP increased by 7% per year, exceeding that in Sweden and Belgium and ranking fifth in Europe (below Germany, the UK, France and Italy). Only then did post-Franco Spain initiate political liberalisation (transition to a multi-party system) and joined the EC.

Chile, Argentina, Uruguay, Brazil, Peru and some other South American countries also changed over from the State-capitalist institutional model to the neo-liberal model of an open market economy system. This involved: (1) privatising mining, oil and gas and other basic industries with 60%–90% State control, as well as transport, communications, banks, etc.; (2) reorganising the national banks into independent institutions providing preferential loans for the government and State-owned companies; (3) lifting restrictions on the registration of foreign firms, lowering tariff barriers, creating export incentives using tax exemptions, reducing transportation tariffs, etc. rather than direct subsidies; (4) weakening control on prices on the national market; (5) reducing profits taxes and supporting small business and market competition.

The reforms were necessitated by a severe financial and economic crisis resulting from the low level of competitiveness of State-owned plants, their inability to accommodate to rapid market changes and continuous renovation of production and the low efficiency of expensive government programmes of the "Grand Project" type. By the early 1990s, Uruguay, Mexico and Argentina succeeded in discharging the budget deficit (three quarters of which was due to State-owned plants) and bringing annual GDP growth rates up to 5%–6%.

The reform in Chile started the in pre-Pinochet period. In the 1950s, the country excelled in having a high proportion of middle classes, South America's lowest income polarisation, well-developed legal enforcement mechanisms and a lack of mass corruption. The high (annual 10%) rates of economic growth in the authoritarian government system were attained by selling property (with the State controlling 85% of the mining industry and 60% of arable land) to effective owners ensuring real investments (only 10% of shares were distributed among the workers).

Despite the immense natural wealth, reforms in other South American countries were far more difficult. Liberalisation of foreign trade, attracting foreign capital and national currency devaluation were unable to eliminate social differences or political instability. As a result, rapid growth in the 1970s (11.5% p a) was followed by inflation in the 1980s in Brazil. In the consistently monetarist Mexico, the trade deficit and growing current dollar liabilities brought about financial collapse and decimated output between 1994 and 1995. As a result, annual capital inflows decreased from $32 to $9 billion.

In the course of reform, Mexico succeeded in bringing down inflation, stabilising the exchange rate and attracting more foreign investments (generally long-term investments in the form of share and bond purchasing). Crediting was extended for consumer durables (e.g. motorcars, refrigerators, television sets) using credit cards, checks, etc. And yet annual output did not increase by 2%–3% per year until the 1990s, the competitiveness of domestic firms and the national savings were at a low and the deficit of trade in the balance of payments was growing. Direct foreign investments accounted for only one quarter of foreign capital. The strain was aggravated by severe wage restrictions, reducing terms of government securities and growing election expenditure. Only the U.S. term loan ($30 billion) prevented full economic failure. Nevertheless, real earnings dropped to the 1970s level, the peso value went down by a third, unemployment rates increased rapidly and the deficit of the balance of trade with the USA amounted to $16 billion in 1996. Moreover, Mexico was deprived of independent foreign trade. New demands are met with imports, and loans cannot be the basis of independent development.

In the 1980s in Brazil, economic liberalisation resulted in dramatic social strains. New hard currency was introduced in 1994. The rate of exchange is now steady, inflation is down and foreign investments are growing rapidly. However, real incomes per capita are still lower than in 1980, with inferior national investment and competitiveness of many goods. In 1998, Brazil was confronted with another financial crisis with only the multimillion IMF loan saving the economy of this major state.

In Bolivia, the restricted government role in the economy was instrumental in reducing inflation (over 25,000% in 1988). However, consumption per head has been declining and the difference between rich and poor growing. In South

America in general, despite increased GDPs and exports, the balance of payments showed a deficit of 4% or even more than 5% of GDP in some countries in the 1990s.

These are all distant countries, of course. Yet learning should also involve lessons other than one's own or those of immediate neighbours. Later in the 1990s, the UN Commerce, Trade and Development Organisation (UNCTAD) and the World Bank agreed on the need to consolidate and enhance market regulation by the State using both legal and economic methods. Superior achievements are evident where the public and private sectors complement and reinforce each other.

Liberalisation in the more developed countries in the 1980s and 1990s was only initiated after creating the appropriate macro-economic conditions. The primary effort involved structural reform. The economic system came to be dominated by research and technology, by intensive production and by information, consulting, financial and travel services. The share of mining, agriculture and other traditional industries (e.g. textile, footwear, meat) decreased dramatically. Thousands of mines, quarries and metal works were closed in the USA, Germany, the UK and France. In some Southeast Asian countries, such as South Korea, mandatory sales of earnings in foreign currency (also from non-commercial transactions) to authorised banks were abolished, import trade liberalised and domestic markets opened to foreign capital only when the manufacturing industries became competitive in international markets in the early 1980s.

Economic liberalisation was preceded by the introduction of detailed economic legislation, including joint-stock, financial, banking, budgetary, trust and leasing (almost 10,000 laws) and enforcement mechanisms, including accounting standards, a system of control, attachment and sales of debtors' property, etc.

Most of the decisions taken by leaders of financial departments, banks, insurance companies, joint-stock ventures and other firms in the CIS countries are inconsistent with laws in developed countries. Many (e.g. the issue of fare securities, export of non-declared foreign currency, transactions evading registration with a bank and/or tax department) are punishable under criminal law in other countries.

Liberalisation in foreign countries was facilitated by the establishment of large commercial systems (e.g. *dzaibatsu* in Japan, *chebols* in South Korea) through which the government conducts its legal tax and credit regulatory economic activities, including depreciation accumulation and its use. The remaining small and medium-scale businesses are either connected with large corporations or act in the market segments that do not determine economic growth or are not attractive for big business (e.g. utility services, public catering, retail trade). Prior to the establishment of competitive and strictly legitimate corporations, the State generally retained key positions in the banking sector, power engineering, transport and the MIC (in particular in South Eastern Asia, France and Italy), financing national research and investment programmes (e.g. Japan, the USA), developing 5-year plans (South Korea, France), etc.

Liberalisation also implied the creation of an extensive middle class and State-sponsored training in up-to-date management. Thus in Taiwan (the world leader in hard currency reserves despite its insignificant mineral resources), until the 1990s, the government controlled all the basic industries (30% of capital assets), banks, imports, oil-product processing and sales. Special programmes provided incentives for management training and business development via authorised banks. Only after an efficient and legitimate business sector was established in the 1970s did it proceed with liberalisation of import and currency exchange.

It should be noted that, even after liberalisation reforms, the extent of State regulation in the USA, Japan and the EU countries in some respects exceeds that in many CIS countries, including Russia. Now, at the end of the twentieth century, the share of hired labour in the USA (almost 80%) and their wages as a percentage of GDP (over 45%) is much higher than in the CIS.

The CIS countries have a far greater share of incomes of "single entrepreneurs" – the "shuttles", stall vendors, brokers and other "new" Russians, Ukrainians, Tajiks, Georgians, etc., whose returns are never reported. The USA and the EU have strict regulations concerning power supply and general bank deposit insurance, and budget subsidies (within scientific and technological services, development of infrastructure, soil conservation and similar programmes) account for almost 30% of the final price of agricultural produce.

While the participant countries of the OECD have surmounted economic decline (with GDP increasing by almost 2%–3% towards the end of the 1990s), each new liberal policy cycle raises unemployment rates (8% and even 12% in some countries). No improvements are evident in environmental hazards or the difference between poor and rich countries, which is responsible for much of the terrorism and severe social conflicts seen in the world. Whether life is better in the market jungle or in the State-borne zoo remains to be seen.

The CIS countries can draw at least three conclusions from the Western experience of reforms. Firstly, the success of reforms is unthinkable without political stability and strong government authority. Secondly, the success of reforms is illustrated by real economic competitiveness rather than current rates of inflation. And finally, this success depends on effective group integration.

Reforms in Central and Eastern Europe. The liberal-monetary type of reform is typically employed in Eastern Europe and the Baltic countries. The "precepts" were formulated by the former Czech Minister of Economy W. Klaus and other economists. This type of reform is often referred to as "shock treatment". Yet this term is hardly applicable in Hungary, where radical changes were even initiated by J. Kadar, or in Serbia, Croatia, Slovenia and, of course, Poland, where the private sector had never been ousted in rural areas and trade. Only the former

GDR was able to carry out basic reforms in 2 years thanks to the massive injections from the FRG's federal budget.

What are the specific features of the liberal-monetary method employed in its purest form in the Czech Republic, Poland, Hungary, Slovenia, Slovakia and the Baltic countries and in Moldova and Kyrgyzstan in the CIS (and in Georgia, Armenia and Kazakhstan after 1995)?

1. Simultaneous liberalisation of prices, foreign trade (lifting of export licences and quotas and of duties on most goods); introducing convertibility and devaluation of the national currency; elimination or drastic reduction of subsidies to inefficient production units.

2. Tight financial and credit policy using IMF loans to reduce the budget deficit and rates of inflation; stabilising the national exchange rate adjusted to the dollar, mark, ECU, etc.; and control on price and income dynamics.

3. Overall privatisation, including land and other types of immovable property and involving the restitution of expropriated property and privatisation checks payable to the person named depending on contributed work. In this case, privatisation is not focused on increased public revenues, but rather on finding effective proprietors not intending to resell or to run dividends but to organise innovative production and increase the company's value.

4. Incentives for foreign investments, international co-operation and TNCs, focusing on international markets and the lifting of barriers to foreign trade rather than asking for foreign aid.

In the Czech Republic, Slovenia, Poland and some other countries taking this road, 2–3 years after the "bubble" demand, subsidised prices and closed markets were eliminated, and GDP went down, prices soared, devaluation avalanched and unemployment rates increased. By 1994, however, the market was defrozen, real prices for goods, services and assets decreased again and production came to follow the new market pattern. By 1995, the equilibrium market economy system led to the rise of GDP, investments, exports and real earnings.

This model of reform, however, can only be effective under certain conditions.[14] Among the most important are: political stability (two to three major parties with realistic programmes rather than clans, tribes and groups of uncertain leadership, demagogic appeal and idle promises), the introduction of civil society (a generally accepted national ideology, complete and correct information, stable direct-enactment laws with proper enforcement mechanisms), a market infrastructure (communication providing access to international markets,

---

[14] Kornai, J. (1992): The Socialist System. The Political Economy of Communism. Princeton; Kornai, J. (1996): Trends of Post-Socialist Development: General Review. Voprosy Ekonomiki 1 (Корнаи, Я. (1996): Тенденции Постсоциалистического Развития: Общий Обзор. Вопросы Экономики 1) [Cited here from Russian edition]

advanced banking and insurance systems with appropriate legislative support, stock market, distribution network, business education, expert consulting services, certification, auditing and leasing centres) and, most importantly, honest and initiative business operators, managers and farmers.

Such conditions were available in only a few of the former USSR republics. The first attempts to use liberal laws to create another Switzerland in Latvia in 1995 therefore resulted in a series of banking failures. It should be noted that the Baltic republics had been privileged over the CIS countries in terms of earnings from mass re-exports of Russian raw materials, transportation of petroleum products via their ports (the most important source of revenue), duty-free trade with Scandinavian and some other countries, foreign employment with no visa requirements (e.g. for Estonians in Finland), etc.

In addition, Eastern European countries did not embark on the path of spontaneous reform. They never attempted the free distribution of State property (excluding assignment to local authorities and the Church or restitution to previous owners). Considering the challenges of preliminary valuation with the lack of stock markets and inadequate investment resources, the government refrained from privatisation of major factories until effective owners emerged. Small and medium-scale plants were sold rather than given to their workers free of charge.

The government controlled earnings by indexing wages (lower than inflation rates), firms' deposits and bank accounts (to prevent loss of savings hindering the propensity to save), listing the goods and services excluded from free pricing and establishing limits for price increases (prior notification and approval).

Keeping positive real interest rates (the nominal one was more than the inflation rate) was of primary importance for the proper investment climate.

Unlike the situation in the CIS countries, fixed exchange rates were introduced. While all the exchange transactions were carried out in the banking system, for some years restrictions on the circulation of hard currency prevailed in domestic markets, including annual quotas on purchasing foreign currency by private individuals. Under the high inflation rate, they applied automatic adjustment – devaluation against some hard currencies or currency baskets (in the Czech Republic, 78% in 1990 and 8% in 1995; in Poland, 17% in 1991 and 12% in 1992, 8% in 1993 and an additional 1.8%–1.6% a month).

In addition, each of the countries allowed for specific national conditions. Thus the Czech Republic had a typically high share of heavy industry and the MIC (like Russia, Belarus, the Ukraine and Kazakhstan), overall co-operation in rural areas (unlike Poland) and no actual experience of reform as compared with countries such as Hungary. The most important factor in Czech experience is a radical change in the economic climate, abolishing State surveillance and subsidies (prior to legal privatisation), protection barriers and hence privileges for foreign investors. The government authorities were no longer entitled to command the economy, but were still responsible for the underlying rates of inflation and stable rate of the koruna. W. Klaus repeatedly emphasised that foreign aid begets corruption and inaction and that foreign investors pursue their own interests. Support from the international community should involve providing access to markets and contribution to joint projects rather than loans. Among the major prerequisites to progress in reform are correct information, political support by the public and orientation towards individual efforts rather than government directives. In 1995, the Czech Republic was the first Eastern European country to have a convertible national currency and whose citizens were free to purchase real estate elsewhere, to obtain foreign loans, etc. Nevertheless, privatisation created some serious complications in the late 1990s.

Poland had the shortest period of decline – 2 years. As in the Czech Republic, the leaders explained to the public the inevitable decrease in GDP, the price rise and the budget deficit in the initial phase of reforms. Special emphasis was placed on the private sector created with domestic and foreign private investments rather than State-owned property. Towards the end of the 1990s, Poland had Europe's highest growth rates in industrial production (mainly manufacturing) and the MIC (6% p.a.). However, there are 3 million unemployed (almost 15% of the labour force), while the top 20% in terms of wealth have incomes four times as great as the bottom 50%.

Hungary leads Europe in foreign investments per head (over $500 as against the average of $50) and the amount of foreign debt (over $20 billion). General Motors (the USA accounts for 40% of foreign investments) and Suzuki built motorcar works (new construction projects also constituting the base of the private sector here), and General Electric bought the major electric light bulb factory Tungsram. However, GDP growth rates in Hungary and Slovakia are lower than in Poland, the Czech Republic, Slovenia and Croatia and in the Baltic countries, choosing less radical reform models.

As part of its monetary policy, the government issues money covered by gold and currency reserves. The principal concern in this case is optimal GDP structure (15% public demand, two thirds individual consumption, 17%–20% capital investments), financial stability of banks, auditing of joint-stock companies, compensation of previous deposits with items of State property (e.g. land, apartments) and securities, taxes on all earnings (except ploughed-back profits) and vigorous action against arrears and non-repayment of loans.

However, even with current growth rates, most Eastern European countries will not be able to regain their 1989 GDP levels before the end of this century (industrial output halved between 1989 and 1993, as was later the case in the CIS countries). By 1999, only Poland and Slovakia were successful in this respect. According to a *Times* survey in 1995, only 18% of Poles, 12% of Hungarians and 33% of Czechs believed that their quality of life had improved in the past 5 years.

It was only in Slovenia, where reforms had started as far back as the 1950s, that living standards approached those in the EU countries. In the Czech Republic, leaving other former member states of the Council for Mutual Economic Aid (CMEA) far behind in terms of privatisation and integration in the European economy, the average worker's salary in 1997 was one fourth that in Germany.

The Baltic countries enjoyed success with the liberal model of reform. GDP halved between 1990 and 1993, but then went up again (0.6% in 1994, 3% in 1995, 5% in 1996 and so on in Latvia). Inflation rates varied in 1995 between 20% (Latvia) and 35% (Lithuania), but then decreased to annual rates of 10%–17%. Export trade with the CIS countries expanded, with external and internal debts being comparatively small (particularly so in Estonia and Latvia). Average wages are higher than in the CIS countries.

On the other hand, the Baltic countries enjoyed the advantages lacking in the CIS countries: profits from the transit of goods to their ports and re-export of non-ferrous metals and oil products from Russia (the most important revenue); the proximity of the friendly and highly developed Scandinavian countries offering trade and investment preferences (e.g. Estonia with a population slightly over 1 million was granted almost the same amount as Russia); and the best developed infrastructure and agrocomplex in the former USSR. Nonetheless, services now account for more than one half of GDP, with an unfavourable balance of trade with the West. Agricultural output has been reduced, while the revival of industries, in particular mechanical engineering, is highly problematic in view of the lack of access to the CIS markets.

In summary:

– Economic liberalisation has been the predominant strategy in developed countries between the 1970s and 1990s. This experience has been used to advantage in Eastern and Central European countries.

– Liberalisation in developed countries did not consist in shock therapy but was gradual, taking 10–20 years for the new economic structure, advanced economic legislation, structural elements of administration and a class of loyal entrepreneurs and modern managers to emerge.

The essential features of efficient liberal reforms are: (1) a competitive economic system; (2) a developed middle class of entrepreneurs and managers with a market-oriented mentality; (3) advanced economic legislation with relevant enforcement mechanisms; (4) access to comprehensive, valid and daily marketing and financial information for all economic agents. Only under these conditions can the government ensure a reasonable response to monetary economic levers.

2.3 Institutional Reforms

Institutional models of reforms. The institutional model of reform involves the key role of central authority, providing some forms of public economic planning, distributing budget funds, regulating prices and wages, supporting priority and critical industries and major individual companies and enhancing social justice with progressive taxes on high incomes and benefits for the needy. The new structures evolve gradually within government target programmes. The whole process is typically anti-shock and evolutionary, taking due account of the challenge of reorganising the human mind and accommodating new realities.

The theoretical basis of such reforms in the 1990s was found in neo-socialist (social-democratic) and neo-Keynesian theories proposing that the government should not abandon regulation of the economic system but rather its previous monopolistic role as owner and production administrator. Some foreign authors, in particular in the USA, Japan and Western Europe, have shown that financial stability will not resolve the long-term structural problems associated with public transport, communications, science and technology, social infrastructure, the fuel and energy (FEC) and agrarian-environmental complexes, research-intensive industries and the intellectual and human potential of society.

Resolution of the problems will require immense investments that private firms cannot afford, particularly in the CIS countries. The government may organise shared financing of priority programmes from the budget, non-budget funds, and national and international commercial structures with appropriate guarantees.

In the institutional model, the government remains both the principal investor and the principal purchaser of research-intensive products and technologies. The limited individual effective demand during the painful period of reform will be compensated for by State-sponsored projects to build roads, pipelines, airports, terminals, irrigation systems, etc.

The government still holds the basic complexes (e.g. power systems, railways, integrated petrochemical plants) which, due to their special significance, low profitability and long pay-back period, either cannot be sold or are not particularly attractive to private owners.

The government will identify the priorities of personnel training and technological renovation of production, supporting them with tax exemptions, subsidies (grants), preferential loans, technology and information transfer.

According to the proponents of institutional reform, the government's functions under the new conditions should include: (1) socio-environmental, economic and legal support for citizens, using relevant legislation and enforcement mechanisms; (2) effective management of State property and its privatisation processes as well as of natural resources – the essential national wealth; (3) overall macro-economic regulation of the public economy aimed at progressive change in its structure, development of human potential, science and high technologies and foreign trade; (4) creation of a favourable investment climate to channel the profits, private savings and foreign investments into national economic priorities; and (5) social security for the disabled and those not easily able to adapt to market conditions.

Reforms in Western countries. Many components of the institutional approach were used in the New Deal proposed by F.D. Roosevelt during the U.S. crisis in the 1930s. In his speech on 7 April 1932, he invited the nation to focus on income redistribution, to abandon the unrewarding elitist approach and to adopt plans basing on "essential elements of economic power", accounting for the "man lost at the bottom of the social pyramid". Speaking in Chicago in July 1932, F D. Roosevelt emphasised the "planned action" and "equity in national wealth distribution", and in San Francisco in September of the same year, he stressed the "adjustment of production to consumption", the "adaptation of the existing economic system to public needs ... even though this will mean certain limits to certain persons engaged in business."

At short notice, inviting the collaboration of competent specialists, laws were issued concerning industrial reconstruction and de-monopolisation, agricultural regulation, seasonal labour camps for unemployed young people, public construction works for highways, stadiums, schools and hospitals and the completion of building projects, including two aircraft carriers. There were emergency banking laws, and the Social Insurance Act of 1935 was the first in the USA to introduce old-age and unemployment benefits. Special emphasis was placed on the national patriotic ideology of overcoming the crisis as the main enemy of New America. It was then that foundations were laid for the roads, sports and educational infrastructure the USA are justly proud of. Over 3 million young people, instead of roaming the streets, were offered vocational and pre-conscription training in labour camps.

Of course, the USA of the 1930s differ from the CIS countries of the 1990s. The U.S. economic system was fairly efficient, labour productivity was high and there was no question of extensive food imports, severe inflation or a budget deficit. On the other hand, the decline of production (to 49%), huge-scale bankruptcy, growing crime and social conflicts indicated the limitations of a self-regulated market.

Sweden's model of economic regulation by the government along social-democratic lines gained great prestige in the CIS countries. This involved a policy of total employment (82% of the labour force employed by the early 1990s, with unemployment rates kept under 1.6%), sponsoring new jobs and vocational training (35% of adult Swedes trained, with education costs accounting for 7% of budget expenditures – as much as defence costs), controlled wage differentiation (the same salary for the same work irrespective of firm activities, with 2:1 earnings ratio in favour of builders, metallurgists and chemists), free social care, subsidised housing and education, high benefits drawing on Europe's highest high-incomes taxes and, finally, the social consensus (strikes or lockouts only permitted under collective contracts negotiated by branch rather than local trade unions).

With all the attractions, in the mid-1990s the system resulted in deteriorating labour activities, flights of capital, decreased competitiveness of goods and devaluation of the krone. In 1975, income per head in Sweden was 11% higher, and in 1996 6% lower than the average in the OECD countries. Sweden has been excluded from the list of the world's ten most developed countries. Major corporations such as Volvo, SAAB, Alfa Laval, Erickson and Electrolux are locating their production in countries with lower labour costs. Superior living standards cannot be ensured by income re-distribution alone. Sweden had to reduce the world's highest individual income tax, which was inhibiting interest in hard or highly qualified work.

Even more instructive is the case of Uruguay. In the 1920s, it was among the world's richest countries, one of the first to introduce the 8-h working day, free secondary education and state pensions. However, the Government then began to re-distribute agricultural export gains, channelling them into inefficient urban development and industrial projects. This resulted in increased fiscal deficit and national debt and interrupted economic growth, so that by the late 1980s the country ranked only 43rd in the world in terms of income.

Reforms in China and Vietnam. The most important success in institutional reform was achieved in Asia. Asian experience is of particular interest for the CIS countries. Firstly, in the twentieth century, the Asian/Pacific region has (along with North America and Europe) become one of the world's three economic poles. The contribution made by Western civilisations to the world's GDP decreased from 64% to 43% between 1950 and 1997, while Japan and China are now listed second and third in the world (below the USA) in terms of overall GDP. Secondly, the region is the CIS's immediate neighbour in the south, with China, Vietnam and other countries in Indochina having similar economic systems before 1990. China's trade with Russia in the 1990s amounted to almost $8 billion and is expected to grow 2.5-fold early in the 21st century.

The specific Chinese method of reform inspired by Den-Siaoping can be summarised as follows:

1. Denationalisation, starting with the agroindustrial complex (AIC), light industry and trade, ensuring tangible public gains even in the initial stage of reforms and attracting peasants, craftsmen and minor traders. The branches typically have low capital intensity, short capital circulation periods and extensive family contracting.

2. The major industrial sector of the economy is still controlled and planned by the State, but a consistent 10- to 15-year programme of commercialisation and

privatisation of enterprises is underway. The intermediary elements – ministerial departments – have been retained to govern the economy. Above all, production units are allowed to independently plan production, supplies, sales, wages and management structure.

3. A special role in filling the market, preventing mass unemployment and creating a middle class is played by rural enterprises engaged in the production of consumer goods, building and services and established with private savings rather than by privatisation of State property. In the 1990s, 9 million plants in villages and rural districts with 100 million jobs accounted for 60% of the overall output of goods and services, including sales, storage and processing of agricultural produce.

4. Foreign capital is attracted on an immense scale (over $180 over 17 years), but mainly in the five special and isolated economic zones, focusing on the export trade rather than competing with domestic producers (with two different types of currency). Foreign investments in the 1990s contributed over 15%, with more than 100 affiliated foreign banks and over 270,000 joint venture companies. Export trade accounted for 45% of GDP, demonstrating the high extent of economic openness, while currency reserves exceeded $86 billion in 1997.

5. Progress in reforms is secured by the strong party and government bureaucracy and the official national ideology of transition to the market economy system for the sake of China's national glory.

China's path of reform is not to be opposed to the liberal-monetary one. The country plans a more rigid monetary policy to bring inflation rates down to 5%–10% p.a. The People's Republic of China introduced a dual-level credit system involving non-public banks and rural crediting co-operation and stock and insurance markets. The contribution of the directive planning system to GDP decreased from 95% to 5%, and a general rate of exchange has been set (with the dollar equivalent to 8–8.5 yuans). Reduction of the budget deficit, banking procedures meeting international standards, lower import tariffs (from 35% to 15%), reformed State-owned plants – all these factors will contribute to the convertibility of national currency. Free or floating prices are set at 90% of consumer and 80% of producers' goods, including a normative level of return. Pricing follows a pre-set formula. To control inflation, extensive use is made of discount rate regulation, the State purchase of MIC products at fixed prices and sales of goods from the State reserves for the purposes of market stabilisation.

Neither are the achievements to be idealised. One half of the 30,000 State-owned plants are unprofitable due to obsolete technology and low-quality management, despite low wages and budget subsidies for engineering updating. Their aggregate debt amounted to $620 billion in 1996. The rate of return of private firms is far superior, particularly in the 37,000 joint-venture companies (with founding capital of $40 billion). Output per 1 t standard fuel in the People's Republic of China is still lower than in the USA and almost one ninth of that in

Japan, and labour productivity and the quality of production cannot be compared. There are frequent upward flights of inflation, high rural unemployment rates, decreasing cultivated areas per head and poor protection against natural disasters. As estimated by the World Bank, over 300 million Chinese spend less than $1 per day.

On the other hand, during the 20 years of reform (in the 1980s and 1990s), China demonstrated an average annual GDP growth of over 9%, coming second in the world (and first in coal mining, yarn, textiles, bicycles and washing machines). It supplied food to 1.2 billion of its inhabitants, leading the world in grain, oil, fat and cotton. Real earnings increased almost 2.5-fold in urban areas and over 3.5-fold in rural areas, with public savings never devaluated. Housing space per rural dweller more than doubled (from 8 to 19 m^2). The volume of foreign market exceeded $250 billion (with a favourable balance of trade with the USA of $40 billion), and this mixed-type economy (the share of the State sector decreased from 98% to 40%, with the co-operative sector accounting for 50%, and the 15 million private businesses for 10%) moved from 32nd to 11th in the world in this respect.

China borders on four CIS countries (the common frontier with Russia alone extends for over 4000 km), and their economic systems are largely complementary. That is why special attention should be paid to the Chinese experience, in particular with regard to regional autonomy policies ("making a living by one's own hearth"), sustained links with emigrants (bringing in 80% of foreign investments), contracted government financing for State-owned plants on terms (fixed payments scheme for 5–10 years), flexible taxation, entrepreneurship in the armed forces (along with strict discipline) and auction trade with foreign firms.

Towards the end of the 1990s, unprofitable State-owned plants have been extensively sold to private individuals, including foreigners, with local government authorities acting as intermediaries. Joint-stock workers-controlled companies are being established. Factories are assigned to private investors in discretionary trust (without sale). As a result, in 1997 the enterprise sector contributed over 60% of industrial output (with the public sector accounting for almost 40%) and 80% of new jobs. Drastic cuts are being planned in the number of major plants financed by the budget.

In Vietnam in the 1990s, prices were liberalised, land ownership was transferred to peasants, private business was legalised, and privileges and protective measures were ensured for foreign investors. At the same time, Vietnam retained the one-party system and State ownership in heavy industry, transport and communications, and the government still has controlling stake in many privatised plants and commercial banks.

Devastated by war, the country succeeded in bringing inflation rates down to 10% p.a., stabilising the national currency and attracting $13 billion foreign investments (mainly from Asian countries, France, Germany and Australia). The country has come to act as a major rice exporter (2 million t per year). The high GDP growth rates (9% p.a.) suggest future improvements, particularly now that the country has joined the strong integrative group ASEAN (annual income per head in the 1990s was only $200, 50% of that in China and India, 20% of that in Thailand and 5% of that in South Korea).

Institutional reforms in another and previously even more backward Asian country, Laos, caused the annual income per head to rise to $350 (from $90 in 1976).

China and countries in Indochina are much different from many CIS countries as far as the conditions of reforms are concerned. The greater part of their populations are peasants preserving their skills of careful manual work. South Asian nations are typically thrifty (domestic savings accounting for 35% of GDP in China and 17% in Vietnam, with earnings lower than in the CIS). The ethnic diaspora (55 million native Chinese) contributes the major portion of foreign investments (80% in China). Their recent experience of war and domestic strain encourages the traditional consolidation and discipline.

Reforms in other Asian countries. Although the Asian countries largely engaged in institutional reforms (Turkey, Taiwan, Malaysia, Thailand) still lag behind developed European and American countries in income per head ($2500 vs. $13,000 p.a.), they were prominent on the list of world GDP growth rates per head between 1985 and 1996 (third and first at 1.9%). Considering the immense and rapidly growing demographic potential (2850 million), the region (including Japan) is expected to act as the world's primary economic driving force in the 21st century. It has taken over from England (in the nineteenth century) and the USA (in the twentieth century) to acquire a reputation as the world's industrial workshop. On the other hand, of the 209 states marked on the World Bank's economic map, GDP fell in more than 60 African, Asian, South American and, regretfully, CIS countries between 1985 and 1997. These countries generally employed the pure market model accompanied by a high share of public expenditure, administrative bans and corruption among the swelling bureaucracy. Income differences between the rich and the poor countries increased from 13:1 in the 1960s to 60:1 in the 1990s. Incomes decreased in African countries south of the Sahara and came to a halt in the Middle East and North Africa (except Tunisia and Egypt). There were severe financial crushes in Indonesia and some other countries.

In this context, a matter of specific interest is the experience in Japan and South Korea. The programme of reform in Japan was devised with active contributions from the proponents of institutional reform in the U.S. scientific community, in particular V. Leontiev. The administrative command system existing in Japan in the 1930s and 1940s was not abolished but rather transformed along democratic lines. With Constitution of Japan (which was actually imported, mainly being devised by U.S. General McArthur), historical traditions and national mentality were embodied in multiple components of the economic system. The economic model demonstrating high performance between the 1950s and 1990s utilised the experience of the Planning Council in guiding the accelerated development of heavy industries in the 1930s and 1940s, with industrial branch associations acting as intermediaries between the Council and production bodies in the course of preparing and fulfilling targets.

Government control of securities issued by the major corporations (almost 40% State-owned shares in the 1950s and 1960s) ensured the preparation and State-financed implementation of major research engineering and export programmes. The economic planning administration at the Prime Minister's office devises the macro-economic strategy of 5-year forecasting plans, annual White Books of economic targets and monthly analytical notes. These provide guidelines for the Ministry of Foreign Trade and Industry, which collaborates with the Ministry of Finance and co-operates with business associations in developing the specific programmes of major applied innovations, resource-saving and environmental technologies, micro-electronics, robot engineering, etc. In doing so, proper consideration is given to specific national challenges such as unbalanced trade with the USA and Europe, the increased proportion of elderly populations and barriers to the yen rate growth.

Over 70% of the shares in major corporations in Japan are held by institutions (e.g. banks, insurance and investment funds) rather than private individuals. In contrast to the USA, the focus is on long-term access to international markets rather than maximum running profits.

Although eightfold greater than in the pre-war period, income per head is still one third that in the USA (considering the price differences and lower living space standards). The pace of economic growth has subsided significantly in the late 1990s. This, however, is actually indicative of a new phase of development rather than a crisis of the institutional system. Higher wages affected the competitiveness of Japanese goods in international markets, with consequently extended exports of capital. The biggest audio-video engineering corporation, Akai Electric, supported by Mitsubishi Electric and Semitech (Hong Kong), brought the contribution of production facilities outside the country up to 70%–80%, with a simultaneous development of the R&D centre in Japan. The bankruptcy of several large financial companies later in the 1990s did nothing to affect the continuous growth of gold and currency reserves.

In South Korea, the government regulates the market economy system in collaboration with the three major corporations – Samsung, Hyundai and Kia. Small businesses are generally operated under franchising or holding agreements with large corporations. The middle class constitutes almost 70%, with only 10% of families having earnings below the average. The national planning system involves collaborative ministries responsible for science and technology and investment policies, as well as business associations and trade unions. The principal concern is with independent law courts and enforcement mechanisms. Hand in hand with the advanced social security system go the increased load of work (6-day working week with a 10-day vacation). Unemployment rates are under 2%, and inflation is at a minimum. The annual GDP increase of 6%–9% was also instrumental in the transformation of this country with its population of 45 million, backward and devastated by the war and having no important natural resources, into a industrial world leader (in shipbuilding, motorcar and electronics industries in particular) over one generation (20–25 years).

South Korea ranks the 11th in the world in terms of GDP, with annual income per head exceeding $8500, thus excluding it from the list of developing countries – clients of the World Bank (income per capita under $4860).

Towards the end of the 1990s, growth rates fell, the loss in the balance of trade grew and the major corporations are now investing in offshore zones and countries with lower wages. In 1997, the country was exposed to a financial crisis, with the national exchange rate falling by one third. This is indicative of the exhausted potential of the government economic regulation model. It was necessary at the start of reforms when co-ordinated efforts and mobilised resources were required. The situation changed with the adjustment to more developed economic systems, expanded competition with other Asian countries, an enhanced role of trade unions and public democratisation. The pattern of decision-making by the central government and related diversified corporations brings more red tape and inhibits initiative, flexible thinking and the willingness to take risks. South Korea, Japan and some other Asian countries are now in need of comprehensive reforms.

Among the strongest proponents of institutional principles of reform in the CIS were Uzbekistan, Turkmenistan, Azerbaijan, the Ukraine and Belarus.

Prospects for institutional reforms in the CIS. Three attempts at institutional reform have been made in the territory currently integrated in the CIS. First, A.A. Stolypin and S.I. Witte planned a peaceful evolution towards international economic standards 25 years after the 1905 revolution, using national resources (e.g. land privatisation, free market), and foreign investments and experience. Long-term loans were to encourage the newly emerging middle class in rural areas, involving opening up of virgin and abandoned lands, State-administered industrialisation and general entrepreneurship. Looking back, we can appreciate the ideas of local government (*zemstva*), co-operation between small producers and national identification in the course of reform. Between 1912 and 1914, Russia as a whole, including Transcaucasia, the Baltic and Turkistan, attained superior growth rates of the public economy, profits, exports, welfare and population.[15]

Another attempt, in many respects anticipatory of current reforms in China, Vietnam, Laos and Mongolia, was made during the NEP. The Tenth Congress of the RKP(b) in 1921 decided to consolidate the single-party system (political dictatorship), retaining government control over the command keys of economy (land, heavy industry), while legalising small business in production and trade, inviting foreign capital (concessions) and introducing State enterprises (commercialisation and financial autonomy for trusts and syndicates). Of great interest is the experience of financial stabilisation (initiated by G. Sokolnikov) based on the introduction of alternative hard currency (*chervonets*). By 1926, the consumer market was saturated and the private sector accounted for 40% in industry, with one quarter leased plants.[16]

On the other hand, no savings for a large-scale programme of accelerated industrialisation were accumulated during the period. This predetermined the abandonment of the NEP and transition to the administrative command system.

The third reform was initiated during *perestroika* and ended in complete failure. In 1988, public money revenues of the population increased by 13%, fourfold more than labour productivity, with the budget deficit amounting to 10% in 1989 and 4.5-fold more money being issued compared with 1985. Consequently, the consumer market deteriorated and gold and currency reserves were eaten up; mass plunder of State property ensued and a criminal economy emerged.

Reforms in that period, both in the USSR and in the People's Republic of China, were aimed at enhancing the human factor against the restricted central planning and command economic administration. Yet the results were different. In the USSR, no clear theoretical justification or ideology of reform was offered to the people; the reform neglected the basis, i.e. ownership. The "full administration rights" gave directors the chance to transfer State assets to false accounts of small plants, co-operatives and "youth science and technology centres" without personal liability for firm management. While emphasis in China was placed on economic interests (effective private ownership and liability, free economy zones, profits for investment), it was generally political in the USSR (*glasnost*). Reform

---

[15] For more details see: Maksimov, S.I. (1992): Reconstruction and Challenges of Economic Reform. Publishing Office of Saint-Petersburg State University, Saint Petersburg (Максимов, С.И. (1992): Перестройка и Проблемы Хозяйственной Реформы. Издательство СПбГУ, Санкт-Петербург) [In Russian]; Sirotkin, V.G. (1991): Great Reformers in Russia. Znanie, Moscow (Сироткин, В.Г. (1991): Великие Реформаторы России. Знание, Москва) [In Russian]

[16] Bogomazov, G.G. (1983): Shaping the Foundations of Socialist Economic Mechanism in the USSR during the 20s and 30s. Publishing Office of the Leningrad State University, Leningrad (Богомазов, Г.Г. (1983): Формирование Основ Социалистического Хозяйственного Механизма в СССР в 20–30-е годы. Издательство ЛГУ, Ленинград) [In Russian]

in China started in the consumer sector, attracting millions of peasants and resulting in rapidly increasing yields and obvious improvements. In the USSR, it was decided to begin with industries, generally focusing on military and space engineering. The reform was only supported by a thin layer of intellectuals and commercial intermediaries, and at the first signs of problems, many of them left for foreign universities and offshore zones.

Following the 1998 financial crisis, monetarism has almost become an expletive in some CIS countries. It has been a virtual scapegoat for all the errors of reform. But monetarism deals with the laws of money circulation without assuming the role of a general theory of reform. M. Friedman and other monetarists were prepared to recognise the expediency of cash issues during the conversion of the war industry and accept temporary inflation for the sake of future economic growth. Changes in the strategy of reform later in the 1990s, rather than rejecting monetarism and market-oriented transformations, were designed to reinforce the role of the government and democratic institutions in such transformations.

The CIS countries are building an original model of economic development, with due account paid to positive foreign experience in monetary and institutional reform, regional integration and, more importantly, their own cultural traditions and social and economic characteristics. In this context, denationalisation and privatisation of State property in the CIS countries should be a matter of special discussion.

Field of Debate

1. What does sustainable economic development mean? Why will it assume a special significance for society in the third millennium?

2. What does structural economic reform mean? How does it differ from simple changes in economic legislation and forms of production management?

3. What is the purpose of reform in the CIS countries? Can it be conceived as a retreat to pre-1917 capitalism?

4. What are the twentieth-century forms of market economy? Can transition to a market economy system be described as the eventual goal of reform?

5. What are the main stages of economic history in the twentieth century? What is the informatisation of production and society as a whole? What are the main strategies and benefits of informatisation?

6. Are economists justified in maintaining that the CIS countries are moving from a planned to market-based economy? How can the need for planning be demonstrated in the new conditions? How does it differ from the previous system? What are the basic characteristics of the market planning model?

7. What are the main strategies of economic development on the eve of the third millennium? Describe the costs and benefits of development in the CIS countries in the twentieth century. What gains are still valid?

8. What are the principal models of economic reform? Can they be the same for all countries?

9. What is the liberal monetary strategy of economic reform? How were reforms implemented in Western, Central and Eastern European and Baltic countries?

10. What is the institutional model of reform? How are reforms implemented in Western and Asian countries? How can the achievements of reform be explained in China, Vietnam and some other countries? What area of their experience might be useful in the CIS countries?

11. What is the essential significance of adjusting the strategy of reform in the CIS countries towards the end of the 1990s? What arguments do you consider as most convincing?

Chapter 3

DENATIONALISATION, PRIVATISATION AND ECONOMIC SECURITY IN THE CIS COUNTRIES

3.1 Denationalisation: Rational Level

Denationalisation – liberal model. Denationalisation of the economy, i.e. the State waiver of the right of day-to-day administration of economic activities of enterprises (e.g. planning the range and output of products, resource supply, sales management) has been at the basis of reform in all the CIS countries without exception. In particular, this involves privatisation, i.e. transfer of ownership or assignment of trust in state property to legal entities or private individuals by sale of shares, sale of entire enterprises at auctions or in tender trade, lease (with an option to buy out) or trust (contracts of discretionary trust).

The science and technology revolution that began in the middle of this century conclusively demonstrated the failure of a system operated by a single owner – the State. Its principal fault was the banishment of individual entrepreneurship and economic initiative to the underground economy. This undermined the basic engine of social progress – human interest – giving individuals and working collectives neither the chance nor the need to develop and implement economic innovations on their own initiative and responsibility and thus hindering the sustainable development of society.

Concentration of resources in a vast land placed under central control did ensure military strategic parity with the USA while impeding the basic productive force of society – the working people. Whole generations were deprived of the desire and opportunity to work wholeheartedly. Government surveillance failed to create a rational economic structure. One striking example is illustrated by comparison of the Ukraine and France. They are not dissimilar in terms of population, size and economic potential, and yet while being far ahead in raw materials produced (14-fold in coal, tenfold in iron ore and threefold in steel), the former lags far behind in finished products (15-fold in motorcars and three- to fourfold in total industrial output).

Market economy gives top priority to the interests of producers and the encouragement of business activities, restricting government intervention to strategic tasks. Firms represent the basis of the market economy rather than the government's milk cow. This is recognised in all the CIS countries. However, the State's role in the transitional economy is perceived in different ways.

Liberal economists describe the four basic functions of the State under the new conditions as: (1) developing economic legislation and supervision of its enforcement and performance under contracts, protecting owners' rights; (2) regulating money circulation (limited issue of money) and the financial and credit system in general (setting basic discount rates, rules of issue and circulation of securities, regulating banking and other financial activities); 3) providing for free competition (e.g. anti-monopoly legislation, business ethics); and 4) national security (defence of national frontiers, environmental control and conservation of natural resources, protecting the nation's health and cultural and moral potential, as well as science, education, rule of law, etc.). Figuratively speaking, this conception views the government as a football referee – ever present in the field, strictly controlling compliance with general regulations, while never sponsoring the players or instructing them as to the manner or amount of scoring.

According to some foreign (e.g. A. Ocklund, M. Friedman, G. Sachs) and Russian economists (e.g. E. Gaidar,[1] G. Iavlinski, A. Illarionov, A. Uliukaev), economic transformations in the CIS are inconsistent because the State fails in the above-mentioned functions, while engaging in unchecked distribution and re- distribution of resources and property. This creates dependence and corruption. A firm's prosperity does not depend on competitiveness but rather on its intimacy with the powers that be, membership in a financial group, tax exemptions and customs privileges, and access to available export and budget resources. All these are fully consistent with tradition in many CIS countries' system of tribal and ethnic relations, of dependence on the leader rather than the market.

Human initiative and activity are applied not to production but to the distribution of what has been produced by others. This prevents equity in consumption, creating a new hierarchy based on authorised privileges, intimacy with the authorities, access to distribution centres and the underground economy. Only private (non-State) ownership can secure economic freedom and responsibility.

These conclusions can be justified as follows. The CIS countries have not yet developed the codes (e.g. tax, trade, land, budget, labour, housing) clearly defining the relations of the State, firms, regions and citizenry. Many laws concerning firms of various ownership types, corporations, non-profit

---

[1] Gaidar, E.T. (1996): Days of Defeat and Victory. Vagrius, Moscow (Гайдар, Е.Т. (1996): Дни Поражений и Побед. Вагриус, Москва) [In Russian]

organisations, natural monopolies, pension and other funds, accounting, securities market, trust, etc. are either missing or inadequate in the current conditions. The lack of direct enactment necessitates multiple legally binding ordinances (decisions, instructions, written administrative orders from tax, customs and other State agencies) often conflicting each other and the laws and granting unfounded privileges to individual firms, etc. Each formal contract is accompanied by a series of agreements, often verbal and hidden from government authorities. The unreliable enforcement mechanism (e.g. economic courts, arbitration) often forces businessmen to use the services of illegal bodies.

In some CIS countries, denationalisation of the public economy is well under way. Thus, in Kazakhstan in 1997, the number of administrative agencies halved, with 25 ministries, councils and other State departments instead of 48. The oil and gas ministry was replaced by the State-owned oil company Kazakhoil. In the new government structure, the President has only two assistants – for national security and the national economy, including investments, securities, planning and control of strategic natural resources. Russia has likewise reduced its civil service staff.

The most consistent economic liberalisation in the CIS is being carried out in Moldova on the IMF's advice. The government abolished the planning system in production and sales, actually abandoned regulation of prices and foreign trade and cut the share of State-owned and municipal enterprises to 8%. Foreign loans were used to support the stabilisation and almost complete convertibility of the national currency (lieu) and to control inflation. Yet denationalisation failed to ensure economic growth and social development. The new market entities – banks, exchanges, investment funds – are still incapable to act as market regulators. Industrial production almost halved between 1990 and 1998, and many high-technology plants were closed down. Average monthly wages comprised only one half of the minimum consumer budget, with the rich earning almost 14-fold more than those in the poor public segments and the considerable number (30% in rural areas) of unemployed. There was a substantial devaluation of the lieu in 1998.

The CIS needs a model of its own. Later in the 1990s, many economists, even in the West, concluded that market transformations of the economy in the CIS are impossible without government regulation. As J. Krecel, J. Macier and G. Graber observed in their monograph *Market Shock* (Vienna, 1995), the market is not a general and predominant economic category, but rather an important institution, along with the government, legislation, science, traditions and culture in each specific country (as first pronounced by Veblen late in the nineteenth century). Austrian economists highlighted the mistake of indiscriminate applications of liberal economic theories, idealising the regulating potentials of the market. Each country should establish a market economy in its own way, starting from a theoretical analysis of both international experience and specific national characteristics.

The basic characteristics governing the CIS countries' need for their own model of reforms can be described as follows.

Limited experience of the market economy. The classical market was first established in 1861, on emancipation of the peasants, the most numerous social class. At the same time, slavery was abolished in Bokhara and some other areas. However, with the World War in 1914, administrative command restrictions were imposed on the market. Even taking into account the NEP (in the 1920s), modern CIS countries had only been exposed to the market for slightly over half a century, and then only at intervals, as distinct from the 300–400 years in the West.

Therefore, CIS countries different from other European countries and China in that they had a smaller proportion and different composition of entrepreneurship. In her analysis of social structure, T. Zaslavskaia[2] identifies the following: business owners proper, engaged in professional profit-making, independent assets management and economic decision-making on their own risk and responsibility (accounting for 1.2% of those economically active in Russia in the mid-1990s); the "self-employed", including farmers, craftsmen, traders, etc. employing no hired labour (1.1%); business managers and owners (1.4%) combining private business with hired work (5.2%); managers having no shares in their firm (2.0%); and hired workers (88.6%). Thus the business segment in Russia accounts for only 10%–12%, mostly in undeveloped forms, and for much less in Belarus, the Ukraine and Central Asia. In Hungary and the Czech Republic, businessmen and managers, largely professionals, account for 17%–19%, and in some European, North American and Southeast Asian countries for over a quarter of the labour force.

This by no means implies that CIS citizens are incapable of efficient market-oriented activities. In Imperial Russia, Russian (Eliseev, Putilov, Riabushinsky), Tatar, Azerbaijan, Armenian and other merchants and factory owners contributed to successful international competition.

Specific irrational mentality. We would now like to discuss the six basic differences between the Western (generally Protestant) and Eastern (Orthodox Christian and Islamic) attitudes to economic activities (mentality).

1. To a Protestant, private earnings provide a measure of private industriousness, practical behaviour, care for the family and an instrument with which to win the respect of others. Most CIS nations traditionally believe that "money never makes you happy", and Russian Orthodox ascetics and Moslem dervishes, for example (for which there are no analogies in the Protestant tradition), never accepted

---

[2] (1995): Humanitarian Culture as a Factor of Transformation in Russia. Conference Proceedings. Saint Petersburg, 30 ((1995): Гуманитарная Культура Как Фактор Преобразования России. Материалы Конференции. Санкт-Петербург, 30) [In Russian]

tangible wealth. Of course, the "new" Russian, Kazakhs, etc. have abandoned tradition, and yet in most CIS countries a rich neighbour still attracts a great deal of suspicion and envy rather than the desire to learn and imitate. "Honest work will not gain mansions of stone" and "No cheating, no selling" – these are examples of Russian folklore about good commerce.

2. Rationalism as an ethical standard is based on the priority of the individual, subjective opinions of usefulness, private choices about preferences and freedom in their realisation, i.e. individual autonomy. This is what underlies the theory of reasonable expectations, predicting human behaviour in specific situations by private interest. Historically, CIS nations always regard the individual as a member of a family, tribe, clan, community, artel, etc., a citizen with no individual legal status. A social man is only free within the choice made by the community which he belongs to, its traditions and priorities. Someone who sticks out in the crowd, i.e. who displays initiative deemed unnecessary by the majority in operating a business or a private farm, even now faces the risk of being spurned or even confronted directly.

3. The Western enterprise style and the general structure of life in Western Europe, North America and even Japan involve continuous calculations of cost and benefit, punctuality ("time is money") and thrift. The vague geography of the CIS nations, the immense natural wealth and vast vacant lands often make these "virtues" either impossible or unimportant. Their single desire seemed to be "one victory for all". The humble appearance of Protestant and Old Believers' churches and their clergy provided an obvious contrast to the golden cupolas, precious icon frames, splendid robes of the bishops, glorious palaces of past and present Oriental rulers and the grandiose ensembles of the mosques. Accuracy and speed were never favoured in the vast expanses. "God will give and God will take" – such was the attitude to human or material loss.

4. The repeated invasions, draughts and other natural calamities have never favoured the long-term planning abilities inherent in Western business people.

5. The mentality in most CIS nations is averse to the interest-charged relations regarded as normal in Protestant ethics. Thus the Koran is explicitly prohibitive about money-lending, while prescribing mandatory aid to the indigent. People disapprove of paying one's own expenses in company. There is a widespread tradition of *khashar*, i.e. collective work to build a neighbour's house. Charity is symbolised in Russia in the monastic order of Sergius of Radonezh, a disinterested ascetic calling for national unity, while in the USA it is the Rockefeller Memorial, a gift to New York City.

6. The CIS nations have never been law-abiding and have been guided by their consciousness, traditions or public opinion rather than legal acts. The concept of private property has never been as important as in the West. God, rather than His sinful children, was the possessor of all beings.

Thus the prevalent Russian Orthodox and Islamic religions preach similar business ethics, and these are very different from the Protestant tradition. While commerce (excluding interest loans prohibited by the Islamic doctrine) is not forbidden, abundant wealth is not laudable, and communal and state interests are superior to individual ones; mutual aid and the just distribution of wealth are superior to rivalry and individual success, and spiritual values to all material ones.

According to V.O. Kliuchevsky and N.A. Berdyaev, the endlessness, vagueness, the yearning for infinite horizons gave birth to a specific "breadth of soul". No one could clearly identify his or her belongings or irrevocable rights, which resulted in the typical dependence on authority. Long-suffering and humility alternated with riots, meaningless and ruthlessness, and there were miracles of creation in the brief critical periods with contempt of regular and careful work. P. Florensky remarked that ethics and religion tended to outweigh legal principles. Russian nature and history defy long-term planning. The Roman saying that what can be done today should never be put off until tomorrow can be splendidly contrasted with the Russian saying that "Work is not a wolf to take to the woods". Such traditions present an important economic institution.[3]

On the other hand, group differentiation by economic culture in the CIS is related more to social conditions and mentality characteristics rather than to national genetics. Thus, among the Muhammadans, the Sunnites and Ishmaelites in one nation accommodate to market conditions better than Shiites, in the same way as German Protestants adapt better than Catholics. Similarly, there have been far more successful businessmen owners and first-guild merchants among Russian Old Believers and Baptists never exposed to serfdom, with overall literacy and temperance dating back to the eighteenth century, than among the Russian Orthodoxy.

A common feature of the CIS countries is their traditional multinational and multiconfessional composition, the bulk of the populations either situated along civilisation lines – Russian Orthodox and Catholic (the Ukraine, Belarus), Slavonic and Roman (Moldova), Christian and Islamic (Georgia), Islamic and Confucian-Buddhist (Kazakhstan, Kyrgyzstan) – or combining their characteristics (Russia). Some CIS countries border on nations speaking either the same (Moldova and Romania, Azerbaijan and North Iran, Tajikistan and Afghanistan) or similar languages (Russia, the Ukraine and Belarus; Uzbekistan, Kyrgyzstan and Kazakhstan), which facilitates international trade and cultural

---

[3] Kliuchevsky, V.O. (1987): Works in 9 Volumes, Volume 1. Mysl, Moscow (Ключевский, В.О. (1987): Сочинения в 9 Томах, Том 1. Мысль, Москва) [In Russian]; Berdyaev, N.A. (1990): The Sources and the Meaning of Russian Communism. Nauka, Moscow (Бердяев, Н.А. (1990): Истоки и Смысл Русского Коммунизма. Наука, Москва) [In Russian]; Florensky, P. (1994): Works in 4 Volumes, Volume 1. Mysl, Moscow (Флоренский, П. (1994): Сочинения в 4 Томах, Том 1. Мысль, Москва) [In Russian]

relations. The CIS nations actually merge ethnic groups, nations and peoples, generally Slavonic, Turkic, Ugro-Finnish, Mongolian and Iranian.

The greatest relative ethnic diaspora is the Armenian one, and the greatest in absolute figures the Russian one (about 13 million in Belarus and Ukraine, over 6 million in Kazakhstan, 1.7 million in the Baltic countries, over 1.5 million in Uzbekistan, more than a million in Kyrgyzstan, over 500,000 in Moldova and 300,000 in Azerbaijan, Georgia and Turkmenistan each). Russians are generally engaged in industry, building, science or information science.

It might be well to point out that members of CIS national diasporas quite often hold key positions in business. This supports the view that national identity does not necessarily imply national isolation or hostility; an original national culture cannot prevent the recognition of neighbouring cultures, and human beings can be related in culture as much as in blood. The critical point is that of the age-long economic, cultural and spiritual relations between the CIS nations and their common mentality rejecting the bourgeois focus on tangible earthly wealth.

Time and again we have tried to deal with this issue in view of repeated predictions in the foreign literature about the future war of civilisations – Christian, Islamic, Confucian-Buddhist. CIS integrative experience also holds universal significance for world peace.

On the other hand, some CIS countries have yet to complete ethnic and political integration. We cannot ignore the East-West conflicts in the Ukraine and Belarus due to historical orientations towards Poland or Russia, the three *zhuzes* in Kazakhstan and regional conflicts in Kyrgyzstan (determining the two-chamber parliamentary structure), Georgia and Moldova (e.g. the Dniester region never being part of Romania).

The special role of the State, lack of civil social traditions and independent, strong legal power. The absolute State power typical among the CIS nations was related to indefinite frontiers, the continuous risk of invasion by foreign civilisations and, in the south, by the need to build, maintain and defend irrigation systems. History in Russia, Georgia, Armenia and Central Asia demonstrated that only a strong and predominantly absolute authority could guarantee family survival, if not welfare. Since the days of Peter I and distinct from other countries, all major enterprises had been State-owned until 1917. Non-public social controlling agencies (*zemstva*) never attained the level of their counterparts in the West.

Prior to the creation of civil society, legal economy and political stability in the CIS countries, the State will have to perform a much broader range of functions than Western democracies, employing legal authoritarian methods, among others. Otherwise, this legal authority will be replaced by other forms of authority in handling the conflicts related to defaults, non-repayment of loans, failure to perform liabilities under contracts, protection of business owners' property, etc.

In Russia, Transcaucasian republics and some other CIS countries striving to prematurely copy international experience in government administration in the 1990s, the criminal structures, instead of keeping within their traditional spheres (drugs, arms, gambling, prostitution, bribery), created an autonomous "shadow" economy with independent "tax" and defence systems. They control the most profitable legal businesses – commercial banks, export trade in oil and other raw materials, and food and car imports. The misappropriations from fictitious businesses, unchecked collection of money from the public financial pyramids, unpaid taxes or loans, etc. are transferred to bank accounts abroad to return in the form of "foreign investments" in stocks of firms with substantial export potential (e.g. aluminium, rare and non-ferrous metals, timber, chemicals). According to the Russian Academy of Science Analytical Centre, 35% of capital assets of privatised enterprises have been appropriated by criminal entities. They control more than 40,000 firms and banks. According to the Ministry of Internal Affairs, half of the criminal gains is spent on bribing civil servants. More than 1 million people, mostly former legal enforcement staff or riot police and athletes, are employed in commercial firms' security and private detective agencies. They hold 3 million registered firearms and far more non-reported ones. According to the Federal Service of Security, underground money circulation in Russia currently accounts for 40% of GDP, as compared to 5%–10% in developed countries.[4]

The same is true of some of the other CIS countries. A psychological predisposition to violating laws was evident in significant public segments acting as permanent earners for "shop-leaders", speculators and civil servants allocating government funds. According to sociological surveys in the 1980s, only 3%–9% of respondents expected moral injunctions, dismissal, etc. due to minor theft at work. This means that, even in the Soviet period, public opinion ceased to act as a factor of social control and public censure. We would do well to bear in mind that the laws of that time suppressed any private initiative, even that causing no social damage.

In the context of reform, the mass media are vigorously promoting the consumer society and wealth as a symbol of success. On the other hand, the socio-economic structure is still unable to provide the legal means of gaining the advertised symbols for most public segments. As E. Durkheim, R. Merton and others have demonstrated using Western examples, this creates a persistent mechanism governing antisocial behaviour, generally among the young or among ethnic minorities suffering discrimination. Thus almost 70% of respondents in some CIS countries in the mid-1990s preferred public order with a somewhat restricted democracy to democracy per se.

Essentially differing bases of reform in different CIS regions associated with ethnosocial and economic conditions, and high transportation costs. The latter

---

[4] Kryshtanovskaia, O. (1995): The Mafiosi Landscape in Russia. Izvestia 178 (Крыштановская, О. (1995): Мафиозный Пейзаж России. Известия 178) [In Russian]

costs are due to very long distances (Russia, Kazakhstan, the Ukraine), lack of or blocked lines of communications with international markets (e.g. Georgia) and poor roads. As a result, prices in different regions of Russia in the 1990s differed 20-fold for production resources (e.g. electric power, cement) and three- to fourfold for food.

Conditions in some CIS countries, as opposed to the Czech Republic, Hungary or the Baltic republics, do not allow any general model of reform. Thus Russia chose a federal system, while Moldova incorporates the autonomous Gagauz and Dniester regions, and the Ukraine incorporates the Crimea. Other CIS states are unitarian, although the distribution of rights between the centre and regions in matters of ownership, taxes, budget, local infrastructure and social development remains the main problem.

In most European countries, competition ensures a balance between cost and return, at least within a single branch. This is not the case in the vast CIS areas, especially with the far lower mobility of labour and the very long list of triage economy regions (e.g. the North and Far East of Russia, Aral, Caspian, Pamir, some Caucasian regions).

Lack of traditions of private land ownership (with the exception of Moldova, West Ukraine, Belarus and Transcaucasia) and stable middle classes. The prosperous peasant households running rational businesses were either destroyed by collectivisation (particularly in Russia, Kazakhstan and the Ukraine) or emigrated (Tajikistan, Turkmenistan, Kyrgyzstan). The bulk of rural populations are now represented by lumpens plundering the collective property and spending government money channelled to the agroindustrial complex.

Private ownership of land, as demonstrated in Hungary, Poland and some other countries, is a prerequisite for the revival of agriculture and sustainable food supplies and for the market economy in general. In our opinion, however, immediate introduction of totally private ownership of land in Russia and some other CIS countries would reduce food supplies in the agroindustrial sector (to be discussed in Chap. 6).

The bulk of the MIC was represented by huge plants and focused on close co-operation with other republics and the member states of the former Council for Mutual Economic Aid. Almost 70% of workers in Russia, Kazakhstan and some other CIS states (25% in the USA and 5%–10% in Germany and Japan) and 85% of research workers (up to 50% in the USA and up to 15% in Germany and Japan) were associated with war and space industries, including mining and processing of raw materials. This initially non-productive complex with no experience in marketing and cost-saving is now at the centre of access to international markets of finished products and services. The rational conversion (not to be confused a sudden reduction of government purchases) will be the central element of reform (to be discussed in Chap. 6).

Unlike other European, Asian and American countries with the exception of Yugoslavia, reforms in the CIS are carried out in the context of conflict-charged divisions of the territories and property of the previous union state, although not to the extent that this is occurring in the Balkans. The republics had no experience of independent macro-economic regulation activities or access to international markets, all the less so as the USSR was largely autarchic in terms of culture and economy (percentage of international trade in GDP amounting to 5%–8% as against 30%–40% in other European countries). Moreover, CIS reformers did not have enough time: when the USSR disintegrated, the gold and currency reserves were exhausted, external national debt and inflation reached a dangerous point and food supply conditions in major cities and political confrontations were critical.

The reformers had no reliable information about the competitiveness and actual credibility of enterprises, international market demands, etc. Unlike China, Vietnam, the Czech Republic, Poland, etc., the CIS countries lacked the leading political force and the clear-cut national ideology of reform. With effective democratic institutions in the CIS countries (e.g. parliament, courts), democracy as a social system with private and group interests co-ordinated by trans-group interests of the majority is at an initial stage. All these prevent automatic economic self-regulation to promote business initiative.[5] The State, at least in the transitional period, is to remain as an economic unit and arbitrator, co-ordinating the interests of society, regions, firms and households. Of special importance in this connection are the policies on structure, science and technology, prices, foreign trade and regional and social policies pursued by the government.

Structural policy. The CIS countries cannot afford synchronous restructuring in all branches of the economy. The government therefore has to resort to the strategy of unbalanced growth, i.e. selective support of the branches and industries capable of maintaining and expanding the markets in their own countries, within the CIS, and on an international scale.

Otherwise, as experience indicates, spontaneous market forces will break the economy into the three loosely associated units: (1) raw material-based branches generally focusing on distant countries supplying the equipment and luxury consumer goods for the well-to-do; (2) electric power generation and production of foodstuffs and elementary goods for the domestic market (with the cut-throat competition with the import market and hence reduced output); and (3) high-technology branches losing the markets and, due to the lack of current assets, the chance to buy the required supplies and accessories abroad, including other CIS

---

[5] The need for a creative, non-typical approach to the issues of new quality was justified by L.I. Abalkin (cf.: Abalkin, L.I. (1996): The Economic Reality and Abstract Schematics. Voprosy Ekonomiki 12 (Абалкин, Л.И. (1996): Экономическая Реальность и Абстрактные Схемы. Вопросы Экономики 12) [In Russian]), D.S. Lvov, I.V. Iakovets, O.T. Bogomolov, V.I. Kirichenko and some other prominent economists

countries. Spontaneous liberalisation eventually results in decline into a colonial-type economy exchanging non-renewable natural resources and the products of faulty and labour-consuming industries (e.g. metallurgy, chemical, cement, cellulose) for high-technology goods and services.

How, then, have the countries listed by World Bank experts among the liberal economies managed to survive without government interference into industrial policy?

They have managed to survive because they operate a competitive market mechanism determining price dynamics by the balance of demand and supply. In the CIS countries, the fuel and energy complex (FEC), transport, metallurgy and other basic industries are of monopolistic type. Thus 10% of companies in Russia (four fifths raw materials and power-engineering) accounted for three quarters of the 1997 output, for instance. The industries govern their monopolistic price mechanisms in a process chain, and the overall price rises even with significantly lower demand. In research-intensive industries, power resources account for almost 40% of overall costs, while in Western resource-importing countries the proportion never exceeds 4%–5%.

The CIS countries have no mechanism to transfuse capital into more efficient spheres of production. This is due to the high proportion of defence industries retaining their mobilisation capacities even with no government orders, undeveloped stock market, high-risk loans, etc. Capital is concentrated in the trade and finance sphere with high turnover rates and a low proportion of capital assets not to be withdrawn even by expropriation.

The CIS countries have neither a middle class capable of independent and cost-effective economic decision-making, nor an army of managers having complete knowledge of international market demands and able to respond adequately. Thus, for every four business units in Russia in 1997, there was only one manager with up-to-date qualifications, and there were even fewer in other CIS countries.

Economists estimate the costs of creating proper conditions for market regulation in the CIS comparable with the EU countries (including housing for workers migrating to top-demand regions) at $2 trillion. Such investment is unlikely in the nearest future. In addition, developed countries never rule out government economic intervention. Since 1997, France has been implementing a rescue plan for the textile, footwear and clothing industries involving an annual FF 2 billion reduction in compulsory payments by private firms. In turn, these firms were obliged to maintain 35,000 existing jobs and to employ 7000 young people. Actions to save major private corporations have recently been taken by governments in the USA, Japan, the UK, the Netherlands and some other countries with a liberal economy.

According to some economists, in the CIS context, the State should act both as the initiator of reforms and creator of legal standards of behaviour for market agents and as an immediate protagonist in economic processes (e.g. government orders for science and technology and research-intensive products, administration of public property, securities and controlling stakes of shares, budget resources for projects of national importance and long pay-back period).[6] D. Lvov[7] demonstrated the conception of legal fixing of considerable parts of natural resources and the infrastructure as public property. In this case, the national dividend, i.e. business returns of public corporations and charges on the commercial use of national property (e.g. public tenders for leasing of natural resources, energy, transport, communications), is regarded as the main source of public revenue and investment.

The building blocks of the government's structural policy are planning and the mechanism of tenders for investment projects accounting for priorities in the maintenance and promotion of essential technologies and competitive industries. In Russia and other CIS countries, these are: aerospace and nuclear engineering, some classes of military engineering and high-purity metal works, instrument-making and lathe building, quantum electronics, microwave and laser engineering and biotechnology.

Industrial planning under the market economy, as demonstrated in Japan, South Korea and some other countries, has three prominent features. Firstly, rather than mandatory tasks, it involves forecasting (indicative planning) and target programmes supported by the government with effective budget financial resources, risk hedging and privileges, rather than merely good intentions. Secondly, a plan is drawn up from co-ordinated positions of the government, regions, financial and industrial groups (FIGs; in the last years of this century actually controlling the economy in most CIS countries) and trade unions. And thirdly, the plans involve nationally significant targets (e.g. promoting export potentials, people, science, small business, business infrastructure) rather than gross output.

Regulating prices and natural monopolies. Controversies abound in the CIS countries concerning the shock-therapy liberalisation of prices in Russia, Moldova and Kyrgyzstan early in 1992 and later in the other countries. Theoretically, pricing cannot be taken out of government control until a competitive economy is created. The situation, however, required urgent action. The USSR's dependence on the West for food supplies, resulting from the lack of

---

[6] Bogomolov, O.T. (Ed.) (1996): Reform as Viewed by American and Russian Scientists. Moscow (Богомолов, О.Т. (Ред.) (1996): Реформы Глазами Американских и Российских Ученых. Москва) [In Russian]; Kirichenko, V.I. (1997): Ekonomist 1, 21 (Кириченко, В.И. (1997): Экономист 1, 21) [In Russian]

[7] Lvov, D.S (1997): A Theoretical Core of Social and Economic Development in the Country. Ekonomist 1, 7 (Львов, Д.С. (1997): Теоретическое Ядро Социально-Экономического Развития Страны. Экономист 1, 7) [In Russian]

appropriate reform in the Soviet period, could be tolerated no longer. Despite enormous blocks of fertile land, 30–45 million t grain was imported every year. In the 1960s and 1970s, the imports were financed by oil exports, and after the oil price dropped, by sales of gold and reductions of currency reserves. In 1990 and 1991, the country was actually bankrupt in foreign currency, with the Vneshtorgbank (Foreign Trade Bank) declaring default of payments on its accounts. The absence of food reserves, the inability to pay for imported goods and the refusal by collective and State farms in 1991 to deliver grain at fixed planned prices – all these could have resulted in starvation and general chaos. A price leap transforming the latent inflation (general deficit of goods) into an open one resolved the problem. Import trade in grain was reduced dramatically in 1993, and the market was saturated. However, in some CIS countries, price liberalisation resulted in the devaluation of private deposits. Major cattle-breeding complexes using imported fodder had to be closed.

Some CIS countries extended price liberalisation for several years. Thus, in the Ukraine, government price regulation of many classes of raw materials in mining, chemical, metallurgical, woodworking and light industries involved a declaration to the Ministry of Industry in collaboration with the Ministry of Economics, particularly in the cases where domestic wholesale prices exceeded export, indicative (recommended) or international ones.

In Russia, even after liberalisation, over 15% of prices were regulated in 32 Federal entities, and over 25% were regulated in five. Almost one quarter of regional budgets is spent on subsidies to enterprises. Some regions introduced tariffs for alcohol imported from other Federal entities and, in addition, duties, excises, taxes and deductions to non-budget funds amounting, according to A. Uliukaev, to 1%–1.5% of GDP.[8] Following devaluation of the rouble in 1992, many regions introduced price and tariff regulations in medical services and communications, listing the socially relevant commodities (bread, sugar, milk and meat products, fuels and lubricating materials) for which price rises would be controlled.

It will be some time before demand restrictions will form the basis for market equilibrium in the CIS countries. This will require co-ordinated regulation of prices and resource production by all economic partners, starting from the efficiency of production and distribution for the producer and of purchase and use of the product for the consumer.

The major challenge of price regulation in the CIS countries, however, is public control of natural monopolies, e.g. electricity generation, railway transport, gas complex, communications. The lack of competition and inadequate control resulted in price rises that were too sharp, impairing productivity and consequently decreasing competitiveness in some basic branches. Thus, between

---

[8] (1997): Эксперт (Expert) 6, 22 [In Russian]

1991 and 1995, the rise in freight railway tariffs in Russia was three times that of prices on industrial products, which made exports of timber from Siberia and coal from the Kuznetsk basin unprofitable, breaking the schedule of co-operation between the CIS countries and the Far East. With the same amount of traffic and half the network length, the Russian Ministry of Railways employs 2 million as against 213,000 employed by U.S. railways. Productivity of labour amounted to 90%–92% in 1988 and 30%–35% in 1995 as against respective U.S. levels. Prices for electricity exceeded those in the USA and some European countries. Prices for gas are now almost the same (e.g. \$57 per 1000 m^3 in Russia and \$60–\$80 in Germany). By contrast, a 20% reduction in electric power generation was accompanied by a 40% increase in personnel.

What cannot be tolerated is the artificial breaking up of natural monopolies by region or on other principles. A monopoly ensures protection of domestic markets and access to international markets, accumulation of potential investment resources and both technical and economic security. No good has come of breaking up Aeroflot into 400 independent air companies, most of them incapable of providing for flight security or plane park updating. Future textbooks on economic history will undoubtedly highlight the abolition of the State monopoly on alcohol in Russia. As a result, corresponding revenues reduced from 30% to 3% of the budget, the well-equipped branch was brought to the verge of decline and there were 15,000 victims of poisonous imported or underground products of inferior quality. The only beneficiaries were organised crime and its agents in the civil service. Later in the 1990s, measures had to be taken to cut the number of air companies and restore control over the alcohol market. But building is far more difficult than destroying.

No privatisation of natural monopolies can be tolerated in the present context. The State owns railways in the USA (Amtrak) and power systems in other countries. This enables promotion of the unrewarding but vitally important regional infrastructure. Additionally, prices on power resources and tariffs, as well as standard minimum wages, tax and social deductions, and the rule of costs and depreciation accounting accepted in liberal economy countries, permit the regulation of almost half of consumer prices.

Government regulation of natural monopolies in the CIS should provide for:

1. Separating effective natural monopolies from other corporations included into their networks and bound to function on competitive lines. Thus the Gazprom system incorporated, along with fields, transport and distribution networks, 200 unprofitable state farms, works, etc. In the railway system, 55% of the staff are engaged in transport operations and the rest in auxiliary or subsidiary works, industrial production, building, "branch" training, health and other systems. As a result, 70%–75% of costs are independent of the volume of traffic (as against less than 30% fixed costs in EU countries).

In the course of restructuring, the number of Gazprom staff will be cut by one third, with all the subdivisions not involved in basic production reorganised as independent legal entities. The integrated power system (Russian joint stock company "EES Russia") will function as the organiser/operator of the integrated market and power transmission manager. Power stations, as the owners of generating facilities, should have access to the competitive wholesale market, as experience in the UK demonstrates. The monopoly involves transport rather than production. Reorganisation of extracting enterprises as subsidiaries with autonomous current accounts would mean demonopolisation of deposits.

2. Public access to information on costs and revenues of natural monopolies and the abolition of quasi-money in payment settlement. Tariffs are currently arbitrary, containing – in addition to the investment component – the costs of purchasing newspapers and television channels, football sponsorship, recreation centres outside the country, etc.

Gazprom first prepared a consolidated statement of assets and liabilities complying with international standards in 1997. However, only one half of the accounts are paid by customers, including 94% in clearing transactions, commercial papers or barter exchange rather than cash. But taxes are calculated on the basis of tariffs rather than actual revenue. Among the important clients that refused to pay are the army and other public services. As a result, Gazprom provides a quarter of incoming taxes and is still the government's debtor. As sales of products and debt securities, real money is handed over to intermediary firms (the Russian joint stock company EES having more than 300), and tariffs and prices are further increased. Thus neither the monopolies nor the economy as a whole can be regulated without recourse to money transactions.

3. Creating effective agencies and a legal framework for regulation. The U.S. control commission for power engineering of 1200 members exercises control over monopolistic costs and prices. The CIS countries have yet to identify and differentiate the rights of similar central and regional commissions as government agencies, ensuring access to financial documents, establishing a well-defined administration procedure for State-owned shares and thus making the market transparent for public control.

4. Gradual cancellation of cross-subsidising with losses in one sector covered by profits in others, both sides consequently losing incentives to save. Public energy supplies in the CIS countries are generally priced several times lower than industrial prices, with passenger traffic subsidised by cargo traffic. In coal mining, profits of effective pits are spent on subsidies to unrewarding and often hazardous mines rather than their own development. Not all CIS countries use tenders for State-owned shares for trust to the best managers.

Due to the absence of meters, consumers cover the expenses of others rather than their own. It is not incidental that urban water consumption per capita in the CIS is two- to fourfold that in EU countries. Nor can double payments for electricity by industrial plants be justified (i.e. the right of consumption of energy and amount of energy consumed). On the other hand, there is no price differentiation by time of day in most CIS countries as opposed to the UK, for instance, where electricity is almost five times less expensive at night than during peak daytime hours.

Reorganisation of natural monopolies is not easy, but it is necessary. Half of the mines in Russia are unprofitable and have no promising markets. As the price for gas contains no definite transport component, there is no realistic price differentiation by region; pipe access is inhibited both for the oil industry having to burn associate gas and independent gas companies. The EES Power Inspection impedes the creation of efficient local systems. An independent gas distributing system would allow for mainline terminals in thousands of housing estates still heated by firewood. A simplified railway system needs to provide for efficiency in all respects. The government would benefit from partial compensation of passenger subsidies from the budget, thus reducing cargo tariffs and increasing output and traffic and, consequently, taxes collected.

Wages per unit productivity in Russia are almost half that in developed countries, with domestic prices for basic fuels, construction materials and crude chemicals 1.5 – to threefold higher than international standards due to resource concentration within a limited range of export traders, banks and other monopolists.[9] Government support is required not only in basic CIS industries, but also in the light industry, particularly textile, where output fell three- to fourfold compared with 1990 and markets were open (in Russia and some other countries almost 60%) to import goods of less than superior quality. The industry typically has a short period of capital circulation (1 month between the input of raw materials and sales) and high profits (almost a quarter of the USSR's budget revenues). They need privileged seasonal loans to purchase the raw materials and low energy prices (their share in costs increasing from 3% to 20% between 1990 and 1997) to recover current assets, a reasonable protectionist policy and tax exemptions on reinvested profits rather than financial aid.

The abandonment of price regulation by the government with no developed wholesale market will not open the way for market mechanisms. Thus, after the total price liberalisation in Russia in 1995, the share of goods at prices considerably higher than international ones increased from 24% to 58%, including petrol, diesel fuel, etc., of which there are abundant supplies. At the same time, regulated prices (for crude oil, gas) are 62%–75% of international ones, which is fairly adequate considering the savings of transport from Siberia.

---

[9] Stroev, E.S. (1997): Corrective Maintenance of Economic Reforms and Development of a New Concept of Budget Policy. Voprosy Ekonomiki 1 (Строев, Е.С. (1997): Корректировка Экономических Реформ и Разработка Новой Концепции Бюджетной Политики. Вопросы Экономики 1) [In Russian]

Total liberalisation of prices and international trade in the period of the transitional economy is highly problematic. The ambitions of some CIS countries to attain the world price levels should be accompanied by the application of new technologies and compliance with the cost and quality standards followed by the key TNCs generally governing international market prices. Reasonable price ratios between the industries, as developed countries demonstrate, should first be negotiated by producers' and consumers' associations and then fixed by the mediating government. A hasty conversion to world prices would only benefit the extractive industries (due to rent charges) and the chemical metallurgy complex (due to low environmental fees).

Regulating foreign trade. The CIS countries abolished the state monopoly in foreign trade in the 1990s and are applying for membership in the World Trade Organisation (WTO), which will result in the lifting of many discriminative barriers in international markets in return for the substantial cut of customs duties and cancellation of subsidies to producers. Some countries, e.g. Armenia, have fully liberalised foreign trade. Kyrgyzstan was the first CIS country to join the WTO.

On the other hand, the Ukraine has set minimum indicative prices on exported goods (e.g. metal, chemicals), banned exports of customer-supplied raw materials for alcohol, tobacco products, petrol, furs, etc. with subsequent re-importing and established minimum customs valuation rates for some goods. The measures to protect the domestic market (97% of tobacco products imported illegally or made of customer-supplied raw materials evading taxation), however, were opposed by the EU, which demanded the lifting of export barriers for pelts and live cattle and the abolition of some import duties (averaging 4% only).

The average import tariff level is 10% among the WTO members compared with 15% in Russia (with a planned 20% reduction by 2000). WTO membership requires complete abolition of import duties on aircraft equipment and some other goods and of subsidies to domestic firms; public tenders for WTO members with the State purchasing over $300,000; free access to CIS services markets (including finance, insurance, etc.); a lower extent of protection for the agroindustrial complex; and no new import restrictions during negotiations. Nevertheless, the lack of a reasonable protectionist policy in the period of reform would fill some CIS commodity markets (e.g. textile, some foodstuffs, domestic equipment) with imports, consequently reducing employment and public revenue.

It should be noted that developed countries will only resort to complete liberalisation of international trade when their own goods attain a superior competitive quality. Thus Japan, for example, plans to liberalise its capital market by 2001, while retaining control over major corporate transactions. Until 1998, there was no free (unlicensed) sale or purchase of currency by firms and no unlimited private export. The confiscation tax (amounting to 76% of capital appreciation for 2 years) inhibited foreign access to real estate and capital markets. Japanese international investments exceeded $50 billion, with foreign investments in Japan lower than $4 billion. Prohibitive duties restrict imports of agricultural produce to the EU countries and of sheet and high-grade metal from Russia, the Ukraine and Kazakhstan to the USA, Chile, Thailand, etc.

A co-ordinated CIS international trade policy should involve:

1. Complete abolition of export quotas, licenses and tariffs (excluding armaments and strategic raw materials)

2. Abolition of import duties on machinery not manufactured in the CIS, their reduction for accessories (in electronics, radio-engineering, computer and some other industries), possibly combined with import quotas on metal, textile and chemicals from the CIS, and temporary CIS duties on competing goods

3. Imposing non-tariff barriers (e.g. specifications, quotas on domestic goods with government purchasing). Interestingly, in 1997 the Czech Republic required that importers of foodstuffs and consumer goods (accounting for 30% of total imports and increasing the loss in the balance of payments to 8.6% of GDP) should deposit 20% of sales on 6-month interest-free deposit accounts.

It cannot be regarded as normal that, although available CIS producers competitive according to the "price/quality" criterion (e.g. the Quant plant built in 1992 ranked among the world's ten best), over 90% of computers purchased in 1995 and 1996 with the Federal budget in Russia were imported from outside the CIS. Restricted foreign contributions to share capital in major corporations would seem expedient.

What is most important to support domestic producers is, rather than protection from competition, privileged government innovation crediting guarantees for private investors orientated towards exports or replacing imports.

The centre and the regions. As international experience indicates, small countries with democratic traditions and an open economy but not abounding in natural resources often attain high levels of economic and social development by joining integrative groups, e.g. Denmark, the Netherlands, Luxembourg, Austria and Singapore. This is favoured by their lower levels of bureaucracy and administrative expenditure, the proximity of authorities to the citizens and private and corporate interests.

More sizeable states such as Germany transfer more rights of local economic regulation to individual regions (or *Länder* in Germany). A similar path was taken in the 1990s by unitarian states – the UK (in 1998 establishing parliaments in Scotland and Wales), Spain, and Belgium; and there is increasing pressing in this context in Italy, France, etc. A united Europe is generally conceived of as a union of regions rather than states.

Under the U.S. Constitution, the states confer on the Federal Centre powers in the spheres of national defence, international politics, macro-economic regulation and national security. The remaining areas, including local tax and economic legislation, social and pension security and rule of law (except for infringements of Federal significance), are equally divided among the states and their legislative and executive authorities. Only the judicial system acts in the entire U.S. territory. Amendments to the Constitution are only effective upon ratification by state legislative assemblies. The centre can only interfere without being requested to do so by the states in cases of danger to the Republican form of government. Prefixed Federal taxes are target orientated (e.g. administration, armed forces, Federal programmes), with government control of expenditure.

In the CIS, the question of the relationship between the centre and the regions is an important one not only in Russia, the Ukraine and Kazakhstan but also in the smaller states such as Georgia, Azerbaijan, Moldova, Tajikistan and Kyrgyzstan, with regional divisions guided by economic, geographic, social and ethnic principles. The regional focus has been considered as a strategic goal in Russia, the Ukraine and some other republics. However, the distribution of authority among the regions and the centre, particularly in budgetary, tax, social and economic policies, is far from complete, with the regions unable to control execution of the budgets. The centre is still monopolistic, with the vassals doing their utmost to obtain more resources or privileges.

In Russia, the rights of Federal and regional authority are characterised by individual items of joint administration under special contracts and agreements. In addition, the centre may confer more power on some regions in a relationship of dialogue and compromise. Some regions introduce quasi-money, ban exports of specific classes of raw materials or take other actions in an attempt to divide the integral economic space. There are no provisions for Federal equality; the constitutions of some republics belonging to Russia therefore contain clauses contradicting the Russian Constitution. An integrated and co-ordinated tax and budget policy requires consolidated Federal entities. The current situation in which seven entities act as donors and over 80 as recipients from the Federal budget cannot be described as normal.

Government support in economic development is necessary for regions with special economic conditions. In Russia, there are 27 such (completely or partially) Federal entities – republics, territories, regions and national districts (60% of the area, 8% of the population, 20% of the national income). In the first few years of the 21st century, they will account for 70% of gas output in the CIS. Due to district wage coefficients and other benefits, prime costs here are 20%–30% higher, with transport costs accounting for 55%–60% (average, 12%–15% in Russia). As a result, over half of the plants are unprofitable, with a non-competitive quality of products. As many of these plants govern urban development policies, their closure will endanger general living conditions. On the other hand, the share of centralised capital in total investments, according to the special Federation Council report, decreased from 80% to 10%–20% between

1989 and 1996, and total investments in the single industries, infrastructure and prospecting were four- to eightfold lower.

Regional policy for regions functioning under extreme conditions should involve conversion to shift operation, special shipment financing (investments being "frozen" for a year), traffic discounts and, more importantly, a reasonable range of competitive plants and the relevant social and other infrastructure.

3.2 Advantages and Disadvantages of Privatisation

Privatisation and its purposes. Most countries have been carrying out privatisation of public property in the last decades of the twentieth century. In the 1970s and 1980s, almost every second enterprise in the infrastructure and basic industries of many European and South American countries was controlled by the State holding controlling interests in relevant joint stock companies. In the 1990s, the pace of privatisation was accelerated in the fuel and energy and petrochemical complexes (Italy, Spain, Mexico), railways (UK), telecommunications and communications (e.g. France, Germany). In Central and Eastern Europe, privatisation was most substantial in the Czech Republic, Hungary, Poland, Slovakia and Slovenia. In China, only one thousand of the 76,000 plants will be supported by the State on privatisation in the unprofitable public sector.

The pace of privatisation in CIS countries is described in terms of employment distribution by segments of economy. By 1998, the states could be divided into the four groups. In Kyrgyzstan, Uzbekistan and Moldova, 24% of workers were employed in the public sector, in Russia and Kazakhstan 33%, in Turkmenistan, Tajikistan, Armenia, Georgia, Azerbaijan and the Ukraine 40%–47%, and in Belarus 65%. At the same time, the proportion of self-employed workers (farmers, entrepreneurs, free professions) increased in all CIS countries: from 16% to 29% in Azerbaijan, from 20% to 41% in Armenia, from 2% to 9% in Belarus, from 4% to 22% in Kazakhstan, from 13% to 48% in Kyrgyzstan, from 13% to 15% in Moldova, from 2% to 10% in Russia, from 19% to 27% in Tajikistan, from 16% to 18% in Turkmenistan, from 17% to 21% in Uzbekistan and from 2% to 9% in the Ukraine.

The statistical data suggest similar trends with different rates in all CIS countries. Moreover, small-scale privatisation (in trade, services, local industries) is almost complete. In 1998, the State contribution to retail turnover exceeded one quarter in two CIS countries only (Belarus and Turkmenistan), amounting to a mere 2%–8% in eight.

The private sector accounts for over three quarters of GDP (8% in 1990) in Armenia and almost 70% in Russia, with 55%, i.e. about 127,000 State-owned enterprises privatised (only 30,500 remaining in Federal ownership). In the Ukraine, privatised enterprises accounted for 36% of industrial output in 1996, but in 1997 the sale of State controlling stakes in major combines was initiated, e.g. Nikolaev alumina (the republic's third earner of foreign exchange), Zaporozhski automobile. By contrast, only ten State-owned plants were privatised in Belarus between 1993 and 1996.

However, privatisation is not a goal in itself but rather a means of improving production efficiency. An effective owner should (a) be capable of increasing the share in the market of goods and services, (b) make bigger profits with lower costs and better quality and (c) invest the profits in innovations.

International experience indicates that, in most industries, a private owner is far more active in finding new markets and saving sources, better focused on customers' demands, more flexible in decision-making and more effective in finding new investment sources and rational strategies and in pursuing "tougher" policies to protect capital against inertia or theft.

All these benefits of privatisation, however, can only be realised under certain conditions. The new owner must provide for high-quality management. The property that is sold must be suitable for effective use. Market mechanisms must facilitate equal competition and promote production (via tax, customs and investment policies). In Russia and some other CIS countries, the mechanism of privatisation was orientated towards the quickest possible abolition of State ownership and the promotion of all conceivable owners and public revenue rather than efficient production.

Russia was the first CIS country to initiate extensive privatisation, actually completing the task in small and medium-sized business. There are over 120,000 joint stock companies, and the sales of controlling interests in 136 major corporations by Federal and in 6000 by regional state property funds have now almost been completed. Of the 40,000 open joint stock companies, 69% were established in the privatisation process and 31% have been newly established.

The model of privatisation differs essentially from those employed in West and in Eastern Europe. The performance criterion was derived not from economic efficiency or market development but from the pace (a presidential decree allowing several months for the process) of abolishing State ownership. Commercialisation and incorporation of State-owned enterprises occurred in parallel with rather than prior to privatisation. Reorganisation, the necessary prerequisite for the transfer of ownership in the Western model, was set aside for the time being. Strong foreign investors could not obtain information on the items of privatisation, nor were they allowed to make investment tenders. The programme was overwhelmingly political and populist.

Property valuation used the outdated book value rather than the market value, without accounting for intangible assets, rights of natural resource use, trade mark or firm price. As the "sale of the century" progressed, the price of assets calculated per unit output (according to the World Bank report on "Foreign investments in Russia: trends and promise") was 25-fold lower than in the USA in telecommunications, and 40-fold lower in oil production reserves. Annual gains from exports to countries far abroad ($5 billion), even without considering sales to CIS countries, allow Gazprom's assets to be estimated at $50 billion. However, in 1994, the Goskomimushchestvo (Federal Committee on State Property), eager to fulfil the fiscal privatisation plan, evaluated all the items up for privatisation in the country at about $ 3 billion.

The use of vouchers not made out to named individuals as a major means of payment (accounting for 80% of receipts) in the initial stage of privatisation led to "self-privatisation", with zero public revenue and very limited gains in capital assets. These benefited the export-orientated industries and those in permanent demand in domestic markets (unless they sold their vouchers or shares) and, more importantly, the commercial structures buying up the vouchers to gain control or resell. Among the losers were the government, who had to compensate for the losses with extra taxes, and the bulk of the population not employed in profitable privatised enterprises and, in addition, losing their bank savings.

The government granted major rights of privatisation to enterprises (and to directors) and local administration. In doing so, no system of financial, corporate or public control was established, contrary to normal market economy practices. While formally obtaining only 10%–15% of shares, the administration has actually gained control over joint stock companies' products and cash flows and the private "subsidiaries" receiving bulk profits. As a result, workers had to sell their shares to the actual owners of enterprises. Quite often now, the parent company is penniless, delaying payments of taxes, wages, utilities fees (e.g. water, power) and thus endangering living conditions in whole urban areas, aggravating the non-payment crisis, etc. At the same time, such administration-controlled companies (affiliated firms and subsidiaries), including those incorporated abroad and in offshore zones, with minimum share capital (to evade liabilities) can purchase controlling interests in the major company, rent the premises at a nominal price, sell products and property, purchase real estate abroad, etc. In cases of bankruptcy (quite often planned in advance) of such privatised enterprise, the directors' mafia takes up strategic positions, buying up dirt-cheap the joint stock company it has ruined. Rights of administration are actually denied to the workers, who fear dismissal and have no access to the necessary information.

Justified valuation and a long period of sale of shares are necessary to prevent the collapse of the stock market. Thus, during privatisation of one of the world's biggest petrochemical complex Eni (Italy), for example, only 20% of stocks worth $6.25 billion were offered on the market. Privatisation of European telecommunications and telephone companies was prolonged for 3 years (1995–1997) to establish the competitive market.

As mentioned before, in Russia the valuation of property and nominal share prices (as shown by 1992 balance sheets of enterprises) ignored the revaluation of fixed capital, location, know-how, land lot size, etc. Hasty auction sales and the lack of dependable laws to protect property rights during nationalisation; etc. resulted in supply far exceeding effective demand. There were many cases of assets undervalued 100- to 150-fold, as the subsequent rise in stock prices demonstrated. In the initial stage, the industrial potential in Russia was valued at slightly over $1 billioin. This deprived the budget of revenue and the enterprises of investments, State property was plundered and consequent criminal proceedings were initiated.

At the same time, the shares issued by newly created joint stock companies were almost tenfold those of nationalised enterprises.

No reason can be found for the privatisation model using vouchers not made out to a named individual, particularly in view of the absence of detailed and dependable legislation concerning joint stock companies, securities and stock markets. The overwhelming majority of the public in Russia had no experience of securities and thus could not profit from their privatisation checks at all (by selling them, exchanging them for investment fund stocks, buying shares in enterprises by private subscription or at auctions). Most vouchers were bought up for a nominal amount by financial firms for the purposes of reselling rather than production development or renovation. Directors often deliberately transferred cash to the accounts of false firms and delayed wage payment to facilitate the purchase of employees' shares. Secondary issue and investment tenders with pre-selected participants contributed to the concentration of ownership within a limited range of speculators. There were no legal provisions for reserve capital, published balance statements, unrestricted access to statutory documents for all shareholders, etc. As a result, "voucher-type" privatisation was regarded by the majority as fraud, determining the increasingly negative general response to reform.

Privatisation certificates in Armenia (with a market price of $10–15, the equivalent of an average monthly wage) were for the most part sold to smart financial dealers. Since an item was considered privatised if at least 25% of the starting price was paid up, the new owners could actually buy them for next to nothing. Equal rights for citizens in property purchasing proved false. However, restructuring of the enterprises accounting for 70% of output as public joint stock companies made it possible to abandon state subsidising.

Some CIS countries intend to use the West European privatisation pattern, with 51% of shares retained by the State for several years, to be realised gradually with the introduction of the "gold stock". In this case, working collectives obtain no more than 3%–10% of shares.

In Armenia, prior to privatisation the balance price of enterprises was raised 13.6-fold, amounting to over $0.5 billion, i.e. only one third that in the much larger Russia. Only 20% of stocks were passed over free to staff. Privatisation first involved the plants immediately associated with agricultural processing and end products, to be followed by supplies and components. Energy, transport and other basic industries (25%–30% of total productive capital) were still controlled by the State.

The constitutions adopted by the CIS countries since 1994 provide for two types of ownership: State (public) and private, including private collective (economic partnerships/associates, societies, co-operatives). Thus the Republic of Kazakhstan Law on the Protection and Support of Private Enterprise, for example, envisages both a private person (individual private enterprise) and a group of private persons or legal entities (e.g. lease, joint, co-operative enterprise, economic partnership and joint stock company, association) acting as private owners and registered as private enterprise. Legislation in the Republic of Kazakhstan regards individual activities involving collective (shared, joint) ownership performed on behalf of a legal entity and with liability as to property as collective enterprise. Thus private property of an individual in the private-type enterprise with the status of a legal entity or without it (individual) is distinguished from private shared, i.e. collective property.

In Uzbekistan, provisions for private enterprises involve two types of private enterprise: with or without the status of a legal entity. Private enterprises with the status of a legal entity may establish branches, subsidiaries and representatives. In this case, the private enterprise is defined as an economic initiative complying with existing laws, operated by private individuals for their private benefits (profits) on their risk and liability as to property and, where needed, employing hired labour. Thus legislation in Uzbekistan defines "private enterprise" as a single type of legal organisation – the individual private enterprise (private individuals) or legal entity-type enterprise. Employment in a private enterprise (including branches, subsidiaries and representatives) is limited, as compared to the collective-ownership type, to 200 people in industry and construction, 50 in other branches of the productive sphere, 25 in the service sphere and 15 in trade.

There have been multiple cases of abusive privatisation in many CIS countries. Thus a controlling stake of shares in the joint stock company Kazkhrom (a chromium mine and two ferroalloys plants) in Kazakhstan was sold to a bank established by the London-registered firm Transworld at $36.8 million, one fourth of its annual profits. A controlling stake in an aluminium plant was sold in a public tender at $20 million. Deals of this kind were later prohibited.

In the new phase of reforms in Russia, some plants and banks having significant debts to the budget or non-budget funds in taxes, investment loans, etc. transferred their controlling stake of shares to the State to make up for the debts. Upon restructuring, they can be offered for privatisation again at true market prices. In all cases, the question was of exercising the right of ownership in strict conformity with the laws rather than expropriation.

Forms of privatisation in the CIS countries. Among the principal forms of privatisation in the CIS countries are auction sales of State-owned and municipal enterprises, investment tenders, lease or hire purchase and assignment in discretionary trust to foreign or domestic companies with options for buying out in the future.

Auctions were widely used in the privatisation of major enterprises reorganised as joint stock companies. With this type of incorporation, the amount of issued stocks corresponded to the value of assets. The stocks were acquired with investment checks (vouchers) or monies. As a result, the joint stock companies appeared in mixed ownership: part of the shares (almost 60% in Russia) were held by the staff (at a substantial discount or even free), others (10%–20% or even 40–60% in basic industries) were kept by the State and others (averaging up to 30%) were obtained by outside investors (banks, investment funds, financial companies).

In the Ukraine, where *tender trade* in large packs of shares is operated, first the consulting and investment firms are selected to sell the stocks and then the buyers are invited (generally strategic investors rather than small proprietors).

Thus 30% of shares in the Nikolaev alumina plant were offered to outside investors, 26% were retained by the State, 30% were bought out by the lessee board, and only 8% were sold at a voucher auction (managers offered the options to buy 5% more). Such customised schedules govern privatisation of all major enterprises, no more than 51% of share capital remaining in State ownership (in addition, the "gold stock" gives the right of veto in strategic decision-making). A total of 54% of shares in the joint stock company AvtoVAZ were sold to strategic investors, 5% for cash in the stock exchange, 26% kept by the State and only 7% exchanged for privatisation certificates. On the other hand, small enterprises were sold at voucher auctions.

In Moldova and some other CIS states, vouchers (e.g. government wealth bonds) were named and invested in appropriate investment funds rather than sold on the open market.

Investment tenders provide additional public revenue and, more importantly, investments for renovation. Tenders are invited in all CIS countries. Thus, in the Ukraine, more than 100 major works (Dnepropetrovsk and Mariupol metallurgical, Okean shipbuilding, Kharkov electrical engineering, Rovno radio-engineering, Ukrelektromash, Polymer, Radon, Krasnaia Zvezda, etc.) were privatised by tenders from foreign investors.

In Kyrgyzstan, an international tender was invited (involving the AK-TIuZ mining/concentrating combine, chemical/metallurgical, Ainek plate glass, oil extracting, rawhide, liqueur and spirits works, Bishkek chemical and worsted/wool combines), with the shares offered by the State Property Board in lots to be sold by public auction at least 25% of the starting price. The unsold shares were offered the following day at a private auction to the highest bidder at a fixed price. Potential buyers were offered information and visits to the plants.

This strategy is generally appropriate in terms of market-price privatisation by effective owners, as well as using the gains (the winner depositing the amount within 15 days) in new loans, banking credit line securities, etc. A very promising strategy involves State purchasing of technological lines to be leased to small and medium-sized businesses. In 1997 and 1998, 76 major mechanical, food, electrical engineering and mining plants were transferred to foreign investors in this way. This resulted in the industrial privatisation rate exceeding 80%.

The Ukraine only started actual privatisation in 1995, 3 years later than in Russia. The privatisation certificates were made out to named individuals and could not be bought or sold but only invested at the place of work (at a nominal price), in a certificate fund or any enterprise privatised by auction. To compensate for the lost private deposits in Sberbank (Saving Bank), compensation certificates were issued and already used in purchasing 30% of shares (they can be sold to investors). As tenders are operated by certificate funds rather than private agents, legal entities play the decisive role. The Ukraine Stock Exchange only trades in stocks that have not been sold in tenders. Privatisation of regional monopolies is co-ordinated by the Anti-monopoly Board. All these are intended to attract real investments in production and to control the State shares in industrial property, preventing associated buffer structures.

The privatisation programme in Azerbaijan involves all branches of the economy, including oil refining. Not liable to privatisation are communication lines, roads, tunnels and bridges, water resources, etc. Privatisation is also implemented in investment tenders invited from joint stock companies, FIGs and holdings and using privatisation certificates.

In Turkmenistan, foreign investors are involved in the privatisation of over 2000 items in trade and public catering. However, there were cases of public tenders replaced by private distribution of pledged stocks (e.g. in Russia in 1996) and violation of investment obligations. In such cases, privatisation was void and the property was recovered by the lawful possessor.

Lease buyout generally establishes collective ownership. This ownership type involved about 6000 major and medium-sized plants in the Ukraine in 1997 (out of a total of 9080), and most of the 33,000 small plants were reorganised as close joint stock companies, limited companies or co-operatives. However, lease of major enterprises to staff proved inexpedient. Such was the case of the world-wide Baltic Shipping agency, which abandoned most of its vessels and almost went bankrupt due to unsatisfactory management.

Assigning major plants in basic industries in *trust* to foreign companies was the principal form of privatisation in Kazakhstan. Key plants were thus assigned to foreign corporations in metallurgy, chemistry and power engineering, chromium, aluminium and uranium production, the Republic's biggest oil refinery in Chimkent, sizeable petrochemical complexes, the world's fourth richest gold field, etc. Foreign investors were entitled to extract and export strategic raw materials, precious metals and stones. Kazakhstan made big profits in this customised privatisation involving international capital.

Following a series of failures and even scandals (e.g. associated with mining rights in the Vasilkovski gold field, management of the Karaganda metallurgical combine), Kazakhstan proceeded to a system of public tenders, inviting some companies of world-wide repute as managing companies. Thus the joint stock company Kazakhstan Electricity Systems Management Company was assigned in a 25-year concession to the National Grid Company (UK), the world's most important private high-voltage lines proprietor and manager. The latter, listed among the world's 100 largest, is to pay the government a bonus of $30 million and to invest over $1 billion in line updating and new construction, new and reconstructed control centres, integrated automatic energy recording and a control system, etc. The Swiss/Swedish corporation ABB was also granted a 25-year right of management of the national energy system. The corporation repaid the government's wage debts and will invest $200 million in systemic development for 3 years.

Deutsche Telekom will hold 49% of voting stocks in the State-owned Kazakhtelecom for 9 years with subsequent renewal for 6 further years. In this case, the German investor will repay the pressing debts and reconstruct the telecommunications system, with profits only to be expected after 10 years. In exchange, the investor receives 15% of net profits and remuneration for management services by end results. The Canadian/U.S./U.K. consortium obtaining gold mining rights will, in addition to bonus and investment liabilities, pay licence fees for the 80% share in the field and lease. As a result, Kazakhstan made substantial budget revenues and prevented failure in several industries. On the other hand, a radical change occurred in their contacts with related industries in Russia previously supplied with the major portion of raw materials (e.g. iron ore, alumina, chromium, uranium, coal).

In Azerbaijan, the U.K. company Transworld Metals received the USSR's most important producer of raw materials for aluminium production, the Glinozem association in Giandj, in a 10-year discretionary trust.

As CIS experience indicates, privatisation alone will not ensure increasing efficiency of production. Everything depends on the quality of management. The initial stage of privatisation should therefore be followed by reconstruction of the management system for public and collective property as well as small-scale businesses.

Control of State property. Under market conditions, the State retains ownership in natural monopolies (in the form of controlling interests in joint stock companies) and strategic branches (joint stock companies with 100% state capital and State-owned works – non-profit and generally State-financed organisations). State contribution is required in essentially important branches attracting no private capital due to low profits and a long pay-back period. These include many research-intensive industries. Federal ownership in Russia in 1998 involved 13,000 unitarian and 20,000 other enterprises.

Administration of State controlling interests requires qualified managers working under contracts and a clear-cut legal framework. In 1998, such controlling interests were held in 5000 joint stock companies in Russia, and these were administered according to non-remunerative principles by ministerial staff or directors. Consequently, annual revenues in the form of dividends amounted to a mere $20 million, several times less than tax arrears.

Revising privatisation results will only make sense if new proprietors fail to perform their obligations concerning investment, etc. Reselling of State controlling interests is only expedient upon realistic market valuation and appreciation following restructuring for improved competitiveness. Privatisation here should involve enterprises of special strategic significance. Placing them in the hands of criminal authorities cannot be tolerated. According to domestic and foreign experts, privatisation in Russia transferred over half of assets and 80% of voting stocks to the control of criminal or pseudo-international capital, illegally exported by people with criminal backgrounds (almost 20 methods of such exports are currently employed in CIS countries).

Nevertheless, these misfortunes should not cast any doubt on the role of trust companies as a legal form of administration for sophisticated complexes, using joint State administration of controlling interests in all components of the process. International economic history has clearly demonstrated the consistent transition from family businesses (e.g. Ford, Krupp, Dupont) via joint stock companies controlled by institutional investors (e.g. banks, pension and insurance firms) to team management-type companies (referred to by J. Galbraith as the technostructure). Control has been increasingly separated from ownership. The CIS countries therefore need a model trust law.

Public property funds are designed to assess the specific trust performance and decide on strategies for the subsequent development of heavy industry in the CIS. In Kazakhstan, enterprises in metallurgical (Karaganda combine, Sokolovo-Sarbay mining association, Pavlodar aluminium plant, Aktiubinsk and Ermakovo ferroalloys works, the Djezkazgantsvetmet, Don mining and concentrating combine), chemical (Chimkent and Djambul works), chromium (30% of world reserves) and phosphor industries were assigned in trust to foreign companies generally established for the purpose and registered in offshore zones (e.g. Japan Chrome, Aiwedon, Whitesven). While the contract is valid (5–10 years), they can take loans (guaranteed by their governments) with gains not exceeding 1% and, if they are successful, they are offered options to buy the enterprises.

Due to unique supplies of raw materials and good promise for privatisation, the shares in such trust companies appreciated and were able to solve some urgent financial problems. Nevertheless, Russian-Kazakh TNCs in the industries could be more efficient than selling basic industries to outside investors.

The concept of regulated investment activities in the Ukraine involves government support in priority strategies and branches – the fuel and energy complex, promotion of energy- and resource-saving technologies, export-oriented production, the agroindustrial complex, medical and microbiological industries, etc. In this case, purchase of considerable (over 25%) amounts of stocks requires authorisation by the Anti-monopoly Board. This will prevent financial brokers from monopolising commodity markets and changing profiles of enterprises, thus affecting national interests. The monopolistic Ukrgazprom system will incorporate independent regional enterprises, and the oil industry will be divided into four regional associations for oil mining, transport and refining and sales of petroleum products (with geological surveys and oil mains under integrated administration).

Financial and industrial groups. Revival of the CIS economy along new lines will require the development and implementation of national, regional and intergovernmental development programmes, above all in the agroindustrial complex (from cropping and cattle-breeding to sales of final products), housing, transport, research-intensive and export-oriented branches. Instead of budget financing, the government can support such programmes by facilitating the establishment and development of FIGs contributing to the implementation of the programmes, financial security and risk insurance.

FIGs have become increasingly prominent in the world economy in the 1990s, particularly in high technologies. Mergers include major corporations such as Lockheed and Martin Marietta, Boeing and McDonnell Douglas, Westinghaus and Hughes (USA); Airbus and Dasso (Europe), etc. A total of 100 major corporations in the USA account for 60% of GDP, 45% of employed staff and over 90% of R&D. In addition, the majority (78%–96% in Germany, France, Italy and the UK) are diversified. The State offers tax exemptions in FIG internal turnover and import of raw materials, supplies and equipment, mitigated anti-monopoly laws and contracts for contribution to government programmes.

The basis of industry in developed countries is represented by major corporations using organisational and legal methods in their administration of integrated technological complexes and collaborating with subsidiaries and independent firms in small and medium-sized business. In fast developing countries such as India, South Korea, Thailand and Malaysia, corporations account for over a half of GDP.

Special attention in privatisation was drawn to sustained processes in research-intensive export-oriented production and engineering for domestic markets. Thus during privatisation of the Thompson group (France), integrated development, production and service complexes were sustained, including those outside the country, in domestic electronics, means of communication and military engineering. The bulk of gains from privatisation ($12 billion in 1995 and 1996) was used for investment and repayment of debts in the public sector rather than discharge of the fiscal deficit.

On the other hand, private property has been transformed rather than ejected. In Japan, over 70% of stocks in major corporations are held not by private individuals such as Morgan or Rockefeller, but by banks, investment, insurance and pension funds and municipalities. This seems the most promising path for the CIS countries.

The intermediate elements of administration in the CIS countries were previously represented by Chief Committees at ministerial departments, in the 1990s laying the foundations of State-owned concerns, corporations, associations etc., demonstrating a high extent of co-operation and self-organisation. Their hasty liquidation and separate privatisation of research centres, design bureaus, pilot and series production plants, trade shops and wholesale depots resulted in massive rupture of effective co-operation, elimination of specialised processes for networks and components, cancellation of long-term development and production projects for sophisticated technology products, in particular electronic and automated equipment and instruments. In order to survive, some plants were re-orientated towards export of rare and non-ferrous metals (both strategic reserves and scrap), export production of elementary junctions and international development applications (in shipbuilding, automobile, transport, electrical engineering and even clothes industries) with the research/production cycle over 6–12 months (original production requiring at least 1–2 years, which is not feasible without adequate financing).

Reorganisation of major State-owned enterprises as joint stock companies in the CIS countries has met with only limited success. Controlling interests in almost one third of these in Russia were transferred to the staff actually only interested in retaining their jobs and receiving increased wages rather than investments in renovation that may yield results many months later. Almost half of the enterprises are now controlled by financial groups interested not in profits (taxable) and much less in investments in production, but rather in controlling financial flows, including depreciation of fixed capital and timely reselling at a profit.

Later in the 1990s, ownership came to be concentrated within major banks and State-related FIGs (in particular in the fuel and energy complex), as well as foreign strategic investors and local administration. Thus, in Russia, the KAMAZ owners are represented by the Government of Tatarstan, ZIL and Moskvitch by the Moscow City administration, the Ruskhim FIG by the Nizhni Novgorod regional administration, etc. Property is redistributed by remit, including budget, and by secondary stock issues.

In the Ukraine, the State holds controlling interests in 26 joint stock coal and three mine-building companies.

The leader on the list of key (in market capitalisation) Eastern European companies is Gazprom (almost $92 billion, 91st in the world), followed by Lukoil and RAO EES Russia. Among the ten leaders are Mosenergo, Surgutneftegaz and Rostelecom. No companies in other CIS countries are listed, and the figures included are far below world leaders such as General Electric ($223 billion), Royal Dutch/Shell (UK/Netherlands), Microsoft, Coca Cola, Intel Nippon Telegraph and Telephone (Japan) and Exon (USA). Among the 500 major European companies, there are seven members of the Russian fuel and energy complex and the Rostelecom.

Among the major financial groups with billion dollar turnover in 1998 were ONEKSIM (e.g. GAZ, Diamonds Russia-Sakha, Kuznetsk and Magnitogorsk metallurgical combines, Moscow aircraft industrial association, Surgutneftegaz, Purneftegaz, Sakhalinmorneftegaz, Novokusnetk and Ural aluminium plants, Oktiabrskaia railway), Menatep (Iukos, Nafta-Moscow, Apatity, Bereznikovski titanium-manganese and Ust-Ilimsk timber combine, Sibvolokno, Nitron, Moscow cotton-printing factory, the Paris Commune, Kirovograd and Sredneuralsk copper smelteries, Uralelektromed, Plastics Research Centre, Karbolit, Zhilevski and other plastics works, Mospishchekombinat and some other facilities for food production and wholesale trade, Mospromstroimaterialy, Montazhspetsstroi and other building firms), Alfa (three big tea-packaging plants, four sugar factories, detergents, cosmetics and medicine combines, Tverkhimvolokno and some trade firms), Gazprom (e.g. over 80% of the gas industry, Leningrad Metal Works, Perm Motors, Aviadiesel, UralAZ, NPO/research and production association/Iskra, welding electrodes and propylene plants in Tiumen, Ufa, Perm) and Lukoil (17 firms for mining, processing and sale of oil and petroleum products in Siberia, the Urals, the Volga region and North Caucasus).

Judging by the list, financial groups are conglomerates led by major banks or natural monopolies involving various branches, but above all they are export oriented, maintaining stable sales in the CIS market or are associated with public opinion arrangements. Thus Lukoil, for instance, holds large stocks in the newspaper Izvestia, TV-6 (television channel) and Bank Imperial. The financial groups focus on a closed cycle (research centres – raw materials extraction – processing – sales – investments) in each specific branch. Following the financial crisis in 1998, some finance groups led by banks (e.g. Incombank) were almost crushed, failing to repay foreign loans used in unsuccessful exchange operations rather than production development. Far more promise is shown by offer the financial and industrial groups led by special managerial companies undertaking less risky industrial projects.

To attract investments for process updating, the joint stock company Russian Metallurgy was established in 1995 with State stocks in both stable (Severstal) and critical combines (Magnitogorsk), contributing to share capital (51%) and profit tax exemptions. In some cases, FIGs trade in Federal blocks of shares.

For more efficient administration of State-owned shares, resources should be channelled to specific projects selected in business plan evaluating rather than to cover losses, and blocks of shares should be assigned in discretionary trust to regional companies proposing better investment, supply and sales administration plans. Business structures will perform consulting and mediating functions. Allocations for the social sphere should be distributed in municipal channels to create new jobs via employment agencies and for the purpose of social security, while closing unpromising mines via social security agencies. To date, depersonalised allocations in Russia, Kazakhstan and the Ukraine, where the problem is urgent, almost never attain their targets.

In some CIS countries, the lack of detailed legislation of joint stock, financial and trust companies, Public Property Board functions, property funds and anti-monopoly structures permits mass-scale deceit of private investors and transformation of directors into actual enterprise owners while not responsible for final results.

One typical example was quoted in a Russian newspaper. The NPO Aviatechnologia developed and applied a process to manufacture aluminium discs for motorcar wheels superior to international ones. However, the foreign firms who had bought up the vouchers purchased controlling interests in Russian aluminium combines, converting them to tolling (processing imported alumina and exporting finished products). The law provides for only 20% voting stocks of those in State ownership. As a result, aluminium prices in the domestic market were 30% higher than international prices ($2.4 vs. $1.8 per kg). Purchase (via the State-owned Mashinimport) of less expensive raw materials abroad was blocked. Railway tariffs were higher in Russia than via Amsterdam. Thus a private monopoly replacing government administration endangered a profitable market contract.

In such circumstances, FIGs can serve as the principal keys of macro-economic regulation, acting as partners for national, regional and international authorities on the one hand, and small and medium-sized businesses on the other. Importantly, FIGs cannot be structured according to uniform standards.

FIGs in developed countries contain firms with various profiles. Contracts of assignment in trust with directors and managers involving a FIF and its business units will ensure proportional inside and outside shareholding, market conditions, co-operation schedules and research and technology production standards. Separation of ownership from control, the participation of top executives in profits and assets (e.g. options for future share purchasing at a fixed price, deferred buyout of assets and production rights, leasing) are currently in common use. Using this experience in the CIS countries is very important for the development of small and medium-sized business.

3.3 Development of Small-Scale Business

Criteria for defining small-scale business. Small business is a special field of economy in terms of staff composition and the sphere and results of activities. This involves:

– Private entrepreneurs not registered as legal entities (not incorporated).

– Independent (not subsidiary) firms not holding key positions in the market or exceeding the limits of business size while operating business in production or trade. In this connection, small business excludes broker and dealer companies, exchanges, and crediting and financial organisations.

Government (public) support can only be obtained by formally registered small businesses (licensed entrepreneurs, firms included in the State register on registration with local State authorities, opening current accounts with any commercial bank and reporting to a tax body).

Guides to the business size of production in small and medium-sized business differ in different countries.

In Japan, small and medium-sized businesses include legally independent companies employing no more than 300 staff or having fixed capital of less than 100 million yen in manufacturing, building, transport, communications or utilities; less than 100 staff (or 30 million yen fixed capital) in the wholesale trade; and less than 50 staff (or 10 million yen fixed capital) in the retail trade and services.

In Germany, an enterprise is defined as large-scale (with certain volume of sales) if it employs more than 250 staff, medium-sized if it employs between 11 and 250 staff and small if it employs less than ten.

In the CIS countries, output is not used as a guide to business size, which is hardly justifiable. Only employment rate is considered (including part-time and contracted workers on time rate). Depending on the specific branch, employment limits for a small-scale business are set at between 15 and 100 staff.

On the other hand, an intermediary firm having no production facilities and using the tolling system will make multimillion (dollar) profits with a minimum number of employed staff.

Throughout the nineteenth and early in the twentieth century, big business was ousting the small, washing away and stratifying the middle class. The economic law of the concentration of production, however, as experience indicates, is fairly ambiguous. Since mid-twentieth century, small businesses have been reviving and the middle classes increasing, while no evidence can be produced for the overall proletarianisation and total interweaving of the State and monopolies – the last step on the road to socialism as an integrated public factory. This was prevented by the science and technology revolution, opening the way for decreasing size and dispersion of labour tools on the base of machine/computer integration. This revolution also gave a dramatic impetus to the human factor best used in small teams and to the relevance of environmental restrictions on the concentration of production. On the other hand, concentrated production is still essential in mass-scale manufacturing of standard networks and components, large-scale R&D and investment projects, with small business being largely corporate regulated and controlled.

The USSR built the world's biggest blast furnaces, turbines and chemical combines. They have proved unprofitable with current environmental fees and market transport tariffs. No less damage, however, is done by the impact of deteriorating technological systems.

In developed European, North American and Asian countries, small businesses account for 4%–60% of GDP. Thus only 4000 of the 20 million firms in the USA employ more than 500 staff, for instance, and only several hundred employ more than 10,000 staff. A total of 16 million do not use hired labour at all, functioning as individual enterprises (over 13 million), partnerships (over 2 million) or co-operatives or limited firms with complete overall self-employment. The proportion of small businesses is small in manufacturing (about 20%) but predominant in the retail trade (55%), building, services and wholesale trade (over 80%). The average number of staff in the EU countries and Japan is less than 100. Small business has three development priorities:

1. Small markets (individual and small-scale production of goods and services) not providing sufficient return for big business

2. New market sectors, primarily innovative ones, still neglected by big firms (if successful, a small firm can either sell the business or licence, or be incorporated)

3. Contracting or subcontracting to manufacture specific components (aggregates) or provide services to big business

The small business priorities in the CIS countries include agricultural manufacturing, production of consumer goods, medical equipment, construction materials and high-technology industries. In many foreign countries, however, they also involve waste control and other environmental activities, transport, communications, repair and construction works, tourism (including hotels, motels, camps management), services (information and reference, advertising, marketing, legal, consulting, publishing and printing, social and cultural), housing and utilities (e.g. cleaning, development, repair and maintenance).

Small businesses are most abundant in Armenia, Georgia, Uzbekistan and Kyrgyzstan (as the number of firms per million adults indicates). In Russia, the number of such firms grew more than fivefold between 1989 and 1998, amounting to over 2.6 million. Half emerged during the privatisation of State-owned enterprises, with over 1 million new private businesses, including 30% in trade and public catering, 14% in agriculture, 13% in industry and 11% in building. Small firms employed 13 million staff (the proportions differing considerably across the regions – from 31% of total employment in Moscow to 2% in Mordovia). Small business accounted for 10%–12% of GDP (four- to fivefold less than abroad) and 11% of investments.

Macro-economic effect of small-scale business. Small business offers some micro-economic benefits: low proportion of overheads, better flexibility to meet customers' demands and changes in market conditions, etc.

A typical European small firm is a family business operated over generations. For every 30–40 employees there are one to two managers. Accounting is handed over to a consulting firm, while engineering advice, legal and other services are provided by a branch or regional association. Filing and recording are computerised. Equipment is generally leased and serviced by the manufacturer. The land lot and office area are often rented, and store supplies restricted to 2–3 days' demand. Contracts for delivery are obtained from a permanent partner or in tenders for all producers whose orders are available in the computer network. Orders are obtained in the same manner. Each worker is ordered by the firm's management on his own liability for damage etc. and stamps his private number on each component. The firm uses an original trade mark. The average profitability in small business varies between 10% and 15%.

Even more important are the benefits offered by small business to the economy in general. Among them are:

– Preventing monopoly, promoting a competitive environment, increasing the number of economic decision-making centres (due to the extended range of economic agents, the number of such centres grew 12- to 20-fold in the CIS countries in the 1990s).

– Improving employment rates: Because the costs of one job (required investments per worker) are 1.5- to twofold lower in small than in big business (no need for new infrastructure, e.g. roads, power lines), there are smaller unemployment benefits, etc.

– Use of local supplies and materials, including reclaimed ones, unfit for big business.

– Employing people with limited working abilities (registered disabled and retired people, mothers with young children, students), offering them out-of-house or close-to-home work.

– Reducing government environmental expenditure by dispersing sizeable complexes (e.g. a complete metallurgical combine is replaced by dozens of small works with electric furnaces of the same aggregate capacity).

– Reducing average transportation distances by reducing distances to sources of raw materials and markets.

– Development of small towns, villages, kishlaks, auls and other communities with no space for big business.

– Consolidating people and improving the social psychological climate in teams in which the leader combines scientific and technological management with administration, makes effective and flexible decisions and maintains emotional and psychological contact with all employees.

– Creating and developing the middle class.

Privatisation in the CIS countries has not yet created a broad middle class with specific social roles in stabilising society and defending the nation, national traditions and the reform process. The class is described by three basic characteristics: (1) average income for this particular country, ensuring adequate living standards of medium-developed countries (monthly $1000–3000 in the late 1990s); (2) economic independence associated with productive work and real estate in home country; (3) obedience to law and patriotism governed by social identification (the interest of civil society perceived as their own).

Examples of middle classes were the well-to-do peasantry at the turn of the century (largely in Russia, the Ukraine and Trancaucasia) and qualified engineering staff and highly skilled workers in major industrial centres. Their potential, however, was never used either by the Reds or the Whites (collectivisation and mass repression of hostile forces). This public segment was revived between the 1950s and 1970s, with earnings approaching Southern European standards but with no immovable or other property. They were the principal losers in the reform process in terms of both material and moral wealth. In some CIS countries, research work is paid at rates several times lower than the work of ordinary bank clerks, foodstuff factory hands or street sellers.

The "new" Russians, Ukrainians, Kazakhs, Georgians, etc. cannot be described as middle class either. Their proportion of the total population is small (2%–4%), their earnings are of a semi-legal and quite often criminal nature and spending generally involves entertainment or purchase of real estate abroad. There is still hope from their children – the "newest" Russians, etc. – trained in management schools abroad. Farmers in most CIS countries have failed to constitute a significant force, the remaining potential middle classes either accommodating to ugly market realities or joining the extremists.

Soviet economic science of the 1930s–1970s actually ignored personal factors of economic behaviour, reflecting the general technocratic trends in politics and the ignorance of the productive force described as the main factor by classical Marxism. On the other hand, A. Smith, A. Marshall, G. Keynes, I. Schumpeter, M. Weber, J. Galbraith and many philosophers and economists in Russia early in the twentieth century realised that the doctrine of economic laws and categories cannot be applied in practice without knowledge of the economic skills, social psychology and ethnosocial background of economic behaviour, perceptions of ownership and types of economy.

Basic theories of enterprise were developed between the eighteenth and twentieth centuries by R. Quantillon, F. Quesnay, A. Smith, J.B. Say, A. Marshall, I. Schumpeter, F. Hayeck and A. Chaianov, among others. A. Smith described only the proprietor as an entrepreneur. Indeed, ownership determines as much the mode of production and distribution of the product as the role of individuals, motivation of economic behaviour, independent thinking, orientation towards long-term savings and capitalisation rather than current consumption. Both State and collective ownership are implemented in the private authority and responsibility of an entrepreneur-manager. In this sense, any type of effective ownership is private. Only public property is anonymous, combining private appropriation of the surplus by millions of "carriers" and State officials not elected by the public and not ultimately responsible for performance.

The more sophisticated production management system and the transition from regional and national to international markets in the second half of the twentieth century enhance the role of professional managers who are not the (single) owners. The percentage of property under their management varies between 70% and 80% in different countries.

Entrepreneurs as a specific social group in the CIS countries represent the four public segments: former party and economic functionaries (the nomenclature) currently key shareholders and senior executives in firms, concerns, associations, etc; professional financial, industrial, trade and engineering managers (often former researchers, engineers, economists, etc.); small producers – farmers, craftsmen, co-operators, lessees; and past and present dealers in the underground economy buying up privatised property, including shops and workshops where they were previously the actual owners.

In the modern economy, entrepreneurship is defined as productive in the same way as the work of factory workers or peasants is. This does not imply similar interests of hired labour and owners. However, the workers will no more welcome the owners' bankruptcy, or the latter the impoverishment of their workers. Stable development of the economy under public control co-ordinates basic interests of the general public.

Privileges for small-scale business. According to the World Bank, half of small businesses are ruined within 1 year after registration, with 7%–8% surviving for 3 years and 3% for 5 years. In Russia and other CIS countries, less than 30% survive for 1 year (many being established for a couple deals and often dubious).

After rapid growth in 1992 and 1993, the rates of small business subsided. A survey by the Institute for Strategic Analysis and Business Development indicates that small business is hindered by high taxes, the shortage of current assets and investment capital, difficulties with sales and the lack of a stable legal framework for property and business security. According to a Russian Commercial and Industrial Chamber survey, 83% of responding small firm directors blame non-payments and violation of contracts, 55% intolerable taxes, 44% shortage of own capital and expensive loans and 44% high prices for power resources. As a result, more than half have no investment programmes whatever, while 15% devise 1-year, 17% 2-year and only 11% 3-year or longer-range plans.

What small business needs is not charity but rather a form of redistribution for their social effects. A government programme for FIGs provides 2-year interest-free loans to entrepreneurs submitting well-justified business plans. The State authorities distribute the loans, supervising target use and cost accounting. Discounts are offered for renting land, and tax exemptions are granted to low-profit firms.

The EU initiated financing programmes for small and medium-sized businesses on the community level. Direct venture-crediting is provided to small firms holding promising positions in the market or producing innovative goods. Five-year loans may amount to as much as 50% of initial capital and 50% of maintenance costs. Within the risk capital programme Eurotech, a network of 13 European funds was established, offering about 200 million ECU for investments in small and medium-sized high-technology businesses. Financial aid is given to small enterprises engaged in priority fields, contributing to environmental projects or functioning in the spheres of structural challenge.

International organisations help to promote business in the CIS countries. The International Association for Development (a World Bank branch) together with Japan and the Government of Kyrgyzstan sponsor the Private Business Reconstruction and Development Fund. The Fund is operated by a French bank and an American consulting firm. The Dresdner Bank (Germany) issued tight credit (8.5% p.a.) to the Federal Fund for the Promotion of Small Business in Russia (secured by a Russian commercial bank and an insurance company in Germany). Small firms can have equipment on credit agreements (e.g. agricultural manufacturing, dentistry, beauty parlours), with a tender-winning firm checking against overstated prices and imported equipment competing with Russian equipment.

In addition to *funds for the support of small business*, the infrastructure includes *business incubators* (non-profit organisations sponsoring training and advice for new business owners on the issues of accounting, taxation, loan taking, marketing, etc.), *commercial and industrial chambers* and business development agencies (seeking partnership agreements, checking reliability of potential partners, marketing research), *technoparks* (lending premises or equipment, providing computing and other customised services), *leasing firms, mortgage banks, venture* and *security funds*, associations of small businesses (shop unions and professional guilds providing information, legal, expert and consulting services, personnel training, patent and licence protection, etc.).

Among the principal forms of direct and indirect support to small businesses are:

– Government and municipal purchases within appropriate programmes.

– Simplified registration, accounting, reporting – including tax statements (especially for individual business owners and low-profit firms employing less than ten to 15 staff), taxation by objective indicators (e.g. sphere of activities, production area, location) rather than running earnings.

– Accelerated depreciation to accelerate capital circulation and reduce taxable profits (with depreciation standards lowered where needed to cut prices).

– Free access to government science and technology and marketing information, options for leasing land lots and premises other than dwellings, partial reimbursement of real expenditures for marketing research, quality and design improvements, participation in exhibitions, personnel training, etc.

– Preferential loans, credit guarantees, insurance, venture financing from special funds.

– Investment crediting (deferred taxes on the purchase of new equipment), tax exemptions for ploughed-back profits, VAT exemptions for the purchase of fixed and intangible assets (in priority spheres and depressed regions), no advanced payment of taxes.

– Assistance in developing the infrastructure for small business and *franchiser operations* – large (franchiser) and small (operation) firms contracting to invest a portion of assets and operate in compliance with the franchiser's process requirements and under its trade mark. In this case a small firm uses a well-known trade mark, equipment (hire-purchased or leased) and process technology, while the counterpart trains the staff and supervises performance.

In the CIS countries, as opposed to other countries, small business has a minor share in the production sector, a wide range of products (generally combining production with trade and intermediary services), a different origin (most medium-sized firms emerging in the privatisation process) and, more importantly, a low extent of co-operation with big business.

Some small firms, often led by former research workers, have found their niche in the market. Thus one such firm manufactures quite competitive stationery, and another developed and patented a process for new thermo-electric materials already purchased by some well-known international firms; the Bit Software firm (50 employees) developed an visual symbol identification software for Cyrillic-script documents.

But such cases are few in number. Small business still needs and deserves government support.

Prospects for collective property. A special sector of private business comprises worker-owned companies. The incorporating process in Russia allowed for staff to acquire controlling interests in most joint stock companies. This, however, was no tangible benefit for sizeable joint stock companies; their percentage was reduced to 60% or, excluding the shares held by small groups of senior executives, to 20%–25%. Membership of all major shareholders on boards of directors and their control over directors' functions are still not the rule in the CIS.

Some authors of monographs published in the 1980s and 1990s[10] advocated the distribution of shares among the workers participating in administration and management, providing that most decisions on production, investments and finance were made by managers rather than shareholders' meetings. Over 12% of employees in the USA hold shares in their companies, including 25% in prominent corporations such as Lockheed, Motorola, Procter and Gamble, Polaroid, and even controlling interests in some (e.g. United Airlines, Publics Supermarkets). However, in the UK and France, the total percentage of staff holding shares is less than 10% and in Poland 20%. Investments, shared assets and profits are non-taxable.

Almost 40% of large companies in the USA invite their staff to participate in decision-making, including on the general firm level, e.g. on improving working conditions. Increasingly popular is the system of profit distribution among staff exercising qualified administrative control. Many strategies encouraging competition, motivation and team work so popular in the former USSR are used to advantage in Japan, South Korea, Sweden and some other countries. However, economic democracy must not restrict competitiveness and redistribution of capital to more profitable spheres or prevent cancellation of unpromising jobs and staff dismissal. According to the National property centre, the proportion of collectively owned firms in the USA is not expected to exceed 20%–25% (generally in small and medium-sized business).

The CIS countries should learn from the Yugoslavian experience of the 1950s–1970s, when workers' management not associated with privatisation degenerated to formal meetings. In the USSR during the 1980s, staff had a right to elect senior executives. This resulted in deteriorated labour discipline and professional administration. Appointment of a director is the prerogative of owners; day-to-day administrative decisions are the responsibility of managers; and the

---

[10] Blazi, G.R., Kruz, D.L. (1996): The New Proprietors: Employees as Owners of Joint Stock Companies. / Translated from English. Delo, Moscow (Блази, Дж.Р., Круз, Д.Л. (1996): Новые Собственники: Наемные Работники – Массовые Собственники Акционерных Компаний. / Пер. с Англ. Дело, Москва) [Cited here from Russian edition]

distribution of work and earnings for shared jobs should be handled by working collectives, providing that they are actually in charge of equipment in their specific sections and responsible for the use of materials, timely supplies and quality of production. Our experience of reforms indicates that authority and responsibility cannot be separated at any level.

Most CIS countries did not favour the idea of staff sharing major State-owned enterprises. Thus, while incorporating a State-owned fuel association (GPO) holding two thirds of the market for petroleum products in Moldova, for instance, the staff acquired less than 12% of public property with credit orders, 8% was sold by auction and 80% remained in State ownership. The GPO was divided into close-end joint stock companies with ten competing commercial structures. This ensured more benefiting supplies using direct links with oil refineries in the Ukraine and capital investments (including private) in the Iuganskneftegaz in Russia, etc.

3.4 Economic Security and Choice of Future Strategy for Reforms

Efficiency criterion for structural reforms. Depending on political orientation, economists in the CIS countries differ significantly in their views of the impact of reforms in their countries. Government supporters highlight the following:

Saturation of the consumers' market and commodity market in general and the elimination of shortages deformed the economy and public opinion for decades, entailing queues, disregard by producers of consumers' demands and low quality of products. While counting of available commodities across the regions is not common practice in all CIS states, on the whole the extent of market saturation with basic consumer goods increased from 30% in 1991 to 90%–95% in 1998.

This, however, was not due to increased supply but rather to decreased effective demand. According to the CIS Statistical Board, retail turnover of formally registered enterprises at comparable prices diminished by an average of 17% between 1992 and 1995, and the volume of services by 30% per year. In most CIS countries, this trend only began to change in 1997 and 1998.

Privatisation of State-owned enterprises, creation of the class of private entrepreneurs and farmers. Towards the end of the 1990s, the share of non-State enterprises in total retail turnover, including consumer's co-operatives, grew to two thirds in Belarus and Turkmenistan and 88%–95% in other CIS countries.

There have been increasingly more non-State pre-school, medical and health institutions and educational establishments. The percentage of private dwellings in the CIS countries increased during the privatisation process from 30% to 75%, and the process is almost complete in Kazakhstan and Uzbekistan.

On the other hand, as mentioned above, massive privatisation did not result in the emergence of a middle class of effective proprietors.

Reforms are generally associated with *international trade expansion*. Indeed, the CIS economy has become more open, and export outside the CIS is broader, although still largely based on raw materials and energy supply, while import trade mainly involves consumer goods and equipment.

Inflation and consumer price rises slackened between 1996 and 1998. In some countries, standard income rates grew faster than prices, with subsequently increased spending on non-food products and services and private deposits in commercial and saving banks. National currencies were stabilised.

On the other hand, many countries faced the challenge of non-payment, including delayed wages. The excess of public expenditure over revenue has not been surmounted and the external and internal national debts are increasing, while dollar/national currency exchange rates are declining, particularly in Russia, the Ukraine, Moldova and Belarus.

Government opponents offer different information, demonstrating the inefficiency or even failure of reforms. They point out the reduced GDP (compared with the pre-reform level in 1989) and industrial and agricultural outputs; the crisis of investments and major construction; the deterioration of living standards and increasing income differentiation; growing unemployment; lower birth and higher death rates, including in the able-bodied age-groups; the adverse impact on culture, education and public health; and the decline of science and research-intensive industries.

Nevertheless, neither the "positive" nor the "negative" data are sufficient to judge the success and social costs of reforms. A strong underground sector has emerged in the CIS countries. Some economists believe that at least 30% of products and proceeds are not reported to statistical boards, banks or tax inspectors. The registered unemployed are often engaged in kiosk and market trade, sometimes thousands of kilometres from home. Transactions in cash, including hard currency, and "shuttle" trade with Turkey, China, etc. are never reported. Many small and medium-sized firms never report at all, preferring to pay penalties and keep trade secrets. Some major works without a kopeck on their current accounts operate large-scale business via subsidiaries and offshore firms.

According to the Ukrainian Centre for Economic Research, the share of the "shadow" sector in the Ukrainian economy increased from 36%–40% in 1994 to 60% of GDP in 1996, outstripping the more developed countries (5%–10%) and even South America (30%) and Nigeria (50%). The population accumulated about $10 billion in cash, more than all foreign loans for the 5 years of independence.

The CIS has yet to develop a framework to estimate the performance of structural reforms. Due account should be taken of international standards for national estimates, findings from representative public opinion studies, including public surveys, and valid indicators that are difficult to falsify such as electricity consumption, mainline traffic, birth and death rates, etc.

International statistics have accumulated extensive experience in cross-country comparison. The six most commonly used basic indicators are: GDP, balance of payments, capital investments, unemployment, inflation rates and labour costs per unit output as a measure of productivity. Among the 15 best-performing developed industrial countries in the early 1990s were Austria, Norway and the USA in terms of GDP; the USA, Austria and Germany in capital investments; and Canada, Japan and Switzerland in inflation rates. The cross-index calculated from the sum of scores (15 for the first place on this scale, 14 for second place, etc.) ranked the USA only tenth in 1991 and first since 1994. However, these simplified estimates ignore the social costs so important in structural reforms.

Statistical compendiums in the CIS countries contain a special section, and Russia published a special statistical yearbook in 1995 as an interim overview of reform. The publications, however, are more factual (e.g. privatised items, new joint stock companies and farms, auctions and investment tenders, issued vouchers) than analytical. In addition, increased outputs and extensive international trade combined with inadequate environmental standards, low wages and wasteful use of irrecoverable natural resources cannot be described as the benefits of reform.

The performance criterion for a comprehensive structural reform in CIS countries will be governed by the interests of people, our children, grandchildren and great grandchildren rather than current politicians. This criterion will focus on the main productive force of society, on human abilities and demands, entrepreneurship, the scientific and cultural potential of the nation promoted by balanced economic and environmental change and justice.

A framework for this criterion will involve the following indicators:

I. Resulting components of quality of life

– Demographic dynamics (expanded reproduction of populations governed by available natural resources, socially conditioned mortality – infant death, homicide, suicide, accidents, infections, average lifetime)

– Public health (sickness and disability rates, including those connected with working and living conditions)

– Ecology (proportion of the population living in unfavourable environmental conditions)

– Effective employment (proportion of employed, including those in favourable working conditions, in the total labour force, as well as those unemployed for longer than 12 months)

– Education (proportion of school and college students among the young, holders of higher education certificates and scientific degrees among the working population, average duration of general and vocational training)

– Access to well-arranged housing and social services (proportion of dwellings, schools and hospitals providing the range of public services, families with private houses or flats, number of rooms per family member, services provided by mass media, travel operators, cinemas, theatres and museums, libraries, communications, public transport, children's institutions per 1000 people)

– Disposal real incomes (minus taxes, etc. and accounting for inflation), the differences between them and their relation to the subsistence minimum

– Level and structure of consumption of goods and services (by reasonable standards in each particular country)

– Business activity and ethics (proportion of registered entrepreneurs, number of firms per 1000 population, frequency of non-performance under contracts, including international contracts, corruption rates as estimated by independent experts)

– Innovative activity (inventors and innovators, patents and publications, including foreign ones, per 10,000 population)

– Legal order/rule of law (crime and crime control, particularly grave offences)

– Subjective quality of life (index of optimism from firms and households – using public surveys and migration balances, including highly qualified staff)

II. Critical factors in quality of life

– Rates of economic growth (GDP dynamics structure)

– Investment activity and renovation of production (shares of savings in private earnings and in GDP, gross and net investments, updated range of products, processes and equipment)

– Competitiveness of the economy (the country's contribution to international markets of core products and services, proportion of research-intensive and hi-tech products, as well as ready-made goods and services in total output and exports, equipment and technologies in imports, net trade and payment balances)

– Resource consumption in production and productivity of labour (consumption of energy, raw materials, water and timber calculated from GDP in corresponding branch complexes, outputs per hectare agricultural land, GDP production per worker and able-bodied person)

– Fiscal stability (inflation and national exchange rate, fiscal deficit, internal and external national debt as a percentage of GDP)

– Involvement in world economic relationships (foreign markets as a percentage of GDP, foreign investments as a percentage of the total amount, short-term foreign travel and foreign visitors as a percentage of the total populations)

Theoretical backgrounds for performance estimates and choice of models are represented by welfare economies, a special field of economic science examining the costs and benefits of modern society, the rationales of administrative decision-making in terms of purely market-based indicators and, more importantly, interests of social groups and society as a whole.

The theory can be traced to the eighteenth-century work of A. Smith (*Theory of Moral Sentiments*, 1759; *Wealth of Nations*, 1776) criticising mercantilism and viewing the emerging market not as a goal in itself but as a means of increasing the common good.

An invaluable contribution to the field was made by K. Marx in conceptualising comprehensive personal growth as the principal performance criterion of society and its productive forces. Economists predicted revolutionary changes in technology (with a corresponding change in the economy), ensuring not only enough food for the people, but also new levels of education, public health and personal growth. In this connection, the spiritual component is prominent in the political economy.[11] In addition, social change will not mean simplification, standardisation and unification, but rather more sophisticated economic and social conditions and their diversified arrangements. Feckless defamation of Marxism is as unwarranted as unrestrained praise.

Theoretical propositions of welfare economics and the efficiency of investment in human capital were formulated in the twentieth century by W. Pareto, A. Pigou,[12] L. Robbins,[13] P. Samuelson, C. Arrow and J. Hicks, among others.

G. Becker (Nobel prize-winner in 1992), J. Minzer, T. Schultz, E. Denison and others argued that investments in human capital (education, promotion of initiative, mobility, social communication skills, physical and mental health) do not reduce GDP but constitute the most efficient type of investment, although the return period is long. The key concept was of integrating economic and environmental ethical performance criteria of reform to elaborate the theoretical

---

[11] Marx, K., Engels, F. Works, 2nd Edition. Volume 1, 555 (Маркс, К., Энгельс, Ф. Сочинения, 2-е Издание. Том 1, 555) [Cited here from Russian edition]
[12] Pigou, A.(1932): Economics of Welfare. London
[13] Robbins, L. (1932): An Essay of the Nature and Significance of Economic Science. London

background for a comparative analysis of useful goods. In this case, the wealth of society is determined by the quality of life of individual citizens who were the best judges of their wealth. Any reform in an economic system is meant to meet private interests. The best possible production and exchange conditions are defined in terms of individual preferences rather than government motivations. A. Entel and T. Gossen quantified the relationship between the growth of household earnings and their distribution, the movement of the composition of consumption towards spiritual values. Accordingly, the UN human growth index used in statistics involves three principal country indices: average lifetime, literacy and per capita income.

In this context, economic growth is regarded as a development model with long-term GDP growth rates always exceeding population growth. The reform process, however, will necessarily involve a transformative decline resulting, as J. Kornai argued,[14] from the reduced non-market demand and investment activity of the State, as well as inadequate financial institutions and uncertain ownership rights.

Economic security. The main target of the CIS countries on the threshold to the 21st century is *national security* – the long-term perspective of society and the State ensuring the satisfaction of individual material and social demands at a medium level of development. National security involves defence (protection of State frontiers), interior (protection of individuals and their property against unlawful encroachments), cultural (preservation and development of national traditions facilitating personal growth), environmental and economic components. In this context, State security is not regarded as a goal in itself but rather as a condition of private (personal) security and social stability. The conception of national security defines the country's role in regional and international communities, public consensus and reform ideology.

Early in the 1990s, countries were classified strictly by economic indicators as highly developed or pre-industrial. First- and Third-World countries were differentiated by the following basic indicators: (a) per capita GDP ($4500 and $450 p.a., respectively); (b) proportion of individuals with at least secondary education (85%–90% and 23%–25%); (c) agriculture and forestry as a percentage of total GDP (10%–13% and 50%–55%) and employment rates (15%–18% and 70%–75%, respectively); (d) share of urban population (65%–70% and 10%–15%); (e) extent of economic openness – share of exports (23%–26% and 15%–20% of GDP); (f) share of manufacturing exports (12%–15% and 1% of GDP); (g) share of savings (23%–25% and 10%–11% of GDP); (h) share of

---

[14] Kornai, J. (1992): The Socialist System. The Political Economy of Communism. Princeton; Kornai, J. (1996): Trends of Post-Socialist Development: General Review. Voprosy Ekonomiki 1 (Корнаи, Я. (1996): Тенденции Постсоциалистического Развития: Общий Обзор. Вопросы Экономики 1) [Cited here from Russian edition]; Kornai, J. (1996): Sustainable Growth as the Top Priority. Voprosy Ekonomiki 10 (Корнаи, Я. (1996): Устойчивый Рост Как Важнейший Приоритет. Вопросы Экономики 10) [Cited here from Russian edition]

government expenditure (30%–32% and 11%–13% of GDP); (i) birth (annual 16–20 and 45–50 per 1000 people) and death rates (8–10 and 20–22) governing population growth; and (j) contribution of the middle class to the economy.[15]

Former USSR republics were assigned to the so-called Second World. While not inferior to developed countries in education and culture, they were not to be compared in income. Their economic security was first endangered in the 1970s, with competitiveness collapsing in basic branches (the share of machinery, equipment and transport facilities in exports to developed countries fell from 5.8% in 1975 to 3.5% in 1985), resource consumption growing (energy consumption costs in GDP in Japan, Italy, etc. decreased threefold between 1970 and 1985 and doubled in the USSR) and independent food supply no longer feasible (particularly with regard to grain). The USSR/USA differential in GDP output per head in the early 1990s was greater than in 1913 (21.8 vs. 17.8%).[16]

Towards the end of the 1990s, the world economy has changed considerably. Economic growth subsided in developed countries with high proportions of government expenditure, taxes and social benefits (e.g. Sweden, France, Germany). Total GDP growth rates in developed countries in the 1990s are lower than between the 1960s and 1980s. By contrast, Asian countries with high proportions of investments in GDP (South Korea, Indonesia, Thailand and Malaysia) have been overtaking the First World. Growth rates increased in agrarian countries with extensive domestic markets and increasingly open economies (India, Brazil, Argentina and Mexico). Conditions deteriorated in the countries orientated towards exports of raw materials (e.g. Nigeria, Algeria, Zaire) and confronted with dramatic civil conflicts.

The central problem in the CIS is how to prevent falling back into the Third World, triggered by the disintegration of the USSR. According to a UN Economic Commission report, in four of the eight CIS Asian countries, per capita incomes per head are far below $100 (the poorest EU member state Greece having $7300 and Switzerland over $36,000). Even in the comparatively safe Moldova, two thirds of households have no running water or other modern conveniences.

Russian economists proposed a set of national economic safety indicators (the figures in brackets stand for the world average or threshold and mid-1990s Russian values):[17]

– Per capita GDP as a percentage of the world average (100% and 25%)

---

[15] See: Gaidar, E.T. (1996): Anomalies of Economic Growth. Voprosy Ekonomiki 12 (Гайдар, Е.Т. (1996): Аномалии Экономического Роста. Вопросы Экономики 12) [In Russian]

[16] Ibid.

[17] Glaziev, S. (1997): A Groundwork for National Economic Security – an Alternative Course of Reform. Rossiiskii Ekonomicheskii Zhurnal 2 (Глазьев, С. (1997): Основа Обеспечения Экономической Безопасности Страны – Альтернативный Реформационный Курс. Российский Экономический Журнал 2) [In Russian]

– Share of manufacturing industries in industrial production (70% and 50%)

– Share of machinery in industrial production (20% and 15%)

– Investments as a percentage of GDP (25% and 13%)

– R&D costs as a percentage of GDP (2% and 0.5%)

– Share of new products in machinery (6% and 2.6%)

– People with income below the subsistence minimum (7% and 20%) (according to UN estimates, there are 20% households below the poverty line in Greece and Portugal, 50% in Bulgaria and Rumania and over 80% in some CIS countries)

– Average lifetime (70 and 64 years)

– Income difference between the richest and poorest 10% of households (eight- and 12.9-fold)

– Criminal offences per 100 people (five and six)

– Unemployment rates calculated according to the WTO procedure (7% and 9.2%)

– Annual inflation rates (20% and 17%)

– Internal national debt as a percentage of GDP (30% and 33%)

– Expenditure on interest and body of credit payments as a percentage of tax revenue (25% and over 100%)

– External debt as a percentage of GDP (25% and 31%)

– Share of external borrowing in budget deficit covering (30% and 45%)

– Foreign/national currency circulation ratios (10% and 50%), including cash payments (25% and 100%)

– Money stock as a percentage of GDP (50% and 12%)

– Share of imports in domestic consumption (30% and 53%), including food (25% and 30%)

– Regional differentials in terms of the subsistence minimum (1.5- and fivefold)

Among the greatest risks for national security in the CIS countries are: low GDP per capita, inadequate R&D investments and expenditure, low renovation rates in production, high proportions of poor households and income differentials by households and regions, growth of external and domestic national debts, dollar-dominated money circulation and import-dominated domestic markets.

Summary of reforms in the 1990s. Evaluation of the outcome of reforms in the CIS countries can use generally accepted macro-economic indicators – GDP, industrial and agricultural outputs, investment scale, real household income (accounting for cash earnings and prices) and external national debt.

However, the starting levels and conditions of reforms differ in different CIS countries. In some (Georgia, Armenia, Azerbaijan, Russia, Moldova and Tajikistan), armed conflicts have affected the reform process, and a final analysis should account for both absolute values (including comparison with the pre-reform 1991 levels) and the pace of recent change (see Table 6).

By living standards (as quoted in the annual World Bank report), group 1 (over $1600 per year as in medium-developed countries such as Peru, Columbia and Tunisia) includes Russia, Belarus and (far below) the Ukraine. Group 2 ($900–$1040 per year as in some South American countries) includes Kazakhstan, Uzbekistan, Moldova, Turkmenistan and Kyrgyzstan. Far below ($440–$570 as in China, India and Egypt) are household incomes in Georgia, Azerbaijan and Armenia; and the lowest incomes, approximately the same as in Zambia, Benin, Equatorial Guinea and some other poor African countries, were registered in Tajikistan in mid-1990s.

The differences are primarily due to different starting conditions. In 1991, the average income per capita was at its highest (although below that in the Baltic republics) in Russia, Belarus, the Ukraine, Transcaucasia and Moldova.

In the 1990s, however, the ratios changed significantly (see Table 6). Living standards collapsed in all the CIS member states. Thus real income per capita in Belarus in 1997 comprised 65% of the 1991 level, for instance. Household incomes in Tajikistan in after the disintegration of the USSR decreased by a factor of 100. Income reductions in Armenia, Georgia, Turkmenistan and Uzbekistan between 1992 and 1995 were so drastic (more than tenfold) that the UN classification refers to them as developing countries. Only in 1997 did real incomes improve in all the CIS countries (1%–7% and almost 30% in Azerbaijan). And yet conditions deteriorated again in Russia and some other CIS countries in 1998.

In 1998, earnings of inhabitants in four CIS countries were growing faster than prices. As a result, the real cash earnings rate increased by 16% in Azerbaijan, by 8% in Armenia, by 22% in Belarus and by 8% in Kyrgyzstan. On the other hand, the financial crisis has entailed a decrease in cash earnings in some of the CIS countries, reducing the real earnings rate by 12% in Moldova, by 18% in Russia and by 6% in Ukraine.

In the past 3–4 years, GDP and industrial output reductions were evident in all the countries involved in market reform. As mentioned before, these were due to reduced State purchases (above all in war industries), closure of non-competitive production facilities (due to increased imports on foreign trade liberalisation) and lower investment rates and consumer demand due to reduced budget subsidies and purchasing power of the population.

Table 6

Macro-Economic Developments in the CIS Countries in the 1990s (in %)

Country	GDP production			Industrial output (as a % of the preceding year)				Agricultural output (as a % of the preceding year)				Investments (as a % of the preceding year)				Real household incomes per capita		Real wages	
	1996 (% of 1991)	1997 (% of 1996)	1998 (% of 1997)	1995	1996	1997	1998	1995	1996	1997	1998	1995	1996	1997	1998	In US $ in 1996	Reduction from 1991 to 1996 (times)	1996 (% of 1995)	1997 (% of 1996)
Azerbaijan	35	105.8	110	83	94	100	102	95	106	93	104	57	180	167	145	480	3	116	137
Armenia	60	103.0	107	102	102	101	97.5	105	109	94	113	–	103	90	...	570	10	134	106
Belarus	65	110.0	108	88	103	117	111	95	100	95	100	59	92	120	116	2110	2	105	114
Georgia	33	111.0	103	91	103	108	97.3	110	110	106	92	103	110	187	200	440	7–8	...	190[1]
Kazakhstan	50	102.0	97.5	92	101	104	97.9	73	103	98	81	63	65	119	113	1040	5–6	103	108
Kyrgyzstan	50	110.0	102	82	111	147	108	98	102	110	104	182	130	65	47	900	5–6	101	101
Moldova	50	101.0	91.4	94	100	98	89	104	95	109	89	83	85	94	100	920	5–6	104	106
Russia	65	100.4	95.4	97	96	102	94.8	92	97	100	88	90	82	95	93	2230	2	100	104
Tajikistan	30	101.0	105	95	80	97	108	72	85	104	106	75	...	90[1]	...	370	100	104	105
Turkmenistan	75	85[1]	...	93	120	70[1]	...	90	96	90[1]	...	...	...	104[1]	...	920	10	...	113[1]
Uzbekistan	84	105.0	104.4	100	106	107	105.8	97	100	104	104	104	100	117	115	930	17	...	150[1]
Ukraine	50	97.0	98.3	88	96	98	98.5	96	90	98	92	65	85	93	105	1630	5–6	104	100

[1] Estimated.

The decline was far greater and longer than in Eastern European countries, since the rupture of established relations could not be remedied by contracting with adjacent well-developed countries, as was the case in countries such as Slovenia, the Czech Republic, Hungary and Poland. The most dramatic fall of GDP (two- to threefold, unprecedented in any twentieth-century country in peacetime) occurred in Kazakhstan, Kyrgyzstan, Moldova, the Ukraine, Azerbaijan and particularly in Georgia and Tajikistan. Only in 1997 did GDP output per capita begin to grow in the CIS countries (0.9%), along with productivity (1.6%). The greatest increase in GDP was evident in Kyrgyzstan, Belarus and Georgia (see Table 6). There was no GDP growth across the CIS in 1998 due to its reduction in Russia.

Future economic growth largely depends on investments. In five CIS countries they increased in 1997, mainly due to foreign capital.

According to international standards, the economic safety margin of external national debt is 40% of GDP. This limit was exceeded in 1997 in Tajikistan (151%), Turkmenistan (114%), Armenia (49%), Azerbaijan (68%), Moldova (105%) and Kyrgyzstan (63%).

Thus the 1991–1997 data indicate an ambiguous outcome of reform. On the one hand, none of the CIS countries have completed their reforms in terms of sustained improvement in basic macro-economic indices. None of the CIS member states have yet regained the former USSR's levels in terms of GDP, industrial and agricultural output, investment and, more importantly, real income of households. On the other, all have made certain achievements in the reform process, deserving careful study and generalisation.

Starting from the data for the period between 1995 and 1998, the countries can be divided into four groups:

Transcaucasian republics, Kyrgyzstan and Uzbekistan indicate stabilised or increased production and investments, with sustained economic growth to be expected in the last few years of the twentieth century, even though industrial production in Azerbaijan and Armenia and the fiscal situation in Georgia are still far from stable. Uzbekistan alone will enter the 21st century with more favourable industrial production dynamics than in the past.

Kazakhstan shows stabilisation and Belarus increased industrial production, although many indicators of economic security are still inadequate.

Russia, Moldova, the Ukraine and Turkmenistan are only midway towards stabilisation, with industrial outputs and some indicators of living standards still declining in the late 1990s.

The situation in Tajikistan is most critical by all indicators. Some improvements were only evident in 1998.

Special features of reforms in individual CIS countries. A specific path of reform was chosen in *Uzbekistan,* third in the CIS in terms of population (24 million, 60% under 25, and 50 million expected by 2010) and fourth in terms of GDP (after Russia, the Ukraine and Belarus). The republic ranks the third in the world (below Russia and Turkmenistan) in natural gas reserves (5.5 million m^3) and fifth in production (1.5 million t per year) and second in cotton fibre exports and has major resources of non-ferrous and noble metals (fourth in the world in the supply and sixth to seventh in the mining of gold, 8% of world output of uranium, etc.); moreover, it is becoming increasingly prominent in explored oil reserves (estimated at 20 billion barrels in Central Asia). All these enabled Uzbekistan to increase international trade turnover and attract substantial investments from the USA, Turkey, etc. not only in the extraction of raw materials. In less than 2 years, an up-to-date automobile plant was built with South Korean assistance. Uzbekistan's GDP in 1997 exceeded the pre-reform level; the country has independent supplies of oil, gas, grain and some other agricultural products, and construction of three sugar refineries is in progress. The purchasing price for cotton (State purchases accounting for 40% of total procurement) meets the international standard ($1000 per ton, added value excluded). The balance of trade with other CIS countries is favourable, and the inflation rate is less than 1% per month.

A special characteristic of Uzbekistan is the one-party government system. President I. Karimov identified the basic specific features of the republican model of reform integrating institutional (neo-Keynesian) and liberal-monetary (neo-classical) approaches:[18]

– The overall de-ideologisation of economic and social relationships, i.e. primacy of economics over politics and extensive use of effective foreign investment (even when undermining the country's current balance of payments).

– An evolutionary, gradual reform strategy, avoiding "shock treatment" and excessive social stratification. In the first phase of price liberalisation, the rationing of necessities was maintained, to be followed by wage adjusting, government purchases and enterprise subsidies. The second phase will involve the new national currency (the sum), persistent price liberalisation and tighter credit-monetary, budgetary and anti-inflation policies and extensive target support for some public segments (almost half of the budgetary expenditure is socially oriented).

– Gradual and charged (non-free) privatisation in contrast to other CIS countries. Reimbursement of previous government investments provided for reconstructing the privatised enterprises, financing the investment projects (above all export-oriented ones), replacing consumer imports and promoting research-intensive

---

[18] See: Karimov, I. (1995): Uzbekistan in the Course of Intensifying Economic Reforms. Tashkent (Каримов, И. (1995): Узбекистан на Пути Углубления Экономических Реформ. Ташкент) [In Russian]

sectors. Particular emphasis in this connection was paid to auctions, competitive sales and tenders involving foreign capital, as during the privatisation of tourist facilities in Bokhara, Samarkand, Khiva and Tashkent, for example, and primary and secondary securities markets.

Some Uzbek economists argue that voucher-based privatisation means the assignment of public property at a purely nominal price to casual holders, resulting in levelling, loss of control and a chaotic national economy. Privatisation in Uzbekistan was first initiated in trade, services and public catering, including the associated land lots. The focus was on encouraging family business, including small-scale wholesale, and preferential and foreign currency credit. Extensive privatisation of major enterprises began in 1995. As early as 1998, employment in the private sector was over 70%. However, the loss of Russian vegetable and fruit markets resulted in increasing unemployment (e.g. almost 80% in the Fergana valley).

Turkmenistan, third in the world in terms of natural gas supply per capita and having substantial export potential in wool, cotton, crude minerals, top-grade vines, fruit, medicinal crops, etc., chose to rely on domestic resources with tight government regulation in all spheres of the economy. President S. Niazov believes that "democracy in its pure, sterilised form is no less harmful for a developing society than the distribution system." Turkmenistan will not join any organisation or union with strictly regulated functions, focusing the tactics of economic reform on foreign investment and applying an evolutionary approach to market experience.[19]

Turkmenistan maintains international trade relations with 77 countries. Turkey, Italy and some other countries are contributing to the full-cycle textile combine project; future plans involve export gas lines both to the West and Southeast Asia, and areas under crop are being expanded to provide for self-support. On the other hand, the share of the non-public sector in GDP is insignificant. Land, means of production and other assets of peasant communities replacing the former collective farms have been declared public property as indivisible funds. Despite the abolition of energy charges and some social benefits, living standards deteriorated and the consumer market is still highly problematic in view of the considerable price rise and declining exchange rate of the manat. These are largely associated with the Ukrainian and Armenian failure to pay the gas charges.

Turkmenistan is the only CIS country with no IMF credit involvement, preferring an overall encouragement of the State sector to the liberal-monetary economic policy. The government fixes the rate of the manat at which the firms must surrender the bulk of their gains in foreign exchange, while currency purchasing

---

[19] Niazov, S.A. (1995): Concord and Independence. Herald of the Interparliamentary Assembly 2, 16, 9, 10 (Ниязов, С.А. (1995): Содружество и Независимость. Вестник Межпарламентской Ассамблеи 2, 16, 9, 10) [In Russian]

at this rate is subject to presidential authorisation to be granted exclusively for the repayment of foreign currency loans, repatriation of foreign investors' profits or the settlement of payments for essential imports. An alternative commercial rate is established for inter-bank clearing transactions. This involves a return margin for commercial banks bound to grant preferential credit to state enterprises, their resources often confiscated and the government authorising the writing off of the mutual liabilities of enterprises.

In *Kazakhstan,* branch ministries and government holdings maintained economic control until 1955. President N. Nazarbaev's Decree of Oil (1995) then assigned the mineral wealth to exclusive public ownership, introducing licensing and contracting for exploration and extraction.

Kazakhstan ranks among the first ten in the world in size (2% global land surface, with 0.9% occupied by the remaining four Central Asian countries), while lagging behind in population (17 million, i.e. 0.3% of the global population as against 0.4% in Uzbekistan and 0.1% each in Tajikistan, Kyrgyzstan and Turkmenistan). The World Bank estimated Kazakhstan's GDP at $25 million in the mid-1990s, almost equal to that in Rumania, Morocco or Bangladesh, thus ranking the first in Central Asia and fourth in the CIS.

Economists in Kazakhstan[20] observe that the almost halved GDP between 1991 and 1996 intensified the one-sided focus on mineral extraction and primary metallurgy with declining machine-building and diversified chemical production, the fall in productivity and increasing agricultural naturalisation. Macro-economic stability and the industrial policy depend on active integration in world economic relationships, above all including Russia, Central Asian countries, the Ukraine and Belarus.[21] The World Bank report (1995) ranked Kazakhstan 62nd among 132 countries in per capita GDP ($1560 vs. $1060 in Moldova, $970 in Uzbekistan, $850 in Kyrgyzstan, $730 in Azerbaijan and $660 in Armenia). In

---

[20] Ashimbaev, T.A. (1994): Economics in Kazakhstan on the Road to the Market. Almaty (Ашимбаев, Т.А. (1994): Экономика Казахстана на Пути к Рынку. Алматы) [In Russian]; Bitimbaev, M.Zh., Kanatchinova, A.K. (1994): Rational Industrial Structuring and Problems of Relevant Investments. Almaty (Битимбаев, М.Ж., Канатчинова, А.К. (1994): Формирование Рациональной Структуры Промышленности и Проблемы Инвестиционного Обеспечения. Алматы) [In Russian]

[21] Cf.: Buranbaeva, L.M., Zhulamanov, R.K. (1994): The Conception of Industrial Policy in the Republic of Kazakhstan. Almaty (Буранбаева, Л.М., Жуламанов, Р.К. (1994): Концепция Промышленной Политики Республики Казахстан. Алматы) [In Russian]; Esentugelov, A.E. (1994): Institutional Structural Transformation of Economy in Kazakhstan. Almaty (Есентугелов, А.Е. (1994): Институционально-Структурные Преобразования Экономики в Казахстане. Алматы) [In Russian]; Ospanov, Kh.A. (Ed.) (1993): Kazakhstan – Russia. Current Status and Prospects of Economic Cooperation. Almaty (Оспанов, Х.А. (Ред.) (1993): Казахстан – Россия. Состояние и Перспективы Экономического Сотрудничества. Алматы) [In Russian]

personnel development (UN estimates), Kazakhstan is in the first half of the list of 173 counries (61st).

Since 1995, Kazakhstan has been accelerating the pace of market reforms in a significant manner. Under the constitution of 1995, land can be held in private ownership (as opposed to mineral wealth) and the rights of rent and use can be sold. Energy prices have been liberalised, maintaining the rate of return margin. Significant improvements have been evident in the late 1990s in oil and gas extraction and metal production.

In *Azerbaijan,* President G. Aliev initiated intensive foreign trade and price liberalisation in 1995. However, the choice of a rational model of reform is hindered by the immense losses in the war conflict with Armenia (over 660,000 refugees) and the underground economy dominating in the 1980s and early 1990s, with directors of State-owned enterprises using clan and family connections to act as effective owners offering employment and benefits to their fellow countrymen. Foreign investment facilitated the growth of oil extraction later in the 1990s.

Reforms in *Belarus* and the Ukraine were delayed by change of government, the high proportion of the MIC initially orientated towards co-operation with Russia and other CIS countries, the comparatively low export potential to countries "far abroad" and strong dependency on energy imports.

Belarus almost completely lacks mineral resources except for some crude chemicals. Industry is dominated by accessories (almost 50%, with finished products only accounting for 5% in some industries) and general exports (up to 40% of GDP). The unfavourable balance of trade with the CIS countries aggravated the fall of the national exchange rate and real disposable cash incomes.

On the other hand, according to World Bank estimates (1993), Belarus had the highest GDP per capita in the CIS – $2870 as against $2340 in Russia and $2210 in the Ukraine ($2010 in Latvia, $1320 in Lithuania and $3080 in Estonia). Between 1996 and 1997, industrial production increased and economic co-operation expanded with Poland (in addition to raw materials and chemicals, exports involve tractors and refrigerators) and some other countries. Despite the high inflation rate, the market is still filled due to the former USSR's most advanced agroindustrial complex.

Unlike Russia, Belarus introduced privatisation certificates (vouchers) made out to individuals (depending on work experience, age and special social merits) and with qualified selling rights. Tax exemptions involve profits used in production updating, environmental control, maintenance of the infrastructure (within standard limits), agricultural aid and profits made by joint ventures (with the foreign capital share under 20%). Nevertheless, in the scope of privatisation and price liberalisation, development of small business and market infrastructure,

Belarus lags behind many of the other CIS countries. New vistas are opening in the union with Russia (to be discussed in Chap. 9).

The *Ukraine*, a leader in Europe in terms of population, area and economic potential, has maintained the State planning system. The protectionist policy involves preferential credit for national industries.

The main problem is related to difficulties with sales in machinery and light industry; due to high production costs and lack of competitiveness both in domestic and international markets, agricultural production has decreased in the public sector, and the excess of imports over exports amounted to 5% of GDP in 1997.

The programme of economic reforms included reduced (but not cancelled) financing and subsidies, price liberalisation (while maintaining State regulation of prices for electricity, fertilisers and other chemicals, crude and finished metals, agricultural machinery), abolition of many tax exemptions and higher real estate and income taxes. The budget deficit during the stabilisation period was to be covered with IMF and World Bank loans.

Between 1990 and 1992, the rates of GDP decline and inflation and the amount of budget deficit were comparable with Russia. Yet in 1993, when Russia embarked on a more active monetary policy and the Ukraine delayed reforms, the latter's position weakened, and outputs in fuel and energy, machinery, railway transport, etc. fell. Some splashes of inflation, a budget deficit and a persistent fall of GDP in 1996 and 1997 demonstrated that neither active government intervention nor a purely monetary policy could ensure the success of reform.

Moldova was the first CIS country to join the IMF (in 1992). The republic obtained substantial (as per head) IMF and World Bank loans. Economic liberalisation was supported by the USA, and Moldova has had free access to the U.S. market since 1995. Moldova was also the first country in the CIS to attain financial stability, bringing inflation down to a minimum and stabilising the rate of the lieu.

However, a critical industrial situation persists, posing the risk of total collapse in research-intensive sectors. With the high population density, jobs are increasingly few in number, especially in rural areas. The energy crisis resulted in huge-scale unlawful felling of timber. The excess of imports over exports amounted to 18% of GDP in 1997. Moreover, delayed foreign loans and declining exports to Russia in 1998 resulted in devaluation and money upheavals.

Kyrgyzstan, thanks to the IMF and the World Bank, also has a stable currency and the most significant financial support as calculated per head. Privatisation involved four fifths of enterprises, including all State farms. The liberal model of reform attracted investments in gold mining and extracting industries. Re-exports of Russian and Kazakh metal to China provide significant revenue. Industrial production has been growing since 1996, despite the collapse of research-intensive branches. In terms of GDP growth rates, Kyrgyzstan is far ahead of other CIS countries. Kyrgyzstan was the first to join the WTO. However, the republic has to repay excessive loans.

In *Georgia*, the monetary and fiscal-budgetary policy ensured reduced inflation and stabilised national currency (the lari). GDP has been increasing since 1996, mainly due to services and trade. On the other hand, 61% of the population has incomes below the minimum consumer budget, 40% of the labour force is unemployed, and tax revenues (4% of GDP in 1996) are among the lowest in the world. Due to the unsuccessful budgetary policy, the entire staff at the Ministry of Finance resigned in 1998.

Georgia has preferential foreign credits. Thus an IMF credit of $113 million was granted for 35 years at an annual interest rate of only 0.75% and with a 10-year initial repayment limit. In exchange, Georgia liberalised bread prices, abolished State subsidies for gas and electricity, restructured the internal debt as non-interest obligations with 3-year repayment terms, consolidated budget accounts in the national bank and imposed tighter constraints on government expenditure, increased taxes (e.g. VAT, petrol excise, customs duties) and promoted privatisation. GDP, which had quartered between 1988 and 1995 and additionally decreased by 30% in 1994, began to grow, but structural reforms are still far off. The greatest risks, as E. Shevardnadze pointed out, are posed by mafia-like groups, banking and financial violations, false bankruptcies, erratic use of credit, concealed earnings in foreign currency and their transfer abroad, big business-sponsored production freezes, smuggling and legalisation of criminal gains.

Armenia initiated reforms in its fiscal and credit policy in 1995, involving the reduction of the budget deficit to be covered using non-inflationary sources (above all, external humanitarian aid and IMF and World Bank loans), abolition of state financing and subsidies to enterprises, tight control of the money stock and privatisation of enterprises at auction sales for privatisation certificates and national currency (no more than 10% per buyer). Over 1000 enterprises (70% of the industrial potential) were reorganised as open joint stock companies. Yet the outcome was the same as in all liberal reforms: the reduced inflation and (dramatically) stronger currency were accompanied by avalanche social stratification, overall impoverishment and deteriorating industrial science and technology potentials. It was only Russian credit that ensured operation of the Armenian Nuclear Power Station, stabilising the republic's energy balance. Iran-mediated barter trade helped to restore the gas supply from Turkmenistan. Yet economic security is by no means complete. Armenia leads the CIS in the excess of imports over exports (41% of GDP).

The majority (59%) of respondents in annual public Eurobarometer surveys in Armenia, Kazakhstan and Russia describe the course of reform formulated in the mid-1990s as wrong (27% in Eastern and Central European countries) and only 22% (against 56%) as correct. Only 20% are satisfied with the general national developments in the CIS (43% in EU applicant states), even though incomes increased in the course of reforms in only 18% of the households, while decreasing in 45%. Further material improvements are expected in 34% of households in Russia and only 26% in more wealthy Western countries. In addition, 52% of respondents in the CIS largely related economic development to Russian partnership. Eastern Europe prefers the EU as the principal partner.

The world economic literature often compares the progress of reform in Russia and China. In 1989, Russian GDP was twice that in China and eight- to tenfold that as per capita. While almost all Russian citizens had access to social benefits and subsidies, in China this was only true of the 20% employed in the State sector, the majority surviving on the verge of starvation. During the period of reform (1980–1997), GDP increased fivefold in China and almost halved in Russia (as compared to 1989). The American economist P. Nowlan, in his book on the *Rise of China, Fall of Russia*, even suggested that China will be the world leader early in the 21st century, largely governing the geopolitical situation.

However, as Chinese economists argue, all these things depend on different conditions rather than on models of reform. The social costs incurred in the 1990s by the CIS countries were paid by the people of China during the "Great Leap" and the Cultural Revolution in the 1960s and 1970s. Having permitted market relations in agriculture, Chinese leaders won the support of the majority of the population, enabling them to prolong industrial reforms and maintain the one-party system. This was not the case in the CIS countries.

Adjusting reform strategy. Most CIS countries are completing the initial stage of reform involving denationalisation and privatisation and the elimination of monopoly in foreign trade, creating markets of goods and services and the relevant infrastructure. The outcome is highly ambiguous. On the one hand, there are no food queues, the national currency has gained real purchasing power and millions are buying motorcars and other expensive goods, travelling abroad and operating business at their discretion. On the other hand, the quality of life has deteriorated in the majority of households, tens of millions are below the poverty line, research-intensive production has almost been lost, the national intellectual potential and health are on the decline, and fiscal and investment problems are being resolved with external borrowing to be repaid by our children and grandchildren.

The CIS countries are now confronted with the alternative of proceeding to a 21st-century sustainable development society or returning to the consumer capitalism of the early twentieth century, involving trade of raw materials and work in hazardous environments for consumer goods and machinery. This is the path reluctantly chosen by many Third-World countries. In contrast to the CIS, however, they had no available basic industries, energy or transport infrastructure, qualified engineering, research or working staff.

Analysis of economic developments in the CIS in the 1990s suggests the following:

- A radical economic reform is an urgent necessity in all CIS countries. The attempted delays, for some reasons evident previously and even now in some CIS countries, will only aggravate the situation.

- A return back to the administrative command system with the State controlling over 90% of property is no longer possible in the CIS countries. There is no escape from the fact that, 60 years after the system was established, GDP consumption per capita and average household assets in the USSR were seven- to tenfold lower than in developed market economies, with the share of private consumption as a percentage of GDP less than 30% compared with 60%–70% in the West, and engineering and economic differentials increasing since the 1970s. While economic rates were almost equal in Austria and the Czech Republic, Spain and Poland, Turkey and Central Asian Union republics in the 1940s, they differed substantially in the 1980s.

- The liberal-monetary model of reform can put the fiscal and monetary system in good order, but not the social and economic system as a whole. It uses the experience of Third-World countries striving to slow down the rate of inflation, but having at their disposal neither science nor research-intensive production and thus making no equal contribution to the world economy; as well as that of more developed countries with no need for radical reforms. In most liberal economies, the State maintains regulatory control of prices for energy resources, electricity and basic foodstuffs, e.g. bread in Belgium or milk in the UK. The reduction of inflation and the budget deficit is a necessary but not sufficient condition for the success of reform.

Government policy in Russia and some other CIS countries in the 1990s was not consistently monetary due to the pressure of lobbying groups, unfavourable objective conditions and the absence of a clearly defined and popular programme. The rapid reduction of war expenditures (armaments procurement reducing eightfold in 1992) and government investments, along with the liquidation of private deposits in Sberbank (saving bank) in 1992, account freezing in Vneshekonombank (foreign trade bank), delayed budgetary financing for the army, the MIC, science, education and cultural institutions, etc. – all these cut inflation down to IMF standards, but the costs were too high, resulting in deteriorating national economic structures and general decline towards a semi-colonial economy. Financial stabilisation makes no sense in the absence of an in-depth institutional and structural change, as inflation is governed by unbalanced structure and inefficiency of monopolised economy. The capitalism developed in Russia and some other CIS countries has been described by reformers as "disgusting and horrible", "thievish and socially unjust".[22] A new strategy of reform in some CIS countries should involve institutional targets, reorganising the mechanism of State regulation in the economy.[23]

The institutional model of reforms is not initially focused on reduced inflation. During successful reforms in Turkey in the 1980s and 1990s, annual inflation rates amounted to 60%–70%. In a dual-sector economy, State-owned basic industries are protected against external competition. Advocates of this model in the CIS (left-wing parties) do not propose to privatise extractive industries or to return already privatised extractive industries to government control, above all oil and gas and coal extraction, along with power engineering, transport, communications and heavy machinery. However, they must become profitable.

In other branches, the budget will gradually – for 20–30 years – promote market structures, sponsoring individual target programmes. In this case, price regulation will involve basic foodstuffs, a State insurance company will be established to provide for bank deposits; social health, science, education and cultural programmes will be restored, and minimum wages will be fixed according to the actual subsistence minimum. A dependable legal framework will ensure comprehensive support for entrepreneurship, free choice of a private or collective economy and a clear-cut taxation system with no privileges for foreign investors.

This is not an all-purpose model either. A favourable outcome can only be expected if the monopolistic positions of the governing party are maintained, with a dominant rural population, an independent food supply, a high export potential, foreign investments from sources other than the IMF and active use of monetary methods of financial stabilisation. The strategy likewise entails the risks of deterioration of national economic competitiveness, an unprofitable State sector and a return to totalitarian governance.

The specific quality of economic and social development in the CIS countries requires a specific model of reform, combining rather than rejecting monetary and institutional experiences. This will necessitate: (a) national political stability starting from popular ideology, middle class consolidation and regulated income differentiation; (b) a mixed-type economy with different and equal types of ownership, a strong legal and enforcement framework, and a clear-cut, popular and consistent strategy of reform; (c) encouragement of private saving and investment in the national economy, controlled inflation and budget forming; (d) extensive public investments in research-intensive production, general and

---

[22] Gaidar, E.T. (1995): The Election Test. Izvestia 117 (Гайдар, Е.Т. (1995): Испытание Выборами. Известия 117) [In Russian]

[23] See: (1995): Russian Reforms: Established Interests and Practical Alternatives. Conference Proceedings. Moscow ((1995): Российские Реформы: Установившиеся Интересы и Практические Альтернативы: Материалы Конференции. Москва) [In Russian]

continuous education, personnel development and an improved labour environment; and (e) an aggressive strategy in international export markets, attracting foreign investments in individual projects on mutually beneficial principles.

A centrist strategy of reform that is adjusted to and focused on the consolidated economic security of the CIS countries should be governed by the following principles:

The progressive nature, i.e. the focus on transition to new forms of civilisation based on science, education and information technologies rather than a return to past stages of the spontaneous, self-regulated market.

The dependence nature, i.e. use of past achievements – major research and production complexes representing the meso-economic level of governance fecklessly destroyed by spontaneous privatisation, multiple components of culture, education, health care and science development. The desire to "raze to the ground, and then..." has never benefited anyone and never will. Successful reforms are inconsistent with social violence, extreme actions, propaganda of hostility or attempts to erase the "bad period" from the history books.

The social orientation of structural reforms means inadequacy of merely economic decisions, of the centralised establishment of a market economy without accounting for potential alternatives, the political and social pressure of monopolistic groups (e.g. AIC and MIC leaders, miners). The alternative lies in equity, the fair distribution of the inevitable costs of reform by controlling the income differentials and the emerging underground economy and mafia-like structures in some regions and public segments. This involves day-to-day work to develop public awareness of the meaning, prospects and future benefits of ongoing change. This is especially important in the CIS countries with the age-old faith of the people in the superior ideology, sagacity and moral power of their leaders.

The specific role of the State in transitional processes. While denationalisation of the economy does mean gradual abandonment by the authority of the day-to-day control of production by planning the range, sales, procurement, etc., this by no means involves State property control, appointment of directors of State-owned enterprises, macro-economic regulation, identification of priorities in science and technology and investment policy. The "State's withdrawal from economy", the "abolition of state monopoly", be it tobacco and vodka or strategic resource exports, will result in chaos ruled and fought over by criminal monopolies rather than economic freedom. In Russia, for example, an undoubtedly negative role was played by the conception of "full control rights" enabling directors (on the emergence of the non-public sector of the economy), via a network of specially established "small enterprises" and carefully observing the letter of the law, to transfer their receipts from the use of public property and the property itself to fictitious accounts. The tour de force in science was the government's refusal to inventory research institutes and design bureaus. The hope for an "invisible hand of the market" only encouraged dubious dealers to lend premises or sell the results of their colleagues' hard work to foreign buyers for a pittance.

The pluralism of market economy models, depending on the stage of development and specific features of the national economy (there are significant differences between the Anglo-American, Japanese, Scandinavian and continental European models) and individual regions (particularly important in Russia, the Ukraine, Kazakhstan, Kyrgyzstan and Georgia). The transitional economy should not be confused with a developed market-based economy, and the CIS citizenry excited by unexpected change with the law-abiding public in other countries.

The integrated conception of reform. The market economy sub-systems (State regulation, fiscal and credit framework, corporate management structure, management style and relevant legal framework, employment and social care frameworks) are all interrelated, co-ordinated and complementary. Thus there can be no grounds for constructing a sustainable economic system with the components arbitrarily drawn from various national systems. The total liberalisation of prices (including the natural monopoly sector and socially important goods) is to no avail in the absence of an advanced competitive market and social care framework. Sweden's model of social security without efficient economic and enforcement frameworks only hinders motivation for work.

Role of mass entrepreneurship. *Entrepreneurship* is the activity of an independent economic agent (private person or legal entity) undertaking financial risks and duly registered, involving the use of property and the development, production and sales of goods and services for profits (earnings).

The definition identifies the agent (owner of property or title, lessee or trustee), the subject (investments, innovative R&D, production, sales of goods, commercial, information, social, repair and maintenance and other services), the goal (profit, earnings) and the arrangements of entrepreneurship (available solitary property, liability as to property).

The primary role of entrepreneurship in societal development is to promote initiative among the people not supported by the State (e.g. communities, mafia-like groups), independent of it and free (within legal limits) to choose the spheres of application for their strength and abilities.

Entrepreneurship is a form of expression and growth of the individual and his abilities and demands. Human social demands govern the striving for economic freedom where the choice of ways of implementing working potentials and forms of economic activities is only limited by efficiency. As liberated from poverty, entrepreneurship is increasingly associated with competitiveness, the desire to attract the attention of others and to win respect in society.

Freedom, competitiveness and the dialectically related responsibility imply the inequality of workers' status, an hierarchy based on the difference of abilities and, consequently, outcome of work. The natural and historical process cannot be eliminated by any social system. All the efforts to transform "human material", to create a "new man" by restraining economic freedom and replacing internal motivation with external, State-arranged incentives and guarantees resulted in personal degradation, transformation of independent workers into unreliable lumpens expecting instructions and material benefits from superior authorities. They are typically imitative in work, limited in demands and hostile to those who wish and can work.

Field of Debate

1. What are the specific features of the liberal model of nationalisation in the economy?

2. Why is total economic liberalisation inefficient in the CIS?

3. What is the role of the State in the transitional economy?

4. How should prices and the activities of natural monopolies be regulated?

5. How should foreign trade be regulated?

6. How do you envisage the prospective relationships between the centre and regions in the CIS economies?

7. What is the relevance of international experience of privatisation in the CIS?

8. What part of international experience in privatisation can be used in the CIS?

9. Analyse the outcome of privatisation in the CIS.

10. What role do FIGs play in the current economy?

11. What privileges are offered to small business in the CIS countries? What should be altered in this respect?

12. Write an interim report of the first stage of privatisation in the CIS countries, with special emphasis on economic security indicators.

13. What adjustments can made in the strategy of reform in the CIS countries? Compare various economic opinions.

Chapter 4

FORMING MARKET INFRASTRUCTURE

4.1 Commercial Infrastructure

Infrastructure and its role in modern economy. The *infrastructure* is a system of economic organisations and non-profit institutions providing the firms and people in a given community with the services required for normal business activities and the reproduction of productive forces.

The infrastructure contains five basic blocks. The *commercial* infrastructure, including banks and other financial institutions, exchanges (e.g. stock, commodity, currency), insurance companies, trade centres (wholesale trade, distribution and storage of commodities), expert and consulting, legal, auditing, advertising and marketing firms, ensures the efficient production and sales of goods and services under competition.

Unlike the commercial infrastructure, the *production* infrastructure – railway, motorcar, sea and river, pipeline and air transport, roads, communication system, power system (electricity, heating, gas), water supply and sewage, environmental control – was already available in the centralised planned economy. However, it was carried by the State and generally focused on strategic military targets, neglecting ecology and the internationalisation of production.

The *science and technology* infrastructure involves fundamental science, information networks, public metrological, experimental/testing and leasing centres, patent and licensing services, engineering firms, scientific and engineering personnel training and development, innovative demonstration systems (e.g. exhibitions, competitions) and protection of intellectual property.

The *social* infrastructure – utilities and city services, public health, education, culture, pensions and social security, demographic control. The social security framework is of particular importance in a transitional economy, facilitating the adaptation of the handicapped to change, the formation of a middle class and the preservation and promotion of national culture.

The *institutional* infrastructure involves central and municipal authorities, including local government. This largely determines the development of a democratic civil society, a law-based economy, public attitudes to reforms and the investment climate in the CIS countries.

Infrastructure enterprises are not involved in the production of material wealth – commodities – yet they define the development of a modern economy. Developed market economies are principally noted for the superior standards and open nature of the infrastructure integrated in regional and world markets.

The infrastructure development is very expensive, with a long pay-back period (from internal revenues, excluding the accompanied effect in other branches). An emerging market infrastructure therefore requires active government intervention and the assistance of international economic organisations. International experience indicates that, at later stages, the production, science and technology and, in part, the social infrastructure can be advantageously administrated by non-public corporations.

An essential distinction between the CIS and many Asian, African and South American countries is that an integrated and efficient transport and power infrastructure, along with networks of communication, education, health, etc., had already been established and operated efficiently between the 1930s and 1980s. The costs and environmental effects of the pipelines, railways, etc. had been ignored, focusing on individual major projects rather than the comprehensive development of highway networks, communication systems or urban economy and housing. On the other hand, the former Union republics were far superior to the neighbouring Asian and some European countries in terms of average life expectancy, infant mortality, ratio of doctors and hospital beds to the overall population, college enrolment and scientists per thousand people and several other indicators.

Banking and financial infrastructure. Commercial banks and other financial institutions (investment and other financial funds, mutual funds, leasing firms, etc.) constitute the central element of the commercial infrastructure. In collaboration with and under the regulation of the Central Bank, they maintain the stable circulation of money and goods and of financial transactions in national economy, store of available financial resources, issue short- and long-term loans to economic agents, accumulate and use investment resources and manage corporate financial assets in trust, etc.

The existing banking and financial infrastructure was established in the CIS countries over a period of a few years in the 1990s. In 1996, Russia had almost 2000, the Ukraine 230, Kazakhstan 130, Belarus 40, Armenia 30, Moldova 27 and Kyrgyzstan, Tajikistan and Turkmenistan 15–18 commercial banks each.

The number of banks in the CIS peaked in 1995, but then reduced when licences were withdrawn in cases of embezzlement, inadequate own capital, non-compliance with Central Bank regulations, etc. More than 500 banks were closed in Russia, Armenia, Kazakhstan, Turkmenistan and some other CIS countries.

With high inflation rates, they made large profits in operations with foreign currency, import procurement credits, etc. Economic stabilisation required highly professional market research, assessment of credit risks and management of investment projects. Many banks were not adequately prepared to handle the task. A number of large Russian banks collapsed in 1998 due to the great losses associated with the treasury bills freeze, forward foreign-currency contracts (the dollar rate trebled over a month instead of the predicted 5%) and depreciated blocks of shares securing foreign credit. Some major banks, e.g. SBS-AGRO, were compelled to transfer their controlling interest to the State. Things were better in medium-scale regional banks not involved in extensive risky operations on the stock market.

Mention should also be made of new financial trends in developed economies in the final years of the twentieth century.

The range of financial services has generally been extended. In addition to traditional credit and deposit (short- and long-term loans, demand and time deposits) and payment and clearing operations (accounts balancing and clearing), modern banks provide over 400 services. Among the most important are:

– Investments and securities (purchase, sale, issue and distribution of securities)

– Trust management

– Hedging (against commercial, investment, credit and other risks)

– Leasing (acquisition of property and long-term lease with further buyout)

– Factoring (purchase of outstanding bills for delivered goods)

– Consulting (e.g. investments, creditworthiness of potential partners, financial risk evaluation, creation of financial portfolios, corporate restructuring)

– Investment management (analysis of investment projects, selection of investors, financing, control on appropriate use and performance)

International financial companies are gathering force, handling current and saving accounts and providing a range of financial services on international markets. For small and medium-sized firms that cannot afford to employ highly paid financial managers, they perform the following functions skilfully and at a comparatively low price: accounting (e.g. control of payments on accounts and drafts, receipt of debts, clearing, cash payments), financial information (preparation of financial balance sheets, tax reports and financial plans, portfolio management) and management (investments, administration of property, material assets and projects, issue and distribution of stocks and bonds, broking and dealing services). Financial companies communicate via up-to-date information technologies, ensuring prompt current payments and capital transfer on a world-wide scale and in conformity with national laws.

Financial internalisation requires access by foreign financial institutions to national banking. The World Trade Organisation (WTO), which most CIS countries intend to join, requires an overall liberalisation of the financial market, including the lifting of constraints on foreign currency, foreign banks and insurance companies, the entitlement of both corporate bodies and private persons to open accounts abroad, etc. On the other hand, while opening the way to foreign investments, global internalisation poses the risk of global crises, as recent cases in Mexico and Southeast Asia have illustrated. The prominent financier G. Soros therefore suggests an international financial framework impervious to dramatic change in exchange rates and capital flows to reduce systemic risks in cases of failure in one of the world's 60 international investment and commercial banks.

Bank laws are most liberal in Armenia, Georgia, Moldova and Kyrgyzstan. Substantial tax exemptions are offered to foreign banks in the initial years of operation, and Armenia (like offshore zones) imposes no curtailment on capital flows whatever. The first international bank in Georgia was established in 1997 with Greek capital (51%) and the EBRD (20%), together with the Georgia Union Bank (29%). A Dutch banking group (50%), together with the EBRD, an international finance corporation (10% each) and the Uzbekistan National Bank, established a bank in Uzbekistan. However, the foreign share in the aggregate bank capital in the CIS countries is currently insignificant. In Russia, it amounted to only 5% in 1998 (as against almost 20% in Poland, the Czech Republic and the USA, 55% in Hungary and Venezuela, etc.) but has since grown.

Replacement of the system from the USA, the UK and Japan of rigid specialisation by financial service to reduce the risks (a demand-deposit bank not being allowed to handle long-term investments, and an investment fund not being allowed to accept demand deposits) with a more diversified European model means a transition from service- to customer-oriented specialisation (e.g. corporations, small business, mortgage loans to farmers and other proprietors).

Thus the Pakhta Bank in Uzbekistan specialises in deposit-credit and foreign exchange investment services for the whole cotton base, including contracts and futures, and the Eksim Bank in Kazakhstan specialises in foreign credit servicing, etc.

An important feature is the restoration of land and mortgage banks to attract household and government investments in the AIC infrastructure, area planning and development and housing construction. The tangible assets represented by land and real estate enable not only the money, stocks and bonds, but also mortgages, bills, commodity papers, certificates, etc. to be used in long-term bank investment.

Bank computer networking is in progress, with packet-switched electronic payments and links to local computer networks with office equipment. Office-to-bank and inter-bank transactions via protected networks ensure both prompt payment and minimum uncontrolled cash circulation. Bank networking is under way in Russia, Uzbekistan, Kazakhstan, the Ukraine, Belarus, etc. According to various estimates, household money overhang in Russia amounted to over $30 billion in 1998, twice as much as budget revenues. Since banking deposit growth rates declined when pyramid scheme companies collapsed, only 7% of people now use insurance services, even though 16% of total cash earnings are invested in foreign currency.

The general transition to electronic transactions, money orders, checks, magnet- and circulation microprocessor cards (both debit and credit) will reduce semi-criminal cash and increase tax revenue in the budget.

Banks in some CIS countries (e.g. Russia, the Ukraine, Moldova, Kazakhstan, Belarus) issue plastic "Europay", "Visa" cards, etc., the relevant infrastructure including authorisation agencies (authenticity and overdraft checking), operational processing centres for accounting and inter-bank clearing, cash machines and electronic shopping terminals. Infrastructural costs are compensated for by faster payments, expanded markets of goods and services (using debit and credit cards) and internationalised money circulation.

Particularly important for the CIS countries is the multi-run bank payment processing system, providing on-line banking transaction with immediate communication via reliable networks.

Banking reliability figures prominently on the world financial market. Thus, when overdue loans worth $11 billion accumulated in South Korean banks in 1997, for instance, it was only the Central Bank's preferential loan that prevented the failure of the Korea First Bank, a creditor of the bankrupt steel corporations Hambo and Sammi and the Kia automobile group. Some major banks in Japan were ruined. More than 20 banks collapsed in the Baltic countries between 1995 and 1997, affecting 40% of the financial sector.

Banking stability requires permanent Central Bank regulation of commercial bank lending, conformity with legal reserve requirements and professional qualified staff. To relieve critical conditions in Lithuania, some banks were merged or nationalised, and a special finance authority for "bad loans" was established. Investigations were initiated and criminal lawsuits brought against debtors. The Kyrgyzstan National Bank authorised the Debra agency to manage restructured banks' assets and liabilities and to recover the debts by the collection of payments and loan restructuring, receiving 5% of the sums collected.

Reduced inflation and lower government bond yields will enhance competition and evict banks with inadequate founding capital and low-qualified staff, previously orientated towards speculations with foreign exchange and securities, and preferential credit to their sponsors. Thus, Kazakhstan's Bank and Banking Law, for instance, provides for a minimum founding capital of $1.5 million. Licences were withdrawn from loss-making and small banks, and State blocks of shares in 65 banks were offered by auction. In Moldova, credit companies lost their own capital, and part of obtained loans were either liquidated or reconstituted as branches of major banks. The number of banks in Georgia decreased from 229 in 1995 to 70 in 1997.

Banks' own capital in Russia increased, with ten (e.g. Vneshtorgbank, Sberbank, Oneksimbank) listed among the world's 1000 major banks. On the other hand, a third of banks had capital resources of less than $1 million. In the future, small banks will be merged with major banks, reconstituted as non-banking financial institutions or wound up. Medium-sized banks are prohibited from establishing branches, operating outside the country, dealing in precious metals, etc.

In Armenia, with 46% of bank capital held by foreign owners, ten of the 30 banks failed. To improve private banking reliability in the Ukraine, the Sberbank is not allowed to give credits to legal entities. Banking reliability is governed by the own capital to total assets ratio, depending on financial risk exposure.

All these require the creation of a deposit insurance framework and a demand deposit payment fund (as a percentage of total deposits).

Bank holdings are progressing, including investment funds, leasing firms, depositories, etc. They are essential to encourage investment in real production rather than to promote short-term imported credit and foreign currency transactions.

Bank conglomerates use affiliated shared and mutual investments as well as those provided by non-government pension funds and firms registered abroad to buy up shares in enterprises with superior export potentials, firm positions on the domestic market and closed supply-production-sales cycles. FIGs are thus established, though not always formally registered, incorporating leasing, transport, construction, advertising and marketing, storage, realty (evaluation and trade), expert consulting and other firms.

The bank consortium involving Russia, the Ukraine (Proektinvestbank, Ukrsotsbank and AKB Ukraine) and Belarus (e.g. Belpromstroibank) is helpful in co-ordinating the payment and investment policy and reinforcing the financial infrastructure. Other useful instruments include the emerging joint banks. Thus, in Uzbekistan, in addition to the Uzbek-Turkish UT Bank and Uzbek-Dutch Uzprivatbank, there is also an office of the major Chase Manhattan Bank (USA). There are over 150 foreign bank branches in Russia and the Ukraine, and 20 Russian banks have branches and offices outside the CIS.

The financial service industry, including previously independent banking, insurance, investment and mortgage companies, savings banks, mutual funds societies, etc., is represented by financial corporations involving both banking and other financial establishments, as well as consulting, design, construction, legal and other non-financial firms.

Crediting in the CIS countries generally includes short-term loans to traders and dealers and financial and commercial credit. Long-term loans accounted for only 1%–8% of total credit in Armenia, Azerbaijan, Kazakhstan and Russia. The percentage was slightly higher (16%–23%) only with the high share of the State in banking (in Tajikistan, Belarus, the Ukraine and Uzbekistan) and in Kyrgyzstan due to the State financing of expanded fixed capital investments.

Some CIS countries use loans to cover the budget deficit, which aggravates inflation. Russia (since 1995) and some other states (e.g. Moldova, Kyrgyzstan, Georgia, Armenia) have abandoned the use of direct Central Bank loans to service budget deficits.

Discount rates regulated by central (national) banks have been reduced in recent years due to lower inflation rates and treasury bond yields.

On the other hand, many bank loans were not returned, particularly in countries with predominantly State-owned enterprises.

Due to the absence of working mechanisms of receiving debts and long-term investment incentives, banks in Kazakhstan, Kyrgyzstan, Armenia, Russia and the Ukraine reduced the amount of credit in mid-1990s, thus impairing financial positions of enterprises. Stale (overdue) debts – for goods shipped, works performed, services provided, etc., as well as outstanding payments to the budget or extra-budgetary funds, and delayed wages – are shown in Table 7.

A new business type currently emerging in Russia, Belarus, Kazakhstan and other CIS countries – auditing – involves independent control of corporate accounting and reporting to validate financial information.

In particular, Kyrgyzstan launched a government agency to control conformity with the laws in joint stock companies, investment funds, stock exchanges, etc. engaged in securities business. To qualify for trade, a firm has to submit the prospect of issue, auditing opinion, pass over the shareholders' register to an independent agency and become listed. An automated system provides contra-accounting on the date of transaction.

A unified auditing space is being created in the CIS at the end of the 1990s in compliance with international accounting standards, general issue and distribution regulations, the model law of audit containing, an unambiguous definition of auditing and its types, auditing and licensing requirements, etc.

Since 1998, Russia and some other CIS countries have been employing the international banking risk standards (the Basel Convention), thus improving the international reputation of their banking systems. In contrast to existing practices, control is both consolidated (including branch and subsidiary balances) and separate by risk type, including derivatives futures, options, etc. Special emphasis is placed on inter-bank credit safety, as banks often use loans to cover losses in non-performing loans, unsuccessful speculations, etc.

Table 7

Credit Structure and Overdue Debts on Bank Loans
(1998, end of November)

Country	Total credit	Including		Overdue debts of enterprises and economic organisations on bank loans
		Short-term	Long-term	
Azerbaijan, billion manate (October)	2052	1942	110.5	740
Armenia, million drahm	56.3	36.2	20.1	6.7
Belarus, trillion Byelorussian rubles	72.8[1]	42.1	30.7	3.8[2]
Georgia, million lari[3]	202.6	170.2	32.4	15.3
Kazakhstan, billion tenge (October)	89.0	54.3	34.7	6.5[2]
Kyrgyzstan, million som (October)	1891	1488	403	195[2]
Moldova, million lieu (September)	1591	1428	162.5	...
Russia, trillion rubles (October)	390.9	...	...	37.2[2]
Tajikistan, billion Tajik rubles (October)	22.9	18.7	4.2	2.3
Turkmenistan, million manate	...	...	...	...
Uzbekistan, million sum	...	...	...	...
Ukraine, million grivna (November)	8949[2]	7406	1485	...

[1] Excluding foreign currency loans.
[2] Including household debts.
[3] Commercial banks.

Insurance market and real estate. The administrative command economy recognised the insurance of property (e.g. against fire, natural disasters), life and health. A market economy involves other important insurance cases, including *commercial risk* – non-performing loans, buyers' delay of payment, unexpected complete product price fall (e.g. due to new competitors) and rise of prices on productive resources. A large role in high-technology branches is played by insurance against *technological risks* (accidents, failure to achieve projected results, delay of delivery). Among other essential insurance cases in a market economy are *indemnity* to third parties (e.g. for environmental discharge, traffic accidents, non-performance under contract), *cargo* and *political risk* (e.g. losses due to nationalisation, expropriation, social conflicts, changes in tax and customs legislation).

The former Gosstrakh (State Insurance Authority) ignored these insurance types. Over 1000 non-public insurance companies emerged in the CIS countries in the 1990s. However, due to an inadequate financial base, a lack of qualified specialists (including actuaries to assess average risk, loss, cover and premium) and legislative support, this component of the commercial infrastructure is only at an initial stage. And yet the insurance business is among the most profitable spheres of investment in the EU countries. While banking deposits accounted for only 47% of household savings in 1981, as much as 70% were attracted in 1995.

At the end of the 1990s, some CIS countries adopted insurance laws, even though these were not properly co-ordinated. For reasons of safety, operations of insurance companies in the Ukraine are restricted to insurance and financing for the development, distribution and management of insurance reserves. The minimum founding capital is ECU 100,000, or ECU 500,000 in cases of foreign contribution, provided that at least 60% of insurance capital is paid up in money. Insurance cannot not be started until the share capital is paid up and an insurance reserve fund established, the latter, along with loans, pledged assets, etc. and intangible assets, not be contributed to the share stock unavailable for premium payments. In addition, the insurance company contribution to other companies' stock is limited by total 20% and 5% per company). All these are designed to protect client's interests and secure compensation.

An important instrument in the development of the insurance market is the attraction of foreign companies, given an available national control authority and resolved problems of taxation and foreign exchange regulation. The draft of the Insurance Law proposed by the Interparliamentary Assembly provides for such conflict-ridden issues as free choice of insurance types (e.g. Russian law prohibits simultaneous life, property and indemnity insurance), a reinsurance mechanism (in contrast to international practices, it is restricted by licensing rather than available resources), including insurance benefits charged to costs, organisational and legal forms of insurance companies, etc.

The insurance market is closely associated with the *realty market*, including built-up areas occupied by industrial buildings and structures, and municipal land. Realty engaged in economic turnover will enhance asset value and, consequently, the credit worth of the company. Liquid real estate can be leased or contributed to a joint venture company's ownership capital or used in *mortgage* – loans on property at a much lower interest than on other loans, generally under 12–15% p.a.

The majority of the CIS member states have no detailed mortgage legislation, real estate composition, real estate order of registration and assessment, real estate leasing or trade legislation. At the same time, the mortgaged real property serves as a strong security that reduces the creditor's risk and makes hypothecation credit cheap. In this context, the point is that hypothecation credit, being accessible to foreign farmers and businessmen, is not open to CIS employers and they cannot compete with importers. In order to protect themselves, businessmen from the former Soviet Union have to delay their payments to creditors (i.e. to delay payments for the goods they have purchased in non-interest-bearing credit) and to evade taxes, etc.

The absence of a realty market impairs labour mobility involving the sale of housing in one place and purchase or rent in another, i.e. actually impedes the labour market.

The realty market infrastructure comprises:

– Market pricing and capitalisation (by expected gains), using international methods (e.g. Anglo-American rules employing sophisticated definitions and matrices) and performed by State-licensed realty firms, and land registration and valuation agencies

– Registration of ownership in real estate and rules of purchase and sale (e.g. government and municipal agencies, notaries)

– Developer companies acquiring real estate for reconstruction, development, repair, etc. with subsequent selling or lending

The realty market largely depends on insurance. Regretfully, the common insurance space has been broken in the CIS. Most CIS countries restrict foreign insurance companies, insurance inspection rules differ across the CIS, and many sectors are still monopolised by the State. On the other hand, reinsurance and insurance programmes are progressing in joint oil and gas extraction and transport, etc.

The relevant laws should by adjusted to conform to European standards. Thus Ukrainian law strictly regulates the minimum stock (fivefold higher for joint venture companies than for Ukrainian corporations), money contribution to paid-up insurance fund, etc. Some other CIS countries have no such insurance risk-reducing regulations. There is good reason to consider a common insurance fund for commercial risks due to a drop in international prices on traditional exports (as in 1997–1998) and currency, environmental and other risks, for example.

Stock market. Now, at the end of the 1990s, many major State-owned enterprises in the CIS countries have been reconstituted as joint stock companies. Thus the issue of stocks in Kazakhstan was registered by 3000 joint stock companies. A total of 90% of the stocks were first State-owned and then sold at coupon auctions. Operations with securities were conducted by investment funds and authorised banks. Taxes were adjusted in an effort to develop the stock market.

The same road was chosen by the CIS countries previously delaying privatisation. Azerbaijan first issued State privatisation checks in 1997. An up-to-date infrastructure for the Ukrainian securities market (e.g. stocks, compensation certificates, government bonds) emerged in the late 1990s.

Privatisation of government and municipal enterprises creates a market of securities and real estate, requiring legal provisions for the rights and liabilities of the parties. The CIS countries need to develop laws on State registration of ownership and transactions in real estate, stock registration and government control of issue and distribution in conformity with international law and based on an integrated model. A government register in each region should provide for immovable property, including land lots and a land book for property rights. Thus the State will act as a market agent lending or selling to privatised enterprises its property represented by land lots and other realty types, while regulating and protecting the rights of all the remaining parties. This will bring property into public circulation and reveal its actual market value.

Property duties represented by taxes and real estate revenues comprise 70–80% of the budget in the world's big cities. Land and housing rent, property and rent taxes and receipts from their sales in St. Petersburg accounted for a mere 1% of budget revenues in 1992 and already over 20% in 1997. This will create the prerequisites for the development of another sector of the commercial infrastructure – the stock market.

The *stock market* is a net of stock and currency exchanges, investment funds, trader's offices, registrars and depositories, expert consulting and auditing firms, linked in an information network and engaged, under State control, in the distribution (underwriting) and circulation of securities and the trading of the rights of their future buying (futures and options).

The stock market in the CIS countries can be traced back to the mid-1990s. It is essential for an orientated economy because this is where enterprises and their assets as well as debt instruments are sold and their actual market value is determined. In 1996, Gazprom was the first CIS corporation rated among the 500 major world companies by market capitalisation.

The stock market is an important source of capital for the economic development of the country in general and the corporations whose stocks are priced (quoted) on the market. This involves both credit (to be repaid at a fixed interest and within strict time limits) and investment lines (i.e. on shared-risk principles, with no obligation of repayment or fixed interest). The International Finance Corporation (IFC) keeps a record of prices for over 2000 stocks in 44 countries, calculating the *stock index* for each of the countries, and globally – describing the potential of local investors prepared to take higher risks by stock purchasing, and investments – stocks available to foreign investors. Between 1984 and 1996, *portfolio investments* (profit-making stocks not ensuring a controlling interest or the right to run a corporation) on the world stock market increased from $0.2 to $50 billion.

A country with no available stock market or the relevant index cannot hope to attract solid, reliable investors. Under-priced property has generally been bought in the CIS countries until recently, to be resold quickly at a good profit, saving the effort and resources of production development and renovation (e.g. plants with land lots in the city centre, oil and other mining companies with sizeable crude resources, corporate monopolists in power engineering, communications).

Regular publication of investment indices will attract financial funds' investments, far less expensive than ordinary credit (8–9% instead of 15–20% p.a.).

The stock market also reflects competition between corporations. Top-management and law-abiding firms disclosing realistic financial results will be sure to attract the required capital, with portfolio investors even accepting 2–3% of the stocks, while inadequately managed and generally unreliable firms will have their stocks depreciated and will go out of business or be taken over by more effective owners.

The stock market in the CIS countries opens up new opportunities but also poses new risks. A case in point is Mexico where (as in other developing countries) three quarters of foreign capital was obtained from stocks and bonds sold to private investors on the stock market. As a result, shares in Telefonos de Mexico, for example, appreciated 20-fold between 1990 and 1994. Yet domestic saving was channelled to expensive imports rather than investment. While China saves over a third, India a quarter, Japan 16% and the EU countries 12% of revenue, savings in Mexico, as in most South American countries (excluding Chile), comprise less than 4%. The loss in the balance of payments and capital flight resulted in the collapse of the stock market, stock prices and the national currency and a soaring inflation. The total loss amounted to $150–200 billion in a few weeks. Even more disastrous were the cases in Southeast Asia and Russia in 1997 and 1998.

Let us now consider the agents on the stock market. First and foremost, the *issuing bodies* – economic agents (e.g. firms, the government, local authorities, banks) who need money and obtain it by issuing and selling *securities* – standard papers containing required elements and certifying property rights to be exclusively transferred or exercised on presentation of the paper itself or in appropriate electronic format. On the Ukrainian stock market, there was a drastic rise in the stocks issued by Ukrneft companies, metallurgical (Khartsyz and Nizhnedneprovsk pipe works) and chemical works (Dneproshina, Cherkasskii Azot) and energy suppliers (Zapadenergo, Dneprenergo). Government bond yields were very high. Changes in the market capitalisation of companies issuing shares is described by two stock indices – prime (calculated from a sample of 20 companies traded at 90% of transactions rather than all 120 emission companies) and weighted (both price change and "weight", i.e. total stock price of companies).

A large role is played on the stock market by *investment funds* – financial organisations operating with profit-making securities. Most prominent in the CIS are the voucher (privatisation) investment funds (PIFs) concerned with household privatisation checks (e.g. vouchers, public property checks) certifying their rights in privatised state property. A PIF version in Uzbekistan operates a dividend-security mechanism to protect investors against commercial risks. To concentrate household investments, the PIFs issue their own stocks to be sold at stock shops or on the exchange. The PIFs have to use the accumulated financial resources for shares in several profitable joint stock companies to diversify risks. Unlike the banks, the PIFs must make information accessible to the public and comply with strict regulations to reduce risks; in addition, they may not withdraw resources to Central Bank reserve accounts. However, their development is slow in Russia in spite of $30 billion household "savings", and also in some other CIS countries due to the bitter lessons of MMM-type pyramid schemes.

Among the principal investors outside the CIS are *non-government pension, insurance and mutual investment* funds (the latter investing $130 billion in stock purchases in the USA in 1993 and over $220 billion in 1996). Even more significant resources are held by *trust* funds performing authorised management (on their own behalf) of others' securities and monies intended for stock purchases. This market segment is now generally represented in the CIS by foreign trust funds.

Professional moving of financial resources from investors to those who need them on the stock market is performed by brokers acting on behalf of clients and by *dealers* buying and selling stocks on their own behalf and at their own expense at published prices. Direct arrangements concerning the securities trade and the provision of required services for the conclusion and performance of deals are handled by the *stock exchange*. In the mid-1990s, there were over 300 exchanges in the CIS countries, varying greatly in their relationships with the Central Bank, investment funds and banks, securities quoting rules and transaction taxes. As a result, securities are sold outside the exchange with no proper control, with investments circumventing the banking system and eventual economic integration hampered.

The number of exchanges reduced significantly in the late 1990s. International standard *depositories* provide the certificates and register the rights of securities, and *clearing* centres are responsible for the identification and clearing of mutual liabilities on settlements and delivery of securities by collecting and checking transaction data and relevant statements of account. For instance, the general depository in Kazakhstan has registered changes in stock since 1997. The registration, including the collection, processing, storage of and access to data, is also allocated to specialised services. Telecommunications networking for exchanges in Moscow, Kiev, Tashkent, St. Petersburg and some other CIS cities in a global system with extended access to national stock markets for non-residents lies ahead. An EU financial company licensed in one of the member states can trade in securities in any other as long as it complies with local rules.

Of utmost significance for normal stock market functioning are the development and observance of rules, procedures and regulations concerning the relationships of all parties on the market, including stock issue, ownership, settlements, etc. These are the responsibilities of government supervisory agencies and professional market associations to whom the State has partially allocated regulating functions. The division of functions among the Finance Ministry, Central Bank, securities commissions, government property committees and funds and professional associations differs across the CIS. To ensure further progress on the market, draft laws on audits and auditing standards should be adopted and enforced, and, as international experience indicates, the CIS countries need laws providing for securities issue and circulation, market eligibility, financial reporting and rules for exchange and non-exchange information systems.

Some CIS countries are developing national electronic stock trade systems. The register is kept exclusively by registrars licensed by the government securities commission and provides an investor with complete and unbiased information on securities issued by a company from the date of incorporation. Appropriate standards are developed by a professional association of registrars, transfer agents and depositories. For the time being, depositories can combine their principal depository functions with trade in securities. However, in the future, different risk functions must be distinguished.

The structure of the securities market differs in the different CIS countries. Thus among the prevalent commercial papers in the Ukraine in the mid-1990s were bills (over 40%, generally treasury bills), stocks issued by commercial banks and investment companies, debt instruments, including dollar notes issued to cover the debt to Gazprom. Among the securities circulating in Belarus were government short-term notes (GKO) and treasury bills. GKO and other government stocks issued to cover the budget deficit and taking resources from industrial investment also prevailed in Russia. Corporate stocks will play a crucial role on the stock exchange in the late 1990s. The stock exchange in Moldova quotes treasury bills, national loan bonds and investment funds stocks. The Sberbank (Savings Bank) with its extensive branch system and electronic mail acts as a clearing centre. The exchange established a clearing house and a depository controlled and regulated by the government stock market commission and a three-tiered listing of issuing companies. Government certificates are sold at auction on a discount scheme, including to foreign financial companies.

By President I. Karimov's decree on additional measures for the development of the securities market in Uzbekistan, investors in the CIS countries and elsewhere can purchase stocks, carry out conversion of investments and yields and distribute their own securities. In addition, the issuing price list registration tax has been reduced (from 0.5% to 0.1% of assets), and dividends and proceeds from sales will be exempted from tax for some years. Over 100,000 companies and individuals have opened accounts with the national depository. In contrast to other CIS countries, revenues from trade in securities are not dissolved in the budget but are invested in updating privatised enterprises, in realistic social programmes and in the business fund supporting small and medium-scale business.

The financial market in the CIS countries is divided in the following sectors:

1. Government debt instruments focusing on maximum liquidity with insignificant yields – this essential rule has been ignored in Russia. The market in Armenia involves government coupons (public) and short-term bonds (GKO). The inter-bank currency exchange in Baku (Azerbaijan) trades in GKO with the earnings exempt from tax and the buyers represented not by corporate bodies alone (as in Russia) but also by individuals. The GKO sector dominates on the markets in the Ukraine, Moldova and Uzbekistan.

2. Corporate finance (issue and primary sales of stocks, acquisition, mergers, restructuring) is gaining acceptance in Russia, Kazakhstan, Kyrgyzstan and Moldova. However, access is only allowed for professional financial companies. In the Ukraine, it is promoted by associations of investment business, stock traders, trust companies and investment funds. Investors in Kazakhstan are offered 10%–30% of stocks previously entrusted to private corporations.

Stock trade in this sector is operated by open joint stock companies listed (validated) at the exchange. In the CIS countries, they represent export-based branches such as oil and gas, extractive, metallurgical, chemical and forestry companies, those securing permanent sales on domestic markets (energy, telecommunications, transport, communication) or import-competitive industry (light, food). Development of this stock market segment requires an independent depository net (stock registration and deposit) and clearing standards enabling investors to evaluate the profits, assets, debts and safety of a company.

Allowance must be made for the multiple "mail-box" firms in the sector that have no real assets and perform no operations except laundering illegal gains. There are over a million such companies in 124 countries, generally registered in offshore zones. Thus the world's and Japan's most important corporate trader in securities, *Nomura Securities*, for example, was rated unusually low in 1997. The president, vice-presidents and directors resigned when evidence of tax evasion and criminal contacts came to light. The CIS countries should learn from this negative experience.

3. Stocks issued by FIGs, the blue chips of the national economy. They are interested in having their commercial papers quoted on foreign exchanges and therefore adhere to the international standards requiring detailed financial disclosure. Three quarters of the stock exchange turnover in Russia was accounted for by only seven companies (EES Russia, Mosenergo, Gazprom, Lukoil, Rostelekom, Norilsk Nickel, Surgutneftegaz) worth $25 billion – half the total stock price. While the d/p ratio was low (0.01–0.08), purchase investments ensured significant foreign currency earnings due to stock price rise.

4. Government corporate and municipal bonds sold on the foreign markets. The profit is generally lower than commercial bank interest rate (15%–20% in foreign exchange in the CIS countries) but higher than minimum yields on government securities issue (8%–9% p.a.). In the late 1990s, there have been some successful sales on the European market of such bonds (worth $1 trillion) issued in Russia and Russian Federal entities (e.g. Moscow, St. Petersburg, Tatarstan), Kazakhstan (3-year time limit at 9.25% p.a.), Azerbaijan, by some Russian joint stock companies (e.g. Gazprom, Moscow Telephone System, Tatneft). However, issuing under $100 million is irrational because of high distribution costs, but it is rather difficult to distribute large volume of shares due to the low investment attractiveness of most companies.

5. Liquid bills.

The Interparliamentary Assembly would do well to follow the Geneva Bill Convention by adopting a model law on promissory notes and bills of exchange/transferable bills, providing for a uniform interpretation throughout the CIS of concepts such as *note sum* (nominal price), *draft, security, acceptance, endorsement, endorser and endorsee* and *regression* (interest charged from the date of payment to eventual performance). It would be expedient to distinguish promissory debts from total defaults and establish a *bill court* – a clearing house with legal enforcement functions concerning the lawful rights of the holder of a bill, including seizure or sale of debtor's property, etc. Otherwise the firms can make promissory notes on non-existent goods and services, debts, etc. and then refuse to pay. The stock market should establish clearing houses – bank bill centres to discount the bills ahead of due time and exchange them for their own, safer and more liquid issue. This will enable the firms to buy back their debts in bill form, cutting expenses, accelerating capital circulation and allowing for debt clearance by purchase and merger by execution against property.

A model law defining the concept of *security* itself and a set of guarantees, hedging venture financing, pledge and investor/issuing body relationships will reinforce legal support for long-term investment and allow the removal of fictitious securities and dubious operators from the market.

Over 3500 traders and other professional agents and more than 2700 investment centres, etc. operated on the Russian stock market in the mid-1990s. This obviously excessive number reduced drastically in 1997.

Operations at the stock exchange should be regulated by detailed legislation, a government commission and an operators' association. An example is the Warsaw Exchange admitted to the International Federation, whose membership includes exchanges in New York, London, Paris, Frankfurt, Hong Kong and Tokyo. Eastern European currency-credit and stock markets are controlled by the Central Bank, the currency exchange is incorporated in the stock exchange and banks operate investment funds. Separation of these sectors on the common CIS markets in the absence of a developed telecommunications system will enhance centrifugal trends, resulting in uncontrolled non-exchange stock trade and investments circumventing the banking system.

Equally important on the stock market are valuations other than the current market price (e.g. investment value of future returns, firm value, insurance totals, amortisation and utilisation costs).

The CIS countries need a court of arbitration with strict procedures (expert opinions, speeches by the parties, record of evidence as a procedural safeguard, appeal and annulment options, prominent businessmen invited as arbitrators) and enforcement services (bailiffs).

In addition to corporate stocks, a stable stock market should involve mortgages of land lots, mineral deposits and other types of immovable property.

Goods and services market infrastructure. In the administrative command economy, wholesale trade was generally focused on the distribution of deficit goods. Elimination of the centralised funding and resource distribution system in the CIS countries required a radically new infrastructure involving commodity exchanges, trade centres, bill circulation, term contracting, chartering and controlled foreign trade.

The *commodity exchange* is concerned with standard commodities (e.g. grain, cotton, rice, tobacco, coffee, ferrous and non-ferrous metals, oil and petroleum products, electricity). The functions include the collection of information on demand, supply and prices, the checking and assessment of the parties, standard quality and terms of delivery.

By the mid-1990s, there were almost 400 registered commodity exchanges in the CIS countries. However, the majority traded in non-exchange commodities (e.g. light and food products, housing equipment, machinery, real estate), acting as standard trade firms. The central problem in the CIS countries is to identify the required minimum of large exchanges (e.g. trading grain in Russia, the Ukraine and Kazakhstan) and manage them in compliance with international regulations. There are only 60 major commodity exchanges in the world. Electronic trade via the Internet will enable dealers to make orders and strike deals online, taking world-wide prices of goods into account. In addition, trade will only be operated in *lots* and securities meeting appropriate listing requirements.

The term market involving *futures*, *options* and *forward* transactions will allow for *hedging*. With continuous prices changes for CIS exports (e.g. ores, energy resources, metals, cotton, timber and round wood), futures and forward contracts in the CIS countries rely on dollar rates and GKO returns. However, term contracting is essential for stability and planning in any kind of trade, reducing the risks of changes in the exchange, interest rates, etc.

A critical question is the regulation of bill circulation, including accounting centres, bill courts – clearing houses with legal enforcement functions, entitled to seize or sell debtor's property, etc. Bill circulation will accelerate advanced payment and barter exchange, accelerate the pace of commodity turnover and reduce non-payments.

The *trade centre* is a wholesale company conducting marketing (market research and price forecasting), factoring (storage of goods in warehouses), logistic (selection of rational types and methods of transport and cargo insurance) and intermediary functions (producer-retail trade). This component of the infrastructure is not always efficient in the CIS countries, as exemplified by increasing direct contacts in the second half of the 1990s, since producers prefer to do without intermediaries, maintaining direct contacts with retail trade or opening their own shops.

4.2 Industrial and Environmental Infrastructure

General issues of transport development. The integration of the CIS countries in world economic relationships largely depends on transport development. This governs both the physical access of commodities to new markets and their competitiveness, since transportation costs often account for more than half the price of goods (e.g. coal, timber, ore).

Only three of the 12 CIS countries (Russia, the Ukraine and Georgia) have ocean-related port facilities, only four (Russia, the Ukraine, Belarus and Moldova) border on European countries and only four (Russia, Kazakhstan, Kyrgyzstan and Tajikistan) border on the rapidly advancing China. Most of the problems in transport development can therefore only be effectively resolved by joint efforts based on mutually beneficial co-operation rather than confrontation. The problems include the following:

1. Railway and motor road density, updating and integration in a global Euro-Asian net. Railway density across the CIS is 6.4 km per 100 m^2 as against 49 km in the EU countries, with 34–38 km in the Ukraine and Moldova, 23–28 km in Belarus and Transcaucasia, 7.8 km in Uzbekistan, 5.1–5.3 km in Russia and Kazakhstan, 4.4 km in Turkmenistan, 3.4 km in Tajikistan and 2.1 km in Kyrgyzstan. In addition, a number of bridges need to be replaced and rails laid on

permafrost soils in the reconstructed Trans-Baikal section of the CIS's major Trans-Siberian line.

Considerable scope is offered by the transcontinental mainline from Singapore to Europe via China, Mongolia, Kazakhstan and Russia; integration of railway systems in Georgia and Turkey (via Akhalkalaki), Turkmenistan, Uzbekistan and Iran (Tedzhen–Serakhs–Meshkhed), Kazakhstan and China (to the Yellow Sea port Lianiungan).

Commodity exchange between the EU countries with a population of 340 million, the CIS and Persian Gulf states will benefit from the Baku–Makhachkala–Astrakhan railway and the ferry lines between Germany and St. Petersburg, Lagan (Kalmykia)–Turkmenbashi (Turkmenistan)–Amirabad (Iran) and Olia (Astrakhan region)–Enzeli (Iran).

The density of hard-surface motor roads per 1000 km^2 is almost 15-fold lower in the CIS countries than in the EU. It is slightly higher (290–420 km) in Azerbaijan, Armenia, Belarus, Moldova and the Ukraine, but still far below West European standards (1000 km). Russia has yet to complete the transcontinental highway to the Pacific (the Chita–Nakhodka–Vladivostok section), Uzbekistan the Andizhan–Osh–Kashtar, Kushka–Gerat (Afghanistan)–Kvetta–Karachi (Pakistan) or Termez–Kabul–Karachi mainlines, Kyrgyzstan the reconstruction of the Bishkek–Osh highway and Tajikistan of the mountainous Badakhshan passage to the Karakorum highway connecting China with Pakistan.

The EU is contributing to the highway building projects North–South (from Scandinavia via Russia and Transcaucasia to the Middle East) and West–East (from EU countries via Belarus, Moldova and the Ukraine, and Russia, Kazakhstan and China to Singapore).

According to some economic estimates, the lack of up-to-date railways and highways in the CIS countries is tantamount to an additional 30% tax on all commercial firms. However, this requires shared investment, new road-building technologies and political decisions on the peacemaking issues in the areas.

2. A multivariant pipeline network connecting oil and gas fields in the Pechora, Yamal, Caspian region and Caspian, Barents, Black Sea and other marine shelves with markets in Europe, Southeast Asia, Pakistan, Turkey, etc. Main pipelines in Azerbaijan, Kazakhstan, Russia, the Ukraine and Uzbekistan pump almost 400 million t oil, 700 million t gas and over 20 million t petroleum products a year, and yet the capacity is insufficient for effective utilisation of export potentials in Turkmenistan (50 billion m^3 gas p.a.), Uzbekistan, Kazakhstan, North Russia and Azerbaijan.

The CIS countries are separated from the majority of export markets by third countries controlling pipelines and port facilities. Joint feasibility studies and co-operation in the design, laying and maintenance of the new systems are therefore of prime importance. Only then will export trade benefit the CIS nations rather than foreign transnational corporations. The challenge is aggravated by unnecessary rivalry within the CIS, eventually resulting in the loss or transfer of the systems to foreign firms. Thus, in 1997, Kazakhstan conceded the gas pipeline system to a Belgian company for 15 years, for instance. Russia exports gas to Turkey via Rumania and Bulgaria, while transit via Georgia (with gas lines utilising 10% of the transport potential) would have been much shorter and more cost efficient.

Among the most important projected mains on the eve of the 21st century are:

– Oil pipelines from Azerbaijan (with early 21st-century export potentials in only three fields in Chirag, Azeri and Giuneshli amounting to 40 million t p.a.) to Novorossiisk (via and bypassing Chechnia), Supsa (Georgia) and Jeikhan (Turkey)

– An oil pipeline from North West Kazakhstan (e.g. Tengis) to Novorossiisk (1500 km long, 24 and then up to 67 million t annual transport capacity, costs of $4 billion, pay-back period of 8 years; Russia-Kazakhstan-Oman TNC Shevrol-Mobile, etc. consortium)

– A gas line net from Siberia to the Ukraine, Moldova and Southern Europe, via Belarus to Germany and France, via Finland to Sweden, Denmark and Germany (the North Network with contribution from Norway)

– Pipelines from Uzbekistan and Turkmenistan via Afghanistan to Pakistan (costs: $2 billion) and via Iran to Turkey (3200 km, transport capacity of 30 billion m^3 gas, costs of $16 billion)

– An oil pipeline from Kazakhstan to China

– A gas line from East Siberia via Mongolia and China to the Yellow Sea (4000 km long, costs of $5–7 billion)

– Sakhalin–Japan pipelines

The unregulated status of the Caspian delays exploitation of the oil fields in Kiagaz and Ialama (on Azerbaijan's border with Turkey and Daghestan) and Azerbaijan's navigation in the Volgo-Don Canal. However, the use of "sea-river" class boats on the waterways would benefit most of the CIS countries. The Caspian Status Treaty will provide for shared laying of pipelines, transport infrastructure, river ways and shipbuilding.

A more rational traffic composition by transport type is needed. Water transport is the cheapest, with the exception of pipelines. However, internal waterways traffic decreased in the CIS countries, in particular in Belarus, Russia and Kazakhstan; traffic reduced dramatically in Kazakhstan, the Ukraine, Russia and Kyrgyzstan; and sea cargo traffic declined in the Ukraine. The Baltic Shipping line lost 90% of its stock in the 1990s.

The traffic market is dominated by foreign companies. The CIS countries lost billions of dollars and several tens of thousands of jobs due to the hasty privatisation of shipping lines (Russia), unco-ordinated sea, river and railway traffic, uncontrolled tariff rises and inadequate engineering conditions in port facilities. By contrast, Latvia earns a quarter of its foreign currency earnings from CIS cargo transits via Ventspils, Liepaia and Riga. With respect to the transits, port facilities have been reconstructed in Estonia (e.g. Muuga, Paldiski), Latvia, Finland and some other countries. Almost 95% of freights in Baltic ports are linked to the CIS countries.

A significant task is the reconstruction and improved appeal to customers of port facilities in the Ukraine (Odessa, Ilyichevsk, Reni, Iuzhnyi, Ismail, Nikolaev, Kherson, Mariupol), Russia (e.g. St. Petersburg, Novorossiisk, Tuapse, Baltiisk, Nakhodka, Vladivostok, Archangel), Georgia (Poti, Batumi), Moldova (Giurgiulesht, where the rivers Prut and Danube join) etc. Russia is building new ports in the Baltic (Ust-Luga, Primorsk, Batareinaia) and several Black Sea oil terminals. Total Russian transfers in 1997 (generally ore and oil exports) exceeded the 1989 level.

The increasing share of motorcar traffic in the CIS countries in the 1990s can only be justified for short distances. In addition, public transport is not popular with many firms because of the higher tariffs, which is particularly evident in Kazakhstan, the Ukraine, Russia, Belarus and Moldova, e.g. private freight transport accounts for 80% of total freight traffic. Air freight, and in some countries air passenger traffic, increased in the late 1990s after a rapid decline. Overall growth is expected in all the CIS countries by the end of the decade.

Lower tariffs determine the competitive merits of different means of transport. A number of railways will be converted to electricity (60% in the CIS and the entire traffic in Kyrgyzstan, Moldova, Tajikistan and Turkmenistan relies on diesel locomotives), the rolling stock updated (there are a total of 640,000 lorries, 13,000 river boats, 240,000 buses, 45,000 trolleybuses and trams, 7500 underground rail cars, etc.). Moreover, 70% of engine and car repair facilities are located in the Ukraine, all DC electric locomotives are manufactured in Georgia, Russia has a monopoly on electric car manufacturing, etc. The maintenance of unified standards and specifications requires enhanced co-operation.

Tariff reductions largely depend on the use of the rolling stock. Some CIS countries (Russia, the Ukraine, Moldova) have accelerated car moving in recent years, have reduced the idle time in freight and improved locomotive performance. Russian railways have cut long-distance freight tariffs, particularly for container transport, relying on increased freight turnover, and expenditures, abandoning subsidiary works, shops and other non-profit units.

Motor transport has great reserves. Almost 70% of lorries were idle in the mid-1990s in Belarus, the Ukraine and Kyrgyzstan, with empty runs amounting to

45%. In this connection, due attention should be paid to the experience of Estonia and some other countries, where the lifting of many duties and transport barriers and simplified documentation resulted in increased earnings in the early 1990s.

Some CIS countries intend to cut the cross-financing of loss-making passenger traffic at the expense of freight tariffs.

Power system. An integrated energy system is the most obvious basis for economic integration in the CIS. The integration of 600 heat and nuclear plants and 100 hydroelectric power stations in Russia with major hydroelectric power stations in Kyrgyzstan, Tajikistan, Georgia and the Ukraine, nuclear power stations in the Ukraine and Armenia and heating power centres in other countries will enable savings to be made by manipulating the capacities of heat and hydropower stations, time zone differentials, and joint machine-building and maintenance of the power systems. An integrated energy system will provide a 30% cost reduction per kWh.

One case of the reverse situation can be seen in Moldova. Up to 1990, the republic had been self-supporting in electricity, even exporting it to Bulgaria and Romania. The fuel oil/gas conversion in the Moldavian hydroelectric power station increased the capacity, doubled the service time, radically reduced atmospheric discharge, including transfrontier sulphuric gas and acidic rain, and cut down fuel transport by railway. Future plans involved transition to gas use in motor transport accounting for 90% of national freight. However, in the 1990s, electricity generation was halved, depreciation resorted to imports, depreciation of the machinery, transmitting and distributing equipment was over 50% and public heat and hot water supplies deteriorated.

CIS electricity exports to Eastern Europe reduced from 40 to 1.7 billion kWh in the early 1990s, mainly owing to national transit jurisdiction. While in some CIS countries fuel is burnt all year round in the heating power centres, their neighbours discharge water outside hydroelectric power station dams in the summertime because of the lack of demand. An energy export and transit clearing mechanism was only established in the late 1990s when the European market had been occupied by Western competitors. Eleven inter-state West-East AC transmission lines are inoperative.

The integrated energy policy within the CIS, joint financing and implementing of major energy supply and saving projects and parallel operation of energy systems are in no way inconsistent with the need for independent and relatively small sources of energy. There are oil and gas fields in Moldova, Belarus, Georgia and Tajikistan. Ukrainian gas resources are estimated at 4.5 billion m^3 and oil at 200 million t (e.g. in the Black Sea, at Poltava). Connection to European power systems (the Baltic net, Black Sea energy system and the Western European system integrating 15 countries) will serve common interests.

An integrated standard-frequency energy system will make possible an inter-state wholesale electricity market and standard national energy reserves maintained under co-operation contracts. On completing inter-state settlements in the late 1990s, parallel energy system operation has been restored in Russia, Kazakhstan, the Ukraine and other CIS countries.

Technologies in the 21st century will enable electric and information signals to be integrated in an information-energy mainline. An international electric transmission system will make data communication tenfold faster at costs that are hundreds of times lower.

However, the integration of energy systems in no way affects local sources. Considerable promise is offered by replacing of centralised heat supplies with autonomous ones (e.g. for plants, urban communities), effecting a saving in the costs of wasteful heating systems. The use of automated equipment and new technologies will raise combustion rates from 60% to 90%. Experience in the Moldavian-German joint venture Moldokon suggests that heat supply can be tenfold cheaper as well as flexible, user-oriented and providing an incentive to save energy. The firm provides works on a turnkey basis, from the design, delivery and assembly of equipment, safety systems, thermal agent circulation, filtration and distribution control to maintenance, instalment and personnel training.

Communications infrastructure. In a modern global economy, communications represent both the means of communication and the baseis for administrative decision-making, contracting, scientific and industrial co-operation, civil society, and public access to education and international cultural achievements. The four basic elements are: postal services, electrical exchange (telephone, telegraph), radio and television broadcasting and information networks.

On average, one *post office* in the CIS countries provides services 3100 people, almost as many as in the EU. The figure is almost double (6000) for Uzbekistan, Turkmenistan and Tajikistan. Postal exchange reduced dramatically in the 1990s due to higher tariffs, lower magazine and newspaper subscriptions and inter-state customs barriers. Continuous parcel exchange was no longer needed with full markets. Almost 40% of postal services in the Ukraine were provided by a Ukrainian-Canadian joint venture, but in other countries they are State-owned and generally restricted to pension remittance.

Public *telephone* exchange is still inadequate in terms of current international standards and national demand. There are 36 household subscribers per 100 people in the EU (94 in the USA), 23–27 in the Baltic countries and 12 in the CIS (15 in Belarus, 13–14 in Armenia, Russia and the Ukraine, nine to 11 in Georgia, Kazakhstan and Moldova, and three to eight in Azerbaijan and Central Asian states). However, in the late 1990s, the ratio has been increasing by 3%–5% annually.

Outdated analogue circuits have been replaced by digital ones; optic-fibre and RF relay lines are operated in many countries. In Russia, there were 1 million new subscribers every year in the late 1980s and over 1.5 million in the mid-1990s. Instead of 1000, there are now 61,000 international exchange channels, and 10 million subscribers will be added within the Public Telephone programme by the early 21st century. Operation of the Russia–Denmark, Russia–Japan–Korea and Moscow–Khabarovsk optic fibre and digital radio relay lines will complete the world-wide telecommunications net, ensuring telephone exchange with any subscriber at any place. A total of 20,500 km cable and 17,500 km radio relay lines and automated telephone lines for 8 million subscribers have been put into operation over the last 4 years.

There is a 20%–50% annual growth in telex, facsimile and e-mail communication, and 320,000 telephone subscribers will be added in 1998/1999 in Azerbaijan. A business digital communications system has been implemented in Belarus. There are six corporate cell telephone communications operators in Uzbekistan, with 1000 km optic lines added every year. An extensive telephone development programme is under way in Osh and some other regions of Kyrgyzstan, sponsored by the World Bank, the EBRD and the Kuwait Fund. Regional organisations for co-operative communications are also assisted by other CIS countries, Turkey and, as observers, Denmark, the Netherlands, Baltic countries and Pakistan.

A new sector of telecommunications is represented by individual *videotext* radio call exchange (paging). Pagers are used by one in three citizens in Singapore, one in five in South Korea and one in seven in the United Arab Emirate and the USA. Since they are comparatively inexpensive ($50–150) and service prices were cut in the CIS countries, in particular in Russia, Belarus, Uzbekistan and Moldova, annual growth in this market sector amounts to 50%–100%. Over 1.5 million subscribers are expected in Russia by 2000.

Superior communication levels are provided by *mobile telephones* (cell, zone and radio) connected to mobile land RF systems. Automated roaming services ensure continuous inter-state exchange. Co-ordination is in progress for digital television and radio broadcasting and metrologic support for standard electric communications. However, this market segment is only at an initial stage to date. By contrast, one third of the population in Finland uses mobile telephones for transmitting e-mails and for Internet access, and world totals will amount to 150 million by 2000.

By the early 21st century, 15 million people will be using satellite telephones, providing individual verbal and facsimile communications to any point in the world via 66 light satellites. The messages are encoded and safeguarded. The CIS needs adequate communication in remote regions, oil platforms, on board ships, aircraft, etc. Solar telephone stations can replace expensive lines in areas with a low population density. Members of the Iridium consortium include the USA,

Russia (Khrunichev Space Centre), China and some other countries. The total mobile communications market will be worth $60 billion by 2000, and European subscription already exceeded 50 million in 1998 (with an annual increase of 11%–13%). In Russia, there were already over 1 million cell and individual RF subscribers in 73 regions in 1997. Recent developments include the Federal EPMES-type net, data trunk and packet-switched communications, e-mail, and elements of multimedia and TV-video. International co-operative projects include the global mobile satellite communications system and the International Congress on Telecommunications from the Perspective of National Security (St. Petersburg 1997).

The costs of updating technology are high. Management and reconstruction of telecommunications in Uzbekistan are allocated to Western companies in a 15-year trust for 49% shares in *Uzbektelekom*. During this period, the investor will replace the outdates automated telephone lines (ATSs) and lay new lines with no international credit, government guarantee or rapid tariff rise. The first cell system project in the Ukraine was completed with U.S. investment. In Russia, this is a self-supporting branch, i.e. with no financing from the government budget. There are 107 public joint stock companies based on State-owned enterprises and over 3000 non-public companies (their share in total services increasing from 5% in 1996 to 10% in 1997). Investments exceeded $6 billion over the past 4 years, including $1.7 billion foreign investments and a mere 1% of the budget, with the remaining portion bidden at tender. The international telephone development credit without government guarantees has already been repaid.

Information networks. A radically new stage in communications is represented by information computer networks. Annual turnover on the world market of information technologies (including hardware production) amounts to $2 trillion, rising by 20% every year. It will amount to $3–3.5 trillion by 2000, outstripping the fuel and energy complex/base, the key sector in many CIS countries.

The European PC-based telecommunications market turnover will exceed $1.1 billion. The number of PCs increased by 10 million annually in the last 15 years, with microprocessor capacity 900 times, and information transmission rates several times higher, given the up-to-date Fast Externet modem technology, ISDN information encoding standards and the new asynchronous transmission mode (from 300 bit to 30 kbit and then 150 Mbit/s). Thus the computer has been transformed from a calculating machine into a means of communication, offering the prospects of business partner selection, direct transactions, electronic payments, know-how exchange and joint administrative decision-making. The turnover already outstrips total sales in textile, motorcar and machine-building industries.

The first phase of development in this sphere involved information agencies to distribute standard information on the financial market, bodies issuing new securities, trade and quotation results, potential partners, etc. In addition to foreign companies on the CIS market (e.g. KPMG, Arthur Andersen, Coopers and Lybrand, Dun and Breadstreet, Reuter), there are also national agencies (e.g. Rosbusiness Consulting, Finmarket, Prime, AKM). They will need to co-ordinate their operations within the CIS, provide on-line panel information on regional exchange transactions, national banks decisions, establish a dealing system, etc.

The second phase will involve *local networking* (Intranet) for major corporations and systems integration. Thus, assisted by IBM the Mangistumunaigaz company, which accounts for 40% of oil production in Kazakhstan, integrated the procession of geological, geophysical and hydrodynamic information in each field, with topographic display, including underground and surface lines of communication, and production management, including document circulation, staff movement and financial flows. Some CIS firms with expensive (over $100,000) equipment and multiple remote operational sites (extractive, metallurgical and aircraft industries, transport, trade) use competing platforms (e.g. Oracle) in networking. An important role on the CIS market of information technologies and business restructuring is played by a merger company involving a Moscow Price Waterhouse branch and the Russian systems integrator LVS. Automated management of business processes and close contacts with partners on a world-wide scale have become vitally important for major CIS firms.

The third phase is associated with national *information networks* for inter-bank settlements, science and technology information exchange, etc. The prototypes were developed in all the current CIS countries as far back as the late 1980s. New avenues will be opened up by the optic fibre digital and RF lines Russia–South Korea–Japan (via Khabarovsk), Moscow–Odessa–Istambul–Palermo (via Novorossiisk and Rostov), etc.

Radical changes in the status of firms, marketing and sales management, follow-up services and market transactions proper (communications between economic agents) are associated with global electronic communication networks. A new market agent type is gaining acceptance – the *virtual corporation*, i.e. business networks of independent firms in various countries using information networks for joint management of the development, production and distribution of research-intensive products. In some developed countries, such companies are engaged in health care, integrating databases of medical, insurance and pharmaceutical corporations, and government agencies.

Global information networks will reduce the costs of advertising, marketing and delivery of goods and services as well as their development and production. This is essential for small and medium-sized businesses to allow them to gain access to information on the state of the world market, new requirements and technologies, costs, prices, etc.

In addition to information on trade in standard goods and services, this radically new market involves information resources (e.g. software, video). While creating new jobs, it necessitates new forms of protection of property and commercial secrets, certification, standardisation, control, financing, insurance, etc. These issues, including their multilingual and multicultural aspects, were discussed at the First International Conference on Electronic Commerce in Moscow (in 1997) and at the international congress on "Telecommunications from the Perspective of National Security. Prospective developments in the information and telecommunications infrastructure" (in St. Petersburg in 1998).

Of prime importance are integrated telecommunication and information infrastructures using broadband digital networks and the relevant services. This offers possibilities for business and remote education, health services, etc. The system of 18 servers, six software development and support centres and training facilities in Russia can support a common market of communications and information services in the CIS.

The new information infrastructure is provided by global Internet services. There were 75 million Internet users in 1997, including over 50 million in the USA. Over 40% had secondary education only. Thus not only scientists, managers and advertising professionals, but all public segments can receive messages even without computers being on and without fax or modem facilities. The Internet is most often used in private or business e-mail correspondence. At $20 a month (average Internet use price), the subscriber can send and receive an unlimited number of messages to and from any point in the world. There are over 100 million e-mail users in the USA in the late 1990s. As a result, the share of private correspondence in the total postal exchange reduced by half (from 8% to 4%). The CIS postal system will also have to provide new services and thus find new sources of revenues.

Almost 45% of subscribers use the Internet in *telemarketing*, gaining information on sellers and buyers of goods and services. Internet sales in the USA alone will amount to $200 billion by 2000, which will necessitate a new type of legal support for electronic commerce (a framework for global electronic commerce). The USA, with their obvious competitive advantages in this sphere, consider the Internet as a customs tariff-free, sales tax-free zone, particularly with regard to electronic products and services. The idea is self-regulation only, starting from the "no harm" principle and involving ethics on commercial Internet use. This, however, will eventually deprive CIS countries of a substantial portion of budget revenues and, more importantly, allow the uncontrolled export of capital and information.

Internet use has both advantages and disadvantages, considering that any computer in any country can communicate any type of information all over the world. It was via the Internet that the formulation of the bomb was transmitted that was used in the Oklahoma Federal Building explosion, the most dramatic act of terrorism in U.S. history. Information censorship on each terminal would be too costly and would also inhibit the most significant benefit of global networking – on-line data exchange. The CIS countries have yet to develop a set (e.g. name, address, telephone number) of encoding/decoding rules for business and private information communicated via the Internet and safeguards for corporate intellectual property against unauthorised access by competitors and abusers.

The third major Internet application is co-operative research and production involving multinational science and technology teams with each member working at his or her terminal within an integral schedule and a long-term contract.

The Internet has come to serve as a basis for education by correspondence, enabling millions to be enrolled in prominent educational centres without leaving home. This, however, poses the risks of cultural levelling and standard thinking. The computer simulates reality, replacing it with programming (1/0 combinations). The standard user is unaware of how and why the software has been devised, why it can be operated, who has entered a particular rule, principle or decision-making scheme in the computer and how, when and why. Every country needs both users and development analysts to evaluate software integrity and the political and economic interests of a given firm or state.

In 1997, there were over 2 million Internet users in Russia, with the number rapidly growing in all the CIS countries. This involves new issues of safety with regard to information, trade and private secrets, intellectual property rights, anti-monopoly and tax regulations. The model law on principles regulating information exchange should be used to formulate the laws on trade secrets, personal identification, electronic digital signature and electronic commerce and to refine the computer offence section in the Criminal Code. Annual losses due to the unlawful use of electronic cards in the USA exceed $4 billion, with a monthly record of 100 unauthorised entries in major industrial, transport and energy information networks. The safety of information, financial transactions and electronic payments will be a major challenge for the CIS countries in the 21st century.

Environmental infrastructure. The environmental infrastructure involves a framework for the protection of the air and water basins, land surface, public life and health, wildlife and vegetation against natural disasters (earthquakes, floods, torrents, landslides, droughts) and detrimental economic effects (e.g. flue gases, sewage, penetrating radiation, waste, deforestation and desertification, global warming, technological disasters, genetic shifts). This infrastructure is generally international in character, since pollution transport (e.g. acid rain) is easy, while environmental projects require large long-term investments.

As we approach the 21st century, environmental issues such as global warming due to CO_2 emission (resulting in the thawing of water-supplying glaciers in some CIS republics, elevated ocean levels, droughts, etc.), the destruction of the ozone layer by refrigerator Freon (cancerogenic) emission and mass-scale deforestation (associated with fuel crises in Moldova, Armenia, Georgia and Tajikistan) endanger human survival.

The following environmental issues are of special economic significance in the CIS.

Formulating and implementing comprehensive programmes to restore normal living standards in the areas polluted, poisoned or desertified by economic activities in the spheres of nuclear engineering (Kazakhstan, the Ukraine, Belarus, Russia), industry (open mining, chemical, metallurgy in some CIS countries) and agriculture. The total area in the CIS countries, including the Aral basin, was estimated by the UN at 4 million km^2, equalling that of Germany, France, Spain and the UK all together.

Water supply plays a special role in the social and production infrastructure. Conditions are particularly arduous in the Central Asian region owing to increased population, irrigation agriculture (exclusively cotton-oriented until the 1990s) and the declining level of the Aral Sea.

The problem can only be resolved by joint efforts, since major rivers in the area run across several states. The Amudaria takes its source at the confluence of the Naryn and Karadaria rivers in Kyrgyzstan, crossing West Uzbekistan, Tajikistan and South Kazakhstan to the Aral. As the bulk of the river flow is dispersed, the Aral Sea may dry out so that the area will be exposed to dust storms in the 21st century.

Co-operative efforts by the CIS countries will achieve three goals: (1) compensation of the costs borne by Kyrgyzstan and Tajikistan in regulating the Naryn and Kairakkum reservoirs in the upper reaches, (2) shared measuring and regulating systems to prevent water loss, and (3) shared water balance and water-saving consumption technologies.

The problems are relevant in many nations. One third of the world's population currently lacks adequate supplies of fresh water, and this is expected to rise to two thirds by 2025. The CIS countries could follow common interests by using the water resources of Lake Baikal and the Siberian rivers. The Caspian Sea level has been elevated, flooding the coast. However, an integrated water supply, purification and saving system can only result from joint efforts of all the CIS countries.

Despite the economic slump in the 1990s, there are far more motorcars in the CIS countries (7%–9% total and 10% annual increase in Russia) as well as private lorries and buses (over 1.5 million in 1997). In 1997, per 1000 people in the CIS, there were over 90 private passenger cars in Belarus, Russia and the Ukraine and 35–45 in Azerbaijan, Kyrgyzstan, Moldova, Tajikistan and Uzbekistan. Motorcars accounted for 45% of hazardous atmospheric emission (up to 80% in large cities). As we approach EU levels (almost 500 cars per 1000 people), the challenge will become even more dramatic.

Despite reduced outputs, air pollution was significant due to coal- and oil fuel-combusting electric plants (natural gas being the cleanest environmental fuel). Only 15% of the urban population in Russia has access to clean air, with 40% periodically exposed to five- to tenfold maximum allowable concentrations of hazardous substances. Chemical and metallurgical giants in Azerbaijan, Armenia, Belarus, Russia, Tajikistan and Uzbekistan affect living conditions. Particularly hazardous are the dioxins produced by chlorine reacting with organic matter (e.g. paper bleaching, waste incineration, polyvinyl films), a cancerogenic agent that takes decades to decompose.

Particularly pressing in many CIS countries is the question of earthquake (Central Asian region, Transcaucasia, Moldova, South Russia) and flood control and other emergencies, necessitating special construction methods, services, etc.

Nevertheless, no treatment or control facilities will resolve environmental problems in the 21st century. The only solution lies in the formulation and implementation of international environmental economic programmes of sustainable development in all world regions, including the CIS. Only on a CIS-wide level can economic development and social security be co-ordinated.

4.3 Public Social Protection

Social orientation of reforms. In any economic system, the social infrastructure performs eight basic functions:

– Correlating the numbers of workers and jobs, earnings and prices for goods and services (government statistical agencies, social economic monitoring, macro-economic regulation, employment service)

– Providing normal living conditions for citizens (housing and utilities, power supply, passenger transport, environmental control, emergency service)

– National security and rule of law (army, police, penitentiary system)

– Public health, maternity and child protection, physical training

– Development of the national intellectual potential (education, culture)

– Social care for the disabled (pensions, benefits and homes for the aged, RDPs and the socially disoriented – former convicts, demobilised servicemen, involuntary refugees, alcohol or drug addicts, etc.)

– A system for the prevention and settlement of social conflicts, based on three-lateral agreements between trade unions, business associations and government authorities, both centrally and locally

– Youth education system, including sport

The social infrastructure should be designed firstly to improve the quality of life as a basis for national economic growth, to expand the demand for goods and services and improve its structure; secondly, to develop the national labour force to meet the new conditions and requirements; and finally, to enhance social stability.

The problems involved are typical all over the world. The integral quality of life index, involving real income and consumption, access to housing and consumer durables, mortality rates, environmental conditions, education and crime, has grown in most regions of the world. According to a UN study (1996), it was the highest in Canada, the USA, Japan, the Netherlands and Norway. However, this was accompanied with increasing differences between rich and poor. The aggregate income of 358 multi-millionaires is larger than that of the 2.3 billion poor accounting for 45% of global population. The UN Human Development Report also indicates that 20% of the global population (1100 million) live in total poverty, earning less than $1 a day. As informatisation provides global access to data on living standards in rich countries, this furnishes a breeding ground for terrorists and religious fanatics.

Three social safety frameworks have been used in the world during the twentieth century. In the administrative command system, citizens were actually supported by the State. The low wages and shortages of vital necessities, including housing, were partially compensated for by employment guarantees, free health care and education, low rent and transport fares and low prices for basic foodstuffs. Towards the end of this century, it has become increasingly obvious that the system suppressed individual initiative by restricting the choice of physicians, teachers, housing, etc., resulting in general degradation in the sphere of services and, more importantly, creating a permanent-deficit economy.

Another purely market system is operated in the USA and some other countries. This involves high household money income (85% of GDP in the USA vs. 59% in Russia), relatively low taxes (25% of average income) and high costs of medical services, higher education ($25,000–$30,000 per year), housing and transport. The social transfers (e.g. pensions, benefits) are fairly high (almost 14% of GDP in the USA), but are derived from compulsory payments of both employers and employees. The basic 19-item food basket is 2.2-fold more expensive in the USA than in Russia ($104 and $45 respectively in 1996) and three- to sixfold that in other CIS countries.

While the U.S. economy was progressing in the 1990s, the poor were getting poorer and the rich richer. In early 1970s, average real wages began to decline. With comparatively low unemployment rates, medium-income households had their mothers and elder children employed. However, during the last quarter of the century, the proportion of children in single-parent families increased from 15% to 31%, with a third growing up in low-income households (under $25,000 per year) and a fifth in actual poverty. The percentage of trailer-home families grew from 3.1% to 7.2% over the last two decades. The average income differential by state increased (more than $40,000 in Connecticut vs. less than $15,000 in West Virginia). The low-paid employment segment now includes not only low-qualified workers but also blue-collar workers. Average wages in 1995 amounted to $13,000 for machine-operators and $15,000 for hotel staff, while 68,000 American citizens earned more than $1 million and 7% households more than $100,000 a year (with tax rates reduced from 47% to 32% between 1979 and 1994).

Of course, the poverty line in the USA ($7764 p.a.) is plenty in the CIS countries, even rent, health care (a third of the children have no medical insurance policy), fares and education fees taking up more than half of earnings. More important is the fact that the contribution of the bulk of the citizenry (80%) to aggregate income in the USA, one of the world's richest countries, has decreased over the past two decades, and the proportion accounted for by the middle class (annual income over $30,000) has declined to one third of the total households. In addition, the road to success has been increasingly associated with education. The biggest incomes have been earned not by scientists or inventors but rather by financial tycoons, people in the show business, professional boxers, basketball players, etc.

Due to increased average life spans in well-to-do households, the proportion of impoverished people aged over 65 decreased from 30% to 10.5% between 1970 and 1996. At the same time, the proportion of children in poor (generally large) families grew from 15% to 20%. Between 1968 and 1994, average income grew by 44% (from $74,000 to $106,000 p.a.) in the top 20% of rich households and only 7% (from $7200 to $7800) in the bottom 20%, lagging behind inflation rates (3.3% p.a. in the 1990s). All these indicate the need for a different social safety network in the CIS countries, without imitating foreign patterns.

We should not follow the social safety pattern employed in Sweden, France, Germany, Japan and some other countries either. This system is noted for its high taxes (up to 60% of income in Sweden) and employment, large-family, sickness benefits, etc.. Despite the more evident rule of law as compared to the CIS countries, motivation has deteriorated for employment, professional development and intensive work, resulting in deteriorating national economic competitiveness. Sweden is now the 17th instead of third in the world in terms of quality of life. In 1996, only 47.5% of respondents in Japan were satisfied with their living standards, the proportion of those feeling unhappy (generally due to unemployment risks) increasing from 15.6% to 22.5% over the last 15 years. In France, as in the USA and some other countries, the budget deficit resulted in reduced social benefits.

According to the UN Human Development Report, quality of life in the CIS, one of the world's major regions, deteriorated in the 1990s, with the number of the poor (earning less than $4 a day) growing from 14 to 119 million, i.e. sevenfold. Even in the fertile Ukraine, the average calorie consumption decreased from 3500 to 2800. This resulted in an overall decline in public health.

Real incomes in the CIS. Analysis of available data on quality of life in the CIS indicates that reforms have failed to achieve tangible results. While inflation subsided, minimum subsistence growth rates are higher than those of the consumption basket in total. This means that the price rise involved vital necessities rather than luxury goods. In addition, the CIS Statistical Board (1996) reported the minimum subsistence budget (subsistence minimum) exceeding average household money income per capita 1.8-fold in Belarus and Kyrgyzstan, threefold in Moldova and 2.4- to 5.2-fold in rural areas. Rural household incomes in Russia and Kazakhstan were 1.6- to 1.8-fold lower than the subsistence minimum. Only urban areas in the two latter countries indicated 17%–23% excess of household earnings over the minimum subsistence budget.

Low living standards are illustrated by household consumption patterns. Between 52% and 63% of urban household expenditures in Belarus, Kazakhstan, Kyrgyzstan, Moldova and Russia were allocated to food (two- to threefold that that in developed countries). In parallel, theatre visits over the 4 years reduced 2.5- to fourfold in Armenia, Georgia, Kyrgyzstan and Moldova. Cinema visits were more than decimated in Georgia and the Ukraine, over 20-fold reduced in Kazakhstan, Kyrgyzstan and Uzbekistan, 100-fold in Azerbaijan and fivefold in Belarus, Moldova and Russia.

Eating pattern differentials by CIS country increased. In 1996, an urban citizen could use the available average money income per capita (excluding taxes, etc.) on 33 kg beef or 802 eggs a month in Russia, 22–23 kg beef or 360–580 eggs in Belarus and Kazakhstan and only 14–16 kg beef or 200–300 eggs in Moldova and Kyrgyzstan with their advanced agricultural sectors. The proportions were the same for bread (110 kg in Russia, 48 kg in Kyrgyzstan), milk (164 and 80 l, respectively), etc. Notice that the report omitted the poorer countries. Average per capita consumption of meat and meat products in Russia and Belarus was twice that in Kyrgyzstan and Moldova (4.1–4.4 and 2.0–2.2 kg per month, respectively). Urban per capita consumption of dairy products and eggs in Russia was threefold that in Kyrgyzstan (17.2 vs. 6.2 kg and 14 vs. 4, respectively), even though the IMF estimated reforms in the latter as more progressive than in other CIS countries.

There are significant wage differentials by industry across the CIS countries (see Table 8).

Wages are impressively high in industry in Moldova and Kazakhstan (175% and 155% compared with average agricultural wages), in agriculture in Armenia (96% compared with 42%–43% in Russia and Kazakhstan), in construction in Armenia (208%) and in trade in Moldova (113% compared with 56% in Uzbekistan). They are unacceptably low (less than two thirds of the average) in public education in Armenia, Kyrgyzstan, Russia and Uzbekistan. The lowest (as compared with other branches of the economy) are incomes in science in Armenia and Russia. The CIS countries have set a record in finance sector wages (1.7- to 3.8-fold higher than average). The average wage in the gas industry (470 grivna) in the Ukraine in 1997 was sevenfold that in light industry. In all cases, export-oriented industries (fuel, metallurgy, electric power engineering, chemistry and petrochemistry) paid much higher wages than light and food industries.

Table 8

Average Monthly Nominal Wage by Industry
(as a percentage of average in the national economy, 1998)

	Armenia[3]	Belarus	Kazakh-stan	Kyrgyz-stan	Moldova	Russia	Uzbeki-stan[3]
Industry	127	124	144	148	174	119	139
Agriculture	96	61	39	63	52	40	76
Construction	208	132	125	151	168	135	152
Transport	159	{109	123	139	153	143[1]	138
Communications	177						148
Trade, public catering, supplies and procurement	77	94	82	67	102	93[2]	56
Public education	47	77	75	69	75	61	65
Science and science support	87	112	104[3]	127	131[3]	94	122
Finance, credit, insurance, etc.	379	192	192	295	439	179	183
Government administration	50	136	103	132	158	140	100

[1] Transport.
[2] Trade and public catering.
[3] 1997.

Real wage movement (accounting for price and tax changes) in the CIS countries can be divided into two periods. In 1991–1995, living standards declined dramatically (almost halving) in all the CIS countries, either applying the "shock therapy" advised by the IMF or maintaining the predominant State sector in the economy and centralised price and income regulation. The 1995/1991 real wage ratio was 44% in the Ukraine, 35% in Russia, 16% in Kazakhstan, 11% in Azerbaijan, 10% in Moldova, 7% in Turkmenistan, 3% in Tajikistan and 2.4%

in Armenia. The wage calculated in dollars amounted to $119 in Russia, $84 in Kazakhstan, $65 in Belarus, $55 in the Ukraine, $31–36 in Moldova, Uzbekistan and Kyrgyzstan, $16 in Armenia, $13 in Azerbaijan and less than $7 in Tajikistan.

Thus living standards in some southern CIS regions are almost the same as in the poorest African countries. Over 20% of the population emigrated from Armenia (generally from Erevan and the Spitak earthquake zone), 15% to countries "far abroad" and two thirds to Russia. Basic food consumption in the previously prosperous Moldova fell by 20% and meat by 48%. At the same time, real wages rose in Latvia and Estonia (by 35% and 13%, respectively), exceeding those in any CIS country and approximating $200 a month (they were almost equal in the Baltic countries and Russia in 1991). Real income stabilisation and growth therefore require political stability, a consistent economic strategy and active use of foreign investment. In this context, several problems need to be resolved.

Firstly, increase of the share of GDP accounted for by wages. By GTUC estimates, it amounts to 55%–60% in Germany, other EU countries and the USA and less than 40% in the CIS countries (25% in Moldova and 16%–18% in Azerbaijan, Kyrgyzstan and Uzbekistan). This requires budget balancing by reforms in the social safety net, housing and utilities charges, government procurement, etc. Per capita GDP in Russia was almost the same and in other CIS countries lower than in Poland, Turkey and Thailand, while the share of social benefits in the CIS, including subsidies to municipal utilities companies, was twice that in the above-mentioned countries.

A framework is needed for the distribution of national income and budget resources that is transparent and controlled by the government and local authorities. In many CIS countries, the collapse of real income in most households was far more dramatic than reduced labour productivity and GDP. This means that a large amount of national income was captured by intermediary firms, plundered and transferred abroad, and a considerable portion (50% in some countries) of income was channelled to the underground economy, thus evading taxation. According to the Russian Government's Statistical Board, hidden income amounted to $50 billion (11% of GDP) in 1996.

A transition to target social safety is needed. By WTO estimates, only 20% of social support reaches the poorest public segments (almost 60% in developed countries). In CIS countries, these are primarily the young urban and rural dwellers without either local employment or the necessary education to seek work in major cities. They provide a source for crime recruitment.

While social expenditure in the CIS countries is increasing persistently, despite the reduced GDP, incomes in the target segments are declining. This is due to an excessive range of beneficiaries. Thus entitlement in Russia involves 200 public categories – 70% of the population, including 40%–60% (depending on the region) receiving housing benefits, 60% fare compensations, etc. Benefits to those employed in hazardous industries are still allocated from the budget, even though the plants are no longer owned by the State.

Most CIS countries abolished standard industrial wage co-ordination by trade unions and employers, securing the authorised subsistence minimum and preventing excessive competition and labour conflicts.

The average wage in December 1997 (calculated in $) was 1.5- to 2.5-fold higher than the per capita subsistence minimum in only five CIS countries ($203 in Russia, $139 in Kazakhstan, $108 in the Ukraine, $107 in Belarus and $56 in Uzbekistan), and even in these countries, the main breadwinner's wage failed to guarantee the subsistence minimum for a three-member family. Considering actual family patterns, income exceeded the subsistence minimum in Russia, matched it in Belarus, Kazakhstan and the Ukraine and reached almost 90% in Uzbekistan.

In five CIS countries (Georgia, Kyrgyzstan, Moldova, Azerbaijan and Turkmenistan), the average monthly wage was $45–64, i.e. less than the subsistence minimum. This even fails to provide for the food minimum. Conditions are even worse in Armenia ($29) – Transcaucasian republics prospering in the former USSR – and Tajikistan ($11), the average wage failing to provide for breadwinner's normal food consumption.

By official national exchange rates, in 1997 and 1998 the average wage increased from $35.5 to $43.6 in Azerbaijan, from $27.7 to $30.6 in Armenia, from $86.1 to $94.9 in Belarus, from $111.6 to $126.7 in Kazakhstan, from $8.9 to $11.3 in Tajikistan and from $49.7 to $56.4 in Uzbekistan. Due to the drop in national exchange rates, the average wage fell from $48.1 to $46.9 in Moldova and from $96 to $77.5 in the Ukraine. Following the financial slump in Russia, public savings in December were devaluated by almost 80% compared with July 1998.

Actual survival is only attained with available private garden farms or supplementary earnings, leaving no time for professional or personal growth. For 40 million families and 10 million single households in Russia, there are 16 million private farms and 22 million garden and vegetable plots. In the late 1980s, they accounted for a quarter of agricultural products, and in the 1990s for 90% of potatoes, 77%–85% of vegetables, fruit, berries and honey and 45%–51% of milk, meat and wool.

In many CIS countries (e.g. the Ukraine, Russia, Moldova), there have been long delays of wages, pensions and benefits in the 1990s due to non-payments, low tax revenues and inadequate financial control.

Another challenge is the excessive income differential. This involves the income concentration ratio, Geannie's distribution by deciles and the proportion of household income below the *subsistence minimum* (where physiological demand is met with the least expensive products, with minimum expenses on services, medicine, sanitation, hygiene and linen), minimum subsistence budget (almost twice the subsistence minimum, including clothes, footwear, consumer durables and vacations) and proportion of *high-income* households (on average sixfold higher than the subsistence minimum per member, satisfying all reasonable requirements in terms of food, footwear and clothes, a car, modern house equipment, etc.).

According to the CIS Statistical Board, the top to bottom wage differential by country amounted to 4.6 in 1992, 16 in 1996 and even 19 in 1997.

High-level incomes (in the CIS at least $1000 a month in a household and $300 per member) are indicative of an emerging *middle class* – entrepreneurs and highly qualified professionals with permanent legal earnings ensuring a range of top-quality goods and services at reasonable prices.

The middle class (almost half the population in the USA and EU countries, and one third of the population in developing Asian countries) provides a basis of civil society and labour force and the principal driving force behind the consumer and stock market. Unlike the rich (in the CIS represented by households with income over $1000 a month per member), they are rational about expenses and prices, and unlike the poor, they demand high-quality diversified goods and services.

Income differentials increased dramatically in the CIS countries in the 1990s. According to J. Phillips,[1] the top 20% (party and administrative nomenclature, scientists) accounted for 36% (48% in the USA), the intermediate 60% (including engineers, skilled manual labour, members of prosperous collective farms) for 55% (48%) and the bottom 20% (generally rural population) for 9% (6%) of total income in the USSR in the 1980s. By 1995, the income differential between the top and bottom 10% of households amounted to 13:1, i.e. almost the same as in the USA (15:1) and South America (20:1). In this case, however, the "new" top Russians, Armenians, Kazakhs, etc. were mainly involved in the underground economy or were corporate and bank leaders, while those at the bottom were physicians, teachers and others employed in State-supported branches, the semi-unemployed rural populations and pensioners.

According to the Russian State Statistical Board, the average per capita income differential between the top and bottom 10% of households in 1996 and 1997 was 13:1. In Belarus (accounting for natural non-money revenues), it was 5.6:1. In addition, the top 20% of households in these two countries accounted for 46% and 35% of total incomes, and the bottom 20% for 6.2% and 9.6%, respectively.

When inflation rates decelerated, household income differentials smoothed out in Russia, Kazakhstan, Kyrgyzstan and some other CIS countries. This resulted in dramatic changes in the markets of clothes, footwear, domestic equipment,

---

[1] (1996): Проблемы Теории и Практики Управления (Problemy Teorii i Praktiki Upravlenija) 2, 27 [In Russian]

computers and motorcars. Demand collapsed for luxuries and low-quality consumer goods made in Asian countries outside the CIS and the middle class emerged, represented by entrepreneurs, farmers, managers and other professionals willing to buy goods that were not too expensive but always high-quality (e.g. environmentally sound, fashionable). The financial crisis of 1998 generally affected the middle class – small and medium-scale entrepreneurs, managers, services, advertising and travel firms. Eating out halved. Social differentiation rates rose dangerously. Obviously, social orientation in a transitional economy is inconceivable without a range of complex reforms.

Housing and utilities reform. The CIS countries differ in housing stock structure and public access to housing. Uzbekistan has the highest proportion of ownership of the housing stock (95%). In the mid-1990s, the proportion amounted to 88% in Kazakhstan and Kyrgyzstan, 70%–75% in Turkmenistan, Tajikistan, Azerbaijan and Moldova and 53%–58% in Armenia, Belarus, Russia and the Ukraine.

In terms of housing space per capita, Moldova, the Ukraine, Belarus and Russia are far ahead (19–20 m^2), followed by Armenia and Kazakhstan (15 m^2), with much inferior conditions in Azerbaijan, Kyrgyzstan, Turkmenistan and Uzbekistan (11–13 m^2) and particularly in Tajikistan (less than 10 m^2).

The share of investments in the social sphere in the CIS countries is falling (from 43% in 1994 to 41% in 1996), particularly in Kyrgyzstan (13%), Moldova, Kazakhstan (26%) and Uzbekistan (32%). This is generally due to reduced government financing of projects to build schools, hospitals, etc. Physical outputs declined in Belarus, Tajikistan, Moldova, the Ukraine and some other countries with a history of predominantly government financing.

The situation is different in some CIS countries (Azerbaijan, Kyrgyzstan, Uzbekistan), with almost 90% of housing projects financed by the public using government credit. Housing output is increasing in Armenia. However, there are substantial differences across the CIS. With over 40 flats per 10,000 people in Russia (irrespective of investment source) in the mid-90s, the output amounted to 23–26 in the Ukraine, Uzbekistan and Belarus, 12–15 in Kazakhstan and Moldova, eight to nine in Armenia, Azerbaijan and Kyrgyzstan and two in Georgia.

Every fifth to sixth household in Russia, the Ukraine and Azerbaijan and every fourth in Belarus are on waiting lists for improved housing conditions. Every fifth household in Russia, the Ukraine and Kyrgyzstan and every sixth in Belarus have been waiting for over 10 years. More than 2 million families in the CIS countries live in dormitories and dilapidated or wrecked housing facilities.

Obviously, the problem cannot be handled by the State alone. Private contribution would be far more effective, including house buying, rent market and preferential mortgage credit to less favoured households. While private ownership of housing in the CIS countries has been growing (from 25% in 1991 to 28% in 1996), the rates are too low. It accounts for 86% in Uzbekistan, 79% in Kyrgyzstan, 64.8% in Moldova and only 18% in Russia. Most households own a flat at best, while in developed market economies the ownership share is two thirds.

An interesting scheme to build housing has been implemented in Moscow, where the average housing space is 20 m^2 for each of the 9 million inhabitants. Design and building contracts are offered in tender. The amounts and time limits for preliminary approval are minimised. The costs are cut by 10% each year. With both domestic and foreign investment (almost $4 billion in 1997), annual output amounts to 3.3 million m^2, with one fifth allocated to people on waiting lists free of charge, 35% sold at market prices and the remaining portion used to re-accommodate inhabitants of dilapidated large-panel industrial buildings or by investors. Every seventh working Muscovite is involved in the long-term urban planning project. By the late 1990s, housing prices fell on the liberalised market.

A housing market ensuring an unrestricted choice of domicile within the CIS, governed by employment opportunities, desirable climate, family or friends, relative purchase or rent prices, etc., by no means implies uncontrolled migration of millions of households.

Developed economies have no compulsory registration in one place of residence or another, and passports are only issued for foreign travel. However, the public registration and identification framework is much tighter than in the CIS. The CIS countries are also introducing personal codes entitling holders to employment, bank accounts, credit cards, driving licences, etc. The code permits payments to the pension fund by employers and employed to be checked (determining the amount and actual issue). The same is true of health insurance, etc. Housing purchase or rent, telephone subscription, energy supply, etc. involve individual credit history and solvency checking using this code. When recruiting a new employee, a firm will refer to previous employers. The system used in many countries is designed to enhance private (both criminal and administrative) and, more importantly, economic responsibility.

And yet the greatest challenge is related to rent and utilities payments, public transport fares, etc. Up to now, 70%–90% of the costs in the CIS countries have been covered from the budget in the form of subsidies to housing, energy and water supply and transport services, etc. The system is inconsistent with the principles of a market economy, and in fact with any reasonable economy. The subsidies amount to 30% of the central budget (over $20 billion in Russia) and 50% of regional budgets, exhausting projected investments, e.g. education, public health restructuring, etc.

Low tax revenues result in a chain of arrears. In regions with a very low electricity tariff ratio to prime costs (e.g. in the Russian Primorski Territory), sectoral wages were delayed for months and workers went on strike, affecting public light and water supplies, etc.

Subsidising monopolistic producers failed to induce resource-saving and better quality. Thus daily per capita water consumption in Moscow and other major CIS cities is 600 l, for example three times that outside the CIS, with 55% water, heat, etc. lost owing to failures in central or household systems.

As the subsidies are calculated per m^2 municipal housing space, the biggest winners are the owners of spacious flats, and the losers the households experiencing space shortages or lacking modern conveniences, private co-operative and individual investors, etc. Municipal housing maintenance deteriorated rapidly in the 1990s due to inadequate budgets.

In market economies, all utility service costs are covered by users. In the USA, such payments amounted to 14.4% of GDP in the mid-1990s (6% in Russia), but this was generally related to more space and better quality. Average payments represented 17% of total household earnings (16% in Russia). Despite the opposition of housing stock owners, most urban areas maintain regulated marginal housing rent and municipal waiting lists for low-income households. When tariffs rose dramatically in the Baltic countries in the early 1990s and housing and utility payments exceeded operating costs, margins were set as a percentage of household income. To save costs, some people moved to smaller flats or less prestigious districts. There are tough policies of penalties, cutting off water supplies, eviction, etc.

The principal trends in housing and utility reform not running into opposition in the CIS countries include the following:

1. Allocation of customer's functions to housing stock owners, including the *condominiums* – non-profit associations of the owners (e.g. individuals, local government agencies, departments, financial and construction companies). While paying a unified tariff, they can offer contracts for housing services to any firm. An important task is to equalise their rights with those enjoyed by *housing construction co-operative units* generally paying higher rates and district *housing agencies* placing orders for municipal housing services.

2. Creation of a competitive market of services by abolishing the rigid monopoly of existing repair and maintenance offices. The offices are reorganised as small municipal or privatised firms. Customers select the suppliers of services, signing a contract providing for mutual liabilities for the amount, quality and time of services provided, terms of payment, etc. This involves water and heat meters, etc., and government control of the tariffs set by natural monopolistic owners of pipelines, energy systems, etc.

3. Formulation of official standards including: (a) social housing space (in Russia 18 m^2 per head in a household of three or more members, 22 m^2 in a two-member household and 33 m^2 in a single-member household), (b) individual contribution to total maintenance and repair costs, including utilities (currently 35%), (c) maximum allowable proportion of total household income taken up by

housing and utility expenditure (16%, with 20% expected in 2000) and (d) marginal price of housing and utility services per m^2 total area (differentiated by region).

The standards will permit budget financial resources to be targeted to those people who are actually disfavoured, depending on the social norms and in the form of social safety net issues rather than producers' subsidies irrespective of effectiveness and quality.

4. Application of advanced energy-saving technologies ensuring 30% reductions in costs, including: low-inflammable insulation and waterproofing, updated plumbing, added garrets, boiler conversion, innovative processes in building construction, pipe laying and rehabilitation, street cleaning, etc., as well as special homes for the aged and disabled.

On the other hand, the projected rise in housing payments causes considerable anxiety. Private housing and utility payments accounted for 25% in the 1980s, 2% in Russia in 1993 (price liberalisation did not involve housing rent, etc.), 26% in 1996 and 31% in 1997 (17% in Moscow), with the projected contribution amounting to 70% and then 100% by 2000. The rise is only feasible with a drastic increase in the wage share in GDP (59% in the USA vs. 23% in Russia), advanced mortgage credit for housing purchase and construction and a network of boarding houses with small living areas and all modern conveniences. Real income reporting for social safety issues (ensuring utility payments under 20% of household earnings) is greatly impeded in the CIS. There is no available legal enforcement framework to be employed in cases of non-payment or a municipal housing stock to re-accommodate the more fraudulent non-payers.

The situation allows for an alternative: current payments for standard minimum space with progressive rates per extra m^2, depending on housing quality, i.e. objective recorded data available in engineering inventory bureaus. This will not cause social protest from non-beneficiaries, while requiring special mechanisms for inspection and compensation and, more importantly, for the promotion of a realistic housing market.

Reforms in public health. Public health is among the most important branches of the national economy, determining the general quality of life, national labour potential and genetic complex, and public expenditure on the sick and disabled. In general terms, and particularly in the context of increasing life expectancy, this branch cannot proceed on purely market lines. Data on public health in the CIS are given in Table 9.

The population per physician ratio is 225–265 in Kazakhstan and Russia, 300–315 in Armenia, Kyrgyzstan, Turkmenistan and Uzbekistan and over 450 in Tajikistan. In the first half of the 1990s, hospital beds per 10,000 decreased by 6%–18% in Armenia, Belarus, Kazakhstan, Moldova, Russia and the Ukraine and by 24%–32% in Kyrgyzstan, Tajikistan and Uzbekistan.

Table 9

Public Health across the CIS (per 10,000 people, 1996)

Country	Capacity of outpatient clinical establishment, visits per shift	Hospital beds	Physicians	Medium-level staff
Azerbaijan	137	99.9	39.1	89.7
Armenia	124[1]	69.6	32.9	81.9
Belarus	211	124.0	43.6	112.6
Georgia	207	66.7	42.0	74.9
Kazakhstan	202	116.9	37.8	101.0
Kyrgyzstan	141	90.2	33.2	93.9
Moldova	210	122.3	39.6	103.9
Russia	236	126.1	44.5[2]	111.0[2]
Tajikistan	111	80.2	21.4	61.9
Turkmenistan	91	101.8	31.4	98.5
Uzbekistan	134	83.9	33.2	108.9
Ukraine	189	125.1	45.1	116.5

[1] 1994.
[2] Dentists with medium-level professional qualifications (1.8 per 10,000 people) included in the medium-level staff.

However, the greatest cause for alarm are the increased mortality rates and deterioration in public health across the CIS.

Until 1917, the average life expectancy in Imperial Russia was less than 40 years, increasing rapidly since the 1950s. By the mid-1960s, the life expectancy for women in the USSR was only 6 months and for men 18 months lower than in the USA, with higher birth rates.

The situation first changed in the late 1960s. When epidemic infections such as smallpox, cholera, diphtheria, poliomyelitis and typhus were eliminated, blood diseases and cancer came to the fore. This is where overall vaccination strategies need to give way to a patient-oriented approach. Developed countries have resolved the problem with considerable investments in pharmaceutics, medical technologies and promotion of healthy life styles. In some countries, reduced consumption of fats, tobacco and spirits contributed to a reduction by a third in infarction- and cerebral thrombosis-related mortality rates.

The USSR public health system failed to reduce morbidity rates as far back as in the 1970s. Only in the period between 1985 and 1987 was male life expectancy 3 years longer due to the anti-alcohol campaign. Mortality rates then rose dramatically in the 1990s, owing to alcohol abuse, injuries, accidents, homicide, tuberculosis, etc. Male mortality in Russia is 5.3-fold that in Germany among 30- to 34-year-olds and fivefold that among 40- to 44-year-olds. Thus the average life expectancy fell from 64 to 57 years – to the levels of India, Egypt and Bolivia. In addition, half of male and one third of female deaths are related to alcohol abuse (largely the consequence of the abolition of the government wine monopoly); suicide rates rose 1.2-fold (social disorientation in the reform process), and homicides 1.3-fold (higher crime rates); deaths caused by infections and parasitoses (deteriorating sanitary and epidemiological status) also increased. The increased mortality alone amounts to 2.9 million human working years annually. In addition (according to a survey conducted in St. Petersburg in 1995), 93% of school-age children suffer from chronic pathologies (2700 cases per 1000 children), and 40% of conscripts are reported as unfit for active service.

The *depopulation ratio* (death/birth ratio) increased from 1.14 in 1992 to 1.63 in 1994, indicating that the population in Russia will fall to 145.6 by 2000 and, according to Goskomstat, 141 million by 2010, despite the favourable migration ratio and increased population in Daghestan, Kalmykia, Tuva and some other republics. Russia was sixth in the world in terms of population in 1998 (after China, India, Indonesia and Brazil), but will be ninth by the early 21st century (after to Pakistan, Nigeria and Bangladesh) and, if the trend persists, 11th in 2025.

However, demographic estimates suggest that only 20%–25% of the birth loss is related to deteriorating living standards. Underdeveloped Third-World countries accounted for 90% of births in the 1990s, with illiterate mothers having an average of 6.9 children, and those with 7 years of education or more, 3.9. An 8%–9% reduction in population by 2020 is expected in developed countries such as Germany, Italy and Hungary. In some CIS countries, lower birth rates are related to human losses in the 1920s and 1930s and in the wartime (the proportion of women aged 20–29 accounting for two thirds of total births in Russia reduced by 2.2 million, or 19%, between 1987 and 1994).

As mentioned before, mortality rates (generally in the able-bodied age-groups) due to accidents, homicide or suicide also increased in other CIS countries. Homicide-related deaths (excluding in war action) between 1991 and 1995 increased almost 1.5-fold in Kazakhstan, Kyrgyzstan, Moldova and the Ukraine, several times in Tajikistan and almost doubled in Azerbaijan, Belarus and Russia.

Of course, there is no immediate relationship between public wealth and suicide. The European leader in this regretful indicator (per 100,000) is the prosperous Sweden, and in the CIS suicide is highest in Russia (26.5 in 1991 and 41.4 in 1995), Belarus (21.0 and 31.0, respectively), Kazakhstan (18.3 and 28.5) and the Ukraine, the top-income countries.

Nevertheless, the costs of reforms are related to higher incidence rates in the 1990s, including severe tuberculoses (1.3- to 1.5-fold higher in the Ukraine, Moldova, Belarus and Kyrgyzstan, and 1.7-fold in Russia), diphtheria and viral hepatitis (particularly in the Central Asian region, the Ukraine and Moldova). The infant mortality ratio (per 1000 births) was 13–18 in the mid-1990s in Belarus, Armenia, the Ukraine, Russia and Georgia, 21–28 in Moldova, Azerbaijan, Uzbekistan, Kazakhstan and Kyrgyzstan and 31–42 in Tajikistan and Turkmenistan compared with 4.5–8 in developed countries. Only in Russia did the ratio fall by 15% (1994–1997). Maternity deaths in the CIS countries are five-to tenfold higher than in Europe (12–88 vs. 2–9 per 100,000). Alcohol abuse increased in Belarus, Kazakhstan, Russia and the Ukraine; drug abuse increased two- to threefold in Azerbaijan, Belarus, Kyrgyzstan, Russia, Moldova and the Ukraine; there are 30–60 more cases of female syphilis in Belarus, Kazakhstan and Russia; AIDS has been a regional challenge in the Ukraine and Russia; and congenital anomalies have increased (1.5-fold in Russia).

The critical condition of public health is largely associated with rising prices for medical supplies, charged health services, reduced number of sanatoriums, recreation centres, etc., and the collapse of preventive medicine. Between 1990 and 1995, health centre populations in the Ukraine and Russia reduced by three quarters, with the centres halved. A pressing problem is related to anti-drug operations, drug traffic being deeply rooted in the South.

Extreme caution should be exercised in applying the experience of developed countries. The USA spend over $1 trillion annually on medical techniques and technologies, new medicines and medical services – more than the rest of the world. And yet the UK, Germany, Japan, Canada and France, where public health is controlled by the government in addition to the laws of the market, have attained comparable achievements in terms of incidence rates and life expectancy at far lower costs.

U.S. health care is profit-making and dominated by major insurance companies. According to Nobel prize-winner Rober Lown, 70% of heart disease patients gain little from surgical intervention, and expensive assays and treatments are often designed for higher profits of health care companies. At the same time, a quarter of the population have no health insurance and, consequently, cannot gain free access to health care.

Public health reforms in the CIS countries involve the following strategies:

1. Promotion of healthy life styles, formulating and implementing programmes to control alcohol and drug abuse, infections and epidemics, enhancing government control over the quality of food, fresh water and air.

2. Creation and development of a framework for compulsory and voluntary insurance, inviting employers and in some cases the general public to cover the costs. Government standards are needed to ensure public access to non-charged emergency services, within State-financed health care for children, mothers and pensioners.

An attractive scheme is employed in Latvia, with sickness benefits paid by the employer for the first fortnight (75%–80% of wages) and then from the social insurance budget (with official employment paying social tax in due time).

3. Development of a medical supply network financed by the government (for target categories), health insurance fund and individual investments, with government control over the quality, distribution and preservation of essential reserves.

4. Of special importance in the CIS countries is the quality of management in the health sphere, combining the competitive principles (free choice of physician, State-run or private hospital, etc.) with government financing and allocations by improved cases rather than hospital beds. Professional organisations, insurance companies, etc. should supervise the quality of health services and rational resource management. Advanced scientific applications and technologies and up-to-date managerial strategies will contribute to improved efficiency and resource-saving and, where needed, timely removal of unqualified staff.

5. The family doctor institution of the type established in developed countries. According to estimates, this general practitioner can perform 23% of outpatient surgery and 36%–46% of the ophthalmologist's, ear and throat specialist's and neuropathologist's functions. As a result, additional counselling will decrease from 50% to 10%. The family doctor with a knowledge of inherited and other characteristics in each individual family will save time by early diagnostics and preventive treatment, thus decimating eventual costs.

A system of local administration, insurance companies and a physician contracted for medical services ensures strict control of the quality of treatment, including legal claims (professional liability insurance). Rehabilitation centres, hospices and medical nursing clinics will reduce the demand for standard expensive hospitals. In developed countries, the physician/nurse ratio is 1:5–6 (1.5:2 in the CIS), with an extended range of health managers. Health economics largely determine overall economic efficiency.

Pension reform. An essential component of the social safety net is the pension issue. There were 70 million pension holders in the CIS countries in 1997, including 75%–82% aged, 18–24% disabled or deprived of breadwinners and 0.3%–3% term-of-service retirements. The share of pension holders as a percentage of the total populations, their movements and pension amounts (as a percentage of the average wage) differ considerably across the CIS (see Table 10), while the general allocation principles are the same.

Table 10

**Pension Holders (per 1000 population) and Average
Pension (as a % of the average wage) by Country**

Country	Pension holders		Average pension	
	1995	1996	1995	1996
Azerbaijan	173	163	22	20
Armenia	175	176	30	32
Belarus	256	247	30	38
Georgia	...	221	...	...
Kazakhstan	176	177	24	26
Kyrgyzstan	137	136	37	35
Moldova	215	217	28	29
Russia	254	259	29	28
Tajikistan	103	97	35	43
Turkmenistan	115	104	30	36
Uzbekistan	121	121	38	41
Ukraine	282	284	31	29

These include the following: (a) the relatively low pension age as compared with other countries (55–60 years), (b) the same length of service (35–40 years) required for maximum pension issue, (c) the high percentage of privileged holders (depending on working conditions, etc.), (d) social old-age and disability pensions without the required length of service (2 million people in the CIS countries), (e) pension issue during working period, (f) maximum admissible amount, (g) adjusted price rise compensations and (h) compulsory insurance payments by enterprises and organisations into the pension fund (25% of the wage fund in Kazakhstan, 28%–31% in Kyrgyzstan, Moldova, Russia and Tajikistan and 35% in Armenia).

The CIS countries are confronted with similar challenges in terms of the interests of pension holders. The average pension in most CIS countries is under 30% of the average wage, with 35%–43% in the Central Asian region, except for in Kazakhstan and Belarus (see Table 10), i.e. below the subsistence minimum. Social pensions in many countries are 1.5- to twofold lower than minimum old-age pensions.

Payments are often delayed due to insufficient pension funds, reduced employment in the economy and wage proportion of total income, and insufficient budget financing.

Higher minimum pensions related to price rises (over 80% of the average pension in Azerbaijan, Armenia and Kyrgyzstan and over 75% in Belarus and Moldova) result in levelling irrespective of the past working period.

To resolve the problems, some CIS countries established non-government pension funds. This is typical in Russia, the Ukraine, Belarus and Georgia, where pensioners account for a fifth or even a quarter of the total populations. A gradual rise of the eligible age to 65 years is being debated.

Some promise is offered by an individual (personified) approach in social insurance. A personal account will contain the basic identification, information on work history, wage and other earnings determining insurance payments, etc. There will be no need to collect and submit many documents (including the work record) to social security agencies, information will be validated and, more importantly, the amount paid will be related to insurance (probably in all CIS countries).

A key challenge in improving social protection in the CIS countries is the identification of the real target-groups needing and deserving protection. The use of computerised databases will lead to the introduction of personal plastic cards containing information on benefit category – housing or utility payments, transport fares, medicine, etc. Non-targeted benefits (e.g. family, old-age) should not be financed by the government in the CIS countries in addition to equalising honest people and parasitic cadgers.

The pension reform must be carried out within the next 5–10 years while the small wartime generation is retiring. Avalanche retirements after 2010 will result in pensioners outstripping the work populations. In this situation, a de-personified government-supported pension system cannot be maintained. The only alternative is a cumulative scheme based on personal pension accounts of the type operated in some countries in Europe, Southeast Asia (Malaysia, Singapore) and South America (Chile being the first). A similar reform is being prepared in the USA, Hungary and Poland as well as in Kazakhstan, Moldova and Russia.

Under this scheme, only the minimum social pension and military pensions are allocated from the budget. The remaining portion is accumulated on the personal pension account from payments made by the employer (depending on working conditions) and the employee. The information is entered in computer databases and is strictly confidential, and the future pensioner can check payments on the account at any time.

Non-government pension funds managed by international companies have come to act as major investors, increasing deposits and thus benefiting the national economy. The government exercises strict control over performance and safety. The funds must make substantial investments in more stable government securities rather than related or inadequately performing firms.

In Russia, such funds were worth over $600 million in 1997, providing supplementary pensions 2.5-fold higher than government ones for almost 150,000 individuals. A gradual transition is under way from distribution to cumulative principles in labour pension financing, with employers' and employees' payments accumulated on personal accounts rather than in the common stock (pension fund). This will induce higher legal wages under contract. As pension expenditure in Russia in the late 1990s accounts for 6.5% of GDP, its rationalisation is essential.

The pension reform in Moldova involves the eligible age being gradually increased (3 months per year), i.e. 65 for men and 60 for women by 2005. The average post-retirement lifetime in Moldova for men and women is 12 and 15 years, respectively, and the pension/average wage ratio increased from 38% in 1994 to 62% in 1997.

Educational reform. A number of studies demonstrate that, at the end of the twentieth century, investment in human capital has become the most efficient strategy ensuring both better qualifications and initiative and education of a new generation to participate in the information society. Developed countries in Europe, America and Asia initiated a radical educational reform, focusing on efficiency, access and continuity.

An interesting study of quality of life among the young was conducted in the USA. According to the report submitted to the President, youth mortality rates decreased between 1985 and 1994. The proportion of young people (under 18) starving in low-income households decreased from 13% to 8%. At the same time, there were fewer children in two-parent families (68% vs. 85%; 75% of Whites, 64% of Latin Americans and 33% of Afro-Americans). The proportion of children of single mothers increased from 5% to 32% between 1960 and 1995, and young victims from 8% to 12% (1980–1996). More school-age children used tobacco, alcohol and drugs.

An essential indicator of the human potential and the national economy is the education level. In the USA in the 1980s and 1990s, 85% young people held certificates of comprehensive secondary education. However, according to a study by the International Association for the Evaluation of Educational Achievement on 500,000 schoolchildren in 41 countries, superior achievements in mathematics were evident in South Korea, Japan, Singapore, the Netherlands, the Czech Republic and Austria. They were not so spectacular in the USA, Canada, Israel, Hungary and Slovenia, and even less so in the UK, Greece, Latvia, Iran and Kuwait. CIS students, even though coming top in a number of comparisons in computer science, mathematics, etc., generally performed worse than in the 1980s.

The main reason lies not in the amount size of classes, home work or number of students in a group (the average 43 in South Korea leading the list of successes) but rather in the use of home libraries and computers and family attitudes to education.

In the first few years of reform, the CIS countries used the Soviet educational infrastructure and intellectual capital. However, this resource has been almost exhausted. The following principal trends of educational reform are being debated in the CIS countries:

1. National standards of secondary, vocational and higher education, rules of government licensing and accrediting by such standards for educational institutes and a mechanism of control for the quality of educational services. An accredited educational institute will have to provide up-to-date aids and equipment, including computer and sport/health facilities, qualified teaching staff and student-oriented active training methods basing on recent scientific results. The institutes failing to meet these standards will be closed (including many weak higher schools), reconstituted as departments of key educational institutions or restructured within strictly specified time limits.

2. Allocation of the rights of financial and economic management, including tenders in contracts for maintenance and repair works, school catering, lease of premises, etc. to immediate educational institutions supervised by a board of governors. This involves corporate schools, colleges, etc. with their own current bank account and balance, providing authorised charged services, sponsored, etc. As estimated, and given rational use of resources, building maintenance costs, etc. (accounting for 35%–45% of school budgets) will be reduced by 15%–30%, while supplementary revenues (including parental and industrial sponsorship) will constitute almost half of the teaching staff wage fund.

3. Minimum government educational financing (4%–5% of GDP) and financing of non-charged educational services in all types of educational institutions (including non-governmental) calculated per student. This will secure free choice of educational institutes, with educational allocations following each student to any accredited school, college, etc. The amount will depend on the amount of knowledge the institute provides (in conformity to government standards regularly checked by independent centres employing appropriate tests) and the number of students it thus attracts. This system, combining competition and educational quality control by the government, parents and students, has been successful in many countries.

4. Public access to free education complying to the government standard combined with charged additional services (intensive language courses, music, etc.). A government order for staff training paid out of the corresponding budget and based on staff marketing would be expedient. In this case, the number of students willing to pay for education is not limited, and a non-interest educational credit scheme is devised. This would also involve budget subventions for regions lacking the required resources to meet national educational standards. Some European countries, e.g. the UK, orientated towards a transition to 2- to 4-year public vocational training on leaving secondary school, have introduced

university/college tuition fees. Even rich countries cannot afford to finance higher education completely out of the government budget.

5. Postgraduate education focusing on additional qualifications or development training in new technologies has emerged as a profitable business sphere in the final decades of the twentieth century. Professional specialists can take a part-time development course every year and a full-time course every 3–4 years, paid by the firm (given adequate test achievements), the government (military discharges, unemployed or disabled people) and themselves.

This is particularly important in the CIS countries due to recent reductions in the armed forces and the military-industry complex. Thus the Ukrainian armed forces will be reduced from 726,000 to 220,000 between 1990 and 2005. Over 20% need social care and 15%–20% psychological assistance in converting to civil conditions; 55% are willing to engage in business but lack the required knowledge.

The former system of evening and extra-mural education and branch development centres discontinued in CIS countries will have to be revived on a new basis.

6. A unified educational space in the CIS countries involves unified educational standards, general acceptance of national certificates of education, inter-state undergraduate programmes (especially in small-scale professions and graduate research), teachers' residential programmes and, more importantly, joint development of the educational reform strategies using international experience.

Employment infrastructure. *Employment* in terms of the market economy is described as lawful civil activities aimed at the satisfaction of personal and public demands and generally earning income (e.g. wages). In this context, employment involves nine public categories: (1) hired labour (e.g. working under labour agreements, contracts), including temporal, seasonal, part-time work, etc., (2) entrepreneurs, (3) self-employed professions (e.g. lawyers, notaries, actors, physicians, journalists), 4) those engaged in subsidiary processes and selling their produce on contractual terms (e.g. hunters, beekeepers), (5) members of productive co-operative units and people working under civil legal contracts (e.g. construction, repair), (6) officials elected or appointed on remunerative principles to government or social organisations, (7) military service, (8) students at full-time educational institutes and (9) those temporarily absent due to vacations, temporary incapacity, development training, suspended production, etc. Those citizens belonging to the labour force but not employed, those who have lost their job or those seeking work are considered as unemployed.

Official unemployment rates in 1998 comprised 1.1% of the labour force in Armenia, 2.8% in Belarus, the Ukraine and Russia, almost 4% in Kazakhstan, 3.1% in Kyrgyzstan and 0.3% in Uzbekistan. These are not comparable with

Bulgaria, Hungary, Slovakia and Poland (11%–15%), Finland (17%) or Spain (23%).

However, if considering job seekers outside unemployment services, in accordance with international standards, a totally different picture is beginning to emerge. The unemployed account for 22% of the labour force in Armenia, 17% in Georgia, 15% in Kazakhstan and 9% in Russia and the Ukraine. The average unemployment time continues to grow, and in most CIS countries it is more than 6 months. Almost half of the unemployed in Armenia, Belarus, Moldova, etc. are in the 16–29 age-group, and 11%–16% of the unemployed in Belarus, Kyrgyzstan and Moldova are graduates of higher educational institutes, specialised secondary and vocational schools. Involuntary inactivity often leads to criminal contacts. Unemployment rates are generally accelerated in rural areas (in Kyrgyzstan, Russia, Moldova and some other countries) and among women (73% of the total unemployed in the Ukraine). In the light, machine-building, chemical and petrochemical industries, part-time employment is well-established. In Russia, for instance, almost a tenth of workers have to work part-time or go on vacation, often unpaid.

The unemployment compensation net is only emerging. Only 3.5 million of the 11 million unemployed in the CIS are formally registered, with 10%–60% not receiving compensation. Community work, including urban development and road and housing repair, garden planning, canal cleaning, etc. has not gained wide acceptance due to the lack of prestige and low remuneration. This contrasts with the USA in the 1930s, when, on F.D. Roosevelt's initiative, millions of unemployed built highways, stadiums, dams, planted gardens, etc.

A typical case of the unemployment profile in the CIS in the late 1990s is Moldova. The characteristic features are:

– An increased proportion of general unemployment and dismissal due to closure, reorientation or staff reduction (over a third)

– Predominantly (over half) unemployment among the young – under 30 with comprehensive secondary (complete or incomplete) education and low qualifications

– Predominantly women who are dismissed (almost two thirds) and unemployed (over a half)

– Decreasing re-employment (from 49% to 24%–26%) provided by government employment services, due to fewer vacancies

– Latent unemployment in rural areas, over 40% in industries and transport, and over 50% in construction, with widely practised unpaid or partially paid vacations

– Increasing demand/supply differential in mass professions (190 unemployed for one agricultural officer vacancy, 90 for subsidiary work, 60 for seamstress, 48 for car driver, 17 for computer operator positions, etc.)

– Low proportion of professional re-training (7%–8%) or reference to social work (1%–2%) offered by employment services

A government employment programme in the CIS countries should be focused on the creation of new jobs in small and medium-sized business, particularly for women, young people, the disabled, etc., using privileged taxation and credit. Another important task involves professional orientation and re-training in accordance with the new labour demand structure, computer-aided employment registration, incentives for legal business and other self-employment types. This is where international experience can be most helpful.

In the USA, over 11 million jobs were created between 1991 and 1997, generally in computer science, high-technology, export-oriented industries (e.g. aircraft, computer, pharmaceutics), entertainment and tourism and small-scale innovative business. Among the points of growth identified were the research production parks in California (software producers in the Silicone Valley creating 50,000 jobs in the late 1990s), North Carolina (biotechnology and pharmaceutics), Arizona (semi-conductor computer chips), Utah and Colorado (computers), etc.

On the other hand, extended demand for highly qualified engineers with an adequate knowledge of physics, mathematics and information technologies, managers, specialists in laser and biotechnologies, communication, medical services, robot engineering, show business, etc. was accompanied by unskilled and long-term labour unemployment. Many states therefore established 2-year professional colleges, often hosted by closed military bases. Some companies cover the costs of personnel training at evening colleges or universities.

The social safety net (welfare) reform in the USA means that 4 million citizens for many years (or even generations) entitled to unemployment benefits will look for work in the late 1990s, competing with 38 million Americans already available on unskilled labour markets. Young CIS residents with no up-to-date professional qualifications cannot expect employment in Europe or in the Middle East. In the 21st century, this labour type will be in abundance all over the world.

Radical changes have occurred in the structure of employment in the CIS countries. Firstly, there is no longer 100% employment. The proportion of unemployed working-age groups will grow from 15% in 1985 to 20%–25% by the early 21st century due to women with children. They will have fewer employment opportunities in some countries. Unemployment proportions will increase to 15%–20% in the countries deciding to close uncompetitive enterprises burdening the budget and depriving the economy of investments.

The share of hired labour will decrease. With the wage contribution to total income falling to 40%–45%, the share of business revenues increased to 40%–42%.

In 1999, the private sector was the dominant employer in Central Asian countries, Armenia, Georgia, Kazakhstan and Moldova. Proportions of non-hired labour (the self-employed, business owners, unpaid family members) were larger in Transcaucasian countries (38%–49%), Kazakhstan (42%), Moldova and Uzbekistan (31%); but only amounted to 10%–12% in Russia and the Ukraine and 5% in Belarus. Total unemployment in the CIS countries in 1999 (including job-seekers outside employment agencies) was over 13 million (10% of the economically active population). The proportions were particularly high in Russia (12%), Kazakhstan (14%) and the Ukraine (10%), even though artificially restricted through part-time arrangements.

Employment has decreased in industries and government agencies (due to military reductions and non-government health care, education, etc.) and is increasing in trade and services. According to the Association for Personnel Selection Consulting, the rate in Russia will decrease from 31% to 5% (sixfold) of the total population in the productive sphere and from 10.5% to 5% in government agencies and will increase from 5.5% to 32% in circulation between 1985 and 2005. In addition, there will be greater percentages of the unemployed (20% instead of 15%) and pensioners (18% instead of 14%) and smaller percentages of infants and school-age children (20% instead of 24%).

Overall CIS demand has been falling for mass professions and rising for up-to-date technologies, marketing, management and accounting. In addition, there are much fewer banking and finance vacancies. There is a stable demand for sales managers, lawyers, accountants and auditors, qualified specialists in the mining and chemical-metallurgy complex and computer technologies, and above all for anti-crisis and receivership managers.

In the long run, an effective employment infrastructure in the CIS countries should incorporate the following:

– An employment forecasting and strategic personnel marketing service (forecasting basic professional demand and required qualifications level).

– Government employment control agencies. Their functions in all the CIS countries are generally restricted to registration, allocation of benefits, resource collection (employment fund) and information on projected dismissals and available vacancies. Far less developed are services for small business and community work (building and repair of roads, lines of communication, drainage and irrigation systems; construction and reconstruction of housing, sports facilities, schools, hospitals, etc.; waste control; planning and development of areas, blocks of forests, hillsides; water store purification, etc.). Unemployment benefits are related to the most recent wage, thus both discriminating against new graduates and allow others to engage in illegal business rather than active job seeking.

– Personnel selection agencies. In 1998, there were over 200 such firms in Russia. The range of services in developed countries (as a percentage of GDP) is several tens of times greater. In the UK, for example, there are 15,000 agencies with a staff of 150,000. By corporate request, they can find any profession, qualifications, personal traits, etc..

– A social rehabilitation service for military discharges, the disabled, former convicts, involuntary immigrants, etc., including training, psychological correction, assistance in small business, etc.

Centres for continuous (postgraduate) education, professional orientation and evaluation of labour potentials (at universities and regional employment services).

Infrastructural development is an essential element of the necessary systematic change in the CIS countries. It is closely associated with structural improvements in the economy and the effective financial and budgetary government policy.

Field of Debate

1. What is the infrastructure? What are the characteristics of its development in the CIS countries?

2. Analyse developments in the banking and financial infrastructure in the CIS countries. Does it provide trust, leasing and factoring services? What changes can you suggest in this infrastructural sector? Analyse developments on the insurance and realty market.

3. How is the stock market arranged and what is its role in the modern economy? List the major agents on the stock market and the government agencies regulating stock issue and circulation.

4. What are the benefits of an integrated banking and financial infrastructure and a common stock market in the CIS?

5. Analyse the future prospects of the transport system in the CIS countries and its integration in the CIS infrastructure. What main transport lines are being built and designed on the threshold to the 21st century?

6. How is the energy system developing in the CIS countries? What are the benefits of an integrated energy system?

7. How is the communications infrastructure developing in the CIS countries? Identify the principal phases of telecommunications in the twentieth century. What are the benefits and the challenges of Internet use in the CIS countries?

8. What are the components of the environmental infrastructure? What are its challenges and future prospects in the 21st century?

9. Describe the components of the social infrastructure. What improvements can you suggest during the transition to a market-based economy? What international experience can be useful in this context?

10. What solutions can you suggest for the problem of excessive income differentiation, and how can the middle class be promoted in the CIS countries?

11. What are the main trends in the housing and utility reform?

12. Why is the pension reform urgently required?

13. How have public health and education been reformed?

14. What are the components of the employment infrastructure?

Chapter 5

TOWARDS A NEW STRUCTURE
OF PUBLIC ECONOMY

5.1 Science-Technology Core of Structural Reforms

Basic strategies of structural reform. The USSR had a highly specific technological structure of production, primarily noted for energy- and material intensity (two to three times that in developed countries) and a very expensive social infrastructure. The proportions were maintained through government-subsidised low prices on raw materials, mainly metals and fuels, and transport tariffs, social subsidies to enterprises, government investments in fixed assets and environmental control. As a result, even the internationally non-competitive (due to outdated process technologies) branches, such as machine building, light industry, construction and the AIC, had been profitable prior to transition to market economy.

On conversion to world prices many enterprises suffered losses and could neither export their products nor compete with imports on the domestic market, even though the wages were traditionally low. During the first years of reforms they survived by using their monopolistic positions to raise domestic prices. However, this pre-market structure of national economy cannot be maintained for long because it fails to secure sustained development.

Divergent prices for industrial goods and agricultural products provoke the well-justified rural protest, with a dramatic drop in effective demand opening up two avenues: maintaining lower than world energy prices, subsidising loss-making branches and increasing the money supply, while restricting imports with high duties (the road taken by the Ukraine and Belarus in the 1990s), or price liberalisation with tighter constraints on money supply, abolished subsidies and prohibitive tariffs (Moldova, Kyrgyzstan and Russia). The former inevitably involves high inflation rates, energy shortages and loss of IMF credits, and the latter results in, among other things, rapidly declining production, increasing unemployment and exports of irrecoverable resources, and domestic markets lost by national producers. Both are unacceptable in terms of long-term national interests.

The CIS economy needs a radical transformation of the branch structure of production inherited from the USSR. The structure must ensure cost efficiency, i.e. maximising GDP output per unit labour and natural resources by extending the sphere of services, research-intensive products and final manufacturing stages. National economic safety requires maximum possible food and energy autonomy, reasonable balancing of exported irrecoverable resources and imported competitive goods, and sufficient jobs for the young and those discharged from the military. Realistic integration in international economic relationships is inconceivable without industrial priorities, the relevant infrastructure and co-operation mainly with neighbouring and friendly States in the development, production and maintenance of a wide variety of required equipment. The investment complex and the technology core much needed in every CIS member country can be derived from the military-industrial complex (MIC). This is where radical innovations have been devised to secure highly profitable niches on the world market and to transform national industries.

In this context an overview of structural changes in seven industrial countries in the 1970s and 1980s is helpful.

The *scope of change* was governed by increased share of services in GNP (repair, finance, insurance, real estate transactions, and information, social and private services): by 13% in Japan, 16% in Germany, 11% in France and 8.8% in the USA, with reduced contributions from agriculture (by 9.5%, 4.1%, 6.7% and 1.8%, respectively) and industry (by 13%, 16%, 11% and 9%, respectively), increased share of high-technology branches in industry (computer-, aircraft- and space engineering, office equipment, communications, transistors) and the share of traditional industries decreased (metallurgy, textile, oil refining, metal-working). Accordingly, jobs were transferred from agriculture and industry to financial, municipal and social services, trade, tourism and recreation.

The *focuses* of structural transformation differed in three industrial branch groups defined by high, medium and low growth rates. Significant growth over the past 25 years in France, UK and USA was only evident in high-technology industries, with output in the remaining branches typically reduced.

The fastest structural transformation was carried out in Japan. Growth rates in high-technology industries there (7.2% in 1970–1985) were twice those in G-7 nations (including the USA), largely owing to extended exports and high-technology imports replaced with domestic products (which EU member states failed to achieve).

The input-output analysis suggests five major *factors* governing the scope and focus of structural change: a) ultimate domestic consumption (demand); b) exports; c) import of complete products; d) import of intermediary products; and e) technological transformations.

Analysis of shifts in employment structure reveals the sixth factor: change in the productivity of labour in 33 branches classified into five groups by technology level. The use of fixed prices ensures the high extent of inter-state correlation. Regretfully, this factor is still unavailable in CIS countries.

The primary role in long-term economic transformations (e.g. not related to temporary shortage of raw materials, inter-enterprise arrears) belongs to technological transformations, international trade and economic reorganisation. Thus, the increased share of the financial sector is generally associated with intensified use of services provided by banks, investment, insurance, pension and venture funds.

Technological transformations produce the change in domestic demand for products of different branches. In a market economy both the public and the enterprises use more high-technology products (time- and resource-saving high-quality goods and services) and fewer low-technology ones. This proved to be a more effective factor than foreign imports

High-technology industries are generally stimulated by exports (excepting computer engineering where domestic demand was crucial in all the countries, excluding Germany and Canada). Domestic outputs in medium- and low-technology industries in developed countries (especially the USA, UK and France) were increasingly replaced with imports. Yet, on the whole, this did not play a decisive role in structural transformations.

Productivity growth largely influences employment patterns. Therefore, in high-technology branches employment increased and in other branches decreased slower than did the output. Productivity growth decelerated with initial computerisation in the sphere of services, enhancing the role of this sphere on the labour market.

Analysis indicates significant differences in the intensity of structural transformations in different countries. Due to superior growth rates in high-technology branches, Japan emerged the only country with industrial share in GDP increased. Industrial revenues generally grew in Canada, France and Germany, due to export trade, and in Australia and the USA, due to domestic consumption.

Imports affected domestic production in the USA and some other countries. In two of them, contrary to the general trend, the share of extractive branches increased: agriculture in Australia and oil mining in the UK. Only in Canada and Germany did the share of employment in medium-technology industries increase (car, chemical, rubber and plastics, non-ferrous metallurgy, transport and non-electric machinery).

International classification differentiates between high-technology and low-technology industries. The classifications for high-technology industries are: 1) aircraft engineering; 2) computer engineering and office equipment;

3) communications and transistor engineering; 4) pharmaceuticals; 5) tool and lathe making; and 6) electrical engineering and machinery. The classifications for low-technology industries are: 1) brick and glass; 2) food and tobacco; 3) oil refining; 4) ferrous metallurgy; 5) forest, paper and wood processing; 6) textile, clothing, leather and footwear; and 7) metal work. An intermediary group includes car industry, shipbuilding, agriculture, machine building and non-ferrous metallurgy.

This classification starts from R&D costs per gross output. But it takes no account of indirect R&D costs associated with the purchase of research-intensive devices, equipment and semi-finished products. Current and adjusted price analyses produce different results. Thus, over 25 years the contribution of computer engineering to output increased by a factor of ten at fixed prices and only doubled at current prices (due to a sharp price drop per unit efficiency).

Conclusions about other countries cannot be automatically extended to the CIS. The industrial share in GDP at current prices has been consistently decreasing in the USA since 1997. This seemed indicative of a U.S. "de-industrialisation". Far more important in this context is the employment structure, since industrial productivity in the USA increased by 2.9% annually in the 1980s and only by 1% in other branches.

A significant contribution to the theory of structural transformation measurement was made by V. Leontiev. Input-output analysis demonstrates why high-growth-rate branches include both high technologies and also plastics and rubber, and even non-production branches such as communications, finance and insurance, real estate and business services. Developed economies categorise branches by absolute growth as follows: real estate and business services, personal services, wholesale and retail trade, finance and insurance, communications engineering, computers and office equipment, construction, transport and store, food, and car industry (even though growth rates are typically low in the construction and food industry).

The negative- or both relative- and absolute low-growth-rate branches include: extractive industries, metal work, brick and glass, textile, timber and furniture, and ferrous metallurgy. In this case production and services are not differentiated. Thus, for instance, among the major inputs to General Motors (with 2 million personnel along with their families insured, i.e. over 1% of U.S. population), rather than other industries, are medical insurance and health care companies (annual $2 billion in the 1980s). Over 20% of the outputs are represented by financial services (e.g. sales financing). The share of earnings from repair (including round-the-clock road services) and technical servicing has grown.

International experience suggests that effective structural transformations are favoured by stronger requirements on environmental safety, health care, personnel qualifications, developments in the social infrastructure and national culture, and the lifting of trade barriers. Of particular importance is government contribution to the transfer of technologies from the MIC civilian industries and the imports of high-technology intermediary products (networks, semi-finished products, process lines). Imports also increased in the 1980s and 1990s in such developed countries as USA, Japan, UK and France.

Economic restructuring is not the sum of isolated changes but rather an integral social and economic process involving joint stock and other types of joint ownership, electronic capital transfer and data communication networks and on-line computer-aided decision making. Consequently, commodity prices are increasingly dominated by services (insurance, marketing and management, futures and follow-up, personnel training) rather than by material costs or industrial wages. Added value has been increasingly generated in the sphere of services. Economic classification by sector (productive vs. non-productive) or group (e.g. I, II) is no longer meaningful.

Government policy in this context should be increasingly focused on the infrastructure systems governing effective branch integration (roads and transport, communications, science and education, market infrastructure) rather than individual branches or industries. Investments in wholesale trade, store and information networks are more efficient presently than direct investments in production.

More than one half of the goods priced in developed countries are generated in the sphere of trade. Restructuring in response to advances in science and technology and expanded international trade in the 1970s and 1980s generally involved high and medium technologies. In the 1990s accelerated transformations of technology and structure in services made this sphere follow industries into the realm of international competition and thus become subject to cyclical change. Services represented 22% of total international trade in the early 1990s and over 40% of exports to France, Japan, UK and USA (e.g. including technology transfer, license trade, turnkey building contracts).

The services share in GDP has been increasing in developed countries. The proportion of industrial outputs in GDP fell from 27% to 13% in the USA from 1960 to 1995, from 36% to 27% in Japan from 1970 to 1993, from 32% to 26% in Germany from 1985 to 1993, and to less than 20% in France.

Structural shifts in different branches are governed by different combinations of many factors. High-technology branches depend generally on change and volume in exports, and services (e.g. communications) on internal demand. Textile and footwear industries are most sensitive to imports, i.e. competitive low-wage importers. Central government and regional structural policy is related largely to taxation of investments and budget R&D expenditure. Most significant consequences, including political, are associated with budget financing and credit allocations for structural purposes (e.g. enterprise reconstruction and relocation, structural unemployment benefits, a regional infrastructure for new enterprises).

Very often structural policy in one branch affects another. Thus, for instance, a protectionist import policy (e.g. higher import duties on transistors) will cause a rise in prices for the products with the consequent high costs of transistor-based electronics, decreased domestic demand, expanded exports of complete products and, eventually, adverse effects on trade-balance structure. Policy has become increasingly international. A structural policy cannot be effective without agreeing on, or at least accounting for, its impact on trade in the CIS.

Analysis of the factors governing structural change in gross output in 35 branches in the USA indicates an intensive industrial growth amounting to 2% (7.7% in high-technology branches), including that related to increased domestic demand for finished products +2.4% (+6.4%), increased exports +0.1% (+1.7%) and imports to replace finished products +0.01% (−0.04%). As a result, industrial employment grew by 14.8 million (13.9 million in high technologies, with a decrease of 1.3 million in backward branches), including changes owing to increased domestic demand +19.4% (+14.4%), exports +1.4% (+1.1%), imports −1.8% (−0.5%) and increased productivity −3.8% (−2.7%).

Changes were also evident in CIS national economies in the 1990s. The share of GDP (costs of goods and services produced in branches of economy and intended for final consumption, accumulation and net exports) produced in the non-public sector, including the private one, increased. Small enterprises employing 9.5 million (altogether 45 million earning income in small business) account for almost 14% of industrial outputs in Russia. The share of services increased from 32.4% to 52% of GDP. The proportion of gross profits (enterprises profits, business gains, depreciation accumulation) increased, with the wage share decreasing. Final national consumption costs also increased (to 69% of GDP in Russia), with a lower share of increase in the stock of material current assets (from 13%–15% to 3.3%) and industrial investments (gross national saving amounting to 27%). The GDP changes, production and use structure are illustrated in Tables 11–13.

In the meantime, high-technology branches have been deteriorating. The CIS is being transformed into a region incapable of independent expanded accumulation and exchanging irrecoverable natural resources for imported intellectual goods. This renders sustainable development impossible.

One typical case relates to trade and economic relations with the EU. In the mid-1990s CIS exports to the EU (23 billion ecu) exceeded imports (annual 18 billion ecu), owing to favourable net balance of trade in Russia (over 6 billion ecu) and Central Asian member countries. However, the CIS export structure was dominated by raw materials and metals (crude oil and petroleum products accounting for 27%), with only 25% of imports represented by industrial equipment and technologies. The CIS imports of cosmetics, furniture, jewellery, beverages, domestic electronics (e.g. video equipment, stereo systems) and cars of prestigious make increased several tens of times during the 1990s.

Table 11

Changes in Gross Domestic Product in the 1990s by CIS Country

At adjusted prices, 1990=100%

Country	1991	1992	1993	1994	1995	1996	1998 of 1991 (1991=100%)
Azerbaijan	99.0	77	59	48	42	42	49.7
Armenia	88.0	51	47	49	53	56	70.0
Belarus	99.0	89	83	72	65	66	80.2
Georgia	79.0	44	31	33	35	38	45.5
Kazakhstan	89.0	84	75	66	61	61	69.0
Kyrgyzstan	92.0	79	67	54	51	54	65.9
Moldova	83.0	59	58	69*	68*	62*	57.9*
Russia	95.0	81	74	65	62	59	60.6
Tajikistan	...	100	84	66	58	48	51.5
Turkmenistan	...	100	102	85	78	78	...
Uzbekistan	99.5	89	86	82	81	82	91.1
Ukraine	91.0	82	71	54	48	43	44.8
Across the Commonwealth	94.0	81	73	63	60	57	59.5

At adjusted prices, in % of preceding year

	1991	1992	1993	1994	1995	1996	1997	1998***
Azerbaijan	99.3	77.4	76.9	80.3	88.0	101.3	105.8	109.1
Armenia	88.3	58.2	91.2	105.4	106.9	105.8	103.0	106.7
Belarus	98.8	90.4	92.4	87.4	89.6	102.6	110.0	112.5
Georgia	78.9	55.1	70.7	108.7	103.3	111.2	111.0	108.9
Kazakhstan	89.0	94.7	89.4	87.4	91.8	101.1	102.0	102.1
Kyrgyzstan	92.2	86.1	84.5	79.9	94.6	105.6	110.0	105.0
Moldova	82.5	71.0	98.8	69.1	98.1	92.0*	101.3	95.8
Russia	95.0	85.5	91.3	87.3	95.9	95.1	100.4	99.5
Tajikistan	...	...	82.7	87.3	87.6	83.3	101.7	102.6
Turkmenistan	...	...	101.5	83.3	92.3	100.1	85.0**	...
Uzbekistan	99.5	88.9	97.7	94.8	98.8	101.6	105.2	104.0
Ukraine	91.3	90.1	85.8	77.1	87.8	90.0	97.0	100.2
Across the Commonwealth	94.0	86.1	90.3	86.0	94.7	95.4	100.7	100**

* In % of 1993.
** Estimated.
*** 1st semester.

Table 12

Value Structure of GDP

Country	GDP	Wage	Gross profit and gross revenue mix	Net taxes on production and imports (minus subsidies)
Azerbaijan				
1991	100	52.3	41.2	6.5
1995	100	22.6	69.5	7.9
1996	100	18.8	70.2	11.0
Armenia				
1991	100	53.0	41.1	5.9
1995	100	39.3	55.7	5.0
1996	100	40.0	53.5	6.5
Belarus				
1991	100	41.9	53.1	5.0
1995	100	43.7	42.5	13.8
1997	100	44.8	37.6	17.6
Georgia				
1991	100	53.9	36.6	9.5
1995	100	37.1	56.8	6.1
1997	100	22.6	72.7	4.7
Kazakhstan				
1991	100	42.4	51.4	6.2
1995	100	36.9	52.9	10.2
1996	100	37.1	53.3	9.6
Kyrgyzstan				
1991	100	47.1	47	5.9
1995	100	37.8	52.1	10.1
1997	100	32.2	57.4	10.4
Moldova				
1991	100	58.3	32.1	9.6
1995*	100	45.4	39.9	14.7
1996*	100	44.5	42.2	13.3
Russia				
1991	100	43.7	51.9	4.4
1995	100	43.4	45.2	11.4
1997	100	46.7	37.9	15.4
Tajikistan				
1992	100	57.0	49.3	−7.8
1995	100	29.2	65.2	5.6
Turkmenistan				
1995	100	33.1	55.1	11.8
Uzbekistan				
1991	100	65.2	34.1	0.7
1995	100	42.5	33.0	24.5
1996	100	36.8	45.3	17.9
Ukraine				
1991	100	58.9	44.8	−3.7
1995	100	43.5	37.4	19.1
1997	100	47.6	30.0	22.4

* Excluding the Dniester river left-bank area and the town of Bendery.

Table 13

Structure of GDP Output in Some CIS Countries

Country	GDP	Goods	Services	Net taxes on products (minus subsidies)
Azerbaijan				
1991	100	61.2	33.1	5.7
1992	100	62.9	31.0	8.6
1993	100	59.7	41.8	4.9
1994	100	60.2	42.7	2.0
1995	100	56.4	37.9	7.7
Armenia				
1991	100	70.4	24.9	5.4
1992	100	64.5	29.6	8.2
1993	100	74.7	21.4	5.0
1994	100	79.5	20.7	3.1
1995	100	73.1	26.8	3.6
Belarus				
1991	100	68.5	29.0	4.0
1992	100	68.3	28.6	4.8
1993	100	54.3	47.9	6.2
1994	100	47.4	49.9	9.4
1995	100	50.1	43.5	9.8
Georgia				
1991	100	61.6	31.7	7.2
1992	100	74.6	24.7	1.2
1993	100	75.2	19.8	5.5
1994	100	74.5	24.5	2.1
1995	100	58.0	37.8	6.9
Kazakhstan				
1991	100	66.6	36.5	−0.7
1992	100	65.1	35.5	4.6
1993	100	55.7	44.8	6.1
1994	100	56.4	41.6	3.3
1995	100	42.3	53.4	4.9
Kyrgyzstan				
1991	100	69.8	26.3	4.6
1992	100	73.9	22.3	4.6
1993	100	69.9	27.8	4.6
1994	100	62.5	33.6	6.2
1995	100	59.0	35.4	7.4

Country	GDP	Goods	Services	Net taxes on products (minus subsidies)
Moldova				
1991	100	60.9	32.7	9.1
1992	100	65.5	25.2	11.7
1993*	100	73.5	29.6	1.0
1994*	100	63.2	34.1	6.6
1995*	100	57.8	32.9	11.5
Russia				
1991	100	61.8	36.7	3.7
1992	100	49.6	52.6	1.8
1993	100	48.2	46.2	9.1
1994	100	47.0	49.1	7.8
1995	100	46.2	46.7	8.4
1996	100	43.3	48.3	8.9
Tajikistan				
1991	100	...	...	...
1992	100	77.7	30.2	7.9
1993	100	62.5	27.6	9.9
1994	100	45.3	32.6	22.1
1995	100	59.6	30.8	9.6
1996	100	56.2	31.7	12.1
Uzbekistan				
1991	100	74.3	26.2	–0.3
1992	100	72.0	29.9	–0.9
1993	100	59.3	33.8	9.4
1994	100	58.9	36.2	8.2
1995	100	52.5	37.3	13.2
Ukraine				
1991	100	79.6	30.5	–8.0
1992	100	73.6	33.1	–2.5
1993	100	59.0	48.6	0.6
1994	100	57.2	38.2	10.3
1995	100	51.9	39.8	10.6

* Excluding the Dniester river left-bank area and the town of Bendery.

Restructuring in CIS national economies has the following three inter-related goals: 1) preservation and development of their scientific and technological potential, involving government assistance and conversion in aircraft, rocket space, telecommunications, nuclear and shipbuilding industries, and exports of arms and armaments; 2) establishment of an independent financial base for export-competitive extractive industries (oil, gas, ore, diamond, forestry) and the chemical-metallurgy complex, with intensive processing and comprehensive recovery of raw materials; 3) use of foreign investments to improve the product mix and technologies in backward branches (e.g. car industry, computer engineering). These should be protected against competitive imports within the limits admissible by international standards.

Programs of structural reform have been formulated in many CIS countries. Future plans in Russia include a decrease in the share of extractive industries from 16% to 10% between 1995 and 2010. The Ukraine has devised a 25-year restructuring program.

A rational structure of national economy cannot be created in the short run and through market incentives only. An active government policy is needed, involving reformed taxation, a new budget policy, antimonopoly regulation, and resolution of the investment crisis (discussed in Chap. 7). Structural reform can only be accomplished through a transition from standard external trade to sustained industrial co-operation within the CIS and with other European and Asian countries.

In addition, account should be taken of differences in GDP structure. The wage share in GDP in the mid-1990s varied from 21% to 23% (Georgia and Azerbaijan) and 43% to 46% (Belarus, Moldova, Russia, Uzbekistan, Ukraine); that of taxes from 2% to 8% (Transcaucasia) and 25% (Uzbekistan, Tajikistan) (see Tables 12 and 13). Gross savings in fixed capital were much higher in Uzbekistan (33%), Azerbaijan and Belarus (25%–28%) than in Georgia (9%), Moldova, Kazakhstan and Armenia (16%–18%). At the same time, the government share in final GDP consumption was at its highest in Moldova, Russia, Uzbekistan and the Ukraine (28%–32%), and at a minimum in Georgia and Armenia (5%–10%) with the bulk represented by households (exceeding total GDP in Armenia in 1997, due to foreign aid).

The mechanism of structural transformation in national economy involves elimination of inefficient and unpromising, reorganisation and restructuring of potentially efficient and establishment of new enterprises basing on latest achievements in science and technology, mainly in top-priority branches. The first target has not been attained in any CIS country. Preferential credit and subsidies (budget and non-budget allocations to the AIC and coal industry comprising 1% of GDP) prevent bankruptcy of loss-making enterprises and the associated upsurge of unemployment, while maintaining multiple inefficient jobs, reducing real income among the formally employed and, more importantly, destroying incentives for high-productive work, production updating and adequate management.

Science-technology core of economy. Resource intensity and competitiveness of national economy are determined by its academic and research and development potentials. The *academic potential* is the totality of financial (budget and non-budget), information, personnel, material and machinery, and organisational resources involved in research- (both fundamental and applied), development- (experimental, process, design, organisational) and innovation projects.

Between the 1950s and 1980s a substantial academic potential had been accumulated in the territory currently under the CIS jurisdiction, mainly in physics and mathematics, chemistry and engineering. By contrast to the rest of the world, however, academic research was exclusively government supported (e.g. the U.S. government only covering one third of the costs), with resources allocated to branches (ministries and academies) and institutes rather than individual innovation projects. No consideration whatever was given to actual efficiency. The academic community was not concerned with commercial importance of their work because the grants were not competitive.

The *research and development potential* is the totality of R&D results available for industrial and commercial use. This is described by:

– Total R&D outputs and exports, including the costs of completed and accepted R&D projects, prototypes, computer software and engineering services (expert, consulting, copyright, process and know-how licensing, feasibility studies and business plans, personnel training, innovatory arrangements)

– Total patents, both national and international, for inventions, industrial designs and selective achievements, and utility certificates

– Proceeds from license trade in patents and *know-how* (engineering and commercial information ensuring competitive benefits for the holder, protected against unauthorised access and not publicly available)

– Total outputs and exports of *research-intensive products* protected by patents, with their price containing a significant R&D share (over 10%–15%)

National R&D potential is governed by the available and effectively used academic potential, above all by the extent of its concentration in the more promising technological progress trends, i.e. competitive spheres of R&D activities aimed at urgent short-term goals of national economic development. In CIS countries these include resource and energy saving, environmental safety, telecommunications, biology and physico-chemical foundations for extractive and processing industries. As opposed to fundamental research, these are concerned with GDP increase in a given country rather than more developed economies securing immediate application of scientific discoveries.

Promising R&D trends are represented by *critically important technologies* constituting the technological framework of economy. Critically important in CIS countries are: new processes in oil production, including sea-shelf mining, gas transport, environmentally safe open-cast coal and ore mining, new alloys and construction materials, genetic engineering, fine biological, chemical and electrophysical (including laser) technologies. Up-to-date information- and electronic technologies, e.g. nanotechnology and cryo-nanoelectronics, enhance productivity of labour while reducing the consumption of natural resources.

The four basic trends in high technologies identified in the EU in the late 1990s are: a new generation of cost-efficient and environmentally clean aircraft, educational multimedia (in 1996 there were 3 computers per 100 school pupils in France and 11 in the USA), low- or zero-emission motor cars, and water management and protection technologies. The EU research budget (over 13 billion ecu) also provides for new railway and water transport, anti-viral vaccines and some other projects.

The R&D statistics in EU countries and the USA include detailed data on the structure of R&D costs by application source and focus, their impact on industrial competitiveness and foreign trade, and specialised staff involved (including engineers and calculated per full-time working day). Special emphasis is attached to inventions and patents, innovations and available firms engaged in R&D, promotion and consulting activities. The data provide a basis for trade and payment balances concerning research and technological products, and license export/import ratios.

Special attention should be given in CIS countries to the management and evaluation of the *R&D level of production* in basic national economic complexes – the degree of sophistication and the competitive qualities of products (e.g. the share of up-to-date, research-intensive and export competitive products), processes (mainly the extent of using computers and information technologies, unit supply/material costs, harmful discharge) and production facilities (e.g. average time of using computer technologies used). These are essential for international comparisons and cost-efficiency analysis of R&D programs. It is noteworthy that in the late twentieth century 85% of GDP growth in developed economies is provided by innovatory techniques and technologies and production management and administration strategies, rather than increased mining outputs or outdated standard production.

While abolishing the previous administrative governance of research and branch R&D foundations liquidating, the current reform failed to establish a market framework. R&D organisations in CIS countries have lost the bulk of orders from MIC while material and energy costs, as well as municipal payments, increased dramatically under price liberalisation. Co-operative research arrangements were abandoned, partly because of the lacking business-trip allowances. Some members of the CIS research community emigrated to Russia or far abroad, or else joined commercial structures. The average R&D wage in CIS countries is almost one order of magnitude lower than that of a bank officer.

The R&D potential in CIS countries has been endangered by reduced government purchases and effective industrial demand for innovations, and the rupture of traditional links. There was a drastic decline of R&D output (e.g. completed research and development projects, prototypes, engineering services). The share in total CIS GDP decreased, despite its crucial role for the competitive positions of national economy in the twenty-first century. Indeed, it fell below 1% of GDP in all countries, with the exception of the Ukraine (see Table 14), compared with 3% in the USA, Germany and Japan, and 2% in the UK and France. This is even more alarming against the background of GDP increasing in most countries outside the CIS.

Analysis of the composition of R&D products in the CIS indicates a significant reduction of the proportion of R&D products and services immediately involved in updating (excepting Russia, Azerbaijan and Tajikistan). The reason is the current financing under enterprise contracts rather than from the government budget.

There have been drastic staff reductions, more than by half in Armenia, Tajikistan, Uzbekistan, Belarus and Moldova (see Table 14), generally in branch of research centres and industrial R&D departments. On the whole the number of research workers and development engineers over a period of only 4 years decreased from 1,590,000 to 940,000 (by 40%) across the CIS and from 81% to 68% in Russia. The faculty at universities engaged in research was also reduced.

There are fewer holders of doctorate and candidate scientific degrees now (269,900 instead of 316,300), in particular in Armenia, Kazakhstan (decrease of 40%–45%), Moldova, Uzbekistan and Russia. This involves the outflow of superior qualified staff. Among the reasons are the low remunerations, especially as compared with industries or business, mainly in Tajikistan, Kazakhstan, Armenia, Azerbaijan and Russia.

Machinery and equipment updating has been actually stopped, thus inhibiting new developments. One proof is the lower proportion of active (e.g. machinery and equipment) fixed assets in their total value: from 53%–59% to 34% in Russia and Azerbaijan, and as low as 20% in the Ukraine.

Findings from special surveys indicate that two thirds of enterprises in Russia and some other CIS countries, including over half of the machine-building plants, actually abandoned innovatory activities in 1997. Over 300 competitive technologies have been lost in the 1990s.

Yet competitive positions have been maintained in some physico-chemical technologies, including lasers and electronics, in Russia, electrified welding and super-solid materials in the Ukraine, and non-ferrous metallurgy in Kazakhstan. With this potential dismantled, CIS countries will be transformed as extractive adjuncts to Europe and the USA, and probably to the rapidly advancing Asian countries.

Table 14

Changes in Academic Potential in CIS Countries in the 1990s

Country	R & D output (in % of GDP)		R & D products and services (in % of total R & D costs)		R & D staff (in 1000s of persons)		Degree holders among the staff (in 1000s of persons)		Wage (in % of average) 1995	Share of active fixed assets (in % of total value)	
	1990	1995	1991	1995	1991	1995	1991	1995	1995	1991	1995
Azerbaijan	1.0	0.3	37	40	16.4	13.1	10.1	10.5	109	53	34
Armenia	2.5	0.2*	61	47	17.2	6.3	4.7	2.6	87	42	...
Belarus	2.3	1.0	69	55	59.3	26.9	10.1	9.3	108	64	48
Georgia	1.2	0.1	26	25	33.6	21.5	10.0	10.5	...	...	...
Kazakhstan	0.7	0.3	41	39	27.6	18.0	9.3	5.6	96	49	43
Kyrgyzstan	0.7	0.3	42	14	5.7	3.6	1.6	1.9	121	53	46
Moldova	1.6	0.8	59	26	12.8	5.8	3.5	2.6	137	61	59
Russia	3.0	0.8	59	66	1079.0	641.0	194.0	163.0	85	59	34
Tajikistan	0.7	0.1	40	42	4.4	1.8	2.0	1.6	120	50	29
Turkmenistan	0.7	0.6	43	...	5.7	5.1	1.2	1.7	120	38	36
Uzbekistan	1.2	0.4	65	45	41.3	16.9	13.9	10.8	122	55	44
Ukraine	2.3	1.3	66	54	295.0	180.0	55.9	49.8	101	59	20

* 1994.

Extreme natural conditions (90% of mineral resources located in northern, and in Central Asia and Transcaucasia in mountain and desert areas) and long distances to international market centres govern the higher production costs and the need for additional R&D investments in CIS countries. A guideline can be provided by their proportion in GDP in developed countries, during the 1980s varying between 1.8% in France and 2.7%–2.9% in the USA, Germany and Japan (including non-military: 1.5%–2.9%).

Conversion of the military-industrial complex. The military-industrial complex (MIC) plays a key role in CIS industry. The MIC has been formally independent of other branches, with typically high supplies discipline and production quality ensured by military inspection, along with the low cost-efficiency and high extent of co-operation.

The MIC comprises three branch blocks. Reorientation to exports was comparatively easy in mining enterprises and specialised metallurgy. Manufacturing of accessories and components in CIS countries was most adversely affected by the rupture of economic contacts with rocket-space, aircraft and shipbuilding industries in Russia and the Ukraine. The third block, arms and armaments production, was exposed to a shock treatment of lost orders and co-operative arrangements.

The first conversion program formulated in the 1980s was never implemented because of the non-market orientation. The MIC enterprises were to be involved in the production of domestic and agricultural machinery, only efficient in the context of permanent shortages. In an open economy the MIC-manufactured washing machines, electric razors, and equipment for light and food industries could not compete, either in price or in quality, with the products of TNCs with their international reputations and long experience in the sphere.

Conversion programs of the early 1990s also failed because of inadequate inter-state co-ordination within the CIS. Russia and some other countries attempted to substitute domestic production for supplies from their neighbours, both increasing the costs and impairing the competitiveness. In addition, inadequate budget resources impeded target-program conversion management.

Conversion in the MIC involves reform in the structure and economic relationships with a view of integrating the academic and R&D potentials in a market-oriented national economic complex. Conversion in the short run involves:

– New organisational and legal status of MIC enterprises via corporatisation, with only predominantly military outputs retained in government ownership (as joint stock companies, unitarian enterprises or State works)

– Co-operative arrangements between most manufacturers of accessories and components (especially electronic) and foreign corporations, to maintain and develop their production potential

– Reduced number of military producers, generally through their re-orientation as competitive research-intensive engineering complexes in oil and gas production, mining, chemical and telecommunications and other solvent industries

– Re-focusing defence technologies and military bases on civilian lines, dual-purpose technologies, especially in measurements and communications, office equipment, medical, environmental and transport engineering

– Reduced serial production of arms and armaments for internal purposes, with expanded exports, CIS-wide unification and standardisation, and accelerated improvement of the product mix, employing high-precision computer-aided up-to-date technologies

In the rest of the world MICs have been typically represented by major corporate groupings in the late twentieth century. Super-corporations emerge, enlisting government assistance in their struggle for international outlets, e.g. U.S. aerospace industrial outputs ($125 billion in 1997) increase by 10%–12% annually, with profits (over $8 billion) doubled over the decade.

In CIS countries there has been a division of major research production complexes and property rights. Thus, for instance, under corporatisation in the world's largest rocket-space complex "Energia" (town of Korolev, Moscow region) 62% shares were allocated to the working collective. The shares were bought up (at seven times the initial price by outsiders) under commercial launching contracts (accounting for over half of the revenues), thus posing the risk of lost control.

Over 130 MIC enterprises in Kazakhstan were transformed as joint stock companies or state holdings in the 1990s, e.g. Kopray (machine building and electronics) or Kateg (uranium mining and processing). Research and production associations, e.g. Biomedpreparat (in Stepnogorsk) and Khimprom (in Pavlodar), were maintained and, consequently, the branch management, even though no military orders were forthcoming. Like in other CIS countries, conversion in Kazakhstan initially relied on government financing (firms only affording 5%–6% of the projected 2.9 billion tenge and over 1 billion for 1995–2000) rather than inter-republican co-operation in research-intensive civilian production, entering the world market and replacement of foreign exchange imports of equipment. With inadequate government preferential credit, civilian outputs amounted to several dozen elementary items produced on a minor scale. Due to decreased defence outputs (e.g. by 30% in 1991, 50% in 1992, 80% in 1993), operation of some plants (e.g. one of the two in Tselinnyi mining combine) was discontinued and valued qualified personnel discharged. Civilian proceeds were inadmissibly low due to the high conversion costs and inadequate internal demand.

This problem can only be approached with a joint program focusing on a common market, using the proceeds from development, production and sales of the much needed products in the CIS and their contiguous States' technology systems and medical, environmental and security equipment, rather than mere mass products (the "sauce-pan conversion").

Experience in Germany and other developed countries suggests the establishment of regional designing and building firms to transform the abandoned military immovables (buildings, communications, transport lines, vacant areas) as innovation, environmental and industrial centres working for export- (generally accessories and components) and import-replacing orders. Regional firms would be needed to handle the reclamation of ships, weapons (including nuclear) and armoured machinery, as well as sales (including export) of the released property. Regretfully, many abandoned military bases in Russia, Kazakhstan and some other CIS countries have actually been plundered.

Multiple MIC enterprises in all CIS countries have been completely converted along civilian lines. Thus, for instance, Razdanmash (Armenia) manufactures motor cultivators, water pumps and turbines exported to Turkmenistan and other countries, instead of radar and AA facilities. The ball-bearing plant in Vologda winning the QS-9000 certificate (the highest international standard) provides inputs for Ford (USA) and Daewoo (South Korea), having created 3000 new jobs. The State-owned complex Splav (Tula), having added six more plants in other towns, employs an original cross-cut rolling process for volley tubes in civilian production. The MIC plants in some CIS countries manufacture water-purifying systems (total world sales of this equipment type exceeding $7 billion). But more than half of MIC plants faced the risk of insolvency, having lost government and inter-government support.

Russia initiated restructuring in the defence complex in late 1990s. Production facilities will be cut by one third, i.e. instead of 2000 there will be 400 basic enterprises concentrating the mobilisation capacities and defence orders. The many joint stock companies finding their market niches unassisted by the government will be relieved from mobilisation capacities and the social sphere.

The progress of conversion is closely associated with military reform in CIS countries. Of major economic importance are the following aspects:

– Defining the reasonable and sufficient amount of armed forces, starting from the nature of expected danger, national economic potentials and populations. The armed forces comprised 1.2%–1.3% of the population in the USSR, and 0.5%–0.7% in most CIS countries in the late 1990s. Projected reductions in CIS countries will amount to 0.5%–0.8% by the early twenty-first century, which poses the question of employment opportunities for several hundred thousand people.

– Legal limited sizes of military expenditure in GDP and total budget expenditures. Exorbitant defence expenditure growth will cause lower investments, deteriorating living standards, as well as backwards social and environmental infrastructures. In the 1980s U.S. military spending exceeded 5% of GDP (including an internal force, National Guard), varying between 2% and 4% in most other countries and estimated between 8% and 13% in the USSR. In the 1990s, with the declining national revenues and an urgent need for a range of social programs (e.g. health care, education, science), CIS countries must reduce the proportion to 3%–5%.

– An integrated comprehensive plan of military developments, involving the most effective national security strategies with available resources: enhanced production of up-to-date, mainly computer-equipped arms and armaments on a basis of extensive co-operation and standardisation; personnel selection and military training systems combining professional and called-up service; and shared costs of the military infrastructure and rational administration.

– Rational management of military releases, joint updating and exports of equipment. Thus, for instance, by 1998 military building industries in Russia (with the staff exceeding 20,000) involved 24 major plants manufacturing construction components and equipment, dozens of building and assembly firms, depots, repair facilities, machine-building firms, and 4,500 items of heavy machinery. Their reasonable privatisation will enable defence and civilian orders to be serviced under contracts with significant resource savings.

Restoration of academic links is a special case. The International Russia-EU-USA-Japan centre for science and engineering sponsors 180 R&D projects in Russia, Kazakhstan, Georgia, Belarus and Armenia, worth over $75 million.

The economic mechanism to save the MIC academic potential in the process of conversion and market-oriented reform involves government R&D inventory and regulation of its contribution to total military expenditure. Thus, for instance, to evaluate the potential of research and technological organisations in GDR, Germany's federal authorities established an independent academic board. On its recommendations, 11 branch research organisations were reorganised as national research centres or their affiliations, 22 assigned to the Federal Ministry of Research and Technology, 8 to universities, 4 to federal scientific societies, about 100 branch departments and Lands, and over 100 liquidated. Total R&D staff was reduced 1.8 times, and financing for the remaining organisations provided from the federal and local budgets (with 45% from firm orders). Almost 90% of vacancies were filled by competing staff members. In the U.S. reductions under conversion involved personnel, military bases and serial standard armaments. These were accompanied with only insignificant cuts in R&D expenses and accelerated updating rates.

Unfortunately, authors of reforms in Russia and some other CIS countries appear to be stronger Catholics than the Pope himself. No developed market economy has employed such radical approaches to the MIC or its research potential. Financing of defence R&D was reduced almost five times in the 1990s with no prior notification and with continuous delays without any extra payment, unique research and production complexes liquidated under privatisation, pilot plants removed from research organisations and long-term R&D planning eliminated. The idea was probably of an "invisible hand" of the market taking better-than-government decisions on maintaining or closing some research organisations. No consideration was taken of the unique nature of research as a business sphere, the lacking market for scientific and technological information and innovation in the CIS.

As a result, employment in defence research was almost halved, generally at the expense of more initiative and young workers. Key members of 200 research schools in St. Petersburg emigrated, in many cases only leaving behind a name of the organisation and retirement-age directors. Two thirds of respondents leading 56 organisations described government intervention in research strategy as detrimental, and only 10% as negligible. In addition, capital stock in 98% organisations excludes intangible assets, i.e. past R&D capitalised. These were often sold in private, when on foreign business trips, unlicensed and very cheap, with the sellers unable to confirm their property rights on know-how. The average wage in defence research organisations in CIS countries being lower than, for example, in food industry, the remaining staff tried to earn additional income in small firms, repair and adjustment works, non-standard export-oriented manufacturing or commerce; the retirement share increased drastically.

Only one fifth of science-technology organisations (NTOs) adjusted to the new conditions – with R&D stable outputs and ongoing equipment updating – through exports, orders placed by the oil-gas and chemical metallurgy complexes, or membership in financial and industrial groups. But foreign competition has increased in recent years. Many ship- and machine-building plants can only obtain orders involving foreign developments.

Some international studies indicate that current military R&D focuses on highly specialised technologies not applicable in civilian production. This is true even of basic products such as super computers and related software, or "Star Wars" lasers. Additionally, top-secret military R&D orders are generally placed in major firms not oriented towards mass production. Some authors (A. Difilippo, N. Goldstein, S. Melman) argue that the superior contribution of Japan and Germany (30%), as compared with the USA (20%), to international high-technology exports is due to the fact that, with almost the same numbers of research workers and engineers per 10,000 employed (67.8, 52.3 and 66.2, respectively) and lower government R&D spending (2.15% and 30%), the former win in the lower proportions of military R&D staff (5%–10% compared with 33%) and the greater of industry shares in the R&D budget (69% and

62% compared with 48%). Unlike the USA, the responsibility for industrial policies in the sphere of high-technologies and conversion in Japan and Germany is, according to V. Leontiev, assigned to government agencies setting priorities targets and subsidising major innovatory projects in the civilian sphere. Conversion in defence industry and science, access to world markets, a synergic integration of the MIC in industrial production as an input of up-to-date technology systems for extractive industries, the chemical metallurgy complex, telecommunications, the AIC, medicine and ecology are the crucial elements of structural transformation.

Special co-ordinating policies are needed in CIS military exports. Among the recent trends on the world armaments market are:

1. Decline of total military exports, due to defence budgets reductions in most countries after the end of the Cold War.

2. Enhanced competition in international markets, due to reduced internal demand in most developed countries. Thus, U.S. federal military expenditures at comparable prices decreased by 40% (from $206 to $140 billion) between 1987 and 1997. To prevent a drop in profits, the USA intends to increase the export share of armament manufacturing from 10 to 25%, mainly via new East European NATO membership.

3. Changed positions of exporting countries, i.e. the U.S. contribution increasing from 30% to 52% (over $11 billion), as well as those of France, UK and Germany. The Ukraine was listed among the top ten world exporters in 1996 and 1997. Russia is fourth in the world (behind USA, UK and France) in total sales (8.6% of the world market in 1996).

4. Diversification of production centres, due to softer requirements on standardisation and operational compatibility of armaments. Over 80% of weapon systems adopted in France, 75% in the UK and 90% in Japan are home manufactured, which helps to restore control over foreign policy. Brazil, Argentina, India, Pakistan, and others started national weapons production in the 1980s.

5. Changed positions of importing countries. With decreasing European and North American demand, contributions from the Middle East and Southeast Asia have increased (the UAE alone projecting $70 billion by 2000).

6. More sophisticated commodity market structure: smaller share of individual items and increased share of commodity groups (serial and complex goods), large objects (buildings, enterprises) and programs (object and building complexes) and, subsequently, trade in technologies and services rather than tangible goods.

In the second half of the 1990s arms and armaments exports in Russia outstripped the government purchases, with increased exports of civilian equipment; the latter's share in total MIC outputs amounted to 72%, with every fifth enterprise restricted to civilian production while maintaining production capacities. Long-term developments in the exports of arms linked with military engineering services, personnel training – particularly in Asian, African and South American countries – service arrangements are largely related to restored inter-state co-operation within the CIS.

Every third defence enterprise in the USSR (205 production- and 139 R&D organisations) was located in the Ukraine. The Ukrainian MIC comprised 40% of national plants. The contribution to co-operative production amounted to 20%–25% in tanks and naval orders, and 60%–80% in radioelectronics. Ukrainian developments involved new tank diesels (1200 h.p.), aircraft engines and accumulators, and optics (Arsenal works in Kiev). Arms exports increased owing to radar equipment and accessories for planes adopted in India, Poland, Peru and some other countries (e.g. AN-24, AN-26, MI-8, MI-24), as well as tanks (ordered by Pakistan), transport aircraft, ships, missiles and guidance systems, cartridges and other such equipment. But even with almost 1.5 million people involved in military orders, the Ukraine cannot produce and, consequently, export most arms types independently. The defence budget is insufficient for major projects. Co-operation with Russia (placing 70% of MIC orders) and other CIS countries in new projects, such as T-84 tanks or AN-70 aircraft (joint Ukraine-Russia-Uzbekistan project), will open up fresh opportunities.

Considerable scope is offered for co-operation with firms in developed countries. The Sea Launch (a Ukrainian-Russian-Norwegian-U.S. project for launching communication satellites from an equatorial sea platform) is worth several billion dollars per year. The government companies Ukrspetsexport and Rosvooruzhenie can join their efforts in selling missiles, armoured machines and other items on international markets at agreeable prices. Kazakhstan, Uzbekistan and Kyrgyzstan can co-operate in expanded exports of nuclear supplies and technologies (almost $3 billion in 1997).

To date, conversion in CIS countries has only involved reductions in the MIC, fewer jobs and additional budget stringencies. Yet international experience[1] has shown that, with appropriate provisions, it can provide a source of development for high-technology branches.

Russia has created new conditions for co-operation with CIS countries in this area by extending enterprise rights in the export of products, spare parts and engineering services, and in obtaining development orders. Among the enterprises empowered to sign contracts and provide maintenance services are Rosvertol (MI-17, MI-26 and MI-28 helicopters), Gidromash (N.Novgorod, air

---

[1] Brauer, J., Chatterji, M. (Eds.) (1993): Economic Issues of Disarmament: Contributions from Peace Economics and Peace Science. New York; Lamb, G., Kalal, V. (Eds.) (1992): Military Expenditure and Economic Development: a Symposium on Research Issues. World Bank, Washington

hydraulics), Metrovagonmash (Mytishchi, running gear for AA systems) and Antei (AA systems). Their traditional partners are in Belarus, the Ukraine, Kyrgyzstan, Georgia and Uzbekistan where orders are in short supply.

5.2 Development of High-Technology Industries

According to international expertise, CIS countries account for less than 0.5% of world high-technology outputs (Russia's is 0.3%). But the CIS have maintained the science, personnel and production-base to regain their positions on the lines of up-to-date management.

Aerospace Industry in Russia and the Ukraine produce items such as unique super-heavy vehicles (e.g. Proton), rocket engines and orbital craft. International demand for space freight transport involving space communications, navigation, prospecting, as well as meteorological and environmental complexes is expected to grow five to ten times by 2005–2010, amounting annually to 2000–6000 tonnes. The CIS can fill half the market, gaining annually $8–24 billion. But this will require continuous training of the appropriate personnel (almost halved in Russia presently), as well as international co-operation and long-term contracting.

Aircraft industries in Russia (TU, Il, IaK classes), the Ukraine (An), Uzbekistan and Georgia co-operating with works in Belarus and some other countries were comparable in R&D and production potentials to those in the USA and Europe. Over 25% of the world fleet in the early 1990s were represented by Soviet planes. In the late 1990s production of unique transport planes, such as AN-70 (Kiev aircraft PO /production association/ linked with plants in Tashkent and Russia), TU-204 (equipped with Rolls Royce engines), IL-96 (Pratt and Whitney engines) and A-50 (with long-range radar systems using electronics from Israel), has been started. A certificate was granted to the 2500 h.p. turbo-prop engine Klimov for Il-114, with 2–4 factor fuel efficiency). A new airbus has been designed in co-operation with the EU.

Yet civilian outputs in the CIS decreased almost five times over the 1990s. Air traffic has intensified since 1996, so that the CIS are expected to lead the world on this market by the early twenty-first century. Fleet updating generally involves imported equipment. Thus, Uzbekistan leased and subsequently purchased numerous A-310, Boeing-767 and RS-85 aircraft, a U.S. computer satellite complex and other equipment. Financing was provided by European and U.S. banks. Lease payments to foreign companies in Russia already exceed budget financing to aircraft industries. In addition, foreign contracts with CIS countries generally omit the transfer of advanced technologies, mutual acceptance of certificates and joint production. All these endanger the 4 million jobs in aircraft and related works in the CIS.

Progress in the area will require an extended range of new engines (previous military designs not meeting current fuel-consumption and environmental requirements), airborne electronics and interior equipment (chairs, video, kitchen). New sales arrangements rely on preferential credit to be repaid from traffic gains and secured with the fleet. Export expansion will require government credit guarantees and long-term co-operative arrangements with foreign corporations, to build repair facilities, adopt new technologies and certify planes and helicopters. Within the next 10–15 years CIS countries will need 3000–4000 new passenger planes, not to mention the short-range stock. The major portion can and must be manufactured within the CIS, generally in co-operation with firms in the EU and elsewhere.

Motor-car industry in the CIS offers great promise. In this case the two extremes are dangerous: on the one hand, excessive import duties will spare CIS plants the competition while condemning them to permanent backwardness. On the other hand, loss of government support in the form of preferential loans (to purchase equipment from domestic producers, adopt new types and establish assembly units in other CIS countries for subsequent exports), differentiated customs duties promoting co-operation and imports of accessories rather than outputs, car leasing with targeted credits to the AIC and small business, will result in a CIS market dominated by foreign producers.

A rapid growth of the CIS car market is expected between 1996 and 2001: from annual 720,000 to 1,035,000 in Russia, 25,000 to 105,000 in the Ukraine, 3000 to 22,000 in Belarus, 11,000 to 56,000 in Uzbekistan and 60,000 to 250,000 in the remaining CIS countries. In 1997 Russia produced 1,130,000, the Ukraine 5400 and Belarus 13,900 cars. On the other hand, foreign concerns established in Poland, Czech Republic, Hungary and other adjacent countries (e.g. South Korean Daewoo, Skoda with controlling interest bought by Volkswagen) are prepared to satisfy market demand.

The only new motor-car plant of the 1990s was built in Uzbekistan by Daewoo. This and related republican works will be tax-exempt for 5 years, with duty-free imported equipment and 70% of personnel trained in South Korea. In Uzbekistan the cars can be bought on a 10-year credit at initial 30%. Dozens of satellite plants will be completed by the end of 2000.

The rest of the CIS have been confined to car assembly using foreign accessories (e.g. Korean Kia Motors in the lathe-building plant in Alma-Ata, Ford in Belarus, Daewoo in the car-building plant in Zaporozhie). Future plans include home-made accessories (at least 50%), but as the project involves tax and other advantages, the EU regards it as a dumping effort. The WTO also demands lower import taxes (in 1997 amounting to 62% of customs value in Russia and 35% in the Ukraine).

Competitive positions on the car market can only be attained by adopting new car types (e.g. with diesel engine, electronic fuel control, low emission level) and technologies in the existing plants. Price reductions (feasible with broad inter-state co-operation within the CIS), superior reliability, mobility and easy maintenance of domestic lorries, motor-vehicle trains and buses, will provide the required competitive merits. Co-operative arrangements with foreign companies should focus on license trade rather than expensive import of complete units. This has been demonstrated by individual experience. Thus, the Lvov bus plant produced only 3000 vehicles in 1994, instead of the planned 15,000. No access to CIS, Asian and South American markets can be gained unless petrol engines are replaced with more efficient diesels and service life extended from 6 to 12 years. The plant started production of a double-section city bus for 200 passengers (an *Icarus* analogue with *Renault* engine and gear box), a three-door bus for 120 passengers, a super-comfort long-distance coach as well as mini-buses. But a city vehicle using systems made in the "far abroad" will cost over $70,000. An alternative is provided by co-operative links with plants in the Ukraine, Russia (KAMAZ) and Belarus (MAZ).

Actual competition between similar-type plants in the CIS was first evident in the late 1990s. Thus, for instance, small-size cars, along with the VAZs, are manufactured in, for example, Uzbekistan, Gorki (co-operating with Fiat), Kaliningrad, Kremenchug. The situation requires co-ordination of tax, customs and other privileges across the CIS. Low- and medium capacity lorries made by joint stock company IVEKO-KrAZ (with 35% of the capital stock held by a Fiat affiliation, 35% by Kremenchug works and 30% by the EBRD) compete with the Gaselle (N. Novgorod) and some other types. Given the highly saturated Western markets, maximum possible outputs to reduce the costs can only be attained through the CIS, which is impossible unless cost-efficient associations are established or long-term contracts made.

Up-to-date computer systems enable different car types to be assembled in a single line under a customised schedule. Thus, a comparatively small Valmet plant in Finland manufactures the Saab, Opel and Porsche simultaneously.

CIS plants have been competing rather than co-operating. The sharp rise in prices for accessories forced Tbilisi aircraft-, Kamski motor-car and some other plants to foreign suppliers. This, however, resulted in higher output prices. Consequently, the heavy-load KAMAZs were more expensive in 1998 than their Minsk analogues and almost as much as the higher-quality Tatras. The demand dropped. Due to the KAMAZ failure to diversify production in due time, bus manufacture was started in Minsk (together with the MAN corporation in Germany). The KAMAZ export market is limited by non-compliance with recent EU environmental requirements on engines. To lower the loss-making line (130,000 lorries, several times the actual output) and reduce taxable assets, the KAMAZ had to sell railway cars, yachts and other property. The diesel, tool, foundry and forgery departments were reconstituted as subsidiary enterprises. New shares had to be issued to cover the debt.

Similar complications appeared in Volzhsk, Ulianovsk, Kutaisi, Moskvitch and ZIL plants. On the other hand, plants in Gorki, Minsk and some other CIS towns gained stable growth rates by finding new markets (e.g. Gaselle-type cars and lorries of superior capacity and mobility for small business), extending co-operative links (Gaselle assembly in Moldova and other CIS countries), establishing joint venture companies with leading foreign firms and taking unusual financial decisions (e.g. GAZ corporate bonds).

Shipbuilding. By the early 1990s, USSR shipbuilding accounted for one third of the world output. The CIS contributed less than 0.5% in 1997. This dramatic decline was governed by the four major factors. Government defence orders reduced drastically. The Navy of 800 vessels of aggregate 2.5 million tonnes decreased several times by the late 1990s. The Ukraine sold almost complete aircraft carriers of over 6000 tonnes as scrap metal.

The break-up of the USSR resulted in the rupture of traditional links (over 300 design and production plants contribute to one vessel). The eight more up-to-date shipyards in the Ukraine (e.g. Nikolaev, Kherson, Kerch) rely on external inputs. Many of the more than 200 Russian shipbuilding plants and 44 shipyards were built in the nineteenth century, e.g. Admiralty, North plant and Baltic plant in St. Petersburg. Shipbuilding efforts in Kyrgyzstan, Georgia and Azerbaijan depend heavily on sustained co-operative arrangements with other countries.

A drastic decline in international shipbuilding occurred during the 1970s and 1980s. But things have changed radically in the late 1990s. As estimated by the UK research firm Drewry (World Shipbuilding), due to the extended international trade and the need to replace 6600 ships with more than 15-year using, orders will grow[2] rapidly to over 150 million Regs. (R.t.). Approximately 80% of the replacements will be represented by tankers and bulkers, and the rest by gas-, chemical and container transport vessels and cruise liners.

The greatest demand was for large boats (20,000–50,000 Regs. (R.t.)). Among the competitors were yards in Japan and South Korea (servicing 70% of commercial shipbuilding orders), Croatia, Poland, China, Scandinavia (cruise liners, icebreakers, sea platforms). The world's biggest ship builder now is the Korean Hyundai corporation established in the 1970s and accounting for 10% of the world market (with only 1% contributed by the USA). Since the end of the Cold War, the U.S. Navy has been reduced to 340 ships (with 600 previously planned by 2000) and the number of active shipyards from 24 to 16 (as in the USSR, 90% of vessels were building for the Navy in the 1980s).

Considering the international experience and the national competitive advantages (developed science and metallurgy, comparatively low wages, extensive markets, expertise in the field of titanium- and other special alloys), the CIS should

[2] (1997): Эксперт (Expert) 37, 41–49 [In Russian]

concentrate on sophisticated vessels with multiple mechanics and devices (e.g. special vessels for research, working in shelf, ice, amphibian and fast air-cushion craft), as well as chemical transport, "river-sea" and naval craft, including exports. This will require shipbuilding marketing, reliable forecasting of demand and freight price (average daily proceeds), service time and maintenance costs. The industry needs a special financing framework involving long-term credit with government guarantees ($1.5 billion in the USA) and leasing arrangements.

Concentration of production organised on the basis of competitive centres is indispensable (e.g. St.-Petersburg project of an integral complex of three shipyards). Among the instructive cases of co-operation with foreign firms are the projects of bulker-building in the Ukraine, very promising in CIS conditions "river-sea" vessels in Rostov and sea platforms in Vyborg. On the other hand, the Ukraine-UK project involves only local steel and hulls with imported equipment. Since Russian shipbuilding companies can only obtain tightened foreign credit secured with future outputs, they have to spend annually over $1 billion outside the CIS. Only in the late 1990s were ice-type tankers ordered in Petersburg by Lukoil. (Credit lines to equipment and accessory purchasing, to be repaid by Lukoil, were opened on Russian government guarantees in Germany and Norway.)

Computer engineering. Computer market in the late 1990s exceeded $70 billion. The world list of top ten firms contains three computer manufacturers: Microsoft, Intel and IBM. Personal computer capacity doubles every 3 years, graphic facilities are extended, operation is faster and costs lower. Over 80% of working places in the world are equipped with computers. In the foreseeable future computers will be able to understand and synthesise human speech. The over 100 computer engineering facilities built in the world in the late 1990s are all outside the CIS (e.g. Costa Rica, Israel, Scotland). Over half the U.S. investments in the mid-1990s were channelled to high technologies, including 30% to computer, information and communications firms, and only 18% to consumer goods and services.

The CIS market of information technologies is dominated by foreign companies, even though up-to-date research and production complexes in computer engineering, information systems and fibre optic technologies have been available or almost complete in Russia, Moldova, the Ukraine and Armenia. Thus, Kazakhstan has only 3 computers per 1000 people. The ten major companies only sell Asian- (55%–60%) or "white" assemblies (annually 25,000–35,000). The Schetmash plant in Moldova, previously manufacturing the unique "Buran" equipment, is now idle. The PC plant in Kishinev with 70,000 projected annual output is sold in fragments through auctions. Fifty firms are generally engaged in import trade, including second-hand. The market of servers for local and international networks (Internet) has been monopolised by Compaq, Hewlett Packard, and other corporations.

Computer stock in the CIS requires radical renovation. This is particularly true of over 6000 main-frames acting as national information brain centres. They must be replaced with new computers which are efficient, reliable and compatible with international networks. Foreign corporations, supported by international charitable funds, offer complete equipment at low price. The USA regards the Internet as a free-trade zone, with commercial tariffs abolished for computers, telecommunication facilities and software. But European and Asian countries insist on maintaining government control over electronic commerce and copyright regulations. Transfer of access points to foreign companies will enable both searching national databases and arbitrary data input and output.

Almost one half of PCs sold in the CIS are locally assembled (using imported accessories). Annual sales amount to over 1.5 million, with growth rates declining in Russia (from 50% to 60% in mid-1990s to 20% to 25% in late 1990s, with the average world rate 15%–20%) and increasing in the rest of the CIS. In addition, key firms in Russia, the Ukraine, Belarus and Kazakhstan combine assembly with providing software and multimedia for home users, personnel training, maintenance services, networking and adjustment, as well as distributing services to major foreign corporations. These integrators generally abandon mere sales to develop the computer development programs subsequently implemented and financed from accretions, long-term credit and other investments.

Eastern Europe and the CIS represented only 3% of the world market of information technologies in 1996, with Russia accounting for 40%, Poland, Czech Republic and Hungary 27%, and the Ukraine, Belarus, Kazakhstan and Bulgaria 13%. Yet by the early twenty-first century computer sales will increase several times in the CIS, considering the high education level and developing infrastructure. A joint program should be formulated if this is to benefit economy and science in the CIS, instead of multiplying the profits of overseas TNCs.

Rather than copying past experience of developed countries, the program should focus on recent achievements. The primary question concerns network computer terminals without hard disks, providing immediate access to databases, corporate networks and the Internet. They are far less expensive and easier to operate than PCs, given standard servers, motherboard interfaces and micro-processors. In addition to network and PCs, medium-capacity machines are required by corporations, and super-computer centres in the areas of research, weather forecasting, traffic management, etc. The first such centre in Eastern Europe and the CIS (1 billion operations per second, memory accommodating 9–10 million medium-size books) has been operated in St. Petersburg.

The computer market is built of three basic segments. Government agencies and major joint venture companies in the CIS generally order well-known brand names directly from U.S. companies. Their only rival in the rest of the world is the government-supported Siemens (Germany).

The second segment includes corporate networks (Intranet). With appropriate software, payback period is not longer than 1–2 years, requiring no storing, printing and distribution of paper-supported documents, providing on-line large-file data communication in the area of computer-assisted design and production with suppliers, and ensuring better justified administrative decision making. Network- and video technologies providing on-line exchange of three-dimensional graphics in real time, radically transform the methods of business management.

The third segment, rapidly growing in the CIS, involves household and portable computers (notebooks) used for games, films and concerts (multimedia). In 1997 Internet subscription in Russia increased four times (to over 1 million), including from 25% to 40% in the provinces. As estimated by the Centre for Internet technologies, over 60% requests are related to business, culture, science and education, 22% to sports, recreation and entertainment, and 15% to mass media news. There is one information server in Russia for 3000 people (70 in the USA and Switzerland, 35 in Norway and 18 in Finland). Almost 50% of Russian public information is distributed in the CIS, and 30% in the USA

The contribution of domestic assembly to the corporate and household market segments has been growing (64% of the 1.2 million PCs sold in 1995 and 75% in 1996). This is accompanied by the increased proportion of high-capacity Pentium processors (from 20% in 1995 to 93% in 1997) as well as up-to-date monitors and servers, due to declining sales of outdated models and PCs assembled by obscure Asian firms. Small firms recently making immense profits by reselling of low-quality imports are being forced out by bigger CIS companies assembling PCs (e.g. Vist, P.&C., Compulink, Air-style) manufacturing accessories, selling the software developed by key Western corporations (QEM agreement), implementing sophisticated information systems, providing maintenance services and customised personnel training. The number of computer firms in the CIS has been decreasing in the late 1990s, with large retail nets established in the area. A parallel decrease has been evident in the share of piracy, i.e. unauthorised software use (from 95% in 1995 to 90% in 1997, compared with 27% in the USA).

A functional computer market in the CIS will require knowledge of international experience. The leaders in the world market are not small sole proprietorships, but large public joint-stock companies with "transparent" financial accounting, highly qualified management and high-priced stocks. They can gain the required investments for continuous renovation of both products and processes.

High-technology industries are typically highly diversified, with lower moral depreciation period and higher R&D and costs of building plants. Both hardware (e.g. IBM, Hewlett Packard, Motorola) and software (Microsoft) developments require increasingly efficient processors (over 80% of the market represented by Intel), servers and displays. The costs of a new production plant (Intel operating

15) amounted to $3 million in the late 1960s and $2 billion in the late 1990s, with the existing types and plants losing their value whenever new types or new archiving- and encoding processes are developed. Intel, with its annual profits over $5 billion, is the immediate generator of demand, supporting new PC manufacturers (in particular, financing advertising projects in many CIS firms), exploring new application areas for processors (e.g. video and audio data transmission modems, computerised telephone exchange via Internet, new processes for shopping, listening to concerts). Computer capacities have been extended with new built-in features (e.g. fast buses, peripherals, board sizes, plugs).

Every year Intel spends over $3 billion on R&D and $0.5 billion on market development. Corporations that cannot afford it encounter considerable difficulties. The Apple company, a pioneering PC manufacturer accounting for 80% of the world publishing systems market, almost went bankrupt in 1997. Moreover, the MacIntosh systems, popular among the CIS, are giving way to continuous technologies ensuring immediate data transmission to a preset place in a newspaper or journal issue. IBM, the major computer manufacturer with unique personnel training and management systems in the 1980s[3] (with 100 applicants for every vacancy at the time), was 25th in market value in the USA the 1990s (Intel third and Microsoft second), dismissing 25,000 workers and cutting the R&D budget by $1 billion. This was related to mass-scale non-licensed PC manufacture in Southeast Asia (IBM having spent $10 billion on the developments).

Computer engineering in the CIS will not achieve the required selection of technologies to compete with world giants in the foreseeable future. But some CIS firms have made advances in the final manufacturing stage – hardware assembly (a Russian firm Vist listed among the top 12 European companies in 1997), with some accessories (e.g. printers, displays), and the local language- and environment software versions. Further developments will require a joint manufacturing base (KVANT plant in Zelenograd, enterprises in Moldova, Armenia, Kazakhstan, Kyrgyzstan, Uzbekistan), systems testing facilities and assembly quality management.

Electronics, electrical engineering and power machine building. In developed countries growth rates in electronic industry are five to ten times those of total GDP and return on development and production three to four times higher than industrial totals. Therefore, the annual investments growth amounts to 12%. The USA, EU countries, Japan, South Korea, China and the rest of Asia initiate electronic development programs with almost half the investments provided by

---

[3] Merser, D. (1991): IBM: Development in the Most Successful Company of the World. / Translated from English. Progress, Moscow (Мерсер, Д. (1991): ИБМ: Управление в Самой Преуспевающей Компании Мира. / Пер. с Англ. Прогресс, Москва) [Cited here from Russian edition]

the government. Transistor, micro-electronic, communication and other producers' associations promote technological improvements, e.g. super-large integral circuits (with component size reduced from 1–1.5 to 0.17 μm) and large-diameter siliceous plates ensuring higher-grade equipment at lower costs. The world civilian micro-electronic output now is forty times that of 1975, electronic sales growing by 10%–15% every year, with $1 trillion expected by 2000. Economic developments in Thailand, Malaysia, Taiwan, Israel and many other countries rely on electronics.

By the estimates of EU Organisation for economic research, between 1997 and 2002 sales will increase half as much again for car electronics: built-in satellite navigation systems, radar and other emergency systems, electronic fuel, stability and mobility controls. This will facilitate radical improvements in traffic capacity and safety. To date, the market is dominated by NAFTA members (USA., Canada, Mexico), the EU and Japan.

The highest growth rates among high-technology industries in the USSR were related to communications, computers and accessories, and office equipment. By the early 1990s most CIS countries had available or almost complete up-to-date plants providing a basis for national high-technology economy. Further developments in the area, however, will require maintenance of a joint research base, sustained co-operation and extensive use of international achievements, and effective conversion.

Having adapted to the new environment, some CIS firms started production of up-to-date telecommunications equipment. Among them are the AOs Dalniaia sviaz (gauges, optic cable systems) and Krasnaia zaria (switching systems) in Russia, and the NPO Integral (micro-electronics) in Belarus. The information technology markets have been growing by 30% every year (equipment representing 70%, services 20% and software 10%).

International co-operation has been extended. Firms in Saratov, Izhevsk, Minsk, Kiev and Dnepropetrovsk supply accessories to such major corporations as Motorola. Firms in Germany, Japan and some other countries supported projects of up-to-date telephone stations and related equipment in Russia and the Ukraine. Up-to-date management systems for freight and passenger traffic, large stores, inter-bank, insurance and pension transactions have been developed by the International Business ALLIANCE -JV between IBM and enterprises in Belarus (NII EVM, computer engineering PO, EVM service and Belkom NIIs).

On the other hand, the area was actually inoperative in the mid-1990s in Moldova, Azerbaijan, Tajikistan and some other CIS countries. The number of micro-electronic production facilities in Russia (over 400 plants and research institutes) was reduced six times, with only 75,000 instead of 300,000 qualified staff members remaining in 1997, as estimated by the federal electronic development foundation.

A new technological revolution has been in progress in informatics on the eve of the twenty-first century. During the second half of this century, labour productivity and the extent of sophistication in transistor micro-circuits doubled every second year. The Intel 1997 micro-circuit with a four-fold memory extension will ensure radical reductions in the costs and size of computers and digital chambers with micro-circuits substituted for tape.

Micro-electronics govern the level of sophistication in domestic equipment. The annual 10 million TV sets had met the demand in the USSR. Outputs decreased 15 times in the 1990s. Almost 94% of total sales are represented by imports, mainly from South Korea and Japan, and only 4%–5% from CIS member countries (mainly Belarus). National production was almost discontinued with respect to, for example, video cameras, music centres, with drastic reductions for items such as video recorders, vacuum cleaners, washing machines, watches and cameras, with national outputs outstripping imports only for refrigerators (Belarus, the Ukraine, Russia) and telephone sets.

Some Western experts believe that CIS countries should abandon some industries. Thus, Armenia has been advised to focus on small-scale services and a limited licensed production range, rather than national industrial developments. Yet the CIS have available raw-material, science-and-technology, and industrial resources to restore its electronics and related industries. Traditional outputs included 2-μm resolution electronic components for military techniques. Their exports (being highly labour intensive, they are imported by the rich countries) will allow effective employment of submicron technologies on mass-scale military engineering. Manufacture of TV sets, previously regarded as by-products in military plants, should be converted from analogue to digital technologies, with hard and CD disks instead of tape and a new generation of recording, transmission and equivalent circuits.

Only 15% of the immense potentials ensuring annual outputs of 5.2 million TV sets and 1.2 million tubes have been used in the Ukraine. Meanwhile 80% of Ukrainian accessories and supplies are sold on other national markets within the CIS. The conversion program "Electronics Ukraine-2000" includes the export of competitive TV tubes. But the program will be much impeded unless adequate co-operative arrangements are made with other CIS countries. Due consideration must be given to projected growth in the sales of domestic and office equipment in CIS countries by the early twenty-first century to $100 billion per year, due to higher incomes and updating requirements.

To restore electronic industries in the CIS, diversified TNCs and inter-state programs should be sponsored, involving TV, communications, car- and aircraft electronics and settlement arrangements. Import duties should be abolished for high-quality electronic components (new TV ray tubes, integral digital circuits, image- and sound signal processors, synchronisation and control units, up-to-date micro-processors and micro-computers) and, taking lessons from China and some other countries, protectionist policies formulated for joint production of electronic, television, domestic and audio-video equipment in the territory under CIS jurisdiction.

Domestic producers have been protected at the national level only. Thus, Russia has closed the import market of fibre-optic cable, extending equipment and cable production in local plants (e.g. Chernogolovka in the Moscow region, Sevkabel in St. Petersburg), including those which are Japan licensed. Public communications use switching stations made in Russia under co-operative agreements and in collaboration with foreign companies. Russia started production of competitive optic cable, local network telephone stations, synchronous digital hierarchy circuits, noise jammers, signal converters and billing systems. Leading foreign corporations contributed the equipment, software and know-how to seven new plants manufacturing up-to-date telecommunications equipment for data transmission line connection (e.g. Sineps). Europe's biggest teleport was established in St. Petersburg, a digital fibre-optic satellite longline circuit. The 55% import duty on TV sets in Uzbekistan prompted Sony's annual local output of 50,000 items.

Things are the same in machine building. Ukrainian rocket-space NPO Iuzhnoe (Dnepropetrovsk) has been exporting with profit both up-to-date rockets and wind-driven electric power units. Russian NPO Energomash supplies the world's most powerful 9-tonne rocket engines for the U.S. corporation Lockheed Martin under a $2 billion contract. Russia provides engineering services for 36 countries (e.g. China, Iran, India, Morocco, Greece, Cuba) in nuclear engineering, metallurgy and other industries. The international electrical-engineering concern ABB established over 200 industrial, building and power machinery companies in Russia. But individual cases fail to change the general picture.

Even in a large country like Russia, large-scale, research-intensive and sophisticated production is not feasible without co-operation and domestic market focuses. The 70% drop in electronic and electrical engineering between 1990 and 1997 in some cases caused irreversible technological degradation. Developed economies used to renew high-technology industrial product mix every 3 years and equipment stock every 5–6 years. In the mid-1990s only 4%–5% of industrial investments were channelled to the basic economic branch – machine building. The bulk (almost two thirds) went to the branches either exporting raw materials or promoting foreign capital on the CIS market (TEK, metallurgy, transport and communications).

5.3 The Fuel-Energy and Raw-Materials Complex

Oil and gas and coal industries. Extraction of energy resources (oil, gas, coal and shales) and electrical engineering have been the most competitive branches in the CIS owing to available unique deposits, inexpensive manpower and fairly soft environmental requirements. In the mid-1990s Russia was the second (after the USA) largest energy producer in the world, accounting for 13% of world energy production. The fuel and energy complex (FEC) accounted for 15% of GDP and 45% of export gains.

Mining and production of energy resources will enter the twenty-first century as one of the major economic branches of CIS. Import share in EU energy consumption grew from 43% in 1986 to 51% in 1992, and is likely to increase to 66%–75% by 2020; energy imports will be doubled in Poland, Hungary, Turkey and Southeast Asia.

The fuel and energy complex in the USSR was largely export oriented. Fuel exports increased almost three-fold (from 170 to almost 450 million tonnes), with every third tonne of oil exported. The FEC share in total industrial investments also grew – from 35% to 48%, which affected competitive positions of many other branches. Energy resource consumption per unit output was two to three times that in Japan or the USA. Many regions had no access to the integrated power transmission system. Since centralised planning was abolished, oil exports decreased almost by half for 1991 only and a substantial portion of the market was lost.

In the 1990s CIS countries embarked on different paths of FEC development. Kazakhstan appointed foreign TNCs to govern the branch, so that CIS member countries can only establish FIGs on their approval. Azerbaijan transferred oil prospecting and mining through tender trade to four international consortia (projected worth amounting to $135 billion by 2030). Russia chose to establish integrated-process (e.g. from extraction of crude materials to sales of gas, petrol) companies involving oil companies (e.g. Gazprom, Lukoil, Iuksi, Surgutneftegaz, Slavneft) having State-owned shares and profitable coal companies (generally developing open pits and closing loss-making or hazardous mines).

Thus, RAO /Russian joint-stock company/ Gazprom (40% government stocks, including 30% in trust to RAO) runs 69 fields (25% world gas output), holding licenses for 33 trillion m^3 of gas (together with subsidiary plants), 1.3 billion tonnes of explored gas condensate reserves and 664 million tonnes of oil. Upon restructuring Gazprom incorporates companies engaged in prospecting and drilling (Burgaz), mining (in Urengoi, Nadym, Iamburg, Surgut), refining (six refineries), transport (including Europe's largest integrated gas supply system), gas sales (Mezhregion gas) and joint ventures in consuming countries. Non-profiled firms (e.g. agricultural, machine building) were removed and the social infrastructure enterprises transferred to municipal bodies. This allowed a 100,000 personnel reduction.

Over one third of gas is exported, meeting 20% of demand in Western (e.g. Germany, Italy, France) and 50% in Eastern Europe. This ensures half the yields, which is especially important considering scale of non-payments in Russia and other CIS countries. Beyond the agreed date, free gas supply to former

CMEA members in return for contribution to gas field development will be discontinued. Gazprom provides 25% tax revenues in Russia. Despite the fact that the RAO maintains strong financial positions, even with 68% of current assets represented by debtors' receivables with assets over $100 billion, the share of net sales per ruble of assets decreased from 1.66 in 1993 to 1.20 rubles in 1996. The ROA increased from 3.35% to 5.75% over that period, with the share of net profit in total sales also increased, along with that of long-term liabilities in the total liabilities (from 3.4% to 11%). The world's largest gas line is Yamal–Europe (16,000 km, 82 billion m^3 yields and costs approximately $40 billion). Gazprom has distributed 1.15% stocks in the form of ADR (American depository receipts) on the international stock market and issues Euro-bonds. Considerable savings (25%) have been offered by the substitution of shift methods for expensive urban developments in the North Area.

Since 1997 the government has tightened their controlling interests, including decisions on RAO strategies and dividend distribution, gas prices (reduced dramatically for industrial consumers with the condition of payment to date) and investment projects, as well as indiscriminate longline access for non-member gas producers. This could be a good example to follow for the rest of the CIS. In many of the countries (e.g. Turkmenistan, Moldova, Belarus) Gazprom contributed to investment projects or established joint venture companies. To promote integrated gas-supply transport systems in the CIS, Gazprom set privileged gas prices. The Ukraine leads the list of RAO gas inputs (annual 51 billion m^3) and Belarus ranks fourth, below the Ukraine, Germany and Italy. At the same time, gas exports have been increasing to Hungary (likely to grow three times by 2015), Poland, Italy and Turkey. In 1998 Gazprom established a strategic partnership with a major world corporation Shell.

By the early twenty-first century Russian contribution to CIS oil production will decrease (already 86% in 1996 compared with 90% in 1990), even though new fields have been explored in the Ob River area and West Arctics. Oil output in Kazakhstan is likely to grow from 26.5 to 170 million tonnes by 2010 (world sixth) in the Karachaganak (under an agreement with Texaco USA and in association with British GES, Ajip and Russian Lukoil), Kashagan (Mobile USA in association with Totale France, Ajip Italy, British Petroleum, Shell, Satoil), Tengiz (Chevron and Mobile, both USA), Uzen and Aktiubinsk (China National Petroleum), Mangyshlak (Central Asia Petroleum Indonesia). A rapid growth in oil production is expected in the Caspian shelf fields conceded to foreign corporations by Azerbaijan and Turkmenistan.

Throughout the 1990s Russian contribution to gas production in the CIS grew from 79% to 84% and that of Turkmenistan decreased from 10.4% to 4.6%, owing to transportation and payment problems. In the twenty-first century substantial increases are expected in Russia (Yamal, Sakhalin, Irkutsk region, Yakutia), Turkmenistan, Kazakhstan and Uzbekistan for gas production and sales both in Europe and Southeast Asia via the integrated European and Trans-Asian gas net.

Russia accounts for 60% of coal production in the CIS. Ukraine's contribution decreased from 22% to 19% during the 1990s and that of Kazakhstan from 21% to 19%, due to declining effective demand. Russia discontinued operation in a hundred loss-making or explosive mines, cutting mining employment from 750,000 to 450,000. As a result, productivity of labour grew by 25%, prime costs stabilised and the share of budget subsidies in coal price decreased from 77% to 15%. Yet a social safety net for discharged miners and efficient recovery (mainly in open-pit processes) will be much needed in many CIS countries.

Between 1991 and 1996 outputs in the fuel and energy complex (FEC) in CIS member countries fell by 28%, i.e. one half the total industrial drop. As a result, contribution of fuel and other mining industries to industrial totals in the CIS grew from 20.7% to 15.1% between 1990 and 1997 (from 19.6% to 22.6% in Azerbaijan, 29.5% to 39% in Kazakhstan, 9.6% to 45% in Kyrgyzstan, 22.4% to 29.4% in Russia and 15.4% to 25.7% in Tajikistan).[4] By product, oil production decreased by 32% (with the exception of a 2.7-fold increase in Uzbekistan), coking coal by 40% (contribution declining from 24% to 22%) and gas by 11% (by late 1990s increasing in Central Asia, particularly in Uzbekistan, and Russia and the Ukraine; see Table 15).

In 1998 oil outputs in CIS countries were only 58% of the peak annual outputs in 1988, notably 53% in Russia and Azerbaijan (as compared with 1966 and 1987, respectively). In 1998 and 1999 oil outputs were almost unaltered in Russia (300 million tonnes) and Kazakhstan (approximately 30 million tonnes), while growing in Azerbaijan (11–15 million tonnes). Gas production increased 2%–4% annually in Kazakhstan and Russia, while coal production decreased 4%–5% per year. Electricity generation remained almost at the same level in Russia, while decreasing 3%–14% in Belarus, Kazakhstan, the Ukraine and Moldova in 1998.

In many CIS countries (Russia, Azerbaijan, Turkmenistan, Kazakhstan and, recently, in Uzbekistan) the FEC became the main source of export revenues. The decline in domestic demand was likewise less significant than for other commodities because of the increased number of motor cars.

Electricity production in CIS countries between 1991 and 1996 reduced less significantly than GDP on the whole (by 16% in Uzbekistan, 20% in Russia and 26%–38% in the rest of the CIS), with GDP energy intensity increased 50% again.

---

[4] (1998): On Social and Economic Conditions in CIS Member Nations. Economic Union Intergovernmental Economic Board. Moscow 13 ((1998): О Социально-Экономическом Положении Государств – Участников СНГ. Межгосударственный Экономический Комитет Экономического Союза, Москва 13) [In Russian]

Table 15

Mining and Production of Main Products in the FEC and Heavy Industries in the CIS from 1991–1998

Country	Electricity, billions of Kwh	Oil (including gas condensate), millions of tonnes	Mining			Production							
			Gas, billions of m³	Coal, millions of tonnes	Iron ore (commercial), millions of tonnes	Pig iron, millions of tonnes	Coke (6% hum.), millions of tonnes	Rolled ferrous metals (complete), millions of tonnes	Commercial timber, 1000s of m³	Sawn timber, millions of m³	Mineral fertilizers, millions of tonnes	Synthetic fibres and threads, 1000s of tonnes
1	2	3	4	5	6	7	8	9	10	11	12	13
Azerbaijan												
1991	23.5	11.7	8.6	–	0.5	–	–	0.5	6.5	0.1	0.2	–
1993	19.0	10.3	6.8	–	0.4	–	–	0.2	5.7	0.02	0.03	–
1995	17.0	9.2	6.6	–	0.01	–	–	0.01	2.5	0.002	0.002	–
1996	17.0	9.1	6.3	–	0.004	–	–	0.002	1.4	0.01	0.002	–
1997	16.8	9.0	6.0	–	0.004	–	–	0.16	–	–	0.005	–
1998	17.9	11.4	5.6	–	...	–	–	0.003	–	–	0.001	–
Armenia												
1991	9.6	–	–	–	–	–	–	–	6.0	0.04	–	4.1
1993	6.3	–	–	–	–	–	–	–	3.4	0.01	–	0.05
1995	5.6	–	–	–	–	–	–	–	2.7	0.001	–	0.2
1996	6.2	–	–	–	–	–	–	–	4.1	0.002	–	0.4
1997	5.4	–	–	–	–	–	–	–	2.8	0.002	–	–
1998	6.2	–	–	–	–	–	–	–	...	...	–	–

1	2	3	4	5	6	7	8	9	10	11	12	13
Belarus												
1991	38.7	2.1	0.3	—	—	—	—	0.7	5839	2.8	5.2	443
1993	33.4	2.0	0.3	—	—	—	—	0.6	5284	2.4	2.5	293
1995	24.9	1.9	0.3	—	—	—	—	0.6	4687	1.7	3.3	209
1996	23.7	1.9	0.2	—	—	—	—	0.8	4410	1.6	3.4	181
1997	26.1	1.8	0.2	—	—	—	—	1.1	4600	1.8	3.9	200
1998	23.5	1.8	0.3	—	—	—	—	1.3	...	...	4.1	197
Georgia												
1991	13.4	0.2	0.04	0.7	—	...	0.3	0.8	121.0	0.3	0.1	20.0
1993	10.2	0.1	0.02	0.1	—	...	0.1	0.1	33.2	0.01	0.06	8.0
1995	7.1	0.04	0.003	0.04	—	...	0.01	0.07	18.1	0.01	0.04	0.2
1996	7.2	0.1	0.003	0.02	—	...	...	0.06	20.5	0.01	0.07	0.9
1997	7.2	0.1	0.003	0.01	—	...	...	0.1	20.0	0.02	0.09	0.6
1998	7.1	0.1	—	0.01	—	...	...	0.04	...	...	0.1	0.3
Kazakhstan												
1991	86.0	26.6	7.9	130.0	22.0	5.0	3.4	4.7	1459	1.5	1.5	11.3
1993	77.4	23.0	6.7	112.0	13.1	3.6	2.5	3.4	828	0.8	0.3	1.9
1995	66.7	20.5	5.9	83.3	14.9	2.5	1.8	2.1	445	0.4	0.2	0.003
1996	58.7	23.0	6.4	76.6	13.2	2.5	1.7	2.2	326	0.3	0.2	0.1
1997	52.0	25.8	8.1	72.6	15.0	2.0	1.6	3.9	239	0.2	0.15	0.05
1998	49.8	25.9	8.2	69.8	...	...	...	2.6	...	...	0.02	—
Kyrgyzstan												
1991	14.2	0.1	0.1	3.5	—	—	—	—	6.6	0.1	—	—
1993	11.3	0.1	0.04	1.7	—	—	—	—	3.5	0.03	—	—
1995	12.3	0.1	0.04	0.5	—	—	—	—	4.3	0.01	—	—
1996	13.7	0.1	0.03	0.4	—	—	—	—	6.8	0.003	—	—
1997	12.6	0.1	0.02	0.5	—	—	—	—	—	—	—	—
1998	11.6	0.1	0.02	0.4	—	—	—	—	—	—	—	—

1	2	3	4	5	6	7	8	9	10	11	12	13
Moldova												
1991	13.2	—	—	—	—	—	—	0.6	33.0	0.3	—	—
1993	10.4	—	—	—	—	—	—	0.5	17.4	0.05	—	—
1995	1.2	—	—	—	—	—	—	...	26.7	0.02	—	—
1996	1.4	—	—	—	—	—	—	...	19.2	0.02	—	—
1997	1.4	—	—	—	—	—	—	...	...	0.01	—	—
1998	1.2	—	—	—	—	—	—	...	...	...	—	—
Russia												
1991	1068	462	643	353	90.9	48.9	32.6	55.1	223160	65.8	15.0	529
1993	957	354	618	306	76.1	40.9	27.4	42.7	138193	40.9	9.9	349
1995	860	307	595	263	78.3	39.8	27.7	39.0	92264	26.5	9.6	216
1996	847	301	601	255	72.1	37.2	25.2	38.8	59729	20.8	9.4	130
1997	834	306	571	244	70.0	37.0	25.0	37.8	60000	18.1	9.5	128
1998	826	303	591	232	...	...	...	34.1	...	...	9.3	130
Tajikistan												
1991	18	0.1	0.09	0.3	—	—	—	—	—	0.07	0.08	—
1993	18	0.04	0.05	0.2	—	—	—	—	—	0.01	0.02	—
1995	15	0.03	0.04	0.03	—	—	—	—	—	0.0007	0.01	—
1996	15	0.03	0.05	0.02	—	—	—	—	—	0.001	0.01	—
1997	14	0.03	0.04	0.01	—	—	—	—	—	—	0.01	—
1998	14.4	0.02	0.03	0.01	—	—	—	—	—	—	0.01	—
Turkmenistan												
1991	15.0	5.4	84.3	—	—	—	—	—	—	0.04	0.2	—
1993	12.6	4.9	65.3	—	—	—	—	—	—	0.01	0.13	—
1995	9.9	4.7	32.3	—	—	—	—	—	—	—	0.07	—
1996	10.1	4.4	35.2	—	—	—	—	—	—	—	0.06	—

1	2	3	4	5	6	7	8	9	10	11	12	13
Uzbekistan												
1991	54.2	2.8	41.9	5.9	–	–	–	0.8	–	0.5	1.7	49.3
1993	49.1	3.9	45.0	3.8	–	–	–	0.6	–	0.1	1.3	22.6
1995	47.4	7.6	48.6	3.1	–	–	–	0.3	–	0.01	0.9	7.8
1996	45.4	7.6	49.0	2.8	–	–	–	0.4	–	0.01	1.0	5.7
1998	45.9	8.1	54.8	3.0	–	–	–	0.3	–	...	1.0	11.1
Ukraine												
1991	279	4.9	24.3	136.0	85.5	36.6	28.4	32.8	7600	6.1	4.2	136.0
1993	230	4.2	19.2	116.0	65.5	27.1	20.4	24.2	6600	3.9	2.5	80.4
1995	194	4.1	18.2	83.8	50.7	18.0	15.8	16.6	5915	2.9	2.2	41.3
1996	183	4.1	18.4	70.5	47.5	17.8	15.1	17.0	5180	2.3	2.4	33.3
1997	176	4.1	18.1	76.3	50.0	20.0	17.0	19.5	5200	2.5	2.3	29.0
1998	172	3.9	17.9	77.0	...	...	...	17.8	...	...	1.9	24.5
Throughout the CIS												
1991	1632	516	811	630	199	90.4	64.7	95.8	238231	77.7	28.2	1192
1992	1526	452	781	605	176	86.2	61.2	83.1	206084	62.5	22.2	1024
1993	1434	402	762	539	155	71.5	50.3	72.4	150968	48.2	16.7	754
1994	1303	364	720	476	135	59.1	44.0	56.8	102757	36.7	14.7	476
1995	1261	355	707	433	144	60.3	45.3	58.7	103365	31.5	16.5	475
1996	1229	351	717	405	133	57.6	42.0	59.4	69696	25.1	16.2	356
1997	1146	347	603	393	135	59.0	43.6	62.4	70062	22.6	16.0	358
1998	1187	355	713	383	...	...	...	56.1	...	...	15.4	360

On the other hand, developments in the FEC involve challenges difficult or impossible to handle at the national level. Deteriorating geological and mining environment (e.g. transition to the development of remote, deep, marine or poor fields with hazardous admixtures) continuously requires increased investments. Their shortage in Russia governs the reduced well development and field exploration. Coal outputs in Georgia and Tajikistan have ceased over the 1990s.

The FEC in CIS countries has been increasingly laggard in terms of technology level. Less than 15% oil production employs up-to-date, effective and environmentally safe processes. Oil refinement degree is 63% in Russia, 60% in the Ukraine and 56% in Belarus as compared with 87%–93% in Germany and the USA.

Almost 20% of incidental gas resources are lost in flare. Almost 11% of electricity (14% in Kazakhstan, 23% in Azerbaijan and 31% in Kazakhstan) is lost in energy transmission systems as opposed to only 4% in Germany and Japan. Multiple small and inefficient boiler houses are operated.

Equipment production declined sharply, particularly mechanical supports, winches and mining loaders, boring machinery and gas turbines previously produced under co-operative arrangements between plants in, for example, Russia, the Ukraine and Azerbaijan. As a result, the number of electric power stations put into operation in the CIS have decreased five times during the 1990s.

In the first half of the 1990s domestic energy prices began to approach the world level. Thus, producers' prices (excluding VAT) rose from $1.7 to $40 per tonne for crude oil, 1.9 to 50 for black oil, 3.5 to 125 for diesel fuel and 5 to 150 for petrol; $1.1 to $23 per thousand m^3 for natural gas; $0.9 to $17 per tonne for energy coal and from 7 to 210 cents per kilowatt of electricity. This price revolution was responsible for a sharp decline in inter-state exports of energy resources in the CIS, increases in transport tariffs and prices for metals, chemicals and other energy-intensive products, and mass-scale non-payments.

On the other hand, fuel price rise spurs energy-saving strategies (new technologies, building insulation, waste heat reclamation), autonomous energy supply (simultaneous generation of electricity and process steam for the enterprise and the housing environment) and recoverable energy sources.

Oil exports led to the emergence of Saudi Arabia, Kuwait and United Arab Emirates as the world's richest nations. However, native populations there comprise a few hundred thousand people. Almost 80% are non-resident, non-citizenship labour. Oil transport costs are insignificant owing to the proximity of deep-water ports. Industrial, agricultural or urban developments had been negligible. The situation differs essentially from that in the CIS, which makes so meaningless the search for Eldorado in large countries like Kazakhstan, Uzbekistan or the Ukraine.

The FEC is not likely to be a successful engine of economic development unless co-ordinated solutions are found by CIS countries for a whole range of problems:

1. Creating their own research-and-technology base to ensure inputs of machinery and supplies for geological surveys and boring/drilling works, gusher- and gas-lift technologies in oil production, construction and maintenance of pipelines, all types of electric power plants and coal sections, and extensive co-operation with foreign firms. Since the collapse of the USSR inter-state exports in the CIS have been almost discontinued for oil and gas machinery from Azerbaijan, pipes from the Ukraine and turbine generators from Russia. Due to inadequate co-operation between CIS countries, the MIC failed to reconstruct the FEC, a true hostage of expensive foreign imports. As a result, profitability of oil extraction has dropped from 41% to 2% in Russia throughout the 1990s, with 40,000 wells idle and domestic prices for petrol beyond the world level. Russia imports large-diameter pipes at a price three times higher than that offered by Mariupol and Khartsysk in the Ukraine.

2. Establishing joint investment funds and energy sales and settlements schemes. In the 1980s the FEC was financed from the budget through the oil rent related to the price change on the world market. Today a targeted fund to promote mining and development of small and medium-size fields and improved oil recovery represents the most advantageous possible use of household savings and bank monetary surplus. A co-ordinated policy will be designed to improve foreign contracting conditions, eliminate intermediary firms appropriating export gains, to restructure FEC debts and to cut down prices while abandoning barter exchange. Among other advantages are joint building projects for improved oil refineries, natural gas condensation and electric power plants to cover the deficit (in Khabarovsk, Primorsk and some other regions) and export of electricity to, for example, China, Europe, Pakistan, Turkey. An integrated Europe-Asia energy system can emerge as a twenty-first-century project.

3. Agreed conditions of oil and gas mining in the Caspian, with only 7% shelf exploration already indicating 850 million tonnes of oil and 8700 billion m^3 of gas. The world press has been debating the question of two axes – Washington – Baku – Ankara and Moscow – Erevan – Teheran – competing for major fields in the twenty-first century. But rather than competition, CIS countries should benefit with a co-ordinated policy, using the experience gained by OPEC and other international organisations. Projected twenty-first-century outputs will require a network rather than a single pipeline system. A co-ordinated clearing policy will ensure effective exports to the adjacent regions (e.g. Armenia, Georgia, North Iran, Volga region), to be compensated through other terminals more convenient for long-range exports. Special attention in this context should be drawn to issues of environmental control and bioresources (Russia presently being the only promoter of rehabilitation actions in the Caspian holding 70% of the world surgeon stock) and navigation access to the Volga for Caspian

neighbours. Addition of a less viscid and sulphur-containing Siberian oil will facilitate pipeline transport.

4. Co-ordinated energy and pipelines circuits, giving top loading priority to oil refineries in the CIS and maximising export gains. To date, Kazakhstan and Turkmenia have been using the Druzhba pipeline system via Ukraine and the Russian oil pipelines via Astrakhan and Grozny to Novorossiisk, Atyrau (formerly Guriev) – Samara, Chardjou – Omsk, etc. But their capacities are inadequate for fields in Kazakhstan and the Caspian area regarded among the world's ten largest.

By 2000 Russia will maintain a pipeline ring in the centre of Europe, thus completing its integration into the world economy, along with other related countries. The Baltic pipeline system will provide gas and oil exports from Timan-Pechora province to Scandinavia and via Belarus to Poland. A similar role can be fulfilled by the gas net project from Turkmenistan via Uzbekistan and Kazakhstan and from Siberia to China, South Korea and Japan. The Asian Pacific region accounts for over 60% of increase in the world demand for oil (annual 5%). A co-ordinated policy will prevent competition between this project and gas production in Sakhalin (15 billion m^3 every year). The same is true about pipelines from the Central Asian region and Azerbaijan to Europe.

5. TNCs with CIS participation on the lines of Gazprom with branches or joint venture companies in Germany, Italy, Hungary and some other countries. The major oil corporation Lukoil (50 subsidiaries and joint venture companies in 30 Russian regions and 16 countries), along with local firms, contributes to field exploration and development in, for example, Kazakhstan (Kumkol, Uzen, Tengiz), Azerbaijan (10% in the first consortium and 32.5% in the second – the Karabakh field), Uzbekistan, Turkmenistan, Tunisia, oil refinery updating (e.g. Chimkent, Pavlodar) and pipeline building. Lukoil acts as a project operator and owner of petrol stations (including in the USA).

6. A common anti-monopoly energy-saving policy. In the past few years, due to decreasing production and depreciation of equipment, electricity- and heat intensity increased 1.5–2 times for metallurgy, chemistry and petrochemistry and construction materials. The FEC (30%) and public utilities (20%) provide the most significant fuel-saving potential.

Electric power production. Most power resources are involved in electricity generation. Over half of the major consumers in the UK have a choice of supplier: a generating company, regional electricity company or wholesale market. They can obtain information on energy prices every half-hour and devise their loading schedules accordingly. Every company formulates an energy-saving efficiency standard and either pays fees or gets bonuses, depending on the achievements. Half investments to energy-saving are provided by consumers and every invested pound saves 5.5 pence. The abolition of natural monopoly with an integrated energy system allowed open tenders for energy supply and elimination of direct dependence of company profits on increased energy consumption.

In Norway a government corporation owns longline electricity transmission systems, the distribution department providing services to all suppliers, accounting for annual maintenance costs. The wholesale electricity market is divided into three segments – daily (price differentiation by the hour; 3% sales), weekly (price differentiation by day of the week) and annual (sold at fixed price; 70% sales).

A wholesale electricity market in the CIS will involve:

– An integrated energy system carrying out energy transportation, with direct competitive contracting of major electric power plants and consumers on the wholesale market of electricity and power, i.e. without intermediary re-sellers

– Tariffs regulated by a special energy commission rather than energy system, the existing double rates (both on power ordered for and on energy consumed) replaced by a unified tariff differentiated by time of day and regional energy intensity

– Gradual elimination of cross-subsidising (advantages to individual consumer categories through higher tariffs for wholesale buyers – major enterprises)

– Price differentiation for gas and other fuels exclusively governed by transportation distance and other objective factors

– Expanding of energy system, new transmission lines to energy-deficient regions

– Energy-saving incentives (in Russia and other CIS countries energy consumption per unit production is 4–4.5 times that in USA, Japan and EU member countries) and control of unauthorised energy consumption in background industry (in some countries over 25% consumption covered)

– Significant reduction of energy prices for industrial consumers, provided that payments are effected in due time and in money rather than barter exchange or promissory notes, with energy payments included in real expenses and estimates in budget-carried organisations

– Corporatisation of enterprises in the energy sector, with strategic investors and real market stock valuation and tight government control

A regulated market in the FEC will enhance structural reforms. Economic restructuring in the Ukraine involves stable energy production through extended nuclear power stations capacity, nuclear fuel using domestic uranium, gas supply from Russia, promotion of alternative power (solar and wind driven) and oil sources. The new economic structure focuses on co-operation with the USA, Germany, Russia and other countries, and North African and South American markets of crude materials.

Gas will remain as a basis for power production, with annual 30 billion m^3 expected from transit payments, 18 billion local production and 32 billion purchased in Russia, Uzbekistan, Kazakhstan and Turkmenistan. Among the top ten by total profits in the Ukraine were seven FEC companies: Ukrgazprom, Ukrneft, Zaporozhie, Rovno, Chernobyl and South Ukrainian NPS and Dnieper oil mainlines. Twenty-seven energy-supplying and four generating companies will be reconstituted as joint-stock companies, with investors from Russia and other CIS countries invited to privatisation and to new construction.

By 2010–2015 Russia, with its 12% NPS-generated electricity, in the conception of Ministry of nuclear power production, will have its capacity doubled and increase uranium production 2.5–3 times, to 10,000 tonnes annually. A solid-fuel heating centre with capacity equalling one NPS block will burn 4 million tonnes coal every year, while generating 1 million tonnes slag and emitting 40,000 tonnes sulphuric and nitric oxides. One NPS block will use 40 tonnes fuel every year, with special storage in the area. Within an international program by the late 1990s Russia will put into operation a reactor providing safe energy generation in controlled light-nuclei synthesis. Methods are being investigated for global energy supply using lunar helium-3 reserves (three times the energy value of all oil and gas fields on the Earth) and space electric-power stations' microwave transmission of solar energy on Earth-based aerials. In this context the fact that research staff in the energy sector have halved during the 1990s is very distressing, all the more so as most remaining members are over 50 years of age.

Renovation is urgent in the energy sector since over 40% of equipment has exhausted their capacities. But higher tariffs will not provide investments. International experience suggests capital accrued from stock sales and financial guarantees provided by major banks. These will allow by 2010 replacement of 18 obsolete NPS blocks, complete the much-needed HPS in the Far East (Bureia, Ust-Srednekansk), Caucasus (e.g. Cherekh, Zelenchuk, Zaramag) and some other regions and restore the exports of equipment and services for international HPS projects (recall the Assuan HPS in Egypt, Tabka in Syria, Khoabing in Vietnam, Siangmyngsia in China).

Experience in the Russian Primorski territory has shown that the problems cannot be approached on non-market lines. Privileged tariffs on energy below prime costs of its production were set for 70% consumers in the region, with bulk profits gained by intermediaries trading energy in barter exchange. Regional system capacity halved while the personnel increased by one half again. Wage delays and mass-scale disconnections led to labour strikes.

In the long run the CIS energy system should be converted from irrecoverable oil and gas fuels (the share exceeding 60% presently) to the potentials offered by mountain streams (the waste in the CIS exceeding current annual energy outputs), nuclear power (already extracted uranium and weapon plutonium will yield almost 30 trillion kilowatts of energy, enough to meet a 20-year demand in the CIS), subsurface heat, the sun and the wind.

Wind-driven electric power stations with equipment designed by NPO Iuzhnoe (in Dnepropetrovsk) and manufactured under a U.S. license are operated in the Crimea (e.g. Donuzlav, Aktash). Geothermal energy is available on the Kamchatka and some CIS countries; in the Ukraine it can substitute for 10% organic fuels. Only 10%–15% river energy resources are used in Tajikistan, Kyrgyzstan, Eastern Russia and the Caucasus. Application of new technologies will promote both safe and economic nuclear power stations. Exports of electricity to Southeast Asia may prove far more profitable than long-distance oil lines with oil stolen on the way (for home-made petrol), converted from the Newtonian- to a far from transportable aggregate condition.

Ferrous and non-ferrous metallurgy. Ferrous metallurgy plays a highly important role in the national economies in Russia, the Ukraine, Kazakhstan, Georgia and some other CIS countries. Yet between 1990 and 1997 the production of iron ore in the CIS decreased from 199 to 134 million tonnes (see Table 15) and pig iron from 90 to 59 million tonnes, due to reduced domestic effective demand. At the same time there was a drastic increase in exports. In Russia annual metal exports increased from 10 to 25 million tonnes (15% of total exports). The Ukraine accounts for 30% of ferrosilico-manganese exports to Japan. Russia, Kazakhstan and the Ukraine have become the world's largest exporters of run-of-the-mine sheet and high-grade metals. Importers, especially developing countries, are prepared to trade-off uncertain quality, reliability and time of delivery from CIS countries for discount prices.

Thirty of over 100 big enterprises in the Ukraine are involved in ferrous metallurgy. The industry has been intensifying production and exports throughout the 1990s (increasing 20%–25% every year), owing to large reserves of iron ore, manganese and other crude materials, and the proximity of seaports. The industry is the main electricity consumer. The highest market quotations for the 1990s were demonstrated by Nizhnedneprovski and Khartsyz pipe plants, Ordzhonikidze, Marganets and Poltava mining combines, Zaporozhie and Stakhanov ferroalloy works, Zaporozhie coke-, Enakievo, Donetsk and Dnepropetrovsk metallurgical works and Dneprospetsstal. Some have a CIS lead in productivity of labour.

But the CIS metallurgical positions on the world market may deteriorate in a significant manner in the twenty-first century. First, detailed investigations are needed in the ore base. After the break-up of the USSR, Russia lost almost the whole strategic resource of chromium, manganese, titanium, zirconium, lithium, niobium, tantalus and strontium, with much of the accessible potentials of uranium and bauxites. On the other hand, mining combines in some CIS countries can no longer rely on sustained research support provided by 66 branch research institutions in Russia. Due to outdated technologies, capital and operating costs of ore mining in the CIS are far higher and useful recovery much lower than elsewhere. In addition, the highly inertial structure of the mineral and raw material complex requires radical reform, which in turn necessitates comprehensive studies of available mineral resources and their processing technologies.

Demand for ferrous metals in developed countries is unlikely to increase within the next few decades. The area is in the process of conversion from typical CIS giant combines to automated mini-plants where workers are few in number, to produce highly durable rolled metal using scrap and iron ore pellets (e.g. abandoning the blast- or open-heart furnaces). By the late 1990s the CIS, China and India account for 70% manpower and only 30% metal output. Between 1975 and 1995 manpower in the steel industry decreased by 65% in the EC and by 50% in the USA and Japan, with outputs only decreasing by 10%–15%. Updating costs amount to $30–$35 per 1 tonne metal as compared with $8 in Russia.

There are only a few up-to-date mini-plants with high final costs in the CIS, unlike the USA and UK where 600 workers produce 2 million tonnes high-grade steel every year. To maintain competitive positions, Russian metallurgy should project a manpower reduction from 700,000 to 400, 000 for the next 5 years.

Essential for metallurgy are up-to-date marketing and cost management strategies, and a distribution net across the CIS for small-scale wholesale trade in rolled metal, general metal goods, etc. Owing to excessive growth of prices and tariffs of electricity, coke and heat costs account for 40% of the price for metal (under 24% in Germany) and 19% (9%) of railway fare. Almost 90% of transactions on the internal market are represented by barter exchange, territorial and bank bills, etc. For real money, works have to export their products at low prices, causing anti-dumping claims to be issued against them.

CIS metallurgists have created competition between each other on the external market. Thus, for instance, wage (8%), transport (16%) and depreciation (10%) costs in a cold-rolling shop in Russia were 2.5 times those in the Ukraine (total 14%). Instead of raising the wage and increasing renovation and environmental expenditure, the neighbours began forcing down the prices, in turn triggering anti-dumping processes in the USA and other countries.

Due to problematic sales, outputs of rolled ferrous metals and steel tubes in 1998 decreased 10%–19% in Russia, the Ukraine and Kazakhstan. This impaired the countries' balance of payments and unemployment profiles.

CIS *non-ferrous metallurgy* occupies a prominent place in the world market. Here too the lack of co-ordinated policy deprives the industry of financial resources. Natural uranium is produced in Russia (20% of world market), Kazakhstan, the Ukraine and some other countries. Unique refining technologies in Russia have determined the export prices 5%–10% lower than in the rest of the world. The Elemash works in Moscow Region provides nuclear fuel for 48 nuclear power plants in nine countries – 10% of the world market. The world uranium consumption has been growing by 4%–5% every year, generally owing to new NPSs in Asian countries (e.g. China, South Korea, Iran). However, competitive exports in 1997 led to a 30%–40% drop in the price of uranium, from $15 to $9.

Among the CIS countries developing gold fields are Kazakhstan (Akbakai, Bakyrchik, Vasilkovskoe, Sharaltyn, Leninogorsk), Kyrgyzstan (Jeroi, Kumtor, Taidy-Bulek, Kadamjai), Tajikistan (Darvaz, Taror-Jilau), Uzbekistan (Zarafshan, Zarshitan, Amanaitau, Mardkhanbulag), Russia (Balei, Darasun, Aginskoe, Pokrovskoe, Suchoi Log, Valunistoe, Omolok, Zakandja), Armenia, Azerbaijan and the Ukraine. Gold production will reach 25–30 tonnes by 2000 in Kyrgyzstan, 18 tonnes in Armenia (fourteenth in the world), over 160 tonnes in Russia (fifth in the world after the UAR, Australia, USA and Canada). World demand for gold is expanding (particularly in India, Turkey and other Asian countries), but the price has fallen to $300 per oz. Therefore, gold mining is unlikely to be profitable until up-to-date processes are employed.

Since new fields have been developed in South America, Australia and Canada, prices for copper and lead are expected to fall, with a rise in prices for zinc, silver (the largest ore deposits are in Central Asian republics), aluminium (to $1800–$1900 per tonne), platinum, palladium (Russia is the leading exporter) and probably tin and nickel.

The risk of unexpected change in metal prices can be reduced in several ways. One way is complex processing of raw materials for product-mix improvement. Thus, Uzbekistan ranks third in the world in tungsten resources (over 100,000 tonnes). Russia produces 60% of palladium used in car building and electronics (Japan importing 40% of world output). Prices have risen for magnesium – far superior to aluminium in mechanical strength and light weight. Indium, a by-product of lead and zinc production in the Ukraine, Kazakhstan and Russia, is used in liquid-crystal displays.

The more successful competitors on the market of non-ferrous metals are TNCs, due to the closed-loop production cycle, from raw material input to final output. Thus, only seven TNCs account for half the world production of aluminium. One such TNC, Reynolds (annual net revenue $7 billion), is involved in the production of bauxites, alumina, rolled metal, tins, wheels and spare parts for vehicles and building purposes, and wholesale trade. CIS countries all have the potential for such TNCs. This will allow elimination of the multiple intermediaries, the sophisticated system of arrears, to reduce output prices, in particular at the domestic market, and consequently to expand the demand.

But the potential has not been used yet. Due to disrupted business links, many enterprises in the FEC and metallurgy complex were closed or sold to foreign companies undertaking to cover external and wage debts and deductions to the budget. There were cases of such companies failing to perform investment obligations. Thus, Kazakhstan had to cancel joint-venture agreements for gold mine management in Aktiubinsk and some other units. Nevertheless,, foreign corporations control the world's fourth powerful mine Vasilkovskoe (near the town of Kokchetav), hydropower plants in Shulba and Ust-Kamenogorsk, alumina in Pavlodar and polymetals in Kounrad.

Balkhash combine (30% of Kazakhstan's copper output) with controlling interest held by the staff and companies in Kazakhstan, Russia and Mongolia, was privatised by Samsung corporation (South Korea) undertaking to pay the delayed wage, contribute to the working capital and invest $700 million. Not infrequently, unco-ordinated actions adversely affected CIS countries. The Don chromium deposit in Kazakhstan met 80% of demand at three works in Russia and one in the Ukraine. Their independent entry on the European market forced down the price for ferrochromium, causing anti-dumping procedures, with the main input assigned to a foreign management. Reliable raw material supplies were lost in Verkhnesaldinskoe AO (Urals), the world largest input of crude alloyed titanium (including for *Boeing* and some other U.S. corporations). Co-operative arrangements with other CIS countries are badly needed in a super-strong substance plant in Uzbekistan (e.g. diamond tools for steel, marble, granite).

Large aluminium works in Russia (17% of the world market) and Tajikistan, having lost reliable inputs in Kazakhstan, the Ukraine and Azerbaijan (domestic alumina only satisfies 35%–40% of industrial demand in Siberia and the development of Sredne-Timanskoe deposit will require almost $1.5 billion investment), resorted to external tolling (firms in the far abroad as both provides inputs and owning outputs). As a result, while works in Russia and Tajikistan maintained their competitive positions (annual exports over 3 million tonnes, profitability 20%–25%, production of foil, aluminium pot bands, and other items started), the budget showed heavy losses (aluminium processing representing only 40%–45% of the price), artificial-deficit-boosted alumina prices and the domestic market was constrained (the share falling to 10%–15%).

The market dictates the new economic patterns. Russian works in 1997 abandoned alumina delivery from Nikolaev (the Ukraine) at $210/tonne (with advance payment and not very reliable), Australian imports appearing 25% cheaper, even considering transport costs. Indeed, obsolete technology in Nikolaev dictated labour consumption per tonne of product five times higher, the yield per 1 tonne crude input 50% lower and prime cost, despite the low wage, far higher than Australian ($200 as against $80–$90/tonne). Russian works likewise employ up-to-date technologies only in 14% aluminium production (100% in Australia and 73%–77% in the rest of the world). If metal prices fall and maximum allowable toxic discharge is lowered to the U.S. and Canadian level, the works will suffer losses.

Kazakhstan will emerge as the major CIS aluminium exporter by the early twenty-first century when the plant in Pavlodar starts production on local bauxites and alumina.

The chemical complex. Chemical industries in the current CIS territory were renovated or re-created in the 1970s. Over 90% of industrial potentials are in Russia, the Ukraine, Belarus and Kazakhstan; high-quality synthetic rubber is produced in Armenia, detergents in Azerbaijan, nitric fertilisers in Tajikistan, and fertilisers and synthetic fibres in Uzbekistan. The Ukraine provides a largely monopolistic supply of titanic dioxide, Belarus fibres and tyres, and Kazakhstan of chrome compounds.

The CIS has all the required conditions to promote production and sales of mineral fertilisers, pesticides, plastics and synthetic resins, synthetic fibres and threads, dyes, tyres and caustic soda. By the end of the twentieth century high growth rates will have been attained in medicines, perfumery, cosmetics, fine chemicals (e.g. biostimulators, enzymes, fodder additives, catalysts). But the complex was adversely affected by the disruption of traditional links between enterprises. Production of sulphuric acid, caustic and calcinated soda, synthetic resins and plastics in CIS countries in 1991–1997 almost halved, that of synthetic fibres and threads decreased almost three-fold, and pipes and thermoplastic components, pesticides, film and tape 4–25 times (see Table 15).

The highest reduction rates occurred where basic markets were in other CIS countries: sulphuric acid and thermoplastic pipes in the Ukraine, synthetic ammonia in Georgia, and synthetic rubber in Armenia, Azerbaijan and Kazakhstan. Enterprises cannot afford foreign supplies of raw materials and energy resources. On the other hand, inter-enterprise competition across the CIS forced down export prices for nitric, phosphate and potassium fertilisers, polyethylene and polypropylene.

Due to reduced supplies of new equipment, share of depreciated equipment increased significantly. These result in large volumes of cheap exports of raw materials and expensive imports of complete products. This is especially true for medicines (imports representing two thirds of the market), pesticides and fine chemicals. Growth rates in prices for chemicals in the CIS have been larger than those for industrial products in general, impairing their competitive positions.

Hazardous atmospheric emission caused by stationary pollution sources in CIS countries amounts to annually to 1 million tonnes. Ammonia, sulphuric, fluorine and chloride content in the air in Dzerzhinsk, Angarsk, Berezniki (Russia), Rubezhnoe and Lisichansk (the Ukraine), Grodno (Belarus), Samarkand (Uzbekistan) and other towns often exceeds admissible levels, with the bulk carried in transfrontier pollution. Emission control is unlikely to be successful unless joint efforts are involved, accounting for close inter-relationship of oil refining, chemistry, consumers of chemical products and chemical machinery, sharing investment resources and co-ordinating export plans.

New trends of development emerged in the area by the end of the 1990s. Enterprises in the Ukraine (AO Azot, Neftekhimik Prikarpatia, Dneproshina) head the list in investment attractiveness index. Uzbekistan started production of 170 medicine types (licensed and with equipment provided by a German corporation) and built an oil-chemical combine in Bokhara, and Turkmenistan, a complex in the town of Mary. Russia expanded the output of synthetic fibres, dyes and detergents, polymeric films and other such items. Chemicals, especially fertilisers and heavy chemical by-products of oil and gas refining, rank third (below energy resources and metals) on the list of Russian exports (7% of totals). But rapid changes in prices on the world market (e.g. for ammonia, polyethylene) caused production halts in Volgograd, Stavropol and some other towns.

Large transnational corporations (TNCs) will be instrumental in filling the technological gap, reducing industrial resource intensity, increasing processing yields and improving research-intensive product-mix and environmental safety. Most enterprises in the area (90% of 800 in Russia) were transformed into joint stock companies. But only in a few countries were they integrated as supply-chain processes going all the way from research and raw materials (the CIS holding one third of world reserves) to complete product packed in up-to-date tare. Thus, for instance, chemical concern in Uzbekistan incorporates 4 institutes, 36 enterprises, and foreign-trade, supply and commercial firms. The FIG Neftekhimprom has enterprises in Russia, the Ukraine and Belarus producing more than 100 chemical and petrochemical product types, e.g. elastics and polymers, tyres, rubber. The FIG Interkhimprom specialises in mineral fertilisers and nitric compounds. But almost 80% of FIG outputs were exported in the mid-1990s.

Of special importance for the domestic market in the CIS are industrial developments in agrochemistry, pharmaceuticals, and perfumery and cosmetics. The fast investment payback will ensure a basis for reconstruction in the whole chemical complex. While application of almost 50 kg fertilisers yields 1 tonne grain, 300 kg mineral fertilisers per hectare were applied in 1987 and only 12 kg in 1996. The pesticide market in the CIS is almost totally dominated by imports.

Development and promotion of a new medicine costs $100–$400 million by world standards. For this reason, and also due to the lack of internationally attested laboratories and clinics, medicines prepared in the CIS are confined to laboratories and are not patented abroad. At most, CIS plants are packaging imported preparations. Meanwhile some European and Asian companies have started mass-scale export to the CIS of medicines with expired patents, prepared by world key firms in the 1970s. Imported perfumery and cosmetics represent 90% of the Russian market ($2 billion annually). National products are limited to inexpensive goods in popular demand. Procter & Gamble, Unilever, L'Oreal and other international corporations have launched a massive advertising campaign in the CIS. Yet the CIS has both, the unique medicinal crops and the material and human resources, required for a rich mix of medicines (expected market of

$10 billion by 2000), luxury cosmetics, and other such items. The question is of appropriate management and joint scientific and industrial efforts in all CIS countries.

The forestry complex. There are vast blocks of forest in Russia and Belarus (25% of world resources), and developed furniture and cellulose and paper industries in the Ukraine, Moldova and Georgia. Developments in this area in the 1990s have been confronted with challenges typical for the extractive sector in the CIS (see Table 13).

1. Obsolete technologies determining the low output per 1 m^3 felled timber and predominant exports of round rather than sown timber, high-grade paper, etc. (These extremely rewarding market niches are gradually being occupied by Scandinavian countries, the USA, Germany and Austria). While exporting timber, the CIS has been increasingly importing furniture from not at all densely forested countries such as Italy and UK.

2. Strategic foreign investments not always successful. Thus, the cellulose and paper combine in Vyborg failed, even though the controlling block of shares had been purchased by a U.S. company. A 2–2.5-fold increase in world prices for cellulose in 1995 was followed by a drop posing numerous problems in many joint venture companies.

3. Higher transport tariffs and other costs made unprofitable timber exports from Siberia within the CIS and to the far abroad, encouraging the Baltic countries to increase their exports significantly.

To resolve this problem, the social sphere (accounting for 30%–40% of costs in timber procurement establishments and railways) should be transferred to local administration, which in turn will require putting in order the taxes and accelerating the housing and municipal reform, and diversifying production in wood-felling settlements.

4. The area needs an intermediary administrative unit responsible both for exploitation and reforestation. A strictly commercial approach resulted in closure of nature-protecting mountain blocks of forest in some CIS republics. A good lesson can be taken from Russian exporters establishing an association to protect their interests at external markets. Another innovation is a timber-exporting shipping company intending to order 50 large transport vessels for export trade in the Asian Pacific region.

Co-ordination at the CIS-wide level will attract national unemployed labour to timber procurement in Russia, in turn promoting national production of building components, cardboard tare and some other products in short supply. Reconciliation of extractive and manufacturing branches of economy in the CIS is of both economic and political importance. The former are still interested in expanded exports facilitated by overall economic liberalisation, reduced customs tariffs and national exchange rates and eliminated constraints on capital flows, and the latter in decreased competitive imports requiring higher customs duties, fixed exchange rates, protectionism, government regulation and support. The conflict of interests, as experience in some developing market economies has demonstrated, impairs political stability.

The new pattern of national economy should accomplish the following objectives:

– Enhanced growth of research-intensive branches securing sustainable economic growth in the twenty-first century, qualified jobs for the young, equitable integration in the world economic relationships, and further progress of science and education

– Development of extractive branches through up-to-date environmental technologies, focusing on the interests of coming generations, co-operation with both foreign corporations and domestic manufacturers, including machine building

– Transition to co-operative external trade, i.e. joint development, production and sales of goods and services, involving foreign firms, partnerships and associations on a CIS-wide scale for a joint R&D, environmental and foreign-trade policy

Co-ordination is of the utmost significance in the agro-industrial complex (AIK) including: firstly, agriculture; secondly, agricultural machinery, fertilisers, fodder and additives; thirdly, related manufacturing (food and light) industries; and finally, the relevant infrastructure for store, transport and sales of products and provision of financial, consulting and other services.

Field of Debate

1. Describe the meaning and the main trends of structural reform in the CIS. How does it differ from that carried out in other countries? How can the impact of reform be assessed?

2. How are the academic and R&D potentials, and the R&D production level differentiated? What trends favour R&D promotion in CIS countries? What are the guidelines for critically important technologies?

3. What can be done to maintain and develop the R&D potential in CIS countries?

4. What factors govern effective conversion in the military-industrial complex? What lessons in developed industrial countries can be helpful in this context? In what way can inter-state co-operation in the CIS facilitate military reform and conversion in defence industry and research?

5. What actions can be taken to maintain employment in CIS aircraft industry?

6. What are the prospects for motor-car industry in the CIS? What is the role of CIS-wide co-operation? What co-operative arrangements with corporations in developed countries will be helpful in this context?

7. What are the prospects for shipbuilding in the CIS? How is shipbuilding financed under market conditions?

8. Describe the computer market and its segments. What are the characteristic features of high-technology industries? Why is their development preferable to exclusive imports? What are the most effective co-operative arrangements at the CIS level in computer engineering and electronics? What product types hold the greatest promise in CIS countries?

9. Describe electronics and electrical engineering as CIS basic machine-building industries. How can crisis in the industries be approached in terms of international experience, by protecting domestic producers while allowing for reasonable competition?

10. What are the twenty-first-century prospects for energy mining in the CIS? What problems in the sphere ought to be handled with co-operative efforts within the CIS and in collaboration with other members of the international community?

11. How can electrical engineering be converted to market-oriented economic methods? What factors should be considered when comparing thermal-, hydro- and nuclear power stations for efficiency? What promises are shown by energy reclamation and saving in the CIS?

12. Describe world developments in ferrous and non-ferrous metallurgy by the end of the twentieth century. What are the relevant goals to be attained by CIS metallurgy? In what areas is CIS-wide co-operation most urgent?

13. What are the main problems of development in the chemical and forest complex in your country and in the CIS as a whole? How are they solved?

14. What are the factors governing the conflict of extractive and manufacturing interests in the CIS? Why is structural reform necessary for sustainable economic development in the CIS?

Chapter 6

CHANGES IN THE AGROINDUSTRIAL SECTOR

6.1 The CIS Agroindustrial Complex Towards the End of the Twentieth Century

Agrarian sector in CIS economies. The agrarian sector figures prominently in CIS economies. It employs a much greater proportion of the public than in other European and North American countries, or Japan (especially in Central Asian and Transcaucasian republics), largely governing the social and political developments, preservation of traditional national values and the basic natural wealth – land and its fertility – as well as the national demographic potential.

The contribution of the agroindustrial complex (AIC) to total GDP is significant (30%–60%), ensuring national food supply at reasonable prices, political stability and national security.

The AIC outputs, with the exception of cotton and some industrial crops, though unimportant for markets in the "far abroad", represent an essential portion of commodity turnover within the CIS. Kazakhstan, Russia and the Ukraine are potentially large exporters of grain; Kyrgyzstan, Kazakhstan and Belarus of meat; the Ukraine of sugar; Belarus of potatoes, cabbages and root crops; and Moldova and the Central Asian and Transcaucasian republics of fruit, vegetables, wine and tobacco.

Nevertheless, despite the vital necessity of the agrarian sector for all nations of the former USSR and the fact that the need for radical transformations in the AIC had been among the reasons for the transition to market economy in all CIS countries, the agroindustrial sphere has deteriorated rapidly over the 1990s. The very transition to market reproduction conditions has aggravated structural crisis in the AIC.

To avoid continued movement "in the spiral of age-long drama", as Academician A.A. Nikonov put it,[1] agrarian reforms in all Commonwealth member states

---

[1] For an extended discussion of the history and the lessons of agrarian reforms in Imperial Russia and the Soviet Union see: Stroev, E.S. (1994): Methodology and Practices of Agrarian Reform. Kolos, Moscow (Строев, Е.С. (1994): Методология и Практика Аграрного Реформирования. Колос, Москва) [In Russian]; Nikonov, A.A. The Spiral

without exception and in the Commonwealth in general must acquire a new quality, promoting a society of sustainable development, all the more so while the physical, human and intellectual potentials are still available.

What then explains conditions in CIS agroindustrial complex as the twenty-first century approaches?

By contrast to developed industrial countries, most (eight) CIS republics between 1991 and 1997 demonstrated increased employment rates in agriculture, forestry and fishery: from 23.3% to 40.7% in Armenia, 35.9 to 46% in Kyrgyzstan, 35.9% to 43% in Moldova and from 44.7% to 58% in Tajikistan (see Table 16). Many urban industrial enterprises there have either cut radically or discontinued production, whereas in rural areas extended household plots help to wait until the hard times are over. Agricultural employment also grew in Russia (from 13.5% to 14.4%), Turkmenistan (from 42.4% to 45.7%) and the Ukraine (from 19.3% to 21.8%). Slight reductions were only evident in Azerbaijan and Uzbekistan where agrarian employment had been at a maximum (32.1% and 42.7%, respectively), and in Belarus. In Kazakhstan the rate almost stabilised. Only in Belarus and Russia does the share of agrarian employment remain under 20% now.

Table 16

Employment Distribution by Commonwealth Member Countries and Industries (in %)

Country	Agriculture, forestry and fishery			Industry and construction			Services		
	1992	1997	1998	1992	1997	1998	1992	1997	1998
Azerbaijan	33.5	32.1	27.5	22.4	15.3	12.5	44.1	52.6	60.0
Armenia	30.0	40.7	40.7	34.3	21.9	20.4	35.7	37.4	38.9
Belarus	20.0	17.6	17.0	39.9	33.7	34.7	40.1	48.7	48.3
Georgia	31.7	51.7	57.8	24.7	10.1	7.9	43.6	38.2	34.3
Kazakhstan	24.9	23.6	24.2	30.1	20.5	17.8	45.0	55.9	58.0
Kyrgyzstan	37.2	46.0	47.3	22.5	14.4	13.4	40.3	39.6	38.8
Moldova	35.8	43.0	41.9	27.4	15.0	14.7	36.8	42.0	43.4
Russia	13.9	14.4	12.9	40.5	34.2	31.2	45.6	51.4	55.9
Tajikistan	45.9	58.0	63.9	20.0	14.2	11.4	34.1	27.8	24.7
Turkmenistan	43.3	45.7	...	20.2	18.5	...	36.5	35.8	...
Uzbekistan	43.5	40.0	40.1	21.6	19.0	19.0	34.9	41.0	40.9
Ukraine	19.7	21.8	21.5	37.0	29.6	27.0	42.3	48.6	52.0

of Age-Old Drama: The Agrarian Nation and Russian Politics (18th–20th Cent.). Moscow (Никонов, A.A. (1995): Спираль Многовековой Драмы: Аграрная Нация и Политика России (XVIII–XX вв.). Москва) [In Russian]

Changes in employment determine differences in proportions of rural populations (see Table 17). In five countries they accounted for more than a half (Moldova, Turkmenistan, Uzbekistan, Kyrgyzstan and Tajikistan), growing in all of them over the 1990s. In three republics (Kazakhstan, Georgia and Azerbaijan) rural populations represent 44%–47%, in three more (Belarus, the Ukraine and Armenia) 31%–34%, and only in Russia is it under 27%. Throughout the 1990s urban population has increased only in Belarus (stabilising in Georgia and the Ukraine).

Table 17

Proportions of Rural Populations by CIS Member Countries (in %)

Country	1991	1992	1993	1994	1995	1996	1997
Azerbaijan	46.5	45.8	46.6	47.3	47.3	47.3	32.1
Armenia	30.6	30.6	32.4	32.4	32.4	34.2	40.7
Belarus	33.3	32.4	32.0	32.0	31.1	31.1	47.6
Georgia	44.4	44.4	44.4	44.4	44.4	44.4	51.7
Kazakhstan	42.5	42.6	42.6	43.8	44.0	44.2	23.6
Kyrgyzstan	61.4	62.2	62.2	63.6	64.4	64.4	46.0
Moldova	52.3	52.3	53.5	53.5	53.5	53.5	43.0
Russia	26.2	26.4	26.8	27.0	27.0	27.0	14.4
Tajikistan	69.8	69.6	71.4	70.2	72.4	72.9	58.0
Turkmenistan	54.1	55.3	56.4	55.0	56.1	55.6	45.7
Uzbekistan	59.7	60.2	60.6	61.6	61.3	61.6	40.0
Ukraine	32.7	32.4	32.3	32.4	32.4	32.5	21.8

In eight CIS countries employment extended in services, to over 50% in Azerbaijan, Kazakhstan and Russia.

Despite increasing employment, total agricultural outputs in CIS countries reduced by 35% during the first 5 years of the decade, including by 64%–68% in Tajikistan and Georgia, 46%–50% in Azerbaijan and Kazakhstan, and 33%–38% in Russia, the Ukraine, Moldova and Kyrgyzstan. Almost 30 million hectares agricultural area have gone out of agricultural production, including 5 million hectares arable land. Fertility has been impaired by inadequate fertiliser application and erratic agrotechnics, with semi-desert, saline, swamp and waste lands extended. The aggregate planted area continued to decrease in 1997 in Azerbaijan (by 11%), Armenia (by 4%), Kazakhstan (by 15%), Russia (by 3%), Tajikistan (by 23%) and Turkmenistan (by 6%).

Market reform in the AIC in most CIS countries failed to achieve production growth, even though rural producers are now free to sell their produce, acquire the necessary inputs and distribute the gains at their own discretion. Only 25% of reduced production in the public sector (by 53%) was compensated for by growth in the private sector (with 10% contributed by household gardens and 3% by farms). This was accompanied by a significant decline in share of agricultural output to be sold (as opposed to consumed by producers; two times for vegetables, 1.6 for potatoes, 1.4 for livestock and 1.3 for milk).

As a result, with extended employment, per capita agricultural outputs declined, especially for sugar beets, meat (from 68 to 39 kg), milk (from 368 to 260 kg) and eggs (from 284 to 180 pieces). Data for the production and consumption of meat, milk and eggs by CIS countries are shown in Table 18 (1996). In 1997 consumption of meat and meat products fell in Russia (to 49 kg) and the Ukraine (to 34.7 kg); milk and dairy products in Azerbaijan (to 144 kg), Kazakhstan (to 196 kg), Moldova (to 154 kg) and the Ukraine. A survey in a sample of households indicated that consumption in terms of calories (generally animal proteins) reduced in all republics during the 5-year period, with the exception of Belarus (from 2.175 to 1.788 ccal per one member in Armenia and from 2.221 to 1.932 in Azerbaijan).

Table 18

**Production and Consumption of Meat (kg), Milk (kg)
and Eggs (*n*) per Capita in mid-1990s**

Country	Production			Consumption		
	Meat	Milk	Eggs	Meat	Milk	Eggs
Azerbaijan	11	300	63	16	364	79
Armenia	13	114	51	27	120	70
Belarus	61	477	334	59	364	295
Kazakhstan	53	226	79	50	205	70
Kyrgyzstan	40	193	35	39	186	33
Moldova	30	172	141	25	158	107
Russia	36	247	216	51	235	208
Ukraine	41	310	171	37	230	162

The bulk of agricultural outputs in the CIS are produced in Russia (50.1% in 1991 and 48.3% in 1996), the Ukraine (22%), Uzbekistan (7%), Belarus (6.8%) and Kazakhstan (6.4%).

Belarus has the highest per capita agricultural outputs (in percent to average in the CIS – 160% in 1991 and 187% in 1996), whereas it is almost at the bottom of the list in soil fertility. Per capita outputs are beyond average in Moldova (127%), the Ukraine (123%) and Kazakhstan (111%). Average lag decreased in Uzbekistan (76% in 1991 and 86% in 1996) and Armenia (42% and 71%). Severe losses in agrarian sectors in Tajikistan and Azerbaijan were caused by military operations (see Table 19).

Table 19

**Agricultural Production per Capita in CIS Member Countries
(in % of average in the CIS)**

Country	1991	1992	1993	1994	1995	1996
Azerbaijan	72	59	51	51	51	55
Armenia	42	38	47	56	62	71
Belarus	160	160	170	169	171	187
Georgia	50	48	43	31	68	77
Kazakhstan	121	134	130	122*	115*	111*
Kyrgyzstan	89	92	86	81*	81*	87*
Moldova	132	122	134	120	132	127
Russia	95	95	94	96	94	93
Tajikistan	60	48	46	39*	38*	33*
Turkmenistan	105	99	109	103	88	91*
Uzbekistan	76	77	77	81	88	86
Ukraine	119	120	124	121	125	123
CIS	100	100	100	100	100	100

* Estimated.

Thus, CIS countries, with their most fertile vast lands (in some cases securing several harvests per year) and big rural populations, are still unable to meet public consumption standards. In the black-earth Ukraine, a potential granary for Europe, over the first 5 years in the 1990s per capita consumption of meat and meat products decreased by 44%, fish and fish products by 82%, milk and dairy produce, eggs, vegetable oil, fruit and berries by 31%–33%.[2]

How can this be explained?

Of course, agrarian crisis can be traced to historical attitudes to the rural sphere as an inexhaustible supply of material, financial and human resources requiring no preservation, management or renovation. Not infrequently, wars have been won and industrial reforms and scientific and technological revolutions carried out at the expense of peasantry. Consequently, the agrarian sector has lived up to its reputation as the "black hole". This is where a suction pump has been applied and, through price disparity and monopolistic pressure on a more competitive branch, revenues are still being pumped out and resources plundered in the Commonwealth agroindustrial complex.

Nor should the long-term rule of the administrative command system be disregarded, the enforced and thoughtless collectivisation and multiple rural

[2] (1996): Экономика Украины (Ekonomika Ukrainy) 10, 10–11 [In Russian]

reorganisations, which undermine the peasant's autonomy, initiative and enterprise while failing to build a framework for development.

On the other hand, the fussy market liberalism leaving the agroindustrial sphere face to face with only slogan-based processes of privatisation aimed at reorganising collective and state farms as private, and with monopolistic monsters in the FEC, financial sphere and external market, has not met with success.

As seen in Table 19, only three republics, Belarus, Armenia and Georgia, attained notable improvements (as compared with CIS average), with the first focusing on preservation and the others on elimination of collective farms. At this stage closer examination of GDP dynamics in the agrarian sector would be helpful.

Industrial development in the agrarian sector. Some data for changes in the physical gross output in agriculture, fishery and forestry over the period of reform are shown in Table 20.

As Table 20 indicates, the greatest losses in GDP occurred in Azerbaijan, Georgia, Tajikistan and the Ukraine, in the latter exclusively governed by internal factors. On average in the CIS gross agricultural output in 1997 comprised 67% of the 1991 level, including 86%–88% in Kyrgyzstan and Uzbekistan, 75% in Belarus, 67%–68% in Moldova, Russian and the Ukraine, and 50%–55% in Azerbaijan, Kazakhstan and Tajikistan. The early 1990s level was only exceeded in Armenia (by 12%) and Georgia (by 8%).

Agricultural outputs continued to decline in 1998 in Russia, the Ukraine, Kazakhstan, Moldova and Georgia, due to reduced areas under crops (by 24% between 1990 and 1998, notably by 48% in Kazakhstan and 60% in Russia), livestock (as compared with the 1980s, in 1998 cattle stocks reduced by 60% in Kazakhstan, 53% in Russia and 56% in the Ukraine), low yields of agricultural crops and livestock productivity.

Because of the draught in 1998, average grain yields per hectare decreased 43% in Russia, 36% in Kazakhstan, 15% in the Ukraine and 23% in Belarus. The result was that grain production) constituted 21% in Kazakhstan, 40% in Russia and 51% in the Ukraine, as against the respective peaks in 1992, 1990 and 1989.

Fishery in the USSR provided a vital public supply of inexpensive and very important proteins. The Soviet sea-going fishing fleet was among the largest in the world. In the 1990s some portions of the fleet and port facilities were taken by the Baltic states. Many countries expanded their economic zones, imposing big fishing charges for foreign vessels, and fuel prices and tariffs went up tremendously. As a result, fish of the North- and East seas has become a rare dish in CIS inland areas, with not infrequent cases of export trade on the high seas, evading statistics and taxation. Fishing in the Aral has been undermined by environmental disaster – the drying up, and in the Caspian by depredation of sturgeon for caviar (abolished state monopoly boosting the exports and a forcing down the prices). Commercial fish-breeding in lakes in Moldova and some other countries has been inhibited by increased energy prices and decreased feed inputs from other CIS republics.

Table 20

GDP in Agriculture, Fishery and Forestry (in % of preceding year)

Country	1992	1993	1994	1995	1996	1996 (in % of 1991)	1997 (in % of 1996)	1998 (in % of 1997)*
Azerbaijan	77	77	80	88	101	42.6	93	104
Armenia	58	51	105	107	106	63.3	94	113
Belarus	90	92	87	90	103	67.1	95	99.6
Georgia	55	71	109	103	11˙	48.6	106	92
Kazakhstan	95	89	87	92	101	68.7	98	81
Kyrgyzstan	86	84	80	95	106	58.1	110	104
Moldova	71	99	69	98	92	61.0	109	89
Russia	86	91	87	96	95	62.2	100	88
Tajikistan	73	83	87	88	83	45.0	104	106.5
Turkmenistan	91	102	83	91	100	65.0	90*	...
Uzbekistan	89	98	95	99	102	82.9	104	104
Ukraine	90	86	77	88	90	47.1	98	92
On average throughout CIS	91	98	87	93	95*	94.0	99	91

* GDP in agriculture, at comparable prices.

As a result, fish and other sea products between 1991 and 1996 almost halved in Russia and Kazakhstan, decreasing 2.5-fold in the Ukraine, four to six times in Azerbaijan, Turkmenistan and Uzbekistan, and several tens of times in Georgia, Moldova, Kyrgyzstan, Tajikistan and Belarus. Rivers, lakes and seas are now dominated by poachers.

Outputs have grown by the end of the 1990s. Private firms are ordering up-to-date vessels and implements. Twenty-first-century prospects for the area will derive from new fish-breeding technologies in inland waters and enhanced inter-state reproduction control, particularly in the Caspian and Pacific seas.

New technologies are badly needed in *forestry*, as well as environmental and fire control systems. At these conditions highland regions and ethnic minorities in the Far North would benefit by woodland's bounty (mushrooms, berries, nuts, medicinal herbs), shooting and hunting, timber procurement and processing.

Table 21

Gross Output of Grain Crops by CIS Countries
(post-procession weight; all kinds of production units; million tonnes)

Country	1991	1992	1993	1994	1995	1996	1997	1998
Russia	89.1	106.8	99.1	81.3	63.4	69.3	88.5	47.4
Ukraine	38.7	38.5	45.6	35.5	33.9	24.5	35.4	26.5
Kazakhstan	12.0	29.8	21.6	16.4	9.5	11.2	12.3	6.4
Belarus	6.3	7.2	7.5	6.1	5.5	5.8	6.4	4.8
Moldova	3.1	2.1	3.3	1.8	2.7	2.0	3.2	2.5
Uzbekistan	1.9	2.2	2.1	2.5	3.2	3.6	3.8	...
Kyrgyzstan	1.4	1.5	1.5	1.0	1.0	1.4	1.7	1.7
Turkmenistan	0.5	0.7	1.0	1.1	1.0	1.0	0.7	...
Tajikistan	0.3	0.3	0.3	0.2	0.2	0.5	0.5	0.5
Azerbaijan	1.3	1.3	1.1	1.0	0.9	1.0	1.1	0.9
Georgia	0.6	0.5	0.4	0.5	0.5	0.65	0.9	0.6
Armenia	0.3	0.3	0.3	0.3	0.2	0.3	0.3	...
CIS as a whole	155.5	191.4	183.9	147.5	122.0	121.2	154.8	91.3

Developments in *agriculture* differed in plant and livestock sectors across the CIS. *Grain* crops play a crucial role (see Table 21). With an overall reduction, areas sown in grain crops have grown (from 53% to 54% of total area). Yet outputs remain low (18.2 metric centners/ha in 1992, 17.5 in 1993, 15.2 in 1994 and 12.8 in 1995). Public grain inputs were only provided through a drastic extension of commercial industrial crops, with per capita levels maintained and even improved in Turkmenistan (2.7 times over the 1991–1997 period), Uzbekistan (one sixth), Georgia (1.5), Kyrgyzstan and Armenia (1.2 and 1.3 times, respectively).

Most CIS areas sown in *cotton* are in Uzbekistan (57%), Turkmenistan (20%) and Tajikistan (almost 10%). Reduced public effective demand and machinery, fuel and fertiliser supplies in the 1990s resulted in reduced sown areas (by 12.14% in Uzbekistan and Turkmenistan between 1991 and 1997, and by 28% in Tajikistan) and outputs. Thus, between 1991 and 1996 gross output of raw cotton decreased three times in Tajikistan and Turkmenistan, by half in Azerbaijan and by 28% (from 4.6 to 3.4 million tonnes) in Uzbekistan. Over the same period gross output of another important raw material – *flax fibre* decreased by 42% in Russia, 36% in Belarus and almost six-fold in the Ukraine.

For purposes of food autonomy areas sown in *potatoes* and gross outputs were increased (e.g. 1.5–1.7 times in Armenia, Uzbekistan and Kyrgyzstan, 1.3 in Moldova and the Ukraine). But the use of important lands, including irrigated, for non-marketable (generally meant for household needs) and not labour-consuming crops is unlikely to be efficient in terms of market economy. Between 1990 and 1997 gross output of *vegetables* increased in Belarus, Georgia, Armenia, Kyrgyzstan and Russia, *fruit and berries* in Kyrgyzstan, Russia, the Ukraine and Uzbekistan (largely in plots and gardens for household consumption or small retail trade). At the same time, marketable products declined, notably *grapes* (four times in Azerbaijan, almost by half in Kazakhstan and by one third in Georgia). Gross output of *sugar beets* decreased in Russia and the Ukraine because of the reduced sown areas.

Considerable agricultural achievements have been evident in some CIS countries by the end of the 1990s. There are no "nation-wide campaigns" recruiting students and labour in harvest time now. For the first time in decades Russia can do without mass-scale grain procurements from outside the CIS. Rural areas are guided by profits rather than "top-to-bottom" directives. Consequently, rice output increased 5.5 times and sugar beets 14 times in Kyrgyzstan, sunflower in Moldova and South Russia, and buckwheat in Belarus.

This, however, is a far cry from the "green revolution" transforming the agricultural sector in many other countries. Agricultural yields are inferior. Thus, recent yields of grain and leguminous crops were 13–16 metric centners/ha in Armenia, Azerbaijan and Turkmenistan, 12–14 in Russia and 5–9 in Tajikistan. In 1997 they varied between 9 and 26 metric centners/ha. Meanwhile grain yields per hectare are over 18 centners in India and Turkey, 42–45 in Saudi Arabia and China, 35–45 in Finland and Sweden and even higher in other European countries.

Feed shortage and deteriorating effective demand governed reductions in *livestock farming*. Between 1992 and 1998 cattle stock in CIS countries decreased by 25% (including 30% in Belarus, Kazakhstan, Russia and the Ukraine accounting for 90%–95% of livestock outputs in the CIS), pigs by 34%, and sheep and goats by 40%. Yields in the livestock sector decreased too. As a result, despite the extended livestock in the household sector and farms (cows by 25%, pigs by 9%, sheep and goats by 1%), per capita production in CIS countries decreased from 62 to 39 kg in meat, 338 to 261 in milk and 272 to 181 pieces eggs. Particularly low are the levels in Transcaucasian countries, Tajikistan, Turkmenistan and Uzbekistan (10–24 kg meat, 76–159 kg milk, 11–60 pieces eggs). In 1997 outputs across the CIS decreased by 9% in meat and 6% in milk, notably in Kazakhstan, the Ukraine, Moldova and Russia.

Food exports and imports. CIS member countries are complementary in terms of agricultural specialisation. The largest CIS exporter of grain (fifth in the world) is Kazakhstan, with 99% average annual exports (2 million tonnes) going to Belarus, Azerbaijan and Central Asian republics. The Ukraine and Moldova export grain in high-yield years, also mainly to CIS countries. Russia exports over half the total of barley and wheat (on average 500,000 tonnes) outside the CIS, including the Baltic states.

The main exporters of meat and meat food by-products are Kazakhstan (approximately 32,000 tonnes in 1996), Moldova (27,000 tonnes), Russia (23,000 tonnes) and Belarus (14,000 tonnes); butter – Belarus (13,000 tonnes), Russia (approximately 6000 tonnes), Moldova (1,400,000 tonnes) and Kazakhstan (approximately 1000 tonnes). In all the cases between two thirds and 100% go to CIS countries. Throughout the 1990s exports have declined dramatically for early vegetables, fruit and grapes from the Central Asian region and Transcaucasia to Russia, Belarus, and other countries. Major exporters now are South European and South East Asian countries, and even the USA Russian urban citizens buy oranges and melons from Brazil, pears from Argentina, tomatoes from Spain, and carrots and onions from Holland. All these, for ages cultivated in CIS countries, are now non-competitive because of the high prime costs, non-compliance with gathering, storage, packaging and transportation rules, inadequate selection and high risks of failure in delivery and payments.

In the mid-1990s food imports in Russia met three quarters of public demand for poultry, sugar and frozen fish, over half for margarine and dairy products and one third for butter and meat. Contribution of food imports is over 60% in Moscow and Saint Petersburg, and one third across Russia. The related lost gains are estimated at $40 billion each year.

The same is true about other CIS countries. In 1 year Azerbaijan imported $250 million worth meat products, butter, wheat and flour, and sugar, mainly from the far abroad (e.g. 98% meat and over 70% flour), with agricultural exports there actually non-existent. Armenia imported 94% meat, 99% potatoes and sugar, and over 90% grain, flour and vegetable oil from outside the CIS. Naturally, inter-republic imports in the CIS have been restricted for citrus and other fruit, grapes and other traditional agricultural products. Consequently, for example, tea exports from Georgia decreased several times.

It is hardly normal that Kazakhstan imports twice as much milk fats as it exports, Kyrgyzstan has come to act as a net importer of vegetable oil, Moldova of sugar, etc. In 1997 imports of meat and meat products extended 2.6 times in Belarus and 3.5 times in Kazakhstan, and poultry 1.4 times in Russia. Vegetable oil imports in these countries extended 2.4–5.2 times, butter 2.4–3 times, etc.

To protect their agricultural producers, foreign countries have made active use of non-tariff methods (e.g. special requirements on certification, environmental safety, packaging, storage time), as well as quotas, customs duties, subsidies to food exporters (almost $6 billion in the West), government investments ($240 per hectare arable lands in the USA as against $50 in Russia). Import tariffs for basic food products account for 5%–20% of the price (30% for chicken) in CIS countries, as compared with 50%–210% in Czech Republic and almost 100% (for milk) in Poland.

At the same time, capital investment to the agrarian sector in the 1990s decreased dramatically (from 18% to 3% in Russia, from 22%–26% to 8%–9% in Belarus,

Uzbekistan and the Ukraine, 34% to 11% in Moldova and 28% to 2% in Kazakhstan – i.e. 14 times!). A vicious circle has been created: imports of finished goods (rather than new technologies) undermines competitive positions of domestic AICs, while a rapid decrease in investments to supplies and machinery impedes their restoration. Devaluation of the ruble and some other currencies in the CIS in 1998 resulted in a sharp price rise and a consequent reduction of food imports. This benefits neither Russia requiring imports of meat and some other products for Moscow and big cities in the North and East, nor the importing countries (notably France, the USA, Ireland, China, Holland, Denmark) losing extensive export markets. Russia had to reduce customs duties for foodstuffs, while the USA and EU member states provided humanitarian aid and issued privileged food purchase credits. But such urgent actions are unlikely to solve the existing problems.

Membership in the World Trade Organisation will not prevent CIS countries from taking tough positions to protect their interests. Thus, Russia in 1998 increased import duties for eggs (annual national output 238 pieces per capita, as compared with 160 in Poland and 215–230 in Germany, Sweden and Finland), some vegetables and dairy products. Higher duties for pre-packed (not loose) tea contributed to higher employment rates in domestic factories. While domestic poultry outputs has increased, per capita consumption remains inferior (6 kg as compared with 14–15 kg in 1990 and 40 kg in the USA).

Food safety is unlikely to be attained in the CIS through prohibitive duties alone. Imports of new technologies should be encouraged and new competitive production facilities built. The latter have been established in Tajikistan and some other CIS republics with the assistance of international economic organisations. Enhanced bloodstock farming, changes in the feed mix and new machinery ensured profitable broiler production in Novgorod, Orel, Sverdlovsk and some other regions of Russia. Under an Italian licensing scheme, Kemerovo region has actually provided food inputs for the next 5 years, with gains from the project covering the investments. Implementation of the food program has provided one third of regional tax revenues.

To date, CIS agroindustrial complex must accomplish the following:

– Using the latest achievements in selection, irrigation and amelioration, up-to-date technologies and comprehensive mechanisation, to reduce agricultural employment in a radical manner, employing the released labour in the rural infrastructure, small and medium-size enterprises in labour-intensive areas, i.e. services and urban development (urbanisation being essential for Central Asian republics)

– To transform rural quality of life, involving up-to-date water and energy supply (gas supply, autonomous heat supply), telecommunications, modern housing and hard-surface roads, schools, health and culture centres

– To develop local government agencies dealing with rights of ownership of immovable property, rural infrastructure, public social care and environmental safety while abstaining from direct interference with economic matters such as sowing or harvesting, sales, etc.

– To increase yields and productivity in the livestock sector in a significant manner, to meet the agrarian demand while preserving and improving land fertility and releasing some lands for national parks, touristic zones and other purposes

– To ensure farms' financial stability, efficiency and competitive positions on the world market

All these goals will require radical agrarian reform.

6.2 Agrarian Reforms

Changes in agricultural enterprises. By the end of the twentieth century total populations were almost equal in the CIS and the USA, with comparable rural proportions – almost 30% (26% of total 370 million in the EU, and 24% in Russia). Yet their AICs differ by all other parameters. Agricultural area in the CIS is much larger (over 460 million hectares as compared with 187 million hectares in the USA and 140 million hectares in the EU). CIS agricultural outputs are far lower (approximately $100 billion as compared with $225 billion in the USA and $290 billion in EU member states), i.e. almost one fifth per hectare, although CIS agricultural output accounts for a slightly greater proportion of GDP. CIS agriculture has much fewer active enterprises (700,000–750,000 compared with 2100 in the USA and 7200 in the EU), generally engaged in agricultural production while those in the foreign counterparts also handle machinery, fertiliser, feed and services delivery, along with processing, storage and sales.

The data show once again the inefficiency of the collective/state farm system with the peasant actually alienated from land and management. Changes in CIS agricultural enterprises in the 1990s have been proceeding along the following lines:

– Transformation of collective and state farms as economic partnerships, co-operatives, limited-liability or joint stock companies

– Establishment of farms and their associations through allocation or lease of agrarian shares

– Additional land allocations to extend household plots, orchards and vegetable gardens

– Organisation of new firms, including with foreign contribution, notably in AIC services, processing and sales areas

Different CIS countries employed these strategies in different proportions, depending on the prevalence of extensive (e.g. North Kazakhstan, Siberia) or intensive (irrigated or ameliorated) agriculture.

Armenia has the greatest number of farms among the CIS countries (including Russia). In 1992, over a period of a only a few months, land privatisation was completed there, involving division of collective and state farms' lands, livestock and machinery. This actually saved the republic from starvation. Peasants are free to purchase seed and fertilisers, distribute water resources, and negotiate with machinery owners. Effective marketing and production co-operation has been initiated. As average farm size is approximately 1–2 ha, emphasis is placed on intensive land use for vine and fruit to be processed as wines, brandies and preserves. These require new orchards, high-yield and frost-resistant grades, and improved processing technologies. Trade representations have been established in 11 cities in Russia, the Ukraine and Belarus.

Armenia did run into difficulties with agrarian reform. Due to low procurement prices and conflicting interests of State-owned bottleries, as well as competitive Iranian spirits, vine outputs decreased from 257 (1981–1983) to 159,000 tonnes in (1996) and their processing increased more than five-fold. Farmers distil grapes into home-made vodka, selling it without paying taxes. Rather than guaranteeing the success of reforms, particularly in highly mechanised branches (e.g. grain, cotton), privatisation only provides the necessary prerequisites.

The CIS republics where reform was confined to formal reorganisation of collective and state farms as joint stock companies and partnerships and the farm sector stabilised and even began to decline after an initial growth, were confronted with deteriorating livestock and productivity, yields, R&D production levels and, more importantly, soil fertility. Small-scale private business has been extended, using manual labour and outdated technologies. Major farms made losses due to the rising prices for energy resources, machinery and fertilisers, and monopolistic actions of processing enterprises and commercial banks.

Over 45% of outputs in the Ukraine are produced at individual gardens and incapable of competing with imports. The government banned allocation of financial and material resources from budget reserves to enterprises in cases of non-repayment or non-target use of credit.

Over 80% farms in Russia suffered losses in 1997. Stocks of cows, pigs, sheep and goats decreased by 8%, 10% and 15%, respectively. Consequently, meat production has declined by 10% and imports from the far abroad has increased six-fold during the 1990s. Farms account for less than 2% and individual subsidiaries for 40% meat and milk outputs.

However, the outcome of well-justified and comprehensive reform demonstrated by federal entities, such as Orel, Belgorod, Moscow and Tiumen regions, starting from reasonable balancing of individual and State interests – the latter, regretfully, only represented by regional authorities presently – suggests a new vision of reform in Russia, a country traditionally known to follow impressive leaders.

The Press in CIS countries represents very different prospects for agrarian reform: from actual return to the State-directed collective/State farm system (prevailing in Belarus) to free land sales and purely capitalistic relations.

The debates were particularly vigorous in Russia where the controversy about the Land Code, with special legal and economic matters replaced by political declarations, has emerged as a touchstone of government's social responsibilities. Yet even in the Russian Federation a more balanced approach has been coming to the forefront, accounting for typical agrarian relations in the republics and focusing on multivariant AIC economics, combining large- (e.g. joint stock companies, agrofirms, agroconsortiums) and small-scale commodity production.[3] These will ensure: equity of State, co-operative and private ownership; independent rights of working collectives and individuals to select organisational and legal forms of management; and privileges for rural commodity producers in purchasing controlling stocks of shares in privatised processing and servicing enterprises in the AIC. Incentives have been provided to voluntary, self-regulating and self-financed co-operative units (e.g. unions, associations) producing, processing, storing and selling their produce, including exports, and providing material and technological, maintenance, R&D, financial and credit, and other services.

Moldova initiated a system of distributed shared ownership by related families and other member of rural communities, with periodic re-assessment of individual shares depending on individual contribution. Thus, fields can be extended to allow for crop rotation, prime costs reduced and marketability improved. Contrary to rural expectations, the government provides no financing, leaving the farmers to their own devices in building the relevant purchase, sales and infrastructure.

Kyrgyzstan has large cotton-growing farms, along with private farms exporting mutton and wool via their associations. Between 1995 and 1998 cotton output was half as much again than in other CIS countries, with superior yields.

As mentioned previously, Armenia has the greatest number of farms (316,000) each slightly over 1 ha in area. The largest farms (average 448 ha) are in Kazakhstan: over 40,000 in 1996. Farming has been comparatively successful in Kyrgyzstan (30,000 farms of average 59 ha) and Moldova (33,000 farms of average 2 ha). The number of farms in Russia (280,000, 43 ha) stabilised with no effective government support.

---

[3] Stroev, E.S. (Ed.) (1997): Conception of Agrarian Policy in Russia for 1997–2000. Moscow (Строев, Е.С. (Ред.) (1997): Концепция Аграрной Политики России в 1997–2000 Годах. Москва) [In Russian]

Georgia places a special emphasis on mutually beneficial arrangements between tea producers and processing plants. Tea and packaging quality deteriorated under privatisation and therefore markets were lost in Russia and Central Asian republics.

During the second half of the 1990s farming employment in the CIS has amounted to 1.6 million only, i.e. 5%–6% of total agricultural. Average farms in Moldova and Armenia had 1.3 ha land and one farmer, and in the Ukraine and Belarus 20–22 ha and seven workers. At the current mechanisation level such farms are unlikely to be competitive in grain crops, cotton, and other production. In Russia with an average of 43 ha and five workers many farms have found themselves in distress with the promised government support unavailable.

Extended holdings of privately owned livestock, including on farms, cannot compensate for the decline evident in large facilities. In 1998 meat production in CIS countries was 5% lower than in 1997.

In the second half of the 1990s the number of farms continued to grow in Armenia, Kyrgyzstan, Moldova, Uzbekistan and Kazakhstan, stabilising in the Ukraine, Russia and Belarus.

In most CIS countries individual farms meet the bulk of demand for potatoes, vegetables, fruit and berries, milk and wool (see Table 22), even with inferior marketability and productivity.

There are exceptions, of course. In Orel region a decline in the farm sector in 1995 and 1997 was followed by a rapid growth – 10% every year. Farming lands extended (from 50 ha in 1993 to 80 ha in 1997) and an unusual strategy was employed where large farmers' associations and strong farms used the share distribution mechanism to annex distressed former collective enterprises.

On the other hand, private farming has not yet emerged as a significant force in Azerbaijan (5700 farms), Belarus (3000), Tajikistan and Turkmenistan, Uzbekistan (19,000 farms of average 15 ha) and the Ukraine (35,000 farms of 23 ha).

So collective and state farms dominate the agrarian sector in most CIS countries with the exception of Armenia and Kyrgyzstan. There are significant variations in size, from 1–2 to 450 ha, related not only to land shortage (Armenia, Moldova) but also to differences in agrarian policy.

Large marketable production of grains prevails in all CIS countries, with the exception of Armenia and Georgia, potatoes only in Uzbekistan, vegetables in Moldova, meat and milk in Belarus, Moldova, Russia and the Ukraine; large poultry farms figure prominently in Belarus, Kazakhstan, Russia, Tajikistan, Turkmenistan and the Ukraine.

Table 22

**Household Production (including farms)
as a Percentage of Total Agricultural Outputs (1997)**

Country	Grain (%)	Potatoes (%)	Vege-tables (%)	Meat (%)	Milk (%)	Eggs (%)	Wool (%)[1]	Agricul-tural wage as a % of national average
Azerbaijan	33	94	98	95	98	93	66	74
Armenia	97	99	100	99	99	99	99	85
Belarus	8	85	81	28	40	38	81	62
Georgia	82	98	97	99	98	100	94	...
Kazakhstan	17	88	80	77	87	47	58	51
Kyrgyzstan	58	88	87	96	93	99	90	52
Moldova	48	98	38	66	77	61	85	66
Russia	7	92	78	57	49	31	50	46
Tajikistan	44	77	65	76	83	36	62	60
Turkmenistan[1]	4	90	34	64	78	58	61	92
Uzbekistan	54	35	67	89	92	70	72	57
Ukraine	11	97	83	65	61	63	40	58

[1] 1996.

Changes in the organisational and legal status left rural producers' well-being almost unaffected. The wage is less than half the modest average national economic levels in Russia (see Table 22), 51%–58% in Kazakhstan, Kyrgyzstan, Uzbekistan and the Ukraine, and 85% in Armenia only.

The point is that avalanche privatisation and "farmisation" in the CIS environment are unlikely to create large-investment (per hectare land) and therefore highly efficient market farms. This has been demonstrated by the East European experience. The transition to small-scale commercial farming in Bulgaria (under restitution arrangements most lands, even in highly profitable farms, were assigned to former owners and their successors) resulted in declining agricultural production and even bread lines. Land fragmentation of the stock in Romania in the early 1990s resulted in an economic slump. Even in Poland with no mass-scale collectivisation, transfer of 96% sown area to peasant ownership brought a decline in production from the 1989 level and a technological lag.

This was not the case in the Czech Republic, where 95% former collective farms (60% land) were not eliminated but broken up into smaller units and reorganised as voluntary bodies of private land owners with clear-cut shares in co-operative property and exit options. Farms (of average 67 ha) comprise only 10% of cultivated area. In Hungary independent farmers also account for one tenth of outputs only, in the co-operative sector involving transformed co-operative and other large farming units. All Central and East European countries, including eastern parts in Germany, have recently focused on large farms (200 ha or more), agrocombines, poultry farms, production co-operatives and other associations in the environment of private ownership of land and government regulation of the market infrastructure.

Private land ownership. Private, i.e. not necessarily individual but rather non-public, ownership of land and other kinds of immovable property is essential to overcome the alienation of peasants from land, restore individual responsibility for its fertility in the interests of generations to come, and provide a basis for agricultural financing via land mortgaging and assignment to more effective owners. Experts estimate the potential value of agricultural lands in the CIS at over $10 trillion. The amount would secure immense investments required for machinery updating in the AIC, as well as seasonal credit on future yields.

The most radical decision regarding land was taken in Armenia. Each of the 800 rural communities elected a land committee of venerable fellow villagers. The committees sorted half a million hectares of arable lands and hillside hayfields among the peasants, workers of the rural social sphere and town dwellers willing to come back to their native villages. The holding depended on family size (average 1.3 ha). The bureaucracy were removed from land division. The government maintained control of seed-growing and pedigree stock farms and of stocktaking and land cadaster. At the same time irrigation fees were introduced and micro-credits (up to $1000) were issued on land certificates in a co-operative bank according to an approved business plan. As a result, credits were repaid in due time, salinated and swamped arable lands reclaimed and land sales have been very rare.

In Kazakhstan private ownership was established for house, suburban and garden plots, as well as those intended for housing and installations (subject to designated use). Agricultural lands were subject to long-term leasing (up to 99 years), with sale, mortgage and inheritance options. Thus, the State has maintained ownership of large blocks of grain in the north of the republic.

An instructive case of agrarian reform is Moldova. Members of collective farms have received only half of the 2.6 million hectares of arable lands, orchards and pastures. A certificate entitles one to inherit and sell one's share. As opposed to Romania, land is allocated to current rather than previous owners.

Minimum parcel price was set ($5000/ha), to be raised for lands used in crop rotation by fertility and location score. As the plots are modest (1 million farmers having between 1 and 2.5 ha), co-operative arrangements are encouraged.

Finally, half the agricultural lands are not subject to privatisation. The State maintains ownership of large producers in the most profitable area, i.e. vine growing and wine making.

Some economists in CIS countries argue that if the land, natural resources and immovable property are not traded, it prevents true evaluation of production costs and prices, market pricing of assets and securities, sustained money circulation, extensive use of foreign investment and mortgaging. But free purchase and sale of land is not a universal panacea. It is not permitted in countries with developed agriculture sectors such as the UK, Holland or Israel, let alone China, which is providing food for 21% of the world community with only 7% of the world's arable lands.

CIS countries could make advantageous use of Russian experience in privatising land parcels of non-government enterprises. Standard price is set at the amount of ten annual land taxes, differentiated according to the government land cadaster. A parcel can be contributed to capital stock, provide a base for secondary issue of securities or pledge on investment credit, with the surplus sold at a market price. A parcel can be sold of government bonds. New infrastructural units (e.g. water- and gas lines, electric cables) cannot be laid in the area unless appropriate compensation is paid to the owner. Almost 85% of proceeds from land sales are channelled to regional and local budgets. But the use of existing roads is free of charge, and municipal services have unrestricted access to infrastructural units in the area.

A very interesting case is represented by agrarian reforms in the Orel region, where the latest achievements in social and legal reform technologies are being implemented, focusing on peasantry, agricultural producers and workers in the real sector of the agrarian sphere. There is no question of whether private ownership of land is or is not necessary. In the Orel regional conception of agrarian reform, private ownership is viewed as a framework of *legal powers* ensuring minimisation of transaction costs. Therefore, the purely political problem of opting for or against private ownership of land has been approached here from the purely economic perspective of increased returns for effective owners, based on effective management and, more importantly, the *movement of formal shares in land and property to the hands of effective workers*. This is what governs the new set of co-operative and integrative relationships, in their turn developing a set of agroindustrial financial corporations to resist monopolistic dictation, control price disparity and promote the interests of the effective private owner – the farmer.

In the short run the question of private ownership of land in Russia is likely to move from the political perspective to optimisation of resource and income turnover.

In most CIS countries private ownership of land only extends to individual plots, buildings and market gardens. The basic block can be had on short- and long-term lease, life hereditary possession or permanent use, but only subject to appropriate experience and qualifications, and designated use. Special attention is attached to the land cadaster and monitoring, rational land management and registration of land rights, and compliance with legal provisions. Land payments (taxes, rent, lease and ownership rights, compensations for lands taken out of agricultural production) are channelled to finance the aforementioned procedures, land protection and fertility improvements. Admittedly, however, none of the CIS countries have yet built a qualified framework of land cadasters, which inhibits both land and agrarian reform, and general progress towards a civilised market of resources of which land is the basic one.

It is therefore beyond question that private ownership of land and its use to create a new class of independent, skilled and initiative workers will contribute to the resolution of agrarian crisis in the CIS. As regards the causes of this crisis, mass media in CIS countries have developed certain stereotypes.

One is the disparity, i.e. the unfavourable balance, of prices for AIC's products and material and machinery inputs. Indeed, prices for machinery, fertilisers, fuels and forage have been growing faster than those for agricultural outputs. Yet the balance has been more favourable in the CIS than in countries with advanced AIC: to purchase a tractor or a combine, a farmer in the USA has to sell three to four times the amount of grain sold by his counterpart in the CIS for the purpose. The only exception is the amount of milk needed to buy mixed feed in the CIS.

Another stereotype is related to farmers' contribution to output value. Indeed, because of the multiple emerging intermediaries, and requirements to packaging and storage quality, it decreased two to three times over the 1990s, but this was not always reasonable. Yet grain producers here still gain 15%–25% of bread price as compared with 10% in the USA The lower contribution than that in the USA of farmers to milk and poultry prices is related to the higher transport and pre-sale costs. Retail prices in Russia selling over half the agricultural produce within the CIS have approached or even exceeded the world level, with much lower purchasing power.

The final stereotype concerns the low level of government subsidising to the AIC and the high loan interest level. Indeed, the subsidies have been reduced significantly. Yet, according to Russian economists' estimates, they still account for over 8% of output price in the AIC (20% in the USA). The interest rate in the CIS is higher than in the USA, but prices for Farmgate in the USA fall frequently, whereas the price growth percentage in the CIS has been higher than interest. The immense investments in irrigation, amelioration and road building in the USSR in the 1970s and 1980s were not efficient because of inferior quality of works.

The primary concern in the AIC is not the lack of money but inefficiency – mainly managerial, mass-scale thefts and inadequate performance – and the absence of proprietary interest in work. To resolve the problem, land must be transferred to peasants not by word but by deed. AIC expansion in China, Japan and South America did not begin until the land problem had been solved and investment used in mortgaging.

But private ownership of land is unlikely to be effective unless the three conditions mentioned in relation to reform in the Orel region are satisfied.

First, this involves the cadaster, i.e. assessment and registration of the allegiance and type of use for all land parcels. Thus, in the Ukraine in 1996, with 60% of lands in State, 37% in collective and only 3% in private ownership, average price of 1 ha agricultural land was set at approximately the level of Iowa (USA). The size of individual land share in a non-government agricultural enterprise was represented both in cost and standard cadastral hectares. Upon withdrawal, the owner is entitled to compensation in kind. The land market involves hire-purchase options for farmers, purchase and sale of farmstead plots, and auction sales of rights to rent land. Standard land price in Russia is set by government authorities in the federal entities at no more than 75% of the market price for plots of similar designation. Local government agencies can further specify the number of assessment zones, their limits and prices within the ±25% standard margin.

The second condition involves specifics of land utilisation in various CIS regions. Per capita agricultural area varies in CIS countries between 10 ha in Kazakhstan or 8.8 in Turkmenistan, and 1.4–1.5 ha in Russia and Kyrgyzstan, 0.7–0.9 ha in Tajikistan, the Ukraine and Uzbekistan, and 0.4–0.6 ha in Armenia and Georgia. The same is true about irrigated and drained lands. Therefore, agrarian policy in countries such as Russia, Kazakhstan and the Ukraine cannot be the same in all regions.

In this context an interesting case is Tatarstan, focusing on individual gardens co-operating with collective farms lending land and machinery, and with local government agencies responsible for road building, gas supply, etc. Unlike independent farms, these require much less investment and permit employment of retired labour, without breaking the established system. In Russia in general, farms use 2% of arable lands while contributing 25% of the agricultural output. In Tatarstan they were helped prevent a production slump in the 1990s with comparatively low food prices. Tatarstan and some other Russian federal entities advocate effective private ownership of land.

The most important agrarian reform scenario, however, involves tight control by the central and local government.

The right to sell land can be assigned to a State land bank, with commercial banks, following the U.S. example, bound to sell debtors' land within 2 years rather than enjoying indefinite ownership.

A privileged right to purchase land can be assigned to neighbours, to be followed by fellow villagers, and only then to other buyers having special qualifications and experience. Denmark and some other countries lacking land specify the size of a plot per household. Some states in the U.S. and provinces in Canada, Ireland, New Zealand and elsewhere prohibit the sale of land to foreigners unless specially authorised by the government.

To ensure designated utilisation, lands can be classified (taking a lesson from Denmark) as urban, suburban and agricultural, with exclusive government authorisation for change of category.

Speculations in real estate can be restrained in particular with taxation. Thus maximum land sale tax in the USA (100%) is imposed where the owner has been in possession for less than a year, and minimum (30%) for over 10 years.

However, even under the above-described scenarios the peasant cannot be left face to face with land. Effective management requires a market infrastructure and up-to-date technologies.

Government regulation of agrarian economy. Agrarian reform involves the elimination of the government's direct interference with the functions of AIC enterprises (e.g. sowing planning, harvest management, distribution of outputs). Yet the role of the government in market regulation will be reinforced. The functions of central and local government authorities, as international experience has shown, should include:

– Indicative functions: implicit, recommended planning of production and financial flows in the AIC, using taxes, transport and energy tariffs, customs and credit policies

– Registration of rights in land plots, promotion of the land cadaster system, control over effective land use and market exchange, preservation of land fertility

– Financing of agrarian science, pedigree-stock and elite-seed farming, reproduction of forest and fish resources, development of rural social and engineering infrastructures, child food industry, as well as staff training and development

– Directed repayable financing of national and regional (particularly in depressive regions) programs of start-up support to farms, small businesses, credit, insurance and sales co-operatives, agrocombines and other units for production, processing, storage and sales of agricultural produce, including exports

– Promotion of an AIC financial and credit system with high payment liquidity and self-paying and using up-to-date banking and telecommunications technologies, including leasing and mortgaging investment and insurance companies, co-operative banks, etc.

– Management of agricultural procurement for the national and regional food reserve (e.g. seed, forage) funds in competitive (tender) trade

– Organisation of the assessment of financial State and solvency of rural enterprises, provisions for equitable competition (including imports), outside management and bankruptcy arrangements for insolvent enterprises (including insurance against the risks of natural disasters) for the purpose of their transfer to more effective owners

– Promotion of a common agrarian market in the CIS, shared development, production and sales of up-to-date agricultural machinery

As a naturally non-monopolistic and seasonal branch, agriculture is unlikely to be competitive on the short-term credit market and therefore requires special support. In a developed market economy, such as that of the USA, agricultural liabilities have amounted to 14% of annual outputs in the 1990s (8% in Russia).

A framework for economic regulation of the agrarian market and creation of food resources involves the establishment of corporations with government contribution for contracted raw-material and food procurements for central and regional funds at prices ensuring the covering of relevant costs and reception of gains; agricultural co-operative banks and insurance funds; machinery leasing firms; directed financing funds for new technologies, elite seed- and pedigree cattle and poultry farming, amelioration and other forms of economic support to producers, including commodity credit (e.g. fuels, spare parts, fertilisers) and futures contracts.

Thus, Kazakhstan in 1995 eliminated compulsory government deliveries. Wheat is sold via the agroindustrial exchange and its branches. Information on prices is published regularly, and their level is controlled by a special commission. The bulk of grains are exported via commercial channels rather than via inter-republic agreements.

On the other hand, the government of Moldova issued credit to the bread department for grain purchases at fixed price. But the producers responded to the market demand in CIS countries with higher prices. A rational regulating mechanism can only be built within a common agrarian market.

Inter-government support is also required for radical renovation of AIC's R&D base and industrial, communications (roads, communications, energy systems) and social infrastructure. All these also require joint efforts. The total stock of machinery and mechanisms included 1 million items by the mid-1990s, with 100,000 intended for the AIC. No other country, including the USA, has endeavoured to undertake independent machinery development and production.

The same is true about new plant- and animal breeds. Under the "green revolution" between 1970 and 1975 wheat yields doubled in developing countries, with India leading the world in gross outputs (60 million tonnes), closing to the USA output (63 million tonnes).

Seasonal credit is essential for the AIC. For years credits were given out of the budget, to be written off subsequently. Commodity crediting (e.g. fuels, fertilisers) proved inefficient because 85% of AIC enterprises made losses while the remaining sold outputs in barter exchange, or sold for cash in circumvention of the bank account or else via others' accounts. Restructuring of debts as rural bonds with taxation advantages was only beneficial for exchange speculators. Overall rural indebtedness to all budget levels in Russia amounted to $12 billion in 1997.

The only alternative was a transition to bank loans with real contracting. The chances of their repayment in some CIS countries are almost 100%. A privileged budget credit (on 25% Central Bank rate) is advanced on a competitive basis to commercial banks issuing loans to solvent debtors only. In the late 1990s Kazakhstan has been implementing a 3-year micro-credit program to create new rural jobs and to promote small businesses and farms (with the assistance of the Asian Development Bank and some other international organisations). Some countries have abandoned monthly taxation in a seasonal branch such as agriculture.

A survey in a sample of household budgets indicates a considerable portion of rural money incomes gained from agricultural sales (almost 50% in Kyrgyzstan, approximately 40% in Azerbaijan, between 20% and 30% in Kazakhstan, the Ukraine and Moldova, and 15% in Russia). To increase rural household incomes in the CIS, a common framework is needed to market agricultural produce via sales co-operatives, wholesale food markets, agroexchanges, fairs and auctions, wholesale depots and agroindustrial firms, supermarkets, trade centres and shops, including those owned by agricultural enterprises. This framework has to replace government deliveries.

Market regulation in the new environment involves forward and futures trade, i.e. contracting for future outputs at agreed prices and within specified time limits. This enables the producer to plan the revenues a year in advance, reducing the risks of broad yield-related price fluctuations (thus, high yields in 1997 resulted in a dramatic and unexpected price drop for grain). Among the important market regulators are international grain, cotton and other agroexchanges, and associations of selling firms (e.g., a grains union). The agencies will inform the producer of the state of the market, the crops in special demand (e.g. currently including brewing barley, hops, soya) and reliability of commercial firms (including the "black list" of unfair partners).

Mortgaging is gaining wide acceptance, involving local government agencies, trade (commodity or money) credits to the agrarian sector issued by selling firms, machinery distributors, processing enterprises, consumer's co-operatives, etc. In this case, unlike government authorities, the market considers the whole range of available information among the market agents.

The new technology structure. A *technology framework* is the totality of inter-related and co-ordinated technological processes matching the engineering and staff qualification levels and securing the outputs. For ages the agricultural technology framework relied on household manual labour and tradition-based individual skills and signs. The framework ensured public food supply and exports (pre-revolutionary Russia had been the major exporter of, for example, grain, wool and butter) at the pre-industrial stage only, with at least 90% of populations employed in agriculture.

Collectivisation created the prerequisites for a new technology framework, basing on electrification, mechanisation and chemisation, while employing conventional cropping and animal-breeding machinery. The framework relied on extremely cheap labour, machinery and combustibles and lubricates, confiscation by the State of marketable products at low fixed prices, permanent labour inspectorate functions performed by multiple administrators and experts, with the workers little interested in the outcome. Harvesting machinery was designed for low yields and repeated repair. AIC material and machinery inputs were created with government investments in the form of budgetary capital investments and credits written off every year.

Agrarian reform requires a radical transformation in the technology framework.

A guideline for new machinery efficiency is envisaged in profit rather than output maximisation (e.g. fulfilment of compulsory deliveries) in the environment involving market prices for machinery, fertilisers, fuels and services, and a radical cut in budget investments to the AIC. In the 1990s the investments to AIC (in percent of total investments into economy likewise decreased dramatically) reduced 13–14 times in CIS countries. With all the differences in agrarian policies, the tendency was the same. Due to a rapid decline in effective demand for obsolete machinery – unreliable, fuel-consuming, requiring multiple spare parts and repair services – between 1991 and 1996 tractor production decreased by a factor of 82 (from 178,000 to 8000) in Russia, 15 (90,000 to 6000) in the Ukraine, 3.5 (6000 to 27,000) in Belarus, 9 in Moldova (660 to 7 items) and 14 in Kazakhstan (34,000 to 2500).

The technology framework in market agrarian economy focuses on independent and interested proprietors with, for example, high and diversified mechanical, agronomic and repair skills, needing no outside supervision to set and maintain rational standards of seeding, fertiliser application, watering, livestock feeding, as well as other activities, using both the traditional experience and, more importantly, the latest scientific achievements. No remedy for agrarian crisis is likely to be successful unless this proprietary class has emerged. The new proprietors will need new machinery, no matter how expensive, but efficient and requiring no continued repair or other outside services.

The new technology framework involves high accuracy and discipline levels, and strictly co-ordinated elements of production (e.g. seed grades, fertilisers, herbicides, pesticides), in their turn requiring extensive use of computer and electronic technologies, including navigation for precise determination and ranging of each tractor, motor car, etc. Therefore, no imports of individual components (cattle breeds, potatoes processing lines, tomato gathering machinery) are likely to be effective where all others (feed ration, potato types, tomato cropping methods) remain unchanged.

The new technologies rely on an individual approach to each individual plot (e.g. soil composition, ground water depth, surface gradient) or animal (e.g. separate rations by breed, age, purpose, upkeep), and accurate forecasting of weather conditions, potential pests, diseases, and other such situations. In addition, machinery will be designed to maximum possible rather than average output in a given environment.

A transition to the new technology framework means that agricultural machine-building in the CIS cannot be confined to updating available tractors, combines etc. A new range of machinery will be required. On the eve of the twenty-first century more developed countries have been extensively using information technologies based on computers, global information systems and remote, including space, probing. Faithful data of the humus, phosphorus and potassium content in soils, moisture and potential yields will enable strict measurement of fertilisers, herbicides or irrigation to be applied to each field section. This will ensure maximum yields and resource-saving, with minimum possible environmental pollution.

Agricultural machine-building in the CIS has not yet been adjusted in the new environment. Only in Belarus, owing to tractor supplies to Pakistan and some other countries, and Uzbekistan, manufacturing original high-rostrum tractors for maize, sunflower and other long-stemmed crops, did production not fall below 20%–30%. In the rest of the CIS, plants utilise only 2%–10% of their potential. In Russia agricultural machinery outputs decreased 12 times over the 1990s, with almost 90% of the plants showing budget losses. The major combine manufacturer Rostselmash has been on the verge of failure. Markets in the Ukraine, Kazakhstan and Turkmenistan are dominated by foreign corporations. Therefore, jobs and tax revenues are lost in CIS countries, with potential dramatic increases in the costs of spare parts and services. Agrarian countries with no developed machine-building industries are doomed to vegetative life. Only 10%–15% of rural demand for new machinery have been satisfied in the past few years.

This will above all require joint development and production of a new generation machinery for the AIC (approximately 900 field and 2700 processing types), with broad inter-republican co-operation and purchases of relevant licenses and accessories (e.g. hydraulics, electronics, engines and conditioners of interior comforts) outside the CIS.

Another task involves restructuring in the plants, abandonment of excessive capacities, including mobilisation and lower loss levels (minimised outputs ensuring compensation of fixed costs).

Proper use should be made of strategic foreign investment. Among the examples are the Russian-Canadian combine plant in Chelyabinsk and Kazakhstani-U.S. ones in the Akmolinsk region.

Reorganisation is required in the system of payments for machinery. The U.S. export combines credit to Turkmenistan, with 85% of costs covered by U.S. state-owned Eximbank and 15% by the manufacturing corporation. International experience strongly suggests the need for a leasing system in the CIS.

Leasing involves a long-term hiring-purchasing arrangement, long-range commodity credit and provision of engineering and other services to the lessee. Leasing companies established with commercial banks, AIC organisations and agricultural machine-building enterprises acquire rights of ownership of machinery and give it to producers on constrained specialised credit (generally for depreciation time).

Leasing has some obvious advantages as a form of investment in the AIC. The AIC will have the machinery with annual payments during 5 years, and foreign financial structures during 7 years in grain at fixed prices. During the period, the property will be shown at the balance sheet of the leasing company, thus sparing the agrarians the taxes and improving their liquid assets. The spare parts and sophisticated repair works will be provided on guarantee. The expanded market will enable the plants to expand production and reduce machinery costs. The loan interest will be lower than standard owing to the lower credit risk (the leased subject serving as security). Given careful maintenance, the lessee will have the machinery at a low price when the lease expires.

All these are essential for small businesses and farms. The government leasing fund for agricultural updating in the Ukraine grants domestic-made machinery on payment deferred for 5 years at 50% of national bank's discount rate. Over 100 leasing companies operate in Russia. Major commercial banks (SBS-Agro, Inkombank, National Reserve Bank, Alfa-Bank) established subsidiaries to handle leasing arrangements, rent of machine-and-technology stations, etc. By the twenty-first century the number of such companies is expected to grow ten-fold. A databank of equipment types and prices enables machinery to be supplied to the AIC at lower than lessor's prices.

Regional leasing companies are gaining acceptance. Among their main subjects in the AIC are motor cars, tractors, combines, bakeries, as well as meat and milk processors.

In our opinion, CIS countries need an inter-state fund for the encouragement of leasing in the AIC, involving industrial (machine building) and agricultural ministries, agrarian and mortgage banks, leasing and insurance companies. Their basic function is envisaged as insurance of leased property and recovery of leasing payments, to extend leasing terms and reduce insurance risks. The government will only secure partial damages.

Progress of agrarian reforms is closely related to developments in the branches responsible for end products on agricultural raw materials, primarily food and light industries.

6.3 Development of Processing Industries of Agroindustrial Complex and Food Safety in the CIS

Food safety. According to expert opinion, food safety is unlikely to be accomplished unless at least 80% vital food outputs are produced locally or in friendly neighbouring states in the amounts meeting food standards. So the question is not of reduced imports. The major exporter of grain, such as the USA, also buys grain in Argentina and some other countries at lower prices. Exports of grain and flour from Stavropol and Kuban territories to Transcaucasia would be easily combined with imports from Kazakhstan and other countries to the Russian East.

Yet the 1990s scenario of selling agricultural inputs to buy high added value products is unacceptable as financing of foreign agricultural producers to the detriment of domestic ones. In this context reduction of grain imports (40 million tonnes annually in the 1980s) seems highly ambiguous, as they are replaced with food imports of far higher added value (flour, macaroni, meat products, confectioneries) and, in addition, delivered by foreign rather than domestic vessels. The price of such imports almost equals receipts from oil sales.

During the 1990s food imports from the far abroad have been extended, whereas inter-republic imports in the CIS have declined (five times from Kyrgyzstan). Only Russia increased intra-CIS imports by 2% (21% from outside the CIS, including 25% in poultry). Due to the low mechanisation levels and obsolete technologies, imports from distant countries are less expensive than those from immediate neighbours, even for CIS countries with high per capita outputs. As a result, CIS rural labour is idle and currency gains are channelled to food inputs rather than to investments.

Under a real economic integration, *food safety is assessed in terms of the whole economic group rather than individual countries.* Thus, annual sugar consumption in Russia varies between 4.0 and 4.8 million tonnes, with Russian plants manufacturing 3.1 million tonnes, i.e. one half, using domestic beets and the remaining half with imported raw inputs (generally sugar cane). Imports amount to 250,000 tonnes (including 90% from the Ukraine). Sugar autonomy is not likely to be attained because between 1991 and 1997 the area sown in sugar beets decreased from 1.3 to 0.9 million ha, with reduced yields and sugar content.

Due to higher energy and transport tariffs and wages, outdated equipment (expected to be fully depreciated by 2000) and part-using (less than 30% of capacities), prime costs of sugar are much higher in Russia than in the Ukraine.

To protect domestic plants, Russia imposed a 10% VAT and a 25% import duty for sugar from the Ukraine. Imports from neighbouring countries fell by a factor of 10. But the fiscal revenues did not increase as the Ukraine introduced the VAT for Russian goods. Third parties gained access to the market, buying up shares in plants in both countries. In 1998 the VAT was abolished and a duty-free quota imposed (600,000 tonnes annually). Proposals to secure food safety involve joint market regulation (in most countries 70%–80% of the sugar market are government-regulated, with only 20%–30% free sales), purchase of shares in Ukrainian plants by Russian import firms and establishment of transnational companies (TNCs); otherwise, sugar industry in Russia will deteriorate within the next few years and prices for this important product will be determined elsewhere.

The same is true about salt. Owing to reduced explored reserves and neglected hydrochemical conditions in lake fields in Astrakhan region and Altay territory, salt extraction in Russia more than halved over the 1990s. Of 9.5 million tonnes of salt (2 million tonnes of inputs to food industry and agriculture) 90% are imported, mainly from the Ukraine.

In Russian import losses have been largely determined by the lack of a common agrarian market, settlement impediments, frequent non-performance of delivery terms and prices overstated by multiple intermediaries. Thus in the 1990s Russia expanded cigarette outputs and crude tobacco imports (domestic raw inputs contributing less than 1%). Yet imports from CIS countries almost halved. Kyrgyzstan, Uzbekistan, Moldova and Azerbaijan were ousted by India, Greece, Italy and Indonesia.

Development of food industry. In the first half of the 1990s meat, milk and confectionery outputs in CIS countries declined due to decreased effective demand, disrupted economic relationships and competitive imports. Only the bread output increased, to substitute for more expensive foodstuffs.

Things changed by the end of the 1990s. Food industry in Russia is represented by seven of the 20 most dynamic companies on the "Expert-2000" list, eight of the 20 top per capita sale firms and six of the 20 top profit-making companies. Confectionery outputs in 1997 increased by 5%, margarine by 20%, beer and non-alcoholic beverages by 10%, etc. Among the factors governing the revival in the area with extensive inputs within the CIS, age-long traditions (notably in wine making and bread baking) and an immense market, are the following:

1. Increased public demand for less expensive and high-quality domestic products (e.g. due to shorter transportation and storage times, absence of conserving agents). Thus, the percentage of discarded cheese, meat preserves and cereals

imports (34%–64%) is more than double, and fish products and butter (32%–65%) half again that of domestic produce. Meat products from Moldova also appeared superior to distant imports.

Relative stabilisation of output prices in the area is also related to reduced price gap between industrial inputs for AIC and AIC outputs. Large grain-producing farms and potatoes and other vegetables produced in farms and household garden plots provided inputs here. Livestock reductions enabled improvement of feed patterns and productivity, notably in suburban areas. An additional impetus for the AIC was provided by national devaluations and consequent changes in the import/domestic price ratio.

2. New distributing channels for agricultural products. Procurement companies (excluding consumer's co-operatives) only dominated grains markets (1996) in Azerbaijan, Belarus, Turkmenistan and Uzbekistan (62%–93%), while retaining under one quarter in Kazakhstan, Moldova and Russia, and one third in the Ukraine. The government only maintained the procurement of potatoes in Azerbaijan (85%) and Uzbekistan (42%), vegetables in Uzbekistan and Azerbaijan (47%–50%), as well as cattle and poultry in Belarus (61%) and Russia (53%). The bulk of enterprise inputs were provided by market structures confined to discount prices in the competitive environment.

3. Large corporations and holdings emerging in food industry. Originally most of the stocks (85% in Russia) were allocated to working collectives, which made the area unattractive for foreign investment. In the mid-1990s the "brand name" status gained acceptance on the market. Thus, over a period of 4 years the Wimm-Bill-Dann corporation in Moscow region increased juice outputs from 8 to 100 million litres, winning the juice and dairy market in the centre of Russia. Confectionery joint stock companies Krasnyi Oktiabr and Babaevskoe purchased some regional factories and established major holdings. Similar processes have been evident in meat, liquor and spirits and confectionery sectors in the Ukraine and some other CIS countries.

Food industries in developed countries are far more concentrated. Corporations such as Nestle, Unilever and Mars manufacture global products. Increasing recent mergers ensure lower production and marketing costs. Thus, the Guinness and Grand Metropoliten alliance (UK) controls 5% of the world market of alcoholic beverages (over 150 names with annual sales of 14 billion pounds).

4. Higher import duties and tighter government control over the imports of items such as alcohol and tobacco, encouraging foreign investment. Thus, higher import duties for margarine (from 5% to 15%) in Russia made the importers reduce contract prices and increase advertising expenditures to maintain their positions on the market. With the import share eventually growing (from 45% to 65% between 1995 and 1998), some corporations decided on building factories in Russia. This strategy was chosen by TNCs Mars (a factory in Stupino), Cadbury Schweppers (a factory in Chudovo, Novgorod region), Stollwerck (a factory in

Pokrov, Vladimir region) and some others. Every conceivable encouragement should also be provided to investment in the AIC related to advanced technologies.

In Kazakhstan Turkish firms built a macaroni factory in Petropavlovsk and a dairy in Ust-Kamenogorsk. In Georgia a joint venture for the development, production and sales of mineral water (the republic has over 2000 natural springs) with a Dutch firm started bottling and marketing the famous Borjomi (outputs decreased 100 times: from 700 to 7 million bottles between 1993 and 1995). Coca-cola and Pepsi-cola built plants in some CIS republics.

5. A primary concern is intra-CIS co-operation on the market of alcoholic and non-alcoholic beverages. Outputs from Moldova have traditionally accounted for 70%–80% of the Russian wine market, and Georgia and Armenia for over a half the mineral water market. But the alcohol market (estimated at $12 billion) was captured by background producers using forged labels of Armenian brandies, Georgian and Moldavian wines, popular vodka types and even Borjomi mineral water.

A drastic increase has occurred on the market of juice and other non-alcoholic beverages (annual per capita consumption 8–10 l as compared with over 100 l in EU countries). Moldova, Transcaucasian and Central Asian republics have unique opportunities for extended production of fruit and vegetable juice for Russia and Belarus, using available spring water.

6. CIS countries have yet to build a sector of deep-freeze pre-fabricated products (e.g. pizza, potato dishes, bakery, soups, fish, vegetables, salads, sandwiches). Extended use of microwave ovens and motor cars, and female employment, expanded the market in EU member countries between 1995 and 1997 from $48 to $54 billion (expected $69 billion by 2002). Individual family members increasingly buy pre-fabricated products to suit their own tastes and cook dinner in a few minutes. The child and dietetic food sector has been extending rapidly. Promotion of these market segments, involving strategic management and broad co-operative arrangements, will provide a new impetus to the AIC.

In 1998 and 1999 food imports to Russia and some other countries were reduced, due to the fall in national exchange rates. This contributed to improved competitiveness of local products, including those using foreign investments. Russia increased the output of items such as unskimmed-milk produce, beer, vegetable oil, macaroni, cereals. There was evidence of growing outputs in Belarus, the Ukraine and Armenia. Yet total meat production across the CIS constituted only 17% of the peak year (between 1979 and 1990), and that of unskimmed-milk produce 23%.

Light industry in the CIS. Light industry has sustained raw inputs (cotton, flax, wool, leather) and multiple enterprises with sustained high profits and turnover rates. Almost all enterprises have been privatised in Armenia and Russia, over

90% in Kyrgyzstan and 70% in Belarus. However, this area, like high-technology industries, has found itself in grave distress. Textile outputs in CIS countries decreased fivefold in the 1990s (10-fold in Kazakhstan and the Ukraine, 5-fold in Armenia and 200-fold in Georgia). Per capita outputs fell from 43 to 8.5 m for textiles and from 2.9 to 0.3 pair for footwear (1996), lagging far behind reasonable consumption levels. In Russia light industry production fell seven-fold, with 20% utilization of capacities and 75% of enterprises potential failures.

In 1998 textile, knitwear and hosiery outputs grew only in Armenia, Belarus and Tajikistan, and those of footwear and Belarus and Kazakhstan. Yet textile outputs in CIS countries amounted to only 22% of those in 1989–1990, including 7% in the Ukraine and 16% in Russia; footwear dropped to 7% (5% in the Ukraine and 6% in Russia).

The primary cause of this crisis is related to the disruption of traditional, though largely irrational, economic relationships. Cotton imports fell from 1.2 to 0.2 million tonnes. Until the 1990s they derived from the compulsory single-crop system in Uzbekistan, Turkmenistan and Tajikistan, causing extensive chemical pollution, drying up in the Aral and actually depriving Karakalpakians of their land. Uzbekistan (fourth in world output and second in export of cotton) processed only 10% of the fibre, the remainder being transported northward at low prices, with 70% of the profits going outside the republic.

Reduced cotton output due to the elimination of the single-crop system and conversion to world prices took textile manufacturers unawares. The obsolete equipment had been designed to maximum lineage (the top-down planned parameter) of a limited range of standard textiles not in popular demand. Attempts to gain inputs in barter exchange, e.g. for Enisei combines, failed. Low-priced cotton inputs were resold on international markets and never reached national textile industries. TNC agreements between cotton, textile and clothing manufacturers have not yet been implemented.

Another challenge relates to uncontrolled imports, including the "shuttles". The proportion of domestic-made clothing and footwear on the Russian market declined to 20%–30%. Almost 75% of clothing, knitted wear, footwear and other such items are purchased on informal markets. In Kazakhstan and Kyrgyzstan the proportion amounts to 80%–95% (generally via the "shuttles" from China, Pakistan, Turkey and other countries). The enterprises are compelled to surrender over 90% of the profits in taxes and to cover machinery, electricity and infrastructure costs, and cannot compete with "wild" imports. Only in 1997 did "shuttle" commodity turnover begin to decline in Russia ($13.4 billion imports, $1.2 billion exports). The 1998 devaluation accelerated the process, giving domestic firms a chance to regain the market subject to technological updating and significant cost reductions.

Another challenge confronted by light industry is the loss of working capital caused by inflation, excessive taxation and loan interest, delayed settlements and advanced-payment requirements in the CIS. These resulted in extended use of inputs supplied by the customer, with, for example, a textile factory retaining only 20%–25% of output costs. Rather than as direct input from the Central Asian region, cotton has been increasingly supplied without advanced payment via intermediaries in the Baltic republics, EU and USA.

The *revival of light industry* will require above all re-profiling of unpromising and loss-making enterprises, machinery updating and competitive and resource-saving technologies ensuring fast customisation to any profitable order. The area needs up-to-date marketing and modelling services. These will require targeted investment programs involving promotion of related sectors such as cotton, linen and synthetic threads and dyes, as well as credits to reinforce working capital.

Establishment of branch associations and syndicates – voluntary share associations selling outputs and raw material inputs – will enable cotton, leather and wool to be ordered a year in advance and thus improve contracting terms. The Rostekstil concern of 400 enterprises and Moscow Cotton Chamber provide continued process lines and investments to production of wool fibre, threads and cotton (expected annual outputs of 100,000 tonnes) in Astrakhan region, Kalmykia, Daghestan, Krasnodar and Stavropol territories. But joint programs with other CIS countries and prominent foreign firms would be far more effective.

At an initial stage in the development of new technologies and management techniques, orders of foreign firms can be filled, with their pattern-, material and technology inputs, a practice currently in extensive use at clothing and leather-footwear enterprises in Russia, Belarus, the Ukraine, Moldova and Armenia. The wage accounts for 30% of clothing prime costs, average hour wage rates amounting to almost $4 in Portugal, $7 in Greece, almost $20 in North Europe and under $1 in CIS countries. For this reason almost 90% imports from CIS countries to Germany use German companies' trademarks, patterns and supplies. Similar outputs of light industry in Belarus account for 75% of totals.

Reorganisation in light industry is largely related to macro-economic policy in CIS member states, above all budgetary, financial, investment and taxation policies.

Field of Debate

1. What are the roles of agriculture, fishery and forestry in GDP output and public employment in CIS countries? What statistical data and trends of development describe the AIC in the 1990s?

2. What are the causes of agrarian crisis in CIS countries? What are the remedies? What are recent developments in grains, industrial crops, potatoes, vegetables and livestock?

3. What are the AIC percentages of farms and household plots in CIS countries? What can be done to accomplish rational proportions of large and small enterprises in the

AIC? What are the differences in the AIC structure in different CIS countries, e.g. in Armenia and Belarus? What is the world experience in the area?

4. What can you suggest to resolve the question of private ownership of land? What are the pros and contras?

5. What is the role to be played by the government in regulating the agrarian market? Discuss the program of agrarian reforms on the eve of the twenty-first century formulated in CIS countries.

6. What are the basic characteristics of the new technology framework in the AIC? What relevant changes would be expedient in terms of labour qualifications and efficiency?

7. What is the meaning of national food safety? What is the import contribution to the food market in CIS countries? What are the reasonable limits of protectionism with regard to domestic producers?

8. What are the prospects for developments in basic food industries in the CIS? What new trends on the world market should be considered in this context?

9. What are the reasons of the very critical conditions in CIS light industry? What remedies can you suggest?

10. What is the importance of intra-CIS co-operation for transformations in the AIC? Analyse the basic co-operative strategies.

Chapter 7

MACRO-ECONOMIC POLICIES IN CIS MEMBER STATES

7.1 Budgetary Policy

Government budget in a transitional economy. The *government budget* is an account of public revenues and expenditures for a specified period, approved by legislative authority. Until the twentieth century, the government budgetary policy involved tax collection exclusively for the maintenance of the State machine, including defence, public security and foreign affairs. For the rest, classical economic science relied on automatic mechanisms of self-regulation in the market economy. However, economic crisis in the 1930s demonstrated that, though effective for small-scale commodity production, this mechanism was inadequate in modern, highly socialised industrial economies.

Neither were the administrative command practices efficient, with the bulk of enterprise revenues remitted to the budget and then redistributed on extra-economic lines by the Communist Party and government authorities, generally for military purposes, aid to foreign communist parties, etc. Between the 1960s and 1980s the Soviet Union earned over $600 billion from exports of oil (at rapidly increasing prices) and some other natural resources. But the immense gains and the self-supporting budget failed to promote an up-to-date infrastructure (e.g. roads, communications, schools).

Since the 1930s developed market economies have been implementing the Keynesian theory, using budgetary funds to generate changes in aggregate demand, to increase employment, prevent inflation, ensure sustainable economic growth and promote the public sector in science, education and health care. Active use of the budget has been made to finance national and regional, and later on, international, scientific and technological, social and economic, and environmental programs. A *discretionary policy* suggests that increased government purchases of goods and services influence the economy in the same way as does increasing investments, i.e. encouraging production and employment. Of course, extended budgetary expenditure will drive up taxes, but this adverse effect is insignificant according to this logic, being offset by decreased private consumption and savings.

Equal increases in government spending and taxes, according to Keynesian logic, will transform itself into higher national income. Therefore, neither *fiscal deficit* (excess of government expenditures over receipts) nor increased (within reasonable limits) *national debt* are to be feared. The limits are represented by production efficiency indicators because large taxes inhibit business activity and the government property created through the budget is less effective than private.

Available methods of macro-economic analysis permit to calculate the parameters of *automatic stabilisers*, i.e. effects of the amount and structure of government expenditures and revenue on GDP and change in business conditions. An appropriate budget policy is essential in the period of structural reform. CIS countries, however, have yet to develop a unitary approach to the optimal budget.

In the conception proposed by radical "market adherents", chances of surmounting the crisis are the greater the less the government interferes with economic matters. A. Illarionov and some other economists maintain that economic growth is inversely related to the public consumption and redistribution of national product through the budget, since public expenditures are less effective than private and the budget deficit has to be financed with Central Bank credits (increasing inflation), external loans (increasing export debt) or internal credits (withdrawing private investment resources). These economists believe that high public expenditures (over 60% of GDP) contributed to economic decline in Sweden, whereas dramatic cuts in expenditure, including financial aid and subsidies (from 36.3% of GDP in 1979 to 13.8% in 1995) and notably from the central government (from 14% to 5%), governed unprecedented growth in China.

In Bulgaria in the early 1990s 45%–48% of GDP were re-distributed through the government budget, with the budget deficit reaching 11%–15% of GDP and annual inflation rates between 73% and 334%. In 1994 and 1995 government expenditures were reduced to 44% of GDP and the deficit fell to 6.7%. As a result, the slump in production (7% every year) was followed by its growth (2%). But then in 1996 the socialist government proceeded with increasing public expenditures. To cover the budget deficit, the Central Bank had to buy up government bonds rejected by commercial structures. Issuing money surged, and the public started purchasing hard currency and withdrawing bank deposits. Central Bank's currency reserves were exhausted and IMF credit was delayed. In an effort to prevent panics, the Central Bank raised discount rate to 300%, which only resulted in a production halt. In 1996 the exchange rate was decimated and inflation rate exceeded 20%. The GDP decreased by 10% and real household incomes two to three times (to $30 monthly). Bulgaria emerged as Europe's poorest country, with the consequent social explosion and change of government. When numerous enterprises were sold in military, metallurgical and some other industries in late 1990s, the budget deficit fell to 3%–5%. This helped to reduce inflation.

According to liberal economists, stabilisation is not likely to be accomplished unless government spending has been reduced to 30%–31% of GDP and the rapid growth (5%–7% annually) to 20%–25% of GDP, as was the case in Singapore, South Korea, Thailand, Chile and Taiwan. Government spending in Russia, including pension and other allocations not formally passed through the budget, amount to 35%–36% and the budget deficit to 12%–15% of GDP (1996–1998). As estimated by the Institute for Economic Analysis (A. Illarionov), total government expenditures, including external and internal loans, credits guaranteed by central government and municipal authorities, and tax credits, exceed 50% compared with 33%–36% in the USA and Japan, and 25%–29% in Turkey, Mexico and Brazil.

Under the administrative system, a great part of national added value was concentrated in the budget, and then was re-distributed by the party and government authorities. But in this case rigid instructions had been formulated and strictly observed as to the budget forming and using.

In the years of reform, the public budget size (in % of GDP) decreased significantly, with the major portion of value added retained by self-supporting firms. But CIS countries have not formulated a budget code starting from the present-day financial law. Developed foreign countries operate a fiscal framework for budget discharge, with revenues entered in a single account and spent in strict compliance with the parliamentary Budget Act for the current year. This enables precise computer accounting. In CIS countries budget reserves are often circulated in commercial banks with uncontrolled account balancing by departmental instructions and eventual inappropriate use. This is particularly true for the non-budget government funds consolidating substantial tax revenues.

Insufficient reserves (only 60%–70% of the planned amount in CIS countries) caused the cuts in expenditures generally specified by financial bodies, depending on the persistence and strength of one department (region) or another, rather than strict legal rules. As a result, recipients never know the amount they can command and sometimes make the orders they cannot afford. Moreover, arrears of social transfers and payments on government purchases acting as periods of *multipliers,* payments in other sectors of economy, are four to five times longer.

Another view suggests that the national debt increased within reasonable limits and at a low rate will resolve many problems today that can emerge as insoluble tomorrow. With appropriate control on effective spending of financial resources, the debt will not weigh heavily on generations to come. The idea that national debt is intolerable is only another myth, as some economists argue.[1] Some systems analysts believe that government expenditures between one fourth and one third of GDP will stabilise the market economy, preventing economic

---

[1] Cavanaugh, F.X. (1996): The Truth about the National Debt: Five Myths and One Reality. New York

decline. The biggest economic crisis in the USA occurred in 1929 when the percentage of government expenditure in GDP was low (8.5%). It was then raised to 25%–30%, never to fall again.

In CIS countries the share of government spending in GDP varies between one third and two thirds (see Table 23). Within this range the rate of economic growth is governed by the structure rather than the amount of public revenues. Excessive expenditure to cover the costs of the State machine, army and interests paid for national debt (expected to exceed the amount of new borrowing in some CIS countries by 2000) will inhibit the growth. On the other hand, financing of profitable investment projects, science and education will promote economic growth given a reasonable monetary policy. Such a budget will only induce negative rates of economic growth with irrational public expenditures exceeding 55%–65% of GDP. The question is of loans effectively used in projects providing higher returns than cost of capital rather than rejecting of external and internal debt. What is detrimental to the transition economy is not the debt itself but the high-interest loan (160% per year on the Russian government bonds market in 1996–1997) used to patch up holes in the budget or repay delayed wages, pensions, etc.

Experience in CIS countries suggests a direct relationship between the amount of budget deficit and the rate of economic growth. In 1995 Kyrgyzstan, Tajikistan and the Ukraine demonstrated the highest deficits (6%–7%) and Belarus and Uzbekistan the lowest deficits (2%–2.5% of GDP). Consequently, macro-economic indicators in 1996 and 1997 were the CIS highest in Kyrgyzstan and lowest in Tajikistan. The government budget in Belarus showed no loss whatever in 1997, but the comparatively rapid GDP growth was accompanied with a rapid growth of inflation and arrears for goods and services provided by enterprises in Russia, the Ukraine and Kyrgyzstan.

These resemble the developments in the Asian "dragons" and Czech Republic with their minimal budget deficits in the 1990s. Large foreign investments and re-orientation on Western markets in Czech Republic resulted in imports exceeding exports, weakening national currency and growing unemployment. These made the "Father of Czech reform", W. Klaus, resign.

In South Korea some major projects and loans proved inefficient. At the first sign of crisis speculators fled, taking away $30 billion In 1997 and 1998 the outstanding debts totalled $150 billion and foreign currency reserves $10 billion; some major corporations failed and the exchange rate dropped by one third. The IMF advanced an economic reanimation credit ($57 billion), advising to cut economic growth by half (from 6% to 3%), deny privileged credit to local monopolies, curtail excessive production capacities and initiate bankruptcy proceedings against insolvent companies and banks. Similar circumstances in Indonesia in 1997 resulted in a five-fold decrease in the national exchange rate.

Table 23

GDP Structure and Use in CIS Countries (in % of 1997 totals)

Country	GDP structure			GDP use				
		Net taxes on production and imports	Gross profits and mixed revenues	Final consumption		Gross accumulation		Net exports/ imports of goods and services
	Wage			Households	General government	Fixed capital	Change in working capital	
Azerbaijan	19	11	70	76	12	37	1[***]	−27.1
Armenia	40[*]	6.5[*]	53.5[*]	101	11	18	2	−33.1[***]
Belarus	45	17	38	56	19	25	0.1	−4.1
Georgia	23	5	73	75	8	19	4[***]	−14.5[**]
Kazakhstan	37	10	53	71	12	17	2.6	−2.4
Kyrgyzstan	32	10	57	67	17	12	−2	−7.9
Moldova	45[***]	13[***]	42[***]	69	26	20	9	−20.2[***]
Russia	47	15	38	51	22	20	3[***]	2.7
Tajikistan	29[**]	6[***]	65[***]	65	12	24	9[*]	−10.1[**]
Turkmenistan	...	...	...	...	...	...	...	...
Uzbekistan	37[***]	18[***]	45[***]	60	21	35	−9	−0.2
Ukraine	48	22	30	57	22	18	3.4	−3.8

[*] 1994.
[**] 1995.
[***] 1996.

CIS countries should take both national and, more importantly, international lessons. International experience has shown no simple unambiguous way to an "economic miracle". No formal reduction in government expenditure will do the job. A special budget policy is required, involving specific consideration of the structure of budget expenditures, and the nature and maximum size of budget deficit.

CIS countries have pursued very different budget policies over the 1990s. The largest deficits in 1997, discharged with external borrowing, were evident in Moldova, the Ukraine, Kyrgyzstan and Russia. By contrast, Azerbaijan, Uzbekistan and Kazakhstan chose to restrict the deficit substantially rather than use it to force economic growth as did some countries in the second half of the 1990s.

The budget revenues differ significantly in structure. Some countries prefer to fill the budget with indirect taxes (the VAT and excise duties) which are easily collected but inclined to raise the prices and consequently restrict the demand (Uzbekistan, Turkmenistan, Kyrgyzstan, Moldova, Belarus). This permitted the

Central Asian and Transcaucasian republics to minimise (4%–7%) the proportion of household income tax in budget revenues (see Table 24). The highest profit tax shares were demonstrated in Uzbekistan and Russia.

Among the important budget receipts in some CIS countries are customs duties and other proceeds from foreign trade (Azerbaijan, Belarus, Russia, Tajikistan and the Ukraine). On the other hand, land tax and receipts of privatisation were insignificant in the mid-1990s. General proportions of tax revenues in budget totals in 1997 vary from 71% to 76% (Kazakhstan, Tajikistan, Kyrgyzstan) and 8% to 87% (Russia, Belarus, Uzbekistan).

Budget expenditures were dominated by the social and cultural sphere, including pensions (allocations to the pension fund exceeding 35% of budget expenditures in the Ukraine). At the same time, expenditures for national economies and science over 25% of the budget were only evident in Russia, Tajikistan, Turkmenistan and Uzbekistan (see Table 24). Maximum military expenditures were observed in Armenia (17%) and Russia (10%). Some countries failed to provide annual expenditure statistics. Kyrgyzstan and Tajikistan headed the list of expenditures for the State machine and public security (over 15%). Amount of interest paid for national debt accounted for the highest proportion of budget expenditure in 1998 in Russia, causing a severe financial slump.

Budget deficit and State debt. Different CIS countries used different methods to discharge the budget deficit: firstly, for precarious money printing, raising prices for goods and services and depreciating bank deposits and other household savings (the method prevailed in early 1990s); then, external non-tightened (not channelled to specific investment projects) loans advanced by the International Monetary Fund (IMF), other international organisations and foreign governments, and distribution of government and regional bonds on European and other international markets; and finally, issue of government securities (e.g. treasury bills, government bills, foreign currency bonds).

The government securities market in CIS countries was meant to cover the national debt and cover the budget deficit without an additional issuing of money emission. Access to the market was provided for *non-residents*, i.e. foreign portfolio investors. However, after the 1997 financial crisis in Southeast Asia, the investors (representing 30% of the market) sold the government bills, converted the proceeds into hard currency and invested them in less risky spheres. To prevent the collapse of their national exchange of the type occurring in countries such as South Korea, Brazil and Thailand, Russia, for example, had to raise government bill yields, thus increasing the national debt costs several times, to an inadmissible level. Moreover, Central Bank's interests as the major market operator (sums earned from transactions) not necessarily favour the budget.

Table 24

Budget Policy Indicators by CIS Countries (in %)

Country	Budget deficit In % of GDP				Budget deficit In % of total revenue		Revenue structure (1995)				Total tax reve- nues in 1998**	Expenditure structure (1995)				Natio- nal bank refun- ding rate
	1995	1996	1997	1998**	1997	1998**	VAT	Excise	Corpo- rate profit (in- come) tax	House- hold in- come tax		Natio- nal econo- my and NTP	Social and cultu- ral sphere	Defen- ce	State machi- ne	(in %, end of 1998)
Azerbaijan	1	3.6	3.2	3.0	18.5	18.9	5	5	17	...	78	4	15	...	...	12
Armenia	...	2.8	3.0	2.2	19.4	11.9	18	3	25	7	83	10	30	17	7	54
Belarus	4	1.3	4.0	0.6	...	1.5	28	8	22	9	76	...	...	...	...	50
Georgia	...	0.7	3.3*	3.0	...	28.1	...	...	...	...	75	...	...	...	...	43
Kazakhstan	4	0.7	0.3	3.3	3.9	21.3	12	3	12	11	76	17	37	...	...	18.5
Kyrgyzstan	12	4.5	3.8	2.2	24.6	12.2	28	12	16	11	80	11	62	3	17	25
Moldova	5	8.5	7.8	2.9	25.9	8.2	29	10	20	10	75	...	24	9	11	21
Russia	3	4.4	4.2	3.7	18.0	16.7	22	6	27	8	84	29	27	10	8	60
Tajikistan	...	...	2.8	4.1	14.0	26.9	12	13	16	6	75	30	29	5	15	56
Turkmenistan	1	1.0	10–14*	...	4.0	...	31	8	25	4	...	41	28	...	...	35
Uzbekistan	3	...	2.5	...	6.8	...	19	27	39	...	...	34	44	4	9	...
Ukraine	7	4.7	7.5	7.2	25.5	12.8	22	2	23	8	74	11	39	4	10	43

* Estimated.

** January to September.

The budget deficit in Russia has been covered with federal bonds (25%–40%), loans from international financial organisations (up to 25%), foreign commercial banks and firms (10%), governments (over 5%), bills and bonds (25%). In Uzbekistan 20% of the budget deficit was covered with government bills.

In 1997 budget deficit in Armenia, Kyrgyzstan, Moldova and the Ukraine was under 3% of GDP. In Russia and Tajikistan it appeared significantly higher. Tax revenues in most of the countries constituted over three quarters of budget revenue.

CIS countries employed various methods to reduce budget deficit. Many were severely criticised by economists, e.g. in Russia: additional printing of money, hard currency purchase to support the certain level of exchange rate, rise of prices for energy resources and tariffs for communications and transport services, cuts in government capital investment to budget expenditure, delayed payments on MIC orders, and planned Army, education and science costs.

Preferable strategies to increase budget revenues should involve transition from voucher-based to money privatisation, sale of insolvent enterprises, abolition of customs privileges to individual exporters and importers, partial sale or lease of military testing areas, tighter customs and bank control over exports and imports, shutting down of potential tax-evasion channels, competitive or interest-charged budget deposits in commercial banks. These will enhance the importance of the *treasury* as an independent government organisation for customs, tax and departmental accounts. Another useful organisation would be a government investment bank contributing to the financing of top-priority projects and supervising the designated use and eventual repayment of credits.

Equally important would be the cuts in government administrative costs, subsidies to loss-making enterprises, excessive armed forces, outright credits to the AIC or unfeasible social programs. These are still substantial in Russia, although decreasing from 71.5% of GDP in 1992 to 45% in 1995. Subsidies to the national economy amount to 12% of GDP as against 1.3% in Estonia and 3%–4% in Hungary, Poland, Slovakia and Slovenia.

By the end of the 1990s, budget deficit decreased in all CIS countries except the Ukraine, Armenia and Turkmenistan (see Table 24). But the tabulated data exclude wage arrears (37% of total budget expenditures in Russia, 57% in the Ukraine and 170% in Kazakhstan in the autumn 1997) and the debts of State-owned organisations in utilities. The deficit in Belarus and Tajikistan was covered with Central Bank loans, i.e. precarious money issue, and in some other countries with external loans (100% in Georgia, 75% in Kazakhstan and Tajikistan, and 40%–50% in Russia, Kyrgyzstan and the Ukraine).

Budget policy estimates should not be confined to the formal amount of deficit. Due account must be taken of changes in hard currency reserves, national debt, government contribution to loans issued by commercial bank wage arrears due to insufficient budget financing, cash proportion in taxes collected, change in tax arrears and total amount of taxes (in Russian budget taxes count 45% of GDP, with 32% eventually collected against the rational economic level of 25%–28%).

International experience has shown that in the absence of a reliable framework for national debt payments, budget deficit presents grave problems in economic growth. In Russia, according to A. Illarionov, government budget deficit fell from 13.8% of GDP in 1992 to 7.2% in 1993, then rose to 10.9% in 1994 and fell again to 3.7% in 1995. GDP negative rates changed accordingly (14.5%, 8.7%, 12.7%, 4%). At the same time, the share of interests paid for national debt and pay-off had been growing (from 3% in 1993 through 11% in 1994 and to 25% in 1998). GDP growth was the fastest (4.5% annually) in the countries showing minimum (under 3%) or zero budget deficit.

In Russia (and increasingly so in Armenia, Kyrgyzstan, Georgia and Moldova) this problem is aggravated by the export debt. The USSR in 1985 appeared in a very stable financial position: 60 countries owed it over $140 billion, including $46 billion due in 1995, with the Soviet debt slightly over $50 billion On the collapse of the USSR, Russia became liable for the whole amount of debt, since 90% of USSR exports had come from Russia. As subsidies to the Union republics represented one third of the budget, many politicians claimed that Russia was entering a Golden Age. Similar beliefs were entertained in other republics.

The reality was quite different. Financial deterioration started in 1990. The republics nationalised Union enterprises which could not survive without centralised financing and, to support them, immediately initiated unchecked of common currency (book rubles) in 15 centres. Household money incomes in the USSR increased from $619 billion in 1990 to almost $1200 billion in 1991, wiping off all consumer goods. In 1991 and 1992, 14 countries (except Estonia), including non-members of the economic union (the Ukraine, Georgia, Moldova and Azerbaijan), proceeded with uncoordinated issue of clearing rubles, advanced credits to enterprises within their jurisdictions, provided them (actually appropriating) with inputs of raw materials and energy resources from Russia. The bulk of the rubles were converted to foreign currency which the Central Bank sold impetuously, exhausting its gold reserves by 1992. The unprecedented financial chaos was supplemented with multibillion forged advice notes from Chechnya and large-scale (bribed) conversion of clearing rubles to cash. Thus, for instance, when introducing the national currency, Estonia sold the available rubles to speculators instead of transferring to Russian Central Bank as had been agreed. The infringements upon elementary economic laws – a genuine civil war in finance – could only be surmounted with the exports of Russian strategic reserves, the almost incredible national patience and the separation of CIS monetary systems in 1993.

The disintegration of the Soviet bloc dispelled the hopes for due recovery of debts from Cuba, Ethiopia, Nicaragua, Somali, India, Vietnam and some others have been paying off at extremely low rate (accounting for the ruble drop) and generally in foodstuffs (e.g. tea, rice). The more realistic expectations regarding Iran and Libya failed because of the embargo.

Between 1985 and 1990 the former USSR debts increased to $71 billion, with the bulk due in 1992 and 1993. This was due to a drastic fall in oil prices (from $30 to $10 per barrel) with still expanding imports of grain. Credits obtained during the period had been wasted on ineffective and incomplete projects. The government relied on the "peaceful dividends" – cold war savings – amounting to several hundred billion dollars. But no significant assistance of the Marshall Plan type was forthcoming to Russia and other CIS countries. What could be obtained generally went to cover the sponsors' advice, training trips (not always effective) and humanitarian aid. As a result, by 1998 Russia held the world lead (twelfth in 1995) in export debt ($130 billion, including $17 billion of interests on Soviet debts), with only 22% due to governments (Paris club) and 78% to 600 private banks (London club). The long-negotiated restructuring involves deferred payment of fixed amount of interest rather than debt write-off. After 1999 annual payments on export debt may amount to $10–$13 billion, i.e. almost half the budget receipts.

By the end of the 1990s, creditors' debts were far in excess of the debtors' in all CIS countries, notably in Kazakhstan, Russia and the Ukraine, indicating a grave non-payment crisis. All the countries, excluding Belarus and Russia, also had an unfavourable balance of payments to enterprises in other countries. Enterprise debts to the Russian Energy and Fuel Complex have been growing in the Ukraine, Moldova and Kazakhstan.

The myth of "saving" the subsidies to CIS countries was likewise dispelled. They largely represented input producers' returns of a portion of taxes gained from the sales of related outputs in Russia and the Ukraine (e.g. textiles, clothing). In addition, Russia's geopolitical position in the world prevents its leaving to the mercy of fate the neighbouring republics with their 25 million Russian residents. CIS members' debts to Russia have approximated $6 billion by 1996. Yet the costs of resettling the people and reinforcing the new frontiers would be far higher.

Russian financial crisis in 1998, exerting strong adverse effects on CIS and some other economies, was governed by several factors; among them were the populist decisions on social allocations, taxability reduced by the slump in production, ineffective tax system, irrational use or theft of budget resources, dominance of speculative investors at the stock market and, above all, the pyramid scheme of government bills with inadmissibly high (by expert estimates, prior to the government bills freeze speculative investors had transferred outside of Russia $80 billion, almost five times more than their initial investment). An additional factor was provided by the drop in oil prices to the lowest level for the previous 25 years.

The economic romanticism focusing on Western assistance and the neglect of neighbourly economic integration have been over. Government budgets in Russia and other CIS countries will have to be discharged with available resources. Budget revenues can be increased through a radical reconstruction of the tax system, improved tax collection, recovery of illegal exports of capital, better export patterns, more rational imports and partial sale of corporate stocks to foreign investors. Almost all of U.S. ferrous metallurgy and half the oil companies in the 1990s are held by foreign investors. But no dirt-cheap sales of large, highly profitable enterprises are allowed, as opposed to, for example, in Russia and Kazakhstan, with controlling interests in the largest men's clothing manufacturer, Bolshevichka, in Moscow, which sold for $5.5 million, or the world's largest platinum and nickel exporter, Norilsk, which combined for $130 million.

The cuts in government spending, and notably in the cost- and socially inefficient subsidies, will ensure both the reduced budget deficit and financial stabilisation. In a transition to the market economy an increasing share of allocations to housing and utilities, agricultural and transport sectors, as well as subsidies and price-disparity compensations, will pass not through the national but rather the local budgets in regions, towns and districts.

A pressing problem in many CIS countries is the restoration of the government monopoly in alcohol production and trade. In the 1980s it was instrumental in financing the education and public health. "Liberalisation" in Russia and some other CIS countries in the 1990s resulted in the revenues transferred to shadow and criminal business.

Alcohol output halved in the first half of the 1990s, while the annual imports (smuggling excluded) amounted to 200 million litres. Thirty plants produced industrial spirits for production use. As the outputs fell by only 14% in 3 years and related chemicals 1.6 times, there is every reason to suggest hidden vodka production. Every year domestic and imported imitations killed 15,000 people. Government regulation of this market was restored in the late 1990s.

The IMF policy unambiguously orients CIS countries on the liberal-monetary model of reform. Having obtained the systems transformation credits and rehabilitation and reserve loans, they can only count on EFF credit with initial financial stabilisation completed (e.g. budget deficit under 5%), land purchase/sale mechanism created, etc. Even greater opportunities for IMF developing customers are provided by SDK credit with only interest paid for a long period. But these will require both further economic liberalisation and approval of other IMF members in Asia, Africa and South America, the major SDK recipients presently. As huge IMF economic stabilisation credits are to be advanced to Brazil, Indonesia and some other countries in the late 1990s, the IMF decided on the advisability of tighter government control on finance.

It should be noted that Estonia, with five loans from the World Bank alone between 1992 and 1995, subsequently abandoned IMF credit for more advantageous arrangements.

A bright case in discharging the budget deficit was demonstrated by the USA. By 1974 the national debt was one third that in 1946 (falling to one third of GDP), largely because the government regulated incomes, depreciation rates and monopolistic prices. But U.S. macro-economic policy in the 1970s and 1980s relied on borrowed assets. By 1993 the budget deficit approached 5% and the national debt 70% of GNP. The federal government borrowed almost 85% available financial resources at the capital market. Nobel Prize winner J. Buchanan concluded that Western democracies can only survive in an environment of growing budget deficit. In EU member countries budget deficit was over 5% and the national debt 62% of GDP in the early 1990s.

However, the rational planning of budget receipts and outlays (5–7 years in advance) advised by competent non-government organisations (Congressional Budget Administration in the USA) made it possible to use the national debt for an up-to-date R&D, social, production and market infrastructure. In the 1990s the budget deficit began to decrease. The USA expects to cancel it by the early twenty-first century by cutting the current expenditures for the administration and the Army, as well as the unemployment benefits and international aid. Nevertheless, social and educational as well as environmental and R&D programs will be maintained, including advanced military engineering.

The former USSR borrowing, including written-off State bank loans and compensation for household deposits in Sberbank (Savings Bank), amounted to over 110% in the mid-1980s and over 130% in early 1990s. What matters, however, is not the amount borrowed but rather the terms (time and price) and use. Regretfully, the national debt served to encourage criminal economy and mass-scale misuse of financial resources. For this reason CIS budget policies as we approach the twenty-first century must above all focus on optimisation of the budget structure and legal regulation of the very processes of composition and discharge.

The first consideration is the absolute "transparency" and control over budget expenditures, responsibility to recipients for its adequate discharge, reliable statistics, and adjustment of the relationships between the budget and private firms; otherwise, legal market economy is not likely to be developed.

Consolidated budget structure. A *consolidated*, i.e. combined, summarised budget includes three budget types: national, regional (e.g. of federal entities, regions, khakimats) and municipal (of towns, villages, auls, kishlaks), as well as special funds not passing through the budget. A rational composition of this budget is essential for the countries with autonomous entities (Uzbekistan, Tajikistan, Georgia, Moldova, Azerbaijan, the Ukraine) or regions essentially different by economic development level and income structure (Kazakhstan, Kyrgyzstan, Belarus), let alone the Russian Federation.

Relations between budgets of different levels involving the passing of most receipts through the central budget and back to their sources are irrational. Certain types of receipts should be initially assigned to regions, with taxes classified as republican, regional or municipal.

International experience indicates the two ways of inter-budgetary regulation. In Germany taxes are distributed in certain proportions. Thus, private income tax and corporate tax are constitutionally divided in equal proportions between the federal and land (local) budgets, with 15% of the first tax going to municipalities (communes). The value added taxes (VAT), under the federal law are distributed between the centre and the lands in the 65:35 ratio. The *tax potential* (total incoming taxes to regional and local budgets) and budget demand (by uniform per head standards depending on population density) are calculated for each land. In the horizontal transfer system the lands that collect more taxes than required by standard expenditure must transfer the excess amount to less favoured regions.

In the USA the problem is largely solved by assigning different taxes to different budgets. Customs charges, social and health insurance fees, excise duties and a portion of income tax are assigned to the federal budget, whereas those related to property, sales, car registration, mining and a share of income and inheritance taxes go to the state and local agencies. The law specifies the maximum allowable rate of taxation. Federal authorities finance over 500 target programs. Subsidies and grants account for almost 25% of revenues in poorer states and almost 45% in some municipalities. Transfers in the USA are generally strictly targeted. By contrast, the EU European Regional Autonomy Charter requires depersonalised transfers with independent regional planning of their use.

Budget federalism in Canada also relies on objective estimates. Income tax and the bulk of purchase and services taxes are assigned to the federal and budget property and mining taxes to local ones. Thus, the local government authorities are interested in attracting owners and resource developers. At the same time, the social infrastructure is levelled out with centralised transfers to the poorer regions. The amount is determined by the difference between national average GNP and that in a given region, and the population.

Things are different in Russia and other CIS countries. Thus, the Orel region is among the dependants (26% of budget expenditures provided with centralised transfers). At the same time, the region transfers 40% of collected taxes to the centre, i.e. eventually acting as a donor to the federal budget. Orientation on self-financing and targeted financial support to enterprise restructuring in 1997 made it possible to increase industrial outputs by 13% (electricity generation, machine building, metal working, ferrous and non-ferrous metallurgy), consumer goods by 28% and budget revenues by one third (largely due to income, profit, property taxes and the VAT). In addition, expenditures were increased by 30% for education, 14%–20% for public health and social security. At the same time, the increased investment share in gross regional product (from 13% to 14%) and the use of foreign investment contributed to the reduction in industrial subsidies out of the budget and completion of some important projects.

Considering international experience, the basic trends in optimisation of the consolidated budget pattern in CIS countries can be described as follows:

– Preparation and legislative formulation of the budget standards describing local demands with budget's objective indicators rather than personal contacts or political interests as has been common practice to date. This will require identification and careful consideration of both favourable and unfavourable objective factors governing social and economic developments in a given region

– Calculation of regional tax potentials from objective data to prevent dependent attitudes (expecting automatically increasing transfers from the central budget with lower tax revenues)

– Assignment to autonomous entities of a certain portion of collected taxes or certain tax types instead of personal agreements with relevant authorities

– An integrated financial support fund for less favoured regions, instead of the existing diversified and almost unchecked system (e.g. budget credits, financing of basic industries, the social sphere, target programs) characterised by financing from several sources for some regions and none for others which are not less important

All these trends will induce the local government authorities to finding new sources of income rather than "knocking out" some advantages from the centre. In the late 1990s territorial budgets in Russia have represented almost 70% of financing to national economy, 80% to education and 88% to public health. The regions contribute over half of the consolidated budget. Yet the overwhelming majority of federal entities (64 in 1994 and 81 of 89 in 1997) have no balanced budgets and receive centralised transfers, in some cases 1.5–1.8 times in excess of their own revenues. This situation cannot be described as normal.

The bulk of credit resources of CIS countries are now concentrated in the capital cities (80% in Moscow). Such monopolisation is regarded as illegal in the USA and some other countries.

Improvement of budgetary procedures. A pressing problem in CIS countries is related to the *budget code* strictly regulating the formulation, approval and discharge procedures. International experience would be helpful to identify the basic principles underlying the rationalisation of budget procedures.

The primary concern is budgetary realism, starting from objective estimates of the fiscal system and revenue potentials rather than unjustified and overstated departmental or regional expectations. To attract the votes and public sympathy or to indulge specific financial groups, some CIS parliaments and governments have included in budget expenditures the items that notoriously could not be financed out of the revenues. This resulted in failure to implement the broadly advertised investment and social programs, non-payment lines, etc. Particularly, often sequestrations involved budget supported organisations, including the Army, electricity supply and other utilities. A realistic budget will encourage the recipients to use realistic financial plans and estimates, and to look for additional incomes and savings.

Reductions in government budget expenditures should start from the structural change, i.e. cutting the number of dependants rather than automatic "sequestration", i.e. reduced allocations to all. Thus, reductions in military expenditure should involve the closure of dispensable units and bases, providing normal financing to the remainder. To prevent the degradation of science and education, eligibility for budget allocations should be identified via the government accrediting of key scientific centres and institutes, giving others the opportunities for self-support, merger with more competitive structures or dissolution.

Of special importance is complete or partial financial autonomy in the social sphere, cancelling outright subsidies to inefficient branches of economy. Thus, loss-making and hazardous mines have been closed in Russian coal industry, with the share of non-public enterprises increased from 8% to 50% and social-safety subsidies rather than damages paid to released labour.

Legal standards will assign to executive authorities responsibilities for strict compliance with the budget law, and to budget-supported organisations for effective resource management. This will require the transfer of financial resources from commercial banks to the treasury, government and municipal bank accounts, detailed itemisation and transparency of budget assignments, and permanent control over budget discharge by legislators and controlling agencies. Thus, for example, the U.S. military budget contains 1200 items as compared with a few large sections not allowing for detailed control in the corresponding budgets of large CIS countries.

The budget code must include strict specifications of competitive sales (tenders) for government procurements (e.g. for the Army, schools, hospitals, institutions) and building contracts, with favourable terms (with equal price and quality) for domestic firms, including small and medium-scale firms. These specifications will exclude the persistent bribery, price overstating and payment for non-performed works. International experts estimate CIS countries as almost the most corrupt (only excluding some African and South American countries), the situation deteriorating since early 1990s. Comparatively low-paid officials in CIS countries have the opportunity to get almost unchecked allowances, bonuses, benefits, subsidies and social privileges out of the budget resources.

Budget regulations will ensure a sharp reduction in discounts and deductions in composing budget revenues; among them are treasury tax exemptions (over

$6 billion in Russia in 1996), government financial guarantees and sponsorship. Some CIS countries have made extensive use of credit for financing working capital to repay budget debts, remission of budget arrears and debts to defence, public security etc. The remissions (Finance Ministry self-payments) amounting to one fifth of the total financing will improve budget discharge for the time being, while disorganising money circulation (replacing money with "securities").

Additionally, a reasonable budget expenditure level will favour direct investments to promote the infrastructure and highly effective and rapidly (in 2–3 years) repaid joint projects with private investors, purchase of high-technology products, export credits, etc. Some economists argue that the share of expenditure to the structural and industrial policy should be increased (notably so in Russia, Kazakhstan and other highly privatised economies) to 1%–1.4% of GDP and total government investment (including the social sphere) to 3%–3.5% of GDP.

Tight control should be imposed on the effective management of State controlling interests in industrial enterprises. Thus, in 1996 no dividends came to Russia's budget from joint stock company Integrated Energy System, Lukoil and Rosneft, reporting $3.5 billion profit each, even though the State holds 51%, 22% and 75% shares there, respectively.

Some CIS countries have started improving of their budgets. The Ukraine proposed to establish central executive agencies by functions rather than branches. This will permit at least 15% cuts in the number of departments and their staff. Under the presidential decree "Provisions for the Government budget and strict fiscal and budget discipline" (1997) budget supported organisations will be financed according to figures planned, and non-public ones subject to credit or with a certain block of shares transferred to State (municipal) ownership. In cases of non-performance of liabilities, in front of the budget, the contract with enterprise (organisation) management will be cancelled.

Solution of budget problems in many CIS countries will be facilitated by the establishment of a free and yet government-regulated market of precious metals and stones, and notably gold.

Strict regulations are required in external borrowing. Rather than grain or other consumer purchases, government borrowing should be aimed at long-term structural reforms, preferably to be repaid with exports. Access to the world financial market can only be provided for regions ineligible for government subsidising. Certain limits will be set both on the amount borrowed (less than 20%–30% annual budget revenues) and interests paid (less than 10%–15% of own revenues).

Azerbaijan has drawn special attention to feasible investment projects, including small and medium-scale business. These only will ensure eligibility for budget allocations.

Reforms in the finance and budget system in Moldova involves a treasury/fiscal framework for government expenditure and revenue management, fixed budget rates and standards, public cost reports to prevent overstated and unlawful expenditure, reduced number of central and local government agencies, and cancellation of government-guaranteed credits to market agents.

Some CIS countries will face the challenge of outstanding external debt in the early twenty-first century. In Moldova it already exceeds annual GDP, including running FEC revenues. The excess is even higher in Tajikistan. Armenia obtained the CIS biggest (per capita) World Bank credits. Even though the amount of debt is acceptable, the time limits need some revision. Effective national debt management depends largely on the credit and monetary policy.

7.2 Credit and Monetary Policy

General conception of credit and monetary policy. The *credit and monetary policy* involves government actions aimed at changing the amount of money circulated through emission open market operations, regulating the discount rate, authorised commercial bank reserves, and requirements on the issue and circulation of securities (e.g. shares, bonds, drafts, treasury bills). The policy regulates the rate of inflation, i.e. depreciation notes and book money not convertible to gold, decreasing of their purchasing power relative to goods and services due to excessive printing money. An explicit inflation in a market economy is evident in the rise of prices for goods and services (balancing the supply and demand), and an implicit one in the commodity deficit and replacement of money with barter.

In CIS countries, as in the rest of the world, there has been no common opinion between the liberal-monetary and Keynesian schools about the conception of credit and monetary policy. The monetary theory advocated by Nobel Prize winner M. Friedman (Chicago University, USA) and his colleagues involved a self-regulation of the market, impaired by government intervention. Economic analysis in this theory is generally confined to the changes in money stock; hence the quantitative monetary theory equation:

$$M \times V = P \times Q,$$

where M is the aggregate money supply (monetary aggregate M2), including total cash (monetary aggregate M0) and on deposit, current and special accounts of corporate bodies, physical persons and local budgets; V the velocity of money; Q the quantity of real goods and services produced over the year; and P the average price level for goods and services.

When describing demand on money, monetarians also consider the expected change in yields from money savings, bonds and stocks, and household and corporate expectations concerning the inflation level. With this logic, demand on money is largely determined by fixed income, and money supply by monetary equations, with no immediate relation to functioning of economy. Inflation in this theory is a purely monetary event inhibiting rather than enhancing economic developments; a temporary and minor inflation growth during the period of structural reforms can be tolerated. An economic crisis is generally caused by unjustified printing of money authorised by the government in a vain endeavour to increase aggregate demand and reduce unemployment. The monetary rule requires persistent but moderate growth of money supply irrespective of the phase in the economic cycle and accounting for velocity of money. Control of money circulation is the main economic function of the government, with all other attempts to interfere with natural competitive processes doing more harm than good.

The neo-Keynesian conception presented in the work of Nobel Prize winner V. Leontiev and some other prominent scholars started from a monetary policy reflecting general economic conditions and focused on economic growth rather than inflation control. In this theory, money demand is not stable and depends largely on speculative attitudes and expectations of market agents, and cannot provide the guideline for macro-economic policy. This is derived from equations of the real commodities markets rather than money markets. The government should not rely on market spontaneity, in a situation of economic decline, accepting accelerated inflation rates to enhance the demand for goods and reduce unemployment. Special emphasis should be placed on the reduction of the *real interest paid* (interest rates adjusted to inflation rate) to encourage investments. By contrast, with excessive rates of economic growth relative to projected demand and resources ("flush" economics) the interest rates ought to be raised. In this case both industrial investment efficiency and employment will decline. The interest rate level will determine the state of the money market.

Proponents of this conception in Russia, the Ukraine, Belarus, some republics in the Central Asian region and Azerbaijan advocate increased issuing of money combined with tighter government regulation and real pressure on prices of natural monopolies' goods and services. They believe that the "self-supporting" budget and suppressed inflation in CIS countries will cause industrial stagnation (restricted growth) and exhaust the resource and investment basis of reform. Issuing new money in this context is not an evil but rather an emergency action. It can be channelled via centralised allocations to specific investment projects on discount or outright lines, or to privileged consumer crediting of housing and commodity purchases. Investment banks with participation of the State will evaluate, select and credit competitive projects through the budget. Favourable credits issued by the Central Bank to Finance Ministry may be useful to cover the budget deficit and bridge the "cash gaps" (difference of reception and payment dates, including external loans). The newly created Investment Committee will be in charge of the capital budget (assigned in Russian Federal budget as far back as 1997 but never actually financed).

A similar monetary and credit policy was operated in 1993 and 1994 in the Ukraine, Georgia, Armenia, Tajikistan and Turkmenistan, in 1995 and 1996 in Turkmenistan and Tajikistan, between 1996 and 1998 in Belarus, and for some years in Uzbekistan, Azerbaijan and Russia. The effects are very difficult to assess because some of the countries in question were exposed to armed conflicts and others never pursued a consistent policy. One typical case is Belarus with economic growth rates higher than average across the CIS and inflation twice what had been planned (over 5% a month) in 1997. Intensification of the money stocks through credits to government projects ensured timely wage payments and increases while rapidly shifting down the exchange rate and wage calculated in dollars (from 103 to 75 per month). President A. Lukashenko has seen a problem in a combination of market forces with a government regulating mechanism.

Some prominent Russian economists (e.g. D. Lvov) and politicians argue that the share of moneys in total turnover and GDP in Russia (12%) is far lower than that in the UK (94%), USA (110%) and some other countries, with GKOs and other speculative securities representing 70% of the finance market. When effective demand declines in a classical market economy, producers will cut the outputs and prices for goods and services. In underdeveloped market economies in the CIS, the prices are not cut and the shortage of goods is replaced with a crisis of effective demand among the households, losses of corporate working capital (as distinct from the fixed capital, never re-evaluated or adjusted) and an avalanche growth of inter-enterprise arrears. Reduction of interest rates accomplished through an immense budget strain and curtailment of social programs in the CIS environment has not promoted industrial investment growth, since the firms have not enough finance for efficient operation even with the low rates.

In another conception, attempts to ignore general laws of international economics "in an isolated country", based on global protectionism for domestic producers and reinforced government role in economics, have generally resulted in decreasing competitive strength. Therefore, as the 1990s Ukrainian Vice-Premier V. Pinzenik put it, we ought to "dispel the myths of reform".

Myth 1: Macro-economic stabilisation only being feasible in a developed market economy, CIS countries should first control the declining outputs using government regulation. This view indicates the lack of will or ability for reform. In CIS countries it is represented by construction firms which cannot compete with firms in Turkey, Slovenia, Macedonia, Finland, Bulgaria or Estonia in quality and rates; machine builders whose machines, with all the low wages and cheap raw inputs, are more expensive than better-quality imports. No disease can be treated with methods that caused it, and one cannot swim by keeping away from water.

Myth 2: The monetary policy being incompatible with output stabilisation, credit should be increased to loss-making enterprises in the AIC, MIC, etc., in particular in cases of strong parliamentary support. This will result in a non-payment crisis (with the directors, instead of renewing the product mix, selling the output to notoriously insolvent buyers and then delaying the wage, hoping to shift the debts to the government, provoking, among other things, economic protest and hunger strikes), increasing fiscal deficit and prices, and continued changes in the economic policy.

Myth 3: Inflation being a non-monetary phenomenon caused by inefficient production structures, the increased government expenditure on current consumption will contribute to economic restructuring. CIS experience indicates the reverse: additional issuing money with a certain lag will inevitably cause a price rise.

Myth 4: Liberalisation of prices involves their multiple rises. This actually occurs when an implicit inflation (absence of goods, or goods sold under the counter) becomes explicit. A competitive market will subsequently restrict the price rise.

Myth 5: A tight financial and credit policy will restrict investment activities. Actually, it is the excessive use of budget funds (leading to budget deficit) for prestigious construction projects that undermines investment efficiency. They should be financed from corporate profits, household savings and accumulated depreciation funds with certain government support.

Myth 6: The fall of national currency is the result of hostile scheming. The rate should be fixed, for example, by closing currency exchanges and extending obligatory sales of hard currency at the official exchange rate. But a patient's temperature cannot be decreased by breaking the thermometer. Devaluation of national currency supplemented with the lifting of quotas and licensing, reduction of duties and government support of exports will stabilise the rate far better than mere administrative control.

On the other hand, macro-economics will not and cannot produce unambiguous rules or universal remedies; there is no single macro-economic model of reform, a magic monetary wand to solve any problem in any country. What is actually needed is a range of long-term monetary and non-monetary actions which account for specific conditions in a given country.

Standard monetarist strategies (price liberalisation, credit tightening, sharp reducing of government investment, reduction of real household incomes) are unlikely to produce definite results (increasing supply of goods, closure of loss-making enterprises and reduced wage funds, increasing fixed investments with depreciation and profits, reduced costs and commodity prices) in the same manner as a switch turns on the light. In this case the "black box" between the "input" and "output" (e.g. current and voltage) defies analysis.

This can only be justified as a short-term approach where a rapid change is required as, for example, in winter 1991–1992 when municipal food supplies were cancelled via previous government and party channels in the CIS. A long-term macro-economic approach is unlikely to be successful unless the three factors are available: market orientations and rational expectations among the majority of citizens, an developed market infrastructure ensuring fast and correct market signal transformation, and standard or at least comparable situations in regions, branches and social groups.

Light can be turned on by just pressing a button only because there is an available electric circuit of standard voltage; otherwise a micro-economic approach would have to be employed, involving investigation, identification and comparative analysis of individual domestic inputs. CIS countries, unlike Poland, Chile or even the Baltic republics, had no available information, storage and transportation systems, popular business ideologies, developed business legislation and a legal framework to enforce debtors to repay the debts, buyers to pay for the goods, or insolvents to declare themselves bankrupt. Huge differences in engineering and organisational levels by regions and branches and in the style of thinking by ethnic and social groups render the macro-economic approach with its levelling principles unfeasible in the long run.

The monetary policy has been efficient in the Baltic states. An interesting experience involved the use of currency to control money circulation with the national exchange rate directly related to the dollar, German mark or hard currency basket, and an unrestricted and fixed-rate currency exchange conversion between banks, and between banks and their clients. In this case, independent central banks advanced no credit to the government and commercial banks without reliable coverage, providing 100% currency supply for cash circulation and bank deposits without extensive issuing of Government securities. This prevented a "dollarisation" of money circulation (hard currency generally used in foreign trade) and limitation of running currency transactions and multiple exchange rates, reducing the inflation (under 1% per month in 1997 and 1998) and interest rates (to 15%–25% annually). Cancellation of subsidies resulted in the closure of loss-making and low-profitable production units. Real household incomes decreased sharply, in particular in rural areas, due to the loss of markets in the CIS countries. But the favourable net balance of payments was maintained through transit of goods from CIS republics, re-export of petroleum products and non-ferrous metals, and EU advantages.

The liberal-monetary strategy of reforms in CIS countries is associated with IMF credit. The IMF issues systemic transformations credit (programs of transition from the command to market economy) on the following four conditions: reduced budget deficit; inflation level (to simple monthly figures); money stock growth rates; and interest rates outstripping inflation. An IMF agreement opens the door for credits advanced by the World Bank, other international organisations and foreign investors.

A reserve credit is issued on more rigid terms, including liberalisation of exports and prices, further reduction of budget deficit, abolition of certain administrative restrictions, subsidies, non-market privileges, foreign investment guarantees and corporate bankruptcy proceedings. Among the first recipients were Moldova and Kyrgyzstan (meeting most IMF requirements), Russia, the Ukraine and Kazakhstan. "Stand-by" rehabilitation credits to Georgia and Armenia, where the financial crisis was particularly severe, contributed to their economic growth in the second half of the 1990s.

But on the whole, as experience in Moldova has shown, even the scrupulous observance of monetary guidelines is unlikely to result in economic growth with the firms remaining uncompetitive. The economic program for the next stage of reforms in Russia by the early twenty-first century has been focused on a socially oriented market economy. Yet the government regulation is reinforced regarding the flow of funds and the banking system, natural monopolies, and stock and currency markets, along with government allocations to restructure some basic banks and enterprises.

Inflation in CIS countries. Inflation rates in CIS countries are shown in Table 25. The sharpest price rise (hyperinflation) was evident in 1993 and 1994 in Georgia, the Ukraine, Armenia, Turkmenistan and Tajikistan. The issue of money increased the money stock by 20%–28% and prices by 31%–48% every month. By the end of the 1990s, in compliance with IMF requirements, the money stock was stabilised; thus, excessive printing of money causes inflation.

Characteristically, large budget deficits during the period (7%–12%) were evident in Russia, Moldova and Kyrgyzstan, but they were covered with foreign credit (notably in Georgia and Armenia) and increased internal debt rather than via the printing of money. In Turkmenistan, Belarus and Kazakhstan the fiscal deficit was lower (see Table 24) and inflation higher due to printing of money.

Increasing inflation expectancies accelerate velocity of money, in its turn whipping up prices. In Armenia the rate increased almost 20-fold between 1990 and 1995. In Uzbekistan, Russia, Turkmenistan and some other countries during the high inflation period money circulation accelerated by 15%–20% every month; the people tried to spend as much as possible between the price rises. The highest money circulation rates in the mid-1990s were evident in Transcaucasia (see Table 25).

According to A. Illarionov and some other economists, in none of the CIS countries did printing money cause sustained growth. The tight monetary policy (restricting the money stock growth to 4.9% per month) was among the GDP reduction factors in the Baltic republics and Kyrgyzstan in 1992–1994, and in Georgia and Armenia in 1995. But this was followed by sustained growth. This did not occur in the countries accepting the monthly 15%–20% growth of money stock.

Table 25

Changes in Consumer Prices (in % WRT of preceding year) and Velocity of Money

Country	Price index (times)								Average monthly inflation rate		Velocity of money			Cash outside banks (M0) in % of money stock (M2) in 1997
	1992	1993	1994	1995	1996	1990–1996, 1000s of times	1997 (in %)	1998 (in %)	1996	1997	1990	1993	1995	
Azerbaijan	10.1	12.3	17.6	5.1	1.2	3.0	104	99	0.6	0.04	1.5	3.8	15.5	72
Armenia	8.3	110.0	50.6	2.8	1.2	4.0	114	109	0.5	1.7	0.8	2.5	18.8	51
Belarus	10.7	12.9	23.2	8.1	1.5	79.0	164	173	2.8	4.2	2.0	5.1	9.6	...
Georgia	8.5	114.0	65.7	1.6	1.1	...	107	104	1.1	0.6	2.8	10.0	26.2	...
Kazakhstan	16.1	17.6	19.8	2.8	1.4	47.0	117	107	2.1	0.9	2.1	5.9	11.6	66
Kyrgyzstan	9.5	13.1	3.8	1.5	1.3	...	125	112	2.5	1.2	5.2	13.4	7.4	...
Moldova	12.1	12.8	5.9	1.3	1.2	3.2	112	108	1.2	0.9	3.5	9.5	7.5	...
Russia	26.1	9.4	3.2	2.3	1.2	3.0	115	184	1.7	0.9	1.4	6.6	8.1	36
Tajikistan	10.1	22.4	...	5.4	3.7	...	172	143	2.9	8.3	1.3	2.2	10.0	...
Turkmenistan	8.7	17.3	28.1	12.0	9.0	970.0	...	...	15–20	4.5	2.8	8.0	13.0	...
Uzbekistan	5.1	13.3	16.5	4.2	1.8	17.0	...	...	4.0	2.0	1.1	5.9	10.5	...
Ukraine	21.0	103.0	5.0	2.8	1.4	117.0	116	111	2.8	0.7	1.3	5.9	10.5	49

The proportion of money in GDP in CIS countries is low indeed. But this is explained largely by the shortage of competitive domestic goods. As the Say law formulated as far back as the nineteenth century, if you have not enough money to buy the required goods, it means that you have not produced enough goods and services to meet the market demand. He who cannot earn money has a lack of it. In addition, the shortage of national currency in CIS countries is related largely to the circulation of foreign currency.

In 1998 the percentage of cash circulated outside the banking (M_0 in percent to M_2) decreased in Armenia (from 53% to 40%), Kazakhstan (from 54% to 47%) and Kyrgyzstan (from 64% to 54%). By contrast, it increased significantly in Russia (from 27% to 42%). The withdrawal of many foreign investors and suspended loans from international financial organisations inevitably contributed to increased emission. This materially affected currency markets in all CIS countries, especially in Belarus and the Ukraine.

On the other hand, with stable conditions on the consumer market (balanced increase in household incomes, expenditures and bank deposits, as well as the share of hard currency purchase in total incomes) the Central Bank may increase the money aggregate M2 faster than the price rise. This will mitigate the money market. Yet, as a U.S. joke goes, drinks should be removed at the height of the party lest merry drinking turn into a brawl. This is especially true with part of the drinks under the table. In the Ukraine, for instance, the Finance Ministry maintains that one half of the money stock is circulated outside banks. The share is even greater in Azerbaijan, Armenia and Kyrgyzstan (see Table 25).

This means that a purely monetary policy is inefficient in the CIS environment. As IMF Executive Director M.Camdessus admitted, "second generation reforms" require government control in all spheres of economy. As is seen from Table 26, increasing of money stock in the mid-1990s was the fastest in Georgia, Turkmenistan and Belarus (seven to nine times). Monetisation ratio (money stock relative to GDP) decreased, notably in the Transcaucasian republics and Tajikistan. This enhanced inflation.

A comparison of money circulation indicators in CIS countries and the Baltic republics would be useful here. The lower printing money rates and the growing monetisation ratio (in the CIS only accomplished in Kyrgyzstan) determined the lower inflation rates (see Table 26).

Market economics have typically higher ratios than the CIS M_1/GDP ratios. In the mid-1990s they amounted to over 100% in Japan, 57%–62% in the USA, Italy and Germany, and 25% in Turkey, as opposed to the CIS maximum 10%–13% (Belarus, Uzbekistan, Russia, Kyrgyzstan and Moldova) and minimum 4%–8% (the Transcaucasian republics and Turkmenistan). Velocity of money amounted to 1.0–1.6 in the UK, China, Czech Republic and Germany, and 3.2–

4.0 in Poland, Turkey and Vietnam, as opposed to 15–26 in the Transcaucasian republics and 8–10 in Russia, Belarus and the Ukraine.

Table 26

Volume of Printed Money,
M₁/GDP Ratio and Inflation Rates
between 1993 and 1995 (average annual rates in %)*

Country	Money stock growth	M_1/GDP ratio	Inflation rate
Latvia	29.3	14.7	52.5
Estonia	38.1	1.0	53.5
Lithuania	66.8	1.5	130.7
Moldova	143.7	–21.4	267.7
Tajikistan	152.5	–34.1	212.6
Kyrgyzstan	196.6	18.1	313.4
Russia	197.0	–26.6	390.6
Azerbaijan	367.7	–35.2	935.5
Uzbekistan	401.8	–38.2	653.9
Ukraine	413.9	–25.3	887.2
Armenia	530.6	–47.9	1684.0
Belarus	723.9	–20.2	1242.0
Turkmenistan	793.8	–19.5	1905.0
Georgia	921.9	–50.3	2371.0

* Illarionov, A. (1996): Theory of "Monetary Deficit" as a Reflection of Payment Crisis. Voprosy Ekonomiki 12, 49 [In Russian] (Илларионов, А. (1996): Теория "Денежного Дефицита" как Отражение Платежного Кризиса. Вопросы Экономики 12, 49)

By the late 1990s monetarist strategies drove inflation under 1% in Azerbaijan and Georgia and other countries. On the other hand, Turkmenistan, Tajikistan and Belarus have not yet solved the problem (see Table 26).

Due to the financial slump, since September 1998 inflation has been building up in Russia, Belarus and the Ukraine. Average monthly price rise rates across the CIS amounted to 5%–7%. These rates demonstrate the general nature of the laws of money circulation and the principles underlying the monetary and credit policy. Yet with underdeveloped competition, poor roads and communications, high taxes and production costs, the demand and supply curves will not intersect in accordance with the classical market theory, and the equilibrium price will not be determined. The price rise will reduce the demand rather than increase the supply. Compensation of price reduction through expanded production in the CIS environment is unfeasible, unprofitable and not necessary in some branches.

Business responds to inflated costs with reduced and more primitive output (the only high return sectors being mining for crude exports, environmentally hazardous processing, implementation of foreign developments and production of non-transportable goods for the domestic market) and price rise (as long as available effective demand will permit).

In our opinion, therefore, differentiation should be made between general macro-economic money circulation laws for any market economy, and methods of governing the economy on the whole, based on specific business behaviour in a given country.

In the rest of the world, inflation is primarily "demand" driven due to the excess of demand over supply with increased real money stock (aggregate M2). In a developed market economy a self-control mechanism is operative basing on supply growth (increasingly profitable production). In addition, the government employs a macro-economic policy – *monetary* (e.g. limited issue of money, credit to commercial banks, exchange of cash for government bonds, deposit loans), *budgetary* (e.g. reduction of government investments, arms procurements, expenditures on science, and education, deferred payment on external and internal debt) and *currency* (stabilisation through foreign credit) policies.

These proved effective (reducing inflation rates) in many CIS countries. But at a certain inflation level (G.A. Iavlinski refers to it as the structural and institutional background), non-payments grew, wages and pensions were delayed, domestic-oriented production deteriorated and competitive scientific and production teams collapsed. As a result, the monetary policy was mitigated when confronted with the risk of social upheavals and inflation often regained previous levels.

In fact, inflation in CIS countries is generally cost- rather than demand driven, i.e. due not to monetary but rather to structural and institutional causes – the resource-intensive, monopolistic and import-dependent production (e.g. energy resources in Belarus, the Ukraine, Moldova and Armenia, food in Russia) and poor infrastructure. The main spring of inflation is represented by energy and transport prices approaching the world level, aggravated by branch monopolies. Therefore, the monetary and credit policy is only effective as a component of rather than an alternative to a macro-economic policy. This is the principle governing the medium-term program for 1999 and 2000 in Russia.

Pricing is an important target of government regulation. Its instrument in the USA and EU countries is the standard procedure of cost accounting and depreciation accumulation, minimum wage rates, tax and social deductions, customs tariffs and, most importantly, co-ordinated prices for energy resources, railway tariffs, etc. Thus, almost a half of the consumer price structure is subject to regulation.

Crisis of payments and way out. Real market economy involves currency (generally national) used as a universal equivalent and issued by the Government via the Central Bank, with the amount of circulated paper money depending on the commodity stock and money velocity.

Most CIS countries, however, are only quasi-market economies, i.e. only nominally market based. Money circulation involves the four money classes. Real moneys, i.e. national currency going through the banking system (money aggregate M2) accounts for only 15%–20%. "Black cash", i.e. hand-to-hand circulation outside the banking and tax systems and, in fact, any book form, represents 10%–15%. The third class, U.S. dollars and other hard currency, comprises almost 40% in some CIS countries, also largely functioning as "black cash". As the bulk of hard currency savings are "stocking deposits", CIS countries are acting as creditors for the USA and other rich countries by trading important crude inputs, rather than for new technologies, for paper-supported portraits of eminent foreign figures which, unlike foreign credit to the CIS, offer no interest.

The fourth, especially hazardous class is quasi-money (partial substitutes) generally issued not by the government but individual departments, banks, local administration agencies and enterprises. Among them are: a) *non-payments*, e.g. unpaid invoices, pay-rolls, authorisations for tax or social payments (in 1997 amounting to 40% of GDP in Russia); *barter* (exchange of goods for other goods and services); c) *commodity bills* (debtor's receipts secured with enterprise outputs); d) *financial bills* (fixed-term payment obligations for a fixed sum) issued by a commercial bank or any other non-public commercial structure on bank security.

By estimates of the Russian Chamber of Commerce and Industry, every third enterprise is involved in barter exchange and quasi-money is employed in almost 80% of non-export sales in metallurgy.

All these partial substitutes represent private money issued by regional or commercial structures rather than the government. Their value as instruments of payment is far lower than that of standard money and related to the economic and political importance of the issuing body. Thus discount rate (allowance for payment in cash) on bills varies between 10%–20% and 50%–60%, depending on the guarantor. All these partial substitutes enable the banks to earn high gains (up to 10%–20% for issued financial bills), firms to evade taxation (barter and bill transactions are not reported at real price) and executive authorities to enter term payments (e.g. utilities). But in the long run they all lose because of the lack of sustained money circulation and financial markets.

An important channel for increasing money supply is offered by Central Bank purchasing (via commercial banks) of foreign currency and government bonds. In this way the accumulated financial resources is partially appropriated by the government, which reduces the banks' opportunities for and interest in crediting the real sector of economy. In addition, the amount of overdue loans in CIS countries has been growing and production efficiency declining. Therefore, even with the decreasing yields, investing in government bonds and foreign currency are more profitable and less risky than financing of industrial enterprises. In this context foreign increasing of money supply will not do the job: instead of reaching the producer, the money will be converted to hard currency or "circulated" by banks via bond purchase or short-term consumer loans. Improvement of money system in CIS countries will require, firstly, reducing the budget deficit and securities issued to cover the deficit; secondly, a realistic debt recovery mechanism, including selling assets of insolvent enterprises; thirdly, a reliable (with compulsory insurance) mechanism of attracting household savings to specific investment projects; fourthly, mortgaging, leasing and other long-term loans on tangible property; and fifthly, adopting and enforcing the laws to prevent the quasi-money (especially financial bills) and non-payments.

Non-payments and other impediments to circulation of money in CIS countries are largely related to the lack of budget-, antimonopoly and tax policies. The budget is often entitled to deduce enterprise debts due to non-acceptance (without payer's consent) and impose penalty for delayed payment, while payment on government purchases for goods, works and services are delayed with no interest paid.

Natural monopolies in many CIS countries, with the government's consent, raised output prices (gas, electricity, water, transport and communications) far in excess of those, for example, in the agrarian sector, thus increasing overall inflation rates and undermining the competitive positions of domestic manufacturers on external markets. But in doing so the government delays payments for energy and carriers' services to the Army and other budget-supported organisations.

And finally, very often taxes are taken from revenues reflected in financial statements but not actually gained yet, e.g. VAT on invoices, at price to be paid by the government itself many months after. In some countries taxable profits include adjusting of past inventories to inflation, or changes in stock due to shares price rise and other gains not associated with real money receipts. As a result, the firms enlist intermediary services to conceal the deals or at least evade taxation.

Thus, the non-payment crisis in the CIS is not an isolated event caused by low fiscal and contracting discipline, but rather a way of life for a non-competitive economy in spontaneous transition to the market with an obviously weak State. It was the State that paved the way for a background monetary system when effecting payment in vouchers, fiscal notes, credit security and authorisations, commodity bills and checks, to be followed by bills, bonds, deposit, commercial and trust certificates. These conditional, negotiable moneys force out the normal ones because they are not taxable. At first they offer an instrument of payment with no competitive marketable products available. But quasi-money is a habit extremely difficult to get rid of because it has to be accepted instead of taxes.

Non-payments have emerged as a specific type of credit in many CIS countries, as a way to price cuts.

Non-payments and quasi-money (in the amount comparable to total GDP in some CIS countries) involve several kinds of money, unrealistic pricing, unreliable financial settlements and contracts, flow of capital to crooked quasi-market exchange and barter links. These benefit the government officials, speculators and organised crime groups.

To surmount the critical non-payments will require a realistic budget (budget debt resulting in three to four times greater inter-enterprise arrears), a reasonable monetary and currency policy, legal relationships between the government and financial institutions and, more importantly, enterprise restructuring, elimination of uncompetitive structures – the "black holes" of economy.

Acceleration and improvement of settlements are largely associated with *plastic cards* employed within an international framework involving, firstly, providing cards banks (issuing bodies); secondly, accounting banks (acquirers); thirdly, holders of individual and corporate cards; fourthly, trade and service enterprises with accounting centres; and fifthly, technical operators (processing companies) providing an accounting interface for the whole range of agents in this payment system. Russia, the Ukraine, Kazakhstan, Moldova and Azerbaijan were among the first CIS member countries to employ the system. Every system can provide the channelling and authorisation of hundreds of thousands or even millions transactions (payments), calculating and transmitting to a computer centre data on inter-enterprise financial arrears. Thus, corporate book settlements can be accomplished in a few seconds on a single document (slip), and even with the customer outside the country, payments for goods and services on his account are guaranteed.

Currency policy. As a component of the credit and monetary policy, the currency policy is of particular importance for CIS economies to be integrated in the world market. This involves the setting and supporting of the *exchange rate* (price of national currency expressed in others) and rules of operation on the currency market. The currency policy is aimed at internal and external macro-economic equilibrium (balances of trade and payments), enhancing the confidence in national currency, preventing illegal outflow of capital and increasing foreign currency accumulation. National gold and hard currency reserves must provide financing for imports of goods and services (at least for 2–3 months), performance of international liabilities and reserves in cases of financial emergency.

The first challenge confronted by CIS countries involved a market framework to regulate the exchange rate accounting for changes in basic macro-economic indicators (GDP, inflation, budget deficit, balance of payments). Due consideration should be taken of independent external factors influencing the exchange rate. Thus, almost a half of the government debt securities in the

Ukraine in 1997 (30% in Russia) were held by non-residents. The upheavals on the world markets causing cash shortage resulted in mass-scale sales of securities and conversion of yields to dollars. The grivna rate fell and the national bank had to quickly raise the discount rate and mandatory reserves rate and tighten the accounting and settlement procedures for grivna accounts in foreign banks. Strict control was imposed on contracted imports following inter-bank hard currency purchases, allowing to control the flow of capital. Maintaining the grivna exchange rate within a specified currency corridor was facilitated by the Central Bank interventions (hard currency purchase or buy-off with no demand/supply equilibrium).

Attempts at administrative exchange rate setting and constraints on currency exchange fared poorly. Thus, in Uzbekistan, with sufficient hard currency reserves in 1996, the exchange rate of national currency – sum/dollar – was overstated. As a result, imports of Western goods at a low rate were intensified, to be resold in Kazakhstan with the proceeds converted to dollars. Exchange restrictions in Belarus developed a wide gap between the official and market rates, increased the share of "black" market turnover, decreased returning back of currency from abroad and intensive speculation with national currency outside the country. Similar problems were posed in Turkmenistan. For this reason CIS currency policies by the late 1990s have been increasingly oriented to national currency rates controlled by central banks and planned devaluation relative to hard currency, depending on current inflation rates (monthly 1% in the CIS as opposed to 3% annually in the USA). These will eliminate several exchange rates (e.g. for commercial and non-commercial transactions and travel), mandatory sales of all foreign currency revenues, restricted purchase for imports or payment on current transactions, as well as foreign transfer of legal revenues and dividends. Moldova and subsequently some other CIS countries, in compliance with Sect. 2, Clause VIII of IMF Regulations, have introduced qualified national convertibility, i.e. abolishing some restrictions on current payments and transfers (excluding the flow of capital).

Azerbaijan established an inter-bank currency market in the form of a unified computer space also involving non-residents (banks with prevailing foreign capital), with shared transaction risks. The manat per dollar rate started to rise.

Hedging of currency and other financial risks is gaining acceptance in the CIS, involving time contracts for future purchase at a previously agreed price (futures).

CIS prices for goods and services calculated in hard currency are gradually approaching the world market levels. The fairly painful transition for uncompetitive enterprises and the general public process will create the prerequisites for a real credit and monetary policy. But this will also pose new problems.

Relations between the State and financial groups. In market economies the macro-economic policy is formulated and implemented by the parliament (approving the budget and tax laws), central bank (reporting to the parliament), government and financial-industrial groups. Such groups also emerged in the CIS in the 1990s, but they are very different from those outside the CIS.

Financial oligarchies in developed countries emerged in the course of long-term market operations, to be merged with the government at a much later time. In the CIS the groups were created under the low-price privatisation of state property and by the end of the 1990s largely relied on budget moneys, government bonds and loans to the government. In many cases such oligarchies were established by former party and government officials and their teams.

In the rest of the world financial groups were first established in national economies, gradually gaining access to the world market. In the CIS their wealth had been initially derived from export/import transactions and services to foreign TNCs. Foreign corporations first emerged in metallurgy, chemistry and machine building, gradually monopolising the markets (while vigorously opposed by the government throughout the twentieth century) and extending their financial operations. In the CIS they started with monopolising extractive industries, trade and finance. As a result, the unified money circulation was broken and monopolistic gains went outside the country. The accumulated resources, instead of reinforcing bank credit, are converted to hard currency. The global economic advantages, rather than promoting the international division of labour and accelerating the exchange of new technologies, are employed in speculations on international finance markets, exploitation of international capital flows and off-shore (tax-exempt) zones.

The CIS have no operative trade and finance code regulating the relationships between the State and major banks, some specifically established as "pocket banks", i.e. owned by a group for uncontrolled cheap and not necessarily justified loans advanced to themselves to the detriment of other holders and involving budget financial resources.

A similar case in 1997 and 1998 resulted in a grave crisis in Southeast Asia. In South Korea large vertically integrated corporations led by their "own" banks ("chebolei") controlled the government, fed up key politicians, obtained privileged credit and prevented competitors' access to the market, including small and medium-scale business. When *Kia* corporation trebled the outputs on such credit, irrespective of actual demand for motor cars, and thus appeared on the verge of failure, the government came to the rescue, buying up the controlling interest. On the other hand, South Korea continued to lag behind Japan, Germany and the USA in science and technology. The crisis was triggered by the decline in South Korean competitive advantages associated with low wages.

The laws of money, and notably currency, circulation are universal for all countries. Many challenges in current economy in the CIS had been faced in other, currently highly developed, countries. In the nineteenth century U.S. banks were often established by mercenary state legislators, with no qualified personnel or starting capital. The banks issued precarious debt instruments, promising gold and silver, and then vanished or presumably opened exchange stations in inaccessible, impenetrable places. Only in 1863 did the Congress passed the National Banking Act, with several hundreds complementary laws over the next century. The federal government safeguards commercial bank deposits (amounting to $100,000) and exerts rigid control over their financial stability and compliance with basic rules of current (check) and savings accounting.

Taking the lesson, CIS countries could create a reliable framework to prevent the financial "pyramids" carrying no real financial operations but paying the interest for a certain period, to attract more credulous investors. Throughout the 1990s such unreliable or even fraudulent companies have robbed millions people in Russia, Czech Republic and the Baltic states, even causing a severe political crisis in Albania. Regretfully, the Russian government let a similar GKO pyramid scheme be created between 1994 and 1997, with the resulting price rise, collapse of many banks and enterprises and real wage drop.

By the end of the 1990s, upon elimination of centralised crediting of enterprises (with the exception of the AIC and coal industry) and covering of the budget deficit by borrowing from the Central Bank, inflation dropped in almost all CIS countries (see Table 25), along with stabilising of the national-currency and decreasing of discount rate. The biggest achievements in this area were attained in Kyrgyzstan, Moldova, Russia, Kazakhstan, Georgia and Armenia. These were evident in decreasing growth rates by such indicators as M0 (currency), M1 (M0 plus demand and other checkable deposits) and M2 (M1 plus household and corporate time deposits). But all these indicators undermine the former sources of bank profits. In the monetarist theory, reinforcement of national currency by reducing on money supply will culminate in growing investment, brisk production, increasing of employment and real incomes of the population. This was not the case in CIS countries. The growth of foreign investment in extractive industries and stabilisation of relevant export outputs leave unaltered the general picture rapidly deteriorating by the end of 1997. This created a new surge of reproaches addressed at the IMF as the principal monetary policy agent and requests of additional money issues to relieve the critical non-payments endangering economic and social stability in some CIS countries.

Yet the criticisms have not always been justified. Rather than formulating macro-economic policies for indebted countries, the IMF, like any creditor, focuses on secure repayment of loans. With all its importance, the monetary policy is only a component of the reform program and reduced inflation is a prerequisite rather than principal content of structural reform. Neither further reductions of interest rate overlapped with an even greater reduction in production efficiency, nor additional money issues are likely to ensure the progress of reform.

Most CIS countries demonstrate the tendencies identified by the Russian Bank and RF Goskomstat (State Committee on Statistics). M_1/GDP ratio (money aggregate M2 relative to annual GDP) dropped sharply (from 80% in 1991 through 18% in 1993 and to 13% in 1997). But rubles only represent 40% of payments. Another 30% are effected in hard currency ($45 billion, including over two thirds in cash) and the remaining 30% in bills (10% issued by banks and 20% by other commercial and government agencies).

Then the household money savings generally supplemented with bank deposits and that of enterprises decreased. This resulted in an increasing disparity of real money circulation (in the financial and export sectors and settlements with the public) and quasi-money (in non-export sectors), and the producers giving a significant share of earnings to financial and trade intermediaries in conversion of quasi-money to real money (e.g. or payments of wages, import, taxes).

Additionally, many CIS countries have to overstate the hard currency exchange rates relative to actual price parity of domestic currency. A dollar in the USA can purchase much less than for domestic currency at the exchange rate at home country. This artificial devaluation in the CIS benefits the exporters maintaining their otherwise problematic competitive positions on the world market owing to resource-intensive production and obsolete technologies. Manpower (at least in Russia, Belarus, the Ukraine and Kazakhstan), considering the labour productivity level and output quality, is not less expensive than in Southeast Asia, South America or Turkey. Therefore, regularisation of monetary policy is unlikely to be successful unless production efficiency is improved radically, which will require the resolution of investment crisis and separation of the public interest from that of individual financial oligarchies. Economic conditions in Russia, in particular when associated with fall in export prices, decreasing tax collection and increasing amount of interest paid for the government debt, called for a gradual devaluation of the ruble to improve the balance of payments. But this was contrary to the interests of some financial groups with mature credit and forward contracts for currency sale. The government attempted to support them, imposing a moratorium on debts and spending the currency reserves to maintain the ruble exchange rate. These resulted in a three-fold spontaneous and avalanche fall of the ruble.

In the mid-1990s yields from GKO, currency and short-term bank credit transactions were 2.5–4 times that of production investments. Unless the ratio is altered, the stock market will not promote production and the savings will not turn to investments. The government must consider but not follow the interests of financial groups; otherwise, no economic development would be feasible.

7.3 Investment Policy

Investments in transition economy. *Investments* are the physical and intellectual values (moneys, securities, movable and immovable property, rights on land use and natural resources use and other property rights, and intellectual property protected with patents and copyright) deposited for economic objects over long periods of time in order to gain profits and/or social environmental effects. *Real investments* represent the savings used to form capital assets and new production capacities. They involve the costs of purchased machinery, equipment and new technologies, building and installation works, and increases in production stock. In the past few years increasing proportions of investments in developed countries have been used in personnel training. These exclude investments in securities distributed on the stock market; the latter only involves transfer of property rights on existing assets. Investments represent the costs advanced, i.e. in a short run only involving increased demand for investment (including construction) goods and services, as well as consumer goods for the builders. In this sense they are to be distinguished from savings reducing current demand. Therefore, in a short run the investment policy is designed to compensate inadequate consumer demand with increased investment demand, while preventing excessive withdrawal of resources from current production to "grand projects" (whether in a communist or any other social system) requiring large expenditures without producing new wealth in the short run.

In the long run, investments will increase both demand for and supply of real goods and services. When planning capital investment, business operators estimate the *marginal efficiency*, i.e. the costs of added capital relative to expected gains, accounting for investment risk. They are concerned with payback period (giving priority to shorter PP projects), expected cash-flow gains minus costs by month and year, potentials for risk minimisation and insurance costs. Increased amount of investment will reduce the marginal efficiency, as "the cream" must alternate with less efficient projects. But with efficiency approaching to the interest rate, investments in securities and hard currency are more profitable and less risky than those in real assets.

A macro-economic investment policy should create a favourable environment for capital investment by influencing the efficiency, risk and interest rate.

In international practices, investments are calculated as the difference between the output value and the amount of current consumption (CIS statistics refer to this indicator as gross savings). Investments in a broad sense reflect total savings, including capital investment in production, social sphere, human resources, individual housing construction, securities, bank accounts and even "stocking" savings.

Higher potential investments (savings, in percent of GDP) are accompanied with higher average annual GDP growth rates. In the mid-1990s the biggest domestic investments were evident in China (42% of GDP), Thailand (40%) and other "economic dragons" in Southeast Asia (36%), and in Japan (30%). These countries also attained the highest economic growth rates (7%–8%).

By World Bank estimates savings in developed industrial economies average 20%–23% of GDP (22% in Germany, and 16% in the USA). Therefore, average GDP growth rates there in the 1990s were lower –1.5%–1.8% annually.

In developing countries savings average 17%. With fast (as compared with Europe and Japan) population growth rates, annual GDP growth amounts to 3%–4% and only 1.5%–1.8% per capita.

In this context CIS countries keep aloof. The amount of domestic investments in Russia and other CIS countries in the 1990s was estimated by the World Bank at 27%–30% of GDP (21% in 1996). But GDP in the CIS has only been growing since 1997, and then very slowly – less than 1% annually. Thus, the question is not of the low investment potential but rather of irrational use of savings to purchase foreign currency and securities rather than invest in production, science and technology.

An investment process in CIS countries is unlikely to be adequate unless the following requirements are met: firstly, political stability, low risk of investment loss due to expropriation or civil conflict. By the end of the 1990s this requirement has been satisfied in almost all CIS countries; secondly, the low – under 1% a month – inflation level, otherwise the long-term investment profits are deflated. This has also been accomplished in most of the countries; thirdly, the interest rate should not exceed inflation rate by more than 8%–10% annually (the interest rate in stable-currency economies). Additionally, the national currency rate should be fairly stable, matching the real purchasing power relative to other currencies. Progress in this area is likewise evident. Thus, in 1993 the rubles-per-dollar equivalent could purchase four times and in 1997 only 1.3 times the goods bought for a U.S. dollar in the United States (estimated in over a thousand goods and services classes). The growth of the relative power of national currency benefits not the exporters (with their goods appreciated on the world market) but the investors.

Yet the two remaining requirements have not been satisfied in many CIS countries by the end of the 1990s. One concerns the risk level and protection for tangible and intellectual property. The high risk is due to the incomplete, unstable and very inadequate legal enforcement framework, persistent non-performance under contracts, lack of adequate insurance and fair competition.

Another problem concerns the inadequate risk/profit level in the real sector as compared with financial sector. This is related to excessive taxes (e.g. including mandatory charities, crime control, bribes) and the low investment management level – inability to select efficient projects and technologies and control the expenditure.

Resolution of the risk/profit problem will translate to production investment the household savings, exported currency and depreciation accumulated.

Investment crisis. Analysis of changes in the scale and structure of investment activities in CIS countries in the 1990s suggests the following conclusions:

1. The total amount and GDP share of investment reduced significantly, with capital investments (invested to fixed capital) across the CIS in 1997 amounting to a third of those in 1990 and the share of gross saved fixed capital in GDP decreasing from 28% to 21% over the period. In 1997 capital investments continued to decline in Russia, the Ukraine, Moldova, and across the CIS in general. Particularly low are the savings contributed to GDP in Georgia, Moldova and Kazakhstan (see Table 27). Capital investments in Armenia, Georgia, Kazakhstan, Moldova and Russia decreased 9–20 times between 1990 and 1996. Investment activities are fairly intensive only in Uzbekistan and Azerbaijan, with the share of capital investments in GDP approaching the level of developing Asian countries. In 1997 and 1998 capital investments increased significantly in five CIS republics: Azerbaijan, Georgia, Belarus, Uzbekistan and Kazakhstan.

2. Capital investments in many CIS countries in the 1990s decreased to a greater extent than did GDP. These involved housing (more completed projects in 1996 and 1997 in Belarus, Kyrgyzstan, Uzbekistan and Tajikistan), construction projects in education and public health sectors. (Progress has been made in the past few years in Uzbekistan, Kyrgyzstan and Belarus.) But even more significant reductions occurred in industrial construction. Its share in total capital investments across the CIS decreased from 67 to 63%, being the lowest in Georgia (see Table 27), while recently growing in some countries (Azerbaijan, Kazakhstan, Kyrgyzstan). High percentages of machinery, tools and equipment in capital investments are typical for Moldova, Belarus, Kyrgyzstan and the Ukraine (see Table 27).

The low level of investment activity in CIS countries is indicative of the lag in capital investments in GDP. In the mid-1990s it amounted to 17%, including 4%–9% in the Transcaucasian republics and Tajikistan. Only Uzbekistan (30%) and Kyrgyzstan (21%) approached the level of developing Asian countries.

Extremely unfavourable for investment activities are reduced outputs of construction materials, e.g. cement, brick and slate, with a parallel rise in prices. In most CIS countries the outputs decreased faster than industrial totals.

The share of industrial construction in total capital investments also decreased – from 67% in 1991 to 57%–59% in 1994–1996. This is particularly true about Armenia and Moldova.

3. Structure of capital investments by industries increasingly oriented on exports of raw materials and imports of consumer goods. Thus, in Azerbaijan between 1991 and 1995 the share of investment increased from 73% to 89% in the fuel and energy (among all oil and gas) complex, while decreasing from 6% to 1% in machine building and from 15% to 3% in the agrarian sector. Machinery share in capital investments decreased 15 times (from 15% to 1%) in Kyrgyzstan, 6 times

Table 27

Indicators of Investment Process by CIS Countries (in %)

Country	Share of gross saving in GDP		Share of machinery in capital investment	Share of government capital investment	Share of foreign investment	Sources of capital investment			Share of industrial capital investment	Share of long-term credit	Capital investment	
	1990	1996				Budget	Enterprise assets	Foreign investments and joint ventures			in % of 1990	1997 in % of 1996
Azerbaijan	20	28	23	38	63	2	23	71	83	8.0	93	167
Armenia	43	19*	15	43	23	30	13	21	64	0.3	5	90
Belarus	22	25*	38	70	1	20	47	4	57	20.0	34	120
Georgia	23	9	19	50	80	17	13	57	33	...	5	187
Kazakhstan	39	18*	32	41	40	7	67	26	73	16.0	11	119
Kyrgyzstan	22	20*	36	25	80	6	19	63	88	22.0	49	65
Moldova	23	16*	39	36	6	12	69	11	71	17.0	14	94
Russia	29	21	23	24	5	19	62	4	62	3.0	25	95
Tajikistan	...	20*	23	80	...	...	...	...	65	5.0	5	90**
Turkmenistan	...	33*	...	...	16	...	...	...	...	...	...	104**
Uzbekistan	31	33*	29	70	14	27	46	20	62	15*	59	117
Ukraine	23	23*	34	53	1	13	83	1	67	11.0	20	93

* 1995.
** Estimated.

(from 18% to 3%) in Moldova and more than halved (9% vs. 20%) in Russia. Import dominance has also made unprofitable investments in light industries considered as principal in many CIS countries. Their share in total investments decreased from 3%–4% to 1% in the Ukraine and Russia, from 9% to 1% in Kyrgyzstan, from 13% to 8% in Uzbekistan and from 20% to 9% in Moldova.

Only one third of the power stations were put into operation as compared with 1991 and one seventh of the ferroconcrete structures and assembly facilities.

4. Radical changes in investment sources illustrated by the role of corporate own and borrowed (through share issue and distribution) capital relative to centralised financing. On average across the CIS own capital represents two thirds of total investments. Yet the firms are still unable to make to long-term loans.

On the whole across the CIS in 1996 and 1997 the Government budget share in total investments in fixed capital decreased from 20% to 19% and that of enterprise own capital from 64% to 61%.

Only in four CIS countries (Uzbekistan, Tajikistan, Belarus and the Ukraine) does the bulk of capital investments represent the government sector. In Russia and Kyrgyzstan it only accounts for 25%.

The budget share among the sources of investments have decreased accordingly, notably in Azerbaijan, Kazakhstan, Kyrgyzstan and Moldova. Own and borrowed capital of enterprises and organisations constitute the principal source of capital investment in the Ukraine, Russia, Moldova and Kazakhstan (see Table 27).

5. To date, bank loans do not act as significant sources of capital investments. Only in Belarus and Kyrgyzstan does long-term credit exceed 20% (see Table 27). In Armenia, Russia and Tajikistan it only amounts to 1%–5%.

6. The role of foreign investment differs considerably in different CIS countries, generally going to oil/gas and ore field development. By 1998 the share of direct foreign investment in fixed capital (excluding stock purchase) was over 70% in Azerbaijan, 68% in Kyrgyzstan, 57% in Georgia, 26% in Kazakhstan and Armenia, and only 1% in the Ukraine.

Thus, the differences between CIS countries in the scale and composition of investments are very significant. But the common critical conditions include reduced money savings and enterprise equipment updating rate, rising prices on investment goods, deteriorating domestic construction complex and failing national investment programs. In the 1990s, increasing share of investments in transport and communications associated with foreign trade (from 8% to 38% in Armenia, 9% to 20% in Belarus, 6% to 26% in Georgia, 5%–7% to 13%–18% in Kazakhstan, Moldova, the Ukraine and Uzbekistan, and from 9% to 16% in Russia) were accompanied by reductions in the agrarian sector (from 15%–34% to 1%–10%), education, science and health care.

Investment crisis has intensified in all CIS countries, even where a boom of foreign investment in, for example, oil and gold mining had started in the early 1990s. Thus, total investments (in adjusted prices) in Russia decreased by 13% in 1995, 19% in 1996 (70% between 1991 and 1996) and 5% in 1997. Particularly low is the investment activity in manufacturing industries (in 1996 total under 9% of the 1991 level in machine building, 6% in construction industry, 3% in light- and 16% in chemical industry, with over 50% in gas production and over 100% in oil refining).[2]

Inadmissibly high are the time of using equipment (24 years in 1991 and 28 years in 1996), depreciation (up to 70% in 1997) and average age (almost 15 years in 1997).

Investment crisis has the four principal implications: reduced competitive positions on the world commodity market (by quality and cost level); increased accidents and, consequently, repair and maintenance costs of worn stock; reduced economic growth potentials, in particular in advanced research-intensive branches; and decreased demand for construction and installation works, machinery and R&D outputs.

Among the factors governing the investment crisis are:

1) Decreasing utilisation of industrial productive capacities (by almost 65% in 1993 and 40% in 1996, including under 30% in machine building and light industries), due to decreased effective demand

2) Decreasing return on fixed assets (from 6 to 2% between 1993 and 1996)

3) Decreasing return on sales (from 26% to 10% between 1995 and 1998, with an increasing share of loss-making enterprises – from 27% to 47% in industry and from 24% to 37% in construction)

4) Increasing tax burden on enterprise profits, along with non-payments (including transfers out of budget), necessitating increasing of working capital rather than long-term investment

5) Increasing government borrowing on the financial market (from 42% to 105% as per ruble investment in the real sector in 1995 and 1996)

Experience in reforms has shown that investment process is unlikely to be successful in a transitional economy without government support. According to Russian Economic Ministry, creating of competitive economy will require $140 billion Neither the budget nor foreign investments will provide that amount. Private domestic long-term investments are needed, in turn requiring government guarantees and shared contribution (at least 20%) as well as reduced discount rate and controlled inflation, among others involving non-monetary strategies.

---

[2] Statistical data by Goskomstat (Government Statistical Board) and calculations by A. Vodyanov. (1997): Эксперт [Expert] 1, 16 [In Russian]

During the 1990s the share of private consumption in GDP has grown significantly in CIS countries (from 41% to 50% in Russia), along with that of exports, due to reduced investments. Moreover, the government has cancelled industrial investment, including even target R&D programs, only retaining social projects. Long-term commercial bank loans in the countries, with their limited opportunities of purchasing equity, decreased to 3%–4%. Enterprises will reduce the proportion of revenues channelled to production developments (from 31% to 20% in Russia between 1993 and 1998), even using accumulated to current consumption. All these endanger both structural reform and updating, and even accident-free industrial production in general.

Reduced investment activities in the CIS have been related to declining outputs and price increases for inputs to construction industries, and reduced budget financing to capital construction. Capital investments from all financial sources have decreased more than five times over the 1990s in the four CIS leaders by total output (Russia, the Ukraine, Kazakhstan and Belarus), regaining the 1960s level.

Privatisation of State property has led to capital investment by private and collective enterprises and organisations. Between 1994 and 1998 their contribution to total investment in CIS countries grew from 50 to 75%. This illustrates the rates of development in the emerging mixed economy. But it is the government policy that will determine the periods of the resolution of investment crisis in any transition economy.

Government investment policy. The Government investment policy in a transitional economy must pursue three major objectives: 1) increased savings by developing domestic production, reducing the costs, extending the national market, and liquidating or restructuring loss-making enterprises; 2) transformation of available savings to investments through taxation reform, an effective and controlled market of capital, and reduction of and insurance against investment risks and improved foreign investment environment; 3) an investment-use framework, including investment funds, leasing firms, as well as design and construction corporations with a network of diversified supplies and sub-contractors.

The investment policy cannot be limited to the decreasing of discount rate (cost of loans). In CIS countries this reduction is generally accompanied by reduced-deposit interest rate. This impairs the propensity of savers, to credit the economy, the more so as the more profitable investment spheres in export-oriented branches have already been monopolised, with the remaining ones both unprofitable and risky. The reduced Central Bank discount rate in CIS countries resulted in a corresponding reduction of interest rate on bank deposits and their declining share in total household savings. The savers refused to save and to credit the economy on such terms. The logic of regulating investments through interest rate, as conceptualised by Keynes and employed in the West, is inoperative in the CIS environment.

The primary objective of the investment policy is the increased corporate and households savings. Table 23 represents investment potentials in CIS countries. The GDP is divided into three major parts: 1)*wages* (remuneration for workers in moneys or in kind, and employers' allocations to social funds); 2) *net taxes* on production and imports (compulsory outright payments levied by the government on enterprises in relation to the production and imports of goods and services, as well as the use of production factors excluding enterprise subsidies – current outright payments to domestic producers, sellers and importers of goods and services); 3) *gross profit* (a part of value added remaining at enterprises' disposal after paying wages and net taxes) and *mixed incomes* of households associated with non-paid labour spending (e.g. housing construction and repair, individual gardens).

As is shown in Table 23, the wage share in GDP is the highest (43%–46%) in Russia, Moldova, the Ukraine, Belarus and Uzbekistan. These countries have the greatest opportunities for translating household savings into investments. The tax share is the highest (19%–25%) in Tajikistan, Uzbekistan and the Ukraine. These republics have great opportunities for government investments. Superior gross enterprise profits (over 50% of GDP) can be used as the primary source of capital investment in Turkmenistan, Kyrgyzstan, Kazakhstan and the Transcaucasian countries.

However, investment potentials only describe potential capital investments from various sources. Real investment is governed by the use of GDP. *Final consumption* represents the value of goods and services consumed by the population (individually or collectively). This involves *household consumption* (purchasing of consumer goods and services, as well as free consumption of those provided by the government and non-profit organisations) and *government consumption* (expenses for budget supported organisations of administration, defence, science, public health, social security, education, culture and arts, services to individuals and the public). As is shown in Table 23, the lowest share of government consumption in the mid-1990s (5%–12%) was typical for the Transcaucasian republics.

CIS countries differ essentially by *gross savings* (share of disposable income not spent in final consumption of goods and services) and *net savings* (goods and services purchased but not consumed in a given year). This involves *gross fixed capital savings* (i.e. purchase of fixed capital less depreciation and exit, along with outlays on improved returns of lands and forests, prospecting and protection of mineral and other natural resources, patenting, license trade), *changes in current assets stock* (inventories of raw materials and supplies, goods in production, produced goods and goods for resale) and *net purchase of valuables* (e.g. precious metals and stones, and works of art).

The greatest share of investment in fixed capital for future GDP generation was evident in Uzbekistan (33%), Azerbaijan (28%) and Belarus (25%). It is in these republics where the highest economic growth rates can be expected by the late 1990s. Contributions of real investments to GDP are far lower in Georgia and Moldova (see Table 23). But Azerbaijan, Armenia and Kyrgyzstan typically demonstrate great excess of imports over exports (13%–19%). This means that the investments are generally generated with increased external debt rather than internal resources.

In 1997 and 1998 GDP, i.e. total gross commodity consumption (household spending on goods and services), corporate capital investments, government purchases and net balance of foreign trade (export/import), increased in many CIS countries. The growth rates are expected to reach 2%–4% within the next few years. But this increase in GDP has been largely attained with increased household-, and to a lesser extent government, consumption with decreasing net investments and net balance of foreign trade (e.g. imports, largely involving food, furniture, domestic equipment, growing faster than exports).

The government investment policy is designed to encourage corporate and household savings and their use as investment. By various estimates, to make CIS economy consistent with the requirements of information society and scientific and technological revolution, ensuring the competitive positions of the principal branches on the world market, will require between $3 and $4 trillion in the next 15 years, with at least 60% provided within the CIS. For this purpose fixed capital savings will have to be raised to 30%–35% of GDP.

The Anglo-American economic school prevailing in the West proposes sophisticated mathematical equations describing, for example, saving through credit and deposit interest rates, contribution of government purchases and various investment multipliers. Yet no less important for the investment policy in CIS countries is another conception developed by Austrian (J. Schumpeter, F. Hayeck), German (L. Erhard), Chinese (Den Siao-ping) and Japanese economists and politicians and emphasising the human and institutional rather than purely monetary factors.

Thus, J. Schumpeter saw the basis of successful enterprise functioning in the development and implementation of innovatory technologies and management strategies in production, control and marketing. Therefore, the primary task of politics is the account and co-ordination of various social group interests, changing the stereotypes of human thinking and economic behaviour. The post-war German Economic Minister, L. Erhard, attached special importance to the ideology of reform: promotion of free entrepreneurship and individual responsibility for the national reconstruction and implementation of individual potentials and initiatives. Leaders in China and Japan also related their investment policies to the revival of the spirit of thrift and entrepreneurship for the sake of national revival. As a result, saving rates in Germany during the reconstruction period (1948–1970) amounted to 40%–50%, and in Japan to 70%, while decreasing from 28% to 20% in Russia between 1990 and 1997.

Not only is the amount of investments essential, but also their rational use (selection of most efficient projects, reduction of construction time, demand-oriented utilisation of capacities). But at this stage of development in the CIS excessive resources are invested in prestigious office premises, villas and motor cars rather than new technologies. Environmental investments in the CIS account for less than 0.5% of GDP as opposed to 3%–4% in developed economies. Likewise, absolutely inadequate are investments in the human potential.

In the past few years CIS countries have initiated new investment institutions. Seven commercial banks in Azerbaijan, supported by an UK management company, have issued *consolidated bonds* (in electronic form) with annual yields of 12%–18%, with joint liability of the issuing bodies (a risk-control factor) and tax-exempt gains (for physical persons). In Russia a similar *investment consortium* of 15 major banks and corporations offered re-drawing overdue enterprise tax arrears as obligation bills and, with government support (of one third of financing), using them to finance approximately 50 investment projects worth $15–20 billion. Among the large investors in some CIS countries are *shared non-government pension, venture* (risk), *mortgage* and other funds accumulating resources of enterprises, banks, local government agencies, international organisations and, most importantly, the public.

Financial institutions have been consolidated. Thus, only 90 banks remained in Kazakhstan in 1998 as opposed to 220 in 1996.

Special emphasis should be placed on translating savings to investment. Over 79% of household income in CIS countries was spent on goods and services (over 50% on food), 5%–6% represented taxes, pension and insurance payments, only 3%–4% bank deposits and securities, and over 20% converted into hard currency. Even excluding the "shuttle" and travel outlays, the remaining one third "stocking" currency savings would provide a large amount of investments.

In Russia converting into hard currency accounted for 11.5% of household incomes in 1992 and almost 25% in 1998. Net savings in cash exceed $22 billion deposit share in total savings peaked in 1996 (60%), declining afterwards due to reduced interest rate and a new tax. The banking crisis resulted in the transfer of most commercial bank accounts to the government-secured Sberbank. In most CIS countries personal deposits in savings and commercial banks grew (in 1997 by 2.1 times in Kyrgyzstan, 1.5 in Armenia and Belarus, 1.2–1.3 in Kazakhstan, Moldova, Tajikistan, Uzbekistan and the Ukraine, and 1.1 in Russia).

In European countries, with PC- or telephone-based bank services, the number of private investors is expected to grow from 600,000 to 2 million by 2001. However, EU member states differ substantially from the CIS both in the income levels (varying between monthly $1000 in Portugal and Greece, $2,500 in UK, and $6000 in Switzerland) and expenditure patterns. Outlays there are dominated by housing and utilities (28%), followed by transportation, education, recreation and medical care (22%–35%), with food ranked third (15%–24%) and clothes and footwear fifth (5%–8%). Food expenditures comprise over half of the family budget in CIS countries.

Along with increased household incomes, individual consumption should be decreased among the top rich segment, via taxes on property and luxury imports, higher utilities, and targeted social care for the really needy. Prohibited domestic foreign-currency settlements will encourage its transfer to central and commercial bank reserves.

Translation of savings to investment will be likewise facilitated with privileged credit for housing and dachas, purchasing domestic cars (as is the case in Uzbekistan), computers and domestic equipment.

Of particular importance is privileged credit to new business owners on personal property. In the case of creditors' debts exceeding the price of such personal property, the debtor will be involved in bankruptcy proceedings.

The bulk of personal savings in developed economies is transferred to share investment funds and bank trusts exclusively authorised by the Central Bank. Associations of securities market operators have been established in CIS countries to control their members' activities. To improve this market sector in the Ukraine, licenses for the use of household savings are only issued to banks of over 3-year standing, with ownership capital over 500,000 and capitalisation of 1 million ecu. Municipal loans (first issued in Dnepropetrovsk in 1995) offer secured yields and can be used in tenders and auctions.

Special actions to improve investment fund performance were taken in some CIS countries.

The investment potential is adversely affected by increased proportion of loss-making enterprises. In Russia between 1995 and 1998 it grew from 30 to 45%–50% in industry and construction and to 60% in transportation. In ten of the regions almost two thirds of the enterprises are unprofitable. Almost one half of enterprises' current assets in the balance sheet are represented by buyers' debts and bills that cannot be sold at book price. Almost 60% of enterprises in Belarus are making losses. Re-registering of economic agents revealed so many false firms that the totals almost halved.

7.4 Role of Foreign Investment

Why are foreign investments required? The low level of both internal and inter-state investment have made most CIS countries rely largely on foreign capital. By 1998 the greatest share of foreign investments was reported in

Azerbaijan, Georgia, Kyrgyzstan (65%–80%) and Kazakhstan. It was slightly lower (15%–20%) in Turkmenistan, Armenia and Uzbekistan. In Moldova and Russia it remains less than 5%–10%, and in Belarus and the Ukraine even lower (see Table 27).

The bulk of investments goes to extractive and mining industries, gas and oil pipelines, telecommunications and market infrastructure (e.g. banking, trade). In Azerbaijan foreign investments in oil and gas production contributed to CIS highest growth of capital investments since the early 1990s. Investments in Georgia involve, for example, transport, as well as manganese and copper production, and in Armenia gold and silver mining, as well as oil and gas prospecting. Kazakhstan is the CIS leader in absolute foreign investments ($3–$4 billion per year), with 75% channelled to basic industries (oil, gas, metallurgy). Uzbekistan has not only obtained investments in the production of uranium, gold, as well as precious and rare-earth metals, but also in manufacturing industries.

Among the major investors in CIS economies are the USA, EU member countries, Japan, South Korea and Turkey. Russian contribution to total crediting in CIS countries amounts to 20% (including energy debts), including only 1% to investment, with 7% in the Ukraine. One third of the foreign investment market in Russia is represented by the USA, 15% by Switzerland and one third by EU countries. Some projects require international investment pools, e.g. the Bureia GES project worth $2 billion, contributing to energy inputs in the Far East, on the one hand, and closure of hazardous coal mines, on the other.

As estimated by V. Garmash,[3] between 1992 and 1997, CIS countries obtained $54 billion worth of credit (with almost $34 billion going to Russia) from international financial organisations and donor countries. On the other hand, Russian credit to other CIS countries amounted to $5.6 billion (14% of total). Add $2.6 billion energy debts of CIS countries to Russia (the Ukraine accounting for 80%).

By the amount of foreign investments CIS countries (except Azerbaijan and Kazakhstan) lag far behind other transition economies. In late the 1990s such investments have been estimated at $100 billion in China, $10 billion in Hungary and $20 billion in the CIS. Due to political risks, wear legislation and business plans, CIS countries are at the bottom of the list of 150 states in investment climate. Per capita foreign investments amounted to $300 in Estonia, $100 in Latvia and slightly over $50 in CIS countries. Private foreign investors expect at least 20%–25% annual profits in the CIS, while gaining no more than 7%–8% at home. This is the price of investment risk.

On the other hand, foreign investments in the CIS has grown by the end of the 1990s. The EBRD, together with some private banks, issued credits to small business, investments are growing in the FEC, metallurgy, chemistry and

---

[3] (1998): Финансовые Известия (Finansovye Izvestia), 24 March [In Russian]

pharmaceutics, cellulose and paper, confectionery and some other industries. In Russia the EBRD contributes to 70 projects (31% in the finance sector, 29% in oil, gas and gold mining, 19% in transport and 5% in telecommunications).

The EU advanced gratis grants to Uzbekistan for the reconstruction of agricultural enterprises. On the same lines food aid projects were implemented in Armenia, Tajikistan, Azerbaijan and Kyrgyzstan. The Transcaucasian countries have also received seed, fertilisers and agricultural chemicals, as well as resources for the reconstruction of railways, mills and bakeries. But charity is not unlimited input.

Do CIS countries need foreign investments? If so, what kind? How can appropriate investors be attracted? These questions have constituted the subject of recent controversies.

Investors are entitled to choose the amount, forms and focuses of investment, to use and hold the targets and effects of investment and to transfer such rights to other physical or corporate persons in compliance with the law. *Direct* investments involve purchasing of controlling interest, or at least blocks of shares (25% or more) and joint management of relevant enterprise. *Portfolio* investments involve the purchase of stocks without contributing to the management.

Foreign investment in CIS countries can be classified into four groups. The first group contains international economic organisations – the World Bank, and European and Asian banks for Reconstruction and Development (EBRD and ABRD).

The World Bank issues privileged (35-year) credits to governments, local government agencies and reliable banks in the countries having per capita GDP under $865 per year. Armenia between 1992 and 1997 obtained credit ($24 per head) for the implementation of business projects involving non-profit enterprises and development of the stock market; Azerbaijan for structural reforms, Russia ($13 per head) for the transformation of coal industry, and the Ukraine ($7) for bank equipment.

The second group contains the TNCs (accounting for over 50% of world investments). They formulate long-term plans of access to CIS markets, establishing their 100%-capital enterprises and joint ventures. The TNCs act as strategic investors. The main benefits here are represented in shared experience in management, international marketing and up-to-date technologies and machinery.

In the mid-1990s credit was largely advanced by governments and international organisations. In Georgia the EBRD, together with the World Bank International Finance Corporation, financed the reconstruction of heating power stations, the airport, Poti port facility, etc. The Ukraine obtained several billion dollars to "cover the fiscal deficit and encourage economic growth", coming in third in the world (after Israel and Egypt) as the largest U.S. aid recipient. But non-targeted credits are generally inefficient, only adding to external debt. World Bank investments are focused on specific projects with promising business plans. Decreased IMF contribution to total foreign investments (exceeding 80% in CIS countries in mid-1990s) is indicative of the progress of reforms.

Foreign investments should not only bring money but also facilitate structural transformations and improve CIS competitive positions on the world market. Strategic investors have been increasingly represented by transnational financial and industrial groups capable of both providing capital and managing production. Thus, the Swiss-Swedish corporation ABB started production of energy-saving turbines in Russia, a $500 million project of a chemical combine in Uzbekistan. TNC Procter & Gamble purchased controlling interests at domestic enterprises and started production of detergents, and Rond Poulinque of previously imported cigarette filters and medicines. Essential for Kyrgyzstan previously importing all of the petrol was the oil refinery built by a Canadian company. Foreign investors purchased controlling blocks of shares to reconstruct Russian paper mills in Segezha, Kotlas and some other towns.

But the TNCs are not interested in promoting rivalling high-technology industries. The tobacco industry is among the leading investment targets in manufacturing (over $1 billion, excluding Russia). Tobacco TNCs have built new factories in Kiev, Samarkand and Saint Petersburg, manufacturing cigarettes with purely national names such as Kozak, Getman or Otaman.

The third group involves financial investors (investment funds and banks) interested in purchasing high-yield and low-risk securities but offering no production technologies. Their resources help improve the national balance of payments, repay the tax and wage debts, and cover the budget deficit. But the high proportion of short-term, speculative portfolio investors will hold the budget and the stock market and the market as a whole (and notably the government securities sector), as well as the national exchange rate and banking system, hostage to situations of foreign exchange.

With underdeveloped stock markets, only 3%–4% of world portfolio investments (roughly totalling $400 billion) goes to CIS countries, mainly Russia and the Ukraine. This cushioned the impact of the world financial crisis in 1997 as compared with Malaysia, Thailand and Brazil. But some Russian issuing bodies spending too much on international audit and credit rating to distribute their stocks on international markets suffered considerable losses due to fall of shares price.

Administrative constraints on capital flows will not be efficient here. Foreign investors, with their life-long habits of measuring risk and return, will withdraw capital from rigidly controlled long-term markets at the first signs of crisis, say, in Hong Kong. The best alternative would be to shift the focus on domestic investors and impose reasonable constraints on external portfolio borrowing.

By expert estimates, several hundred billion dollars worth of capital has been exported from the CIS. This means that credits and investments to CIS countries from developed countries use CIS money at an interest far higher than on foreign bank deposits. Bringing back of fugitive capital would solve the investment problem. As experts in Coopers and Lybrand (USA) estimate, Russia alone has lost $60 billion worth of capital during the 1990s, several times more than obtained as trade credit and bank deposits (soaring five-fold), the "hot money" of portfolio investors and direct investments in the form of addition to capital stock and credits (one third only).

The fourth investor group involves small and medium-scale businesses having no large financial resources and thus orienting on trade and intermediary operations ensuring quick gains at small costs. This sector requires special control, in some cases being represented by dubious firms given to fraud, tax evasion and non-performance. Only 15% of the companies competing for access to the Russian market can be regarded as reliable, 44% finding themselves in financial distress, 22% failing and 19% criminal (as reported at the international conference on "Business and Security", 1997).

Thus, there is no and cannot be any unambiguous answer to the question of whether foreign investment is or is not required in CIS countries, or how they are to be attracted. The required investments should involve up-to-date technologies, machinery and accessories not manufactured within the CIS, and advanced management strategies. Regulations in foreign investment should be differentiated as follows: firstly, by invested capital structure; secondly, by target branches and regions; and thirdly, by investment conditions (e.g. sharing of profits from joint projects, credit interest rate, investment periods, responsibilities for personnel training, new jobs).

Investment climate. The inflow of foreign investment has been typically evident in the regions with available developed infrastructure and clearly defined business proceedings. In Russia 67% of investments in 1995 and 83% in 1997 went to Moscow, and in the Ukraine to Kiev, Odessa and Dnepropetrovsk region. Some TNCs consider the Novgorod region with neither oil and gas wells nor gold mines as the key investment target in the CIS, due to the favourable local legislation.

Investment climate is the expected return/risk ratio in a given country (region) relative to other capital employment spheres.

Comparative studies of investment climate by countries in the 1990s indicate that the key factors governing foreign investment inflows are political and economic stability, stable economic legislation in force, an enforcement framework ensuring compliance with the laws and performance under contracts, organised crime and corruption levels, and property rights protection.

These are followed by national currency stability, secured convertibility to hard currency, investments and profit exports, and financial reporting compliant with international standards.

Next come the quality of labour force, the qualifications and disciplined behaviour, combined with relatively low wages enabling up-to-date technologies to be employed to produce competitive outputs.

Only then do investors consider the tax and other privileges, mainly profit tax rates, opportunities to purchase immovable property, depreciation rates, etc. Therefore, most EU investments have been channelled to Germany, UK and France, even though Greece, Ireland, Spain and Portugal offer much higher tax deductions. Yet, the emerging common economic space, infrastructure and currency union have been stabilising general political and economic conditions and risk level with cost and tax considerations coming to the forefront.

Agreements to prevent double taxation have contributed to the attraction of foreign investments. Thus, a Russia-Germany agreement permits firms with German capital (irrespective of the amount) to deduce from taxable profits all interests paid (including non-banking institutions) and advertising costs (real expenditures depending on real market conditions), as is done in Germany. Thus, international law is given priority over national law. Similar agreements have been made in many CIS countries. But to implement them, financial and tax agencies in CIS countries must learn to analyse both corporate balance sheets and market prices, lest the firms overstate their expenditures to evade taxation.

Legislation regarding foreign investments should include a stabilising "grandfather clause" (a minimum 3– to 5–year safeguard against deteriorating tax, currency and customs environment for a given investor) and a listing of exemptions from national non-resident regulations (e.g. restrictions on land purchase, strategic activities). Bilateral agreements for the encouragement and mutual investments protection are of considerable importance, including tax privileges, lifting of customs barriers and elimination of double taxation. Over 100 such agreements have been made in CIS countries in the late 1990s.

Of fundamental importance for CIS countries is the abolition of duties and the VAT on imports of research-intensive high-technology machinery, structures added to capital enterprises and joint venture capital stock, and facilitation of VAT reimbursement for output exports.

Strong foreign investors prefer specific capital investment spheres. Among them are energy machine building and lathe building for German companies, telecommunications and communication media for Japan, the textile complex for Italy and Turkey, non-ferrous metallurgy for Canada and Australia, oil and gas production for the USA and forestry for Finland.

Insurance against political risks matters here. Thus, a corporation engaged in private investments abroad (the USA) insures (through the government budget) risks to the amount of $200 billion per project. This permitted to expand exports and create 225,000 jobs in the USA. Regretfully, such funds have not gained acceptance in the CIS to date.

According to foreign experts, investment attractiveness of developing countries is governed by ten major factors: economic growth rates (GDP growth); political stability (risk of upheavals, crime levels, civil conflicts); market size (population by per capita GDP); dependence on foreign assistance and potentials for independent development; external debts (in percent of GDP); national currency convertibility and profit export opportunities; inflation rate and national currency stability; internal accumulation of capital level (in percent to GDP); developed infrastructure (transport, communications, information); legal support (e.g. property leasing and purchasing procedures, business registration and insurance, tax stability, price change constraints, exit of obsolete capacities).

Economic globalisation involves control on managers and government officials in each country, exercised both by national legal agencies and firm owners, and foreign investors and buyers. In this context *corruption* comes to act as an insurmountable obstacle for fair economic integration.

Considerable attention has been focused recently on bribed privileged loans and large orders, tax evasion and violation of financial operating rules, with cases of imprisonment or large fines involving the Fiat Board of Directors president, South Korean Hanbo steel corporation's sponsor (with three bank presidents, Minister of Domestic Affairs arrested and the company going bankrupt), prominent figures in the Deutsche Bank and Volkswagen, two cabinet ministers in France and a major financier in Spain.

Considerable interest has been placed on corruption control in the USA. Along with other police actions, they use the tax declaration mechanism (reporting the sources of big expenditures). In the 1980s all customs operations in Indonesia were held by a Swiss firm ensuring simplification and adequate management. Having no need to bribe the officials, foreign investors contributed almost $150 billion to the national economy.

Foreign investment is unlikely to be successful unless due account is taken of local traditions and customs, and differences in business culture. The U.S. business manuals emphasise the importance of friendly personal contacts in CIS countries (adding that a friend is not necessarily a boon companion), and respect of actual achievements in the firm and country in question. Firms are advised to have an authorised representative for on-site negotiations and decision making. Admittedly, negotiations in CIS countries are more emotional and open-minded, and vehement protests almost never mean refusal of further co-operation. In turn, while training their foreign trade personnel, CIS countries should consider international differences both in legislation and business ethics.

Forms of attracting foreign investments. CIS countries employ various strategies of co-operation with foreign companies. Caspian shelf development projects in Azerbaijan involve *output sharing agreements* between a State oil company and foreign consortia (e.g. British Petroleum, the French Elf Aquitaine, the Norwegian Statoil). This secures steady profits for both parties, whereas consortia ensure large investments with no individual dependence. Thus, for example, in the Lenkoran-Talysh-Deniz sea-field development project (worth $1.5 billion) Azerbaijan will contribute 25% and the principal foreign operator 65%.

A similar contract between the public company Azergyzil and a U.S. corporation involves exploratory development in nine ore fields. If deposits in excess of the predicted are discovered within the next 15 years, the investor's contribution may be reduced from 40 to 10%.

International flotation of government bonds is largely unrelated to specific investment projects. The *euro-bonds* have been successfully distributed by Kazakhstan, Russia and some of its regions, and other CIS member states. Credits here (in the mid-1990s covering 50% of budget deficit in Georgia, Kazakhstan, Moldova and the Ukraine, 80% in Kyrgyzstan and 100% in Armenia) are less expensive than bank loans but the external debt surges. In the late 1990s access to the euro-bonds market (e.g. almost 45% eventually distributed in the USA, 15% in the Middle East) has been gained by key banks in Russia and Kazakhstan (e.g. Kazkomertsbank with almost one third of stocks in foreign holding) and corporations. The euro-bond market totals $1 trillion and borrowing is less expensive than distribution of ADR on the U.S. market or currency credit advanced by CIS banks.

Assignment in trust to foreign companies of enterprises or whole branches with the related infrastructure has been typical in Kazakhstan. Approximately two thirds of industries here, including, for example, lead and zinc, copper- gold- and uranium mining, metallurgy and electricity generation are held in trust with buy-out options. A contract generally involves repaying of enterprise debts to subcontractors, to all government budget levels and to staff within 3 months, a bonus paid to the owner (government) and implementation of the investment program. In cases of non-performance, the contract is cancelled. In 1998 Kazakhstan suspended privatisation in oil and gas complexes, criticising the actions of some foreign investors attempting to conceal taxable gains.

Uzbekistan invites investment tenders for *concessions* (15-year with renewal options) in activities such as mining.

In some countries *government-secured credit* has been gaining acceptance. But there have been frequent cases of irrational use of them by enterprises. Thus, for instance, Kazakhstan's government had to go to court to take back investments.

Purchase of stocks and debt securities by portfolio investors represented the major portion of foreign investments in Russia and the Ukraine in the late 1990s. But these investors are inclined to leave at the first sign of crisis. Thus, for instance, of 37% non-resident GKO holders in Russia in October 1997, only 12% remained in November.

The main form of direct investments in CIS countries are *joint ventures*. In 1997 there were over 20,000 joint ventures, including 17,000 in Russia. But as privatisation of State property advances, direct investments in joint ventures declined. On the other hand, joint ventures have been soaring in the Ukraine where tender trade in blocks of shares was only initiated in late 1990s. Commercial banks and investment companies authorised by the State property fund to operate tenders provide financial security for contract performance. In the 1990s investments generally went to food industry (20%), domestic trade (17%) and the financial and credit sector (9%), the major investors including the USA, Netherlands, Germany, UK, Cyprus and Russia. In the late 1990s tax and customs privileges have encouraged investments in combine- and tractor building (Iuzhmash, Kharkov Tractor, Malyshev, Serp i Molot and other works), motor car, engine building and oil and gas industries.

A joint venture offers cheap labour, less rigid environmental requirements and local raw materials. But not infrequently joint ventures have been used only for duty-free imports or to "stake out a claim" on the market. Thus, of 2400 industrial joint ventures in Uzbekistan, only 50% were actually operative, with their falling to 27% in industries while soaring up to 59% in trade and services. Joint ventures contributed 41% to total imports and less than 6% to exports. Most joint ventures in Armenia (Iran, Russia and the USA being the key investors) involved shops, photographer's studios, etc.

In Russia joint ventures account for only 3%–4% of total industrial output. Their share is greater in imports (11%–12%) than in exports (9% in 1997), which impairs the balance of payments. Only later in the 1990s did Japanese and Swedish corporations start joint ventures in high-technologies industries (e.g. communications engineering, optical electronics). Note that it was in Russia where at the turn of the century R. Diesel initiated mass-scale engineering, the Nobel brothers a range of chemical works, and so on. It is the pioneering projects that are of prime importance for CIS economies.

The stock market is generally described in terms of *capitalisation* (ratio between value of national shares traded at stock market and GDP, i.e. generated output). It amounts to almost 200% in Singapore, 120% in Brazil, 80% in Mexico and only 13% in Russia with its 40,000 joint stock companies, i.e. stock price a little over monthly output. Consequently, the market value of the companies is only 0.7–0.8 of fixed in balance sheets (even less in other CIS countries), as opposed to 2.5 in Poland and Hungary. Moreover, 97% of capitalisation represents only three industries: oil and gas (51%), power engineering (38%) and telecommunications (8%). Investment in other branches will only come upon successful transformations at the micro-economic level.

7.5 Tax Policy

Tax policy and its purposes. A *tax* is a compulsory payment lawfully and systematically raised by the government and local authorities from physical persons and corporate bodies to create appropriate budget revenues. Taxes are classified in three types by *origins*: those included in prime costs (e.g. land tax, mining and natural resources fees, allocations to social funds); those paid from profits (income, property and other taxes); and implicit, paid by the consumer in excess of wholesale price (e.g. the VAT, excise duties, retail tax). Taxes are also differentiated by *taxable objects:* taxes on production and sales, transfrontier transport of goods and services (customs duties and charges), wage fund, consumption (sale, VAT, excise duties, purchase of vehicles and use of roads) and legal actions (e.g. registration of corporations, issue of licenses, patents). Thus, taxes in a broad sense include not only payments to the tax inspectorate but also customs and stamp duties.

Tax policy is the totality of actions performed by the government and local authorities to calculate, collect and use taxes. Under constitutions adopted in CIS countries, the lists of taxes, their amount and collecting procedures can be established only by legislative and representative authorities. In this case the government will delegate a portion of rights to fix local taxes to the regional (autonomies, administrative territorial entities, i.e. regions, territories, khakimates) and municipal levels (i.e. towns, villages, auls, kishlaks, prefectures, okrugs/areas). Taxes are collected by executive agencies, social funds (pension, social and health insurance, employment) and customs offices.

Taxes reduce corporate and personal real incomes, and notably their consumption and savings. At the same time government expenditures through taxes extends the aggregate demand (through government purchases and social allocations) and investments. In the economic theory, tax policy exerts a significant influence on economic developments, acting on consumption, accumulation, demand, investments and business activities, but numerous qualifications are involved.

Firstly, there is a tax budget margin beyond which business activity will decline, an increase of personal income through intensive legal work will no longer make sense and market agents will escape in the "shade", evading transaction records, transferring funds abroad, etc.

Then, due account should be taken of the time lag between the change in taxes, consumers' and producers' economic behaviour and GDP output. For instance, a cut in the tax on investments will increase their amount, consequently extending production and taxable base. But a cut in taxes will cut budget revenue today, while positive effects can only be expected some years after, thus generating financial resource shortages for schools, hospitals, etc. Moreover, different social and ethnic groups have different attitudes concerning the use of increased revenues to increase demand or accumulation. Some groups will use saved taxes in business development, whereas others may prefer to buy a prestigious car or other luxuries.

Additionally, uncertain implications of the tax policy are determined by the alternative nature of economic decision making. An increase in implicit taxes on goods will not reduce their consumption if the demand is price stable (e.g., the demand for sugar from the Ukraine when the VAT had been imposed remained almost unaltered). On the other hand, a tax can crush the sales of goods and services if the demand is elastic (e.g. flights, cinema, theatre) or can be satisfied outside the country (jewellery and furs, fashion clothes) or on the "black market" (vodka).

Thus, the tax policy performs three basic functions: *fiscal* (providing for fiscal revenues); *regulation* (i.e. promoting certain spheres of activity, regions, industries, resource inputs); and *social* (re-distribution of incomes among the classes and groups of population).

Formally, the tax system in CIS countries is not different from that in developed economies. The list of basic tax types is the same (profit tax, VAT, excise, retail tax, income tax for physical persons, property tax, mandatory allocations to social funds, customs duties). Foreign countries also operate a three-tier system including national (federal), regional (i.e. states, cantons, lands, provinces) and local (municipal) taxes. Neither do taxation rates differ substantially. Thus, the VAT amounted to 15%–18% in EU countries and 20% in the CIS, profit tax varied between 40%–50% and 30%–35%, capital gains (securities, dividend value) 25% and 15% and income tax between 22%–55% and 12%–35%, respectively.

However, tax systems in CIS countries are purely fiscal, i.e. aimed at increasing government revenues by all and every means, while providing a powerful instrument of government macro-economic regulation and promoting targeted business in developed foreign countries.

The regulation function of taxes in developed economies involves:

– Providing tax exemptions for re-invested (ploughed-back) profits, with only withdrawn from business gains and capital considered as taxable

– Encouraging private investment in production, and notably in high technologies, via tax incentives, including for physical persons

– Encouraging independent (of the government) financing for social developments via tax exemptions for investments in pension, charity and other social funds, education fees, receipts of non-profit organisations accredited with local government authorities and confirming their social relevance

– Providing tax exemptions for small businesses, notably those creating new jobs in depressive regions and priority spheres, employing registered disabled and other persons requiring social support or rehabilitation

– Encouraging exports through preferential trade areas, R&D subsidies (e.g. direct subsidies for equipment and electricity charges for export-oriented goods are prohibited by WTO regulations), and privileged tightened credit to purchasers (if the goods are purchased in the issuing credit country)

Regretfully, CIS countries have made poor use of tax incentives, since this requires advanced legislation (detailed justification for all incentive types) and, more importantly, a reliable system of control and legal enforcement. As estimated by foreign economists, the best incentives for production involve the profit tax under 20%, VAT under 10% and social and income taxes under 35% of total wage fund. But then the GDP contribution to the government budgets in CIS countries must be almost halved.

On the whole, between 1990 and 1997 the largest per capita foreign investment among East European countries went to Hungary (roughly $1500). The amounts in Poland, Estonia, Czech Republic and Slovenia varied between $400 and $800, with Bulgaria (approximately $100), Russia ($50) and other CIS countries ranked at the bottom of the list. Due to a reasonable tax policy in Poland, two thirds of the investments were channelled to motor-car, electrical engineering and chemical industries consequently accounting for 90% of Polish exports.

A tax policy starts from setting the tax margin in GDP. In EU countries this amounted to almost 39% in 1980, 42% in 1992 and 42.2% in 1996. This means a gradually increasing tax burden owing to increased government expenditures, notably social. Tax levels are the highest in countries with intensive social policies, generally government-financed public health and education and high pensions and benefits (e.g. 55% in Sweden, 52% in Denmark, 49% in Finland, 47% in Belgium). The lowest tax contributions to GDP among EU member countries are indicated in Spain and Ireland (35%). It should be noted that actual tax collection amounts to 90%–95% of planned sum in EU member countries.

The tax margin in GDP had not been large (16% in 1990) in the USSR, with almost all enterprises in State ownership. It had to be increased substantially when most of the enterprises were privatised. Moreover, GDP fell much lower than did the minimum allowable government expenditure. In the 1990s contributions of taxes and social allocations to GDP grew to 25%–30%, i.e. 1.5–2 times, in most CIS countries. However, given the high proportion of non-payers, taxes for law-abiding enterprises amount to 75% of added value, impeding investments and covering working capital. High tax proportions exclude many commodity prices from the competitive environment. Thus, the tax share in petrol and diesel fuel prices in many CIS countries amounts to 55%–60% as opposed to 20% in the USA and EU. The market mechanism does not regulate tax-dominated prices or create the conditions for resource-saving technologies because the enterprises lack the required investments. Price reduction through implicit tax cuts would reduce transport and energy tariffs, consequently improving industrial competitive positions and within some time increasing tax collection through industrial developments.

The highest proportion of net production and import taxes in GDP in the mid-1990s were evident in Uzbekistan and Tajikistan (roughly 5%), the Ukraine (19%), Russia, Belarus, Moldova and Turkmenistan (12%–15%). They were significantly lower in Kazakhstan and Kyrgyzstan (10%), and notably so in the Transcauoasian republic (3%–8%). The Ukraine led the list by the aggregate tax budget.

A tax policy should involve a mechanism for restructuring enterprise debts due to objective causes. Reduced inflation will crush the amount of book profits to be taxed in advance in some CIS countries. Penalties for delayed tax payments in Russia in 1996 amounted to 0.3%–0.7% for each day, several tens of times in excess of inflation rates. Having fallen into an insolvency trap, a firm would never get out. In Moldova, and then in some other CIS countries, restructuring of debts to the budget involves deferment of payment on accrued debt for several years and penalty reduced to the National Bank interest rate, but only subject to the current payment schedule. In this case joint stock companies shall deposit with the government the new issue of shares, and other firms their immovable property. No fine can be charged to companies not receiving payments on filled government order in due time. Debt "clearing" would cancel many debt types.

A tax policy is only likely to be efficient with sufficient tax collection. This requirement is not always met in CIS countries, due to the high proportion of barter exchange and other non-monetary and non-banking settlements. Moreover, joint liability must be established for firms and their controlling holdings, as well as for intermediary managers of money flows under contracts of commission. Some firms will enlist the services of such intermediaries to understate their export and other gains. Operations in the CIS by offshore firms generally registered in Cyprus, Liechtenstein, Canaries, Bahamas and some other islands also need regulating. The Greek billionaire A. Onassis claimed that he had not paid a cent in taxes thanks to offshore operations. Such opportunities should not be granted to the "new" eastern European private investors who have established a genuine tax-evasion framework using fictional creditors, suppliers and buyers in tax-free zones.

Total tax debts in Russia by 1998 almost equal two annual budgets. Many firms registered in Cyprus (where profit tax is 4.25%) or as U.S. limited-liability companies (not liable to taxation) never contribute to the fiscal budget, while complying with the letter of law. Almost 40% of total debts to the federal budget in 1997 were represented by only 80 major motor-car (e.g. Avtovaz, Kamaz) and oil and gas corporations maintaining contacts with central and local government authorities.

Most companies in foreign countries enjoy *tax deductions*.

First of all, taxes can be legally reduced by increasing the allocations to non-taxable funds (e.g. depreciation, pension, charity). There are also tax privileges for investments to depressive regions, exporters, etc. Small businesses are taxed at lower rates (e.g. under 25% in the UK for companies showing annual profits under 750,000 pounds). In some countries the profit tax can be consolidated for a corporate group, thus restricting the total taxable base. There are also the carry-back (current loss deduced from previous profit) and carry-forward (current loss deduced from future profit) systems. The resulting average taxation level is lower than basic (maximum).

Privileges in CIS countries are generally rather personal than legislative, i.e. granted by special executive decisions. This distorts the tax policy.

Principal tax types. Table 24 reflects the roles of different taxes in budget revenues.

The value added tax (VAT) has a special budget importance in some CIS countries. Russia has abolished all the privileges, so that all goods are taxed at a unified rate of 20%. The regions may impose retail taxes (up to 5% of prices, excluding, for example, bread, milk and children's food).

The VAT and retail tax are classified as indirect, i.e. paid by purchasers rather than producers. The taxable base – turnover – has been extending consistently in all CIS countries. Therefore, some economists maintain that the central government budget should be largely composed of the VAT and excise duties (i.e. on the basis of the economy as a whole) and local budgets with income and property taxes for physical persons and legal entities under their jurisdictions.

The VAT is calculated as a surcharge on the sale price, with suppliers' taxes subsequently deducted from the purchaser's taxes. As a result, the taxable object is only represented by the added value, wage fund and profits, rather than total gains. The VAT is raised at each stage of supply chain, thus sharply appreciating such sophisticated products as aircraft, vessels or motor cars with production processes involving multiple inter-enterprise transfer of supplies, components and units.

VAT deductions vary across the CIS. Thus, the Ukraine offers VAT exemptions for exports of goods and services, coal production, electricity generation, culture and education, entertainment, sports and many construction services.

Excise duties in many CIS countries are imposed not only on alcohol and tobacco, like elsewhere (tea, coffee and salt are added in Germany), but also on the sales of private passenger vehicles, carpets, jewellery and other items. The high excise rates for legal outputs benefit secret vodka manufacturers whose products appear far less expensive. Using international experience, the number of manufacturers and wholesale traders in basic excise-due goods – alcohol and tobacco – should be reduced dramatically, with tighter control on sales and tax payment.

The range and rates of excise-due outputs differ considerably across the CIS. Thus, the list in the Ukraine, along with wines and spirits and tobacco (between 50 and 85% of prices), includes, among other items, natural leather, sugar, carpets, furs and jewellery, porcelain and cut glass (30%–45%), private passenger vehicles (depending on power) and lorries (35%), tyres for private passenger vehicles (85%), chocolate, coffee, beer and colour TV sets (20%). Consequently, excise duties and the VAT account for almost two thirds of budget revenues (approximately 45% in Belarus in 1997).

The *profit tax* in CIS countries is lower than in developed foreign countries (30%–35% vs. 45%–50%), as well as the *tax on capital gains* – dividends, interests, stock rise (10%–15% vs. 20%–25%). But CIS countries have a far more extensive taxation basis, i.e. expenses to be covered out of profits. Thus, for example, international taxation generally excludes justified and documented personnel training, advertising, charities, insurance and interest paid. In CIS countries only short-term credit interest is included into prime costs (generally at the central bank rate +3%). Particularly unfavourable are the taxes on sales (in some cases taxes exceeding real profits). Of fundamental importance for long-term industrial investments is a transition to a new depreciation policy. Following the experience in some other countries, standard machinery life should be reduced and accelerated depreciation procedure facilitated for new technologies and R&D.

Market economies offer tax exemptions for corporate reserves designated for risk insurance and innovatory financing (given appropriate justification and documentation).

Moreover, in Russia and some other countries taxes used to be imposed on shipment (invoice), prior to actual settlement on accounts. Having no finance reserves, firms have to require advance payments, thus being discriminated against relative to foreign competitors.

Real profit tax rates are higher in countries with high inflation rates. The difference in prices of supplies and accessories on dates of purchase and actual use is regarded as taxable gain. This is most unfavourable for machine-building works with long process cycles. Some economists argue that declining enterprise efficiency in the CIS and problematic profit tax collection will contribute to its replacement with indirect taxes.

The *income tax* for the public is designed to bridge the excessive income differences. This will involve tax exemptions for a portion of income required to meet basic household needs. In some foreign countries "family" declarations are submitted, describing rather than individual breadwinner's the aggregate household income per family member. Regretfully, the non-taxable income in all CIS countries is far lower than the subsistence minimum generally not legally specified.

All CIS countries operate differentiated income tax rates. But these largely involve the "middle class" of wage-earning professionals. On the other hand, high-income tax rates are far lower in CIS countries than elsewhere, e.g. maximum 35% in Russia compared with 53% in Germany in 1998. At the same time, CIS professionals earning Europe's medium-sized wages ($1000–$2000 per month) pay higher percentages in taxes. The same is true about small business.

On the whole the share of income tax in budget revenues in CIS countries (average 10%) is substantially lower than elsewhere (35% in UK), and that of profit tax (30% and 5%, respectively) far higher. Yet the proportions are unlikely to be altered unless public incomes are driven up to the average European level, with appropriate reporting. In all CIS countries the amount of retail turnover (in particular including street markets) is far in excess of total reported proceeds.

Of vital importance in regulating the income tax collection is the assignment of individual fiscal codes to taxpayers, to be used in automated computer systems providing tax and debt recovery and processing unified reports of all economic agents and individual business operators. The system is being established in Moldova and some other countries to replace the current mailing of income reports to district tax inspectorates. In Saint Petersburg in 1997 over 5 million personal accounts were opened for 1 million persons with more than one income source, with 10 million reports mailed. The new income declaration format will facilitate the procedure.

Compulsory *allocations to social funds* (e.g. pension, social and health insurance, employment) in some CIS countries are passed through and in others outside the budget. In Russia they amounted to 40% of the wage fund. In the late 1990s payments for supporting police, educational institutions, as well as the social and cultural sphere were abolished. In the Ukraine, along with allocations to pension, social insurance and employment funds (39%), 12% of the enterprise consumption fund is assigned for Chernobyl follow-up operations (approximately 6% of government budget).

In some CIS countries allocations to different social funds are assigned separately. A single social tax to be further distributed among the pension and other funds in legal proportions would reduce administrative costs substantially.

An individual personal code will enable the financial resources to be transferred to personal pension accounts rather than a common stock. A computerised system using the code will provide information on real household budgets from the central car register, real estate registries, banks, customs offices, employers and supermarkets. Where expenditures are out of proportion with revenues and individual earnings cannot be documented, the tax and social allocations will be imposed. In Estonia the procedure involves compulsory individual documentation for as long as 6 years after the date.

By late the 1990s some CIS countries have reduced allocations to social funds (the Ukraine from 52% to 32% of wage fund). But inter-republic contradictions in this area have not been resolved.

The *property tax* (e.g. land, real estate) has not been prominent in CIS countries. On the other hand, the taxable object here is much more obvious than, for example, income or profit. Property taxation promotes better its use. Thus, a land tax in the agrarian sector (starting from cadaster valuation) would replace all other taxes, facilitating reporting and control. Some CIS countries intend to abandon income control in small business, with the tax calculated by objective factors (e.g. area, location and trade list for a shop, seats in a café, places in a car park, equipment items in gambling establishments).

This will involve real market prices rather than book ones, to be fixed by special local government agencies. To date, registration of land and realty owners in a variety of methods is the responsibility of land, financial and taxation bodies, inventory offices, etc. Almost 90% of duties in CIS countries (excluding customs and social) represent the four types: the VAT (over 40%), excise duties, and profit and income taxes, with property and land taxes accounting for only 5%. The proportions should be changed in a radical manner. One can conceal "under-the-counter" earnings but not a splendid mansion or office.

Some CIS countries intend fixing a single *land tax* for a year. This will be calculated from the price and cadastral value of a land parcel, replacing all other duties in the agrarian sector.

Mining and natural resource use taxes contribute only 3%–5% of budget revenues. An increased share of property and resource taxes would promote business in the spheres where the value is added through qualified labour rather than exploitation of natural resources.

By the end of the 1990s the proportion of property and resource taxes has grown substantially in some CIS countries. Thus, the Ukraine imposed a tax on corporate and personal property, initiating the re-evaluation of fixed capital and reduced standard depreciation rates.

Tax reform. Tax reform is essential at the second stage of reforms, with the fall in production checked, inflation rates reduced and issues of economic integration and structural policy coming to the forefront.

In the late 1990s Moldova, Russia, Kyrgyzstan and some other CIS countries have been introducing new tax codes. The basic improvements in the tax system involve:

1. Shorter general tax lists. Thus Moldova only retained five of the previous 30 taxes and charges: profit, property, income, the VAT and social. Regional and local government authorities in some CIS countries arbitrarily fixed compulsory charges for public security agencies, schools and roads. Many taxes hardly cover the collection costs and complicated enterprise reporting, or are obviously of a non-market nature (i.e. taxes on wages above permitted standards, frontier crossing, sales at prices under prime costs, for the maintenance of loss-making industries).

2. Change in the taxable basis. A market economy involves entry as corporate costs and non-taxable of: loan interest, advertising, representation, insurance against commercial risk, marketing and some other costs, as well as reserves. Many CIS countries maintain the pre-market system of entering the production rather than transaction costs in prime costs.

3. Abolition of tax advantages granted by executive authorities to individual persons on arbitrary rather than legal lines. Due to such advantages CIS countries only collect 50%–65% of the planned amount of taxes, thus increasing the burden on law-abiding taxpayers. In Russia in 1996 almost 75% of arrears were represented by 70%–80% major corporations maintaining special contacts with government authorities. For similar reasons the budget lost over $30 billion in the mid-1990s. Yet complete abolition of advantages would be inexpedient in the AIC, machine-building and construction industries emerging as the engines of economic growth.

In the USA the Republicans proposed to replace all income taxes for physical persons and corporations with one fixed tax on consumption in excess of a non-taxable minimum (at a rate of 25%), not to be extended to invested (ploughed-back) profits. Estimates have shown, however, that a single tax will not permit co-ordination of the interests of the budgets, the public and the economy.

4. Mandatory declarations for the purchase of valuables, increasing top-income taxation while cutting down taxes for the middle class of professionals and business owners.

5. Enhancing the regulation role of taxation. This primarily involves accelerated depreciation calculated for assets groups rather than individual units, including R&D, machinery updating and natural resource management. This will reduce taxable profits and in 4–5 years, instead of the current 14–18 years, repay the investments to production renovation and development.

An interesting experience was demonstrated in Kazakhstan and Uzbekistan, with direct investments exempt (completely for a few years and partially after) from income and property taxes. Such incentives will rapidly increase fiscal revenues.

Some CIS countries abolished taxes on earnings (e.g. for the maintenance of roads, social and cultural institutions). With low inflation rates, even a 5% tax will prevent the producers from selling their products at a normal international market return (3%–4% of total sales), impairing their competitive merits over the advantages.

On the other hand, taxes on "imputed income", i.e. fixed charges (similar to trade license fees), calculated from dozens of indicators describing the property and functional organisation of a small firm, in some regions ensured the rapid growth of business activities and jobs and, consequently, income taxes.

Tax privileges for preferential-trade areas (duty-free imports of supplies and materials, tax-exempt exports of goods and services) have been efficient in Belarus, Moldova and the Ukraine.

Of fundamental importance is the taxation mechanism for small business. Complete elimination of existing advantages would result in withdrawal to background economy. Real earnings cannot be recorded in small business. Some countries plan taxation by economic potentials (e.g. production space, location, operating range), i.e. productive factors rather than outputs. Thus, the Tula region experimented with consolidated profit, land, property taxes and local charges in a single fixed tax by utilised resources.

6. Using the experience in EU member countries, constraints should placed on inter-republic tax competition compelling some companies, notably the TNCs, to be registered in the countries offering more favourable tax advantages rather than at the place of operation.

Economic integration is not likely to be successful in the absence of a co-ordinated tax mechanism. The recent multiple and uncoordinated tax changes in Kazakhstan, the Ukraine, Belarus and other CIS countries have impeded reasonable decision-making, profit and loss accounting and long-range planning for counterparts both in the "far abroad" and "near abroad".

The primary concern is the exclusion of double taxation, unifying the tax listing and co-ordinating the rates, as well as the taxation basis. Thus, for instance, since 1995 the tax on trade amounts to 5% of turnover in Belarus and 25%–35% of profits in other CIS countries. In Russia corporate after-tax profits comprise less than 19% (26% in 1991) and tax share in prime costs over 30%, varying between 20% and 40% in other member countries. Aggregate higher-income tax rates amounted to 70% in some countries, with the resulting flight of capital abroad, to offshore zones, or background economy.

A tax code basing on the model version approved by CIS Interparliamentary Assembly would systematise appropriate enforceable enactments, providing a comprehensive, stable and unified framework for tax advantages and grants, deferments and inspections. Reductions will generally involve the non-development oriented taxes inhibiting industrial co-operation between firms in the CIS, duplicating each other, involving high reporting and controlling costs and, more importantly, purely fiscal, providing no incentives for industrial developments.

Unification and stabilisation of the tax system will require a taxable margin. As mentioned previously, the actual fiscal tax revenues in CIS countries are far lower than elsewhere. Moreover, the law-abiding firms have to give up almost all the added value, impeding further development, while background economy yields nothing whatever. With 4000 legal tax standards in Russia in 1998, mostly established by departmental instructions rather than legal provisions, every third of the 2.7 million registered firms evaded taxation. The new tax code will substantially restrict the roles of legally binding (issued by executive authorities) enforceable enactments, ensuring legal protection of taxpayers' rights, reducing the tax range and facilitating the calculations.

The taxation reform is designed to restrict the tax range, establishing a clear-cut and simple tax system. Conversion to international reporting standards will provide for the correct calculation of corporate debts, flow of moneys, income, real estate and other assets, creating a transparent and independent of the management procedure for shares registration. Only then would tax payment be easier and more profitable than evasion. In addition, the tax code will protect taxpayers' legal interests, preventing unlawful prejudice by tax agencies currently inclined to arbitrary interpretation of laws and failing to provide access to required information for the payers.

7. A unified mechanism for debt restructuring, retention and sale of debtor's property. In this case firms are granted a 5-year deferment of debt payment with a simultaneous cut in fines or penalties, as well as cancellation of current account freeze. On agreement with local tax inspectorates and social fund affiliations, the firms undertake due settlement of current payments. They are offered training support and advice for reorienting, restructuring, up-to-date management and marketing (see Chap. 8).

Joint stock companies in this case shall issue additional shares as security to the government and other creditors. The debt can also be converted as securities to be sold at a discount. The government will recover the debt immediately and then the holders of securities will settle the debtor's accounts. In some cases the debts incurred by subsidiaries are repaid by holdings. A contract of trust with the manager of the corporate debtor can be cancelled unilaterally (with no lawsuit initiated).

Retention upon non-performance of tax obligations first involves non-productive assets (foreign currency, securities, motor vehicles), then outputs, and finally other assets. This is more effective than bankruptcy inevitably involving deferred payment of overdue tax payments.

8. Taxation reform includes a new mechanism to check tax payments. *Tax census* involves re-registering of all enterprises with tax agencies, forbidding simultaneous use of one registered office by more than one entity. This reduced the number of market agents, e.g. by half in Belarus.

Taxable objects in this cases are represented by consolidated entities rather than individual and formally independent firms. Thus, while joint stock companies AvtoVAZ in 1996 and 1997 increased car output to 700,000 items, the incoming money accounted for only 1.5% of the gains, the balances appropriated by all kinds of intermediaries not at all willing to pay the taxes. An even lower proportion was deposited in the accounts of the world's largest producer of platinum and other precious metals, Norilsk combine. Consequently, while outputs and exports expanded, budget receipts decreased on a formally legal basis, being entered on accounts of other firms in the same holding.

Taxation reform intends to change the economic environment for the firms as the basic component of CIS economy.

Restructuring of firms in a changing economic environment involves: 1) development and realisation of property rights (separating the powers of sponsors, owners, managers and lessees, promotion of contract law and liability for non-payment, implementation of mechanisms for bankruptcy and re-nationalisation of privatised property where new owners fail to perform); 2) a mechanism for the management of state property and regulation of natural monopolies (replacing "right of management" with market relationships of trust, lease or rent, with an institute of government representatives in mixed joint stock companies and a regulating framework for prices, tariffs and flow of funds in natural monopolies); 3) promotion of corporate management and co-operative arrangements in large and small business (with financial responsibility centres and business networks, control over change in stocks by independent depositors, franchising); 4) conversion to international standards of financial, administrative and tax registration, separation of commercial secrets and information accessible for shareholders, investors and creditors; 5) improvement of firms' investment attractiveness by purchase of land lots and registration of intangible assets, including know-how; 6) improvement of management basing on strategic planning, certification of products and technologies, comprehensive quality control, computer networking, strategic marketing and administrative decision-making justification mechanism; 7) a radical change in personnel management – from registration of personnel movements to comprehensive personnel development.

Towards unity of economy. The USSR economic system represented an ineffective but unified and controllable structure. In the 1990s it broke down into three little related blocs with different patterns and problems. This was due to the lack of target programs of transition to socially oriented market economy, as opposed to the post-war developments in the former totalitarian (Germany, Japan, Spain) and many colonial countries.

One bloc was represented by joint stock companies in the fuel-and-energy, chemical-metallurgical and forestry complexes, and some engineering industries (aircraft, rocket-and-space, nuclear, shipbuilding, turbine) discovering their niches on international markets. These were former state enterprises (the State maintaining controlling interests or blocks of shares in some joint stock companies) led by former directors or important party and economic officials often ignorant of up-to-date management. The competitive advantages were associated with unique natural resources (e.g. world's richest reserves of gas, platinum, palladium, forest), low (even considering the productivity) wages, lax environmental requirements and a government-approved decline of the national currency. But these merits have been increasingly outweighed by the high energy prices and expensive social infrastructure (e.g. Norilsk combine maintaining a large Arctic city) and transport (due to remoteness of non-freezing ports and international transits).

This bloc produces competitive outputs gaining "quick" money. Nevertheless, it cannot be described as really market based because the management's gains are largely derived, instead of new technologies and cost reduction, from monopolistic prices on the internal market and trust- (State property management), taxation and financing (e.g. budget subsidising and guarantees on commercial credit, tolling) privileges owing to personal contacts with government authorities. In addition, this bloc has been increasingly isolated from national economy with foreign TNCs monopolising the sales (aluminium, non-ferrous metals), technologies (oil mining, cellulose and pulp), research-intensive machinery inputs (shipbuilding, aircraft electronics and engineering), gaining controlling interests and paying director's remunerations via foreign bank accounts.

The second bloc is represented by the former state enterprises that are uncompetitive on the world market, exchanging their outputs for quasi-money (e.g. barter, precarious bills) and probably for this reason obtaining no real support from government authorities. Some firms, re-orienting on imported raw materials, technologies, equipment and design, find their niches on the internal market due to low prices (food, and notably meat and dairy, flour and cereal, confectionery, construction materials, pharmaceuticals, perfumery, motor-car factories). These items attract foreign capital.

In a pseudo-market economy, a firm is only likely to be efficient when ignoring the traditional rules of business. Thus, for instance, Novolipetsk metallurgy combine produces 15% of Russian steel, with 75% exported. The joint stock company earns $2 billion every year, paying taxes and wages in due time, sharing the management of Lipetsk Tractor and some other major works, and financing a range of social programs in the region. Nevertheless, the main money flows have been passing through a foreign firm holding 37% of the shares and monopolising both inputs and outputs. Contrary to the laws in force, the joint stock company refused external audit and denied membership in the Board of Directors to unwanted investors, even those holding half the shares. Despite the reduced prime costs, the reported rate of return fell from 40% to 5% over a year. Informal contacts with local and federal government authorities were used extensively in financial management.

A most dramatic case was represented by high-technology industries governing CIS long-term developments in the twenty-first century. They have lost the domestic market and could not gain access to the world market dominated by foreign TNCs with their excess capacities and transportable outputs. Many electronic, optical and instrument-making facilities, factories manufacturing domestic equipment from TV sets to washing machines and vacuum cleaners, and large department stores are on the verge of collapse. Many directors have preferred assured earnings from the lease of fixed assets and sale of former state strategic supplies to careful market research, search for partnership arrangements and technological updating.

Light industries in Russia, the Ukraine and Belarus have lost their historical chance at realistic alliance with previous suppliers in the southern republics, joining their efforts to oppose the expansion of consumer goods from Turkey, China, and other countries. Not infrequently the republican cotton inputs were re-exported at a profit while domestic labour received no wage. Yet clothing factories in Moscow, Saint Petersburg and some other cities provided cases of market-based management and maintained their independence. Ignoring multiple offers, they started work for export orders, using foreign patterns and updating their machinery and technologies. Their example was followed by some textile factories. On the other hand, many actually failing and obsolete factories, plants and department stores are still acting as parasites on new commercial structures having no premises of their own.

The department stores represent the third, market-oriented bloc of economy, the initially private-owned firms. They feature numerous specific characteristics. Most sponsors and directors here are intellectuals (scientists, teachers, engineers, students) having no previous experience in personnel, bank and finance management, while being free in their choice of business contacts and areas. They have been acting as entrepreneurs, i.e. economic persons combining the owner/manager functions and generally not associated with the management of state property. The firms were established mainly in unstructured and unsaturated market sectors where competition was actually non-existent. These sectors involve finance (commercial lending, securities, sponsorship – establishment and sale of new firms, financial mergers), trade, including dealer, factor (warehouse) and distributor functions, market infrastructure (cell communications, consulting, software).

Surveys conducted by the research and consulting firm Alt and some other organisations indicate the three phases of management in this bloc: investigating, holding and stabilising. In the first phase, fairly high (several hundred percent annually) profits were gained by investigating and establishing new unrelated business ("topics") on a non-saturated, non-competitive and non-regulated – essentially "barbarous" – market. Fortunes were made by sensing the interplay of forces, starting or abandoning business in due time, focusing on the "quick" money in the peak-inflation period. Many, having profited by the collapse of former supply/distribution network, emigrated or abandoned business for politics.

The second phase, with the saturated market, intensified import competition, declining speculative demand and more profitable spheres captured by Mafia-type groups, required structural experiments, financial mergers, large diversified holdings, and buying up and reselling blocks of shares in new companies. Here return was only several tens percent, while business management required both courage and intuition, and substantial expertise. Many well-known companies lost control and faded into the background, e.g. Microdin previously engaged in simultaneous computer sales and car manufacturing.

By the end of the 1990s, the phase of systematic and professional management has emerged. The lower inflation and interest rates reduced profits from gambling in securities and foreign exchange. The key international TNCs gained access to the CIS market. To secure sustained 15%–20% profits, firms in this bloc have to specialise in business processes requiring common management, abandoning the non-profile businesses. Friendly leadership has been replaced with professional managerial teams. Assets management (selection of business strategy, ways of restructuring, appointment of directors) has been separated from operations. Firms have come to establish their own frameworks for management, including finance and budget, investment and innovation, and personnel, employing up-to-date strategies of simulation, forecasting and planning, logistics, controlling and real estate development.

Some economists believe that it is this business type that has been shaping the Eurasian market management style. While this may be true to an extent, one important point to remember is that the third bloc is only a fragment of real production and has often been associated with shadow or even criminal economy.

Field of Debate

1. What distinguishes the government budget role in macro-economic policy in transitional economies?

2. Analyse the changes in the government budget deficit and national debt in CIS countries during the 1990s. How do they affect economic growth? How is the government budget deficit covered?

3. What are the components of budget revenue and expenditure in CIS countries? How can a more rational composition be accomplished? Compare budget policies in CIS countries.

4. What should govern the relationships of central and local government budgets? What does international experience in this area suggest?

5. Why are strict regulations necessary in budget planning, approval and execution? How are they accomplished in CIS countries?

6. How do different economic schools explain the causes of inflation and its economic implications?

7. What are the measures of money component, money, velocity and money stock growth? Analyse their changes in CIS countries and compare them with price growth rates. What are the causes of different inflation rates in the 1990s?

8. What are the causes of payment crisis in CIS countries? What are the remedies? What is the experience of CIS countries in this area?

9. How can the government influence the exchange rate? What governs changes in the rate?

10. Why should monetary policies in CIS countries differ from those in developed foreign countries?

11. What is the meaning of investment crisis in CIS countries? What are the causes and principal remedies?

12. Analyse the amount of savings (investment potential) in CIS countries, sources of capital investments, their amount and composition.

13. What changes in investment policy will be needed in CIS countries? What are the primary concerns in this context? How are savings translated to investments? What international experience would be useful here?

14. Why do CIS countries need foreign investment? What are their main sources and focuses?

15. What are the components of investment climate? What part of experience in other countries would be helpful in the CIS?

16. What are the functions and objectives of tax policy? What basic tax types are operated in CIS countries?

17. What are the basic trends in the tax reform in CIS countries? How can their regulation role of taxes be intensified?

18. Why are co-ordinated tax systems essential for CIS countries? How can they be accomplished?

19. What are the main causes of financial crisis in 1998? Why did it first affect Russia? What program has been proposed to resolve the crisis? How is it implemented? In what way did the crisis affect economic developments in the Ukraine, Belarus, Moldova and other CIS countries?

20. How can the international community contribute to the resolution of investment crisis in CIS countries?

Chapter 8

MICRO-ECONOMIC BASIS OF REFORMS

8.1 The Firm in the Pseudo-Market Economy

The firm as a principal unit of the market economy. Four basic types of economic entities to make management decisions operate under market economy, i.e. the State and local power authorities, households (families), firms, non-profit economic establishments and associations.

A firm is a basic unit of the market economy. The firms produce the bulk of goods and services and, consequently, GDP. Here the bulk of the public wealth concentrates, this being not only the tangible one (productive assets) but the intellectual one (applied research end engineering developments, professional qualifications of employees, management experiences) as well. The firms spend the bulk of living and materialised labour (first and foremost, energy resources and raw materials), thus establishing not only a productivity thereof but an environment condition as well. The Model Civil Code adopted by the Interparliamentary Assembly and made effective in Russia and numerous other CIS countries distinguishes the concepts of "a business enterprise" as an object of economic activities and "a legal entity" as a subject.

A business is a property complex including immovable property (land, buildings, facilities), movable property (e.g. equipment, inventories), rights, claims and debts (accounts outstanding, accounts payable and receivable), industrial rights (e.g. trademark, licences, contracts), intellectual property (e.g. patents, know-how, copyright), cash and securities.

A legal entity is a duly incorporated owner of separate property (based on the rights of ownership, lease or trust) who is in charge of the property and income gained therefrom, liable for its undertakings, enters into a business agreements (contracts) in its name, may act as a party (sue and be sued) in courts and maintains a separate accounting system (balance sheet, profit and loss statement).

A firm is a legal entity performing business activities.

The civil code is a kind of economic activity constitution. It vested the title of tangible and intangible assets in legal entities, thus having recognised their equal rights with the State and individuals, and an opportunity to appeal against illegal actions of the governmental agencies in courts. Although a delay was extended, a barrier was erected against false firms that created financial pyramids while having almost nothing as their own property to secure the obligations undertaken. A clear distinction was made between *transactional* and *intracompany* management decisions; the first are made under a direct impact of market forces, and fixed in contracts between independent economic units, and the latter express a will of the owner or its managers employed, and is fixed in decrees, resolutions, etc.

The rights and obligations of *a founder* who submitted the firm's constituent documents for incorporation, *an owner* and *an employee*, including a manager, were distinguished.

A State-owned firm (with respect to which a designation of "enterprise" was preserved) was recognised as a *unitary* one, which means it belongs to the owner as opposed to a team of employees, brigades or production shops.

For the first time, a clear distinction was made between profit and *non-profit* organisations (i.e. institutions, public factories, foundations, consumer co-operatives societies, associations), whereby a legal basis was established for *a public economy sector* (this accounts for 55% of employees in USA). A direct translation of the English term "non-profit" as "generating no profit" is incorrect with respect to such organisations of special importance to the development of fundamental science, education, public health, culture, environment protection and other areas wherein the goods and services of public nature are directly produced. These organisations gain profits but spend the same for the productive and charitable purposes only, contrary to the disbursements of dividend, bonuses, etc.

A distinction was made between the business *partnerships* – being associations of workers – of individuals liable for their undertakings at the cost of their property, including personal property, and business *companies* based on the consolidation of capitals of legal entities, households, as well as the State and local authorities. In this case, the liability is not extended to the property of partners and is limited to their contribution into the authorised (share) capital.

The foregoing legal principles are important to the economic theory and practice. Based on the foregoing, a system of contracts develops, i.e. voluntary, though registered and protected by the State agencies, undertakings to supply goods, services and works. Long-term contracts entered into before the production (mining) starts, and often before the development of novel goods (e.g. prospecting a deposit) provide for the limits and terms of supply, prices, payment amounts and types, and penalties in case of failure to perform under the contract. In the environment of modern market economy, a system of contracts implements the *planned nature* (the proportionality established deliberately) of the economic development. In doing so, given a voluntary and horizontal construction (between the partners equal in rights and concerned), the plans appear to be much more realistic than those under the vertical command governance when the administrative authorities (e.g. Gosplan) approved the same, which were not liable for any justification of their decisions on their own account.

A new part of the firms is bound up with relationships of economic liability which regulate in detail the indemnity for any damage (including any profit lost) caused to the partners in case of breaching the contracts and other rules of behaviour in the market. This will not reserve any development prospect for the firms that is not related to improving efficiency of their operations.

At last, the firms are destined to find a most reasonable ration between the transaction and intracompany (administrative planning) costs. The *transaction* costs are related to the arrangements for, entry into, and performance of contracts with other firms. These include the costs of marketing, advertising, commercial risk insurance, the legal follow-up of contracts, the contraband cash flows, sales taxes, customs duties, etc. Such market expenses amount to 60% of total costs in the developed countries, which is more than the direct costs of, for example, raw materials, supplies and labour remuneration.

An expansion of a firm's scale, its transformation into a vertical company (starting from the production of, for example, oil to the manufacture and sales of petrol and other finished products) allows to cut down the transaction costs to a great extent. In particular, this applies to the transnational corporations that do not pay VAT and duties when transferring their values within a corporation. It is not by chance that the transnational corporations account for 60% of the global foreign trade. Any firm is a centrally planned system because no advertising, expensive negotiations will be required to place an order at one of its subdivisions; decision by the owners or managers will be sufficient.

However, all the advantages of a firm would not allow transformation of a country's national economy into the single factory and eliminate the independent small-scale business. Although the transaction costs are superfluous in this case, nevertheless, as a firm's scale expands, the administrative planning costs grow which relate to development, communication to the responsible persons, follow-up of the tasks, a multistage procedure of data retrieval and decision making and the co-ordination of effort by multiple offices. Overheads of the small-scale business amount to 50% on average, and those of the large-scale business sometimes exceed 500% as opposed to the prime costs of production.

The losses resulting from a decreased number of centres making strategic management decisions are much more significant. During the twentieth century a range of goods and services has grown by a factor of 100 at the least and now comprises tens of millions of designations. Numerous alternative processes to produce them have grown as high as hundreds of times, as well as numerous consumers who do not restrict themselves to their natural economy products but purchase goods imported from all over the world. The management centres of the corporations, not to mention Gosplan, are not able, even using computers, to look promptly through every potential alternative decision and choose an optimal one. They are forced to restrict themselves to the manufacture of goods of either global and mass production (including standard parts and component products) or special national importance (weapon and life buoyancy systems), whereas the rest is left to the small-scale business.

Numerous legal entities in the CIS countries has multiplied in the 1990s more than by the factor of 10, including by the factor of 20 in Russia (from 120,000 to 2.6 million), whereas two thirds of them are non-government entities. Relying upon the practices of the developed countries, 250 million inhabitants of the CIS must set up 20 million firms which is six or seven times as high as the figure for 1997. This will result in the flourishing of business initiatives, creating millions of new jobs for university graduates. However, the majority of the present firms cannot be deemed as fully fledged subjects of the market economy. Approximately two thirds of them were established in the course of privatisation through the division of manufacturing as well as research and production enterprises. Frequently, the small-scale firms within an enterprise, which saw the world in such an artificial manner, appear to lack vital capacity.

It is possible to point out five primary indicators of competitiveness and adaptation of the firms under the new business environment, i.e. 1) dynamics of market position (a firm's share in the total sales of specific goods and services in the national, regional or global market); 2) a rate of return providing for an extended reproduction (in the CIS, depending on an industry, it cannot be less than 15%–30% as opposed to the total capital and 6%–12% as opposed to the sales); 3) a solvency (prompt payment for labour, trade accounts payable, taxes, lack of overdue debts); 4) a persistent team core (labour environment and remuneration at least at the standard level specific to the region in question, labour fluidity of 10% per year at maximum); and 5) production renovations (e.g. investments in the development and assimilation of new technology).

In Russia, as low as 20% (10%–25% in various regions) of the firms met the foregoing criteria in 1997. They are able to take the lead of the economy and so must be a priority target of foreign investments under the participation or warranty of the government or local power bodies. Approximately 50% of the firms are not competitive, however, though they have stabilised in terms of one or two indicators mentioned previously (most often, a slowdown of their production decline given a low rate of return and acute non-payment crisis). First and foremost, they need some *restructuring*, which means a production and administration structure modification on a modern management basis. Finally, up to 30% of the firms have lost their market positions and exist at the cost of budget subsidies only (coal mines), non-repayment of debt (agricultural complex), non-payments, leasing out or sales of their privatised assets. The best way to terminate their extended agony, both from the viewpoint of the society and the working collective, is to go into bankruptcy that in many cases (especially when the point is any town-forming enterprises (a town was created around the enterprise or that of national security importance) implies a change of the owner only as opposed to the legal entity cancellation. The world practices should be taken into account in all the cases.

Revolution in management. A competitive ability of the U.S. firms in the international markets seemed to decline in the 1970s–1980s and the country lagged behind Japan, Germany and other developed countries in terms of economic growth rate, productivity and export dynamics. American economists proved that a primary reason for that lag was the management inconsistency with the new challenges of the world market. First of all, a former focus on mass production appeared to be out of date. A saturated market calls for a flexible adaptation of the goods and services to the needs of specific customers, whereas increasingly often it is not a mere thing that is deemed to be a commodity, but a sophisticated engineering complex set including the transfer of technology, manufacturing and commercial experiences (know-how) and other service.

The U.S. firms inclined to increase their current profits without due regard to a strategic planning process or administrative level of production. Also, the innovative management dropped behind. Given a high level of fundamental research (the achievements thereof were accommodated by the countries of Asia promptly and free of charge), they failed to secure a proper quality and reliability of goods, high level of technology and protection of engineering secrets. Since the time of President Ford, the personnel management principles concentrated on a clear and detailed division of labour as opposed to the enrichment of a labour content, the involvement of employees in the firm's affairs, their continuous education and improved relationships within the team. Millions of personal computers were often employed as great calculators while an information system and decision-making arrangement were kept the same in essence. The relationships with the suppliers and customers featured a pure market nature, and no use was made of the long-term co-operation capabilities under a single plan. The protectionism towards the native firms in the USA entailed the respective restrictions on the activities of the U.S. corporations abroad.

The 1990s saw the second industrial revolution. The revolution of the nineteenth century that created a large-scale machine industry had been based on the conversion of the engineering facilities, and a production system of twenty-first century was based on that of data streams. Modern computer hardware, technology and software allow integration of the computerised workplaces within a firm, though the same are located in different parts of the world, into a common data network (Intranet) that could be connected to the networks of related firms and banks, and added to the global data network, i.e. Internet. At the threshold of the twenty-first century, Internet turns out to be a new format of production socialisation, a tool of global marketing, technology and know-how transfer, personnel training, international payments and a basis of entry into long-term contracts. The latest inventions reduce a cost of network technology drastically, thus making the same affordable to the small-scale business and households. It seems that a kind of negation will terminate in the twenty-first century. Millions of people will be able to work at home like former peasants or craftsmen, indeed, at a computer instead of a wooden plough or distaff. The second industrial revolution transforming a firm's management quality into a principal competitive advantage of national economy entails, in our opinion, six essential consequences:

1. A business process as a whole could be represented as a system of equations and inequalities, in which it appears to be an object of simulation modelling that allows for each firm to develop a most reasonable mechanism for the purposes of preparing and optimising the management decisions, forecasting, planning and control, capital and cost budgeting, *monitoring* (permanent observation and analysis) the competitive positions.[1]

A network management approach results in a much more controllable and predictable economic process within a firm but requires the application of operations research, linear and dynamic programming, and systems-analysis techniques on a daily basis.[2]

2. The concentration and integration of regional and national markets improved a part and modified a nature of marketing. It appears to be of global nature as even medium- and small-scale firms have to predict a behaviour of foreign competitors and customers. The price competition is increasingly accompanied with a contest for a higher efficiency in using the goods and services. The marketing effort turns out to be more and more aggressive, it is destined not only to examine the prevailing customer needs but also to identify their problems and supply modern products and technology on that basis. The 1990s have seen enormous growth of *benchmarking*,[3] i.e. the target programmed management of administrative projects intended to satisfy the needs of specific customer groups, occupy new market segments, perform large-scale contracts, etc.

3. A structure of the firms evolves. They identify some profit and cost centres implementing an entire process cycle of creating a product (service) or some finished part of it. Profit centres make their own decisions towards the expenditure of resources (concerning the costs charged to their account) and the performance of extra orders (in excess of the firm's task). Such decentralisation modifies radically a management accounting system (e.g. instead of aggregated accounting they have a system accounting for each of the above centres, market segments, investment projects, product types) as well as the functions of a firm's

---

[1] Armistead, C., Rowland, Rh. (Eds.) (1996): Managing Business Processes. New York; Scholz-Reiter, B., Stickel E. (Eds.) (1996): Business Process Modelling. New York

[2] Solomon, N. (1991): Dynamic Strategic Planing Methodologics for Mid-Size Growht Organizations. Oakland; Lucas, M. (1994) Information Systems Concepts for Management, 5th Edition. New York

[3] Polstadas, A. (Ed.) (1995): Benchmarking: Theory and Practice. London

general-purpose subdivisions. Now *strategic* and *financial investment* management predominates. A bookkeeping department consolidates with the economic and planning and financial departments and transforms into an accounting, analysis, forecasting and financial management division. It also serves as an intracompany bank keeping the profit and cost centres accounts, effecting the payments between them.[4]

4. A part of business associations is increasing which consolidates (either in full or in part) the capitals of firms and discharges those management functions which are capable of effective centralisation. The internationalisation of markets, an increasing share of global products (e.g. computer, electronic and office facilities, transportation means, drinks, tobacco and confectionery items, medicines, cosmetics, semi-finished goods) put in the forefront such transnational corporations as *holdings* (a financial centre owns a controlling shareholding in the subsidiaries), *concerns* (all of strategic, investment, innovation, financial and part of production management is centralised), *trust structures* (a TNC's participants assign their shares in trust of a specially established management company on a voluntary basis) or those based on the cross-owned shares.

Late in the 1990s, *virtual companies*[5] started progressing in which the co-operation in setting up an engineering complex (e.g. a computer system) proceeds based on a long-term contract and permanent data exchange via Internet free of any newly established corporation and bulky administration structures. This allows integration of the advantages of the large-scale business (e.g. a customer is offered a complete process system with a full set of services, including warranty repairs and personnel training) and those of a small-scale company (e.g. targeted specialisation, operation management, lower overheads, consolidated employees).

A drastic growth in the diversity of goods and services leaves no chance to the firms to specialise by product. Each of them, sometimes using the same process line, has to produce a diverse range of goods, moreover, in small lots (specialisation by process type or customer group). This improves a part of the associations in the macro-economic regulation of the entire areas of business activity, interindustry complexes, etc. Relying upon the associations, consulting with, and rendering every assistance possible to them, the government can ensure a planned development of the economy.

5. The knowledge, skills and behaviour of employees now predetermine a firm's competitive ability. It appears to be not only a manufacturing and commercial but also *a training complex.*[6] A part of "golden collars", i.e. technician workers who

---

[4] See: Hammer, M. (1996): Beyond Reengineering: How the Process-Centred Organization Is Changing Our Work and Our Lives. New York
[5] Dawidow, W. (1992): The Virtual Companies: Structuring and Revitalizing the Companies for Management the 21st Century. New York
[6] Pedler, M., Burgoyne, J., Boydell, T. (1997): The Learning Company: the Strategy for Sustainable Development, 2nd Edition. New York; Kirk, K., Kirk, L., Newstrom, S.

know the fundamentals of mathematics, informatics, as well as natural and engineering science, is expanding. The personnel training both with or without work interruption (e.g. professional colleges, courses to obtain a certificate, remote education, practical training) appear to be the most efficient type of investment. Over 80% employees in USA, Japan and South Korea have graduated from a secondary school, and half of them are graduates of a secondary professional school.

6. A new (in the opinion of some economists, revolutionary) trend of management theory and practice by the end of twentieth century seems to be *reengineering*,[7] being the systematic and continuing renewal of products and technology based on improving structures of management (especially of product quality and finance) as well as the promotion of long-term competitive advantages related first and foremost to a labour and management culture.

The restructuring of the enterprises in the CIS countries means their conversion into firms of a market type. To this end, however, the economy itself has to transform into that kind of a market type.

Fundamentals of pseudo-market economy. The economy of Russia, Ukraine, Belarus and other countries of the CIS is not of an administrative command type any longer, but it is not of a market type either, at least to the extent specific to the countries of East Europe and the Baltic countries. Here the producers and consumers behave in a way other than they should under a market theory of rational expectations.

Money is not a universal and principal payment means. In Russia, according to the computations of the Central Bank, 40% of the total amount of deals in the mid-1990s fell on antediluvian barter (direct exchange) transactions, 30% was secured by means of money substitutes (e.g. unsecured financial bills, tax clearings), 15% by means of foreign currency (mostly, U.S. dollar and German mark) and only 15% by means of national currency.

A free competition, even though in its oligopolistic form, is missing in main markets. As little as 10% of companies concentrate almost 75% of total sales and 80% of the capital (a monopolisation extent is 7.4 times as much as in USA), whereas 84% of the turnover falls on raw materials, semi-finished products, energy resources and transportation thereof, and only 7% on machinery and equipment. These companies settle their basic problems (i.e. an access to natural resources, pipelines, budgetary funds) not in the market but with the power bodies, including those of the Mafia.

(1997): Training Games for the Learning Organisation. Organisational Behaviour, Human Behaviour at Work, 10th Edition. New York
[7] Stein, N. (1996): Reengineering the Manufacturing System: Applying the Theory of Constraints. New York; Hammer, M. (1993): Reengineering the Corporation: a Manifesto for Business Revolution. New York

A profit is not a goal of the activities carried out by most companies. A majority of them belong to anonymous financial holdings that are almost not concerned about the production management, reducing costs, paying dividends and increasing rate of return. Their goal is to monopolise the cash flows, depreciation funds (in 1996, the latter exceeded $50 million, and in 1997, owing to the revaluation of fixed assets, the same doubled), etc. The goods and services are sold through numerous intermediaries permitted to show the lowest income and taxable profit on their accounts, and to transfer the bulk of proceeds to foreign banking accounts.

The most important kinds of wealth (i.e. land, water, real estate) have no real market value. The administrative revaluation of fixed assets diverted a book value from an actual one. An annual average sales of goods and services per employee amounts to $30,000, whereas this figure is lower that in other countries of the CIS (e.g. $435,000 in USA). At the same time, the labour remuneration is lower than the world levels in several industries to a greater extent than the productivity which is partly compensated for by means of low charges for housing and utilities.

The system of economic liability of market agents for performance under contracts, debt repayment and inflicted damages has been inefficient. Only several hundreds of almost 4000 laws regulating developed market economies have been adopted in CIS member countries, often easily modifiable (and reversible) and not immediately enforceable without multiple instructions, interpretations, etc.

Because of a low professional and geographical labour-force mobility, a labour market does not exist. A housing market is just starting to operate and the manpower education system has been destroyed. A production decline is not accompanied with an appropriate personnel cutback; thus, the unemployment is mostly latent.

A shadow economy accounts for up to 40% GDP, and more than 40,000 firms are under direct control of criminal structures.

Everything mentioned previously provides no chance to import a foreign experience of management and reengineering to the CIS, though one must study those structures anyway. The words of advice by highly remunerated consultants from abroad seem to not be understood. There is nothing to do but wait (nobody knows how long) until the CIS economy becomes a market one or train managers to operate in the existing environment.

A high shadow economy percentage reduces the authenticity of any figure indicating production dynamics, unemployment rates and actual earnings. Judging by electric power output (in which generation and consumption are synchronous and there is no chance to conceal both), industrial output and GDP shrank in the 1990s by one third as compared with a reduction by half as it was held. At the same time, a share of exports in the GDP, as per the data of the Foreign Economic Research Institute of the Russian Academy of Science, increased from 5% to 7%–10% (in view of an actual purchasing power of currencies).

Thus, a pseudo-market economy of the CIS features not only and even not so much a quantitative fall (in many respects, it was predetermined by a reduction of the non-competitive production facilities and excessive output of weapons) as it does negative qualitative variations in the research intensity of production, employment pattern and intellectual potential of the nation.

8.2 Major Trends in Firm Restructuring

Evolution and use of property rights. Formally, most enterprises in Russia, in the mid-1990s, and in most other countries of the CIS in the late 1990s, are non-governmental, i.e. private property. However, most of them have not got a real "master", or an entrepreneur, e.g., an owner who is interested in long-term performance of an enterprise, not only in short-term money benefit. Evidence of that is a low share of reinvested profits, i.e. those spent on production expansion and development. Frequently, directors and their close associates who are not legal owners and have no required qualifications dispose of a firm's assets and earnings for their own benefit. The employees holding a majority of shares do not really decide anything. Outside shareholders whom the directorate regards as undesired persons are sometimes deprived of any necessary information.

To settle those problems, the rights and responsibilities of founders, owners, managers and lessees should be distinguished clearly. *A founder* is an individual or legal entity that incorporated the firm and contributed resources into its authorised capital stock. It is responsible for the correct execution of documents; however, it may either sell or assign its rights of the owner subsequently.

An owner is a registered present proprietor of the capital (e.g. shares, stocks) who has an exclusive right to decide on any modification of the articles of association and authorised capital stock (e.g. a new issue of shares, extra contributions), rearrangement or liquidation of the firm (e.g. opening and closing of branches, divisions), net profit (including dividend) distribution, sale and purchase of major blocks of shares, hire of executive officers (managers) and general strategy of the firm. Any variation in the body of owners, including sale and purchase of shares, must be registered not with the personnel department, as happens from time to time, but with a special governmental agency (land and other real estate) or a depository company licensed by the government (shares and other securities).

A manager (including a director) is in command of the property pursuant to a legal deed (e.g. contract, trust agreement, proxy statement) in which it must be specified which operational decisions (e.g. a production range and level, supplies, sales, personnel recruitment and remuneration) the manager is entitled to make without permission of the owner while still being liable for the earnings, profits, production upgrading and job number dynamics. The development of trust relationships and management under contract is especially urgent for the CIS countries.

A lessee, as opposed to an owner, is liable for its undertakings not by means of all the property, but of its revenues and acquisitions made at the cost of it. Any leased property must be redeemed at its market value (in view of anticipated revenues and prices of similar assets) as opposed to formal book value as it has been thus far. The issues of compensation for improvements in the leased property, rent adjusting subject to inflation rates and property tax payment procedure should be settled.

The property relationships are implemented in *contracts* for delivery of goods and services. A duly executed contract must provide for any kind of potential damage that the parties may cause to each other, as well as the appropriate payment and liability types. Before any contract is entered into with a new partner, its solvency should be verified with the assistance of consulting companies. In case of any delay in payment (an average term between the delivery of goods and the payment for the same is 32 days in the EU countries) a promissory note is to be drawn. All those market economy truisms are often ignored in the CIS countries, though not for the reason of lacking knowledge, but deliberately to conceal commodity flows that are violating the rights and benefits of the owners in the jungle of barter transactions and non-payments.

The State exercises its owner's rights worst of all. Its interests in a joint stock company should be represented not by a director or a ministerial executive officer on a voluntary basis but a skilled professional. Only then will the budget receive the revenues due it, and the natural wealth will be preserved for the forthcoming generations. A right to lease (concession) State property as well as to orders and subventions at the budget cost must be granted to firms only based on a public contest under the requirements announced beforehand.

Transition to international accounting standards. By far, several accounting systems have been operational in the world, among which one could point out the Anglo-American, the West European Continental Systems as well as the Soviet System designed to report to the Government bodies the performance of the targets established by them. The expansion of foreign economic relations compelled many firms of the CIS to recalculate their data according to the Western procedures or even maintain a parallel, dual accounting system. The adoption of common accounting standards by the international community late in the 1990s allows transition to a new, commonly recognised accounting system.

First of all, it stipulated for an open, transparent data on the total value and structure of assets and liabilities (under a uniform classification), equity and share capital, debt, total revenues, gross and net profits, dividend, total staff numbers and payroll. The joint stock companies are bound to publish such data, and the other firms must communicate the same at the request of investors, creditors and shareholders. The data authenticity will be certified by an external audit, and in case the shares are quoted at a stock exchange, by a further financial analysis (listing). At the same time, a commercial secret to be protected carefully are the details of specific deals (amounts of supplies and sales, the addresses, prices, payment terms thereof), engineering processes, production and management organisation, labour remuneration types and cost calculations.

The new accounting standards will establish another procedure of accounting (based on the time of any deal transacted), valuation of assets, including, for example, land plots and buildings (at market value), itemisation of amounts payable, accounting of reserve funds, due payments, and income and profit structure.

Of special importance will be the introduction of the management and tax accounting along with the financial accounting. The *management accounting* (maintained by a special office) is designed for operative decisions to be made by a firm's managers. That is the reason it is maintained in real time (every day) rather than for a previous month or quarter, and is kept separately by product type, intracompany profit and cost centres, investment project and market segment. It is not limited to current cost figures but includes data on labour and material expenditures, output and sales of different product types, prices and other positions of the competition. Everything mentioned previously is a commercial secret. The *tax accounting* is required to plan for a most reasonable structure of business activities allowing reduction of a tax share in the value added subject to the existing laws. It includes the accounting of taxable revenues (e.g. sales, profits, earnings from dividends, deposits), expenses (payroll), property and value added.

The modern cost accounting techniques (e.g. direct costing), when applied in the CIS countries, shows three features:

1. The costs are calculated promptly, though less accurately. A normative technique permits identification of any deviation from the fixed figures and enables appropriate decisions to be made. The conventional techniques supply the data by the middle of the next month only, and everybody knows there is no sense in shaking your fists when the fight is over.

2. The modern accounting techniques permits analysis of the process of forming costs, revenues, and profits, while separating direct costs and an appropriate *gross profit* (sales less claims, direct material and labour costs, manufacturing overheads), total manufacturing costs and *operational revenues* (a gross profit less depreciation costs and company overheads), a total prime cost and a *book profit* (subject to non-manufacturing revenues and expenses).

3. A total prime cost and rate of return for each product, project, etc. Many firms of the CIS are still unaware of which activity types generate profits, and which cause losses to them, as many expenses (research and development, interest on investment credits, advertising, marketing, representation, commercial risk insurance, software acquisition, personnel training) are not included in a prime cost in full. In particular, it applies to the transaction costs that are an increasing percentage of the costs all over the world.

Of principal importance are the government controls over the costs of natural monopolies. For lack of such control, the energy, gas, transportation and other companies and industries included in their prices the expenses for extraneous activity types (e.g. agriculture), acquisition of property abroad, mass media, financial investments, excessive administrative staff maintenance, etc. As a consequence, the tariffs on electricity and railway carriage exceeded the average world rates, which resulted in a reduced competitiveness of the chemistry and metallurgy as well as forestry complexes, aggravated the non-payment crisis and shrank the market. (In the 1990s numerous foreign orders for container carriage via the Trans-Siberian Railroad decreased by a factor of 10).

Enhancing investment attractiveness of manufacturing firms. A central problem of restructuring the firms still is to raise investments to upgrade equipment and technology, including expenses for the refreshment training or substitution of managers and the improvement of professional skills of all employees. As per the surveys data on the five central regions of Russia in the mid-1990s, as low as 10% of the firms performed or outlined some important production upgrading, even in the areas of machinery and instrument engineering.

By the late 1990s, for the reasons of physical depreciation and obsolescence, the equipment and buildings of most enterprises will not be valid as real mortgage for investors and creditors. Any product (except for raw materials) manufactured by equipment more than 10 years old (as per the data of the World Bank, an average equipment obsolescence period is 6 years, and for the research intensive industries the figure is 3 years) is not competitive.

To increase a mortgage value of the assets, it is necessary to add the land plots. The laws of Russia and some other countries of the CIS permit the buy-out of the same to the firms, with a portion approximated for a rental of 10 years. The price of a plot wherein the enterprise is located amounts in European countries to approximately 50%, and under the CIS circumstances could amount to 80%, of the total value of fixed assets.

For many firms, of great importance is the valuation and inclusion of their intangible assets, especially know-how, into a balance sheet. A specific example is a research institute of Saint Petersburg which developed an original measurement device. In the course of setting up a joint venture with a German company to produce the devices, the institute's contribution (premises, water supplies, waste disposal systems, power supplies) was estimated as 10%, and a share of the foreign party (new equipment, precision materials, working capital) as 90%. After the Russian know-how was estimated by an independent foreign agency, the ratio reversed. The research institute consented to include only part of its know-how value into the assets of the joint venture being established, and as a result, the profits were distributed in equal proportions.

The intangible assets taken into account will permit increase of a depreciation fund and, proportionately, decrease of a taxable profit, if an immovable property is subject to taxation rather than the total assets. In this case, of principal importance is the introduction of corporate, and then government, control over the targeted spending of the depreciation fund. As per our data, more than 80% of the aforementioned fund was spent for the current needs as well as the acquisition of non-productive assets (securities, rest houses, elite housing). In many foreign countries, the fund is kept in a separate account and spent for equipment renewal and upgrading purposes only.

When manufacturing any product competitively in the international markets, an important tool to improve an investment rating is product sharing agreements. In this case, an investor using a relevant trading (distributor) company secures the repayment of its capital, a firm retains the title in its products (as opposed to a tolling scheme being widespread in aluminium and other industries where an investor monopolises all types of supplies and product sales).

A government support of investments implies the identification of priority investment areas (technology of critical importance, export products, depressive regions) where the imports of modern equipment is not subject to taxation. The same applies to the duties on imports of any equipment and component parts that are not produced in the country. Indeed, it calls for the development of some centres to estimate a competitive ability of the national economy and its engineering structures as is the case in many countries. However, a simplified procedure whereby the benefits are granted to all the foreign investments, including those aimed at the purchase of domestic enterprises for the purposes of their subsequent shrinking, changing their profile, resale or shutdown, and the duties equally affect both the competitive and developing imports, is only an obstacle to an actual restructuring process.

The firms of the CIS need, first and foremost, a new structure to administer the co-operated supplies that is able to replace the former centralised supply and sale system. In the 1990s, many efficient complexes to develop and produce aeroplanes (Russia, Ukraine, Uzbekistan, Georgia, Belarus), ships (Ukraine, Russia, Kyrgyzstan, Baltic countries), electronics (Ukraine, Russia, Baltic and Transcaucasian countries) and missiles and space vehicles (Russia, Ukraine, Armenia, Azerbaijan and others), as well as cars, disintegrated. In numerous cases the suppliers were monopolists (e.g. silicon of Ukraine, rubber of Armenia).

Then the urgency of the problem declined in view of a production decline concerning the previously mentioned industries, the development of domestic though less efficient production facilities and the reorientation towards some suppliers from remote foreign countries. However, to revive the industry, new forms of co-operation are required for those partners who still need each other. These forms under a modern environment should be based on a mutual interest between the firms. As the practices have indicated, some mere administrative inter-government co-operation arrangements are implemented poorly.

The international practices show the two most widespread co-operation structures, i.e. transnational corporations and business networks (industrial groups). As a rule, transnational corporations were established by major corporations of USA, Western Europe, Japan, and Canada which established new enterprises in the countries featuring cheap raw materials and labour; it is natural that then the enterprises were the property of a corporation as its branches or subsidiaries. In the CIS, some co-operation of different owners is the point in question now rather than any new construction. That is the reason a TNC as a concern or holding is acceptable only in the event that the shares are either purchased (in this way, Gazprom affiliated a fertiliser factory in Estonia) or assigned to repay a debt. The most realistic approach to setting-up a TNC in the CIS is the transfer of shares in trust of a specially established managing company recruiting its managers from different countries. In this case there is no change of an enterprise owner, and only the division of capital occurs. This permits effective management while eliminating any convictions of "national wealth sales" at the same time.

Business networks permit small- and medium-scale firms in different countries to shift from single sale and purchase deals to a long-term co-operation while offering the customers a finished product including technology complexes with a full set of devices and services instead of particular goods and semi-finished products. However, such networks operate successfully only when all the parties perform in strict compliance with the contracts. Any penalty for breaching the contract must be imposed by an international economic court (arbitration tribunal).

A new administrative and legal status of the firms necessitates a modification of their internal structure. If so, a basic cell will be *an autonomous complex team* responsible for the entire cycle of manufacturing a product, a set of parts or rendering a service. For the first time, such teams showed up in the USSR during the first 5-year plans. Then the experience was forgotten, and just in the 1970s an attempt was made to revive a collective labour organisation form. Meanwhile, such teams in Japan, Sweden (Volvo corporation), and then in other countries permitted rejection of the former administrative division of a firm into shops and process areas. The only advantage of the latter is that the uniformity of (e.g. turning, grinding, revolving, boring) equipment facilitated the operations of foremen managing the workers of one occupation. However, nobody was responsible there for the quality of an entire product. A firm's management, instead of strategic issues, co-ordinated the operations of shops and areas, settled numerous conflicts between them and provided for an operational production schedule.

A complex team, headed by either an elected, or appointed upon agreement with the collective, team leader being a foreman will be responsible for the *operational management* (e.g. making of orders to a partner of supply chain, quality control of supplies, distribution of work among team members, service orders, operational planning). A team will hire new employees. The remuneration will depend on a finished product output that avoids making of work orders to each operation and terminates the disputes concerning some "profitable" or "non-profitable" work. Of course, everything mentioned previously calls for high qualifications of the foremen and many skilled workers.

Middle level of management in a firm will be presented by profit and cost *centres*, i.e. businesses, branches and subsidiaries, being responsible for the entire cycle from the delivery of raw materials and supplies to the shipment of finished products, its quality, costs and earnings. The remuneration for executive officers of profit and cost centres will depend on its profits to be calculated as a difference between the revenues (at market or intracompany prices) and expenses. A special inspector (internal auditor) will supervise the cash flow.

The restructuring calls for some fundamental modification of the functions vested in a firm's management. Conventionally, it was responsible for the relationships with government bodies where it had to obtain some less intensive plans, larger budget financial and material funds, as well as the administration of supplies and task distribution among the work shops. At present, various integrated management functions are in the forefront, including the strategic, market (marketing), production, administrative (corporate), personnel, innovative, networking, environmental and financial investment management. All of these functions are the responsibility of the director in case of a small-scale firm (employing up to 25 persons). It is advisable for a medium-scale firm (employing up to 100 persons) to appoint two functional directors, for marketing and production. Major companies appoint professionals for each type of management, and then functional departments, some of which (primarily financial, personnel, administrative, and innovative departments) are headed by directors.

Integrated management. *Strategic management* is a responsibility of a firm's managing director which is discharged with the assistance of a personal assistant or a special headquarters. Firstly, they must assemble a database of the firm's competitive advantages. A technology monopoly secured by means of patents for invention and trademarks permits election of an aggressive strategy aimed at conquering a new market segment through the exclusion of competitors or (in case the latter is impossible) co-operation with them.

Lack of technological advantages given lower costs creates a *defensive* strategy aimed at retaining an occupied market segment based on a price competition while arranging for a technology breakthrough at the same time. In case any advantage is missing at the segment and sales bring a loss, then a planned retreat and appropriation of resources for other purposes are required. That is the reason, for instance, the confectionery factories stopped producing Snickers-like chocolate items with a filler that allowed them to expand the production of modern-packed sweets being in great demand.

Marketing is also a new management area for the firms of the CIS. A forthcoming task will be to assimilate the diversity of techniques intended to study and build a consumer demand, advertising, choose the most rational forms of distribution (e.g. trademark stores, wholesale intermediaries, dealers, direct deliveries to retailers) and its stimulation, after sales service, including the disposal of the products out of use. Of special importance are flexible prices taking into account not only the manufacturing but also transaction costs (wholesaler and permanent customer discounts), a market situation and efficiency of using the goods (royalty prices).

The modern *production management* is aimed at the complex management of product quality based on a targeted impact on the determining factors (design rationality, quality of raw materials and supplies, equipment precision, metrological basis, workers qualifications and attitudes towards labour, process discipline). In doing so, the certification of products and technology is required at internationally recognised centres. A flexible computer-based complex permits prompt readjustment of the production facilities to new orders.

A firm's competitiveness by the end of twentieth century is predetermined in many respects by the development of its human resources. The *personnel management* is intended to be a responsibility of the professionals in labour economics, sociology, psychology, and physiology labour laws. The duties of a personnel management office include the *personnel marketing* (forecasting of staff dynamics, recruitment sources, professional orientation and job advertising, searching for ways of least painful release of excessive employees), *attestation of jobs, personnel selection* (the appraisal of candidate's compliance with office requirements based on documents, tests and private interviews, the entry into employment contracts with selected persons), their *attestation* and *arrangement* (annual, and in case of newcomers, monthly appraisal of labour capabilities, attitudes towards work and its results to shift employees subsequently sent for training, and change in wage levels), *training professional* (initial training, tutorship, training, qualification improvement, practical training), *incentive system* (remuneration system improvements, bonuses, compensations, non-money incentives), labour administration (job rearrangements, labour rating and rationalisation, labour organisation and conditions improvements), *a collective's social development* (involvement of employees in management and profit sharing, competition and creative activity development, conflict prevention and settlement, meals and medical services).

Pursuing an active personnel strategy, the firms select employees at educational institutions, arrange for the professional training on their own premises and enter into long-term employment contracts. When sufficient resources are missing, the firms look for professionals and then single out a core staff (20%–25% of the total personnel) on short-term contracts and a temporary staff engaged for a period of peak loads (for several months, months a week, hours a day).

The innovation management also needs some fundamental rearrangement. It must start from the marketing, i.e. the identification of problems to be solved using innovations, the justification of their sequence, maximum allowable costs and potential developers. Then a manager takes command over the specific innovation projects, including setting tasks, acceptance of work, administration of innovation implementation, protection and, if necessary, sale of intellectual property. Finally, it is required to ensure the payback of the project costs and an improved production research and engineering level.

Financial management is a central link of restructuring. Firstly, the firms of the CIS need to adjust the planning for a cash flow. Such a plan is generally developed for 3 years; while the first year is split by month, and by ten-day periods in cases of major corporations, the second year is split by quarter, and then extended for another year annually. The planning for a cash inflow and outflow permits co-ordination of the flows in time and prevent even temporary insolvency of an enterprise.

Under the market economy, the manufacturing companies carry on extensive financial operations. They issue and distribute shares and bonds, buy and sell government securities, bonds, and shares in other corporations, various currencies, and make out and discount (sell to banks) bills of exchange as well as accounts due from customers before maturity (factoring, forfeiting). Major companies establish their own pension and reserve (insurance) funds, grant loans to customers, especially foreign ones, and to their own employees (e.g. to purchase or build a house).

Utilising international experience, large corporations in the CIS set up special *stock exchange departments* for that purpose (GAZ was one of the first companies in Russia to do so). The small and medium-scale firms cannot afford the same. The qualified financial management is provided by the banks to which some firms transfer their capital in trust. Late in the 1990s, throughout the world, capital of $3 billion was managed in such a manner. As a result, many companies gain a substantial percentage of their revenues from the beneficial deposition of their temporarily free financial resources.

A firm's financial manager (treasurer) is responsible for its relationships with banks, a stock exchange and other financial institutions, a status of the firm's balance of payments, and the control and implementation of specific investment projects. Another manager (controller) provides for the accounting and controlling of the rational spending of funds and utilisation of resources within the firm, the development and execution of capital and current budgets.

The financial management is closely related to the *controlling*, i.e. an intracompany administration system based on the accounting of a contribution by each subdivision and employee of the firm into its final financial results. The integrated management parts are inter-related by means of a prospecting (for 3–5 years or longer) and operating (daily and monthly) planning system including *forecasts* (justified probability suggestions concerning the targets to be achieved by the firm and ways to achieve them), programs (inter-related lists of events ensuring that the target will be achieved and appropriate resource budgets) and schedules (obligatory tasks concerning the release of resources into the production process, delivery of goods and services, gain of appropriate revenues).

The restructuring of enterprises and their conversion into modern competitive firms depends in many respects on the macro-economic stabilisation, while establishing the terms for the economy revival of the CIS countries and their mutually beneficial integration into the world economy at the same time.

8.3 Insolvency and Preventing Insolvency

Insolvency as a phenomenon of market economy. A firm's life cycle consists of several stages. In the course of a firm's establishment and incorporation, of greatest importance is the development of a business-plan with a detailed justification of the feasibility of a new business (a competitiveness of the product or service supplied, a calculation of potential sales levels, most likely price, costs and profits), the investments required, the sources thereof and payback guarantees. A business plan also includes a plan for the firm's organisation (a choice of production technology, equipment, management structure, equipment and material suppliers, and the calculation of numbers and sources of personnel to be employed, especially managers). The quality of a business plan will, in many respects, set a level of the documents required for the incorporation as well. A *memorandum of association* establishes the relationships between the firm's founders (the establishment goals, an amount of contributions and a procedure of paying shares, profit sharing, participation in administration), and *articles of association* defines the firm's area of activity, its production and administration structure.

Depending on the achievements and changes in the business goals, the rearrangement of firms is carried out. It includes their *division* (the liquidation of the former legal entity and the establishment of several new entities based on the division of its assets), *separation* (the transformation of a firm's subdivision into a new legal entity), *acquisition* (the inclusion of the former independent market unit into a firm), incorporation (the conversion of a State-owned enterprise into a joint stock company involving the government, employees and outside investors), and other modifications of the firm's administrative and legal status. Most often, it affects leased enterprises, co-operative societies, limited liability companies and private companies that transform into open and joint stock companies to expand their activity.

The final stage of a firm's life, i.e. its *liquidation*, is implemented pursuant to a resolution of the owners (i.e. in view of the expiration of the memorandum term, achievement of the goals established by the constituent documents, any rearrangements), administrative or judicial authorities (in case it is identified that the constituent documents were executed incorrectly, of any breach of law, and bankruptcy). The bankruptcy is the legal recognition of a firm's insolvency entailing introducing of receivership of its assets to settle creditor claims.

A respectable funeral of the deceased (this is the case for a business incapable to settle its accounts) is necessary so that the living persons can do well. Bankruptcy is a frequent and far from tragic event in the market economy countries. In the late 1990s, under U.S. economic growth, more than 300,000 firms and individual businessmen are going into this situation. As regards the small-scale firms, more than half of them go into bankruptcy or wind up on a voluntary basis just during the first year of their existence, whereas in most cases the owners start a new business subsequently.

The point is that, in essence, the bankruptcy of a firm differs from the death in its common sense. Frequently, the bankruptcy does not imply the liquidation of a firm as a legal entity, but its transfer to the new owners whereupon it is often revived. The purchase of unprofitable firms (indeed, at low price) to restructure and resell them is a most profitable type of business. Bankruptcy is not an instant action. Having received the first notice from its own financial department or creditors, a firm may take urgent steps to remedy the situation. As a rule, neither creditors (in this case they will not be able to recover all of the debt) nor the government and local power bodies (unemployment benefits will grow, a social environment will deteriorate, an output of required goods will terminate), nor the employees themselves are not interested in firm's shutdown. Therefore, the creditors may consent to the debt restructuring (a delay and partial payment in kind, products and securities, and not in money), the employees may agree with a temporary decrease in salaries or purchase of shares, and the power authorities will grant a budgetary loan to the firms of special social importance. (As a result, it is not seldom that the ownership is then assigned to the employees and municipalities.)

The business world knows the five basic types of legislation concerning bankruptcy as the totality of relationships between the business entities to settle a debt.[8] England and its former colonies (e.g. Australia, New Zealand, India, Pakistan, Bangladesh, Singapore), as well as Israel, operate the radical legislation in favour of creditors that is aimed, firstly, at unconditional debt recovery. In the late 1980s France enforced radical legislation in favour of debtors that was targeted to save a debtor firm. In continental Europe (Germany, Netherlands, Scandinavian countries), Japan, and Southeast Asia (South Korea, Indonesia, Taiwan), the laws promote the creditors, though not as positively as in England. In Spain, Portugal, Latin America and Greece, the law permits selling a debtor's assets only after all the opportunities of agreement and debt restructuring are exhausted. In USA the bankruptcy law is notable for its detailed nature and provides numerous *force majeure* (beyond the control of a business entity) events (e.g., a farmer's crop failure) where both the creditor and the debtor are given some extra opportunities to escape losses. The same neutral principle was employed in Italy, numerous East European countries (e.g. Czech Republic, Slovakia) as well as in the European Bankruptcy Convention (1996).

Formally, the bankruptcy institution exists in the CIS countries; however, it has been actually exercised in extraordinary cases only. The main reason was that the government appeared to be a major non-payer with payment for the goods and services purchased and this left no chance to make the firms liable for their debt. In most countries of the CIS, a decision to start the bankruptcy procedure is a responsibility of the government bodies (e.g. committees, agencies). However, they are not able to institute any suit against private firms and especially individual businessmen, and also have no funds to remunerate appointed receivers intended to restore a firm's solvency or arrange for the sale of its assets. The CIS countries apply different criteria (ratios, indicators) to estimate a firm's financial position. Lack of detailed legislation provides no chance to prevent the cases of false bankruptcy, priority debt repayment to particular (generally possessing a criminal "umbrella") creditors only, and also to liquidate unfair business entities the financial accounts of which are deliberately falsified and management is missing. Extensive training and licensing of receivers has not yet been established.

To transform bankruptcy into a real economy rehabilitation media, the Russian law 1998 stipulates the following:

1. The principal criterion of a firm's insolvency is deemed to be not the ratios showing a balance sheet structure (e.g. a liquidity of assets) but a delay in statutory payments (to creditors, suppliers, employees, tax authorities, extra-budget funds) for a term exceeding 3 months provided an appropriate application was filed (a petition for the debtor's insolvency auditing), in case a debt amount is in excess of the minimum established by law.

---

[8] Wood, P. (1995): Principles of International Insolvency. London

2. A decision for the insolvency of any debtor, including individuals, will be made by an economic court (arbitration tribunal), while a deciding vote concerning the choice between the legal entity liquidation or the appointment of a receiver of its assets will be attached to a meeting of creditors, including a tax inspectorate. The insolvency and bankruptcy agency will license receivers, and render a methodical aid in their training, to prevent the cases of bankruptcy, though the government will have the same rights as the other creditor and will not be allowed to recover any debt free of acceptance.

3. A process of declaring a firm's insolvency will be split into four stages:

– A preliminary external audit and financial rehabilitation measures at the request of creditors and with the consent of the firm's management

– The compulsory monitoring of the firm's transactions on the part of *an arbitration receiver* (in the presence of the former management) and sequestration (transfer into the custody) of the assets in case of any attempt to conceal them from potential recovery or to transfer them to some selected creditors

– A turnover of the firm's management and the appointment of *a receiver* (a licensed professional or company) to rehabilitate, and pursuant to a decision of the creditors, sell part of the enterprise as a property complex, dispose of its assets in part or ensure *a cession*, i.e. an assignment of claims and debts to a third party (thus appearing to be a new owner)

– The legal entity liquidation in case all the attempts to restore solvency and escape bankruptcy failed (i.e. there are no parties desiring to buy the assets and undertake its debt) or the debtor's representatives with the relevant documents are absent. (A simplified liquidation procedure will be enforced in this case.)

As follows from the experience of other countries, a time period on the sequestration may extend to 3 months, and that of receivership to 18 months. However, in the cases of major (employing more than 10,000 persons) and *town-forming* (predetermining the employment or the vital functions of the inhabited location) enterprises, the aforementioned time limit may be extended 1 year more to refocus the production facilities, retrain the personnel and create new jobs.

Any non-profit organisation (State-owned factories, institutions) may not be declared as bankrupt, where the government is liable for the debt.

4. Of special importance is a mechanism designed for securing the rights of creditors and employees of an insolvent firm. Its debt will be suspended for every creditor during the receivership period, though interest will be accrued on the debt at a rate of the Central Bank. The previously mentioned delay will not affect any debt related to salaries and wages. In case the assets are sold out, the debt under mortgage (hypothecation) and leasing agreements will be repaid first (after the personnel claims), then come the taxes and the statutory payments to extra-

budget funds. The balance will be distributed among the other creditors pro rata with an amount of debt.

The law establishes which part of the property in possession of private persons and State-owned enterprises will be turned to recover the debt. Numerous publications examine a competitive effect of bankruptcy under a market system,[9] as well as the features specific to a mechanism in USA and to the EU countries,[10] under a transitional economy.[11] A special problem is the bankruptcy of transnational firms.[12]

Monitoring of firm is solvency. To prevent bankruptcy, a firm must observe its key financial economic indicators, analyse them and take appropriate strategic and operational decisions on a regular basis. To this end, the developed economy countries employ 100–150 ratios. The CIS countries should compute 15–20 key indicators under the existing accounting system. Given below is a model list of the indicators:

A firm's competitiveness indicators:

1. A firm's specific weight in the total sales of the goods and services specific to it in a regional, national or international market (%)

2. A specific weight of products provided with an internationally recognised certificate of quality in the total sales (%)

3. A specific weight of export products (%)

4. A specific weight of research and engineering services and high-technology products (with a high share of R&D costs in the product price) in the total sales (%)

Liquidity and debt indicators:

5. A current liquidity ratio (a proportion of cash and liquid securities to an amount of short-term liabilities)

6. A liquidity ratio considering non-payments (accounts receivable to be added to the numerator of ratio 5 less bad debt)

7. Balance of payments (a proportion of overdue accounts receivable to accounts payable)

[9] Lang, L. (1992): Contagion and Competitive Intra-Industry Effects of Bankruptcy Announcements. New York

[10] Mc Bryde, W. Bankruptcy, 2nd Edition. Edinburgh; White, M. (1993): The Costs of Corporate Bankruptcy: A US-European Comparison. Munich; (1994): Corporate Bankruptcy and Reorganisation Procedures in OECD and Central and Eastern European Countries. OECD, Paris

[11] Brada, S. (1992): The Demise of Lossmaking Firms in Capitalist, Socialist and Transitional Economies. Cologne

[12] Wood, P. (1995): Principles of International Insolvency. London

8. A share of equity and borrowed (share) capital in total value of liabilities

9. A current solvency ratio (a proportion of short-term liabilities to current assets value)

10. A debt coverage ratio (a proportion of total liabilities to total value of equity and borrowed capital)

Generally, the short-term liabilities include those to be settled within the subsequent 6 months. The rest of the liabilities are long-term loans.

Efficiency indicators of utilising assets and labour:

11. Return on sales (a proportion of net profits after tax to sales of goods and services, %)

12. Return on assets (a proportion of net profits to book value of assets, %)

13. A working capital turnover ratio (a ratio of sales of goods and services to average current assets value for the same period of time) and an average rate of turnover in days (a quotient of dividing the said period duration in days by the turnover ratio)

14. A return on fixed assets (a proportion of sales and profits to book value)

15. An average shipping period before payment in days (a quotient of dividing a sum of prices of shipped goods by an average daily receipts for the same period of time)

16. A productivity of labour (sales of goods and services per employee, a proportion of profits to payroll)

17. Dividend on one ordinary share in a joint stock company (a proportion of disbursed dividend amount to value of ordinary shares)

18. Rate of shares in joint stock companies (a proportion of share market price to par value)

In 1998 proportions of loss-making enterprises grew in most CIS countries. Even before the collapse of the Russian stock market, they made over 52% in the Ukraine and Kazakhstan, 47% in Kyrgyzstan and 37% in Azerbaijan and Tajikistan.

When analysing the foregoing indicators, their variations in time are of the greatest importance (as compared with the immediately preceding quarter or the same quarter of the past year) along with comparison with the indicators of competitors which are average industry figures in the country and region. In the developed countries, most of those indicators are published each quarter, and share prices daily. In addition to the firms themselves, analysis of them is the business of numerous consulting companies, bank departments and research institutions.

For example, a period of payment for the shipped goods in the EU countries lasts approximately 30 days, an average return on sales amounts to 3%–5%, and that of assets to 13%–17%. A short-term debt generally does not exceed 50% of working capital value (which permits proceeding with operations even after the creditors are satisfied in full). It is deemed that two (three in the most stable-economy countries) units of borrowed capital are allowable as against one unit of equity. In cases of a greater debt the firm is at risk of bankruptcy just because of a temporary decrease in earnings. A firm trying to operate at the cost of its equity only will lose to its competitors in terms of production expansion and upgrading rates.

Anti-crisis management. The development and implementation of programs for bankruptcy prevention, solvency and profitability restoration of a firm is a most pressing and hard macro-economic problem. Such world-wide corporations as IBM and Apple (computers), Chrysler and Volvo (motor vehicles), Woolworth (retail network), Credit Lyonnaise and others had to implement similar programs. In the cases of receivership, a program must be approved by a board of creditors.

The experience gained in the CIS countries makes it possible to single out the basic lines of anti-crisis management under the environment of transitional economy.

1. *Introduction of a modern accounting system, fighting against thefts and labour discipline violations.* Numerous prospective tasks in that area include the promotion of cash flow planning and accounting, intracompany auditing and controlling, and cost budgeting. If the accounting, discipline and elementary order are not established, any other anti-crisis measures will not be successful. The foreign companies that received Djezkazgan Mining and Metallurgy Merger and Karaganda Metallurgy Combine (Kazakhstan) in trust started from setting up a new security system provided with watch dogs, rearranging the finished-product and motor-vehicle accounting systems. All those steps immediately permitted expansion of sales because stealing appeared to be much harder. The factories of Saint Petersburg (Zvezda, Baltika, Turbinnykh Lopatok, Russkiye Samotsvety, Khlebniy Dom) started also with the establishment of an elementary order, i.e. area security, dismissals for the reason of alcoholism, cleanness at the workplace, on the premises and in the yard, purchase of convenient special clothes and uniforms.

2. *Review of a product range based on a marketing data.* It is necessary to stop the production of products out of demand or unprofitable ones and turn the resources to the output of new prospective types of goods and service, having adjusted the accounting of a speed and profitability of their sales. Firstly, they should look for market niches allowing for the utilisation of the resources available. However, if it is impossible, then production *diversification* will be required, which means the arrangements for a profitable business in new areas

that are not related to the former specialisation. For example, Volvo, a Swedish corporation, following a car sales reduction in the early 1990s, closed two assembly factories but started a pharmaceutical production facility.

In Saint Petersburg an optical and mechanical company stopped manufacture of their cameras as they failed in the competition with the imports from Japan, while expanding an output of school microscopes as well as telescopes designed for exports. A subsidiary was established that assimilated a new niche, i.e. the development and manufacture of security alarm systems. Pervomayaskaya Zaria, a garment factory, terminated the output of standard consumer goods for the reason of the competition with imports from Turkey and switched over to sew various articles under orders from Western companies (according to their designs) as well as fashion ware designed for women employed in offices, banks, etc.

Nevertheless, diversification calls for careful computations. For instance, a facility to produce bricks and tiles at Krasnoyarsk Aliminium Factory failed to cover expenses within the scheduled time limit. It seems it would be much more reasonable to adjust the deep processing of aluminium (e.g. thin sheets, foils, beer cans, packing tapes).

Of special importance is the implementation, including with the assistance of foreign investors, of new products allowing set up of a technology monopoly in the CIS market. For example, Mars Factory's command for equipment in Yerevan, which started construction in the 1980s and was completed with the assistance of English, Italian and Swedish firms, has been manufacturing modern control devices, phones and other items. A rated capacity of the factory (3000 jobs) is almost equal to the aggregate output of all the factories of Armenia in 1995. However, the market of the Republic is not sufficient for that capacity.

Sumskoye machine-building company named by M.V. Frunze, a joint stock company, was specialising mostly in chemical equipment for 100 years. However, the number of orders have declined in the 1990s. A principal competitive advantage of the joint stock company is the availability of a large-scale design bureau, a testing laboratory intended for experiments and natural tests, high-qualified personnel and its own metallurgy facilities. With the aid of Italian companies, a closed-loop factory equipped with a computer control centre was erected to produce heavy-weight drilling and flow pipes designed for oil and gas wells, and the complex sets were developed and manufactured for grain storage facilities providing the acceptance from a combine, weighing, accounting, drying, classification and storage of grains as well as those for storage of products such as fruits and vegetables.

The equipment for gas lift production and transportation of oil and gas, well repair, condensate processing and disposal of waste at oil and gas fields has been certified and is in demand in Russia, Uzbekistan, Turkmenistan and other countries (a share of exports amounts to 70%). However, owing to some complexities of co-operation in the CIS, the town of Sumy set up its own production of materials and component parts. Russia, at high costs, set up a competitive production facility for gas pumping equipment, fittings for gas pipelines, compressors and hydraulic piston pumps, though Sumy runs below full capacity.

Given a proper initiative and government support, a market niche could be conquered based on domestic instead of foreign technology. Signal, a Moldavian factory, the production capacity of which was running as low as 10%–12% in the mid-1990s, and the average salary at which was as low as 70 leis ($15), developed, in co-operation with research institute Kbant, a series of security devices which have been sold in Russia, Ukraine and Belarus, as well as an original wind power plant. Instrument engineering factories of Moldova (Mezon, Reut, Sigma, Topaz, Alpha), which performed the important orders of the military industrial complex, may offer some other competitive products provided that a financial industrial group is established. There may be great demand for the equipment of Pischemash, a Kishinev factory, to produce a food fibre preparation patented in Moldova, based on a sugar beet marc, which is helpful in cases of malignant and other illnesses, as well as in cases of poisoning.

Belarus offers a new design of tyres, superseding the French Michelin in terms of some properties. The integrated flexible tractor cultivators of Lipetsk Factory (in co-operation with some enterprises of Minsk) ensure a lower specific pressure on soil and easy control as compared with its U.S. equivalent, John Deer. A bit less comfort is compensated for by low price. Also, road- and pavement-cleaning machines have been developed for the CIS market.

Tashkent Aviation combine upgraded the well-known Il-76 air vessel, having increased its carrying capacity given lower fuel consumption rates and international environmental standards achieved.

Of interest is the history of Voronezh Mechanical Factory, a State-owned enterprise, which employed its experience concerning the space missile technology to develop and manufacture the equipment designed for oil and gas production. Thanks to the high quality and price reduction by one third, the factory won tenders for the supplies of equipment to Russia, Persian Gulf and Indochina countries, and restored the top output figures achieved in 1987.

However, most firms of the CIS do not possess the techniques to carry on marketing research studies, or to develop and implement proper plans and reports. Frequently, even the simplest requirements are not complied with, such as the verification of customer solvency, debt validation by means of promissory notes and price differentiation depending on the payment terms.

3. *Rationalisation of organisation structure of companies and groups* based on the separation or sale or closure of non-promising production facilities and branches, establishment of complexes (e.g. associations, financial industrial

groups) to extend to the entire production process and product sale cycle, and conversion of a company into a holding or a system of profit centres.

Such rearrangement is carried out by the corporations that are well known in the world. In particular, Kia, the third car producer firm in South Korea by size (annual sales exceed $20 billion) faced a threat of bankruptcy in 1997 (its debt approximately $11 billion). Using an extraordinary loan from the government and banks, the corporation decided to sell, divest or merge 23 of 28 subsidiaries, thus cutting down its assets by half, and requested that the employees accept a 50% cut in annual salary on a "voluntary" basis.

Altaikhimprom, a Russian joint stock company, escaped bankruptcy through the establishment of a holding including 17 enterprises, each being responsible for their financial result. In Uzbekistan, Uzselkhozmashholding is known (the production and distribution of unique three-wheel tractors designed for the cultivation of corn, sunflower and other high-stem cultures, 30 and 60 h.p. tractors, and other machines).

The establishment of profit centres is especially urgent for the industrial giants that were the former basis of heavy industries in Russia, Kazakhstan and other countries of the CIS, and found themselves in a particularly difficult situation due to a reduced government defence and investment spending. Thus, Kirovsky Zavod in Saint Petersburg, having lost a government order for combat tanks and turbines for military vessels, was forced to cut down the output of tractors from 23,000 to 890 during 1992–1996. After privatisation, the enterprise survived through the establishment of profit centres that were provided with their account current, and were entitled to operate in the market and pay profits tax. As much as 33 of those profit centres proved their competitiveness. This resulted in drastic personnel reductions. However, the profitable profit centres succeeded in the output of high-quality steel, the production of tractors designed for farmers and machines for the municipalities. A leasing scheme will also allow implementation of new fuel-saving tractors type K-744, which are needed for the farms of Kazakhstan and other grain-producing regions.

Of special importance to the anti-crisis management is to promote a private distribution system, reject numerous intermediary companies, including small-scale firms and co-operative societies which do not produce any parts or production services, though misappropriating a prevailing percentage of the firm's profits and controlling its cash flow.

In general, the foregoing transformations mean a shift from a product-oriented to customer-oriented structure targeted at the search for and performance of orders placed by particular solvent customers instead of at the production of as much products as possible.

4. *Proper arrangement of a financial structure* based on the budgeting of cash flows, revenues and expenses, and the additional issue of securities.

For many decades, Volzhskiy car factory was almost a monopolist in the market of inexpensive middle-class cars in the former USSR. The selling price of a car was five times as much as its cost which was a warranty of high contributions to the budget. Under the environment of great car deficit, any principal car modification was missing (such modification costs approximately $1 billion). The technology was also not upgraded in proper manner as well as the management quality. As a result, the cost of products almost equalled that of a similar class of foreign cars though the quality was lower. (Each car inspected in 1997 by the intracompany quality directorate had 42 defects on the average.) The exports shrank during 1991–1996 from 340 to 132,000 units. Irrespective of the production growth, annual losses reached $400 million during 1995–1997 (including rejected products losses, warranty repair costs and dealer discounts). The amounts due to the federal budget approximated only half a billion dollars.

To prevent bankruptcy, the debt was rewritten as an investment credit for 10 years against an extra issue of named shares. In cases of decreasing prices and increasing sales of new cars equipped with a 16-valve engine, VAZ could repay the debt. In cases of breaching the contractual terms, the deposited block of shares will be the property of the State as a creditor and the latter will be free to sell it to new investors. Such a mechanism is especially important for the town-forming enterprises for which closure is impossible for social reasons.

To escape the transfer of control of a firm over to some new investors, preference shares are issued instead of ordinary (voting) ones. Thus, non-voting shares of the six issue in Krasnyi Oktiabr, a confectionery factory, were purchased by the investors from USA (74%), EU countries, Australia and Russia (approximately 5%). The money is applied to develop the production of sweets at the company's head factory and subsidiaries in Riazan, Kolomna and elsewhere (in total, there are 14 such companies), as well as to set up a distribution network in the CIS regions. As a result, the company competes successfully with the association headed by Babayevskaya factory and foreign concerns.

The same problem occurred to Nairi, a joint stock company of Armenia, for which rubber and water insulation materials are not of poorer quality than those of DuPont (USA) and Bayer (Germany). A rubber reduction cost per tonne from $5500–$6000 to $2000–$3000 allows debt repayment and investment acquisition to develop the production while escaping the transfer of the company to foreign control.

5. *Application of modern management practices.* The development of a micro-economic reform basis calls for the managers who are able to take the lead under the market environment, proficient not only in production technology but also in marketing, financial management, advanced methods of decision support and dealing with personnel.

Each firm needs a team consisting of at least two or three top managers (executives) and five to ten professionals in marketing, modern accounting and finance, administration, human resource development and project management. By the late 1990s, Russia saw as low as 33% professional managers per firm, and the other countries of the CIS saw even lower figures.

The CIS countries make use of different forms to train managers, such as their education at foreign business schools with a proper probation period (part of the costs is usually borne by the international and foreign foundations); their own management schools that are attested and certified, and inviting licensed lecturers from the CIS and other countries; remote education and training being implemented on the premises of a firm with entire manager teams by professionals applying special training techniques (tutors); and the transfer of enterprises in trust with the obligatory employment of local inhabitants.

The modern education techniques include, among other things, an analysis of case studies, business games using computer software of analysis, education course and graduate projects at the orders of particular companies, a system of diversified written and computer tests and group training. Systematic refresher courses both with and without the work being discontinued, especially in the networking, financial and personnel management, international marketing, accounting and auditing, and economic analysis and forecasting, is a must for the specialists of every tier. A high-quality management, labour and business culture is the basis of a firm's competitive ability.

Field of Debate

1. What are the new aspects introduced into a concept of 'legal entity' by the Model Civil Code as approved by the Interparliamentary Assembly of the CIS countries?

2. What are the novelties appearing during recent years in the CIS laws on joint stock companies, small-scale business, business agreements (contracts) between firms?

3. What are the transaction costs? Why does their part grow in the modern economy of the CIS countries?

4. What indicators can you rely on to judge a firm's competitiveness in the CIS?

5. What are the specific features of management in the CIS countries?

6. What is a part of business associations in the economy of the CIS countries? Describe specific examples.

7. What is the restructuring and reengineering of the CIS firms? What are the basic principles of such activities?

8. Which way should you change the environment of activities carried on by the firms in the CIS so that they actually make use of the market economy advantages?

9. What is preventing the actual implementation of the rights vested in private owners in the CIS countries? What are the ways to counteract the development of shadow economy?

10. Which way shall the firms of the CIS countries switch over to the international accounting standards?

11. Which way shall a firm's investment attractiveness be improved in the CIS environment?

12. Which way shall profit centres be established within a firm in the CIS environment?

13. What are the problems and ways of shifting to the integrated (regular) management? What types of the functional management are of special importance for a firm?

14. Why is it the financial management that is deemed to be a basic link of restructuring the firms in the CIS environment?

15. Why is the bankruptcy of the firms an indispensable condition of the successful operation of a transition economy? What are the specific features of the restoring mechanism for the firms under a transition economy in the CIS environment?

16. What are the ways to forecast a firm's solvency in the CIS environment?

17. What is a part of the anti-crisis management in the economic integration of the CIS countries? Analyse the examples of successful anti-crisis management and restoration of a firm's competitiveness in the regional and international markets.

Chapter 9

CIS COUNTRIES ON THE WAY
TO REGIONAL ECONOMIC INTEGRATION

9.1 Regional Economic Integration in Today's World

The region in modern economy. The term "region" has three meanings in modern publications: first, it is the way to identify an administrative-territorial unit (a district, an area (oblast), a hukimat, a vilayet, a borough, a county, other subjects of a unitarian State or a federation) whose administration is responsible for the living conditions of its residents (e.g. energy and water supply, telecommunications, medicare, housing and utilities). A second definition refers to an economic-geographic region, such as Siberia, Far East or northern Caucasus in Russia, or Pridnestrovie or Galicia in the Ukraine, representing an aggregation of administrative entities united by common environmental climatic conditions, industrial specialisation and transportation infrastructure. Lastly, a region in the global economy signifies several neighbouring states sharing common economic traditions and inter-related economy sharing the single reproduction cycle on their territories, including mining and use of raw materials and energy resources, research, as well as developments and production of research-intensive products. Such hyper-regions are: North America, Asia and Pacific Region (APR), Southeast Asia (SEA), western and central Europe, Northeastern and Central Eurasia (CIS territory), and Africa.

The global experience shows that the formation of a community of sustainable development with highly efficient computerised production and a socially driven market economy is related to the elaboration of powerful integrated groupings creating a common economic, technical-scientific, educational and legal environment that they protect by way of customs tariffs, quotas, product certificates and anti-dumping sanctions. Such groupings are: the EU (15 European countries), ASEAN (nine Asiatic countries), and the North-American Free Trade Association (NAFTA): USA, Canada, and Mexico.

In economic publications, based on the extent of the development of mutual exchange of activities, there are four stages of development of international economic relations: 1) formation of relatively independent national economies; 2) internationalisation of production; 3) transnationalisation of economic development and interstate integration; 4) globalisation of economic activities.

During the first stage (which EU countries had undergone as far back as the nineteenth century, and CIS countries have only currently been completing), a single national market is set up, along with the development of foreign trade in goods which are manufactured in excess of demand in a given country, or require lower production costs. Nevertheless, this trade is not dominant (its share did not exceed 3%–5% of GDP in the USSR).

At the second stage of internationalisation, presently experienced by the CIS countries, foreign trade becomes the benchmark for the national economy, following international, and not national, standards and legal regulations, expanding capital flow, technologies and labour force.

Transnationalisation envisages inter-industry labour division, joint development, manufacturing and sales of goods, rapid expansion of mutual supplies of components and parts (as well as offering services), the development of transnational companies and interstate integration on the basis of customs as well as monetary and financial unions. This is specifically the case for the EU and ASEAN.

Globalisation makes transnational companies the basis for manufacturing and sale of global goods (computers, aircraft and automobile engineering, audio and video techniques, telecommunications, medications, makeup, videotapes, soft beverages and canned food); it triggers development of international environmental and technical-scientific programs, objects of private property, economic institutions, and information networks, and the creation of suprastate governance bodies and uniform monetary systems.

By the end of the twentieth century the *regional science* of studying the conditions, forms, methods and results of regional economic integration has become a very important separate branch of science. According to numerous scientists, the economies of countries are gradually turning into the economies of regions at the turn of the 21st century. Three types of integration are shaping up here.

Communities of states with similar political systems and similar levels of economic development (e.g., EU) create suprastate entities to facilitate integration in all spheres of life by reconciling national and global interests. Although EU has concluded special agreements with numerous northern Africa, eastern European, and CIS countries on customs and other incentives, it does not permit free migrations of labour force, or import of competing goods in excess of quotas.

Groupings including countries with different development levels (ASEAN, NAFTA) usually limit themselves by creating a zone of free trade and capital flows, and reconcile financial policies, but do not set up suprastate supervising bodies.

The third type of groupings largely involves developing countries. For example, in the Mercosur group (Argentina, Brazil, Uruguay and Paraguay) the level of mutual trade increased from $4 to $14 billion in 1993–1997, whereas in Latin American Association mutual trade amounts to just 10% of the turnover which is several times less than that in USA. This share is even less in the Economic Community of West African countries. The most successful are groupings with high levels of labour division and relatively low transportation costs.

A specific role is also played by the structure of industries of countries forming an interstate grouping. For example, the EU countries unite economies based on high technologies but lacking essential, according to global standards, raw material resources (e.g. ore, gas, gold, uranium). The ASEAN countries unite their powerful raw resources with high technologies, but the latter, as a rule, are exported from the USA and western Europe. Dependence of Western countries was revealed in monetary and financial crisis of Southeast Asian countries in 1997–1998.

It is only the North American alliance of countries which facilitates free trade in a region rich both in highest technologies and in huge raw materials resources which in part are being saved for generations to come.

The change in economic weights of different countries of the world in the 1990s should be taken into consideration. In 1997, according to absolute volume of GDP, the top 21 places among 209 countries of the world belonged to the USA, China, Japan, Germany, India, France, Great Britain, Italy, Brazil, Indonesia, Mexico, Canada, South Korea, Russia, Spain, Thailand, Turkey, Iran, Austria, Taiwan and Pakistan. This list includes 12 countries from Asia or Latin America.

Region distribution based on population number has also changed. In 1990–1996 the annual increment of the earth's population decreased from 87 to 80 million due to a drop in births in many countries. Nevertheless, the gap between rich and poor countries has widened. The number of people living in complete destitution (less than $1 per day) has increased to 1100 million (almost 20% of population of the earth). One third of population resides in regions short of fresh water; this number is projected to reach two thirds by 2025, whereas the amount of aid rendered by developed countries to developing ones dropped from $55 to $50 billion in 1992–1997.

The biggest concern of ecologists is deforestation and global warming due to carbon dioxide exhaust, methane and other products of fuel combustion. Annually 34 million acres of forest are destroyed by fires and by economic activity that results in the expansion of deserts and semideserts.

The exhaust from carbon combustion products freed into the atmosphere increased from 5.9 to 6.2 million tonnes in 1990–1996. Although 75% of this exhaust is generated by developed countries (the USA is responsible for more than 25% of it), all nations are affected by its disastrous consequences. These include a rise in sea level, resulting in coastal flooding; a decrease in the area of glaciers, which supply water to numerous CIS countries; repeated droughts alternating with floods and storms; and the destruction of the ozone layer that protects living organisms from space irradiation. Destitution in many Asiatic and African countries enhances environmental degradation. Mankind is approaching a point of no return with regard to normal conditions of life. The only way out is to develop and implement international ecological and economic programs of sustainable development of all regions of the world.

The CIS countries by production of GDP per capita are lagging behind the average global level by 50%. Back in 1970s and 1980s the USSR occupied the second place in the world after USA in production of GDP. Republics of Central Asia and Transcaucasia exceed the neighbouring countries in per capita GDP volume. By the mid-1990s the situation changed. According to the assessment of the Institute for Economic Analysis, in terms of absolute GDP volume per capita, Russia occupies the fourteenth place in the world; GDP per capita dropped from 30% to 15% of the U.S. level. Other CIS countries in this indicator are in the second hundred (among 206 countries) being outstripped not only by most of their neighbours and developing countries of Asia, but also by states where rapid economic development began quite recently (e.g. Tunisia, Morocco, Botswana, and Namibia in Africa; Panama, Peru, Ecuador, and Surinam in Latin America). There is a danger that without economic integration CIS countries will end up among the most backward regions of the world in the twenty-first century.

Of paramount importance is not so much the place currently occupied by the CIS countries as the direction they are following now. According to the forecast of the World Bank on global economic perspectives (1997), in the first quarter of the twenty-first century five countries, China, India, Indonesia, Brazil and Russia, will boost their development and will increase their share in world GDP from 7.8% (1992) to 16% at the expense of the shrinking of the share of the currently richest countries from 81.5% to 66%. In that case, these five countries will facilitate the transformation of the surrounding regions.

Regional economic groupings. The key regional trade unions are given below. The end of the twentieth century signifies a dramatic increase in regional economic integration. Creation of ASEAN resulted in the fact that the region occupied first place in the world in rates of economic growth (in excess of 7% and 4% in 1997–1998). These countries, with a population of approximately 500 million and a GDP in excess of $830 billion have dramatically increased their cross-investments and received approximately $35 billion in foreign investments, primarily in oil refining, manufacturing of construction materials, and electronic equipment. Half of the foreign trade turnover (which exceeds $340 million) is made by the republics of the region, and the share of imports from the USA does not exceed 25%.

North-American Free Trade Agreement (NAFTA): USA, Canada and Mexico

European Free Trade Association (EFTA): Norway, Switzerland, Iceland, Liechtenstein

European Union (EU): Ireland, Great Britain, France, Germany, Italy, Spain, Portugal, Finland, Sweden, Denmark, Luxembourg, Belgium, Netherlands, Austria, Greece

Asiatic-Pacific Economic Union (APEU): Australia, Brunei, Malaysia, Singapore, Thailand, New Zealand, Papua New Guinea, Indonesia, Philippines, Taiwan, Hong Kong, Japan, South Korea, China, Canada, USA, Mexico, Chile, Russia, Vietnam, Laos

Mercosur: Brazil, Argentina, Paraguay, Uruguay

South African Committee on Development: Angola, Botswana, Lesotho, Malawi, Mozambique, Mauritius, Namibia, Republic of South Africa, Swaziland, Tanzania, Zimbabwe

Western-African Economic and Monetary Union: Ivory Coast, Burkina Faso, Nigeria, Togo, Senegal, Benin, Mali

South-Asian Association for Regional Development: India, Pakistan, Sri Lanka, Bangladesh, Maldives, Bhutan, Nepal

Andes Pact: Venezuela, Colombia, Ecuador, Peru, Bolivia

ASEAN (Association of South-East Asian Nations): Brunei, Singapore, Indonesia, Malaysia, Thailand, Philippines, Vietnam

Eighteen countries of the Persian Gulf involved in more than 50% of the global trade decided to set up a free economic zone with minimum tariffs and single industrial tariffs.

Asia and Pacific Economic Union (more than 20 countries including USA, Japan, China, Canada, ASEAN countries, and since 1997 Russia and Peru) accounting for more than 40% of population and 50% of global GDP of the world defines the strategy for development of raw materials industries, energy, transportation, telecommunications, human resources, small business, as well as investment priorities, facilitates the streamlining of customs policies, approvals of technical standards and certificates, mutual acceptance and acknowledgement of qualifications. Along with that some more close and narrow economic groupings were created in Northeast Asia which intend to take into consideration the peculiarities in integration for specifically vulnerable sectors (e.g. textiles).

The fourth largest economic block in the world (after NAFTA, ASEAN and EU) is currently the Association of Caribbean States with a population of 204 million and a foreign trade turnover of $180 billion per annum (Colombia, Mexico, Venezuela, and the countries of Central America and the Caribbean, including Cuba). Following the Cold War, the U.S. assistance to Caribbean countries dropped ten-fold (from $226 to $24 million), and these countries are striving to join the single market of America, in line with projections for the twenty-first century, not separately, but as an integrated community.

Creation of NAFTA generated 90,000–160,000 new jobs in the USA just within the first 3 years. By the start of the twenty-first century the USA is planning to include Chile and other Latin American and Caribbean countries in the group. Nevertheless, the integration even with such wealthy countries as the USA and Canada has entailed many challenges both in those countries and in Mexico.

According to the assessments of Institute for Economic Policies, of scholars of Cornell and California universities (Y. Shaiken, S. Faux) the USA lost 400,000 jobs due to the fact that 62% of American companies transferred part of their manufacturing facilities to Mexico where average annual wages, according to IMF, have dropped from $1 to 70 cents per hour over these years (in USA the legal minimum hourly wage is $4.75). The increase of America's exports to Mexico from $18 to $42 billion is largely related to transferring the manufacturing of labour-intensive components to Mexico with subsequent import of finished products into the USA. As a result of the growing import of these goods from Mexico, as well as of fruit and vegetables (by 30%–45%), instead of the previous $2 billion active balance in 1977 the USA ended up with a $17 billion trade-balance deficit. Annually 3.3 million large cargo trailer trucks arrive from Mexico to USA, whereas only 1% of them are inspected at the border. It should be noted that health and ecological standards in Mexico are a lot more liberal in Mexico compared with USA. Of the $2 billion ecological fund promised when NAFTA was created, actually only 1% has been spent.

The *New York Times* published (13 July 1997) assessments according to which it was not the residents of the USA, Mexico and Canada who mostly benefited from the integration, but the 28 largest transnational companies whose revenues increased almost three-fold thanks to relocating jobs abroad. This experience shows that it is not sufficient for effective economic integration just to release market mechanisms. It is crucial to reconcile ecological and social standards beforehand, to bring levels of labour payment much closer to one another, and to set up funds for recovering potential losses.

European Union experience of integration. The population of the 15 countries of the EU amounts to only 7% of global population, but the EU accounts for 21% of global trade (cf. 20% USA, 10% Japan, 2% CIS). The EU is the second largest stock market in the world with revenues of approximately 5 trillion dollars (USA has approximately 9 trillion dollars).

The experience of economic integration in EU countries has been analysed in many publications.[1] Here we identify the principles, forms and methods of integration which are especially interesting for the CIS countries:

1. Objective of integration is a decrease of spending of natural resources and development of human potential on the basis of transition to new technological structure. Macro-economic stabilisation should be combined with regulating of commodity markets, investments, labour force, technologies, information, creation of uniform transportation and energy infrastructure, and monetary system with the potential for political integration.

2. Among key principles of EU functioning are: equality (of countries, legal entities and physical persons), efficiency (joint efforts are only admissible where they result in much better outcome than individual activities), supra-national law (states waive part of their sovereignty in return for consensus principle in making decisions which are compulsory for all; community laws have direct or framework action), dialogue as the basis for decision making (i.e. with trade union, entrepreneurial and other public organisations, local authorities), creation of independent entities expressing common interests (e.g. European Commission, Europarliament, Council of Ministers, Court of Justice), as well as common budget (where 1.2% of the GDP is channelled, approximately half of which is spent for common agricultural policies, and one third is spent for restructuring in backward regions).

3. EU institutions perform both confederate, inter-governmental (Council of Ministers makes final decisions on concrete issues) and federate, supra-national functions (European Commission, Europarliament, European Court of Justice). Decrees of these entities have a direct action as well as a privilege of WRT national laws. Directives of EU executive bodies are reconciled with those laws and are mandatory for concrete countries and companies, whereas recommendations only express opinion of the corresponding EU entity.

The EU Commission supervises foreign trade, economics and finance, agriculture and other industries, controls prices (e.g. for coal and steal), compliance with competition rules, manages the funds for social, technical and regional development, and originates legislative initiatives. Its members represent the EU countries but are not accountable to them, do not fulfil their instructions and cannot be disbanded before the expiration of their authorities.

The Europarliament, which had initially been a consulting body, is currently elected based on direct common voting, it approves the EU budget, supervises the European Commission's activities and adopts stipulations, among other functions.

---

[1] One of the first publications – "Brief Overview of EU" – prepared in 1992 by General Department on Economic Issues and by Legal Department of European Commission jointly with Centre of European Political Studies.

The EU Council of Ministers actually consists of numerous councils which comprise the heads of states (European Council), the ministers of finance, the ministers of agriculture, etc. The number of voices of separate countries depending on their economic power ranges between ten and two. For some decisions (on taxes, labour, immigration, environment) consensus is needed, and other decisions need qualified (two thirds) or simple majority. Expansion of EU resulted in a decrease in numerous issues on which countries exercise their right of veto.

4. Economic and monetary alliance of EU countries started from creation of European Coal and Steel Union (1951) and common investment bank lending and giving guarantees for the development of transportation and telecommunications infrastructure, of backward regions and so on. The co-ordination of budget policies and tax legislation includes a ban on funding governmental bodies and enterprises by way of issuing money, limiting the amount of budget deficit and ways of offsetting it, and limiting of government debt. The EU Commission is in a position to oblige a specific country (which does not take part in voting in such a case) to rehabilitate a situation entailing flow of capital (e.g. to regions with lower tax rates, beneficial terms for lending) and breaking of financial stabilisation. Together with sanctions the funds of "uniting" and national program supporting of financial stabilisation and investment projects are used (especially on development and use of cost-saving information and bio-technologies.

Transition to common currency in compliance with Maastricht Treaty of EU countries envisages achievement of five criteria of convergence: national debt (not more than 60% of GDP), government budget deficit (up to 3%, and 1% beginning from 1999), controlled low inflation, stable exchange rate and interest rates on banking loans. In 1996 these criteria were only complied with by Germany, Luxembourg, Ireland and Austria, with Belgium, Netherlands and France approaching it. Whereas Germany is in favour of profound economic and political integration down to complete denial of budget sovereignty, England supports the idea of Europe of sovereign states with flexible convergence criteria also including level of employment, investment activity and labour productivity.

According to EU plan, beginning from 1999, selected states are to set up European Central Bank, fix national currencies' exchange rates, re-value financial indicators into a common currency, and use it for interbank non-cash transactions. After that, in 2002, national currencies are to be replaced with a common European currency, issuing Euronotes and Eurocoins. It actually means discarding the current functions of central banks and budget systems of EU states.

The European Central Bank is based on federation principle as a system of national central banks having at their disposal major part of treasury reserves. In order to conduct common anti-inflationary monetary policies it establishes the most important interest rates and an amount of compulsory reserves which banks should keep in that central bank. Central bank is independent on political institutions, all national banks are represented in its Council, with each of the banks having one vote.

5. Reconciliation of the national legislation of the EU countries guarantees freedom of movement of labour force, goods and services, capital, as well as of competition. Along with a single external customs tariff VAT has also been unified. Increase in payment for labour resources triggered investments into human intellectual capital. The share of social payments and benefits in 1970–1995 increased from 34% to 40% of GDP (cf. 30% in the USA and Japan), a unified policy of labour and environment protection is conducted. Although there are no limitations on population migration within EU, as well as of housing purchases and receiving of education, migrants from other countries amount only up to 2% of labour force; mostly they are only specialists who are relocating. In employing residents each country gives preference to its own citizens. Cross-accreditation of diplomas is based on general standards of education. EU citizens are entitled to set up companies and offer services in any country, in compliance with the established respective minimum wage and other regulations of labour law. Until recently, permit for residency in another country was given only to economically viable residents in order to prevent the inflow of retired people, unemployed and others into countries with higher social standards. Residence of citizens of the third countries is regulated by national laws.

6. Boosting the development of backward regions is conducted through subsidies for creation of new jobs, development of human capital and infrastructure from Fund for Regional Development and other structural funds (26% of EU budget for 1990s). Their objective is to decrease income differences (in western part of Germany, in northern Italy, in Benelux and Paris region they were by 1.6 in excess of Portugal, Greece, Ireland and some Spanish regions) and unemployment (its level ranged from 4% to 20%). Funding is carried out jointly with national, domestic and commercial sources (EU share is up to 75%) and is channelled for construction of roads and telecommunication networks, water supply, personnel training and small business development (70% of jobs in EU is offered by 14.5 million of companies each staffed up to 500 employees).

7. Unified EU policies in the area of capital mobility, competition, social development, scientific and technical progress, taxation, trade and budgets were formed gradually. At the outset of the existence of payment union foreign exchange of national currencies was limited by current operations: importers had to confirm a real import of goods, and exporters were supposed to exchange their proceeds into national currency on market rate which was kept in narrow range by interventions of central banks. National capital was guaranteed a specific share in a joint venture, and limitations were imposed on a share of profit to be taken out of the country by foreign investor. A free flow of capital was allowed only after overcoming the inflation and strengthening national economies. As early as the 1970s, France, Italy and Great Britain had imposed constraints

during deterioration of their payment balance and depletion of treasury reserves. It is envisaged to set free retail prices, to remove numerous constraints at the resource market only by the end of the 1990s.

There are 12,000 large corporations in EU countries. Anti-trust regulation prohibits them to split between themselves a common market, to make agreements on prices, production limitations, and so on apart from those cases when it enhances technical and economic development, does not deteriorate competition and streamlines customer service. European Court of Justice can facilitate access to a common market for competitors from the third countries in case of the prevailing (more than 50% of the market) EU corporations abuse their position. Major mergers able to decrease competition are under control. There is a ban on State subsidies influencing mutual trade (apart from subsidies for ecology, R&D, resource preservation and structural reforms in backward industries and regions).

Scientific and technical policy is implemented on the basis of 5-year programs covering priority areas: informatics, computer technologies, telecommunications and transportation (42% of appropriations at the outset of 1990s), energy including a nuclear one (22%), industrial technologies, state-of-the-art materials, use of secondary resources, standardisation and measurement methods (16%), health care, environment, living standard (7%), biotechnology and management of agrarian resources (5%), and general projects of scientific and technical co-operation such as human resources development and usage of major testing plants (5%). Study is conducted on the basis of subcontracts, approved plans or directly by EU institutions.

The basis for unified trade policy of EU is a common customs tariff. For the majority of manufactured goods it is altogether insignificant (1%), but there are specific protective practices related to agricultural goods. This policy includes high ad valorem (in percent of commodity value) and variable duties (depending on the dynamics of global prices), fixed minimum prices which guarantee profits to EU farmers and export subsidies enabling them to export goods at prices much lower than the world prices. Also common import quotas (e.g. for textiles, clothes), voluntary export limitations (e.g. aluminium based on agreement with numerous CIS countries), anti-dumping efforts, refunding customs duties, requirements for certification, the rules of goods origin and other technical constraints protecting EU market on the basis of common customs code are valid.

The EU customs regulations envisage a specific order of protection against goods from "non-market" countries which comprise many CIS states, allow to limit valid term of any importer document, to introduce specific conditions and requirements for an indefinite period of time and even to suspend imports without establishing (in contrast to other countries) supplier quotas. This is possible not only at low import prices (whereas the actual value of goods, as has been mentioned, is defined not on the basis of domestic prices of importing country but on the basis of "constructed value" in developed countries), but also at significant volumes of import (irrespective of prices). It is only fair because other integrated groupings apply anti-dumping measures to EU goods even more frequently.

The example of the incorporation of the most developed country of the former COMECON – the GDR – into the Federal Republic of Germany is indicative of the difficulties of integration. Financial aid to new federal lands in 1995 (subsidies, credit and tax privileges) in all channels exceeded DM 600 billion, i.e. 40% of added value in those lands. As a result, the wages there grew from 34% to 70% of the level of the western part of the FRG, whereas labour productivity increased from 26% to only just 54%. Thus, the further expansion of the EU eastward creates serious challenges, since new member states lag much further below the average EU level than did Greece, Spain and Portugal, which "ascended" into the EU in the 1980s. According to the EU program in 1994–1999, the eastern part of Germany, the southern part of Italy, and these three countries have received $180 billion; Greece receives 3%–5% of the GDP, i.e. 400 ECU per capita; and the overall fund for EU restructuring will exceed $40 billion by the end of the 1990s. In order to render similar assistance to countries of Central Europe $50 billion per annum will be required. On average it will be 17% of GDP, including 7% in Slovenia, 13% in Czech Republic, 15% in Hungary, and 34% in Bulgaria and Romania, which signifies a 30-fold increase (from 1.2 to 40 billion ECU) versus the current level. All this will require significant increase of capital injections from EU donors (Germany channels to budget $12 billion annually which equals the overall amount disbursed by the other 14 EU countries), and dramatic downsizing on the aid to its current recipients, and neither of them agrees with that. According to the data from the World Bank, the total GDP of ten eastern European candidates for EU does not exceed the GDP of the Netherlands alone.

Moreover, countries of central and eastern Europe are currently not able to use large structural investments in an efficient way. In the mid-1990s GDP per capita amounted up to $1100 Romania, $1300 in Lithuania, approximately $3000 in Hungary and $6500 in Slovenia. There are great differences in the East of Europe as well where this indicator in the EU countries was 17,300 ECU versus 5500 ECU in six candidate countries. According to projections it is only by the year 2010 when these countries are going to reach 75% of the EU level (including 29% Romania, 36% Bulgaria), whereas Greece amounts to 51% presently. Therefore, EU expansion envisages a lengthy (more than 10 years) transition period and limitations of new member countries' rights to free migration of labour force. Moreover, Spain, France and Germany, in protecting their farmers, insist on retaining social benefits valid for the EU markets of agricultural produce, and import quotas by the end of this century will be increasing by 5% per annum, although this import totals only 1% of sales at the EU markets.

Export

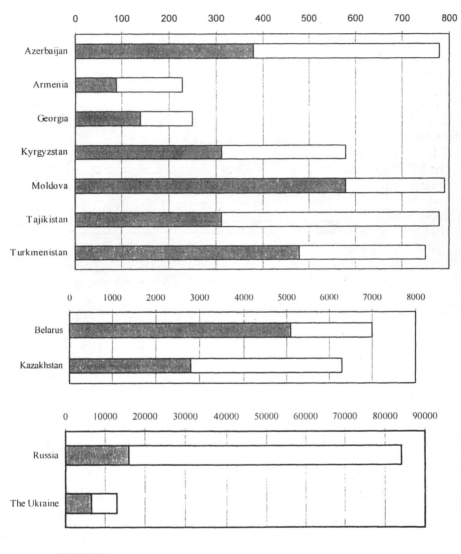

- including to the Commonwealth countries

Import

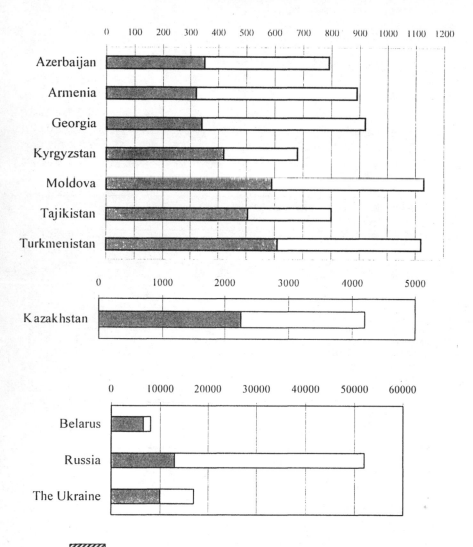

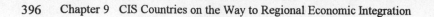 - including from the Commonwealth countries

CIS countries have very small chance to ascend into EU within the next 10–20 years. At the same time streamlined policies can help them overcome unjustified constraints all the more so that new members are liable to adhere to EU common trade policy including tariff, non-tariff and anti-dumping measures in relation to exports from CIS countries.

Thanks to economic integration in 1970–1980s, European Community countries (EC) achieved leading rates of economic growth compared with other countries the world over. But the situation changed in the 1990s. In 1972–1996 the share of EC countries in global trade dropped from 24 to 18%, and by the year 2000 it will decrease down to 14% at maintenance of current tendencies. Primarily it is due to the fact that EC is lagging behind global high technologies (trade balance of EC countries towards this end in 1976–1996 had negative balance of $11 billion, whereas in the USA the surplus balance boosted up from $4 to $22 billion), also in the area of modern telecommunications networks.

Another EC challenge is the insufficient interaction with boosting markets of Southeast Asia as well as eastern Europe. The famous manager P. Barnevick recommends removal of barriers in trading with eastern European countries prior to their ascension into EC, and to open up EC markets for foreign investments, especially for purchasing hi-tech equipment.

At the outset of the 1990s the EC countries were more frequently using proactive marketing strategies at new markets of research-intensive products in order to create new jobs (the number of the unemployed exceeded 18 million in 1998). All this should be taken into consideration in the CIS integrational policies where some countries have deficit in trade with countries which are not members of the CIS (EC members also). Export-import operations of the CIS countries in 1997 are shown in flow charts (in millions of dollars).

9.2 Experience and Problems of Economic Integration in the CIS

General principles of CIS forming. The CIS is an integrated union, one of the world's largest in area and population. At the end of the 1990s, it has produced 4% of the global GDP. If the reforms are successful, this share can grow to 6% by 2005 and up to 11% by 2020. One should remember some essential differences between the CIS-forming process and that of other integrated unions.

In its beginning, the CIS was not a result of integration between originally independent countries, but a way to separate the parts of a uniform country, an attempt to keep the efficient economic relations caused by a common infrastructure, century-long traditions, etc. Russia imported from other USSR republics products manufactured by 102 industries, producing only 40%–60% of the goods (including 18% of weaponry). The research-and-production cycle of building ships, air craft, automobiles, rockets, agricultural and other machinery involved the participation of several republics. However, the rapid and uncontrollable conversion resulted in breaking a lot of these relationships. No attempts to restore the technological chains on the basis of long-term co-operation have proved successful. The trade activities of the CIS countries in the global markets is not co-ordinated either. Joint programs are extremely rare.

Numerous CIS countries, thinking nothing about the expenses, created new production facilities allowing them to do without co-operation. For instance, in Russia (Sterlitamak) in 1998, they mastered obtaining vinyl chloride of ethylene, which enabled it to stop buying it from the Ukraine.

The CIS countries differ from each other in their economic potential. Of their cumulative GDP, 80% is produced in Russia, 8% in the Ukraine, 3.7% in Kazakhstan, 2.3% in Belarus and 2.6% in Uzbekistan. All other seven CIS members together make approximately 3% of the GDP. In these conditions, CIS, and primarily Russia, have failed to create a mechanism of making decisions which would combine the equality of all CIS members and the idea of their unequal economic development level. Due to the absence of such a mechanism, the balance of the current and prospective national interests in every CIS country has been undermined, and no co-ordinated decisions on integration have been carried out.

In the global economy and policy there are three points of view on the expediency of developing supra-national bodies of governance. Keynes, during the crisis of the 1930s, suggested a single World bank, which would actually dictate to national governments their economic policies as a means of overcoming trade and currency disproportions. The Club of Rome of the advanced countries' economic leaders supported this idea in the 1960–1970s, suggesting a concept of steady development in order to rescue the world from the ecological collapse resulting from the unrestricted use of natural resources. This point of view is most popular in the EU countries.

Another concept, developed by Charles de Gaulle, may be considered prevalent in the 1990s. Supra-national regulation, according to its definition, should not essentially limit the sovereignty of separate countries, especial in the currency field. This is what many leaders of the CIS countries think as well.

Finally, the positions of complete national sovereignty are presently protected by few. Even G. Soros, the most daring exchange dealer of the 1990s, has declared the necessity of joint regulation for the global financial market.

The formation of CIS, unlike that of other integrated groupings, occurred during a deep economic crisis, deficiency of financial resources and increased gap between the CIS countries in their economic development level, incomes of the population, and until the mid-1990s, also in methods and speed of market transformations. The largest CIS country, Russia, until now could not and sometimes did not want to support with its resources the integration process. Foreign investments and loans repeatedly exceeded intra-regional becoming for many CIS countries the main source for survival. Trade between Russia and the CIS countries of 1991–1997 fell by almost five times (down to $31.5 billion).

Under these circumstances, leading world powers and numerous countries neighbouring the CIS sharply expanded their influence, aspiring to strengthen subregional groupings unconnected with Russia, making them regular suppliers of cheap fuel, raw materials and stable markets for their goods, drinks and services. Unfortunately, the Russian policy in this regard for many years remained passive, contemplative and not supported with real actions.

A special role in developing economic integration is played by the State. Its help is necessary not only in developing the legal base, but in carrying out specific projects. For example, the transition of metallurgy in Kazakhstan, the Ukraine and Russia to continuous steel pouring (instead of periodic) and conventor furnaces (instead of Martens) will lower the costs by 20–30% and improve ecology. Mining industry and metallurgy require significant long-term investments, impossible without sharing or financial guarantees from the State. Due to their absence, the CIS drastically reduced its capacities in producing concentrates (wolfram, molybdenum, leaden, zinc, tin), and to an even greater degree ore mining (rare metals, fluor-spar, tin, wolfram, copper and bauxite).

Stimulating machinery export requires government credits, insurance of long-term commercial and political risks, and state guarantees at participation in international tenders.

Only economic integration will allow the CIS countries to become equal partners in the global economic community. The experience of the Central European countries earlier that the ex-USSR entering the path of reforms shows that their separate attempts to push their way into the markets of even the nearest western European neighbours proved as a rule unsuccessful. New applicants for a worthy place in the world economy are compelled to deal not with separate countries, but with integrated associations of states, each connected with rigid obligations on protecting common economic space via co-ordination of customs policies, export quotas and discriminatory requirements to the quality of imported goods as well as other items. The natural way out of this situation can be either entering the EU (if one is accepted) on the conditions dictated by it, or founding a new interstate grouping assisting in protecting and developing the domestic market, defending the rights of all participants in the world market in interactions with the EU or other integrated associations. An example of such a new interstate grouping is the experience of the seven leading countries in Southeast Asia.

However, it is necessary to remember that not any group of countries can found a competitive interstate association. This association is feasible under two primary conditions: sufficient resources and high technologies. Otherwise, as is shown by the experience of some states in Africa and elsewhere, the association serves solely the purpose of duplicating backwardness. It is important for remembering for those CIS countries which consider it possible to found interstate associations without Russia.

Integration with the Russian Federation, due to its potential, makes both the CIS as a whole and its internal elements, the customs union of five states (Belarus, Russia, Kazakhstan, Kyrgyzstan, Tajikistan) and the Union of two states (Belarus, Russia), competitive. Other unions between the CIS countries uniting Asian (Kazakhstan, Kyrgyzstan, Tajikistan, Uzbekistan) and southwest countries (Azerbaijan, Georgia, the Ukraine, Moldova) are certainly useful. However, there is a question of their being competitive in the global market. The experience of developed Scandinavian countries incorporated as the Nordic Council has shown that even they could not compete in an information environment and had to enter the EU on the conditions dictated by it.

The CIS countries are not being invited into the EU. At the same time, southern and eastern countries and organisations are wary about the CIS itself. Instead of Russia, the CIS countries are offered alliances with Central European countries within the framework of the Central European Initiative (Belarus, Moldova, the Ukraine), or with Turkey (Turkic states), or between Transcaucasian republics as Caucasian parliament. These offers can result in mutual isolation of the CIS countries and Russia, weakening their positions in the global market.

The CIS countries' reaching distant markets can only be welcomed, but the liquidation of industrial and technological complexes on joint manufacture of planes, ships, computers and complex machines leads to economic primitivisation, throws science and education backward, stimulates export of the exhaustible and unprocessed raw materials instead of finished goods and services, and import of consumer goods and machines instead of new technologies. The global market, figuratively speaking, takes away the fishing line from the CIS giving a fish in exchange. Quite often the fish is far from fresh and occasionally given on credit.

The disintegration of the common economic space in the ex-USSR took place spontaneously and rapidly. Recreation of this space on a new basis when integration does not mean centralised administration and uniformity of economic systems is possible only in accordance with a jointly developed program.

The EU was formed as two basic stages: *the common market* (an incomplete economic union) and the transition to *a complete economic union*. These two stages were reflected in the corresponding names: the European Economic Community (EEC) and the EU. The characteristic features of the first stage which had lasted for 25 years since signing the Roman Treaty in 1957 were the creation of *a free trade zone* (unrestricted exchange of goods inside the EEC), and *the customs union* (removal of internal customs barriers with simultaneous introduction of uniform duties and restrictions on trade with third countries) on the basis of free movement of goods, capitals and labour.

Servicing such an incomplete economic association required a monetary union and powerful international superstructure, the Ministerial Council, European Community Commissions, Europarliament and European Court. They were delegated supra-national co-ordinating functions in managing the programs of the European Community on the consensus basis. These programs served the purpose of structural reforming of the economies and were financed from the consolidated European budget.

Since the Maastricht Treaty came into force in 1993, there began the second stage of the West European integration, transition to a complete economic union. This union is based on fully co-ordinated economic policies and a currency union, all-European currency controlled by the European bank, and on the decisions passed by the Europarliament.

The CIS stands only at the first stage of forming a common market, with not all its members participating in this process equally.

The countries which have signed the CIS Charter and the Ukraine form, in our opinion, a free trade zone. Belarus, Russia, Kazakhstan, Kyrgyzstan and Tajikistan, in joining them, created a customs union. Russia and Belarus went along the path of fullest integration, having founded an economic union.

Why do half of CIS members remain outside the customs union? One argument against integration is the opinion that an association of the CIS countries will be viable solely after the market reforms are over. This leads to the idea that the distinctions in the speed and nature of the reforms, such as the political differences, are an unbreakable barrier on the way to integration. World experience shows, however, that integration is stronger than these handicaps. So, socialist Vietnam with a backward industry and retarded market has since 1995 become a full member of the association of Southeast Asia countries, one of the modern world leaders. In its turn, it sharply sped up the reforms in Vietnam itself.

More inhibiting factors for CIS integration are the contradictions of interests between the mining and processing branches. Exporters of oil, gas and other scarce resources do not want to remove customs barriers inside the CIS, cancel VAT in the country of manufacturing, their products being competitive even without that. On the contrary, manufacturers of finished industrial and agricultural products need a common market and protection against external competitors. It is also proved by world experience. For example, Norway has not entered the EU because its oil and gas can be sold without integration. What will be the way for the CIS countries: high technologies or raw materials appendage of the West? Answering this question means outlining the prospects of integration.

Certainly, essential roles in the differing degrees of readiness of the CIS countries integrate is played also by other factors. For example, the main obstacle to the customs union between Russia and Transcaucasian states is regional conflicts. Entering Moldova and Tajikistan into the customs union on geographical reasons depends on the positions of the Ukraine and Uzbekistan, neither a member of the customs union.

It is noted that some economists in Russia, the Ukraine and other CIS countries protect the development of mutually profitable bilateral connections, but against multilateral economic integration, propagating integration into the world economy within the framework of a European or Asian community. We review the reasons of these economists.[2]

During the years the CIS has existed, the share of traded goods flow among CIS countries in the total volume of foreign trade steadily declined (in 1992 58%, in 1994 40%, in 1997 34%), like Russia's share in the foreign trade of the CIS countries and the share of the CIS in Russian export (from 69% to 19%) and import (from 70% to 27%).

The share of finished products decreases, like that of co-ordinated deliveries of units, parts and semi-finished items; increased gets the number of manufactures for which deliveries from CIS and industrial co-operation are of no importance. The share of machinery and vehicles in the Russian export to the CIS fell from one third to 18%, whereas that of fuel and energy grew from 17% to 46%. Joint manufacture of complex and high-tech products is especially sensitive to delays in payments, customs duties and taxes, and restrictions on capital movement. That resulted in the production of aircraft (Russia-Ukraine-Uzbekistan-Georgia), tractor, computer and other industries being forced away from global and home markets.

Having switched over to world prices, most CIS countries became chronically insolvent and have had a constant deficit payment and trade balance. In fact, the CIS countries want only to receive raw materials at low prices, whereas Russia desires geopolitical control over the communications. This leads to the conclusion that the CIS should become nothing but a purely consultative political body.

However, this pessimistic prognosis has not been proven. The prices in the CIS have really grown to the world level. The average price on Kazakhstan wheat has grown by three times, on Uzbekistan cotton (exported to Russia) by 2.4 times, and on Russian oil, cellulose and paper, wood and timber, fertilisers and cars by 1.2–2 times. Petrol from Belarus, and coal, petrol and diesel fuel from

---

[2] Risovannyi, I.M., Krivoshei, G.Iu. (1996): Integration in the CIS: Challenges and Contradictions. Vestnik of Saint-Petersburg State University. Series 5. Issue 4, 36–41 (Рисованный, И.М., Кривошей, Г.Ю. [1996]: Интеграция в СНГ: Проблемы и Противоречия. Вестник СПбГУ. Серия 5. Выпуск 4, 36–41) [In Russian]

Kazakhstan were sold in the CIS at even higher prices than in the world market. As a result, there started redistribution of commodity flows: Kazakhstan, Kyrgyzstan and numerous other countries have increased export to Russia, but reduced to the Ukraine, the Ukraine to Moldova, etc.

Furthermore, the Russian trade with the CIS countries by the end of the 1990s was better balanced, certain countries have begun to repay the debts with counter deliveries and shares of their enterprises. Positive trade balance in the CIS has been observed in Azerbaijan, Kazakhstan and Russia. Many states can cover the deficiency at the expense of their active balance in the trade with other countries.

The financial crisis which shattered the CIS in late 1998 resulted, however paradoxical it might sound, in better conditions for restoring the economic relationships between the CIS countries. Everywhere, enterprises specialising in import started switching over to internal markets, as the external ones appeared inaccessible due to the currency crash and lack of any credits.

In early 1998 the CIS countries' shares in the general import-export volume grew in comparison with 1997 in six countries: Azerbaijan (from 42.7% to 50%), Armenia (from 34.7% to 42%), Belarus (from 71.3% to 76.4%), Georgia (from 55.5% to 59.7%). Moldova (from 74.9% to 76.3%) and Russia (from 18.9% to 20.7%), and was reduced in only four countries: Uzbekistan (from 44.6% to 42%), Kyrgyzstan (from 50.6% to 43.9%), Tajikistan (from 32.3% to 31.9%) and the Ukraine (from 39.1% to 30%).

Serious problems in CIS functioning due to objective and subjective reasons are obvious. Their overcoming requires one to separate out the basic principles of effective economic integration in the CIS.

The equal and mutually profitable nature of new economic connections, on the one hand, rejects any dictatorship from a more powerful state, and on the other, excludes any opportunity for this State to act against its own national interests. The differences in technical and economic development certainly require additional investments in retarded regions, but they should not be simple alms or non-repayable debts or charity, but rather joint investment projects (with the participation of the accepting country, local authorities and common CIS funds), with the long-term prospect of benefiting the CIS as a whole, rather than a separate region.

Each of the CIS countries, as it was proved in previous chapters, has specific advantages and preconditions for successful economic development. Successful integration means using and developing the potential of each republic and every region. Its results should be visible to all.

Legal considerations of integration. An important precondition of real economic integration is a common legal space including co-ordinated economic legislation, systems for arbitration of economic disputes and execution of international judicial decisions.

In the early 1990s the legislative bodies of the CIS countries of passed a large number of normative acts. In Azerbaijan, the list exceeded 170 titles, including 58 on economic and financial questions, in Armenia 110 (38), in Belarus 280 (108), in Georgia 70 (16), in Kazakhstan 295 (124), in Moldova 140 (49), in Russia 390 (140), in Tajikistan 130 (50) and in the Ukraine 300 (120). Certainly, these data are conventional, as many acts regulated repeated changes in tax systems, laws about enterprises and bank activity, labour and foreign investments. However, analysis of the list confirms that of the several thousand laws regulating the market relationships in developed countries, the CIS has no more than a tenth. Furthermore, the laws frequently did not cause direct action, and required numerous instructions and methodical indications, which reconsidered and often changed the sense of the law itself.

In this connection of special importance is the work of the CIS Interparliamentary Assembly (IPA) in filling the legal vacuum, adjustment and harmonisation of the national legislation of the CIS countries. By early 1999, the IPA had developed and passed over 80 model laws. Among the laws were Civil and Criminal Codes, and laws covering major directions of the integration: economy, social policy, ecology, defence and safety, rights and freedoms of the citizens, humanitarian co-operation, education, science and culture.

The model laws developed by the IPA are highly professional projects. They are written by the best skilled legal forces from each State. They take into account the UN, EU experience that of the leading countries of the world and pass international examination. This simplifies the legal work of parliaments and, mainly, harmonises the legislation of the various CIS countries. For example, in the past 3 years Kyrgyzstan used 33 CIS model acts to pass its own laws, Belarus 22, Kazakhstan 18 and Armenia 17; this list may be continued. Whenever similar laws have already been passed by a parliament, it gets amended in view of the IPA recommendations. So, for example, the basic rules of the model laws "On the Government support of small business" and "On protection of the rights of children during housing privatisation" were taken into account by the Moldovian parliament when they modified and amended the current legislation. Certainly, important is not the quantity, but the quality, of the laws. The Assembly, in essence, has already laid the bases for civil and criminal legislation in the CIS. Moreover, the Belarussian constitutional court in numerous cases, when passing its decisions, leaned on its model laws.

Of special importance for achieving the purposes of economic integration between the CIS states under the new economic conditions was the development of unified civil law. In practice, all three parts of the Model Civil Code were included into the national legislation, the model having been drafted by a working group founded by the Interparliamentary Assembly and its Scientific-Advisory Centre for Casual Law of the Commonwealth, with deputies of the parliaments, scholars and legal experts.

On the basis of the IPA Model Civil Code, the Civil Code of Republic of Uzbekistan, part 1, Civil Codes of Republic of Kazakhstan (24 December 1994) and Kyrgyzstan Republic (February 27, 1996). Under influence of these development, the preparation of the first part of the Civil Code was done in the Russian Federation (passed by the State Duma, Federal Assembly, 27 October 1994).

These codes are already about to be accepted as a whole, and their likeness to the IPA model code is striking. The same can be said about the Civil Code of the Republic of Belarus, and those of republics of Armenia and Moldova (they are still being developed). In the Civil Code of the Ukraine, despite its structural peculiarities, a lot of the standards from the Model Civil Code have been used. Important also would have been its conformity with the international standards of accounting and reporting, contract legislation, etc.

The CIS is about to pass a new system of economic laws, corresponding to the principles of international law. Especially important are the co-ordinated codes, tax, land, labour, housing, water and air, financial investment and budgetary.

The CIS countries' constitutions establish the status of legal state and the principle of dividing the legislative, executive and judicial authority. It assumes that the orders, decisions, instructions, letters and cables from executive bodies, including customs, tax, anti-monopoly and central bank, can be considered only as acts of the official interpretation of laws explaining their sense and contents, but not amending, changing or cancelling any legal acts or establishing new economic rules. However, in the real life directives and instructions of administrative bodies are often used to replace existing laws and court decisions for the reason that the laws are too general, and do not include appropriate enforcement mechanism. Public prosecutors are to defend the law, protecting the economic interests of enterprises regardless of their ownership, reviewing complaints about encroachments on their property and wrongful actions of officials causing them damage, especially when addressing the court or the police is complicated or ineffective.

All CIS countries are interested in similar understanding such categories as tax, object of taxation, taxpayer, tax agents, obligations and courts. Simplifying the tax system on the basis of the IPA models along with tax accounting and reporting, unification of payments into social funds and the responsibility for tax infringements will remove double taxation and many obstacles preventing entering into foreign markets.

However, despite certain achievements, the Assembly could not fully realise its potential due to an overtly rigid mechanism of making decisions, insufficient co-ordination with other CIS bodies and absence of tools for influencing the integration as a common CIS budget. Moreover, passing the same harmonised national laws by various CIS states does not automatically lead to integration, but is only its necessary precondition. Therefore, the activity of the Assembly is closely connected also with co-ordinated ratification of the interstate agreements and CIS contracts.

The CIS legal base by early 1998 consisted of 900 multilateral documents approved of by the councils of the leaders of states, leaders of governments and ministers of foreign affairs. The following agreements concern, for example, documents on economic co-operation:

– On separate branches (e.g. co-operation in machine engineering, the Euro-Asian association of coal and metal, manufacture of grain-harvesting machines, interstate manufacture specialisation and deliveries of sorted and hybrid seeds, the general conditions and mechanisms of developing industrial co-operation, co-operation in chemistry, construction, technical rearmament and restructuring railroads; on a uniform policy in transit and safety of natural gas)

– On major areas of activity (e.g. safety in railroads, information exchange on international economic activities, co-ordination of anti-monopoly policies, exchange of scientific and technical information, co-operation in investments, solving economic disputes, mobilisation readiness of the economy, military economic co-operation, co-ordinated railroad tariffs, goods re-export, peaceful use of nuclear energy, development of exhibition and fair activity, unified statistical base)

– On interstate bodies (e.g. the Economic Court, the Interstate Economic Committee of the Economic Union, the Interstate council on protection of industrial property, the Commission on military economic Co-operation), and industrial, commercial, credit financial, insurance and mixed transnational associations

– On specific joint projects (e.g. car factory in Yelabuga, information station in Baranovitchi, radio station in Vileyka)

However, a significant number of multilateral contracts and agreements subject to ratification or other national procedures are still dormant. Of the 108 documents, only 79 have thus far passed the necessary procedures, and only 7 have been carried out by all signing countries. There is a question as to why only 7 CIS contracts have had any effect for all participants. The fact is that they mainly are simply never presented to the national executive authorities. In addition, the mechanism of preliminary discussion of interstate legal documents is often ignored at sessions of the Assembly.

Naturally, it is not only the problem of examination. The parliaments could initiate ratification in their countries determining the priorities of reviewing the laws suggested by the CIS bodies. Such recommendations have been prepared by the Assembly and presented to the council of the leaders of states. At the same time, the 6-year-long practice of the CIS shows that even ratification is not the final stage of the legal support for integration. Unfortunately, even those contracts which have taken effect do not work, e.g. the contract about the economic union of the CIS countries of 1993. The priority of the CIS international treaty on economic co-operation assumes putting national laws in conformity with its norms. That means that signing of an interstate treaty should be accompanied by taking up specific obligations on changing the national legislation.

For securing the treaties and agreements passed within the CIS framework, it would be sensible to develop a special procedure regulating the order and terms of passing corresponding national legal acts mentioning the specific departments responsible for its implementation. It is necessary to develop a control mechanism for overseeing the work along the lines stated in the CIS documents, first of all in the economic field.

Here the Interparliamentary Assembly could again effectively work together with the Interstate economic committee, and other CIS bodies.

A special role in integration is played by the *Commonwealth bodies*. Its structure comprises 64 chartered and other bodies, with 2300 employees in 1998. A special role among them should be played by the interstate economic committee (IEC) of the economic union.

According to the IEC charter, its functions include:

– Preparation of suggestions on adjusting economic and social policies, perfecting industrial connections and joint investments

– Development of joint programs in development and restructuring of the economy, and infrastructure objects (e.g. transportation, power)

– Organising control over the CIS countries' carrying out their obligations

– Co-ordination of standardisation, product unification, protection of the environment, statistics and metrology

– Co-ordination of payment systems, monetary credit, budgetary, price, tax, international, customs, currency policies, anti-monopoly regulations, etc.

In other words, the IEC could carry both co-ordinating and control functions. However, the IEC Charter has not come into force, and therefore the CIS has no tools for organising economic integration similar to those of the EU.

The CIS bodies' inefficiency caused their being drastically reformed, first of all via uniting the International Economic Committee, the executive secretariat and 62 other executive bodies into a single one resembling the European Committee.

The Interparliamentary Assembly encounters endless difficulties. At the first stage, the principle of the Assembly, one republic – one vote, and the necessary consensus emphasised the common interests of all countries making the legal acts better acceptable for all members of the Interparliamentary Assembly. But now recommendations and decisions on the consensus basis reduces the efficiency of the interparliamentary activity in the CIS. World experience assumes consensus only when obligatory decisions are to be passed. Recommendations get approved by either simple or qualified majority of votes.

Numerous parliaments insist on direct elections to the Assembly, and on proportional representation in it. It is extremely important, while reforming the Assembly or other CIS bodies, to use world experience. For example, elections into the Europarliament are taken in various EU countries according to different rules. Election, for example, of a Luxembourg deputy requires 14 times fewer votes than in Germany.

The western European experience of structural reforms in inter-relation with the interstate integration reflects a strict logic of unfolding these processes. The efforts on integration will not be successful if steps and stages are omitted, with all attention focused on separate elements. In this context, understandable is the failure of a uniform ruble zone in the CIS, in essence a currency union, without such necessary preconditions as free trade, customs union and freedom of moving capitals and labour.

Likewise, it will hardly be possible to advance along the way of real integration with the interstate bodies having no co-ordinating functions delegated to them by the Nation States. The opposite is also correct: it is impossible to transform the CIS interstate bodies into something like the EU institutions without the economic basis necessary for this purpose. So, the CIS IPA, whatever the principle of forming its deputy structure, will never play a role similar to that of the Europarliament as long as the CIS does not have an interstate budget. Making such a budget in the EU is the main function of the Europarliament.

On the basis of world experience, the CIS countries must have their own association model. They need a system of not solely national, but also interstate, "brain" centres, involving the best scholarly force of the CIS. The base of such scholarly associations could become the Interparliamentary Assembly and the CIS executive bodies, the Interparliamentary and Integration Committees of the "big five": Russia, Belarus, Kazakhstan, Kyrgyzstan, Tajikistan, and the Parliamentary Assembly, and the Executive Committee of the Union of Belarus and Russia.

It is important that the existing "couples", "fivesomes" and the CIS bodies as a whole would not duplicate each other, having differentiated functions within optimum co-operation. What is, for example, the differentiation of parliamentary structures in the economic area? The Interparliamentary Assembly should legislatively secure a free trade zone. The Interparliamentary Committee must legislatively support the customs union. The Parliamentary Assembly of the Union of Belarus and Russia has an opportunity to reach the farthest and to have a common budget, like that of the Europarliament, formed with payments and contributions, e.g. from national customs duties and VAT. It is natural that the forms and methods of interparliamentary activity among the "couples", "fivesomes" and the whole CIS should vary. While the Interparliamentary Assembly and the Interparliamentary Committee should develop and accept model and frame laws, respectively, the parliamentary assembly of the "couples" must establish the legislation basis. For the time being, there are no essential distinctions between the Interparliamentary Assembly and the Interparliamentary Committee.

The advantages of the customs union with respect to the CIS as a whole are not clearly revealed. There are successes in special problems of introducing uniform customs declarations, simplified border crossings and a uniform system of control over the ethyl alcohol traffic.

However, the participants of the customs union, Belarus, Kazakhstan, Kyrgyzstan, Russia and Tajikistan, cannot agree about the main questions of the customs regimes and tariffs. The prospects are in no way promising either. The matter is, Kyrgyzstan, without having informed its partners, entered the World Trade Organisation (WTO) in 1998 and immediately changed its custom duties according to the demands of the WTO. For instance, the average customs duty established in the agreement between Kyrgyzstan and the WTO is 10% which is unacceptable for Russia, Belarus, Kazakhstan and Tajikistan. All this puts under a question mark the prospects of the customs union.

In 1997, due to the tariff and tax disagreements, the mutual goods exchange between the "foursome" countries decreased by 30%. At the same time, that between Russia and Belarus grew by 40% and amounted to approximately $10 billion.

In this connection, of special interest is the activity of the Executive Committee and the Parliamentary Assembly of the Union of Belarus and Russia. These bodies develop and introduce unified customs codes and laws on customs duties. Before 2000, their tasks include:

– Unifying the legislation on land ownership

– Adapting standard legal documents on supporting small businesses, protecting domestic manufacturers, developing competitive environment and supporting export

– Unifying the legislation regulating pricing forming, developing commodity markets, as well as standardisation and certification of the products sold in the union's internal market

– Realisation of a uniform tariff policy in transportation, communication and power resources

– Completing forming of a payment union, and then a currency union, to found a union bank

Solving these and other tasks assumes establishing absolutely new bodies of integration.

So, the Parliamentary Assembly of the Union includes equal numbers (20) of parliamentarians from each country, and the quorum requires the presence of not fewer than two thirds of the delegates from each. Decisions are passed by the qualified majority (not less than 75% of votes of the session participants). Such an order takes into account national interests of all countries participating in the union. The sessions take place at least twice a year intermittently in Russia and Belarus. Russia and Belarus plan to enter the twenty-first century as a single united State.

The EU countries have signed only 60, whereas in the CIS there are 1200 agreements, chiefly of recommendationary nature. But the legislation of the various EU countries have almost 1500 acts following from these agreements. In the CIS most joint decisions have never become laws.

Meanwhile, the world practices still wider uses of geoeconomic approach, according to which integrated groupings win in the global competition not by military means (e.g. capturing new territories), and not via protectionist defence (restrictions imposed on foreign companies), but with attacking strategy.

Geoeconomy is a science of the forms and methods of increasing the international competitiveness of states. It recommends for this purpose developing regional infrastructures as well as educational, scientific and technical levels of the economy, technological control and non-tariff obstacles.

Benefits and challenges of integration. To the achievement of the CIS firstly one should attribute the fact that due to a political union and mutual deliveries of vital power resources and food, the young CIS states have created their own authorities, national markets with appropriate infrastructures, became participants in the global economy and developed their foreign trade potential; however, by 1998 only three CIS countries, Russia, Kazakhstan and Azerbaijan, had had positive balances, i.e. the excess of export over import.

Although the CIS has up to now not solved all conflicts in its territory, by the end of the 1990s its countries have become fully sovereign, having overcome the "dependence complex", keeping at the same time a uniform system of transportation and communications, certification and standardisation and statistics.

The main problem for integration remains the increase of international connections over the ones within the CIS (see Table 28), while the basic form of those connections in the CIS remains trade (power resources, raw materials and food), instead of joint development and manufacture of complex high-tech products or designing and investing into joint projects. It was only in Belarus, Moldova and Kyrgyzstan that the CIS occupied a favourable position in the foreign trade. In 1997 the share of the "far abroad" countries in the total goods exchange of the CIS countries grew to 73%, in import to 61%. For 3 years the share of the CIS countries in Azerbaijani foreign trade has been reduced from 62% to 35%, and in Armenia from 52% to 32%. In 1997 four countries exported to the CIS less than 40% of the total (Armenia, Uzbekistan, the Ukraine, Russia), and five countries imported less than 40% (Armenia, Georgia, Russia, Turkmenistan, Uzbekistan).

Before the 1990s, Russia had supplied the countries of CIS with 12%–13% of their industrial products, including one sixth of all machinery, or by two to three times more than to the "far abroad" countries. In 1992–1993, national currencies having been introduced due to the lack of accounting mechanism, co-operation between companies virtually stopped, with only deliveries on interstate agreements left. Then these deliveries began to get reduced, too, because of no money in the budgets and in connection with new suppliers from "far abroad" countries entering the market, who offered goods on credit, without advanced payments, and often with generous commission for assistance. However, with the support of commercial banks direct contacts between companies with payments effected in national currencies began, on barter or (seldom) in hard currency. Nevertheless, Russia reduced import from the CIS (by 8%); its foreign trade is to the greatest degree among all other CIS countries focused on the "far abroad" countries (export 81%, import 73%). However, it is Russia that up to now remains the basic trade partner of the CIS countries.

In the EU the share of mutual trade was in the mid-1990s 61% of the total export volume, in the North American Free Trade Association 45%, but in the CIS, less than 30% (in 1990, 72%). At the same time, the structure of economy has worsened: the FEC share in the total industrial manufacture grew in the CIS during the 1990s from 16.5 to almost 40%, with simultaneous reductions in high-tech products.

At the same time, the necessity of economic co-operation between the CIS countries has not decreased. Russia imports manganese from the Ukraine (80%), Georgia and Kazakhstan, chromium from Kazakhstan, varnish and paints from the Ukraine (over 75%), bauxites from Kazakhstan, Azerbaijan and the Ukraine (up to one third), lead for cables and accumulators from Kazakhstan (70%) and the Ukraine, zinc necessary for car tires, steel sheets and chemicals from Kazakhstan, carbide from Turkmenistan and the Ukraine, and melanine and isoprene rubber from Armenia. It is impossible to replace 130 kinds of furnishing parts from the Ukraine for 100 Russian space factories. The largest Verkhnesaldinsk metallurgical agglomeration in the Urals cannot survive without co-operation with the Ust'-Kamenogorsk titanium-manganese agglomeration in Kazakhstan and Verkhnedneprovsk one in the Ukraine. The Russian participation is expedient in reconstructing or restructuring the Uglegorsk, Dnestrovsk, Tashlinsk power plants in the Ukraine, South-Kazakhstan and Ekibastuzsk power plants.

The specialisation of the CIS countries remains fairly stable throughout recent years. Belarus sells to the CIS members its trucks, tractors, tires, chemical fibres, mineral products and textiles. Almost 37% of the export in the CIS countries are machines, equipment, transportation, etc. (in Moldova this figure is 28%, in others countries much lower). Kazakhstan supplies coal, oil, ore, sheets of ferrous metal, grain, wool and groats; Kyrgyzstan, electric power, alcohol and tobacco; Moldova, corn, tobacco, wines and canned foods; Tajikistan, aluminium, cotton, tobacco and carpets; Turkmenistan, natural gas and cotton; Uzbekistan, cotton, gas, cars, ores and chemicals; the Ukraine, ferrous metal, pipes, grain, sugar, sunflower oil, machinery and furnishing products.

Russia exports to the CIS countries firstly oil, its products, natural gas, chemical products, metal, metal wares, wood, timber and paper. Machines, equipment, and vehicles make only 18% of its export.

This structure attests to the initial stage of economic integration and internationalisation. The total value of the export from the CIS countries per capita was in the mid-1990s only $380, or a world less than in average-developed countries in Europe and Asia. Solely in Russia this figure exceeded $500; in Kazakhstan, Turkmenistan and Belarus it was $300–450, whereas in the countries of the Transcaucasia and Kyrgyzstan it did not even reach $100 (in Uzbekistan, Moldova and Tajikistan $120–170).

Most of the export was unprocessed raw materials, whereas of the import, consumer goods, fuel, energy and other materials instead of equipment and new technologies.

Unlike in the developed and rapidly developing countries, the export of the CIS countries had next to no devices and precise machines (e.g. measuring, control, high-precision units). In not a single CIS country, the share of high-tech products in the export exceeded 1.5%. The total share of five goods groups with the highest value added and most favourable from the viewpoint of creating new jobs, rational use of non-recoverable natural resources and the payment balance was in Belarus and Moldova 38%–50%, in Armenia, the Ukraine and Kyrgyzstan approximately 30%, in Russia and Azerbaijan 13%–15%, in Uzbekistan and Kazakhstan 4%–6%, and in Tajikistan and Turkmenistan these goods were totally absent from their export.

One should pay attention to the differences between the structures of export to CIS countries and that to the rest of the world. In the first case, the share of, for example, machines, cars and ready food is much higher, whereas in the second case mineral and vegetative raw materials prevail. The matter is not only that the markets of finished products, especially if their manufacture does not pollute environment, have for a long time been shared. The CIS countries often need custom-made machinery, e.g. fool-proof, inexpensive, working under any conditions, in sharply differing temperatures and across large distances.

Foreign economic relations of the CIS countries are based on trading goods instead of services, furnishing parts, units, tools within the framework of joint development programs, as well as manufacture and sales of goods, as has become customary in developed countries.

The economic connections of the CIS countries are mostly bilateral instead of multilateral.

According to their contribution in the total trade volume, the CIS countries can be split into four groups. In Belarus, Kyrgyzstan and Moldova, the CIS is the target of more than 50% of their export and import (1997), with the share growing in Belarus. The second group comprises Kazakhstan, the Ukraine, Azerbaijan, Georgia and Turkmenistan. The CIS share in their export is 40%–65%, in the import, strongly reduced (especially in Azerbaijan and Georgia). Armenia and Uzbekistan are oriented basically towards contacts outside the CIS, with regard to import, Georgia and Turkmenistan (see Table 28). The share of other countries in them has become prevailing. Russia's position looks special. The CIS share in its export-import operations is still below 25%; in 1995–1996 it somewhat grew, and in 1997 decreased again (due mainly to the reduction of trade with the Ukraine after the VAT had been introduced).

Each CIS country has its own targets and integration problems. Only two countries, Russia and Kazakhstan, have steady positive balance in foreign trade both inside the CIS and with the rest of the world. Turkmenistan has positive balance inside the CIS and negative with the "far abroad" countries, and Azerbaijan, positive inside the CIS and negative with the whole world (total balance was in 1997 for the first time summed up as positive). Other CIS countries have the import generally in excess of the export: Armenia, Georgia and Moldova both inside the CIS and with other countries; the Ukraine, Tajikistan and Kyrgyzstan at their general negative balance (due to their trade in the CIS) export to "far abroad" countries more than import. In 1997 in 9 of 12 CIS countries import exceeded export, in numerous countries the negative balance being significant (Armenia 41%, Moldova 18%, Belarus, Georgia and Turkmenistan 14%–15%). In 1998, due to the fall in prices of raw materials, the active balance changed in Russia and Kazakhstan, and the deficiency in other countries grew.

Armenia in the 1990s has been characterised primarily by the growth of industrial products sold inside the republic (from 2% to 40%) due to its transition to closed-link production cycles caused by the transportation blockade breaking old co-operative connections.

The share of the CIS countries in foreign trade declined from 85% to 60% (in Russia, from 44% to 33%), and of the rest of the world grew from 15 to 40%. Furthermore, Armenia's role in international division of labour has also changed. Export of radio-electronics and tools, originally shipped mainly to Russia, was sharply reduced due to the fall of demand the CIS market receiving plenty of

Table 28

The Share of the CIS and Other Countries in the Total Exports (E) and Imports (I) of the CIS Countries

Country	Exports as % of the GDP			Imports as % of the GDP			Share of the CIS in total external trade							
							1994		1995		1996		1997	
	1992	1995	1996	1992	1995	1996	E	I	E	I	E	I	E	I
Azerbaijan	57	33	23	76	53	55	42	62	45	34	46	35	47	44
Armenia	40	24	...	61	62	...	73	52	62	50	44	32	39	36
Belarus	60	50	...	58	55	...	59	68	62	66	67	66	73	68
Georgia	50	16	13	99	34	22	75	81	63	40	64	38	56	33
Kazakhstan	77	41	35	89	45	36	58	61	53	69	56	70	45	54
Kyrgyzstan	36	30	29	48	42	51	66	66	66	68	67	58	53	61
Moldova	38	60	–	55	69	–	72	72	63	68	68	62	73	52
Russia	62	26	22	48	22	17	21	27	18	29	18	31	19	27
Tajikistan	47	121	79	71*	129	62	19	43	34	59	43	57	40	63
Turkmenistan	...	...	...	...	...	...	77	47	49	55	67	30	...	...
Uzbekistan	34	32	33	43	29	33	62	54	39	41	21	32	...	...
Ukraine	24	47	46	29	50	48	55	73	53	65	51	63	39	58

* 1993.

superior Japanese, South Korean and western European electronics. The same is true of footwear, textile and other manufactured goods (exported en masse only to Turkmenistan). The export to the CIS countries basically consists of copper and molybdenum concentrate, special rubber (in that, Armenia remains monopolist), cognacs and wines.

Armenia's primary trade partner has become Iran (23% of all exports and import), buying scrap metal and mining products, in exchange for food. The metal works are then re-exported by the Iranian intermediaries to third countries. Developed countries (e.g. Belgium, Germany, SAR, the Netherlands) willingly buy gold and diamonds cut of Russian raw stones. The gold affinage factory built near Yerevan allows the country to produce finished items instead of semi-finished (concentrate and cathode deposit). The State-owned enterprise Shogaki makes and sells jewellery already not of borrowed (tolling) raw materials, but of that purchased for hard currency.

Armenia's legislation regarding foreign trade is the most liberal one among all CIS countries; it has low customs duties, and close contacts with the skilled labour in diaspora. Taken together, that allows it to return to the CIS markets as a supplier of plastic, chemicals, high-quality consumer goods and furnishing parts. Up to now its trade balance has remained negative (the total exports in 1997 covering less than 25% of the import), but the deficiency gets compensated for with loans.

The structure of Russian export into Armenia has essentially changed. Before 1990 the latter received primarily wood, timber (90%–98% of its consumption), machines and equipment, whereas presently it does energy and precious metals, equipment for the nuclear plants and electrical machines. Russia occupies the second place, after Iran, in its foreign trade. The trade is expected to increase sharply as soon as the Abkhazian railroad is restored.

In *Azerbaijan* export oil and other mineral products (48%), chemicals and plastic (6%), textiles and textile products (27%), and ready food, including wine and cognac (approximately 5%), prevail. A significant part (16%) of its export into the CIS countries make machines and equipment, in particular oil pumping (in trade with other countries amounting to only 2%).

The share of the CIS countries in Azerbaijan export in the 1990s was drastically reduced (from 84% to 47%, that of Russia from 48% to 18%). Significant export went solely to the Ukraine (6%) and Georgia (8%). In 1997 export of petroleum to the CIS countries increased by 20%. Among other countries, the first place occupies export to Iran (39%), Great Britain, Switzerland and Turkey (4.7% each). Its most important import partners are presently Iran and Turkey (16% each), followed by Russia (13%), Germany (10%) and Turkmenistan (8%).

However, this reorientation did not relieve the republic of hardships in maintaining the trade balance, due mainly to the trade with the countries of western, central and eastern Europe. Basically, its import includes food and drinks (approximately 40%) instead of machines, equipment and devices (13%).

Azerbaijan was the monopolist in the CIS (95%) in production of sulphanol, the basic component of detergents. It supplied Russia with oil, cotton fibre, early vegetables in exchange for sheets of ferrous metal, petrol and wood. However, the manufacture of machines, electronics and devices in the republic fell sharply. Russia occupies the third place in its export (24%), after Iran (35%) and Turkey (30%).

In the 1990s, *Georgia* has also reduced its trade with the CIS countries, due primarily to the blocked Abkhazian railroad. The Russian share in Georgian trade during 1989–1995 fell from 28% to 7%, or from two thirds to one eighth in the total volume of foreign connections (not counting smuggling, which increased in the same years) becoming significantly less than that of Turkey (10%). With the agreements on joint development of electric power industry in Georgia, restoration of power lines, co-operation in manufacturing transportation machinery, mutual aid in currency and export control, the joint venture founded with the Rustavsk metal works resulted in growth of the goods flow. It will supply Russia with manganese (Georgia has two thirds of its global stocks) and ferrous-manganese alloys, partially with copper, zinc, lead and steel pipes used for oil pumping, allowing at the same time to start work at the Kutaisi car factory which received more than 90% of its components from Russia. Georgia has received a credit against the shares of a joint stock companies Electrovozostroitel (25%) and Tchiaturmarganetz (10%).

The states of the Central Asian region in the mid-1990s entered the economic co-operation organisation founded by Turkey. In 1 year, Turkish export to these countries grew by two to eight times. At the same time, the volume of mutual trade between Russia and Uzbekistan was reduced in 1997 by more than 10%, with the share of machines, equipment and vehicles in the Russian export falling even more.

In the mid-1990s throughout the CIS territory more than 110 Turkish companies operated; of those, 86 in Azerbaijan and Turkic countries of the Central Asian region. The goods exchange with Turkmenistan has grown for 3 years by 16 times. Due to their low quality, export of goods with no quality certificates issued by the Standardisation Institute was prohibited. Certainly, it is impossible to object to mutually profitable co-operation between independent CIS states and any foreign partners, but insufficient attention to developing relations with CIS republics has promoted orientation of the economy towards raw materials.

In the late 1990s *Kazakhstan* and *Kyrgyzstan* have occupied the first two places in the CIS according to their industrial growth. However, that is basically due to restoring the mining and metallurgical with the help provided by foreign companies. Kyrgyzstan, thanks to co-operation with Russia, managed to restore manufacture at numerous machine-building factories. *Uzbekistan's* interest in the

CIS market grew essentially higher after the car and certain other factories had been put into operation. Integrating *Turkmenistan* into the CIS economy in the 1990s was inhibited by the difficulties with sales of gas due to the partners' default and unregulated transportation problems.

The problem of restoring the connections between *Moldova* and the CIS economy in many respects depends on, among other things, the conditions of transit over the Ukrainian territory, taxation of traditional export, prices on energy, orders for machines, devices.

The export of *Ukrainian* products into the CIS countries was in the late 1990s 40% of its total volume (ferrous metal and their products, equipment and electric machines, chemicals and mineral products), whereas the import from the CIS countries amounted to 60% of the total (natural gas, oil and its products, machines and equipment). Furthermore, significant exchange of goods took place only with Russia (approximately 38% of all exports), Belarus (3.5%) and Moldova (1.3%). The share of other CIS countries did not exceed 0.1%–0.8%.

In Ukrainian imports, the Russian share is 44% (Belarus and Turkmenistan, 1.8% each). Its major partners (after Russia) are not the CIS countries, even the ones closest to it, but the USA (5% of exports and 8% of imports), Germany, Great Britain, Switzerland (each of them, 3%–4% of the total export and 5%–6% of the import). Naturally, active participation in world economic contacts is important for every state, but it cannot compensate for the loss of the CIS markets. In 1998, after signing of the contract of large-scale co-operation with Russia, in this respect obvious changes started.

Expanding of the contacts between the CIS countries, which began in the late 1990s, attests to the growth of mutual trips. In a single year the number of trips into Russia increased by 3.7 times (from the rest of the world, by 1.6 times), the share of business trips growing from 6% to 14% (especially from the Ukraine and Georgia). The frequency of the Russians' visits to the CIS countries has increased by 12 times, particularly to the Ukraine, Moldova and Georgia. At the same time, the number of their visits to Latvia, Estonia (especially on vacations) Mongolia, China, USA and Israel decreased.

The economic connections of the CIS countries with Russian regions are very important. For example, Saint Petersburg has signed an agreement of co-operation with the Ministry of Economy of Belarus, founding over 300 joint ventures with its companies, thus supplying the city with food, transit of Belarussian cargoes through the sea harbour, joint R&D on nuclear power, polymers, chemistry and pharmaceuticals. Agreements have been signed also with Georgia, Uzbekistan, Azerbaijan, Kyrgyzstan, Zaporozhsk area, Nikolaev and Dushanbe. Trade houses as joint ventures with participation of commercial banks on the basis of credit clearing and mutual purchases have been opened with Lithuania, Estonia and Uzbekistan. Correspondence relationships with banks of all CIS countries have been established.

The role of regional agro-industrial agglomerations (e.g. southern Russia and northern Ukraine, southern Urals, Siberia, northwest Kazakhstan, Kaliningrad province, eastern Moldova, western Ukraine) is important. However, these opportunities are not used completely. Thus, the Krasnodar and Stavropol provinces co-operate with Turkey to a much greater degree than with the Transcaucasian republics.

The integration of the CIS countries will allow them to establish new contacts with the Baltic states where idle remain the unique capacities of the VEF, RAF, factories in Vilnius, Riga, Panevezys, earlier producing car compressors, nozzles, odometers, rejecting systems and TV channel selectors for the common market along with medicines, jersey, and so on.

The new co-operation scheme is not to copy, but to take into account, the co-operation existing in the USSR. Thus, in 1990 the co-operation enabled Russia and the Ukraine to satisfy 80% of their needs in ready metal sheets (importing 26% and 21%, but exporting 18% and 24% of the total manufacture volume), Georgia and Kazakhstan 30%; Moldova 15%; Kyrgyzstan, Tajikistan, Armenia and Turkmenistan imported 100% of metal sheets. It would be hardly economically sensible to start new production lines with no raw materials handy.

Numerous republics imported 98%–100% of commercial timber (Azerbaijan, Moldova, Kyrgyzstan, Tajikistan, Armenia, Turkmenistan); Belarus, due to the import, covered its needs by 80%, and the Ukraine and Kazakhstan by 40%. This is another branch where self-supplying is not realistic.

Armenia imported 87%, and Moldova 78%, of synthetic tars and plastic, without which modern device and mechanical engineering is impossible. Their manufacture with no raw materials and under the conditions of sovereignty is inexpedient. The same can be said about medicines produced in only five republics.

The Ukraine has reduced purchases of the Rostov combines Niva and Don priced at $20,000–40,000, preferring foreign Dominator and Laverda at $120,000–160,000 apiece. During the warranty period, compared with the machines produced by the ex-monopolist Rostselmash, they harvest the crops more than twice as fast, reducing its losses, fuel consumption, with incomparably better working conditions. However, after the warranty period ends, the Ukrainian combine Park (100,000 machines) will be linked to expensive spare parts. The Rostselmash, due to the reduction of demand, is compelled to stop its conveyor belts, which results in unemployment, also at its sub-contractors in the Ukraine. The mutual profit is in joint development and manufacture of competitive machinery instead of its mass import.

Privatisation creates new opportunities for this. Thus, at the shareholders meeting of the Bratsk aluminium factory a decision was made to direct almost all earnings of the recent years not to pay dividends, but to buy shares of similar enterprises in the Ukraine and Kazakhstan.

Table 28 summarises the general data on the mutual foreign trade between the CIS countries, and Table 29 lists the most important among them. The data confirm the conclusion that these connections continue to decline, becoming bilateral instead of multilateral. Meanwhile, the experience of the eastern European countries proves the hopelessness of such a way to enter the global market. In 1997, for the first time export of the CIS countries to the rest of the world ceased to grow, though their import grew by 15%, basically in consumer goods. The Transcaucasian countries, Belarus, and Moldova, despite the growth of oil export from Azerbaijan, mineral fertilisers and ferrous metal from Belarus, had negative trade balances outside the CIS.

As Table 28 shows, the greatest share of export in the GDP in the mid-1990s characterised Tajikistan (79%) where a lot of enterprises had previously focused on the domestic market and then stopped, the least one (13%) in Georgia, where the greatest damage was done to export of tea, fruit and other such products. Furthermore, in most countries (except Moldova and the Ukraine), the export share in the GDP was noticeably reduced in the 1990s.

Most dependent on import (55%–65% of the GDP) are Azerbaijan, Armenia, Belarus, Kyrgyzstan, Tajikistan and Moldova, but in most countries (except in Armenia, Moldova and Kyrgyzstan) this dependence has decreased in the recent years.

The economies of Belarus, Moldova, Kyrgyzstan, Turkmenistan and Georgia are the ones most strongly integrated according to their export in the CIS. With regard to import, the same can be said of Tajikistan, Kazakhstan, Belarus, Kyrgyzstan, the Ukraine and Moldova.

Note that despite the aggravated economic slump, Russia maintained its position as an integrative core of the CIS even in 1998. The country accounts for most of the export and import trade in Azerbaijan (48% and 45%), Armenia (50% and 79%), Belarus (90% and 83%), Kazakhstan (75% and 84%), Kyrgyzstan (37% and 41%), Moldova (80% and 52%) and the Ukraine (69% and 90%). Russia and Kazakhstan continue with the favourable net balance of trade with CIS countries. Russia's contribution to exports to (77%) and imports from the world countries (65%) is still the biggest among the CIS countries. The Ukraine comes next with 11 and 13%, respectively.

The greatest reorientation from CIS to other countries with regard to export is characteristic of Armenia, the Ukraine and Turkmenistan, with regard to import of Azerbaijan, Armenia, Georgia, Turkmenistan, Moldova and Uzbekistan (see Table 28). However, unfortunately, the CIS market is least import for Russia. It is explained by the prolonged crisis of many branches inside its economy.

Table 29

The Share of CIS Countries in the Total Exports (E) from and Imports (I) into Other CIS Countries (%)

Country	Azerbaijan		Armenia		Belarus		Georgia		Kazakhstan		Kyrgyzstan		Moldova		Russia		Tajikistan		Turkmenistan		Uzbekistan		Ukraine	
	E	I	E	I	E	I	E	I	E	I	E	I	E	I	E	I	E	I	E	I	E	I	E	I
Azerbaijan	–	–	–	–	0.2	0.1	19	29	0.3	0.8	0.8	0.3	1.2	0.7	1.1	1.1	0.8	–	1.0	9.0	0.4	0.1	1.2	0.3
Armenia	–	–	–	–	0.1	–	16	6.4	–	–	–	–	0.9	–	0.7	0.6	–	–	7.6	5.9	–	–	0.3	–
Belarus	1.1	1.5	0.9	0.8	–	–	1.1	1.0	1.4	4.1	1.4	1.3	6.3	9.2	21.3	20	1.3	0.8	–	0.2	2.9	4.5	10	3.4
Georgia	32	8.3	5.4	19	0.1	–	–	–	0.3	0.1	–	0.3	0.5	–	0.6	0.5	0.1	0.2	–	3.6	0.1	–	2.5	–
Kazakhstan	5.3	5.7	0.8	–	2.3	1.3	1.9	0.3	–	–	29	29	1.4	0.4	16	21	7.3	14	16	5.7	21	16	1.2	2.2
Kyrgyzstan	0.4	1.0	–	–	0.2	0.1	0.2	–	3.2	3.1	–	–	1.1	0.1	1.0	1.0	3.2	1.9	0.1	0.3	6.0	3.1	0.1	0.1
Moldova	1.3	2.6	0.1	–	1.9	1.1	0.1	–	0.1	0.3	0.2	–	–	–	2.5	5.7	–	0.1	0.4	0.9	0.3	0.2	3.2	0.6
Russia	38	47	75	45	80	77	44	47	80	79	34	36	79	45	–	–	24	19	13	40	50	64	75	78
Tajikistan	0.6	0.1	–	–	0.1	–	0.4	–	1.8	0.6	2.1	1.3	–	–	1.0	–	–	–	0.9	0.5	14	3.9	0.3	0.1
Turkmenistan	12	4.3	14	31	0.2	–	10	1.7	1.1	5.9	0.8	2.8	0.5	–	0.7	1.2	2.6	6.9	–	–	2.4	2.9	3.7	15
Uzbekistan	1.9	2.1	0.3	0.1	2.1	0.8	2.3	0.4	5.9	3.0	30	27	0.6	0.4	6.9	4.5	58	52	0.3	1.4	–	–	2.4	0.6
Ukraine	7.6	28	3.8	4.3	13.1	20	4.2	14	6.1	3.1	2.4	2.5	8.7	45	48	44	3.3	5.0	61	33	3.9	5.5	–	–

Table 29 specifies these conclusions. Many CIS countries the economies of which supplement each other in many respects, during the late 1990s have had practically no economic relations (Azerbaijan – Belarus, Kazakhstan, Uzbekistan, Ukraine; Belarus – the Transcaucasian countries and those of the Central Asian region; Georgia – the Central Asian region, Russia and Moldova; Kazakhstan – Moldova; Kyrgyzstan – the Ukraine; Moldova the Central Asian region and the Transcaucasia). The transition from multilateral relations to bilateral relations has resulted in subregional groupings rapidly formed inside the CIS.

Integrated groupings within the CIS. In the mid-1990s there appeared well-pronounced differences in the development paces of the CIS countries with regard to economic integration. Three subregional clusters were formed, the Union of Belarus and Russia, the customs union (Russia, Belarus, Kazakhstan, Kyrgyzstan and, since 1998, also Tajikistan), the agreement on deepening integration in the economic and humanitarian areas and the economic agreement between the Central Asian countries (Uzbekistan, Kazakhstan, Kyrgyzstan, Tajikistan). A joint transportation and power infrastructure is about to be created by Georgia, the Ukraine, Azerbaijan and Moldova (GUAM).

The Union of Belarus and Russia is a subject of international law. The charter assumes, among other things, a common economic space, co-ordinated program of market reforms, common infrastructure including the united transportation and power networks, communication, unification of the monetary, budget and tax systems, a common customs space. These goals can be achieved via forming a Parliamentary Assembly, a Supreme Council of the Union, and an Executive Committee on the parity basis. The decisions carried out by the last two bodies are subject to direct execution (with observance of the national laws) by the executive authorities. The parity basis may result also in other branches. Financing joint programs and projects requires creating a common budget of the union. As a result of the monetary systems unification, uniform issuing centre has been scheduled along with the transition to a common currency.

Integration agreement between Russia, Belarus, Kazakhstan and Kyrgyzstan also assumes co-ordinating the basic directions, stages, and terms of reforms, pricing policies, a uniform model normative base for economic regulation, a bank union and other elements of a common economic space. The interstate council, the integration committee as a regularly working executive body and the Interparliamentary Committee adapting model laws serving as the bases for national legislation, constitute the bodies controlling the integration.

Kazakhstan, Uzbekistan, Kyrgyzstan and Tajikistan have created, in addition to the councils of the heads of the states and prime ministers, also a central Asian bank of co-operation and development for carrying out common projects.

The creation of subregional groupings in the CIS is caused by political and economic forces. Regarding political reasons, numerous CIS countries (e.g. Georgia, Azerbaijan, Turkmenistan, Uzbekistan) disagree with supranational bodies created inside the CIS. Uzbekistan votes for bilateral, but against multilateral, agreements on numerous specific questions (e.g. VAT and excise duties decrease at co-operated deliveries, development and use of mobile cellular communication systems).

The CIS cannot force any country to participate in something it abhors. At the same time, nobody can block the movement of other countries to higher levels of integration and more intensive interaction, if it does not result in their isolation from the CIS as a whole.

The subregional groupings have been formed by the countries closest to each other with regard to co-operation. Thus, for Belarus, Russia is the major (59% of the total) export and import partner. For Russia, Belarus is the second most important partner in the CIS (after the Ukraine). One should also remember the ethnic affinity between the Russians and the Belarussians, the absence of international conflicts between them both in the past and in the present, absence of compelled migration and special position of the Russian language. At the 1995 poll, 83% of all voters expressed support for giving it a status equal to that of Belarussian and for economic integration with Russia.[3]

Belarus is also characterised by the active economic co-operation with neighbouring Poland, Lithuania and Germany. With regard to the general living standard (taking into account the incomes from 1 million land plots of up to 1 ha allocated to city dwellers) this country looks only a bit worse than Russia, surpassing it in per capita amounts (1996) of meat (60 and 30 kg), milk (480 and 240 kg) and grain (580 and 420 kg).

The Union of Belarus and Russia in principle proves its efficiency. In 1997 the goods flow between the two countries grew by 40%. In Belarus, GDP was increased (by 11% against 2% in 1996), industrial (by 13%, at joint ventures by 40%), and agricultural production (by 4%), cargo exchange (by 14%) and warehouse stocks were reduced (from 85% to 50% of the monthly production) along with the number of unprofitable enterprises (from 24% to 17%). Due to the customs union with Russia and its lower wages (almost by 50%), Belarus received competitive advantages and increased the export of TVs to Russia (by 80%), tractors and trucks (by 1.5 times). The revenues share from import in the Belarussian budget grew from 5% to 15%. Three quarters of all cargoes Russia ships to Europe pass via Belarus, and the deficiency of its trade balance with "far abroad" countries and Russia has decreased.

---

[3] See: Kozhokin, E.M. (Ed.) (1996): Belarus. A Way to the New Horizons. Russian Institute for Strategic Research, Moscow (Кожокин, Е.М. [Ред.] [1996]: Беларусь: Путь к Новым Горизонтам. Российский Институт Стратегических Исследований, Москва) [In Russian]

The development of new export products with the help of foreign TNCs proved to be justified. They included in the late 1990s a truck corresponding to EU standards, a bus with a new diesel engine (together with MAN, Novy Star, Detroit Diesel) and sixth-generation TVs with new tubes (based on the Phillips). Belarus makes twice as many tractors (in the late 1980s the ratio was reverse) and four times as many TVs as Russia. Furthermore, deliveries of components from across the border are not taxed.

Russia also benefited from integration due to the reduced expenses on transit of goods, increase in export of the materials and units manufactured by the factories in Yaroslavl, Lipetsk and other places. Russian large corporations and banks penetrated the Belarussian market. However, the losses were also huge because of the customs regulations inconsistency (e.g. duty-free transit of cars into Russia, alcohol and other goods arriving from third countries).

Belarus has not managed to stop the inflation (5% per month), though the population's incomes grow faster than the prices after 50% of city families received vegetable gardens. The external trade deficiency results in the minimum gold-and-currency reserves, and the rate of the national currency has dropped.

In 1998 Russia and Belarus outlined a joint capital budget (the parties' shares being 65% and 35%, or accordingly 0.08% and 1.23%, of their national budgets, respectively). It is used to develop the border and customs infrastructure, diesel motor industry based on the FIG Belrusavto according to the Euro-2 standard, joint manufacture of chemical fibre.

One of the most active participants in the CIS economic integration and the world economic connections is presently Kazakhstan with its balance of foreign trade (the export exceeding import) both with the CIS countries and with other countries. In 1997 the CIS countries received 45% of its export (Russia 46%, Uzbekistan 3%, Ukraine 1.3%) and was the source of 54% of its import (Russia 57%, Turkmenistan 7%, Belarus 2.8%). Among Kazakhstan's other distinguished partners are China (approximately 9% of the export), the Netherlands, Great Britain, Germany, Italy, South Korea and Switzerland (each of these countries getting 3%–4% of its export). The diversification of international economic relations is a feature characteristic of Kazakhstan.[4]

In the structure of its export mineral products prevail (35%), non-precious metals and their products (34%), agricultural products (grain), wool and chemicals (8%–9% each), followed by machines and tools, textiles and its products (up to 3%). It imports primarily mineral products (27%), machines and equipment

---

[4] See: Kozhokin, E.M. (Ed.) (1995): Kazakhstan: Realities and Promise of Independent Market. Russian Institute for Strategic Research, Moscow (Кожокин, Е.М. [Ред.] [1995]: Казахстан: Реалии и Перспективы Независимого Рынка. Российский Институт стратегических Исследований, Москва) [In Russian]

(16%), metal and metal works, vehicles, chemicals, food, drinks and tobacco (8%–10% each).

The share of Kazakhstan in the total volume of CIS export made 6%. The deliveries of oil and petrol, natural gas, grain, tractors, coal, ferrous metal bars, tires and wool get reduced. At the same time, the export of raw wool, ferrous metals and cotton to other countries gets increased.

Kazakhstan's import makes 11% of its total volume in the CIS. Its leading partners in import operations have been Russia (70%), Turkmenistan (10%) and Uzbekistan (9%). Furthermore, it has sharply reduced importing gas, oil and oil products from Russia. The imports of natural gas from Turkmenistan has been stabilised. The import of household refrigerators and TVs, leather footwear and cotton fabrics (mainly from Russia and Uzbekistan) has decreased by several times. At the same time, the import of vegetable oil and sugar has grown. Kazakhstan imports from elsewhere 96% of its mineral products, 61% of chemicals and 79% of metal wares.

The principal partners in trade with CIS countries are still Germany, Turkey, China, the USA, Iran, the UK and Switzerland. The top export market in 1996 was worth $123 million, i.e. 21% more than in 1998, with top imports amounting to $95 billion in 1997, i.e. 17% more than in 1998. Reduced exports due to deteriorating world prices for raw materials were evident in all the countries except Armenia. In this connection Russia lost $8 billion, when the exports reduced by 27%, the imports by 12% and the favourable net balance of trade outside the CIS from $28.2 to $21.7 billion.

9.3 Towards a Common Economic Space

Main stages of integration. Any regional economic integration, as world experience shows, implies a few main stages. Firstly, a *free trade zone* assumes cancellation of customs duties and export-import quotas (limits) inside it. Secondly, a *customs union*, means creating a uniform customs service, tariffs, quotas and non-tariff regulations with regard to third countries. *The common market* as a whole means a possibility of freely moving not only goods and services between the participating countries, but all production factors: labour, capital, technologies and information. *Economic union* also assumes co-ordinated macro-economic policy (budget, currency, investment, tax) and a suitable legislation. Finally, *complete economic integration* (a full economic union) means not simply co-ordinated, but also common, economic policy involving the unification of contract, financial, tax, labour, anti-monopoly and other legislation, as well as uniform technical and environmental standards, common currency and a common issuing centre.

The integration mechanism in the CIS has up to now not taken into account these basic distinctions. Many concepts and agreements accepted throughout these years never considered the USSR former republics having become fully sovereign states, each with its own interests. Armenia can by no means become a member of the customs union with unified tariffs and quotas with all duties and other restrictions on imported food, energy and other vital utilities cancelled, when all existing transportation routes have been blocked. Numerous CIS countries agree to free trade and collective safety, but object to any supra-national bodies necessary for an economic and especially defence union to operate.

When integration prospects were planned, quite often the established goals were unrealistic and unattainable at the given stage. A common market and particularly an economic union cannot be formed before the customs union starts working at its full force. It is indicative that even the Baltic countries, closest in their economic and political standing, at the end of the 1990s cancelled uniform duties with respect to agricultural products, at the same time stipulating their right to introduce restrictions on import when the foreign trade balance gets negative, import exceeds export, a special branch or the economic situation as a whole is threatened.

One should not forget also that the term "economic integration" was introduced by the American co-ordinators of the Marshall Plan, and that the first supra-national body in Europe. The Organisation of European Economic Cooperation was founded in 1948, under the conditions of a general post-war disaster and with the purpose of distributing American money. Today, the CIS has no centre capable of financing structural reforms in other countries and consequently it is impossible to envisage a supra-national body paid for not by a kind overseas "uncle", but the participating countries themselves, out of their not very large budget. It is equally impossible to forget that the first European supra-national unity, the Association of Coal and Steel (1951), solved purely research-and-production problems, as did the European Society of Nuclear Engineering (1957). It was only after the first successes in industrial integration did the committee of European communities, European Parliament and Organisation of Economic Cooperation and Development (1960), begin co-ordinating the economic policies of European countries. The idea of a "cavalry charge", resulting in supra-national structures within months, while Europe with its immeasurably greater financial resources had been forming them for years, did not and could not yield anything.

According to the Centre for Researches of Economies of the CIS countries, the council on production facilities location and the economic co-operation of the Ministry of Economy of the Russian Federation, the CIS countries' contribution in Russian foreign trade in 1990–1997 decreased from 46% to 21.5%, the share of goods exchange with former republics in the Russian GDP falling from 25% to 10%. Furthermore, 87.5% of the Russian export and 84% of the import inside CIS concerns three countries only: the Ukraine, Belarus and Kazakhstan. At the same time, the Russian share in the foreign trade of CIS countries exceeds 50%, and in the three specified countries, 70%.

This leads to the conclusion that Russian economic policy largely determines the success of integration. Hesitation and inconsistency of Russian ministries and departments does inhibit the integration process in the CIS.

At the same time, other CIS countries have also contributed to the lack of integration. In 1993–1997 Russia carried out its obligations concerning deliveries of energy to the CIS countries by 70%–75%, receiving in exchange only 25%–30% of the goods stipulated by the contracts. As a result, despite the considerable industrial growth in numerous CIS countries in 1997, (49% in Kazakhstan, 17% in Belarus, 4%–10% in Georgia, Uzbekistan and Kyrgyzstan), their mutual trade was reduced by 8%. The share of Russian investments in CIS countries did not exceed 1%.

Objective analysis shows that at the end of the 1990s, the traditional model of the CIS economic co-operation is undergoing a crisis. The CIS is turning into an amorphous, primarily political formation, with bilateral relations in the foreground, instead of a co-ordinated economic policy. Therefore, according to the estimations done by the Interstate Economic Committee, the CIS countries, with their 25% of the world's natural resources and 10% of its industrial potentials, make the tiny 4% of the world GDP. The CIS share in world export (4%–4.5%), despite an increase in raw material production, gets reduced by the growing share of the products requiring high costs of processing and services exported by other countries.

It is noteworthy that numerous objective factors, causing the fact that the market reforms in the CIS, overcoming industrial drop in most countries and reduced inflation, did not result in strengthened economic co-operation, but quite the opposite, and the situation is still more complicated.

1. The decrease in importance of interstate agreements concerning deliveries and growing direct links between independent participants of the market. The interstate agreements were mainly oriented towards former economic connections, without taking into account the profitability and commercial risks. As is well known, the central government authorities in the USSR fully administrated all natural resources in all republics, imposed the economic structures together with the relationships, guided primarily by the military and political reasons. By the end of the 1990s, most CIS countries have their basic GDP produced by privatised, newly founded private, joint and given in trust to foreign TNC enterprises, choosing their partners on the basis of pragmatic, economic reasons as well as the competition.

Supplies from outside CIS often appear more favourable due to:

– Prices being lower despite the significant transaction costs and salaries. It results from the indirect taxes existing in the CIS, where the VAT of 20% gets charged from every process (i.e. ore, pig iron, steel, bars, hardware). This makes the price of metal, wood, oil, cars and tractors inside the CIS 1.3–1.8 times those in the rest of the world. According to the Government Statistics committee, the price of a metric ton of petroleum, oil, coal and a cubic metre of natural gas when exported from Russia inside the CIS grew by 1.2–1.4 times in 1996 resulting in an essential decrease in export. Finnish gasoline made of Tyumen oil is sold in Saint Petersburg at a price well below the price for domestic production. The price of Russian export is above the world figure in pig iron ($250 and $140 per tonne), assorted metal ($400 and $300 per tonne), steel pipes ($800 and $600 per tonne), cars ($8700 and $3900) and synthetic rubber ($1870 and $1280 per tonne).

– Better conditions of payment on a leasing basis, related credits and factoring. Disintegration of the CIS economy has been a logical consequence of its liberalisation and rationalisation. There had been no common market in the CIS territory and it had to be created anew instead of being restored. Thus, the commodity market is created on a specifically market basis, whereas that of financial services, securities and labour cannot be established without any help provided by the state.

– Complete sets of services, including post-sales maintenance guarantees, spare parts and training of the staff. CIS companies frequently sell "iron", i.e. machinery or sets of engineering specifications, demanding an immediate payment, whereas foreign enterprises sell full technological complexes ready to work, paid for with their revenues, profits (royalty prices) or even on the basis of barter. Russia's share is only 0.5% of tightened credits received by the CIS countries. Because of that, they bought only 2 TU-154s but 48 Boeings last year.

– Incomparably lower commercial risk connected to delays of delivery, failures to pay, liquidation of legal entities or changes in their management. The CIS still has no modern business ethics, the state does not protect contracts and a lot of businessmen work according following the principle: "There are no sales without deceit". Therefore, Roscontract and numerous other companies incurred heavy losses in 1997, having trusted their partners in Kazakhstan, whereas Kazakh companies, in their turn, incurred losses due to the failures of some corporations in Russia.

2. As world experience shows, a real economic integration (as opposed to an economic union or partnership) is possible and effective only when the industrial structure is dominated by the manufacturing industry requiring deep division of labour and being competitive enough to replace import and to exit to international markets. This condition in the CIS is missing, but it is necessary for the national interests of the CIS countries. During the conversion, the countries switched over to producing simpler products, not requiring the previous level of co-operation with suppliers of components, research and technical services. The integration of the CIS mining branches into the world economy reduces the need

of a regional integration, as it is financed by foreign investors using their technology and equipment.

3. The growth of transportation costs, to a large extent caused exclusively by high railroad rates, has made it necessary for the CIS countries to rely on their own resources. The oil fields discovered in Kazakhstan, Uzbekistan and other countries have allowed them to refuse or sharply reduce import from Russia and Turkmenistan. Numerous countries have significantly reduced the crops of technical cultures (e.g. cotton, hemp, linen), grapes and vegetables previously exported northwards, replacing them with grain (e.g. in Uzbekistan, Turkmenistan and Azerbaijan), potatoes (e.g. in Tajikistan, Georgia) and rice (in Kyrgyzstan) for their own needs.

4. Copying the EU experience has proved unjustified in the 1990s with regard to liberalising the commodity and stock markets according to the recommendations provided by the IMF and WTO. Developed countries started that liberalisation only after 30 years of integration, when their manufacturing corporations had achieved competitiveness in the world market. In the 1990s the EU countries and the USA still regulate import of textiles, fabrics, ferrous metal, tools and house electronics. The quantitative restrictions concern approximately 50% of food, 13% of fuel and 10% of textiles. Germany keeps quotas on coal import, Austria on wine and canned meat and France on oil. The liberalisation connected with the forthcoming entrance of many CIS countries into the WTO will make some of their branches unprotected against the stronger foreign competitors.

The new factors must be taken into account when developing a new integration model. However, the difficulties related to them cannot become the basis for refusing multilateral integration; otherwise, the CIS research-technological and also agrarian complexes will decline in the twenty-first century. The West and the East want oil, gas, metal and chemicals from the CIS, but do not need high-tech products and food. If the market for these goods is not created inside the CIS, scholarly and village youth will go jobless, mass unemployment will become inevitable and the economic safety of the CIS countries will be threatened.

The free trade zone as a realistic phase of integration. The most reliable form of integration at the end of the 1990s are *free trade zones*, a regional common market based on uniform customs, research-technological, educational and legal space, monetary union, common market for goods, capitals, technologies and labour not requiring at the given level any strengthening of supra-national administrative bodies. A similar zone had worked in western Europe until the mid-1980s and successfully functions presently in North America and ASEAN countries. This zone in the long term assumes:

1. A common customs space, within which customs duties and quotas on imports and exports are removed, and unified customs tariffs and co-ordinated trade policies with regard to third parties are introduced. The collective protectionist measures mean a voluntary refusal of some sovereignty, as the country loses the

right to independently change the co-ordinated conditions of trade, including those in the agrarian market.

2. A monetary union ensuring mutual convertibility of currencies, free movement of services and capitals, access of financial and insurance organisations of other countries to the market and integration of the stock markets.

3. Creating conditions for developing transnational FIGs (financial and industrial groups), including the unification of tax systems, establishment of a joint investment bank and insurance companies, regulated freedom of labour movement, founding a social fund for improving the situation with employment.

N. Nazarbayev was the author of the idea concerning the Eurasian Union; he suggested numerous measures to maximally simplify the migration of the union citizens and the development of their economic initiative. They include: simplification of granting citizenship in all countries members of the union, free crossing of internal borders without visas and references along the "green corridor", increased limits of unobstructed currency transportation (up to $10,000) and duty-free baggage (up to 100 kg), freedom of subscribing to and receiving periodicals, exchange and distribution of TV and radio programs, other information, mutual recognition of the education certificates and freedom of entering high schools in all countries of the union, and freedom of along-the-border contacts and exchanges between relatives. Creating maximally favourable conditions for smaller and medium businesses in all countries of the union is of special importance.

4. Development of a united transportation and communication infrastructure with uniform tariffs.

Numerous CIS republics can participate in interstate transit of electric power. The RAO EES of Russia has developed the concept of unifying energy systems in the countries/ members of the Black Sea economic association including five power lines more than 1700 km long to be built between Georgia and Turkey in 1997–2010. Intersystem transfer of energy, including that from Russia to Turkey, is controlled by the Gruzrosenergo joint venture. Russia, the Ukraine, Belarus and Moldova together with the EU develop economic and technical specifications for merging the western and eastern energy systems. It will lead to avoiding expensive reserve capacities and to increasing the west-oriented export in 1997–2000 from 5 to 20–25 billion kilowatts per hour.

At the turn of the century, it is planned to develop a transportation infrastructure between Azerbaijan and Georgia, tanker routes between the harbours of Georgia and Romania where in Constance factories to condense natural gas are under construction with American assistance. Under appropriate conditions, all these projects can serve consolidation instead of disintegration of the CIS.

Western European countries strictly adhere to the priority of arrangements within the EU with regard to bilateral contracts. This is the common practice of all free trade zones.

The CIS countries certainly do not have to mechanically copy foreign experience, as the specified zone is created with the lack of modern business culture, no middle class, land ownership and real estate market. Presently, the CIS has no legislative bases necessary for real economic integration, and the new laws adequate to the market economy are only now being written. For example, the fifth section of the CIS charter lists the directions of co-operation in economic, social and legal areas. First of all they include reforming the common economic space on the basis of the market relations and freely moving goods, services, capitals and labour. Then follow co-ordination of social policies, development of joint social programs, of transportation and communication systems, of power systems, co-ordination of the monetary policies, encouragement and mutual protection of investments, standardisation and certification of manufactured products and goods and protection of intellectual property.

Establishing a free trade zone, one should follow the strict logic of this process being expanded. This logic is determined by the development of business relations between companies instead of the number of administrative services and bodies. Decrease in export prices for the CIS goods at the end of the 1990s will in certain cases make these connections inside the CIS more favourable than outside its borders. However, this will hardly be a way to real integration if intergovernmental bodies do not have any co-ordinating functions delegated to them by the nation states.

The agreement on an economic union (1993) between the CIS countries envisages:

– Freedom of moving goods, services, capitals and labour

– Co-ordination of monetary, budget, tax, pricing, foreign trade, customs and currency policies

– Co-ordination of the economic legislation

– Co-ordination of transportation and transit tariffs

– Creation of a common information base

– Unification of cross-boarder documents

The agreement on a free trade zone (1994) was even more specific. It included:

– Cancellation of customs duties, quotas, taxes and payments (except co-ordinated exceptions valid through the transition period)

– Stopping export subsidies from interfering with equal conditions for all competitors

– Taxation of import not higher than domestic goods

– Free transit of imported goods on conditions not worse than for domestic ones

Furthermore, restrictions on exporting the items were allowed, the internal prices on which were supported by the state at a level below the global one and on trading, among other items, precious metals and stones and weaponry, as well as emergency measures in case of suffering payment balance.

However, all these agreements were never followed completely. At the end of the 1990s, the formation of a customs, monetary and economic union between the CIS countries again has become extremely urgent.

The customs union. The customs union is a free trade zone having common customs borders and mechanisms of regulating foreign economic relations with third parties. According to the experts, by 2015–2020, when all main countries of the world enter the WTO and form the global free trade zone, the need of such unions will disappear. However, until then, neither the EU nor other regional unions are going to reject this form of integration. It is necessary to remark that the EU had 20 years between the creation of a free trade zone and the complete abolishment of customs barriers in the mid-1990s, during which time there were uniform rules of competition and currency operations, and uniform business ethics.

The trade turnover between the participants of the customs union of the four (since 1998, five) countries also grew faster, than in the CIS as a whole. However, the rates of growth appeared modest. Export of certain goods from Kazakhstan to Russia (ferrous metal and alloys, copper) and from Russia to Kazakhstan (oil and its products) decreased. The introduction of uniform customs tariff, co-ordination of measures for non-tariff regulation, foreign trade, customs and financial legislation were delayed. Often the parties independently changed the VAT, import duties for third parties and rules of currency control, based on their own interests. The trade between Kazakhstan and Belarus was reduced.

For the CIS countries, it is most important at the present stage to solve the following problems:

1. Unification of import duties, excises and quotas (export duties in the mid-1990s were cancelled by most CIS countries. Up to now, the situation in this respect varies. The Ukraine raised import duties on more than 600 items, e.g. heavy trucks, direct current motors, main-frame computers, cash counters, paper, cardboard, potatoes and the duties on meat and milk products (50% and higher), making the import unprofitable.

Since 1997 Russia has exempted from duties machines, their components and materials (except those subject to excise taxation) imported as contribution into founding capital (according to the constituent documents and balance sheets). However, for the CIS countries more urgent was the introduction of excise taxes and import quotas on alcohol. Moldova, exporting into Russia 60% of the wine and 85% of the vodka, thus incurred heavy losses. In 1997 Moldova itself introduced licensing on alcohol and tobacco import.

Up to now, unification has not been achieved even by the four countries/members of the customs union. Thus, Belarus (unlike Russia) has exempted from customs duties all businessmen carrying out investment projects. That country provided individual privileges to importers, 63 goods were subject to excises different from those in Russia (as a rule, lower) and 460 were exempted from duties. As a result, the flow of cargo into Russia via Latvia was reduced by 50%, the import of alcohol into Belarus from "far abroad" grew after closing the customs along the Russian borders by 410 times, and ethyl alcohol and beer by 30–45 times.

Kazakhstan has lowered its import tariffs for furniture, industrial and agricultural equipment, and cars (from 40% to 2%). Russia has introduced taxes on imported cars (up to 70%) and combines (from 2% to 20%). Kazakhstan's export to Russia due to the customs union grew in 1995 by 60%, in 1996, by 42%, then followed difficulties due to the lack of co-ordination. However, the budget of these countries had received far less than expected.

2. A mechanism of customs bodies' interaction and distributions of the duties for imports to their territory from third countries, development of a common policy with regard to these countries and introduction of a common customs border are very important.

All CIS countries have signed the agreement on simplification and unification of customs procedure at customs borders, providing a list of obligatory data mentioned in the control documents of delivery (the cargo customs declaration) and certificates of origin; however, it is still a long way off from creating a modern computerised system.

Numerous problems regarding mutual trade have thus far not been solved. Thus, Russia in 1996–1997 introduced an import duty on Ukrainian white sugar the wholesale price of which (1.9–2.4 rubles) appeared lower than the cost of the Russian factories (3 rubles) due to lower wages. Therefore, a third of Russian factories stopped and 70% worked with incomplete load. In addition, uncontrollable re-export (import of sugar from the Ukraine in 1996 exceeded its manufacture by three times) and damping by the beet producers (they received sugar from the factories free and exported it through intermediaries at half the retail prices) started. As a result, the import of raw beet at the Russian factories grew multifold, whereas sugar manufacturing of domestic beet was sharply reduced. A whole branch of the AIC was threatened. One hundred ninety-two sugar factories in the Ukraine (in Russia, 92) were about to stop. In 1998 a co-ordinated quota on duty-free sugar import into Russia was created.

3. The common economic space requires co-ordinated taxes, the ideal case being the VAT cancelled for mutual deliveries altogether. Since 1998 VAT and excise

duties are not levied on the goods delivered according to the contracts within the co-operation framework (except oil, gas, gas condensate and alcohol). However, under many contracts some countries (Russia, Belarus, Moldova) collect indirect taxes guided by the principle of the country of origin (the taxes are not levied at import and not compensated for at export), whereas others follow the principle of the destination country (levied at import and compensated for at export).

In the CIS this results in problems. Due to the poorly controllable movement of goods, pseudo-export is the common practice, when goods get exempted from taxes and then sold inside the country. In the CIS countries there are different qualifiers of products and ways to collect excise taxes. Thus, Kazakhstan in 1996 unilaterally changed the VAT offset mechanism for the goods imported from Russia by including it into the costs. That apparently purely accounting operation resulted in a rise in the price of Russian products and decreased their competitiveness. At the same time, Russia and Turkmenistan could not co-ordinate the prices on Turmanian gas transported through Russia to the West.

To solve this problem, in the EU taxes and duties are directed to a central fund, used to indemnify the states suffering losses due to the introduction of flat rates and taxes and to financed common projects. In the customs union between the CIS countries this is not stipulated.

A different way, complete cancellation of the VAT, was used in 1998 by Russia and the Ukraine. Russian export to the Ukraine consists by 80%–85% of raw materials and under-processed goods, the Ukrainian export is by 47% services (mainly, transit of Russian goods), 15% metal, 14% machinery and units, and 13% food including grain. The Ukraine exempted from VAT its export and introduced import VAT in 1996. As Russia levied the VAT on export goods they appeared non-competitive in the Ukraine. Responding to this, Russia introduced increased VAT for Ukrainian goods. Certainly, the trade war brought nothing to both countries except losses. The cancellation of the VAT will lead to expanded co-operation in manufacturing military equipment, new blocks for the Rovno and Khmelnitskiy nuclear power plants (as not only suppliers of equipment and constructors, but also investors) and reconstruction of sugar factories, among other things; however, a bilateral agreement cannot replace a multilateral one.

4. The common policy protecting the domestic market and fighting damping, transition of the CIS countries to open economy on the basis of restricted exports and imports including everything also sharply increased their dependence on the fluctuations of the global market. In the most advanced countries (USA, Japan), the export share in their GDP makes 10%–11%. In Russia in 1992, it reached 62% (the result of a shock cancellation of the State monopoly on foreign trade) and only then started declining (1994: 28%; 1997: 20%). Furthermore, the goods exchange volume in those years grew by 1.5 times (up to $150 billion, or the 15–16 position in the world). The average import rate (14%–15%) by 2000 is planned to get reduced by 20% before 2000 and by one third by 2005.

However, foreign countries are putting obstacles in the way of their competitors from the CIS supplying seamless pipes, thick metal sheets, ferrous silicon and other metalware, calcium, magnesium and uranium. Anti-dumping duties on Ukrainian metal exist in the USA, Indonesia, Thailand and Chile (1998), being drafted in Turkey, Canada and elsewhere. The duties reach 60%, on magnesium (EU countries) 170% and are supplemented with quotas, though the lower price of the goods from the CIS is explained most often by the wage level (the average monthly salary at Severstal in Cherepovets is $350, whereas in the USA it is $4000; the salary share in the production cost of pipes in the CIS is 10%, in the West 60%).

The CIS countries incur heavy losses due to restriction of their export, especially Russia ($1 billion per year), the Ukraine and Kazakhstan. They can be reduced via improving modern management of international economic relations, observing the rules of goods certification and coding, and timely provided data for international audit. Joint associations and cartels would prevent products from being mass delivered on the world markets without valid certificates. Thus, the Taganrog metal works, having sent in 1995 30,000 underpriced low-quality pipes to Italy, became the reason for anti-damping procedure hurting a lot of factories in the Urals. It was only in 1997 that the manufacturers and exporters of ferrous metal from the CIS countries met in Rybnitza (Moldova) for the first time and planned co-ordinating export prices.

Since 1998 commercial and industrial chambers of ten CIS countries, Poland, Yugoslavia, Bulgaria and Macedonia have co-operated in managing enterprise risks and economic safety. This co-operation is extremely important for strengthening the customs union.

5. The co-ordination of the CIS countries' obligations is necessary before entering the WTO. These obligations include four documents: a list of special obligations on the accessibility for foreign suppliers to the national market of services; the description of exemptions from the common rules on granting all WTO members the status of the most favoured nation in foreign trade (no country can receive access conditions worse than others); the import tariff (it cannot be raised after entering the WTO); and changes in the current legislation and international agreements.

For example, the duties for customs clearing and registration of the bargain passports should be levied not as a certain percent of the bargain sum, but at a rate of the actual expenses connected with registration of the documents. The CIS countries should reconsider a thousand laws and agreements, including the customs, tax and criminal codes. Numerous CIS countries get prepared for entering the WTO independently, which is incompatible with the customs union principles. Without a co-ordination of joining the WTO, the main benefits will go to the best developed countries, whereas many CIS companies will lose their share in the market. During the 20 years of international trade liberalisation, its growth increased (by up to 6% per year), but the share of the least developed countries decreased by a factor of 2.

The WTO rules prohibit direct subsidies to industry. In the CIS market of services, foreign suppliers practically do not encounter resistance (except in banking and insurance) or even have better conditions (Russian transportation companies pay VAT, whereas the foreign companies do not). The CIS countries, like in a lot of other places, should limit the activity of foreign financial companies (except for the CIS countries and, on a reciprocal basis, other neighbours). In advertising, tourism, construction and transportation many WTO members oblige foreign companies to place orders (e.g. for 50% of TV advertising) in their territory, to involve local labour, or to transfer know-how to national companies. They limit the level of foreign investments, number of representative offices, legal form of companies and the number of foreign personnel, and the total of foreign suppliers in specific services (the list contains over 150).

The greatest damage related to joining the WTO can be incurred by the consumer, food and machine-building industries of numerous CIS countries. Moldova, getting ready for entering the WTO, introduced licensing import of alcohol and tobacco and foreign trade operations with medicines, chemicals, pesticides and textiles. Countries having unsatisfactory payment balance are allowed by the WTO to introduce import quotas (India, for example, till recently generally banned import of 2500 consumer goods).

New import tariffs require a detailed substantiation in view of the share of the goods in the domestic market, opportunities of attracting modern foreign technologies and creation of new jobs.

It is necessary to take into account special relations of some CIS countries with the EU, Turkey, Iran and China. The EU customs duties on the goods imported from the CIS are on average below 2%. However, the EU, like over 100 other regional groupings supporting the general WTO rules, do not abolish tariff barriers for all goods to the same degree, as they do for those produced domestically. Special attention is paid to non-tariff barriers: standards, certificates and protection of intellectual property.

In the CIS market, there are over 2000 Finnish companies, the only EU country with which the CIS has a common border. In 1996 Russia's share of the Finnish export was 27%, that of other CIS countries 6% and in 1997 it was 9%. In Latvia, where more than 50% of all businessmen at the end of the 1990s were of Russian origin, the share of businessmen considering Russia as their primary market grew from 30% to 42%, and in other CIS countries from 19% to 29%.

The EU rules allow for quantitative restrictions on import and export if their growth threatens national economy. Thus, in Russia the manufacture of carpets and rugs fell in 1993–1996 from 34.8 to 4.8 million m^2 due to the competition of import (from the EU, $300 million). Russian carpets serve five times longer, are well-coloured, and are resistant to dynamic loads and wet laundering; thus, their price is naturally higher than that of Belgian carpets ($4.6 and $3.3/m^2). By 1998, the share of import had reached 90%, and Russia had lost in this branch 40% of jobs and had also introduced import quotas. Similar quotas had been introduced by the EU with regard to American beef, but the Russian action caused the protest.

The export credits permitted by the WTO guaranteed by the State are even more efficient (e.g. the USA provides them with sales of Boeing aircraft, Caterpillar tractors, John Deere combines) and grants for R&D.

6. Co-ordination of the status of free business zones. As has been mentioned already, many CIS companies are registered in off-shore areas, European (Cyprus, Ireland, Gibraltar, island Man, Guernsey and Jersey), American (Virgin, Bahamas, Bermudas, Cayman islands, Panama and others) and South Asian (Mauritius, Maldives, Nauru). Expansion of the rights of local government bodies results in tax oases in the CIS as well. Such zones exist in Moldova, the Ukraine, Belarus and Russia (e.g. in Kalmykia, Altai, Buryatia). The co-ordination of their status will strengthen the role of free business zones as centres of manufacture development, instead of speculative intermediary operations.

An efficient customs union is inconceivable without an effective system of accounts and payments.

The monetary union. The financial background of economic integration, as global experience shows, includes four stages: forming a common financial and credit infrastructure, forming a payment union, creation of a consolidated budget, and transition to a uniform currency. The CIS countries are presently at the first or second stage, and the EU countries have passed to the final stage.

The common financial and credit infrastructure gets created on the basis of commercial banks, insurance and investment companies from other CIS countries, joint banks, stock exchanges and other financial structures. This process started in 1995 on the background of strengthening national currencies.

In the countries of the Central Asian region and Azerbaijan, the minimum founding capital for joint and foreign banks is comparatively small (below $1 million); in Belarus and the Ukraine it is much higher. Joint banks with Russian participation are founded in the Ukraine, Belarus, Kazakhstan, Kyrgyzstan, Turkmenistan and other countries.

The payment union of the CIS countries (the agreement was signed in 1994) envisages as its first stage a system of payments through correspondence accounts with central (national) and authorised commercial or other banks. In addition to the banks, participants of the payment system are the governments of the countries (according to the bilateral and multilateral treaties between them), business units (including those with no legal entity) and physical persons, and residents of the countries (with regard to non-trade operations).

The formation of the payment union is based on the following principles:

– Recognition of the national currency sovereignty and the role of the central (national) banks as issuing centres and the bodies regulating credit and currency circulation rules over the territory of each party

– Prevention of any restrictions on accepting and use of national currencies as payment means for trade and non-trade operations stipulated in the contracts over the territory of each party

– Introduction of the rules for government regulation of foreign trade and currency circulation on operations on sale and purchase of national currency for national currencies of other parties and other currencies

– Guaranteed converting of national currencies into currencies of other parties on socially important payments

– Granting non-residents the right to possess their national currency and use it to pay for goods and services, the payments being of non-trade nature

The participants of the payment system can freely deposit money resources in national currencies of other parties in their internal money market in the order determined by the legislation of the said country. Furthermore, it has been decided to adhere to a uniform currency exchange rate for all external economic operations, to apply the exchange rate determined by the supply and demand in the currency markets of the parties and to carry out co-ordinated measures aimed at stability of the national currencies.

With the purpose of regulating the exchange rates, central (national) banks create and use stabilisation funds in hard currencies and precious metals. The parties guarantee admission into their internal currency markets for banks-non-residents and the Interstate Bank according to their respective national legislation.

Exchange of national currencies for physical persons is carried out by commercial and other banks according to the exchange rate established in the currency market, with the exchange to national currency of other parties having remaining money on the accounts belonging to non-residents is facilitated. Furthermore, the central (national) banks do not bear the responsibility on settling obligations of the commercial banks of the parties. For multilateral co-operation, the Interstate Currency Committee has been founded. For solving the non-payment problem and in order to reduce the volume of barter trade envisaged is the bill introduced into the international economic circulation, accompanied by a mechanism of multilateral clearing via the Interstate Bank and other specialised institutions.

The structure of the monetary relations inside the CIS in the 1990s has essentially changed. The share of bilateral interstate barter clearing fell (from 50% to 15%), that of payments via central banks (from 20% to 5%), the share of non-currency barter remained the same (10%), but that of payments in hard currency grew, like the share providing currency equivalents (from 5% to 15%). What grew most of all were the payments in national currencies through correspondence accounts in commercial banks (from 5% to 55%).

However, the conditions for financial integration have not yet been created. Unlike the EU countries, the CIS lacks uniform regulations of, for example, budget deficit and exchange rate, settlements on trade and non-trade payments are not balanced, the mutual trade is reduced and the role of barter and uncontrollable "shuttles" remains great. The interests of the CIS countries are different: five of them welcome rises in power resource prices, whereas seven greet their decrease. It is necessary to pay the debts of the former Soviet Vnesheconombank to the legal entities inside the CIS (approximately $10 billion) and to introduce mortgage as a means for securing credits.

In the late 1990s the volume of converting national currencies has increased, especially for the Ukrainian grivna, Kazakh tenge, Byelorussian rubles, Uzbek sums and Moldavian leys. Regular operations with them are carried out by a lot of Russian banks (Russian Credit, Menatep and others), currency stock exchanges and financial centres. Thanks to a network of correspondence accounts they can be used in trade. Their stock quotations allow for finding the most favourable variants; however, by 1997 only 10% of all external economic payments were effected in currencies of the CIS countries.

Russia, Belarus and some other CIS countries have opened their currency markets for each other, admitting authorised banks to conduct currency operations on the terms equal with their residents. Measures have been taken to introduce a uniform rate of national currencies for all operations and its alignment within certain limits. At the expense of the trade participants, a reserve fund for covering the losses suffered by the stock exchanges has been created to be used in case they fail. The currency corridor had reduced the scale of financial gamble, which resulted in pushing out the banks unable to efficiently deal in real corporate assets (long-term credits, inter-industry mobility of capital, bankruptcy, merges and acquisitions, and financial services).

However, in general the payment union is not an act of direct action, but only a basis for the bilateral and multilateral mutual payments and currency conversion. In the CIS it has resulted in considerable difficulties. The flow of goods from Russia to many CIS countries exceeds the counterflows. The exchange rates of numerous currencies are adjusted administratively according to political reasons and essentially differ from the market rates. The rates of inflation differ, like the discount rates and the degree of liberalisation in the internal currency market. The freedom of moving currency in these conditions can only lead to flight of capital from some countries into other. It was not by chance that the Ukrainian National Bank limited operations on the "Loro" accounts with real flow of goods and services, forbidding the remains on correspondence accounts of CIS banks to be used as credit resources.

The mechanism *of multilateral payments* (MP) is the one most promising when done on the basis of mutual requirements and obligations within the clearing pool. The pure balance of settlements is thus adjusted, not for each country separately, but for the MP system as a whole via the quota, established depending on the trade volume of the given state within the system. Some of the passive balance gets covered with credits from a special fund and the rest with hard currency, its share increased along with the balance growth. A similar system was successfully used by western European countries in the 1950s and promoted increase of their mutual trade, reduction of barter, growth of gold reserves and solidification of their national currencies.

A model of a similar system suggested by N. Petrakov and G. Shagalov (Institute for Market Problems, RAS), assumes the use of European currency as the media of payments. The fund necessary for the MP system to function in the CIS, according to their calculations, makes 1.6 billion ECU ($2 billion), which is feasible even if the first stage will be participated in only by those countries which have entered the customs union.

Of the greatest importance for putting payments for machinery and equipment into order is the development of *leasing*. In the USA, its share is one third of all capital investments in equipment. The bank then acts as an intermediary, guarantor and sometimes leaser, whereas real mortgage reduces its credit risks. The enterprises in the CIS countries urgently need updating their equipment but have no money to do so. Leasing will become their chance to receive modern machinery, the payment being done only after its launch, reaching the design capacity or making the first profits. The leasing party guarantees complex maintenance and spare-parts delivery. Leasing payments are referred to the costs, which reduce the taxation base. The lessee is exempted from the property tax and customs duties, and improves the assets liquidity and the ratio of its own and borrowed capital. (The object under leasing remains on the leaser's balance, though used by the lessee.) According to the leasing contract, the bank renders financial, tax, legal and information-marketing services. Once the IPA passes the model law on leasing, it will promote the expansion of the market for selling machines and the increased competitiveness of the CIS industry.

Overcoming of *the non-payment crisis* is connected with a reduction of barter which in addition to being unequal is unbalanced. This requires solving a lot of problems.

The first problem is forming currency stock exchanges from national into interstate level. In the mid-1990s these stock exchanges basically secured the internal convertibility of national currencies, the non-residents' access to the national currency markets being limited by law. The Belarus currency stock exchange was still a State institution in 1997: all buyers of hard currency (except those importing energy, grain and other vital products) had to pay the obligatory 10% duty and most exporters had to sell the proceeds in hard currency and Russian rubles at the stock exchange.

However, in the late 1990s, the stock exchanges requiring advance payments and raising high converting fees ceased to be popular. Moldova, Kyrgyzstan, Russia, Kazakhstan and the Ukraine were the first to introduce free conversion of their currencies. The basic exchange started being done out of stock exchange. In these conditions, the internationalisation of the currency market was amplified. The Russo-Ukrainian bank Creditimpex was the first among the CIS non-residents which became a shareholder of the Kazakhstan currency stock exchange. The stock exchanges lowered or even cancelled commissions charged for exchanging currencies of the CIS countries, creating a more rational system of accounts.

The next problem is the mechanism of paying debts. Thus, among the five major creditors of Georgia in the mid-1990s, there were IMF, Turkmenistan (both 25%), the World bank (12%), Russia and EU (both 9%). The debt to Turkmenistan and Russia was formed basically as a result of the negative trade balance of Georgia (excess of import over the export). Without re-structuring this debt (Georgia does not have the money to pay in either hard currency or rubles), further trade is impossible. According to the international rules, the debts (including those binding Uzbekistan, Armenia and Kazakhstan) were restructured on the same conditions for 10 years, during the first 5 years only interest (4% annually) is to be paid. The same principle was used in deferring target payments (to buy Russian goods) to Kyrgyzstan, Tajikistan and Moldova. The largest debt (over $9 billion) is to be paid by the Ukraine (mainly to Russia and Turkmenistan).

One of the ways to pay it is transfer of property and shares of privatised enterprises, or paying the debt with valuable papers. This was what the Ukraine, Moldova, Kazakhstan and Kyrgyzstan did. Up to now, over 60 organisations have been busy "squeezing" mutual debts on various CIS companies. Introduction of uniform rules for circulation of bills and other securities according to international law would lead to eliminating advance payments, to expanded practice of tightened credits to CIS partners for purchasing goods with a guarantee of permanent maintenance of the delivered equipment throughout its life. Only then will CIS companies become equal competitors of foreign corporations in their market.

One more problem is the complete mutual currency convertibility, cancellation of any restrictions on operations with payment balance, creation of a uniform market of securities and free access of foreign financial institutions to the national markets. A similar agreement was signed by Russia, Kazakhstan, Kyrgyzstan and Belarus in 1996. However, the first three countries joined the agreement between the countries are participants of the IMF, which obliges them to allow to their markets companies from any IMF-member country, and to abolish discriminatory currency agreements as well as restrictions on any money transfers not connected with movement of capital and investments. Kazakhstan and Kyrgyzstan were the first permitted non-residents to freely buy foreign currency for tenges and sums. The problems in this respect are faced solely by Belarus, where several exchange rates are established administratively instead of as the result of the intersection of supply and demand.

However, many CIS countries up to now do not support the idea of joint regulation of the currency quotations, which requires a joint control of budget deficit and other macro-economic indicators of the currency union participants, and complete information interchange about the conditions of the financial and banking sectors. Without it, no high-level organisation of interbank accounts and financial co-operation is possible.

In the CIS countries there are isolated markets of government securities, one of largest ones in Russia (approximately $35 billion), in the Ukraine (the secondary market, $3 billion), Kazakhstan, Belarus and Moldova. The Russian bank suggested to CIS national banks swap operations, exchange of national currencies for rubles guaranteed with reserve dollar deposits with subsequent reverse exchange at the fixed rate. It would allow owners of ruble accounts to temporarily invest free financial resources into government securities, getting much more yields than with ordinary deposits.

Prospects of the currency union. The currency union is a natural and logical stage for completing the uniform market. The exchange rates of national currencies WRT the common currency are fixed with a mutual arrangement and the responsibility for the monetary policy and basic interest rate gets laid onto the community central bank. The countries, where the budget and economic conditions do not allow entering the currency union immediately, enter the union on exchange rates. It enables them to plan their trade, prices and investments, without regard to unforeseen changes in exchange rates. It will result in tourism development, the banks pile reserves to a greater extent in their national currency instead of the dollar (of the $380 billion, approximately 60% remain in cash circulation outside the USA, which means that country gets interest-free credit from the whole world).

As is seen in Table 30, recent years have led to a stabilisation of most CIS currencies. However, due to the financial crisis of 1998, the standing of the Russian ruble worsened along with that of Belarussian, Moldovian and Ukrainian currencies.

In less than a year since August 1997, the ruble-per-U.S. dollar rate dropped by 25%. This resulted in a significant fall in national exchange rates in the Ukraine, Belarus, Georgia, Kyrgyzstan, Moldova and Tajikistan. The national exchange per ruble rates climbed up in particular in Azerbaijan, Armenia and Kazakhstan.

Table 30

Exchange Rates of National Currencies
(according to central banks, end-of-the-year rates)

	Per 100 Russian rubles				Per $1 U.S.			
	1995	1996	1997	1998 (late December)*	1995	1996	1997	1998 (late December)
Azerbaijan manats	8.5	74.0	65.0	188	4440	4098	3888	3890
Armenian drams	8.4	7.8	8.2	24.7	402	435	496	522
Belarus rubles	247	279	316	5100	11500	15500	30740	107000
Georgian laris	0.03	0.022	0.022	0.086	1.25	1.27	1.30	1.8
Kazakh tenges	1.39	1.36	1.3	4.29	64.0	73.3	75.6	83.8
Kyrgyzstan soms	0.24	0.30	0.29	1.478	11.2	16.7	17.4	29.4
Moldovian leys	0.09	0.08	0.078	0.396	4.5	4.65	4.66	8.3
Russian rubles	100	100	100	–	4640	5560	5960	20.7
Tajik rubles	6.0	5.6	12.4	49.6	294	328	747	985
Turkmenian manats	4.3	73.1	69.7	253.7	200	4070	4165	5200
Uzbek sums	0.76	0.98	1.35	5.65	35.5	54.7	80.2	110
Ukrainian grivnas	...	0.034	0.032	0.166	...	1.89	1.90	3.43

* Per one deposited ruble.

The uniform currency helps in: lowering commercial risks, simplifying and making cheaper mutual payments, simplifying investments process, comparing prices and increasing company competitiveness in various countries. Furthermore, new currency is introduced instead of the currency already used in one of the countries, let it even be the largest (such as the Euro in the EU).

However, in the CIS this problem will become urgent only after national economies get really approached. Its first stage may be a monetary union with a full liberalisation of capitals flow, currency convertibility, strengthening of co-operation between the central banks, stock, currency and commodity exchanges of the CIS countries, and writing a uniform legal base for issuing and circulation of securities. Only after all that will establishing a common currency institution as a prototype of the CIS Central bank make sense, like a treaty on rigid co-ordination of the economic and financial policies.

It is only at the third stage that one can suggest a uniform currency in clearing settlements and later issuing new uniform bank notes and coins.

It is always easier to break than to build. The CIS countries quickly rejected a uniform currency. Return to former ruble is already impossible. The prospects of transition to a new European currency in the twenty-first century depend on the real successes in the integration. However, the importance of a uniform currency cannot be underestimated. It would mean a revolution in methods of management of assets and securities, a rapid growth of investments and reduction of risks resulting from the instability of the currencies of the CIS countries and the low liquidity of their securities. Simultaneously, it would stop financial gambling connected to the differences in exchange rates of the CIS countries, rates of their depreciation in relation to dollar, return on government bonds and discount rates of their central banks. Instead of gambling, the banks would have to get engaged in organising real investments in promising projects.

It is necessary to remember the consequences caused by introducing the EU uniform currency for the CIS economy. It is not so much about the technical difficulties of recalculating the marks, francs, guilders and other currencies into Euro and not about the temporary fluctuations of the exchange rate at the moment of introducing the new currency than about the strategy for the early twenty-first century. The volume of trade between the CIS countries and the EU is greater than that with the USA. The common currency space will undoubtedly raise the stability and efficiency of the European economy and increase the role of Euro in the world financial market. The CIS countries receive export proceeds chiefly in U.S. dollars, paying in Euro for their import. With the relative fall of the dollar, it can cause huge losses. At the same time, binding the rate of a possible common CIS currency to the Euro will open new prospects.

The Euro is introduced only by those EU countries which have conditions appropriate for this. Probably, for the CIS this way will appear most real, too.

The co-ordination of financial policies between the CIS countries would allow a fuller use of financial reserves for the debts paid in hard currency. These are: control over the export of currency; efficiency of foreign investments; shuttle trade; reducing amount of food and services imported for hard currency; increase in the export of goods with high added value; and joining the WTO (decrease of the tariffs will give the CIS countries up to $3 billion a year). After settling the financial problems with the Paris and London clubs of creditors and with the Ukraine, Russia will be able to sell the liabilities of numerous Asian, African and Latin American countries. The former policy of the CIS countries with regard to restructuring the credit and making new obligations replacing the old ones only aggravated the problem of the national debt.

The export of currency in the past 3 years only from Russia amounted according to different estimations to $25–50 billion, with another $300–400 million taken out by the "shuttles" every month without paying any taxes. Only to Turkey, with its official trade with Russia of $2.5 billion per year, did the "shuttles" bring to Turkey annually $4 billion in cash and approximately $1 billion in goods to be exchanged for consumer goods. Turkey receives even more uncontrollable currency (in percentage to the total trade volume) from Georgia, Azerbaijan and Moldova; China from Kyrgyzstan and Kazakhstan. The currency obtained from exported national wealth and deposited by CIS companies into foreign accounts gets given by the same countries as foreign loans spent for purchasing foreign goods, i.e. it creates new jobs abroad and increases the CIS national debts.

In Russia, the introduced registration of export deals resulted in reducing the share of the profits left abroad from 50 to 4%. Since 1996, the import channel of capitals outflow has been blocked, too: having transferred the currency, the buyer must prove that the goods were really received. In 1998 the obligatory sale by the exporters of 75% of their hard currency revenues was introduced, a flat ruble rate, and the currency stock market started having different sessions for importers and other banks having licenses for work with currency. The purpose of all this is setting limits to currency speculations. Currency control does not contradict the market laws (in France, it had worked until the early 1990s). In the late 1990s the interdependence of CIS financial markets grew. Belarus, the Ukraine and some other countries purposefully decreased the rates of their currencies to make export cheaper and to reduce the negative trade balance. In these conditions, co-ordination of currency policies is a must; otherwise, neighbours will hurry to devalue their currencies.

The growth of the national currency rates causes ambiguous consequences for the economies, complicating export and facilitating import. The decrease of real incomes in export branches requires a reduction in their costs due to new technologies or cancellation of export taxes, VAT and other charges. (This is the way for Russia and numerous other CIS countries.) The growth of import profitability strengthens the necessity of its restriction with taxation and other methods. All this strengthens the necessity of economic integration.

A uniform currency policy would help the CIS countries to create a civilised labour market. In the 1990s migration of the population into Russia sharply increased. The balance (the difference between arrivals and departures) was especially great in the relations with Kazakhstan, Central Asian countries and Transcaucasia, and much lower with the Baltic states, the Ukraine and Moldova. Only to Belarus have more people come from Russia (basically from Siberia and the Far East) than have gone to Russia.

The number of temporary workers has increased sharply, especially of construction workers, miners and transportation workers coming to Russia from the Ukraine, Belarus, Moldova and of merchants from Azerbaijan. In the Donetsk area, according to the local administration, due to the workers' migration into Russia 60% of streetcars and one third of trolleys remain non-operational. Legal provisions for this migration cannot be postponed.

One of the preconditions of free labour movement between the CIS countries is the creation of the housing market. The share of privatised housing in the 1990s grew from 30% to 85%. However, its price in Moscow exceeded the price level in Brussels, Madrid, Toronto and Jerusalem in terms of poor quality. In other CIS capitals and cities it is a few times lower, e.g. in the Ukraine from $220 to $400 (in Kiev to $500) per m^2, which is affordable for the professionals arriving from other CIS regions. At the same time, the average Ukrainian has to work in order to buy a two-room apartment ($8000–$10,000) for 45 years. In other European cities this term does not exceed 3–5 years, and in New York and Tokyo 8–10 years. In the mid-1990s a two-room apartment, according to real estate companies, was priced (in thousands) in Moscow for $35–60, in Saint Petersburg and Minsk for $27–30, in Kiev for $12–16, in Alma-Ata for $9–12, in Bishkek and Kishinev for $4–7, and in Tashkent for $2–3.

Housing could become a profitable area for joint investments. Thus, in Russia the general living area per inhabitant has by 1998 exceeded 19 m^2, but 20% of all apartments have no sewage, 50% lack hot water and 80% are without phones.

The common economic space assumes co-ordinating national budget policies and creating a joint fund for financing common scientific, technical and social economic programs. The EU budget is formed of three sources: payments by the states-members, a part of national taxes (e.g. VAT) and 90% are customs duties levied on the trade with third countries.

For the CIS countries for the time being important is reduction of budget deficit down to a co-ordinated level and establishment of the funds financing the programs of interest for several countries (e.g. ecological, space, scholarly, educational, transport). The common budget since 1997 has existed only in the union of Russia and Belarus. The interstate bank does not work, as its participants have not brought payments into the founding capital. A joint budget is especially important for developing and carrying out scientific and technical programs.

9.4 Towards a Common Science-Technology and Education Space

Co-ordination of the scientific and technical policies. Soviet science has occupied an outstanding place in the world in such areas as mathematics, physics (e.g. nuclear, high energies, new materials, laser, space), chemistry, earth sciences (e.g. geology, oceanology, soil analysis) and biology. There has been a global infrastructure with a certain division of labour between the republics and the new research centres in Siberia, the Far East, the Central Asian region (e.g. Tashkent, Navoi, Tchkalovsk, Ust'-Kamenogorsk), Transcaucasia, the Ukraine and Belarus. However, up to 80% of all research and technical products have been intended for the military field.

The CIS states had to sharply reduce the budget financing of science, as a first defensive, to narrow the circle of fundamental research. The annual budget of a modern laboratory in physics of elementary particles is $500 million per year. Discoveries in this area require several years of work and billions of dollars, which is impossible for a single country.

Co-ordination of scientific and technical policies between the CIS countries would allow one to reduce non-promising research and similar work done at various organisations at the same time. However, the Interstate Committee on Scientific and Technological Development and the International Association of Academies of Sciences, created to promote the common scientific technological space, began their work only in 1996, with their decisions being pure recommendations. As a result, the number of scientific and technical personnel in the CIS countries was reduced by half, having lost its most active participants who had moved abroad or to private business.

In Belarus, having serious research potential (e.g. physics, mathematics, genetics, molecular biology, ecology, chemical synthesis), in 1990–1996 the number of scientists fell from 107,000 to 39,000, basically at the expense of young ones. Field, expeditionary and experimental works, as well as publishing and informational exchange, have been reduced to a minimum. Over 1000 developments ready for manufacture have not been demanded. In Russia, the average age of scientists in 1997 exceeded 55 years, and doctors of sciences are over 57–58 years old. In Kazakhstan, where 270 research institutions (128 academic, 48 high school, 82 branch and 13 factory institutions) operate, the share of research and technical production in the GDP fell in 1993–1996 from 1.1% to 0.3%. The average salary of scientists (as in other CIS countries) is lower than in industry (by one third) and in financial institutions (almost by 50%).

However, in the late 1990s the CIS scientific and technical complex showed some tendencies towards growth. The high level of work in physics, astrophysics, astronomy, mechanics and laser engineering in Uzbekistan is evidence of the fact that 90% of all projects have received INTAS grants. Kazakh scientists have carried out an order of the European organisation on nuclear researches producing beryllium tubes of special design, sold to a Swiss company as the know-how for producing nicotine acid used for medicines and fodder additives. In the late 1990s the CIS countries started reforming their scientific and technical complexes.

Major trends of reforms. Mutual consultations of the CIS countries on their scientific and technical policies lead to making them more efficient. The first thing necessary for preservation and development of scientific potential is a Eurasian innovative system, a set of high-tech industry branches which could become the main consumer and customer of the research and technical products, to lead efficient commercialisation of the newest high-tech technologies.

Even in those CIS countries where the role of the state in economy remains prevailing, it is not anymore the sole or even the main source of financing science. In Belarus, the budget covers 39% of its expenses, extra-budget centralised funds 11% and 46% are covered by customers. If we recall that 25% of the money came back into the budget and social funds as taxes, the self-supporting of applied science will become even more obvious.

According to foreign experts, most significant segments of the R&D market, for which the CIS countries have the necessary potential, are in the early twenty-first century communication and information transfer (the world market is $40 million per year) remote sounding of the earth ($2 billion), launching space crafts into orbit ($1.5 billion) and other such activities. Since 1996 the volume of commercial sales in the space area (with over 100 countries-participants in the market) had exceeded the budget financing.

In the CIS, on the threshold of intensive growth, there is the computer market. It is represented by manufacturers of equipment, merchants-distributors, system integrators for specific projects and operators of general-purpose networks. They have the certain financial resources for conducting long-term programs. The innovative system includes marketing centres studying the prospective demand for innovations. In the USA and EU countries, research and evolving of the innovations market (e.g. also with advertising, demonstration of novelties) and transfer of technologies, consumes more than 10% of all expenses on R&D, whereas in the CIS countries it consumes less than 1%. Joint analytical, exhibition, expert consulting, engineering and other centres will be for the participating countries much cheaper and with shorter payback period.

These establishments are most expedient for capitals and large cities. The factories capable of mass manufacturing, located in the centres of such cities, lose competitiveness.

The development of the technologies market in modern conditions means that the scientific and technical organisations transfer to the customer not the documentation as scientific reports and drawing projects, but technological lines ready to work, new products with all accompanying services (e.g. adjusting, training of the staff) and equipment protected by patents. The payments for such complex R&D products is usually made as a certain percentage of the sales of goods and services produced on their basis, or corresponding profits (royalty price). In this case an isolated research institute or design bureau is not the seller, but a major R&D centre or a design and constructing corporation as the general contractor capable of bearing the responsibility for the innovative project as a whole. World practice knows that such contractors are most often TNC co-ordinating efforts of the experts in different countries. The reform of science assumes approach or association of academic science with university research and branch research with financial and industrial groups (FIG) and corporations.

Preservation of personnel potential in science is especially important. In the 1990s hundreds of thousands of experts have left the CIS countries abroad for permanent residence or temporary contract work. The most capable of them, mainly young people, received well-paid jobs. In Russia, the Ukraine and Moldova whole scientific schools have disappeared. To forbid such migration under the conditions of sharply decreased budget financing of science is impossible. However, as the China experience shows, it is possible to draw back some of the scientists enriched with new experience, if they can receive appropriate conditions and opportunities to head in new directions. In Russia, the experience of joint ventures financed by foreign companies and corporations proved useful. It would be expedient to continue co-operation with the scientist-emigres, to invite them for lecturing. Trips of experts from numerous CIS countries presently having no conditions for developing science to institutes in Russia, Belarus and Kazakhstan with having better life will help in preserving the national scientific elite.

The priority of *macro-technologies*, sets of know-how and production facilities required and sufficient to produce competitive high-tech products are also very important. According to the director of the Russian institute of air technologies, O. Sirotkin, the seven most advanced countries have 46 of the 50 technologies of the sort and hold 80% of the market for high-tech products. The USA receives from its exports $700 billion a year, Germany $530 billion and Japan $400 billion. Russia together with other CIS countries, can compete in 10–15 technologies (air, space, nuclear, shipbuilding and car industry, transportation, chemical and power engineering, special metal processing, special chemistry and new materials, micro- and radioelectronics, computer, information, bio-technologies), with the market capacity of $23 to 94–98 billion in 1996–2010. Each of these technologies requires state and interstate programs, whereas the orders to research organisations on developing separate parts of the whole system should be given out on a competitive basis.

On an interstate basis the creation of a new scientific and technical infrastructure, including systems of automation of R&D, computerisation of manufacture, quality management, standardisation and certification, looks most promising. It is in these areas that the CIS countries lag behind the world level most of all.

The research centres *State accreditation* allows to really estimate the scientific and technical potential of the country and to indicate those organisations which can expect basic budget financing (approximately one third of all expenses on science) and participation in contests for specific innovative projects. In Russia, of 4360 research organisations, more than 1200 have turned into joint stock companies, and others have been included into public centres of science (SCS), those of financial and industrial groups, academy of sciences, and others. More than 40 SCS conduct research along priority and interdisciplinary lines, and also, on a non-commercial basis, consult the government and examine projects; however, many institutes have already ceased to be research institutes.

The reorganisation of financing science is based on allocating financial resources, not to feed the research organisation itself, but to carry out specific innovation projects. The share (contributed by the government and local authorities) credit and venture (risky) financing is especially important, when the money is not credited, but given as a share in a common business. The profit is then formed primarily as a result of the growth of share price in those enterprises which managed to finish developments having market value. Venture funds, also with foreign participation, in the late 1990s successfully worked in Russia, the Ukraine and Moldova.

The CIS countries should select three spheres of R&D activity. In the technologies where CIS countries are traditionally strong (materials, non-ferrous metals, high-frequency, laser and numerous sorts of space engineering), it is necessary to pay special attention to foreign patenting, protection of the intellectual property and sale of the licenses, especially to the rapidly developing countries of the Asian-Pacific region.

Development of *vital technologies* where CIS countries lag behind, but without which it is impossible to keep the economy competitive (computers, information technologies, medicine, ecology, power, agriculture), should be having investments on a co-operative basis. Furthermore, the transfer of defence technologies will become very important. The CIS countries cannot keep the military industrial complex at its former size. They need modern industry capable, in view of international conditions, of flexibly changing the ratio of military-space and civil machinery in their output.

Finally, the third sphere includes the R&D directions not having a decisive importance and significantly handicapped as compared with the level of the developed countries. Here purchasing of foreign licenses can appear much more favourable than feeding idle research organisations.

In Kazakhstan and some other CIS countries the role of the Academy of Sciences has changed essentially. From an administrative department controlling a network of research organisations it has become a community of scholars exempted from administrative functions. Many institutes are thus united with universities, which results in increased quality of training and involves young people in research.

Legal protection of intellectual property. The transition to information society means that the main resource of a country becomes the intellect of its people. In the late 1960s the concept of "intellectual property" was introduced into the theory of law including four parts: author's (rights on literary, musical, art, video and audiovisual products), patent (right on inventions, industrial samples, trademarks and names of places of origin of the goods, selection achievements), computer (rights on software, databases, topology of integrate plates) and license patentless right (e.g. right on know-how). Since 1967 the World Organisation of Intellectual Property has existed.

In the ex-USSR the concept of intellectual property was never applied. Inventors received copyright certificates, which, unlike patents, did not give them exclusive rights to use the development. The transfer of "advanced experience" to other enterprises usually was done free of charge and interested neither the transmitting, nor the receiving, party with regard to its accumulation and use.

For the CIS countries, accepting and following accepted norms of international law on patents, trade and service marks, copyright and adjacent rights, selection achievements, about the legal protection of computer software, databases and topology of integrate plates, and the mechanism of transferring technologies abroad (e.g. including the official registration and listing of contracts, licensing of consulting and intermediary services) is very important. It produces a favourable climate for R&D and other kinds of activity, protection against industrial intelligence, active involvement of advanced foreign technologies and acceptance of the CIS countries into the WTO.

The copyright includes non-property rights (i.e. the right to be considered the author of a product, to give it a name, to be the first to promote the product, to interfere with its distortions) and property rights on reproduction and distribution of the products via, for example, selling of books or tapes, transmissions or via a cable, translating, resale, carrying out architectural, town planning and park or design project. In all cases, except those directly listed in the law (e.g. recording a movie from the TV screen for personal use or reference purposes), the author, including foreign authors (since adhering to the Bern convention on protection of works of literature and art) is entitled to payments. Developed countries often stop transfer of technologies to the countries where illegal copying of, for example, computer programs, trademarks and vidcotapes, is going on, exacting vast penalties.

The property right on a product or a patent can belong to a company (the personal non-property rights remain with the author) only in the event that the intellectual property was created as an official duty following a direct order by the employer. However, even then the author gets paid a compensation for every use of his/her innovation (as a percent of the revenue and when it is impossible to define, as a lump sum).

The patent laws of the CIS countries establish rules of drafting and considering applications for an invention, useful model, industrial sample, registration and certification of patent attorneys, ways of protecting the rights of patent holders and sale of *licenses* to commercially use the patents. Under inventions we mean devices, methods, substances, micro-organism stamms admits, cultures of plants and animals cells, or their use for a new purpose, but only in the event that this technical solution is new (not registered anywhere in the world before the date of the priority application) and practically applicable.

The useful model (this concept is not applied in all foreign countries) is a technical solution with its essential attributes little known and not registered in a given country. Therefore, a copyright certificate on a model can be received much faster than a patent for an invention, thus guaranteeing legal protection of the new item. This allows simultaneous submission of applications for a useful model and an invention.

An industrial sample is an artistic design solution determining the appearance of a product (e.g. model, dummy model, industrial draft). The patent is granted for new, original and industrially applicable (possible to reproduce) samples. Like an invention and a useful model, the sample is entered into the State register.

A special object of legal protection is *know-how*, technical and commercial information (e.g. methods of organisation and management of a facility, carrying out technological and economic operations), little known and protected by its owner against easy access by outsiders (representing thus commercial secret) and promising additional income when used.

The Eurasian Patent Organisation, joined by most CIS countries, provides legal protection of inventions within 20 years on a uniform patent. Its reliability is secured with a system of examination. The application is presented in one language on the basis of uniform requirements and the duty gets paid in stages.

Intellectual property in the world market is protected in three basic ways: by registration of a *trademark* (protection of the name or another designation, distinguishing the products of a given company), *the copyright* (protection of the idea expressed as a script, musical or other creative work) and the patent protecting a technical idea, a way of manufacturing, a technological process, an operational method for a technical system or its electronic components. During recent years, a major object of patent protection has became computer software and topology of integrate plates.

In order to receive a patent, for example, in the USA, the companies and citizens of the CIS countries-participants of the agreement on patenting (the Patent Co-operation Treaty) should first submit an application to the patent establishment of the said country and then to the Bureau of Patents and Trademarks of the USA (U.S. Patent Office). The application to this bureau should be presented within 1 year of the beginning of marketing campaign, publication or demonstration of the object of patenting (premature advertising makes patenting impossible). Furthermore, the application can be submitted even without a working model or any experience of practical use of the technology, even if it goes with insignificant improvements of existing devices and mechanisms or a new way of their use not having an analogue.

In 1988–1996 the number of patents issued in the USA (for 20 years following the application date) grew from 57,000 to 110,000, 20% of which were granted to foreign applicants. They receive significant royalties from the total volume of sales of their products in all countries making use of the patented idea, even when they do not realise them themselves, but only transfer licenses. Large corporations (for example, Texas Instruments) receive incomes from license sales not less than from selling their products.

Small companies, having patented their ideas in timely manner, often receive larger profits than from direct competition against large corporations in the market. Thus, Star Electronics, having patented computer software compressing databases in computer memory, received according to the court decision $120 million from the powerful Microsoft as indemnification for infringement of their rights.

Patenting of intellectual property abroad is aimed at guaranteeing patent cleanliness of export (a chance to freely export without a danger of violating patents of the country belonging to third persons) and sales of licenses abroad. Furthermore, the licenses can be split into simple (they can be sold to several buyers), exclusive (they give the licenser, i.e. the buyer, exclusive right to use the patent in the given territory) and complete (sales of the property rights). The validity of patents is limited by international law to 20 years.

The European patent department in Munich (Germany) grants patents valid in all EU countries. The same order has been introduced in the CIS. It results in removing duplication of patent funds and avoiding repeated and fairly expensive red tape. According to the contract on patent co-operation, national examination bodies present the results of their checks to the international patent offices.

Legal protection of *computer software* (e.g. an objective form of representing data sets and commands intended for computers as initial codes, binary code) and *databases* (data sets as records, accounts and other information systematised so that it can be found and processed with computers) is very important. Legal protection in this case concerns not ideas and principles, but means of their expression. In the CIS countries, most programs get copied and distributed without registration. It interferes with the development of the branch producing in other countries up to 10% of their GDP. Furthermore, the principles of interface organisation (means of establishing and supporting the information exchange between humans and computers), programming languages and algorithms (instructions about a sequence of commands for solving a task) remain freeware all over the world and not subject to legal protection.

In the CIS countries, where the technologies market has not yet been created, the share of public financing in R&D should be higher. A target may be seen in Japan and other Asian countries where the state finances priority scientific and technological programs via, among other means, the budgets of ministries, universities and non-profit funds.

However, one country, in numerous cases even one such as Russia, cannot secure the entire research-and-production cycle without co-operation, ensure the variety of machines and devices, teach the staff in the required fields and invest large sums on long term. Moreover, Russia still has unique patent-information funds, the reconstruction of which in each CIS country would involve huge expenses.

Integration into the science-and-technology community. Integration is impossible without a wide exchange of students, post-graduate students and scholars. Here there appears to be a paradox: studying in the USA or Germany, let alone Istanbul, is cheaper than in Moscow, Saint Petersburg, Kiev or Tashkent. Some countries create independent systems of training. Thus, on the basis of a branch of a Kiev high school, the Tashkent air institute has been founded to train staff and experts of the airport ground services. Regional high schools are developed, where Academy of Sciences, the Agricultural Academy and metropolitan high schools of Uzbekistan have to send scholars. The republic has introduced quotas on training candidates and doctors of sciences for districts, teachers' working hours have been reduced, and an innovative centre "Patent service" has started work providing a variety of services. However, the uniform educational system of the CIS, capable of increasing the efficiency of national schools, has not been formed.

The development of a uniform telecommunication and information network with optical fibre lines linking Copenhagen-Moscow-Khabarovsk-Japan, and Italy-Turkey-Ukraine-Russia, among other countries, is very important.

The concept of reconstructing the common scientific-technological space in the CIS countries assumes making a list of high-tech products requiring co-ordinated financial and material support, and association of personnel potential of many CIS republics. That does not mean returning to former methods of managing technological progress. The basis of the joint strategy in scientific and technological development is not mass standardised production, but the development and acceptance of a whole new basis for resource-saving technologies supporting organised manufacture of small batches and fast updating of a wider selection of goods, competitive and linked to local demands on goods and services and joint export of scientific and technical products.

Joint innovative projects of the CIS countries according to interstate agreements are carried out in the technology of welding, powder metallurgy, earthenware and lasers.

Large economy can result from joint development and manufacture of automatic gas water heaters (not fewer than 3 million pieces are necessary) capable of saving up to 30% of gas and differing from foreign ones with low cost and stability against voltage peaks. All CIS countries need meters for gas and water, economic radiator thermostats and sets for utilising household trash allowing radical improvement of sanitary conditions, especially in hot areas. All this will not only give economy (energy saving is four to five times more profitable than fuel production), but also create tens of thousands of new jobs.

Prospects for such programs get opened by the model law passed by the IPA "On protection of high technologies". It recommends a system of protecting intellectual property (the owner of technology is its discoverer, assignee or employer, if the technology has been created while performing official duties or specific tasks), compensation for the authors and stimulation of inventing and use of high technologies (e.g. tax privileges to the investors in certified technologies, their consumers, soft loans to the authors of technologies and their assignees, refunding of expenses on patenting).

The integration of the CIS countries into scientific-technological area includes:

– Creation of joint ventures and TNC in high-tech industries

– Development of a uniform computer communications system for constant exchange of the scientific and technological information, joint publishing houses and journals in leading areas of science and engineering

– Joint financing and use of unique scientific and technological objects (e.g. launching site in Baikonur, observatories in the Ukraine, Russia, Turkmenistan)

– Creation of international R&D centres (e.g. on welding and related technologies, on the basis of the E.O. Paton Kiev Institute of electric welding)

– Development of interstate scientific and technical programs (e.g. in seismology, ecology) financed from the common budget

– Expansion of the Interstate Council on standardisation, metrology and certification, and of other organisations of the scientific and technological infrastructure

– Signing agreements and conventions directed at creating favourable financial, tax and other conditions for joint scientific and research activity, as well as protection of intellectual property

– Creation of joint training centres, improvement of professional skills and assessment and hiring of researchers and engineers

Furthermore, the CIS countries could jointly participate in international programs. Up to now they have done it separately. Thus, the Russian missile-building association, M.V. Khrunitchev, together with French and German companies, designs a space system of monitoring the environment on-line, which can be used by more than 50 countries. The joint stock company Energy has been carrying out the program of delivering engines for American rockets since 1998, making approximately $1 billion. Numerous promising projects are planned by the Ukraine, and joining the efforts would give greater effect.

It is important for the economic and scientific development in the CIS countries to get connected to the global information network Internet. However, it requires a telecommunications infrastructure including optical communication cables, modern phone stations, information centres with appropriate databases and systems of information protection. It must be their own manufacture of computer equipment (otherwise it will be too expensive), systems of service and training of users. Russia, the Ukraine, Belarus, Armenia and certain other CIS countries have already achieved some success in this respect.

The interstate R&D centre for AIC problems is going to supply the hardware to the CIS countries on the basis of co-operation and information exchange. A uniform fund will help in reimbursement to the developers some of their expenses.

In 1995 the All-Russia Institute for scientific and technological information won the EU competition on designing network structures for processing the global flow of scientific and technological information transfer, linked to high-speed optic cables for data transmission and the international computer network Internet. Joining this network will allow the research organisations in the CIS countries to receive complete information in all fields of knowledge (reviewed are 1.3 million publications per year from 13,000 publishing houses, 130 countries, in 60 languages).

Towards a unified education space. The scientific potential of the twenty-first-century economy, based on knowledge, includes four main sectors: state (centres of fundamental researches in leading technological progress areas and macro-technologies), business (corporate institutes and laboratories), public non-profit (humanitarian, medical, ecological and other research financed by non-profit funds) and education (university science).

In the CIS countries the reduction of budget financing had a heavy impact on high school science. In Russia its share in the R&D total volume fell in the 1990s from 20% to 5%. In the Ukraine, according to the Higher Education Ministry, more than 2000 doctors and candidates of sciences 35–50 years old left high schools; half of the doctors are of pension and pre-pension age. Jobs can be found by only 36% of all graduates from state high schools (in the EU countries this ratio is 50%–70%).

But modern economy, alongside with codified knowledge written as texts, formulas and symbols increasingly needs knowledge embodied in humans: sets of individual abilities, knowledge, as well as innovative skills and personality traits.

As sociological studies have shown, more than 75% of all young people in the CIS countries still aspire to receive higher (35%–40% of those interrogated), secondary or at least initial vocational training. Since the mid-1990s the competition in universities began to grow again, first of all in economic, legal, medical and technical ones.

Numerous CIS countries have started educational reforms. They include:

– Guarantees of equal access for talented youth to higher education. Thus, in Turkmenistan most gifted children are under personal protection of the leader of the state

– Development of diverse educational institutions, including non-government ones. For example, Uzbekistan has more than 400 colleges, lyceums and grammar schools, not only in Tashkent and Samarkand, but also in Urgetch, Turtkul, Andizhan. Regional pedagogical institutes have been transformed into universities. By 2001 there should be established legal, scholarly-methodical and financial preconditions for reforming the entire educational system

– The role of high schools in creation of research-technological parks, development of culture and international consent gets increased; Kyrgyzstan has a Slavic university, and Moldovian high schools include groups with training in Russian

– The structure and programs of training in high schools change with the requirements in the labour market. In Russia, training 5000 managers of the top and 25,000–30,000 of the middle level for the enterprises conducting re-structurisation, with additional training in leading foreign companies and management schools, is planned

The creation of a uniform educational space in the CIS is promoted by the mutual recognition of diplomas.

An important role in creating a uniform economic and educational space in the CIS countries can be played by high schools with international status. Last year, it was granted to many business schools in the USA.

Internationalisation of education passes along three basic directions. Business schools, organised as corporations, have co-founders and shareholders represented by foreign governments and organisations. An increasing number of students and post-graduate students get involved from other countries, which allows expansion and to make more efficient economic co-operation in the future. In training, more and more active place gets occupied by studying foreign markets, experience of joint activity, and peculiarities of the economies and cultures of foreign countries, also with the help of visiting professors.

9.5 Organisational Forms of Integration

Direct links are all-important. Efficient customs and monetary unions create the conditions for mutually profitable bilateral connections of companies, which, in turn, form the basis for the development of real economic integration requiring a common market and an economic union. As most enterprises in the CIS countries are private, the government promotes direct connections in non-administrative but economic methods, becoming the financial guarantee of the vital investment projects. Long-term contracts, consortia, simple partnerships, ventures and joint ventures all are organisational forms of stable direct connections.

Long-term contracts are drafted for numerous years as agreements on deliveries of raw materials, furnishing products and stuff. The leading CIS manufacturers of agricultural machinery (e.g. Rostselmash, Kirov factory) are highly interested in orders from Kazakhstan, the Ukraine and other republics with barter payment (in spare parts or grain). The deliveries of watering systems and agricultural machinery to Turkmenistan in exchange for cotton, melons, early vegetables and fruit are promising. The bank SBS-agro has since 1998 begun crediting processing agricultural products in the CIS countries so that the manufacturers lent money under specific contracts to the producers, supervising the target use of the moneys.

Russian oil companies deliver on the give-away basis raw materials to Kherson, Lisitchan and other oil-processing factories in the Ukraine. The pledge of steady direct connections here is the suppliers' purchasing a part of these factories' shares.

A special role in establishing stable connections is played by local authorities. Thus, the Moscow city government with the participation of the CIS countries establishes a system of large wholesale markets, where agricultural products will be delivered on a long-term basis. According to another project, Moscow will buy fodder in Krasnodar and Stavropol, re-routing it to the feeding complexes in Belarus with subsequent sales of meat in Moscow.

In accordance with the "Agreement on general conditions and mechanism of supporting the development of industrial co-operation" (the unified normative acts "On the order of deliveries and customs clearing of goods", passed by ten states), the CIS countries have developed rules concerning the order of moving, registration and account of appropriate goods. However, there are still latent financial flows, when a company is registered in one country and conducts business in another. In the first case it does not pay taxes because it does not conduct economic activities in the country in which it is registered, and in the other case, the same is true because it is a non-resident. This problem can be solved with a uniform database across the CIS countries, containing the information on companies registered elsewhere, their solvency, revenues, foreign trade contracts and other such characteristics. Up to now, advance payments directed, for example, to a Kazakhstan company with debts to the budget, under the laws of this country gets immediately withdrawn to the budget, export remaining prohibited until full indemnification of the debt. The buyer remains without money and without the products and will hardly ever risk co-operating with any CIS companies again unless the modern contract laws get developed and strictly observed.

The absence of due co-ordination hurts all countries. Therefore, the Ukraine delivers to Russia linking units for space craft. Russia sends to the Ukraine more than 30% of all components for the T-80 tank. Thus, selling tanks to other countries appears impossible without co-ordination with Russia.

Numerous CIS countries, with earlier received technologies and lower prices on raw materials and labour, export military machinery two to three times cheaper than the Russian one. Joint and co-ordinated export would give the CIS countries large additional benefits.

A *consortium* is a temporary joining of capitals for a specific investment project. Thus, the Russo-Ukrainian consortium has since 1997 conducted works on designing a universal carrier on the basis of intercontinental missiles for putting into orbit international communication satellites Teledesic (total cost of 840 satellites is $9 billion). Russian oil companies finance reconstruction of Belarussian oil processing plants in Mozyr and Novopolotzk, which will allow them to increase the depth of oil processing from 53 to 82% and to produce diesel fuel with sulphur contents of no more than 0.5%, according to the new EU ecological standards. Foreign credits get attracted only for purchasing equipment with no analogues in the CIS.

The list of profitable projects for which consortia are necessary is long. Armenia wants a co-operation of power systems over the northern Caucasus and Transcaucasia and restoration of the uniform transportation system; Turkmenistan will welcome the participation of Gasprom and Lookoil in searching and pumping hydrocarbon raw materials along the right bank of the Amu Darya with subsequent sale to Iran and Turkey. High returns are expected on investments into polymetal ores (e.g. copper, zinc, lead, niobium, wolfram) in eastern Kazakhstan.

However, CIS companies do not have sufficient capital for projects with long-payback periods. International consortia developing the deposits Azeri, Tchirag, Gyuneshli, Shakh-Deniz and Karabakh on the Caspian shelf are thus far participated in only by State oil companies of Azerbaijan, some foreign TNCs and the Russian Lookoil (its share is 10–30%).

Consortia frequently turn into permanent alliances. The Russian air consortium started selling and leasing planes TU-204 (done previously by eight companies), having signed contracts on technical support and post-sales servicing. Later, 14 participants of the consortium agreed on a joint development of the foreign trade strategy, management of financial flows, and other such factors.

Ordinary partnership is an agreement on joint development, manufacture and sales of goods and services providing association of assets, contributions and other resources, but without a new legal entity and isolation of its property. The bank participating in the partnership can simultaneously act in it as its debtor and creditor, at the same time working with other companies. Such alliances do not require special registration. In countries with market economy they are considered as a hidden weapon of competition.[5]

Such a union was signed in 1997 between the Sayan aluminium, Nikolaev earthenware, Tajik aluminium factories and the joint stock company Alyuminproduct (Russia). The purpose of this alliance is to attract investments ($200 million) for the modernisation of factories in the Ukraine and Tajikistan and to organise the goods and raw materials flow from mining to the final products (e.g. cans for soft drinks, building profiles). It will result in reduced risks from falling prices on primary aluminium and improve conditions of selling accompanying products (soda, cement, potassium).

The alliance of car factories in Russia and the Ukraine would allow them to develop new models, to exchange parts and to reclaim their positions on the foreign markets undermined by the TNC competition and alliances of corporations in Japan, South Korea and Germany with factories in Czech Republic, Hungary and Poland.

In the late 1990s the share of CIS factories in the total volume of sold car tires increased (from 30% to 50%). Their assortment expanded from 3–4 to 50 kinds and sizes. Shintorg, included in the group of petrochemical enterprises Maxim, acts as the general dealer of the largest Dnepropetrovsk and Byelotzerkovsk factories (the Ukraine).

The alliance between 120 diamond-cutting enterprises in Russia, Belarus, Armenia and the Ukraine, all having modern equipment which at reasonable supply and taxation can well export diamonds for up to $2 billion per year, looks promising.

The alliances are frequently based on personal relations and verbal arrangements of their bosses, protocols on intentions and agreements on joint activity, which are neither registered anywhere nor advertised. Often they found only common clearing and informative-marketing centres, or security services. Nevertheless, such alliances (under favourable tax conditions many of them subsequently turn into FIG) allow their participants to co-ordinate their activities in research and technological, industrial, commercial (trade, warehouse, transport, advertising, broker, lawyer's and consulting companies) and financial fields (e.g. investment, insurance, leasing, factoring, pension funds, settlements and depository centres).

Joint ventures between the CIS countries are much less usual than those with "far abroad" ones. In 1997 Uzbekistan had 100 joint ventures with Russian and 1200 with "far abroad" companies, Moldova 13 and 520, respectively, and the ratio was a little better in Kyrgyzstan (300 and 1350) and the Ukraine (1300 and 2700).

---

[5] Cf.: Lynch, R.P. (1993): Business Alliances Guide: the Hidden Competitive Weapon. New York; Badaracco, J. (1991): The Knowledge Link: How Firms Compete Through Strategic Alliances. Boston

In the late 1990s the number of joint ventures between the CIS countries started growing. joint venture Moldovagas (with the RAO Gasprom), into the founding capital of which Moldova invested main gas pipelines and distribution networks, improved the conditions of gas delivery and created additional jobs. The Georgian-Russian joint stock company Tbisa started developing, manufacturing and installing automated rope and monorail transportation for cities and agriculture, tourism, alpine skiing and mining industry of Transcaucasia, Russia, the Ukraine and Tajikistan. OAO GAS began assembling trucks Gazel at the joint ventures in Kazakhstan, the Ukraine and Moldova. The Kazakh-Kyrgyzstan joint ventures for uranium mining and processing has been founded on the basis of the Kara-Baltic combine.

The results are indicative of joint venture activity in Belarus (1996). Their total number, as well as in other CIS countries, grows, but only 38% really work, with fewer producing goods and services (14%). It is interesting that in Moldova, where the reforms are much more advanced, the corresponding figures are 63 and 56%. While the reforms have not been started, joint ventures are nothing but a way to "fix" a site without significant investments. It is necessary to note the low activity of the CIS countries' capital. In Belarus, their share in the authorised joint venture capital is only 0.3%, with the leading role played by Germany (30%) and Poland (13%). At the same time, approximately 40% of joint venture export were directed to the CIS, first of all to Russia.

Very often joint venture with "far abroad" countries worsen instead of improving the payment balance of a country. For example, the Moldovian joint venture import (in dollars) exceeded their export by more than five times.

In Kazakhstan, the share of the CIS countries' capital in authorised joint venture capital in 1996 reached only 5%. Russia with its 106 joint ventures occupied second place after Turkey (130). However, other CIS countries, needing goods imported from Kazakhstan, conceded in that not only to large European or Asian states, but also to such countries as Czech Republic, Bulgaria or Afghanistan. Furthermore, 20% of joint venture export went to the CIS countries. Unlike numerous other CIS countries, Kazakhstan's joint ventures exported one third more goods than were imported.

Finance-industrial groups. The top form of the developed connections between business units is *a financial and industrial group,* an association of legal entities including financial (e.g. banks, investment funds), manufacturing and trade companies uniting completely or partially tangible and intangible assets on the contract basis with the purpose of technological and/or economic integration, investments and other projects and programs, and increase of competitiveness.

In the late 1990s the world has approximately 40,000 FIGs with approximately 200,000 affiliated companies. They control one third of world production, more than a half of foreign trade, and 75% of licenses on new machinery, technologies and know-how. In the CIS countries, more than 90 FIGs operate, uniting more than 2000 industrial enterprises and research organisations, over 100 banks, bank holdings and other financial institutions. Their total volume of sales, according to experts, exceeds \$25 billion. In the 15 largest Russian FIGs in 1997, the sales volume grew by 1.4, export by 1.3 and investments by 2.5 times. This is where the main points of economy growth and integration are.

Regional FIGs raised labour productivity by 25% in 1 year, the sales volume by 55% and almost doubled export. The Perm FIG Yedinstvo will sell in 1998–2001 an investment program worth \$165 million The FIG Magnitogorskaya stahl (16 enterprises, 260,000 workers, the annual sales volume approximately \$600 million with fixed assets of over \$800 million) has managed to put into operation a unit producing 7 million metric tons of steel sheet per year. The FIG Nizhny Novgorod cars achieved the volume of sales best in the industry and the Interkhimprom, uniting the cycle from supplies of raw materials through sales of ready products, increased its fertiliser output up to 9.6 million metric tons (80% of which are exported).

The main advantages of the FIGs are primarily the possibility of avoiding VAT and customs duties on their products (materials, semi-finished items, parts, units, scientific and technological developments), which move inside the FIG while the final product is being made. However, the CIS countries have thus far no legal and methodological base for consolidating the balance statements across enterprises, banks, insurance companies and investment funds inside FIGs. The corporate law must create conditions for redistribution of resources between the FIG members taking into account their common interests, different depreciation rules, joint payment of taxes, redistribution of equipment and profits of the participants in a uniform investment program. The consolidation of the tax responsibility including VAT, under the condition of clearing the profit and dividends from double taxation, is advantageous for both the FIG and the budgets.

A major advantage of the FIGs is the decrease of credit risks and an increase in the share of long-term loans. The FIG investments in Russia has shown that 55% consist of their own resources, 43% of attracted resources and only 2% of budget-financial resources. Moreover, due to liquidation of duplicating services and rejection of numerous outside intermediaries, FIGs reduce administrative and other overhead expenses. Additional profit is created by the expansion of manufacture into regions with the lowest costs of raw materials, energy, transportation and labour. This profit is spent for researches, development and updating.

Governance structures of FIGs are based on *cross of shareholding* (banks and enterprises are represented on each other's boards), establishing *managing companies* (as a rule, called like the FIG itself) given all FIG shares by its members voluntary in-trust management, *holding* (one of the companies buys up the shares of others, which become affiliates). For the CIS the second variant is presently the one most promising, as the property remains with the legal entities of the country and in case of contract infringements can be withdrawn; however, trust laws in most CIS countries are still non-existent.

National and international FIGs are frequently initiated by large banks signing contracts with the interested parties or buying the shares at the stock exchange or outside it, during investment tenders or auctions. When a FIG includes State-owned enterprises, international agreements get signed. Different are FIGs full, permanent and associated, or temporary participation, vertical (from raw materials to the ready product) and horizontal (diversified and versatile).

FIGs need less working capital. The prices for parts get stabilised and the problem of mutual arrears is solved, and real becomes strategic planning. Thus, FIG Interkhimprom, designing a self-regulating system for manufacture of nitric fertilisers, depends on seven enterprises, two banks (Strategy and National Reserve) and a group of companies Solvalyub with the centre in London, which has an annual trade turnover with Russia of $500 million. However, these advantages are in the CIS countries inhibited by the lack of legal regulations of the FIG managers' responsibility over WRT assets in view of controlling commodity and financial flows and State-owned blocks of shares.

The CIS countries have co-ordinated the basic principles of FIG organisation. As legal entities, they work in accordance with the laws of their place of registration, and they are affiliated with the laws of the country where they are actually based. Investments are regulated by the laws of the country where they are implemented, with attention paid to the agreements on mutual protection of investments. The order of assessing resources brought into the FIG founding capital, profit distribution and indemnifications is regulated by the constituent documents of the FIG itself.

For realisation of their advantages, FIGs require an information centre with a uniform database and a common financial accounting centre which assesses and collects all resources of the FIG, continuously supervising their flows and allocation, production connections of the FIG participants and the competitive positions of its goods. Furthermore, the participants remain independent legal entities instead of structural units of the company, frequently based abroad. For developing FIGs, it is expedient for numerous CIS countries to remove restrictions on bank participation. The laws on mutual protection of investments, insurance of commercial risks and mortgage funds are a must.

The organisational basis of developing a uniform economic space is *transnational corporations* (TNC).

K. Marx was the first to show that in market economy large corporations use planning organisational methods. R. Coase and J. Gelbreit (USA) have established that larger companies lead to lower market uncertainty and reduced transaction costs connected to searching partners, advertising, training, legal support of the contracts and insurance of commercial risks. In the USA approximately 1000 of the largest corporations forming 200 industrial-financial groups co-ordinate and plan the activities of millions of affiliated companies and contractors, following uniform marketing, R&D, financial, investment and personnel policies. Their share in developed countries is up to 80% of all sales. Furthermore, 60% of the shares in the USA are controlled by only the 12 largest financial groups.

In the twentieth century, the TNC became the basic organisational form of international economic integration. In the 1990s 50% of global trade goes on between affiliated and parent TNC companies, carried out along internal (transfer) prices without any customs duties, VAT or other similar taxes. Many TNCs lowered the taxes with mutual transfers of administrative and managerial expenses, license payments and transfer of finished products for resale. Due to this, for example, Coca-Cola had to pay a fine of 15 billion yen to Japan and Nissan paid 17 billion yen to the USA.

Unfortunately, according to the recommendations provided by the experts of IMF, IBRD, OESD and EBRD, branch ministries, formerly being the mesolevel of governance in the USSR, were not transformed into TNC, but simply disbanded, and uniform technological complexes dissolved. Only in the mid-1990s did there begin the formation of, among other entities, international FIGs, including related enterprises, the establishments, organisations, financial and investment institutions via joint stock companies, transfer of shares to trust management or their purchasing by an FIG member, and cross shareholding.[6]

It would be sensible to separate the basic principles of FIGs becoming the organisational and legal backbone of economic integration:

1. Special attention should be paid to supporting FIGs not only in mining, but also in high-tech fields: aircraft, cars, ship building, as well as electronic, electrotechnical and mechanical engineering. It is thanks to the TNC that the small South Korea produces approximately 2.5 times more cars than the CIS (2.6 and 1.1 million, respectively), and ten times more TVs (30 and 2 million, respectively).

2. The anti-monopoly policy should not interfere with establishing vertically integrated FIGs with the close-loop cycle from production or cultivation of raw materials through selling finished products (e.g. oil, clothes, footwear), as only in this case is self-financing of the production complex and real savings on transaction costs, taxes and duties feasible.

3. International FIGs are most efficient if they are created on the bases of voluntary co-operation between companies, creation of consortia, agreements on

---

[6] See: Boiko, I.P. (1995): Business Associations in Market-Oriented Economy. Saint Petersburg, 30–51 (Бойко, И.П. (1995): Объединения Предприятий в Рыночной Экономике. Санкт-Петербург, 30–51) [In Russian]

stabilisation of the mutual delivery prices, tariffs and export cartels co-ordinating sales to third countries. The states and interstate bodies are not to order, but only to promote, this process via transferring the shares to trust management, granting budget credits (no more than 20–25% of the total investments) and guarantees, scientific, technological and commercial information, and dual-purpose technologies.

4. Partners in the CIS countries should be certain of equally benefiting from the FIG. Therefore, it is sensible (with agreements on trade secrets) to submit data regarding costs and economic results of selling mutually delivered goods, to co-ordinate the prices, order of additional profit distribution, formation of common FIG funds and financing for joint projects.

5. At the first stage, at the participants' request, the FIG management can be carried out on the basis of cross the shareholding, and only then with common consent gets a managing company or a holding centre in one of the countries.

FIGs in joint development, manufacture and export of high-tech products, such as planes, their engines, ships, turbines, chemical fibres and equipment for their production, as well as missile engineering, are very important. The point is the reconstructing of the research-and-production complexes, commercial and industrial, agro-industrial, as well as design and building associations, which on the basis of co-operation between the CIS countries can produce goods competitive on the world market.

In recent years numerous agreements have been signed between Russia and the CIS states on co-operation in research and production: with the Ukraine regarding plane engines (6.11.1992), gas turbines (12.03.1992), shipbuilding (15.01.1993), air engineering (8.02.1993), including planes AN-70 and AN-70-T with engines D-27 (24.06.1993), TU-334 and its engines (8.09.1993), and ship gas turbines (18.11.1993); with Uzbekistan on aircraft (17.03.1995); and with the Ukraine and Belarus on chemical fibres and equipment for their production (17.10.1994).

However, as experience has shown, inter-government agreements are insufficient. Creating FIGs acting as independent legal entities is the best approach.

The main features of efficient FIGs in the CIS conditions are:

– Careful improvement of co-operative connections within the joint ventures founded according to the initiative of joint ventures and long-term contracts. Inter-government agreements (if they concern State property) should complete the process instead of beginning it, as the goods exchange share under the inter-government agreements is steadily reduced.

– Presence of uniform technological complexes. For example, Russo-Kazakhstan FIG presumes enriching uranium (Angarsk and Krasnoyarsk), manufacture of nuclear fuel (Ul'ba in eastern Kazakhstan) and assembling heat separation elements for nuclear plants (Novosibirsk and Electrostahl). The FIG will unite the capacities of the Sokolov-Sarbaysk iron ore, Magnitogorsk and Karaganda metallurgical combines. The FIG participates with regard to chromium alloys by the Don ore dressing, Chelyabinsk electromechanical combines, two Russian factories and one Kazakhstan factory of ferrous alloys.

– Minimisation of credit risks, organisation of development and assessment of investment projects, attraction of foreign investors, diversification of securities portfolio with a view to the market demand, and control over the target use of loans.

– The variety of FIG structures. They should not be restricted as one branch and there must not be any limits to the number of their workers or models of share distribution. However, it might be sensible to include into FIGs whole trade houses and export structures interacting with local authorities.

Transnational corporations in the CIS. Most FIGs in developed countries conduct their business in several countries. However, in the CIS countries in 1998, there were no more than ten TNCs. Their development was inhibited by the absence of uniform legal base. Fair objections were raised by the aspirations of Russia and some other states to centralise the flows of TNC goods and finances so that the headquarters and taxes concentrated on their territory. By 1998 only two TNCs (Ruskhim and Nosta-gas-truby) had managed to get the management of state packages of the shares. A transnational corporation under the CIS conditions is virtually an FIG with participants dwelling in various countries and representing mostly non-government companies of various organisational and legal status.

In the late 1990s in developed countries the process of merging TNCs was amplified after the corporation Lockheed bought Martin (1995) and Northrop Grumman (1997; that company itself was founded in 1994 as a result of a merger), Boeing merged with McDonnell-Douglas, and in the U.S. aircraft industry there remained two TNCs instead of the 15 in the 1980s. The federal commission on trade studied a lot of papers checking if these bargains were in conformity with anti-trust legislation and finally agreed they were. The EU committee did the same.

The merging process sped up in the 1990s also in computer, pharmaceutical, food and other industries, and in banking in the EU and the USA. One pharmaceutical company, ACN, moved its headquarters from California to Moscow, bought five factories in Russia, founded an international research centre and ten distributing centres. Without uniting their efforts, similar CIS firms cannot compete against such TNCs anywhere.

However, consolidation of capitals does not belittle the role of middle-size and small businesses. The Japanese economic skeleton is formed by six of the largest FIGs (Mitsubishi, Mitsui, Sumitomo, Daiichi, Kangin, Fuyo and Sanwa), making up 15% of the GDP ($500 billion). Each of them includes a bank (Savings bank, insurance company), a trade house and 20–48 large enterprises. They all have contract or other partnership relations with hundreds of small and middle-size affiliated companies (over 50% of the capital belongs to the founder), with individual shares (less than 50%) or without such on the franchising basis, long-term contracts, and so on. In the group of 175 enterprises belonging to Toyota, the share of the managing company in the founded capital frequently makes up only a few percent, with 40 enterprises' property relations totally non-existent. Nevertheless, the FIG gives them soft loans, transfers technologies, sends experts in management. The gap in payment between the FIG president and an ordinary expert does not exceed 10:1 (in the USA 200:1). Unfortunately, many CIS countries followed the American way instead of the Japanese.

TNCs are most expedient in those branches which in market conditions have already started the development of mutually benefiting direct connections, consortia and joint ventures. Among them there are:

– Nuclear engineering (Russia, the Ukraine, Kazakhstan)

– International air engines (e.g. joint stock company the Perm engines, the Zaporozhye association Motor and over other 100 metallurgical, modular and engine factories, research organisations and banks, working in designing and manufacturing of powerful turbojet and other engines for planes used on local lines, agriculture and sports aircraft, and gas pumping stations)

– Car industry: FIG Belrusavto (founded by the Yaroslav factories Autodiesel, fuel and diesel equipment, Tutayev engine factory, in Belorussia, MAZ, BELAZ, the Mogilyovsk car factory and the Minsk factory of wheel tractors) received a Russian credit until 2005 allowing it to develop a new generation of engines meeting to the standard Euro-2 and to start producing modern truck convoys never made in the CIS before

– Metallurgy: interstate FIGs have been founded for manufacturing gas pipes (Russia, the Ukraine, Kazakhstan), metal sheets (Russia, the Ukraine, Belarus), oil pipes (Russia, Azerbaijan, the Ukraine, Kazakhstan)

– FIG Neftekhimprom (chemistry, petrochemistry, pharmaceutical, tire and rubber-technical industries in Russia, the Ukraine, Belarus, based on the raw hydrocarbon material of the Yuksi corporation)

– Mechanical engineering for chemical industry (Format: Russia, the Ukraine, Belarus)

TNC Trubtrans (13 enterprises in Russia and the Ukraine) by 2000 is going to produce up to 2 million metric tons of large-diameter pipes for oil and gas routes, which will allow the Ukraine to pay the Russian Gasprom; Russia and the Ukraine will found in the late 1990s TNCs Transaluminity, Transtitan, Transitzernotechnica and Transpharmash (pharmaceutical equipment). Such

TNCs are capable of forming transnational information, technological and data flows, influencing the development of stock markets, i.e. to carry out geoeconomic functions much wider than the former ministries and chief directorates. In the late 1990s the petroleum market of the CIS countries will probably become the place of competition for two Russian TNCs instead of ten, Lookoil and Yuksi.

The financial and industrial group Granit developing looks promising, manufacturing and selling systems of AA defence. In Russia, military machinery is exported by the Rosvooruzheniye having an advanced marketing service and guaranteeing State support and export control. However, this corporation is interested primarily in contracts on new developments worth more than $50 million Moreover, the market of $4–5 billion per year is formed by small orders for servicing Soviet military equipment delivered before (its cost is $120–150 billion) which could be done by CIS countries. In Russia, more than 15 manufacturers of military products have already received the right of direct export. A lot of them (e.g. the Sukhoy OKB) have sold a sizeable (up to 30%) part of their shares to commercial banks.

The creation of a free trade zone in the CIS will result in newer organisational forms of enterprise integration.

9.6 The Petersburg Economic Forum

A new organisational form of integration for the CIS countries is the Petersburg economic forum carried out annually since 1997 in Saint Petersburg on the initiative of the CIS Interparliamentary Assembly and of the Federation Council of the Federal Assembly of Russia with support of the Russian president.

Already the first and the second Petersburg economic forums in 1997 and 1998 were participated by more than 3000 people: chiefs of governments and parliaments of the states-participants of the CIS, the subjects of the Russian Federation, representatives of business, businessmen, employees of banking and financial institutions, trade-union and public leaders of the CIS countries, other states in Europe, America and Asia.

Special attention during the forum was paid to the search of new ways and opportunities to expand economic co-operation between Russia and other CIS states with the financial and industrial structures of the leading countries, the strengthening of the foreign investment inflow into the economies of the CIS countries, determining additional sources of assistance for the integration processes underway in these states on the threshold of the new millennium.

The forum is a non-political body with the widest representation of government structures and business, where the parliamentarians of the CIS countries establish direct business contacts with the executive authorities and with business structures. If we throw in the most prominent representatives of the scientific thought, there will appear a unique conglomerate of political and economic ideas, being directly realised in practice. As a matter of fact, the Assembly has created for itself an opportunity for realising those model laws which it develops and adapts. It is not necessary to explain what it means for the economies of the CIS countries, after they have lost the industrial potential of such a state, as, for example, Russia due to the break of economic links.

Moreover, the fact of such a representative and urgent body has given a powerful push to accelerating integration, to restoring the broken off connections and establishing new ones. These connections are of a qualitatively new level, developed not under pressure of a certain Gosplan or ministry, but dictated by the laws of market economy.

During the plenary sessions and "round tables", 1402 investment projects were discussed; the Declaration and 49 resolutions were adapted, and a unique creative situation for the informal search of strategic development bases for the economies of Russia and other CIS countries was formed.

Among the 1402 investment projects declared and submitted to presentation in 1997–1998, 14 were from the Republic of Azerbaijan, 29 from the Republic of Armenia, 58 from the Republic of Belarus, 72 from Georgia, 22 from the Republic of Kazakhstan, 83 from the Kyrgyzstan, 12 from the Republic of Moldova, 778 from the Russian Federation, 65 from the Republic of Tajikistan, 154 from the Ukraine, 5 from Uzbekistan and 80 from separate companies and organisations.

It is necessary to note also the practical result which the forum produced. It included agreements and contracts signed by heads of states, regions, corporations and even separate enterprises. The governments of Belarus and Russia, for example, signed the credit agreements on 500 billion Russian rubles in 1997. In 1998 agreement on intentions were signed to the total of $2.5 billion

We also note the democratic spirit of the Petersburg conference. Besides the political and economic leaders, the discussion tables were attended by experts in a variety of fields. Whereas the official number of the participants was 1200, plus 100 official visitors, the discussion tables were attended by 1936 people who made 400 reports.

The peculiarity of the Petersburg forum was in its direct relation to practice. Three large industrial exhibitions taking place in the city were started simultaneously with its beginning.

Another feature of the forum was its regional orientation, as in Saint Petersburg, where the entire variety of regions led by their governors were represented, not only Russian, but also Armenian, Kazakhstani, Moldovian, Greek, German and those from many other countries.

The example of the Petersburg economic forum shows the importance of involving into integration processes the wide strata of society, including businessmen, scholars and politicians.

9.7 Issues of Economic Integration in International Research

The main distinctive feature of economic development in the twenty-first century will be formation of a uniform world market of goods, capital, technologies, information and labour. Furthermore, the main driving force in this market will become not national states and companies, but regional groupings developed in, among other places, western Europe, North America, Southeast Asia, Latin America and the Caribbean, and transnational corporations. This chapter reveals on the basis of the publications printed in the 1990s (most of them published in the USA and EU scholarly centres) the basic directions and results of research, most important for the CIS countries.

Objective backgrounds, ways and forms of regional economic integration. In the twentieth century, the number of independent states has grown sharply. In 1944, after the Bretton-Woods conference, 44 states founded the International Monetary Fund, and in 1996 their number exceeded 180. Furthermore, the number of the decision-making centres increased as well. The share of the USA in world manufacture and trade during the 1940s–1990s fell from 35–40 to 15–20%.

The states whose participation in the world economy was insignificant (e.g. South Korea, Indonesia, Thailand, Malaysia, Brazil) created regional unions and received an opportunity to protect their interests. At the same time, the countries, which, due to their leaders' political ambitions or for other reasons, have not conceded some of their sovereignty to integrated groupings, have lagged behind in their development.

As noted by B.R. MacLaury, R.O. Keohane[7] and other economists, the technological, social and cultural differences between nations in most areas of the world in the end of the twentieth century have significantly decreased. The government policies traditionally limiting moving of property and people across the border have been relaxed. New types of transportation and communication have reduced the costs of this moving. For 50 years international transactions have been made in stock exchanges at certain times, but now they take place round the clock. In 1964–1992 the volume of production in industrial countries grew in 1 year by 9%, the export by 12% and international bank transfers by

---

[7] See: Kahler, M. (1995): International Institutions and the Political Economy of Integration. Washington, 3–10, 135–138

22%. Eliminated are the distinction between internal and world markets, and international economic relations outlined less by the government than by transnational organisations and companies.

An independent research organisation in Washington, The Brookings Institution, has, since 1994, conducted the special project "Integrating National Economies: Promise and Pitfalls", investigating common problems of regionalism and economic globalisation,[8] generalising the experience of economic integration in the developed countries[9] and states with transition economies.[10] Statistical analysis proves that inclusion into the global economy under the present conditions is the basis of the national sustainable growth. At the same time, natural resources are not enough for this growth. Keeping up with the global standards is necessary in technology, production quality, ecology and education, none of which are possible without a mutual recognition and explicit harmonisation of management rules and regional supranational organisations (federalist mutual governance).

The problems of economic integration increasingly occupy a place in foreign literature. In recent years, numerous monographs were published on general theory of economic globalisation and founding the international economic system,[11] regionalism as a tendency of economic development,[12] financial

---

[8] R.Z. Lawrence (Harvard University) Regionalism, Multilateralism and Deeper Integration; S.M. Collins (Brookings Institution) Distributive Issues: A Constraint on Global Integration; R.N. Cooper (Harvard University) Environment and Resource Policies for the World Economy; F.M. Scherer (Harvard University) Competition Policies for an Integrated World Economy

[9] W. Wallau (Oxford University) Regional Integration: The West European Experience; A. Tanaka (University of Tokyo) The Politics of Deeper Integration: National Attitudes and Policies in Japan

[10] S. Haggard (University of California, San Diego) Developing Nations and the Politics of Global Integration; B. Bosworth (Brookings Institution), G. Oder (Hebrew University) Reforming Planned Economies in an Integrating World Economy; P. Rutland (Wesleyan University) Russia, Eurasia and the Global Economy

[11] Stetting, L., Svendsen, K.E., Yngaard, E. (Eds.) (1993): Global Change and Transformation. Copenhagen; Bergsten, F., Noland, M. (Eds.) (1993): Pacific Dynamism and the International Economic System. Institutional for International Economies, Washington; Segal-Horn, S. (Ed.) (1994): The Challenge of International Business. London; Kenichi, O. (1995): The End of the National State: The Rise of Regional Economies. New York, etc.

[12] Hettne, B., Jnotai, A. (1994): The New Regionalism: Implication for Global Development and International Security. Helsinki; (1995): Regional and Federal Studied. London; Higgins, B.H., Savoie, D.J. (1995): Regional Development: Theories and Their Application. New Brunswick, New York; Gibb, R., Michalak, W. (1994): Continental Trading Blocs: the Growth of Regionalism in the World Economy. New York; Jordan, D.M. (1994): New World Regionalism. Buffalo, Toronto; Cable, V., Henderson, D. (1994): Trade Blocs?: the Future of Regional Integration. London, etc.

integration as a basis of the global market functioning[13] and macro-economic aspects of integration in Europe[14] and other areas of the world.[15]

Numerous works are devoted to the problems of integration in Indochina,[16] Baltic countries[17] and other Eurasian states into existing economic groupings.

The main idea of this flow of publications is that in the information society of the twenty-first century, no national economy can remain competitive on the global market without being really included into the structure of some super region comprising a powerful group of countries, having their own scientific and technical potential and advanced human resources.[18] According to numerous economists, the development of super-regional economy in the twenty-first century will call into question the expediency of the national states in their present shape and result in federations and confederations of a new type.

International political economy as a new branch of economic science. In world economic science there are three basic directions: national political economy investigating the features of social and economic systems formed on the basis of ethnic traditions;[19] economy of separate activity spheres: large and small businesses, non-commercial and public sector, households, industrial and inter-

---

[13] Grauwe, P. (1994): The Economics of Monetary Integration. Oxford, New York; Crauford, M.L. (1993): One Money for Europe? The Economics and Politics of Maastricht. Houndmills; Mitsuhiro, F. (1995): Financial Integration, Corporate Governance and the Performance of Multinational Companies. Washington; Aggarwal, R. (Ed.) (1995): Global Portfolio Diversification: Risk Management, Market Microstructure. San Diego

[14] Tsounkalis, L. (1993): The New European Economy: The Politics and Economics of Integration. Oxford, New York; Willenbockel, D. (1994): Applied General Equilibrium Modelling: Imperfect Competition and European Integration. New York; Delamaide, D. (1994): The New Superregions of Europe. New York; Jones, B., Keating, M. (Eds.) (1995): The European Union and the Regions. Oxford

[15] Kehoe, P.S., Kehoe, T.J. (Eds.) (1995): Modelling North-American Economic Integration. Dordrecht, Boston; Garnant, R., Drydale, P. (Eds.) (1994): Asia Pacific Regionalism: Readings in International Economic Relations. New York

[16] Thager, C.A. (1995): Beyond Indochina: Indochina's Transition from Socialist Central Planning to Market-Oriented Economics and Its Integration into South Asia. London

[17] Sorsa, P. (1994): Regional Integrations and the Baltics: Which Way? World Bank, Washington

[18] Gates, S. (1994): The Changing Global Role of the Human Resource Function. New York; McKenney, J.L. (1995): Waves of Change: Business Evolution through Information Technology. Boston; Gates, S. (1995): The Changing Global Role of the Research and Development Function. New York

[19] Chan-Sup, Ch. (1994): The Korean Management System: Cultural, Political, Economic Foundations. Westport (Connecticut); Voich, D., Stepina, L.P. (Eds.) (1994): Cross-Cultural Analysis of Values and Political Economic Issue. Westport (Connecticut); Bergsten, C.F., Sakong, I. (Eds.) (1995): The Political Economy of Korea — USA Cooperation. Washington; Arase, D. (1995): Buying Power: The Political Economy of Japan's Foreign Trade. Boulder (Colorado); Bebritton, R., Sekine, T.T. (Eds.) (1995): A Japanese Approach to Political Economy. New York

industrial complexes;[20] international political economies as a science about the principles, forms and methods of international economic integration[21] including formation of economic alliances.[22]

In recent years numerous monographs dealing with the ideas of liberal classical political economy have been published.[23] However, the tendencies of strengthening economy regulations with large corporations,[24] international economic alliances[25] and government strategic planning[26] are simultaneously being investigated.

The universal conclusion of most foreign researchers is that "the invisible hand of the market" does not mean rational economic integration and results in an increasing gap and amplified contradictions between rich and poor countries, which threatens a crash of the whole world economic system in the twenty-first century.

Systematic co-operation in regional groupings and their equal co-operation in the global arena secure the greatest economy in transaction costs connected to the international exchange, restricting competition before it reaches dangerous limits.

---

[20] Petrazzini, B.A. (1995): The Political Economy of Telecommunications Reform: Privatization and Liberalization in Comparative Perspective. Westport (Connecticut); Agmon, T., Drobnick, R. (Eds.) (1994): Small Firms in Global Competition. New York; Sommer, S.W. (Ed.) (1995): The Academy in Crisis: The Political Economy of Higher Education. New Brunswick, New Jersey; Blatt, R.G. (Ed.) (1994): Confronting the Management Challenge: Affordable Housing in the Nonprofit Sector. New York, etc.

[21] Isaak, R.A. (1995): Managing World Economic Change: International Political Economy. Englewood Cliffs, New Jersey; Faruqee, H. (1994): International Linkage and Macroeconomic Adjustment. New York; Balasubramanyam, U.N., Sapsford, O. (Eds.) (1994): The Economics of International Investment. Brokfield; Barry, J.R.S. (1995): Globalization and Interdependence in the International Political Economy: Rhetoric and Reality. London, New York; Chase-Dunn, C. (1995): The Historical Evolution of the International Political Economy. Aldershot, Brookfield; Kahler, M. (1995): International Institutions and the Political Economy of Integration. Brookings Institution, Washington

[22] Gutterman, A.S. (1995): The Law of Domestic and International Strategic Alliances: a Survey for Corporate Management. Westport (Connecticut)

[23] McKinnon, R.I. (1993): The Order of Economic Liberalization: Financial Control in the Transition to a Market Economy. Baltimore; Boaz, D., Grance, E.H. (Eds.) (1993): Market Liberalism: A Paradigm for the Twenty-First Century. Washington

[24] Tongeren, F.W. Van. (1995): Microsimulation Modelling of the Corporate Firm: Exploring Micro-Macro Economic Relations. Berlin, New York; Hipple, F.S. (1995): Multinational Companies in United States International Trade. Westport (Connecticut); (1995): Multinational Corporations: Expanding Influence in the 1990s: An Analysis. Washington

[25] Gilroy, B.M. (1993): Networking in Multinational Enterprises: The Importance of Strategic Alliances. Columbia (South Carolina)

[26] Steidmeier, P. (1995): Strategic Management of the China Venture. Westport (Connecticut)

In this connection many foreign scholars, unlike certain ultra-right politicians in the CIS countries, do not consider socialism as a deadlock of development, but objectively examine the positive aspects of the transformations carried out in the CIS states during the Soviet period.[27]

Some of the studies demonstrate the limitations of the bourgeois ideal, the "Misfortune of prosperity",[28] of the paradigms followed by the purely market economy,[29] the necessity of expanding its subject, of choosing new directions,[30] and development of political economy based on ideas of justice and personal development as the highest value in the information society.[31]

Furthermore, it does not concern rejecting democracy and returning to totalitarianism, but instead concerns co-ordinating purely economic, social, moral, ethical and ecological criteria of reforms.[32]

We have listed the works published within 1 year, but they reflect the general tendency of development in humanitarian sciences during the period of the information society being established.

The political-economic theory of integration widely uses the methods of the games theory (games of collaboration and co-ordination) for co-ordinating various interests and developing of joint decisions (dilemmas of common interest and common version). Furthermore, there is an opportunity to take into account not only purely economic parameters of the transaction costs (transaction cost economics), but also political economic factors of integration (demon-side theory of international regimes).

In the late 1990s the flow of publications on organisation and regulation of international economic relations grew significantly. The problems of globalising

---

[27] Crawford, B. (Ed.) (1995): Markets, States and Democracy: The Political Economy of Post-Communist Transformation. Boulder (Colorado); Ito, M. (1995): Political Economy for Socialism. New York; Arestis, P., Marshall, H. (Eds.) (1995): The Political Economy of Full Employment: Conservatism, Corporatism and Institutional Change. Aldershot

[28] Cohen, D. (1995): The Misfortunes of Prosperity: an Introduction to Modern Political Economy. Cambridge (Massachusetts)

[29] Stokes, K.H. (1995): Paradigm Lost: a Cultural and Systems Theoretical Critique of Political Economy. Armonk, New York

[30] Banks, S., Hanushek, E.A. (1995): Modern Political Economy: Old Topics, New Directions. Cambridge, New York

[31] Zajag, E.E. (1995): Political Economy of Fairness. Cambridge (Massachusetts); Hennipman, C. (1995):Welfare Economics and the Theory of Economic Policy. Aldershot

[32] Wittman, D.A. (1995): The Myth of Democratic Failure: Why Political Institutions Are Efficient. Chicago; Haggard, S., Kaufman, R. R. (1995): The Political Economy of Democratic Transitions. Princeton; Levine, D.P. (1994): Wealth and Freedom: an Introduction to Political Economy. Cambridge; New York

separate branches,[33] the importance of direct investments for formation of global economy and corresponding political economic settings[34] are especially examined.

The CIS countries may urgently use the diaspora capital (it concerns Armenia primarily) and the knowledge of recent emigrants for developing their international businesses[35] and their experience in regulating international economic relations.[36]

However, international economic integration of TNC activity is particularly important, which in the early twenty-first century will become the point of focus for the organisational planning management of the leading sectors in global economy,[37] most of all in high-tech spheres.[38] For the CIS countries, the experience of the state, including tax, TNC regulation and control over the transfer price formation, is particularly important.

Structural reforms as a precondition of economic integration. In recent years numerous monographs have been published on the general theory of structural reforms[39] and their peculiarities during the transition period,[40] including those of

---

[33] Yang, X. (1995): Globalization of the Automobile Industry: The USA, Japan and China. Westport (Connecticut)

[34] Chan, S. (Ed.) (1995): Foreign Direct Investment in a Changing Global Political Economy. Houndmills

[35] Selmer, J. (Ed.) (1995): Expatriate Management: New Ideas for International Business. Westport. (Connecticut)

[36] Jakson, J.H., Davey, W.S., Synes, A.D. (1995): Legal Problems of International Economic Relations: Cases, Materials and Text on the National and International Regulation of Transnational Economic Relations. St. Paul (Minnesota)

[37] Hauward, J. (Ed.) (1995): Industrial Enterprise and European Integration: From National to International Champions in Western Europe. New York; Estabrooks, H. (1995): Electronic Technology Corporate Strategy and World Transformation. Westport (Connecticut); Pearce, R.D. (1993): The Growth and Evolution of Multinational Enterprise: Patterns of Geographical and Industrial Diversification. Aldershot; Brookfield

[38] Sally, R. (1995): State and Firms: Multinational Enterprises in Institutional Competition. London, New York; Jansson, H., Sagib, H., Sharma, D. (1995): The State and Transnational Corporation: a Network Approach to Industrial Policy in India. Aldershot; Feldstein, M., Hines, J.R., Hubbard R.H. (Eds.) (1995): Taxing Multinational Corporations. Chicago

[39] (1995): Reason and Reform: Studies in Social Policy. Dublin; (1994): Assessing Structural Reform: Lessons for the Future. OECD, Paris; Barth, D.C., Roe, A.R. (Eds.) (1994): Coordination, Stabilization and Structural Reform. JMF, Washington; Merring, R., Litan, R.E. (1995): Financial Regulation in a Global Economy. Brookings Institution, Washington

[40] Cook, P., Nixson, F. (Eds.) (1995): To Move to the Market?: Trade and Industry Policy Reform in Transitional Economies. London, New York; Lazeaz, E.P. (Ed.) (1995): Economic Transition in Eastern Europe and Russia: Realities of Reform. CA, Stanford; Kornai, J. (1995): Highway and Byways. Studies on Socialist Reform and Postsocialist Transition. MIT, Cambridge (Massachusetts)

Russia and other CIS states.[41] In a lot of them the inconsistency of reforms in Russia, the Ukraine, Belarus and other countries is discussed, as well as the weakness of their theoretical substantiation and difficulty of integration.

Pessimists believe that by the early twenty-first century, the scientific and technical base of the CIS states will be destroyed finally, thus making their effective integration impossible. According to this viewpoint, Russia will cease to be a serious military and economic force not only globally but also regionally. The West wants social stability over the open spaces in Eurasia, a market for consumer goods and machinery for its infrastructure and mining in exchange for resources and accommodation of ecologically harmful industries (most of all, in Russia, Kazakhstan and Turkmenistan, which have the smallest population densities).

However, most foreign authors consider reforms in Russia and other CIS countries radical and irreversible under the condition of eliminating mistakes in privatisation and conversion, and real struggle with the criminal economy. The concern is that the alternative to equal-rights regional integration will be chaos and growing extremism.[42]

Foreign scholars are recently paying increasing attention to the Chinese model of reforms. Furthermore, they especially emphasise the problems connected to the relations of the State and society, including democratisation within a one-party system,[43] the centre and provinces,[44] as well as financial[45] and external economic policy[46] developing, with which China, as is universally recognised, has achieved considerable successes. China, according to the leading foreign economists,

---

[41] McFaul, M., Perlmutter, T. (Eds.) Arrow, K.S. (Foreword) (1995): Privatization, Conversion and Enterprise Reform in Russia. Boulder (Colorado); Leitzel, J. (1995): Russian Economic Reform. London; New York; Rowen, H.S., Wolf, Ch., Zlotnik, J. (Eds.) (1994): Defence Conversion, Economic Reform and the Outlook for the Russian and Ukrainian Economics. New York; Lieberman, J.W. et al. (Eds.) (1995): Russia: Creating Private Enterprises and Efficient Markets. World Bank, Washington

[42] Nelson, L.D. (1995): Radical Reform in Yeltsin's Russia: Political, Economic and Social Dimensions. Armonk, New York; Smith, D. (Ed.) (1995): Challenges for Russian Economic Reform. Washington

[43] Chih-yu. (1995): State and Society in China's Political Economy: the Cultural Dynamics of Socialist Reform. Boulder (Colorado); Chen Feng (1995): Economic Transition and Political Legitimacy in Post-Mao China: Ideology and Reform. Albany, New York; Wekkin, C.D. (Ed.) (1993): Building Democracy in One-Party Systems: Theoretical Problems and Cross-Nation Experiences. Westport (Connecticut)

[44] Yong-Nian, Z. (1995): Institutional Change, Local Developmentalism and Economic Growth: the Making of Semi-Federalism in Reform China. Princeton, New York

[45] On Kit Tam. (Ed.) (1995): Financial Reform in China. London, New York; Naughton, B. (1995): Crowding Out of the Plan: Chinese Economic Reform. Cambridge (U. K.), New York

[46] (1994): China: Foreign Trade Reform. World Bank, Washington; (1994): China. 3000 Largest Foreign-Funded Enterprises. Beijing

forms its own management style taking into account the laws of the market and national traditions.[47]

Of doubtless interest for the CIS countries is the experience of successful reforms in the countries of Latin America and Southeast Asia generalised in numerous monographs.[48] Although the initial conditions of reforms in the CIS and in these countries has differed, it is possible to view many problems of the social price paid for the reforms, of the inter-relations and contradictions between the political and economic democracy, as common.

Furthermore, Cuba has played the same role in accelerating the social and economic reforms in the Caribbean and Latin American countries, as Soviet Russia had in shaping socially oriented market in Europe and the USA. It is only by the end of the twentieth century that these countries have found hope for structural reforms on the basis of integration.[49]

Science-and-technology and educational backgrounds of integration. In numerous studies based on vast material it has been shown that during the transition to an information society, for efficient economic integration it is not sufficient to remove barriers and to enter payment unions. The main thing is associating the scientific, technical and educational potential, as well as development and implementation of joint programs of human resources[50] and high-technologies development.[51]

It is only on this basis that one can ensure in the twenty-first century the competitiveness of a national economy.[52] Foreign researchers have long arrived at the conclusion that even large countries cannot solve this task in isolation.[53]

---

[47] Broadman, H.C. (1995): Meeting the Challenge of Chinese Enterprise Reform. World Bank, Washington; Young, S. (1995): Private Business and Economic Reform in China. Armonk, New York; Wazner, M. (1995): The Management of Human Resources in Chinese Industry. New York

[48] Pozwat, M., Malik, W.H., Dacolias, M. (Eds.) (1995): Judicial Reform in Latin America and the Caribbean. World Bank, Washington; Smith, W.C., Acuna, C.H., Camarra, E.A. (Eds.) (1994): Democracy, Markets and Structural Reform in Latin America. New Brunswick, New York; Dornbusch, R., Edwards, S. (Eds.) (1995): Reform, Recovery and Growth: Latin America and the Middle East. Chicago

[49] Edwards, S. (1995): Crisis and Reform in Latin America: from Despair to Hope. World Bank, New York

[50] Minti-Belkaoni, S., Mulkey, O. (Eds.) (1995): Human Resource Valuation: A Guide to Strategies and Techniques. Boulder (Colorado); Aseda, S., Wei Chiao Huang. (Eds.) (1994): Human Capital and Economic Development. Kalamazoo (Michigan)

[51] Halana, D. (Ed.) (1993): Critical Technologies and Economic Competitiveness. New York

[52] Rapkin, D.P., Averty, W.P. (Eds.) (1995): National Competitiveness in a Global Economy. Boulder (Colorado); (1994): Growth, Competitiveness, Employment: The Challenges and Ways Forward into the Twenty-First Century. White Paper. Luxembourg

Unfortunately, in the CIS states it is still not understood by everyone. Integration is often reduced to attempts to supply to the neighbours the goods marked to be sold in the global market, to get missing resources cheap, to improve the payment balance via delaying payments and paying of credits. These policies give only temporary benefits, without solving the radical problems of increase in national economies' competitiveness: the poor quality of goods, backwardness of technologies and discrepancy between the qualification and organisation of local labour and modern requirements. The economic growth with them unsolved remains quite often "a desert mirage".[54]

For certain CIS countries the experience accumulated by developing countries in getting high technologies and developing human resources[55] will be interesting. It is necessary to use special forms of integration for the partners with various potentials[56] in order to avoid their resistance and to achieve a general rise. Some studies assert that the economic integration of the CIS countries is a demonstration of Russian hegemony, a attempt to restore the USSR in its former shape, which obviously contradicts Western interests. However, most publications objectively assess the meaning of this integration for overcoming chaos and social conflicts over the Eurasian open spaces, for including the CIS states into the world economic system and for counteracting extremism in all its forms.

This problem occupies a special place in the Brooklyn project.[57] Interesting are the offers on joint program of health care as a beginning of economic integration.[58] It is not less important to create a uniform labour market, which would ease the unemployment in the southern regions of the CIS without lowering the quality of life in safer areas[59] and create a uniform system of technical standards.[60]

---

[53] Kramer, R.S. (1993): Organizing for Global Competitiveness: The Geographic Design. New York; Garone, S.J. (Ed.) (1993): Productivity: Key to World Competitiveness. New York

[54] Salomon, J.-J., Lebenau, A. (1994): Mirages of Development: Science and Technology for the Third Worlds. Boulder (Colorado)

[55] Galhari, R.M. (1994): The High Technology Firms in Developing Countries: the Case of Biotechnology. Aldershot, Brookfield; Wogart, J.P., Aasha, K.M., Arun, N. (1993): Technology and Competitiveness: the Case of Brazilian and Indian Machine Tools. New Delhi

[56] Georgakopouls, T., Paraskevopouls, C.C., Smithin, J. (Eds.) (1994): Economic Integration Between Unequal Partners. Brookfield

[57] S. Ostry (University of Toronto), R.R. Nelson (Columbia University). Techno-Nationalism and Techno-Globalism: Conflict and Cooperation

[58] R.N. Cooper, International Cooperation in Public Health as a Prologue to Macroeconomic Cooperation

[59] R.G. Ehrenberg (Cornell University). Labour Markets and Integrating National Economies

[60] A.O. Synes (University of Chicago). Product Standards for Internationally Integrated Goods Markets

Of paramount importance for efficient integration is a uniform conversion program, the results of which depend on the place the CIS countries will occupy in the global economy in the future. Many studies deal with this problem.[61]

The conversion theory is developed mainly in three fields: financial and investment,[62] as a factor of economic growth[63] and as a global socio-economic problem.[64]

Financial basis of integration. Ultimately, the rates of regional integration, as world experience has shown, are determined not by administrative measures and not political decisions, but the real economic connections between the business units. According to most foreign researchers, the co-ordination of the central banks' activities,[65] development or the accounting and insurance system,[66]

---

[61] Ouagrham, S. (1993): Le Desarmement et la Conversion de L'industrie Militare en Russie. New York; Cooper, J. (1993): The Conversion of the Former Soviet Defence Industry. London; Anthony, I. (Ed.) (1994): The Future of the Defence Industries in Central Eastern Europe. Oxford, New York; Rowen, H.S., Wolf, C., Zlotnin, J. (Eds.) (1994): Defense Conversion, Economic Reform and the Outlook for the Russian and Ukrainian Economics. New York; McFaul, M., Permutter, T. (Eds.) (1995): Privatization, Conversion and Enterprise Reform in Russia. Boulder (Colorado); Khrutski, K.E. (1995): Arms Trade and the Future of the Russian Defense Industry. Commack, New York

[62] Hartley, K. (et al) (Ed.) (1993): Economic Aspects of Disarmament: Disarmament as an Investment Process. New York; (1994): Critical Issues in Defense Conversion. Centre for Strategic and International Studies, Washington; Renner, M. (1994): Budgeting for Disarmament: the Costs of War and Peace. Washington; O'Prey, K.P. (1995): The Arms Export Challenge; Cooperative Approaches to Export Management and Defense Conversion. Brookings Institution, Washington

[63] McCorquodale, P.L. (et al.) (Ed.) (1993): Engineers and Economic Conversion: from the Military to the Marketplace. New York; Brauer, J., Chatterji, M. (Eds.) Arrow, K.J. (Foreword) (1993): Economic Issues of Disarmament: Contribution from Peace Economics and Peace Science. New York; Payne, J.E., Sahu, A.P. (Eds.) (1993): Defense Spending and Economic Growth. Boulder (Colorado); Murphy, S.T., Rogan, P.M. (1995): Closing the Shop: Conversion from Sheltered to Integrated Work. Baltimore

[64] Cassidy, K.I., Bischak, G.A. (Eds.) (1993): Real Security: Converting the Defense Economy and Building Peace. Albany; Clandon, M.P., Wittneben, K. (Eds.) (1993): After the Cold War: Russian-American Defense Conversion for Economic Renewal. New York; Chatterji, M., Lager, H., Rima, A. (Eds.) (1994): The Economics of International Security. New York; Dumas, L.J. (Ed.) (1995): The Socio-Economics of Conversion from War to Peace. Armonk; New York; Sandler, T., Hartley, K. (1995): The Economics of Defense. Cambridge (U. K.), New York; Cansler, J.S. (1995): Defense Conversion: Transforming the Arsenal of Democracy. Cambridge (Massachusetts)

[65] Frazer, W.J. (1994): The Central Banks: International and European Directions. Westport (Connecticut); Deane, M., Pringle, R. (1994): The Central Banks. London; Solomon, S. (1995): The Confidence Game: How Unelected Central Bankers Are Governing the Changed Global Economy. New York; (1994): The Future of Central Banking. New York

formation of the modern banking system including credit, investment, venture, leasing, selling and other companies,[67] and elimination of obstacles for the movement of capital[68] represent the basis for economic integration much more significantly than any administrative supra-national bodies. This is especially important for transition economies.[69]

Successful agrarian reforms are based on a specialised banking sector,[70] principally new bio-technologies[71] and the co-ordination of agrarian policies within integrated groupings.[72] In many respects it determines the total political climate of integration.

Financial aspects of integration are increasingly more often addressed by the economists of the CIS countries.[73]

American and European economists suggest the ways of developing the international financial system allowing supervision of the course of economic reforms in the CIS states.[74] Especially marked are the new opportunities of capital market globalisation at the end of the twentieth century.

Financial reforms in the countries of Eurasia are dealt with in numerous special studies.[75] Authoritative consulting companies think that a decrease in inflation and strengthening of national currencies in the CIS countries under the condition of political stabilisation creates conditions for private investments. There are, for the first time since 1995, published reference books for investors and

---

[66] Hoschka, T.C. (1994): Bankassurance in Europe. New York; Caprio, G., Folkerts-Landau, D., Lane, T.D. (Eds.) (1994): Building Sound Finance in Emerging Market Economies. IMF, World Bank, Washington

[67] (1995): Banking Federation of the European Union. Annual Report. Brussels; Revell, J. (Ed.) (1994): The Changing Face of European Banks and Securities Markets. Houndmills

[68] Welfens, P.J.J. (Ed.) (1994): European Monetary Integration: EMS Development and Integrational Post-Maastricht Perspectives. Berlin, New York; Cassis, Y., Feldman, G., Olsson, U. (Eds.) (1995): The Evolution of Financial Institutions and Market in Twentieth-Century Europe. Aldershot (U. K.)

[69] Borish, M.S., Noel, M., Long, M. (1995): Restructing Banks and Enterprises: Recent Lessons from Transition Countries. World Bank, Washington; Masahiko, Aoki, Hyung-Ki Kim. (Eds.) (1995): Corporate Governance in Transitional Economies; Insider Control and the Role of Banks. World Bank, Washington

[70] Bisotra, R.L. (1994): Agricultural Development through Cooperative Banks. New Delhi

[71] (1995): Agricultural Reform and Its Impact on the Fruit and Vegetables Sector in OECD Countries. Paris

[72] (1995): The Common Agriculture Policy beyond the Maastricht Reform. Amsterdam, New York

[73] Gaidar, E.T. (1995): Reform and International Money. Cambridge (Massachusetts)

[74] Shabo-Pelsoczi, M. (Ed.) (1994): The Global Monetary System after the Fall of the Soviet Empire. Aldershot (U. K.), Brookfield (Utah)

[75] Millineux, A. (Ed.) (1995): Financial Reform in Central and Eastern Europe: Lessons from the West, Poland and Further East. Comack, New York

businessmen working in Russia.[76] Previously, similar directories were printed for the countries with the investment risks reduced to the maximally admitted level.[77]

Managing economic integration in the CIS conditions. The interstate governance is an especially complicated problem. As global experience shows, economic integration is accompanied by founding international organisations: global (e.g. International Monetary fund, World Bank, World Trade Organisation) and regional ones having imperial aspirations. However, the real result of integration depends not on the number of these organisations and the formal centralisation of economic decisions, but on the scale and depth of co-operation between national economies.[78]

It is possible to separate the major principles of governing regional integration:

1. The international organisations should not have rigid administrative structure and numerous staff. Flexible management based on agreements signed in accordance with the procedures accepted beforehand is most efficient in this case.

2. Forming of administrative structures as well as distribution of powers between the interstate and national bodies is a slow and gradual process. In its initial stage, when the advantages of integration remain unclear and mutual suspicion is strong, centralisation should be minimal. While the co-operation process develops, the differences between its participants get obliterated, information exchange about its results goes on and new rights get voluntarily transferred to interstate institutions. Arranging other connections between companies and citizens of the countries, i.e. the success of integration, allows subsequent reduction in the administrative power of the central structures.

3. The development of federalism elements is determined not solely by economic, but primarily by political, factors: by the social climate and comparative standards of living in the countries participating in integration, the ratio between different groups (particularly in the leading CIS countries) interested in co-operation with the neighbours (mechanical engineering, high technologies, MIC) and oriented towards exporting raw materials and importing consumer goods from "far abroad" countries.

Therefore, the interstate structures should co-ordinate the policies not only with the governments, but also with associations of businessmen, trade unions and regional authorities. As a result, the North American group NAFTA (North-

---

[76] Goleppolsky, T.C., Johnstone, R.M., Kashin, V.A. (1995): Doing Business in Russia: Basic Facts for the Pioneering Entrepreneur. New York; (1995): The Ross Register of Siberian Industry: A Directory to Resources, Factories, Products, Mines, Banks and Stock Exchanges. New York

[77] Engholm, C. (1995): Doing Business in Vietnam; for Investors, Marketers and Enterpreneurs. Englewood (New Jersey)

[78] Kahler, M. (1995): International Institutions and the Political Economy of Integration. P. 18, 22, 80

American Free Trade Agreement) is eliminating barriers between Mexico, the USA and Canada in movement of goods and investments, but (unlike in the EU) does not introduce uniform standards in wages, working conditions and ecology.

The political logic (not only in the CIS but in other regions as well) quite often appears stronger than economic.[79] Thus, the EU up to now has to surrender to the requirements of national farmer organisations and to use non-market methods of regulating the food market (e.g. subsidised prices, import quotas).

4. The members of an economic community should have real advantages as compared with other states in the common market. The larger the participant number and the stronger the distinctions in their specialities, the more significant are the advantages of integration and the difficulties in managing them. This problem is solved by choosing a core of the commonwealth (a group of the countries which have agreed on a closer economic union with corresponding interstate structures of a confederate or even federate sort) and division of the connections between its members and corresponding institutes into general (multilateral), plurilateral and bilateral.

Furthermore, it is necessary to precisely separate the problems requiring consensus (agreement between all participants), qualified (two thirds majority) or even simple majority of votes based on the conclusions of independent experts (an arbitration court). In numerous governing bodies, the officials representing participating countries are later not subordinated to them and cannot be replaced before the end of their term. The projects of the national bodies' decisions on current questions get submitted to the participating countries which can present their objections in strictly limited time. On numerous questions, especially concerning labour, migration and ecology, it can be done also by regional authorities. After the specified term expires, the decision is considered passed (without ratification in places, i.e. on the basis of "silent consensus") and binding. In 1996 the EU countries discussed in connection with its expansion the question on cancellation of the consensus principle (the right of veto) when certain problems are to be solved.

Micro-groupings inside the CIS can increase the danger of its disintegration and amplification of contradictions between its participants. However, membership with limited rights and obligations, as world experience shows, is quite feasible, especially if a transition period and the final term for complete inclusion of newly accepted members into the economic and social union has been fixed.[80]

---

[79] Martin, L.L. (1993): The Rational State Choice of Multilateralism. In: Ruggle, J.G. (Ed.) Multilateralism Matters. New York, 91–121

[80] Kahler, M. 1) (1995): International Institutions and the Political Economy of Integration. Washington, 125–130; 2) (1993): Making Sense of Subsidiarity: How Much Centralization for Europe? London; Baldwin, R.E. (1994): Towards an Integrated Europe. London

Furthermore, it is necessary to avoid disguised protectionism in relation to separate goods, which becomes discrimination against the countries importing these goods.

5. The methods of governing economic integration differ from ordinary ones in many respects, and the general principles of administrative law are inapplicable. The ratio between centralisation and decentralisation, national independence and federalism elements is determined by the depth of economic integration, distinctions in economies of its participants, in the model of reforms accepted by them, national legislation, ethical norms and traditions.

A lot depends on the ratio between the interstate and direct (inter-company) economic connections, real benefits of the integration and losses due to strengthened foreign competition, but mainly on disseminating information about the advantages of integration in administrative bodies and among the population. However, in any case the spheres of primary and even exclusive national competence (e.g., issuing of residence permits to non-working aliens) have been established. At any level of integration, national independence and the right of governments to independently solve most of their problems, to protect national interests, is not disputed.

A special role in managing integration is played by monitoring, joint supervision over economic processes based on uniform methods of counting expenses and the results,[81] unification of technical, ecological and social standards, co-ordination of legislation across countries,[82] and the main thing, development of precise procedures to finally solve complicated problems and to control carrying out the decisions.

The interstate administrative bodies are not to be guided mainly by the force of ordering (power-oriented approach, judicial model), but by developing and following co-ordinated rules for international economic relations and joint projects (rule-oriented model).

The decisions of interstate bodies are divided into obligatory (international law having priority over national) and recommendations. However, in the latter case also the system of economic privileges and sanctions, permanent control and information on failure to follow the recommendations, widely applied interstate courts and arbitration guarantee the observance of the decisions. In the CIS this problem has not yet been solved and many decisions of the CIS exist only on paper.

---

[81] Haas, P.M., Keohane, R.O., Levy, M.A. (Eds.) (1993): Institutions for the Earth: Sources of Effective International Environmental Protection. Boston, 402–405

[82] Elster, M. (1994): The Impact of Constitutions on Economic Performance. Washington, 24–28

Furthermore, the specificity of the object under governance and the CIS countries should be taken into account. For example, when general finance gets regulated, contribution of the investors is to be considered, i.e. the principle "one country one vote" is inapplicable, although the most significant investor cannot receive more than 50% of votes, thus imposing his/her will on the others. Payment union becomes necessary while the number of the participants in international bargains, and hence the volume of payments, grows.

Government, administrative functions are most important for managing international transportation, communication, fuel and energy, and coal-metallurgical complexes.[83] When solving social problems, on the other hand, most important are agreements, as imported foreign labour and cheaper goods can significantly worsen the standing of local workers (such problems have arisen, for example, in certain areas of the Ukraine and Russia).

The methods of management in bilateral (Australia-New Zealand, USA-Canada), tripartite (NAFTA) and multilateral (ASEAN, EU, Latin American and Caribbean communities) communities differ greatly. Studying their experience is of special interest for the CIS.

Field of Debate

1. What is regionalism? What basic regional economic groupings are there in the modern world? What are the advantages of regional economic integration?

2. What experience of the European Union development might be expedient for the CIS?

3. What is it possible to call CIS achievements in recent years?

4. Why has the CIS not completely justified the hopes, assigned to it? What are the reasons of the crisis in the CIS in the late 1990s? How is it possible to solve the problems faced by the CIS?

5. Why are there internal grouping in the CIS? Does the commonwealth of Russia and Belarus help or inhibit the CIS development?

6. What is a free trade zone? What is its role in regional economic integration?

7. What is a customs union? What are the results and prospects of the customs union between Russia, Kazakhstan, Belarus, Kyrgyzstan and and Tajikistan?

8. What is a monetary union? What are the prospects of introducing a uniform currency in the CIS?

---

[83] Ruggic, J. (1993): Multilateralism Matters: the Theory and Praxis of an Institutional Form. New York, 170–172; Hoffmann, S., Keohane, R.O. (Eds.) (1991): The new European Community. Boulder (Colorado), 102–104

9. List the basic stages of regional economic integration development. In which is the CIS now? What are the basic directions of co-operation development between the CIS countries which have been planned for the late 1990s?

10. What should be done to create a uniform scientific-technological and educational space in the CIS?

11. What is the role played in regional economic integration by FIGs and TNCs? In which areas of your country's economy can they be most useful?

12. What should be done to develop direct connections between the CIS companies?

CONCLUSION

The analysis of the results of social and economic development in the CIS countries during the 1990s allows for the following basic conclusions:

The CIS countries have very real competitive advantages, allowing them to enter the world community in the twenty-first century as equal participants forming one of the leading world centres of economy, science and culture. Among these advantages there are: 1) unique natural resources (over one third of the world reserves); 2) extensive territories and broad home markets; 3) comparatively cheap, skilled and educated labour; 4) intellectual property: new technologies and experience in manufacture, export of high-tech products (only in Russia is it assessed as $400 billion), significant scientific potential (approximately 1.5 million scholars or more than 15% of all scholars in the world); 5) common industrial infrastructures and experience in co-operation, and lots of common welfare traditions and history; 6) significant capacities in numerous industries and agriculture.

During the economic reforms, there has been denationalisation of the economy and privatisation of enterprises, and market mechanisms and market infrastructure, formed is the new middle class of businessmen and managers have been created; also, foreign economic relations have been developed. The reforms strategy has been refined: the countries oriented towards the liberal monetarist model strengthen the government regulation, whereas those using primarily State economy accelerate the processes of privatisation and evolving the capitals market. The transition to socially oriented and regulated market economy becomes irreversible. *Centrist positions in economic science and policy become amplified,* and the middle class begins to be formed as the basis of social stability.

However, industrial stabilisation occurs mainly due to mining raw materials and manufacture of simple products according to ecologically dangerous technologies for export to developed countries. According to UNESCO, by 2000, two thirds of the earth's working population will use information technologies. Approximately 80% of the GDP revenues in developed countries is received with scientific and technological innovations. The global market of high-tech products amounts to $2.3 trillion, the CIS share in this market being below 0.4%. In Russia, per capita expenses on information technologies (according to the corporation Intel) are 35 times lower than in the EU countries and 70 times lower than in the USA (in relation to GDP, 0.5, 2 and 4%, respectively). In other CIS countries, the situation is even worse: they lag behind not only the most developed countries, but also many Asian ones. The Russian per capita GDP is approximately ten times lower than that in developed countries, other CIS countries having even less.

If present tendencies get kept, the CIS countries are threatened with curtailing their research-and-production potential in the most promising branches, transition of the most valuable natural resources under foreign control, loss of a chance for independent steady development and unemployment growth. The world consumption of raw materials (unlike that of high-tech products) will by 2015 get increased by only two times, and its prices will be subject to even more significant fluctuations, which will not make it possible to satisfy its export countries with large populations.

In 1998 the financial crisis cut the CIS countries' GDP by 3.5%, industrial production by 2.5%, agricultural sector by 9%, investments in the capital assets by 3%, freights by 8% and retail trade commodity circulation by 2%, as well as the real earnings.

The crisis aggravation was caused by both internal (the decrease in prices for exported raw materials, developing markets money escape) and external (the drought of 1998, mistakes in financial policy, poor management, slow structure reforms, currency control and corruption prevention ineffectiveness, ineffective integration measures in the CIS) reasons.

As a consequence of the aforementioned particulars, in 1998–1999 Russia and numerous other CIS countries have vastly corrected their reforms policy. That means, firstly, the improvement of state economy regulation (which bears mainly economic rather than administrative character), particularly state regulation of cash flows and domestic and foreign investments in substantial production, which includes, first of all, high-technological branches and infrastructure, and agricultural industrial complex; secondly, high-social orientation of the reforms to be reached; and thirdly, the acceleration of budget and taxation reforms to provide budget income growth by means of black economy reduction and implementation of hard control over the expenditures, especially foreign credits, rationalisation.

At the same time, neither peoples nor CIS governments are going to release market reforms and the policy of democratisation and global economic system integration.

Market reforms in the CIS countries are an opportunity and necessity of economic integration on a new basis, *securing a steady development of their economies and societies* as a whole. The CIS size and specialisation of its national economies are optimal for a common market guaranteeing profitable manufacture. Moldavian vegetables, Central Asian and Transcaucasian fruit, North Kazakhstan coal, metal, grain and meat, Russian and Uzbek gas and wool, Byelorussian refrigerators and computers, most sorts of machinery, as well as tourist and resort services with paying demand are most profitably and sometimes only possibly sold in the near as opposed to the distant foreign countries. This is promoted by the uniformity of the transportation infrastructure and the ethnic groups immeasurably facilitating management and economic relations.

The financial crisis has assisted the CIS internal market development. In 1998 the CIS states' share in total external trade circulation calculated in hard currency units decreased. However, that was caused mainly by the CIS currencies' devaluation depreciating the commodities; nevertheless, in 1998 the CIS countries' mutual real commodity circulation value increased.

Economic integration feeds and stimulates itself. Thus, the free trade zone and the customs union founded by the CIS countries objectively put their participants in a privileged situation in relation to other countries. FIGs on the basis of national enterprises of the countries participating in the customs union do not pay internal customs duties and are in a more favourable position than the FIGs from other states. Thus, the basis of economic integration of the CIS countries becomes mutually advantageous for direct connections between non-government enterprises. Development of modern management, study of national cultures and experience in reforms from other CIS countries will allow them to join the global market not as a raw materials appendage, but as an equal partner, *the fourth centre of the global economy,* alongside North America, the EU and Southeast Asia.

A special role is played by the CIS geopolitical situation: it is located between the most developed countries of the Asian-Pacific region, with already more than half of mankind and the EU.

In the nineteenth century Rudyard Kipling wrote that the East and the West could never come together. In the twentieth century confrontation between the two civilisations has not been infrequently dangerous. In the next century the settlement of this conflict could be immensely influenced by Russia and other CIS countries that account for almost 300 million people representing more than a hundred nations of Christian, Islamic and other cultures. Presently, these countries are still at the historical crossroads and need the centrist conception of sustainable development to be worked out. That will be assisted also by the new direction of the economic theory and actual economies of the CIS countries, as outlined in this book.

LITERATURE

1. Akulai, E., Rodionov, A. (1996): Analysis of Business Developments in the Republic of Moldova. Kishinev [Акулай, Е., Родионов, А. (1996): Анализ Развития Предпринимательства в Республике Молдова. Кишинев]

2. Ashimbaev, T.A. (1994): Economics in Kazakhstan on the Road to the Market. Almaty [Ашимбаев, Т.А. (1994): Экономика Казахстана на Пути к Рынку. Алматы]

3. Baigeldy, O. (1998): This Holy Word – Freedom. Almaty [Байгелди, О. (1998): Это Священное Слово - Свобода. Алматы]

4. Berdyaev, N.A. (1990): The Sources and the Meaning of Russian Communism. Nauka, Moscow [Бердяев, Н.А. (1990): Истоки и Смысл Русского Коммунизма. Наука, Москва]

5. Bliakhman, L.S., Krotov, M.I. (1996): Structural Reforms and Economic Integration: Experience and Challenges in the CIS. Publishing Office of the Saint-Petersburg State University, Saint Petersburg [Бляхман, Л.С., Кротов, М.И. (1996): Структурные Реформы и Экономическая Интеграция: Опыт и Проблемы СНГ. Издательство СПбГУ, Санкт-Петербург]

6. Boiko, I.P. (1995): Business Associations in Market-Oriented Economy. Saint Petersburg [Бойко, И.П. (1995): Объединения Предприятий в Рыночной Экономике. Санкт-Петербург]

7. Bolbochan, Iu.I. et al. (1993): Small-Scale Enterprise in Transition to the Market. Kishinev [Болбочан, Ю.И. и др. (1993): Малое Предпринимательство при Переходе к Рынку. Кишинев]

8. Bogomazov, G.G. (1983): Shaping the Foundations of Socialist Economic Mechanism in the USSR during the 20s and 30s. Publishing Office of the Leningrad State University, Leningrad [Богомазов, Г.Г. (1983): Формирование Основ Социалистического Хозяйственного Механизма в СССР в 20–30-е годы. Издательство ЛГУ, Ленинград]

9. Bogomolov, O.T. (Ed.) (1996): Reform as Viewed by American and Russian Scientists. Moscow [Богомолов, О.Т. (Ред.) (1996): Реформа Глазами Американских и Российских Ученых. Москва]

10. Cheban, N.I. et al. (1997): Securities Market in the Republic of Moldova: Current Status. Prospects. Kishinev [Чебан, Н.И. и др. (1997): Рынок Государственных Ценных Бумаг Республики Молдова: Состояние. Перспективы. Кишинев]

11. (1997): CIS Economics. Issue 1. Progress of Economic Reforms in CIS Member States. Moscow [(1997): Экономика СНГ. Выпуск 1. О Ходе Экономических Реформ в Государствах – Участниках СНГ. Москва]

12. (1997): CIS Economics. Issue 2. Structural Changes in Economics in CIS Member States between 1991 and 1996. Moscow [(1997): Экономика СНГ. Выпуск 2. Структурные Изменения Экономики в Государствах – Участниках СНГ в 1991–1996 гг. Москва]

13. (1998): Commonwealth of Independent States in 1997: Statistical Yearbook. Moscow [(1998): Содружество Независимых Государств в 1997 Году. Статистический Справочник. Москва]

14. (1999): Commonwealth of Independent States in 1998: Concise Abstract. Moscow [(1999): Содружество Независимых Государств в 1998 Году. Краткий Обзор. Москва]

15. Dadalko, V.A. (1996): Economic Reform in the Republic of Belarus. Minsk [Дадалко, В.А. (1996): Реформирование Экономики Республики Беларусь. Минск]

16. Dubov, A. (1997): The Russian Capital Market and Foreign Portfolio Investors' Operations There in 1996 and 1997. Moscow [Дубов, А. (1997): Российский Рынок Капиталов и Деятельность на Нем Иностранных Портфельных Инвесторов в 1996–1997 гг. Москва]

17. (1996): Economic Forum of European Regions for Cooperation, Security and Sustainable Development. Moscow [(1996): Экономический Форум Регионов Европы за Сотрудничество, Безопасность и Устойчивое Развитие. Москва]

18. Eltsyn, B.N. (1998): Address of the President of the Russian Federation to the Federal Assembly. Moscow [Ельцин, Б.Н. (1998): Послание Президента Российской Федерации Федеральному Собранию. Москва]

19. (1993): Foreign Capital in the Economy of Kazakhstan. Almaty [(1993): Иностранный Капитал в Экономике Казахстана. Алматы]

20. Gaidar, E.T. (1996): Days of Defeat and Victory. Vagrius, Moscow [Гайдар, Е.Т. (1996): Дни Поражений и Побед. Вагриус, Москва]

21. Heine, P. (1991): The Economic Mentality. / Translated from English. Novosti, Moscow [Хейне, П. (1991): Экономический Образ Мышления. / Пер. с Англ. Новости, Москва]

22. (1995): Humanitarian Culture as a Factor of Transformation in Russia. Conference Proceedings. Saint Petersburg [(1995): Гуманитарная Культура как Фактор Преобразования России: Материалы Конференции. Санкт-Петербург]

23. (1996): Integrative Processes in CIS Countries. Saint Petersburg [(1996): Интеграционные Процессы в Странах СНГ. Санкт-Петербург]

24. Karimov, I. (1995): Uzbekistan in the Course of Intensifying Economic Reforms. Tashkent [Каримов, И. (1995): Узбекистан на Пути Углубления Экономических Реформ. Ташкент]

25. Khrishchev, E.I. (1997): Firm Management. Kishinev [Хрищев, Е.И. (1997): Менеджмент Фирмы. Кишинев]

26. Korotchenia, I.M. (1995): Economic Union of Sovereign States: Strategy and Tactics of Development. Saint Petersburg [Коротченя, И.М. (1995): Экономический Союз Суверенных Государств: Стратегия и Тактика Становления. Санкт-Петербург]

27. Kuntsev, P. (1997): The Period of Transition: Realities and Promise of Economic Development. Bishkek [Кунцев, П. (1997): Переходный Период: Реалии и Перспективы Экономического Развития. Бишкек]

28. Maksimov, S.I. (1992): Reconstruction and Challenges of Economic Reform. Publishing Office of the Saint-Petersburg State University, Saint Petersburg [Максимов, С.И. Перестройка и Проблемы Хозяйственной Реформы. Издательство СПбГУ, Санкт–Петербург]

29. McNoton, D., Karlson, D.J., Dits, K.I. et al. (1994): Banks in Developed Markets. Volume 1. Finansy i Statistika, Moscow [Мак-Нотон, Д., Карлсон, Д.Дж., Дитц, К.Т. и др. (1994): Банки на Развивающихся Рынках. Том 1. Финансы и статистика, Москва]

30. Miasnikovich, M.V. (1995): Formation of Market Economy in the Republic of Belarus. Minsk [Мясникович, М.В. (1995): Становление Рыночной Экономики в Республике Беларусь. Минск]

31. Miasnikovich, M.V. (1997): Finance and Industry Groupings in Transitional Economies (Cases of the Republic of Belarus and the Russian Federation). Publishing Office of the Saint-Petersburg State University of Economics and Finance, Saint Petersburg [Мясникович, М.В. Формирование Финансово-Промышленных Групп в Переходных Экономиках (на Примере Республики Беларусь и Российской Федерации). Издательство СПбГУЭФ, Санкт-Петербург]

32. Mobius, M. (1995): Investor's Manual of Developing Markets. Moscow [Мобиус, М. (1995): Руководство для Инвестора по Развивающимся Рынкам. Москва]

33. Musakozhoev, Sh.M., Meimanov, K.M. (1997): Economics in the Kyrgyz Republic. Bishkek [Мусакожоев, Ш.М., Мейманов, К.М. Экономика Кыргызской Республики. Бишкек]

34. Nazarbaev, N.A. (1996): On the Threshold of the 21st Century. Almaty [Назарбаев, Н.А. На Пороге XXI Века. Алматы]

35. Nazarbaev, N.A. (1996): Five Years of Independence in Kazakhstan. Almaty [Назарбаев, Н.А. (1996): Пять Лет Независимости Казахстана. Алматы]

36. Nazarbayev, N.A. (1997): Eurasian Union: Ideas, Practice, Perspectives. 1994–1997. Moscow [Назарбаев, Н.А. (1997): Евразийский Союз: Идеи, Практика, Перспективы. 1994-1997 гг. Москва]

37. Orazov, M.B. (Ed.) (1997): Foreign Trade Policy of the Neutral Turkmenistan. Ashgabat [Оразов, М.Б. (Ред.) (1997): Внешнеэкономическая Политика Нейтрального Туркменистана. Ашгабат]

38. Ospanov, M.T. (1996): Tax Reform and Harmonisation of Taxation Terms. Saint Petersburg [Оспанов, М.Т. (1996): Налоговая Реформа и Гармонизация Налоговых Отношений. Санкт-Петербург]

39. Rakhmatov, M.A. (1996): Issues of Business Development in Uzbekistan. Kazan [Рахматов, М.А. (1996): Проблемы Становления Предпринимательства в Узбекистане. Казань]

40. Rozhko, O. (1992): Privatisation in the Social Sphere: Problems of the Initial Phase. Kishinev [Рожко, О. (1992): Приватизация в Социальной Сфере: Проблемы Начального Этапа. Кишинев]

41. Rybak, G. (1995): Tax Regulations in Small-Scale Business in Terms of Transition to the Market: Starting from Industrial Developments in the Republic of Moldova and International Experience. Kishinev [Рыбак, Г. (1995): Налоговое Регулирование Малого Предпринимательства в Условиях Перехода к Рынку: На Материалах Промышленности Республики Молдова и Зарубежного Опыта. Кишинев]

42. Sirotkin, V.G. (1991): Great Reformers in Russia. Znanie, Moscow [Сироткин, В.Г. (1991): Великие Реформаторы России. Знание, Москва]

43. (1998): Six Years of the Commonwealth: Challenges and Prospects: Proceedings of Minsk Conference 2–4 March 1998 [(1998): Шесть Лет Содружества: Проблемы и Перспективы: Материалы Конференции 2–4 Марта 1998 г. Минск]

44. Staritsyna, L.V., Khrustiuk, L.G. (1996): Issues of Improvement and Functioning in the Banking and Credit System in the Republic of Moldova. Kishinev [Старицы-на, Л.В., Хрустюк, Л.Г. (1996): Проблемы Совершенствования и Функционирования Банковско-Кредитной Системы Республики Молдова. Кишинев]

45. Stroev, E.S., Bliakhman, L.S., Krotov M.I. (1998): The Economics of the Commonwealth of Independent States on the Eve of the Third Millennium. Nauka, Saint Petersburg [Строев, Е.С., Бляхман, Л.С., Кротов, М.И. (1998): Экономика Содружества Независимых Государств Накануне Третьего Тысячелетия. Наука, Санкт-Петербург]

46. Stroev, E.S. (Ed.) (1997): Conception of Agrarian Policy in Russia for 1997–2000. Moscow [Строев, Е.С. (Ред.) (1997): Концепция Аграрной Политики России в 1997–2000 гг. Москва]

47. Stroev, E.S. (1994): Methodology and Practices of Agrarian Reform. Moscow [Строев, Е.С. (1994): Методология и Практика Аграрного Реформирования. Москва]

48. Stroev, E.S. (1994): The Market and Development of Regional Productive Forces. Orel [Строев, Е. С. (1994): Рынок и Развитие Производительных Сил Региона. Орел]

49. Stroev, E.S. (Ed.) (1998): The Petersburg Economic Forum 17–21 June 1997. Collected Papers. IPA Council Secretariat, Saint Petersburg [Строев, Е.С. (Ред.) (1998): Петербургский Экономический Форум 17–21 Июня 1997 Года. Сборник Материалов. Секретариат Совета МПА, Санкт-Петербург]

50. Sutyrin, S.F., Kharlamova, V.N. (Eds.) (1996): International Economic Relations. Saint Petersburg [Сутырин, С.Ф., Харламова, В.Н. (Ред.) (1996): Международные Экономические Отношения. Санкт-Петербург]

51. (1998): The Petersburg Economic Forum. Herald of the Interparliamentary Assembly 2, 3 [(1998): Петербургский Экономический Форум. Вестник Межпарламентской Ассамблеи 2, 3]

52. (1998): The Petersburg Economic Forum: "Round Table". Meetings 19 June 1997. Issues 1, 2. IPA Council Secretariat, Saint Petersburg [(1998): Петербургский Экономический Форум: Заседания "Круглых Столов". 19 июня 1997 г. Выпуски 1, 2. Секретариат Совета МПА, Санкт-Петербург]

53. Usmanov, Kh.M., Usmanov, M.Kh. (1997): Anti-Crisis Management in Tajikistan Economics. Dushanbe [Усманов, Х.М., Усманов, М.Х. (1997): Антикризисное Управление Экономикой Таджикистана. Душанбе]

54. Weber, M. (1990): Selected Works. / Translated from German. Progress, Moscow [Вебер, М. (1990): Избранные Произведения. / Пер. с Нем. Прогресс, Москва]

55. Zaslavskaia, T.I., Ryvkina, R.V. (1991): Sociology of Economic Life: Essays on Theory. Nauka, Novosibirsk [Заславская, Т.И., Рывкина, Р.В. (1991): Социология Экономической Жизни: Очерки Теории. Наука, Новосибирск]

THE COUNTRY INDEX

New in Economics

U. Walz

Dynamics of Regional Integration

1999. X, 209 pp. 7 figs., 11 tabs. (Contributions to Economics) Softcover **DM 85,-** ISBN 3-7908-1185-8

The long-run effects of regional integration are analyzed in this book. Most importantly, it investigates on the basis of a model of endogenous regional growth the long-run effects of a deepening as well as of an enlargement of a regional integration bloc on regional growth and specialization patterns.

A. Siedenberg, L. Hoffmann (Eds.)

Ukraine at the Crossroads

Economic Reforms in International Perspective

1999. XVI, 437 pp. 22 figs. 52 tabs. Softcover **DM 89,-** ISBN 3-7908-1189-0

Economic reforms in Ukraine since the collapse of the Soviet Union and the beginnings of transformation in 1991 are reviewed, and are compared with the experience of other transformation countries. The approach of the authors is empirical, providing insiders' understanding and evaluation of the reform process.

G. Lay, P. Shapira, J. Wengel (Eds.)

Innovation in Production

The Adoption and Impacts of New Manufacturing Concepts in German Industry

1999. XVI, 188 pp. 61 figs., 6 tabs. (Technology, Innovation and Policy, Vol. 8) Softcover **DM 85,-;** ISBN 3-7908-1140-8

How companies in Germany's critically important capital goods sector are deploying new technological and organizational production concepts to adapt to competitiveness challenges, new production requirements, environmental demands, and policy pressures is examined in this book. It draws on the Fraunhofer ISI's unique nationwide survey of technology use and production in Germany.

F. Meyer-Krahmer (Ed.)

Globalisation of R&D and Technology Markets

Consequences for National Innovation Policies

1999. VI, 182 pp. 51 figs. 11 tabs. (Technology, Innovation and Policy, Vol. 9) Softcover **DM 75,-** ISBN 3-7908-1175-0

In this book the subject is considered simultaneously, on a high level, from different perspectives. In the first part the policy perspective is given. In the second part, the globalisation of R&D and technology markets is considered from the scientific point of view. The third part is dedicated to the firms' perspective.

Physica-Verlag
A Springer-Verlag Company

Please order through your bookseller or from Physica-Verlag, c/o Springer-Verlag, P.O.Box 14 02 01, D-14302 Berlin, Germany;
Tel. (0) 30/8 27 87-0, Fax (0) 30/8 27 87-301, e-mail: orders@springer.de, Internet: www.springer.de/economics